CONCISE COLLEGE TEXTS

"A" LEVEL LAW:
CASES AND MATERIALS

OTHER BOOKS IN THE SERIES:

AUSTRALIA
The Law Book Company
Brisbane ● Sydney ● Melbourne ● Perth

CANADA
Carswell
Ottawa ● Toronto ● Calgary ● Montreal ● Vancouver

AGENTS
Steimatzky's Agency Ltd., Tel Aviv;
N.M. Tripathi (Private) Ltd., Bombay;
Eastern Law House (Private) Ltd., Calcutta;
M.P.P. House, Bangalore;
Universal Books, Delhi;
MacMillan Shuppan KK, Tokyo;
Pakistan Law House, Karachi, Lahore

CONCISE COLLEGE TEXTS

"A LEVEL LAW: CASES AND MATERIALS

Third Edition

BRIAN HOGAN, LL.B.

of Gray's Inn, Barrister, Professor of Common Law,
University of Leeds

PETER SEAGO, J.P., LL.M.

Senior Lecturer in Law, Head of the Department of Law,
University of Leeds

GEOFFREY BENNETT, M.A.

of the Inner Temple, Barrister, Senior Lecturer in Law,
City University

LONDON ● SWEET & MAXWELL ● 1994

Published in 1994
by Sweet & Maxwell Limited
of South Quay Plaza
183 Marsh Wall, London E14 9FT
Computerset by PB Computer Typesetting,
Pickering, N. Yorks
Printed in England by Clays Ltd.,
St Ives plc

A CIP catalogue record for this book
is available from the British Library

ISBN 0421 512105

No natural forests were destroyed
to make this product only farmed
timber was used and re-planted.

The index was prepared by Deborah Harris

Preface

The aim of this book remains what it has been from the outset: to provide 'A' level law students, who rarely have access even to basic legal materials, with at least some of the raw material of the law. We work within the severe constraints of producing an affordable text covering three substantial areas of law. We have also continued our previous policy of providing reasonably substantial extracts so that the student gets a better idea of argumentation and decision-making. More on less rather than less on more.

Developments affecting the sections on Legal System and Contract, though significant, have not been extensive. It is Criminal Law that has been hardest hit. A cataract of case law has made the second edition look distinctly dated and only within the space of three years. In that time there have been seven decisions of the House of Lords affecting both general principles and particular crimes. Nor has the Criminal Division of the Court of Appeal been idle. To some of us it seems that while the rules of the game seem essentially the same the courts are constantly readjusting the position of the goalposts.

We reiterate that we welcome criticism, constructive or destructive, from users of the book. We are tough enough to withstand it and, we hope, sensible enough to take account of it. No criticism or comment goes unanswered and we endeavour to explain why we accept or reject it.

Brian Hogan
Peter Seago
Geoffrey Bennett

Acknowledgments

The extract from Cross, *Precedent in English Law* (3rd ed.), 1977, reproduced by kind permission of Oxford University Press.

Crown Copyright material is reprinted by kind permission of the Controller of Her Majesty's Stationery Office.

Extract from *Bolduc and Bird* v. *R.* Reproduced with the permission of Canada Law Book Inc., 240 Edward Street, Aurora, Ontario, L4G 3S9 Canada.

Extracts from various law reports reproduced by kind permission of: The Incorporated Council for Law Reporting and Butterworth & Co. (Publishers) Ltd.

Extracts from *R.* v. *Stephen Malcolm R.* Taken from Justice of the Peace Reports (1984) 149 J.P. 89 with permission from the Publishers.

Extracts from *R.* v. *Price* © Times Newspapers Ltd. 1989

Extract from *R.* v. *Sulman, R., R.* v. *Adomako, R.* v. *Holloway* © Times Newspapers Ltd. 1993.

Extract from *Winzar* v. *Chief Constable of Kent* © Times Newspapers Ltd. 1983

Table of Contents

PART TWO: CRIMINAL LAW

Table of Cases

Table of Statutes

PART ONE

ENGLISH LEGAL SYSTEM

Chapter 1

Sources of Law and the Doctrine of Precedent

1. THE INTERPRETATION OF STATUTES

Is a horse a "conveyance?" Is a football pools coupon an "instrument?" Is a constable "in uniform" when on his way home he is wearing a civilian raincoat over his uniform and is not wearing his cap? Does it matter? Well, it matters very much if you happen to be charged with taking a conveyance contrary to section 12 of the Theft Act 1968, or forgery contrary to section 1 of the Forgery and Counterfeiting Act 1981, or driving a motor vehicle with an alcohol concentration above the prescribed limit contrary to section 5 of the Road Traffic Act 1988. How "conveyance," "instrument" and "in uniform" are interpreted may mean the difference between conviction and acquittal.

Take the first question. In *Neal* v. *Gribble* ((1979) 68 Cr.App.R. 9) the three defendants, using lengths of rope as bridles, rode off on three horses belonging to X. A little while later, when confronted by X, they abandoned the horses and fled. Had each taken a "conveyance"? Had the word "conveyance" been undefined it would seem that a horse may fairly be regarded as a conveyance; indeed it is the oldest form of conveyance known to man. But section 12 of the Theft Act defines conveyance as "any conveyance constructed or adapted for the carriage of a person or persons whether by land, water or air". It was held that a horse was not a conveyance within the definition; the definition contemplated artefacts but not animals. And even if it were to be regarded as a conveyance, using the rope as a bridle did not constitute an adaptation for the purposes of the section.

This decision, with respect, seems entirely sensible. But would a parachute constitute a "conveyance" within the section? Or roller-skates? And what of the employee who uses a lift reserved for the exclusive use of the managing director?

So it will be appreciated that lawyers are very much in the business of interpretation. It will also be appreciated that

3

while *Neal* v. *Gribble* presents a none too difficult problem of interpretation, provisions of, say, the Income and Corporation Taxes Act 1988 (an Act of 845 sections and 31 schedules) may present problems of interpretation of considerable complexity. So what does the judge do? A short answer might be that judges do their best. Clearly his or her preference is to carry out the intention of Parliament and not to defeat it but where the meaning of a word is unclear or the meaning of a phrase is ambiguous how is the true intention to be determined? It will be immediately apparent that words or phrases take colour from their surroundings so the judge may take account of the context of the Act as a whole and regard may be had to the long title which sets out, albeit in general terms, the aims of the Act.

In addition the judge may use certain external aids. Reference may be made, for example, to dictionaries, to other statutes dealing with a similar subject matter and their interpretation in prior cases, and to certain official reports such as reports by Royal Commissions, the Law Commission and the Criminal Law Revision Committee.

Even so, the judge, having used the internal and external aids available, may conclude either (a) that the intention of Parliament is not clear; or (b) though the intention is clear, it is difficult to see how the language used gives effect to that intention. What is the judge to do? In one case (*Bebb* v. *Frank* [1939] 1 K.B. 558 at 568) Lord Goddard said of a particular statutory provision: "For myself, I am not ashamed to admit that I have not the least idea what [it] means." At such a stage would it be helpful to call on the draftsman (assuming the draftsman is still available) to explain what he or she intended? What reasons can you think of in favour or against such a course? In *Hilder* v. *Dexter* [1902] A.C. 474 Lord Halsbury L.C. declined to give a judgment on the grounds that he had been responsible for the drafting of the statute in question. "My Lords," he said at p. 477, "I have more than once had occasion to say that in construing a statute I believe the worst person to construe it is the person who is responsible for its drafting. He is very much disposed to confuse what he intended to do with the effect of the language, which in fact has been employed." Suppose you had been in Lord Halsbury's shoes. Would you have declined to give a judgment on the grounds that you knew what was the intended effect of the words used?

But why not, at the very least, consult proceedings in Parliament? A commentator, called upon to write an exegesis of a statute for, say, *Current Law Statutes* would inevitably read parliamentary proceedings regarding that statute as an

aid to the commentary on the statute. These may give
valuable insights as to what was intended though the
commentator might properly question whether the words
used give effect to that intention.

Until 1993 the courts took the view that reference to
Parliamentary proceedings was impermissible for the purpose
of resolving uncertainties in statutes. In that year the House
of Lords, in *Pepper* v. *Hart* [1993] 1 All E.R. 42, decided to
move the goalposts. Not surprisingly it was a case involving
taxation. The taxpayers were masters at an independent
school whose children attending the school were charged only
one-fifth of the fees applicable to other students. Clearly a
benefit to the masters and the issue was whether this was a
"taxable benefit" under the Finance Act 1976. The provision
in question was ambiguous and to resolve the ambiguity the
House referred to Parliamentary proceedings which showed
that Parliament's intention was to favour the taxpayers and
not the Revenue.

Pepper v. *Hart* is *not* authority for a general proposition that
legislation is to be construed in the context of statements
made in Parliamentary proceedings about its intended effect.
Reference is permissible only where a provision is ambiguous
and the reference must clearly resolve the ambiguity. In
Pepper v. *Hart* the reference revealed that the Financial
Secretary had given explicit assurances that the benefit in
question was not to be taxable.

Obviously the interpretation of statutes is not, and cannot
be, a precise science. Over the years the courts have adopted
various approaches to the interpretation of statues known as
the Mischief Rule, the Literal Rule and the Golden Rule. It is
perhaps unfortunate that "rule" has been used since it
suggests a formula by reference to which the meaning of
words can be readily determined. It would have been better
to have used "approach" since this is what they are in that
they reflect judicial attitudes to the process of interpretation.
More recently there has emerged the so-called "Purposive
Approach" and this approach is now probably in the
ascendant. Whatever approach is adopted no judge may, like
Humpty Dumpty, make words mean precisely what he wants
them to mean; a judge cannot rewrite a statute to give it its
intended meaning. The judge can only work with the material
provided but it appears that some judges may be bolder in
fashioning the material than others.

Mention must also be made of the Interpretation Act 1978.
The long title says it is an Act "to consolidate the
Interpretation Act 1889 and certain other enactments relating
to the construction and operation of Acts of Parliament." This
sounds very promising but it is really only of marginal

significance.   It tells us, for example, that, unless the contrary
intention appears, that words importing the masculine gender
include the feminine and vice versa; that in measuring
distance for the purposes of an Act, the distance shall, unless
a contrary intention appears, be measured in a straight line on
a horizontal plane; that "England" means, subject to
alteration of boundaries under Part IV of the Local Government Act 1972, the area consisting of the counties established
by section 1 of that Act, Greater London and the Isles of
Scilly. The Act, in effect, crosses a few t's and dots a few i's
but otherwise does not explain how statutes, including the
Interpretation Act itself, are to be interpreted.

A   The Mischief Rule

Historically, the so-called "mischief rule" of statutory interpretation appears
to be the oldest.

Heydon's Case

(1584) 3 Co.Rep. 7a

[I]t was resolved by [the Court] that for the sure and true
interpretation of all statutes in general (be they penal or
beneficial, restrictive or enlarging of the common law,) four
things are to be discerned and considered:—
   1st.   What was the common law before the making of the
Act.
   2nd.   What was the mischief and defect for which the
common law did not provide.
   3rd.   What remedy the Parliament hath resolved and
appointed to cure the diseases of the commonwealth.
   And, 4th.   The true reason of the remedy; and then the
office of all the Judges is always to make such construction as
shall suppress the mischief, and advance the remedy, and to
suppress subtle inventions and evasions for continuance of
the mischief, and *pro privato commodo* [for the benefit of the
individual], and to add force and life to the cure and remedy,
according to the true intent of the makers of the Act, *pro bono
publico* [for the public good].

Magor and St. Mellons v. Newport Corporation

[1952] A.C. 189 (H.L.)

Lord Simonds.   My Lords, I have had the advantage of
reading the opinion which my noble and learned friend, Lord

Morton of Henryton, is about to deliver, and I fully concur in his reasons and conclusion, as I do in those of Parker J., and the majority of the Court of Appeal. Nor should I have thought it necessary to add any observations of my own were it not that the dissenting opinion of Denning L.J., appears to invite some comment.

My Lords, the criticism which I venture to make of the judgment of the learned Lord Justice is not directed at the conclusion that he reached. It is after all a trite saying that on questions of construction different minds may come to different conclusions and I am content to say that I agree with my noble and learned friend. But it is on the approach of the Lord Justice to what is a question of construction and nothing else that I think it desirable to make some comment, for at a time when so large a proportion of the cases that are brought before the courts depend on the construction of modern statutes it would not be right for this House to pass unnoticed the propositions which the learned Lord Justice lays down for the guidance of himself and, presumably, of others. "We sit here," he says, "to find out the intention of Parliament and of Ministers and carry it out, and we do this better by filling in the gaps and making sense of the enactment than by opening it up to destructive analysis." The first part of this passage appears to be an echo of what was said in *Heydon's Case* 300 years ago and, so regarded, is not objectionable. But the way in which the learned Lord Justice summarises the broad rules laid down by Sir Edward Coke in that case may well induce grave misconception of the function of the court. The part which is played in the judicial interpretation of a statute by reference to the circumstances of its passing is too well known to need restatement. It is sufficient to say that the general proposition that it is the duty of the court to find out the intention of Parliament—and not only of Parliament but of Ministers also—cannot by any means be supported. The duty of the court is to interpret the words that the legislature has used. Those words may be ambiguous, but, even if they are, the power and duty of the court to travel outside them on a voyage of discovery are strictly limited. . . .

The second part of the passage that I have cited from the judgment of the learned Lord Justice is, no doubt, the logical sequel of the first. The court, having discovered the intention of Parliament and of Ministers too, must proceed to fill in the gaps. What the legislature has not written, the court must write. This proposition which restates in a new form the view expressed by the Lord Justice in the earlier case of *Seaford Court Estates Ltd.* v. *Asher* (1950) (to which the Lord Justice himself refers), cannot be supported. It appears to me to be a naked usurpation of the legislative function under the thin disguise of interpretation, and it is the less justifiable when it is guesswork with what material the legislature would, if it had discovered the gap, have filled it in. If a gap is disclosed, the remedy lies in an amending Act.

Questions

1. Do you think the judges in *Heydon's Case* would have found themselves more in sympathy with the approach of Denning L.J. or with that of Lord Simonds? Was Lord Simonds saying that Denning L.J. went beyond the principles laid down in *Heydon's Case* or that *Heydon's Case* itself went too far?
2. Denning L.J. was obviously trying to find out what Parliament wished to do and to give effect to that, if necessary by a bold interpretation of the words of the statute. Are there any dangers in such an approach?

B   The Literal Rule

The so-called Mischief Rule derived from *Heydon's Case* is by no means a dead letter and its spirit may now be informing the newer purposive approach. The duty of the court, as Lord Simonds says, is to interpret the words which the legislature has used. This—the so-called Literal Rule—until recently most accurately expressed the judicial attitude to the interpretation of statutes. But as a principle of interpretation the Literal Rule may be stated in different terms as the following judicial views show:

"If the words of an Act are clear, you must follow them, even though they lead to a manifest absurdity. The court has nothing to do with the question whether the legislature has committed an absurdity." *R.* v. *The Judge of the City of London Court* (1892), *per* Lord Esher M.R.

"If the language of a statute be plain, admitting of only one meaning, the Legislature must be taken to have meant and intended what it has plainly expressed, and whatever it has in clear terms enacted must be enforced though it should lead to absurd or mischievous results." *Vacher* v. *London Society of Compositors* (1913), *per* Lord Atkinson.

"A judge must not alter the material of which [a statute] is woven, but he can and should iron out the creases." *Eddis* v. *Chichester-Constable* (1969), *per* Fenton Atkinson L.J.

"The duty of the courts is to ascertain and give effect to the will of Parliament as expressed in its enactments. In the performance of this duty the judges do not act as computers into which are fed the statute and the rules for the construction of statutes and from whom issues forth the mathematically correct answer. The interpretation of statutes is a craft as much as a science and the judges, as craftsmen, select and apply the appropriate rules as the tool of their trade. They are not legislators, but finishers, refiners and polishers of legislation which comes to them in a state requiring varying degrees of further processing." *Corocraft* v. *Pan American Airways* (1969), *per* Donaldson J.

But however the Literal Rule is expressed, and whether in broader or narrower terms, the governing principle is that the words of a statute must be given their ordinary meaning in the context in which they occur. "In

determining the meaning of any word or phrase in a statute," said Lord Reid
in *Pinner* v. *Everett* (1969), "the first question to ask always is what is the
natural or ordinary meaning of that word or phrase in its context in the
statute."

This, then, is the agreed starting point, but the question Lord Reid requires
the interpreter to first ask himself does not provide its own answer. In
determining, for example, whether a telephone kiosk or a bandstand is a
"building" for the purposes of section 9 of the Theft Act, or who is an
"occupier" for the purposes of the Occupiers' Liability Act 1957, how helpful
is it to say that "building" and "occupier" should be given their "ordinary"
meanings?

It seems to be established that the interpretation of statutes is a matter of
law for the judge. Following dicta of the House of Lords in *Brutus* v. *Cozens*
([1973] A.C. 854) there was a flirtation with the idea that the meaning of
"ordinary" words was a matter of fact for the trier of fact to determine. The
courts have now substantially (though perhaps not entirely—see the materials
on "dishonesty" in theft, below, p. 381 resiled from this position. Statutes
must be consistently and uniformly interpreted.

Take, for example, the meaning of "building" for the purposes of the
offence of burglary under section 9 of the Theft Act 1968. "Building" is not
defined except that it includes an inhabited vehicle or vessel (note that a
statute may give a definition to a word not to be found in any dictionary).
Suppose the builder has completed the foundations and one course of bricks
when A enters the site and steals the contractor's tools from what would be
the kitchen of the house when it is completed. Obviously theft (which carries
seven years' imprisonment) but is it burglary (which carries 14 years'
imprisonment)? Common sense appears to indicate (but is common sense a
sure guide?) that the foundations plus one course of bricks is not yet a
building. When does it become a building? Must there be a roof? If so would
a projected hotel not be a building because only 25 of its 50 storeys have been
completed? Are we really to say that one extra brick or one extra state marks
the difference between theft or burglary? Does it matter?

Judges have said that in cases of this sort (and there are many of them) that
it is all a question of fact and degree. Does this formula help? Can you
suggest a better one? Assume two identical and adjoining bungalows are
under construction and at precisely the same stage of construction. A has
entered one and B has entered the other to steal tools belonging to the
builder. The judge in A's case ruled that the structure was not a building and
A has been convicted only of theft. In B's case the judge ruled that the
structure was a building and B has been convicted of burglary. A and B have
appealed and you are sitting as a judge in the Criminal Division of the Court
of Appeal. How would you approach the two cases? Throw up your hands in
despair? Or give a reasoned answer? What would your reasoned answer be?

London & North Eastern Rly. Co. v. Berriman

[1946] A.C. 278 (H.L.)

The respondent's husband was employed by the L.N.E.R. as
a signal fitter's labourer and his duty was to look after the
apparatus connecting signal boxes with signals and points.
His duty, when no specific defect was reported, involved the
routine oiling of the apparatus and on the day he was killed

by a passing train he had not taken his tool bag with him and was involved simply in oiling points. His widow brought an action under the Fatal Accidents Act alleging that her husband was killed in breach of a statutory duty, namely the Prevention of Accidents Rules 1902, Rule 9, which provided that "with the object of protecting men working... on or near lines of railway in use for traffic for the purposes of relaying or repairing the permanent way" the railway company should provide a look-out for giving warning of approaching trains to the men so working. No such look-out had been provided on the occasion the respondent's husband was killed.

It was held by three votes to two that the respondent's claim failed since her husband was not at the material time engaged in "relaying or repairing" the permanent way.

Lord Jowitt L.C. (dissenting)...

The Court of Appeal took the view that 'repairing' as used in the Railway Employment (Prevention of Accidents) Act 1900, must be construed as including the work of maintaining in good working order; I agree with them and I agree with them largely because I can find no satisfactory criterion to tell me at what point that which is called repair as opposed to maintenance begins. It would, I suppose, be conceded that if a nut had worked loose and required to be tightened the work involved would be a work of 'repair,' even although the actual work occupied only a few seconds of time. Oiling and cleaning may take longer than tightening a nut and in the course of oiling and cleaning something which is 'repair' in any sense of the word may be discovered. It might, for instance, be seen that a split pin which had sheared off required to be replaced. To limit the word 'repair' in the sense contended for by the appellants seems to me to make the duty imposed by the statute quite impracticable. At one moment of time a man might merely be oiling and cleaning and at another moment he might be doing something which is repair in the narrow sense of the word—that is in making good something which has developed a fault. It would be impracticable for the railway company whenever he did repair work in this sense to afford him protection which they failed to give him in the course of his oiling and cleaning....

The word 'repairing' is in my view a word sufficiently wide, if the context so requires, to include 'maintaining.' Having regard to the fact that the primary intendment of the Act in question was to provide more adequate protection for railway servants, I think it should be so construed in this case. Accordingly, in my view a man engaged in oiling and cleaning the moving parts of the machinery which enables the signalman to adjust the points is engaged in the work of repair.... For these reasons I would dismiss the appeal.

Lord Macmillan ...

I do not, however, find it necessary to pronounce finally on this matter for in my opinion, even if the system of connecting rods forms part of the permanent way, the deceased was not engaged in relaying or repairing these rods. He was oiling and cleaning them. There is of course no question that he was not doing any work of relaying the permanent way. The critical word for the present purpose is 'repairing.' I am unable having regard to the ordinary usage of the English language, to characterise the work of oiling and cleaning as a work of repair. The collocation of the words 'relaying' or 'repairing' is significant. Relaying is the major operation of renewing what is so defective as to be past repair; repairing is the minor operation of making good remediable defects. There was nothing wrong with the points which the deceased was oiling and cleaning, nothing requiring repair. The engineer who oils his engines would certainly be surprised to be told that he was repairing them. Oiling and cleaning, to my mind, are operations designed to keep plant in good running order and to prevent the development of defects necessitating repair. There may well have been a good reason for limiting the requirement of protection to the case of men engaged in the work of relaying and repairing, for these operations suggest tasks occupying time and requiring concentration of attention, precluding those engaged in them from looking after their own safety. If the word 'repairing' were to be extended to include the simple and routine matter of oiling and cleaning, the railway companies would require to provide persons or apparatus for the purpose of maintaining a good look-out or for giving warning of an approaching train or engine every time one of their servants oiled a single bearing in the system of points and connecting rods and this under the sanction of prosecution and penalties. For it must be borne in mind that while the statute and rule have the beneficent purpose of providing protection for workmen, their contravention involves penal consequences under s.11 of the Act. Where penalties for infringement are imposed it is not legitimate to stretch the language of a rule, however beneficent its intention, beyond the fair and ordinary meaning of its language. I quote and adopt the words of Alderson B.: 'The rule of law, I take it, upon the construction of all statutes . . . is, whether they be penal or remedial, to construe them according to the plain, literal, and grammatical meaning of the words in which they are expressed, unless that construction leads to a plain and clear contradiction of the apparent purpose of the Act, or to some palpable and evident absurdity': (*Attorney-General* v. *Lockwood* (1843)). It appears from the evidence that it has not been the practice of the appellant company, although the rule in question has been in operation for over forty years, to provide a look-out man when oiling is being done. On the other hand when a job of repair has to be done on the points which may take some time, a lookout man is asked for and provided. If it is thought desirable to extend the protection of a look-out to the case of men engaged in oiling and cleaning it is for the legislature to do so, after investigation of all relevant considerations. The present rule in my opinion does not cover the case. I am accordingly in favour of allowing the appeal and restoring the judgment of Stable J.

Questions

1. Which of the two interpretations placed upon the word "repair" do you prefer and why?
2. Can it be said of either interpretation that it was "obviously right" or "obviously wrong"? Was it not the case that there were two equally tenable interpretations of the word "repair"? If so, how is the judge to decide which is the preferable interpretation?
3. Assuming *London & North Eastern Rly. Co.* v. *Berriman* had fallen to be decided *post, Pepper* v. *Hart*, is this a case in which reference to Parliamentary proceedings should be made? Was there a genuine ambiguity as to the meaning of "relaying and repairing?" More of us are familiar with having cars serviced. Is this a "repair?" Could anyone who has had his/her car serviced sensibly say that s/he has had the car "repaired"?

C The Golden Rule

While the first thing to be considered is the ordinary meaning of the word or phrase in its context, it may be that the ordinary meaning leads to an absurd result. Lord Atkinson in the passage quoted above was prepared to say then so be it; it was for Parliament and not the courts to put the matter right. It is unlikely that any judge would now take so very literal a stance. There would probably be general agreement with the view expressed by Lord Reid in *Pinner* v. *Everett* that when the ordinary meaning leads to a result which cannot reasonably be supposed to have been the intention of Parliament, it becomes permissible to look for some other meaning of the word or phrase. This is the so-called Golden Rule that statutes should be construed so as to avoid absurdity. But notice that Lord Reid said this approach was permissible *only* where the ordinary interpretation led to an absurd result and in *Jones* v. *DPP* (1962) he added:

"It is a cardinal principle applicable to all kinds of statutes that you may not for any reason attach to a statutory provision a meaning which the words of that provision cannot reasonably bear. If they are capable of more than one meaning, than you can choose between those meanings, but beyond that you must not go."

Hence in *IRC* v. *Hinchy* (1960) where income tax legislation provided that a person who failed to submit a correct return was liable to forfeit £20 plus "treble the tax which he ought to be charged" the defendant was held liable to pay some £438 (calculated on the basis of his total tax liability for the year multiplied by three) though his return failed to declare only some £14 of taxable income. The trial judge, the Court of Appeal and the House of Lords were all agreed that Parliament could not reasonably be supposed to have intended so extravagant and extreme a penalty but the House, unlike the trial judge and the Court of Appeal, held that it was not possible to attach any other construction to the statute. Simply because the ordinary construction leads to an absurd result does not of itself justify the court coming to some other conclusion.

The principles and practice of statutory interpretation were considered by the Law Commission's *The Interpretation of Statutes*, Law Com. No. 21 (1969). Their general conclusion was that in the hands of the courts interpretation had become too restrictive. They said in paras. 29–33 of their Report:

"The three so-called rules which have been described above do not call for criticism if they are to be regarded simply as convenient headings by reference to which the different approaches of the courts to problems of interpretation may be described. They are less satisfactory, when they, or equivalent propositions in other language, are used to justify the meaning giving to a provision. In our view, the ultimate function of a court in the interpretative process is not simply to decide whether it is bound to follow a literal interpretation on the one hand or to adopt on the other an interpretation reached in the light of the golden or mischief rules. It is rather to decide the meaning of the provision, taking into account, among other matters, the light which the actual language used, and the broader aspects of legislative policy arrived at by the golden and mischief rules, throw on that meaning.

To place undue emphasis on the literal meaning of the words of a provision is to assume an unattainable perfection in draftsmanship; it presupposes that the draftsmen can always choose words to describe the situations intended to be covered by the provision which will leave no room for a difference of opinion as to their meaning. Such an approach ignores the limitations of language, which is not infrequently demonstrated even at the level of the House of Lords when Law Lords differ as to the so-called 'plain meaning' of words. . . .

When we turn from the literal rule to the golden rule, we find that this rule sets a purely negative standard by reference to absurdity, inconsistency or inconvenience, but provides no clear means to test the existence of these characteristics or to measure their quality or extent. When a court decides that a particular construction is absurd, it implies, although often tacitly, that the construction is absurd because it is irreconcilable with the general policy of the legislature. Thus in *R.* v. *Oakes* (1959) (where the Court read 'aids and abets *and* does any act preparatory to the commission of an offence' in s.7 of the Official Secrets Act 1920 as 'aids and abets *or* does any act preparatory to the commission of an offence') the underlying assumption was that the Act was framed to fit in with the general pattern of the criminal law. Similarly, in *Riddell* v. *Reid* (1942) (where the majority of the House of Lords held that the words 'outside the area of the building under construction' in the preamble to the Building Regulations 1926 made under s.79 of the Factory and Workshop Act 1901 could be read in effect as 'outside the area used in the building operations') the finding that a strict construction would be 'narrow and unprofitable' (Lord Thankerton), 'illogical and inexplicable' (Lord Russell of Killowen) and 'paradoxical' and 'generally inconvenient and unworkable' (Lord Wright) can only be explained by reference to the purpose of the Building Regulations and their parent Act. In fact the golden rule on closer examination turns out to be a less explicit form of the mischief rule.

The mischief rule as expressed in *Heydon's Case* (1584) describes on one view a somewhat more satisfactory approach to the interpretation of statutes. But, apart from the archaism of its language, it reflects a very different constitutional balance between the Executive, Parliament and the public than would now be acceptable. Hence, particularly under its fourth head, in its emphasis on the suppression of the mischief and, in effect, adaptation of the remedy for that purpose, it does not make it clear to what extent the judge should consider the actual language in which the specific remedies contained in the statute are communicated to the public. *Heydon's Case* is also somewhat outdated in its approach, because it assumes that statute is subsidiary or supplemental to the common law, whereas in modern conditions many statutes mark a fresh point of departure rather than a mere addition to and qualification of, common law principles. Furthermore, the mischief rule was enunciated before the rules excluding certain material, which might bear on the mischief and 'true reason of the remedy,' had been developed. If a court has inadequate means of discovering the policy behind a statute, a mere exhortation to consider that policy may not be very effective. . . . "

D   The Purposive Approach

"Judicial legislation is not an option open to an English judge. Our courts are not required, as are, for instance, the Swiss courts (see the Swiss Civil Code, articles 1 and 2), to declare and insert into legislation rules which the judge would have put there, had he been the legislator. But our courts do have the duty of giving effect to the intention of Parliament, if it be possible, even though the process requires a strained construction of the language used or the insertion of words in order to do so ... The line between judicial legislation, which our law does not permit, and judicial interpretation in a way best designed to give effect to the intention of Parliament is not an easy one to draw. Suffice it to say that before our courts can imply words into a statute the statutory intention must be plain and the insertion not too big, or too much at variance with the language used by the legislature. The courts will strain against ... leaving unfilled the *'casus omissus,'* per Scarman L.J., *Western Bank* v. *Schindler* [1970] Ch. 1, C.A."

Coltman and Another v. Bibby Tankers Ltd., The Derbyshire

[1987] 3 All E.R. 1068, H.L.

In 1980 a 90,000-ton bulk carrier sank off Japan. The plaintiffs, personal representatives of a member of the crew, brought an action against the defendant, the owner of the ship, alleging that the ship was unseaworthy owing to defect in its hull. By section 1(1) of the Employer's Liability (Defective Equipment) Act 1969 where "an employee suffers personal injury in the course of his employment in consequence of a defect in equipment provided by his employer for the purposes of the employer's business" the employer is made liable. By section 1(3) " 'equipment' includes any plant and machinery, vehicle, aircraft and clothing." The defendant contended that the ship itself could not constitute "equipment" within the Act. The C.A., reversing the trial judge, held that the ship did not constitute equipment, but the decision of the C.A. was reversed by the H.L.

Lord Goff of Chieveley

My Lords, I am entirely in agreement with my noble and learned friend Lord Oliver, that, for the reasons he gives, a ship may form part of the "equipment" of the business of a shipowner, on the natural and ordinary meaning of that word. Accordingly, if the word "equipment" were not defined in the Employer's Liability (Defective Equipment) Act 1969, I would have no difficulty in deciding the present case in favour of the plaintiffs. The real difficulty in the case, as it seems to me, arises from the fact that the word "equipment" is defined in s.1(3) of the 1969 Act, and that the definition expressly includes any vehicle and aircraft, but makes no mention of ships or vessels. This fact provided the basis for the powerful submission advanced on behalf of the defendants that Parliament could not, in these circumstances, have inadvisedly excluded ships or vessels from the definition and must therefore have intended, for some reason, to exclude them.

I have struggled to discover any rational basis for such a deliberate exclusion. The only possible basis which has occurred to me is as follows. It is, I understand, accepted that, in respect of operations on land, the 1969 Act only provides protection for the employee in respect of defects in equipment provided by the employer on the premises, but provides no protection in respect of defects in the premises themselves. It might therefore have been thought that, in respect of operations at sea, a similar distinction should be drawn between defects in equipment provided by the employer on the relevant ship, and defects in the structure of the ship itself. In both cases, whether the defect is in the structure of a building or in the structure of a ship, the employee would, on this hypothesis, be restricted to his rights against his employer as occupier, even where the defect in the building or the ship was attributable to the fault of a third party. In both cases, no doubt, nice distinctions might have to be drawn between equipment on the one hand and the structure of the building or the ship on the other hand; but, since it is plain that in any event such distinctions would have to be drawn in the case of premises on land, it is not necessarily surprising that Parliament should have intended similar distinctions to be drawn in respect of a ship at sea, although it is likely that more difficult questions could arise in the case of ships than in the case of premises on land. If this were to be right, it would explain why ships or vessels were excluded from the definition of "equipment" in the Act, and it would follow that the appeal in the present case would have to be dismissed.

I must confess to having felt some attraction for this approach, as a matter of logic; but I have come to the conclusion that its practical consequences are such that I do not think that it can have been the intention of the legislature so to provide. As my noble and learned friend Lord Oliver points out in his speech, ships or vessels may vary enormously in character and in size, from the Trinity House launch or even a speedboat to a supertanker or a bulk carrier. It is very difficult indeed to imagine that small craft should be excluded from "equipment" provided by the employer for the purposes of his business; but no sensible distinction can be drawn between small and large vessels for present purposes; certainly the approach which I have set out provides no basis for any such distinction. Moreover, it seems to me that, in the case of ships, the distinction between the equipment on the ship and the structure of the ship is not only very difficult to draw in practice, but is artificial in the extreme. In any event, the duty of care imposed under the Occupiers' Liability Act 1957 may apply not only in respect of vessels, but also in respect of vehicles and aircraft: see s.1(3)(*a*). I have therefore come to the conclusion, in agreement with my noble and learned friend, and with Lloyd L.J. in the Court of Appeal, that the definition of equipment in s.1(3) of the 1969 Act must have been included in the Act for the purpose of clarification only, and that the mere fact that ships and vessels were not expressly included in the definition cannot have been intended to have the effect of cutting down the ordinary meaning of the word "equipment" by excluding ships or vessels from that word.

For these reasons I too would allow the appeal.

Questions

1.   Parliament had included within its definition of equipment vehicles and aircraft, *i.e.* vessels which travel by land or air. Had it meant to include ships, *i.e.* vessels which travel by sea, would it not have said so expressly? If this was an oversight, was it right for the H.L. to fill in the gap?

2. Is the word "includes" in section 1(3) significant?
3. Assuming *Coltman* v. *Bibby* had fallen to be decided after *Pepper* v. *Hart*, is this a case in which reference to parliamentary proceedings should be made? Such a reference would have disclosed that it was *not* intended to include ships (see *Dobson*, [1988] Stat.L.R. 126).

E Examples of Statutory Interpretation

Smith v. Hughes

[1960] 1 W.L.R. 830 (D.C.)

Lord Parker C.J. These are six appeals by way of case stated by one of the stipendiary magistrates sitting at Bow Street, before whom informations were preferred by police officers against the defendants, in each case that she "being a common prostitute, did solicit in a street for the purpose of prostitution, contrary to section 1(1) of the Street Offences Act, 1959." The magistrate in each case found that the defendant was a common prostitute, that she had solicited and that the solicitation was in a street, and in each case fined the defendant.

The facts, to all intents and purposes, raise the same point in each case; there are minute differences. The defendants in each case were not themselves physically in the street but were in a house adjoining the street. In one case the defendant was on a balcony and she attracted the attention of men in the street by tapping and calling down to them. In other cases the defendants were in ground-floor windows, either closed or half open, and in another case in a first-floor window.

The sole question here is whether in those circumstances each defendant was soliciting in a street or public place. The words of section 1(1) of the Act of 1959 are in this form: "It shall be an offence for a common prostitute to loiter or solicit in a street or public place for the purpose of prostitution." Observe that it does not say there specifically that the person who is doing the soliciting must be in the street. Equally, it does not say that it is enough if the person who receives the solicitation or to whom it is addressed is in the street. For my part, I approach the matter by considering what is the mischief aimed at by this Act. Everybody knows that this was an Act intended to clean up the street, to enable people to walk along the streets without being molested or solicited by common prostitutes. Viewed in that way, it can matter little whether the prostitute is soliciting while in the street or is standing in a doorway or on a balcony, or at a window, or whether the window is shut or open or half open; in each case her solicitation is projected to and addressed to somebody walking in the street. For my part, I am content to base my decision on that ground and that ground alone. I think the magistrate came to a correct conclusion in each case, and that these appeals should be dismissed.

Fisher v. Bell

[1960] 3 W.L.R. 919 (D.C.)

[By section 1(1) of the Restriction of Offensive Weapons Act 1959 "Any person who manufactures, sells or hires or offers for sale or hire or lends nor gives to any other person—(a) any knife which has a blade which opens automatically by hand pressure applied to a button, spring or other device in or attached to the handle of the knife, sometimes known as a 'flick knife'... shall be guilty of an offence...."

The defendant displayed in his shop window a knife bearing a ticket which stated, "Ejector knife—4s." When a constable entered the shop and told him he would be reported for offering the knife for sale the defendant replied, "Fair enough."]

Lord Parker C.J.   read section 1(1), Restriction of Offensive Weapons Act 1959, stated the facts and continued: The sole question is whether the exhibition of that knife in the window with the ticket constituted an offer for sale within the statute. I confess that I think most lay people and, indeed, I myself when I first read the papers, would be inclined to the view that to say that if a knife was displayed in a window like that with a price attached to it was not offering it for sale was just nonsense. In ordinary language it is there inviting people to buy it, and it is for sale; but any statute must of course be looked at in the light of the general law of the country. Parliament in its wisdom in passing an Act must be taken to know the general law. It is perfectly clear that according to the ordinary law of contract the display of an article with a price on it in a shop window is merely an invitation to treat. It is in no sense an offer for sale the acceptance of which constitutes a contract. That is clearly the general law of the country. Not only is that so, but it is to be observed that in many statutes and orders which prohibit selling and offering for sale of goods it is very common when it is so desired to insert the words "offering or exposing for sale," "exposing for sale" being clearly words which would cover the display of goods in a shop window. Not only that, but it appears that under several statutes—we have been referred in particular to the Prices of Goods Act 1939, and the Goods and Services (Price Control) Act 1941—Parliament, when it desires to enlarge the ordinary meaning of those words, includes a definition section enlarging the ordinary meaning of "offer for sale" to cover other matters including, be it observed, exposure of goods for sale with the price attached.

In those circumstances I am driven to the conclusion, though I confess reluctantly, that no offence was here committed. At first sight it sounds absurd that knives of this sort cannot be manufactured, sold, hired, lent, or given, but apparently they can be displayed in shop windows; but even if this—and I am by no means saying it is—is a *casus omissus* it is not for this court to supply the omission. I am mindful of the strong words of Lord Simonds in *Magor and St. Mellons Rural District Council* v. *Newport Corporation* (1952). In that case one of the Lords Justices in the Court of Appeal had, in effect, said that the court having discovered the supposed intention of Parliament must proceed to fill in the gaps—what the legislature has not written the court must write—and in answer to that contention Lord Simonds in his speech said: "It appears to me to be a naked usurpation of the legislative function under the thin disguise of interpretation."

Approaching this matter apart from authority, I find it quite impossible to say that an exhibition of goods in a shop window is itself an offer for sale. We were, however, referred to several cases, one of which is *Keating* v. *Horwood* (1926) a decision of this court. There, a baker's van was being driven on its rounds. There was bread in it that had been ordered and bread in it that was for sale, and it was found that that bread was under weight contrary to the Sale of Food Order 1921. That order was an order of the sort to which I have referred already which prohibited the offering or exposing for sale. In giving his judgment, Lord Hewart C.J. said this: "The question is whether on the facts there were, (1) an offering, and (2) an exposure, for sale. In my opinion, there were both." Avory J. said: "I agree and have nothing to add." Shearman J., however, said: "I am of the same opinion. I am quite clear that this bread was exposed for sale, but have some doubt whether it can be said to have been offered for sale until a particular loaf was tendered to a particular customer." There are three matters to observe on the case. The first is that the order plainly contained the words "expose for sale," and on any view there was an exposing for sale. Therefore the question whether there was an offer for sale was unnecessary for decision. Secondly, the principles of general contract law were never referred to, and thirdly, albeit all part of the second ground, the respondent was not represented and there was in fact no argument. I cannot take that as an authority for the proposition that the display here in a shop window was an offer for sale.

... Accordingly, I have come to the conclusion in this case that the justices were right, and this appeal must be dismissed.

Questions

1. Was not what was done by the defendant in *Fisher* v. *Bell* within the mischief aimed at by the Act? If so, why did not Lord Parker C.J. apply the Mischief Rule as he had done in *Smith* v. *Hughes* (1960)?

2. Would *Smith* v. *Hughes* (1960) have been decided the same way by applying the Literal Rule? Note that Hilberry J., while agreeing with Lord Parker, said that the men were solicited "in a street" since that was where the soliciting took place. But on this view what would the position be if the prostitute was in the street and solicited a man who was on private premises?

3. Lord Parker admits in *Fisher* v. *Bell* that most lay people (note that most Members of Parliament are lay people) would think it was "nonsense" to say that the defendant was not offering the flick knife for sale. In that case should not the ordinary meaning of the phrase, (*i.e.* the meaning as understood by ordinary people) have been given to it?

4. If the court in *Fisher* v. *Bell* had given to "offers for sale" its "usual" as opposed to its "unusual" meaning, (*i.e.* the technical meaning the phrase has for the lawyer) would Lord Simonds really have regarded this as "a naked usurpation of the legislative function"?

Adler v. George

[1964] 2 Q.B. 7 (D.C.)

Lord Parker C.J.   This is an appeal by way of case stated from a decision of justices for the county of Norfolk sitting at Downham Market who convicted the defendant of an offence contrary to section 3 of the Official Secrets Act 1920, in that, in the vicinity of a prohibited place, namely, Marham Royal Air Force station, he obstructed a member of Her Majesty's Forces engaged in security duty in relation to the said prohibited place.

Section 3 provides that: "No person in the vicinity of any prohibited place shall obstruct, knowingly mislead or otherwise interfere with or impede, the chief officer or a superintendent or other officer of police, or any member of His Majesty's forces engaged on guard, sentry, patrol, or other similar duty in relation to the prohibited place, and, if any person acts in contravention of, or fails to comply with, this provision, he shall be guilty of a misdemeanour." In the present case the defendant had obtained access to—it matters not how—and was on the Air Force station on May 11, 1963, and there and then, it was found, he obstructed a member of Her Majesty's Royal Air Force.

The sole point here, and a point ably argued by the defendant, is that if he was on the station he could not be in the vicinity of the station, and it is only an offence under this section to obstruct a member of Her Majesty's Forces while he is in the vicinity of the station. The defendant has referred to the natural meaning of "vicinity," which I take to be, quite generally, the state of being near in space, and he says that it is inapt to and does not cover being in fact on the station as in the present case.

I am quite satisfied that this is a case where no violence is done to the language by reading the words "in the vicinity of" as meaning "in or in the vicinity of." Here is a section in an Act of Parliament designed to prevent interference with members of Her Majesty's forces, among others, who are engaged on guard, sentry, patrol or other similar duty in relation to a prohibited place such as this station. It would be extraordinary, I venture to think it would be absurd, if an indictable offence was thereby created when the obstruction took place outside the precincts of the station, albeit in the vicinity, and no offence at all was created if the obstruction occurred on the station itself. It is to be observed that if the defendant is right, the only offence committed by him in obstructing such a member of the Air Force would be an offence contrary to section 193 of the Air Force Act 1955, which creates a summary offence, the maximum sentence for which is three months, whereas section 3 of the Official Secrets Act 1920, is, as one would expect, dealing with an offence which can be tried on indictment and for which, under section 8, the maximum sentence of imprisonment is one of two years. There may be, of course, many contexts in which "vicinity" must be confined to its literal meaning of "being near in space" but under this section, I am quite clear that the context demands that the words should be construed in the way I have said. I would dismiss this appeal.

Questions

1. In this case Lord Parker adds two words, "in or," to the statute which were not there before. Is this not a naked usurpation of the legislative function?

2. Since it was clear in *Fisher* v. *Bell* that Parliament meant to penalise the shopkeeper who placed flick knives in his window, could not Lord Parker, on the reasoning of *Adler* v. *George*, have just as easily added two words so that the section would have read "offers *or exposes* for sale"?

3. In which, if any, of the cases in this section should a reference be made to Parliamentary proceedings?

F   The Interpretation of EEC Legislation

Bulmer Ltd. v. Bollinger S.A.

[1974] Ch. 401 (C.A.)

Lord Denning M.R. . . .

5.   *The impact of the Treaty on English law*

The first and fundamental point is that the Treaty concerns only those matters which have a European element, that is to say, matters which affect people or property in the nine countries of the common market besides ourselves. The Treaty does not touch any of the matters which concern solely England and the people in it. These are still governed by English law. They are not affected by the Treaty. But when we come to matters with a Europeran element, the Treaty is like an incoming tide. It flows into the estuaries and up the rivers. It cannot be held back, Parliament has decreed that the Treaty is henceforward to be part of our law. It is equal in force to any statute. The governing provision is section 2(1) of the European Communities Act 1972. It says:

"All such rights, powers, liabilities, obligations and restrictions from time to time created or arising by or under the Treaties, and all such remedies and procedures from time to time provided for by or under the Treaties, as in accordance with the Treaties are without further enactment to be given legal effect or used in the United Kingdom shall be recognised and available in law, and be enforced, allowed and followed accordingly; and the expression 'enforceable community right' and similar expressions shall be read as referring to one to which this subsection applies."

The statute is expressed in forthright terms which are absolute and all-embracing. Any rights or obligations created by the Treaty are to be given legal effect in England without more ado. Any remedies or procedures provided by the Treaty are to be made available here without being open to question. In future, in transactions which cross the frontiers, we must no longer speak or think of English law as something on its own. We must speak and think of community law, of community rights and obligations, and we must give effect to them. This means a great effort for the lawyers. We have to learn a new system. The Treaty, with the regulations and directives, covers many volumes. The case law is contained in hundreds of reported cases both in the European Court of Justice and in the national courts of the nine. Many must be studied before the right result can be reached. We must get down to it. . . .

10. *The principles of interpretation*

In view of these considerations, it is apparent that in very many cases the English courts will interpret the Treaty themselves. They will not refer the question to the European court at Luxembourg. What then are the principles of interpretation to be applied? Beyond doubt the English courts must follow the same principles as the European court. Otherwise there would be differences between the countries of the nine. That would never do. All the courts of all nine countries should interpret the Treaty in the same way. They should all apply the same principles. It is enjoined on the English courts by section 3 of the European Community Act 1972, which I have read.

What a task is thus set before us! The Treaty is quite unlike any of the enactments to which we have become accustomed. The draftsmen of our statutes have striven to express themselves with the utmost exactness. They have tried to foresee all possible circumstances that may arise and to provide for them. They have sacrificed style and simplicity. They have forgone brevity. They have become long and involved. In consequence, the judges have followed suit. They interpret a statute as applying only to the circumstances covered by the very words. They give them a literal interpretation. If the words of the statute do not cover a new situation—which was not foreseen — the judges hold that they have no power to fill the gap. To do so would be a "naked usurpation of the legislative function": see *Magor and St. Mellons Rural District Council* v. *Newport Corporation* [1952] A.C. 189, 191. The gap must remain open until Parliament finds time to fill it.

How different is this Treaty! It lays down general principles. It expresses its aims and purposes. All in sentences of moderate length and commendable style. But it lacks precision. It uses words and phrases without defining what they mean. An English lawyer would look for an interpretation clause, but he would look in vain. There is none. All the way through the Treaty there are gaps and lacunae. These have to be filled in by the judges, or by Regulations or directives. It is the European way. That appears from the decision of the Hamburg court in *In re Tax on Imported Lemons* [1968] C.M.L.R. 1.

Likewise the Regulations and directives. They are enacted by the Council sitting in Brussels for everyone to obey. They are quite unlike our statutory instruments. They have to give the reasons on which they are based: article 190. So they start off with pages of preambles, "whereas" and "whereas" and "whereas." These show the purpose and intent of the Regulations and directives. Then follow the provisions which are to be obeyed. Here again words and phrases are used without defining their import. Such as "personal conduct" in the Directive 64/221, article 3 (E.E.C.) which was considered by Pennycuick V.-C. in *Van Duyn* v. *Home Office* [1974] 1 W.L.R. 1107. In case of difficulty, recourse is had to the preambles. These are useful to show the purpose and intent behind it all. But much is left to the judges. The enactments give only an outline plan. The details are to be filled in by the judges.

Seeing these differences, what are the English courts to do when they are faced with a problem of interpretation? They must follow the European pattern. No longer must they examine the words in meticulous detail. No longer must they argue about the precise grammatical sense. They must look to the purpose or intent. To quote the words of the European court in the *Da Costa* case [1963] C.M.L.R. 224, 237, they must deduce "from the wording and the spirit of the Treaty the meaning of the community rules." They must not confine themselves to the English text. They must consider, if need be, all the authentic texts, of which there are now six: see *Sociale Verzekeringsbank* v. *Van der Vecht* [1968] C.M.L.R. 151. They must divine the spirit of the Treaty and gain inspiration from it. If they find a gap, they must fill it as best they can. They must do what the framers of the instrument would have done if they had thought about it. So we must do the same. Those are the principles, as I understand it, on which the European court acts.

2. CASE LAW

Cross, *Precedent in English Law* (3rd ed.), pp. 38–40

According to the preliminary statement of the English rules of precedent contained in the last chapter, every court is bound to follow any case decided by a court above it in the hierarchy, and appellate courts (other than the House of

Lords) are bound by their previous decisions. This statement is too concise because it does not indicate that the only part of a previous case which is binding is the *ratio decidendi* (reason for deciding). The principal object of the present chapter is to consider what is meant by the *ratio decidendi* of a case when the phrase is used by judges and other lawyers and by what methods it may be determined. This will show what is entailed by "following" or "applying" a case and by being "bound" by a previous decision, although these matters are not discussed until the beginning of the next chapter.

The *ratio decidendi* is best approached by a consideration of the structure of a typical judgment. The contemporary English judge almost invariably gives reasons for his decision in a civil case. Assuming that the trial is by a judge alone without a jury, he generally summarises the evidence, announces his findings of fact, and reviews the arguments that have been addressed to him by counsel for each of the parties. If a point of law has been raised, he often discusses a number of previous decisions. Nowadays it is comparatively seldom that a civil case is tried by a judge and jury. When there is a jury, the judge sums the evidence up to them and bases his judgment on their findings of fact. In criminal cases tried on indictment, the all-important feature from the point of view of a lawyer is the summing up to the jury. The form of the judgments in appellate courts is similar to that of a judge who tries a civil case without a jury. It consists of a review of the facts and arguments and a discussion of relevant questions of law. Several opinions are frequently delivered in appellate courts because appeals are always heard by more than one judge.

It is not everything said by a judge when giving judgment that constitutes a precedent. In the first place, this status is reserved for his pronouncements on the law, and no disputed point of law is involved in the vast majority of cases that are tried in any year. The dispute is solely concerned with the facts. For example, the issue may be whether a particular motorist was driving carelessly by failing to keep a proper lookout or travelling at an excessive speed. No one doubts that a motorist owes a legal duty to drive carefully and, very frequently, the only question is whether he was in breach of that duty when he caused damage to a pedestrian or another motorist. Cases in which the only issues are questions of fact are usually not reported in any series of law reports, but it is not always easy to distinguish law from fact and the reasons which led a judge of first instance or an appellate court to come to a factual conclusion are sometimes reported at length. For example, an employer is under a legal duty to provide his employees with a reasonably safe system of working. The question whether that duty has been broken is essentially one of fact, but the law reports contain a number of cases in which judges have expressed their views concerning the precautions which an employer should have taken in particular instances. When an injury would not have occurred if a workman had been wearing protective clothing it has been said that his employer ought to have insisted that such clothing should have been worn instead of merely rendering it available for those who desired to wear it, but the House of Lords has insisted that observations of this nature are not general propositions of law necessarily applicable to future cases and the decisions based upon them do not constitute a precedent. There is no point in endeavouring to ascertain the *ratio decidendi* of such cases.

The second reason why it is not everything said by a judge in the course of his judgment that constitutes a precedent is that, among the propositions of law enunciated by him, only those which he appears to consider necessary for his decision are said to form part of the *ratio decidendi* and thus to amount to more than an *obiter dictum*. If the judge in a later case is bound by the precedent according to the English doctrine of *stare decisis*, he must apply the earlier *ratio decidendi* however much he disapproves of it, unless, to use the words of Lord Reid, he considers that the two cases are "reasonably distinguishable." Dicta in earlier cases are, of course, frequently followed or applied, but dicta are never of more than persuasive authority. There is no question of any judge being bound to follow them. Even when the *ratio decidendi* of a previous case is merely a persuasive authority, it must be followed in later cases unless the judge has good reason to disapprove of it. It constitutes a precedent, and the difference between a persuasive precedent and an *obiter dictum* is only slightly less significant than that between binding and persuasive precedents. If, for example, a High Court judge of first instance comes to the conclusion that a proposition of law contained in a previous opinion of another High Court judge of first instance is *ratio*, he will be a great deal more reluctant to differ from it than would be the case if he was satisfied that it was merely a dictum, although a judge of first instance is not bound to follow the decision of another judge of first instance.

The law student soon learns to appreciate the importance of the distinction between *ratio* and *obiter dicta* but to realise that the distinction is important itself provides no test for determining which is which. And there is of course no test, in the sense of a formula, capable of being applied to a case which will automatically provide the answer. Take *Felthouse* v. *Bindley* (below, p. 422) for example. The case might be said to be authority for the proposition that silence cannot be construed as assent. But what it really decides is that on the facts of that case John Bindley's failure to reply to his nephew's offer did not bind John; it is not an authority for a general proposition that in no circumstances may silence be taken as assent. Professor Goodhart ("The Ratio Decidendi of a Case," *Essays in Jurisprudence and Common Law*) thought that in determining the *ratio* of a case certain things had to be kept in mind. Of prime importance, he thought, was to discover which facts the judge found and which of these he considered material. Note, it is the facts which the judge considers to be material, *not* the facts which we think he ought to have regarded as material (why?). The judge, however, will only rarely say which facts he regards as material and leaves this for others to determine; but if he does indicate which facts he regards as material and which he regards as immaterial then those facts must be accordingly so regarded. Goodhart then says:

"Having established the material and the immaterial facts of the case as seen by the court, we can then proceed to state the principle of the case. It is found in the conclusion reached by the judges on the basis of the material facts and on the exclusion of the immaterial ones. In a certain case the court finds that facts *A*, *B* and *C* exist. It then excludes fact *A* as immaterial, and on facts *B* and *C* it reaches conclusion *X*. What is the *ratio decidendi* of this case? There are two principles: (*a*) in any future case in which the facts are *A*, *B* and *C*, the court must reach conclusion *X*, and (*b*) in any future case in which the facts are *B* and *C*, the court must reach conclusion *X*. In the second case the absence of fact *A* does not affect the result, for fact *A* has been held to be immaterial. The court, therefore, creates a principle when it determines which are the material and which are the immaterial facts on which it bases its decision.

It follows that a conclusion based on a fact, the existence of which has not been determined by the court, cannot establish a principle. We then have what is called a *dictum*. If, therefore, a judge in the course of his opinion suggests a hypothetical fact, and then states what conclusion he would reach if that fact existed, he is not creating a principle."

Consider *Carlill* v. *Carbolic Smoke Ball Co.* [below, p. 409]. Write down what you consider to be the material facts of the case and its *ratio*. Obviously the sex of the plaintiff was not considered material; only Lindley L.J. tells us that the plaintiff was female but it is clear that he attaches no importance to this fact. Was it material that it was a Carbolic Smoke Ball that was sold to the plaintiff? Lindley L.J. helps here by saying, "What that is I do not know," and since he did not trouble to find out he cannot have regarded it as material. So what was material? That it was a patent medicine? Or is the case authority for the more general proposition that whenever the defendant claims certain properties for his wares, the goods must have those properties? Was it material that the defendants had lodged £1,000 with the Alliance Bank? All the judges mention this fact and lay at least some stress on it. Would the case have been decided otherwise if the £1,000 had not been deposited with the bank?

All cases are subject to this form of analysis. The lawyer is always concerned to determine (i) precisely for what does a case constitute a precedent; and (ii) does that precedent govern the case he has at hand. He will of course attempt to show that precedents he sees as favourable to his case are not properly distinguishable while he will seek to distinguish precedents he sees as unfavourable. To distinguish a case he must show that the facts are distinguishable in a material respect, so material that a different legal consequence must follow.

Chapter 2

The Operation of the Doctrine of Precedent

1. THE HOUSE OF LORDS

London Street Tramways v. London County Council

[1898] A.C. 375 (H.L.)

Earl of Halsbury L.C. My Lords, for my own part I am prepared to say that I adhere in terms to what has been said by Lord Campbell and assented to by Lord Wensleydale, Lord Cranworth, Lord Chelmsford and others, that a decision of this House once given upon a point of law is conclusive upon this House afterwards, and that it is impossible to raise that question again as if it was *res integra* and could be reargued, and so the House be asked to reverse its own decision. That is a principle which has been, I believe, without any real decision to the contrary, established now for some centuries, and I am therefore of opinion that in this case it is not competent for us to rehear and for counsel to reargue a question which has been recently decided.

. . . . . .

My Lords, it is totally impossible, as it appears to me, to disregard the whole current of authority upon this subject, and to suppose that what some people call an "extraordinary case," an "unusual case," a case somewhat different from the common, in the opinion of each litigant in turn, is sufficient to justify the rehearing and rearguing before the final Court of Appeal of a question which has been already decided. Of course I do not deny that cases of individual hardship may arise, and there may be a current of opinion in the profession that such and such a judgment was erroneous; but what is that occasional interference with what is perhaps abstract justice as compared with the inconvenience—the disastrous inconvenience—of having each question subject to being reargued and the dealings of mankind rendered doubtful by reason of different decisions, so that in truth and in fact there would be no real final Court of Appeal? My Lords, *"interest rei publicae"* there should be *"finis litium"* at some time, and that there could be no *"finis litium"* if it were possible to suggest in each case that it might be reargued, because it is *"not an ordinary case,"* whatever that may mean. Under these circumstances I am of opinion that we ought not to allow this question to be reargued.

Practice Statement (Judicial Precedent)

[1966] 1 W.L.R. 1234

Lord Gardiner L.C. Their Lordships regard the use of precedent as an indispensable foundation upon which to decide what is the law and its application to individual cases. It provides at least some degree of certainty upon which individuals can rely in the conduct of their affairs, as well as a basis for orderly development of legal rules.

Their Lordships nevertheless recognise that too rigid adherence to precedent may lead to injustice in a particular case and also unduly restrict the proper development of the law. They propose, therefore, to modify their present practice and, while treating former decisions of this House as normally binding, to depart from a previous decision when it appears right to do so.

In this connection they will bear in mind the danger of disturbing retrospectively the basis on which contracts, settlements of property and fiscal arrangements have been entered into and also the especial need for certainty as to the criminal law.

This announcement is not intended to affect the use of precedent elsewhere than in this House.

Since this Practice Direction previous decisions of the House of Lords have only exceptionally been seriously questioned and only very exceptionally have previous decisions been explicitly overruled. In *Moloney* (1985), below, p. 301) the House defined the *mens rea* of murder in terms markedly different from those set by its previous decision in *Hyam* (1975) but did not take the formal step of overruling *Hyam*. In *British Railways Board* v. *Herrington* (1972) the House stated an occupier's duty to trespassers in terms much more generous to the trespasser than had been stated in its decision in *Addie* v. *Dumbreck* (1929) but the law reporter cautiously noted that *Addie* had merely been "reconsidered." In the *Milliangos* case [1975] 2 All E.R. 801, below, p. 34, the reporter noted that an earlier decision of the H.L. had been "not followed" though it seems to have been overruled. In *Shivpuri* [1986] 2 All E.R. 334, below, p. 293, the House of Lords explicitly overruled its earlier decision in *Anderton* v. *Ryan* [1985] A.C. 560 and in *Howe* [1987] 1 All E.R. 771, below, p. 246, overruled its earlier decision in *Lynch* [1975] A.C. 653.

In *Food Corporation of India* v. *Antclizo Shipping* [1988] 2 All E.R. 513, the H.L. said it would not review a previous decision simply because that decision had given cause for concern unless its review would be relevant to the resolution of the case being heard by the H.L.

Questions

1. Was the House of Lords ever bound by its own decisions? May the House in some future case properly decide that it is bound by its own decisions?

2. Why the "especial" need for certainty in the criminal law? Is it not more important to avoid injustice in criminal cases than in civil cases? Compare the attitude of the Court of Appeal (Criminal Division) in this respect, below, p. 42.

2. COURT OF APPEAL (CIVIL DIVISION)

Young v. Bristol Aeroplane Company

[1944] K.B. 718 (C.A.)

Lord Greene M.R. The question thus raised as to the jurisdiction of this court to refuse to follow decisions of its own was obviously one of great general importance and directions were given for the appeal to be argued before the full court. It is surprising that so fundamental a matter should at this date still remain in doubt. To anyone unacquainted with the rare cases in which it has been suggested or asserted that this court is not bound to follow its own decisions or those of a court of coordinate jurisdiction the question would, we think, appear to be beyond controversy. Cases in which this court has expressed its regret at finding itself bound by previous decisions of its own and has stated in the clearest terms that the only remedy of the unsuccessful party is to appeal to the House of Lords are within the recollection of all of us and numerous examples are to be found in the reports. When in such cases the matter has been carried to the House of Lords it has never, so far as we know, been suggested by the House that this view was wrong and that this court could itself have done justice by declining to follow a previous decision of its own which it considered to be erroneous. On the contrary, the House has, so far as we are aware, invariably assumed and in many cases expressly stated that this court was bound by its own previous decision to act as it did. . . .

In considering the question whether or not this court is bound by its previous decisions and those of courts of co-ordinate jurisdiction, it is necessary to distinguish four classes of case. The first is . . . where this court finds itself confronted with one or more decisions of its own or of a court of co-ordinate jurisdiction which cover the question before it and there is no conflicting decision of this court or of a court of co-ordinate jurisdiction. The second is where there is such a conflicting decision. The third is where this court comes to the conclusion that a previous decision, although not expressly overruled, cannot stand with a subsequent decision of the House of Lords. The fourth (a special case) is where this court comes to the conclusion that a previous decision was given *per incuriam*. In the second and third classes of case it is beyond question that the previous decision is open to examination. In the second class, the court is unquestionably entitled to choose between the two conflicting decisions. In the third class of case the court is merely giving effect to what it considers to have been a decision of the House of Lords by which it is bound. The fourth class requires more detailed examination and we will refer to it again later in this judgment.

[His lordship reviewed previous decisions where conflicting views had been expressed on whether the Court of Appeal was bound by its previous decisions and continued:]

It remains to consider the quite recent case of *Lancaster Motor Co. (London)* v. *Bremith. Ld.* (1941) in which a court consisting of the present Master of the Rolls, Clauson L.J. and Goddard L.J., declined to follow an earlier decision of a court consisting of Slesser L.J. and Romer L.J. This was clearly a case where the earlier decision was given *per incuriam*. It depended on the true meaning (which in the later decision was regarded as clear beyond argument) of a rule of the Supreme Court to which the court was apparently not referred and which it obviously had not in mind. The Rules of the Supreme Court have statutory force and the court is bound to give effect to them as a statute. Where the court has construed a statute or a rule having the force of a statute its decision stands on the same footing as any other decision on a question of law, but where the court is satisfied that an earlier decision was given in ignorance of the terms of a statute or a rule having the force of a statute the position is very different. It cannot, in our opinion, be right to say that in such a case the court is entitled to disregard the statutory provision and is bound to follow a decision of its own given when that provision was not present to its mind. Cases of this description are examples of decisions given *per incuriam*. We do not think that it would be right to say that there may not be other cases of decisions given *per incuriam* in which this court might properly consider itself entitled not to follow an earlier decision of its own. Such cases would obviously be of the rarest occurrence and must be dealt with in accordance with their special facts. . . .

On careful examination of the whole matter we have come to the clear conclusion that this court is bound to follow previous decisions of its own as well as those of courts of co-ordinate jurisdiction. The only exceptions to this rule (two of them apparent only) are those already mentioned which for convenience we here summarise: (1.) The court is entitled and bound to decide which of two conflicting decisions of its own it will follow. (2.) The court is bound to refuse to follow a decision of its own which, though not expressly overruled, cannot, in its opinion, stand with a decision of the House of Lords. (3.) The court is not bound to follow a decision of its own if it is satisfied that the decision was given *per incuriam*.

Young was regarded as settling the question of precedent in the Court of Appeal until Lord Denning became Master of the Rolls in 1962. Lord Denning was never an aficionado of *stare decisis*. He was in *Broome* v. *Cassell & Co. Ltd.*, [1971] 2 W.L.R. 853 to take the view that the C.A. was not bound by a decision of the H.L. which, in the view of the C.A., had been decided *per incuriam* (in effect the C.A. could anticipate that the H.L. would not follow a prior decision). For this he was sternly taken to task by the H.L.: *Cassell & Co Ltd.* v. *Broome* [1972] 1 All E.R. 801. Lord Hailsham L.C. said, at p. 809:

"[I]t is not open to the Court of Appeal to give gratuitous advice to judges of first instance to ignore decisions of the House of Lords in this way and, if it were open to the Court of Appeal to do so, it would be highly undesirable. The course taken would have put the judges of first instance in an embarrassing position, as driving them to take sides in an unedifying dispute between the Court of Appeal or three members of it (for there is no guarantee that other Lords Justices would have followed them and no particular reason why they should) and the House of Lords. But, much worse than this, litigants would not have known where they stood. None could have reached finality short of the House of Lords and, in the meantime, the task of their professional advisers of advising them either as to their rights, or as to the probable cost of obtaining or defending them, would have been, quite literally, impossible. Whatever the merits, chaos would have reigned until the dispute was settled, and, in legal matters, some degree of certainty is at least as valuable a part of justice as perfection."

Lord Denning tried a different approach in *Schorsch Meier GmbH* v. *Hennin* [1975] Q.B. 416. Here a majority of the C.A. held that despite a ruling by the

H.L. to the contrary (*Re United Railways of the Havana and Regla Warehouses Ltd.*, [1960] 2 All E.R. 332) an English court could give a judgment in a currency other than sterling on the grounds *cessante ratione legis cessat ipsa lex* (when the reason for the rule ceases so also does the rule). *Schorsch*, which did not go to the H.L., was followed by the C.A. in *Milliangos* v. *George Frank (Textiles) Ltd.* [1975] 3 All E.R. 801 which did. While the H.L. held that a party was entitled to be paid in a currency other than sterling where the proper law governing the contract was the law of a country with a currency other than sterling, Lord Denning was once again rebuked. Lord Cross said (at p. 837):

"It will be apparent from what I have said that I do not view the decision of this House in the *Havana* case with any enthusiasm. Indeed, to speak bluntly, I think that it was wrong on both points. But as Lord Reid said in *Knuller* v. *Director of Public Prosecutions*, the fact that we no longer regard previous decisions of this House as absolutely binding does not mean that whenever we think that a previous decision was wrong we should reverse it. In the general interest of certainty in the law we must be sure that there is some very good reason before we so act. In the *Schorsch Meier* case, Lord Denning M.R., with the concurrence of Foster J., took it on himself to say that the decision in the *Havana* case that our courts cannot give judgment for payment of a sum of foreign currency— though right in 1961—ought not to be followed in 1974 because 'the reasons for the rule no longer exist.' I agree with my noble and learned friend, Lord Wilberforce, that Lord Denning M.R. was not entitled to take such a course. It is not for any inferior court—be it a county court or a division of the Court of Appeal presided over by Lord Denning M.R.—to review decisions of this House. Such a review can only be undertaken by this House itself under the declaration of 1966. Moreover, although one cannot but feel sympathy for Stephenson and Geoffrey Lane L.JJ. in the embarrassing position in which they found themselves, I think that it was wrong for the Court of Appeal in this case to follow the *Schorsch Meier* decision. It is no doubt true that that decision was not given '*per incuriam*' but I do not think that Lord Greene M.R., when he said in *Young* v. *Bristol Aeroplane Co. Ltd.* that the 'only' exceptions to the rule that the Court of Appeal is bound to follow previous decisions of its own were those which he set out, can fairly be blamed for not foreseeing that one of his successors might deal with a decision of the House of Lords in the way in which Lord Denning M.R. dealt with the *Havana* case. I propose, therefore, to consider this case as though the Court of Appeal had dismissed the appeal from Bristow J. and we were hearing an appeal to use by the respondents to depart from the *Havana* decision under the declaration of 1966."

These cases have settled, so far as the H.L. is concerned, that in no circumstances may an inferior court decline to follow a decision of the H.L. and it is unlikely in the extreme that the C.A. would now seek to circumvent a binding H.L. decision. One possible qualification to this appears from *Harper and others* v. *National Coal Board* [1974] Q.B. 614, where the C.A. held that it was not bound to follow a H.L. decision in which there was no discernible *ratio* and was accordingly bound to follow its own decision in that case.

But the rulings by the H.L. in *Cassell* v. *Broome* and *Milliangos* did not concern the operation of the doctrine of precedent so far as the C.A.'s own decisions were concerned. In a number of cases Lord Denning expressed his dislike for the principle in *Young* and the high point came in *Davis* v. *Johnson* (1978) (C.A.) where three (Lord Denning M.R., Baker P. and Shaw L.J.) of the five judges in the Court of Appeal stated that the Court of Appeal was not always bound by its previous decisions. Lord Denning did so on the broad ground that the Court of Appeal could depart from a previous decision where it was convinced it was wrong. Baker P. and Shaw L.J. expressed the power in more limited terms which appear in the next extract.

In the House of Lords (1978), where the decision of the Court of Appeal as to the merits was upheld, their Lordships were unanimous that the Court of Appeal should follow *Young.*

Davis v. Johnson

[1978] 2 W.L.R. 553 (H.L.)

Lord Diplock. So far as civil matters are concerned the law upon this question is now clear and unassailable. It has been so for more than 30 years. I do not find it necessary to trace the origin and development of the doctrine of *stare decisis* before the present structure of the courts was created in 1875. In that structure the Court of Appeal in civil actions has always played, save in a few exceptional matters, an intermediate and not a final appellate role. The application of the doctrine of *stare decisis* to decisions of the Court of Appeal was the subject of close examination by a Court of Appeal composed of six of its eight regular members in *Young* v. *Bristol Aeroplane Co. Ltd.* (1944). . . .

The rule as expounded in the *Bristol Aeroplane* case was not new in 1944. It had been acted upon on numerous occasions and had, as recently as the previous year, received the express confirmation of this House and Viscount Simon L.C. with whose speech Lord Atkin agreed: see *Perrin* v. *Morgan* (1943). Although prior to 1944 there had been an occasional deviation from the rule, which was why a court of six was brought together to consider it, there has been none since. It has been uniformly acted upon by the Court of Appeal and re-affirmed, notably in a judgment of a Court of Appeal of five, of which Lord Denning as Denning L.J. was a member, in *Morelle Ltd.* v. *Wakeling* (1955). This judgment emphasised the limited scope of the *per incuriam* exception to the general rule that the Court of Appeal is bound by its own previous decisions. The rule has also been uniformly accepted by this House as being correct. . . .

Furthermore, the provisions of the Administration of Justice Act 1969 which authorise 'leap-frog" appeals in civil cases direct from the High Court to this House are based on the tacit assumption that the rule as stated in the *Bristol Aeroplane* case is correct. One of the two grounds on which a High Court judge may authorise a "leap-frog" appeal is if he is satisfied that a point of law of general importance involved in his decision:

"is one in respect of which the judge is bound by a decision of the Court of Appeal or of the House of Lords in previous proceedings, and was fully considered in the judgments given by the Court of Appeal or the House of Lords (as the case may be) in those previous proceedings": s.12(3)(*b*).

The justification for by-passing the Court of Appeal when the decision by which the judge is bound is one given by the Court of Appeal itself in previous proceedings is because that court also is bound by the decision, if the point of law was fully considered and not passed over *per incuriam*.

So the rule as it had been laid down in the *Bristol Aeroplane* case (1944) had never been question thereafter until, following upon the announcement by Lord Gardiner L.C. in 1966 [*Practice Statement (Judicial Precedent) (1966)*] that the House of Lords would feel free in exceptional cases to depart from a previous decision of its own, Lord Denning M.R. conducted what may be described, I hope without offence, as a one-man crusade with the object of freeing the Court of Appeal from the shackles which the doctrine of *stare decisis* imposed upon its liberty of decision by the application of the rule laid down in the *Bristol Aeroplane* case to its own previous decisions; or, for that matter, by any decisions of this House itself of which the Court of Appeal disapproved: see *Broome* v. *Cassell & Co. Ltd.* (1972) and *Schorsch Meier GmbH* v. *Hennin* (1975). In his judgment in the instant appeal, Lord Denning M.R. refers to a number of cases after 1966 in which he suggests that the Court of Appeal has either refused to apply the rule as laid down in the *Bristol Aeroplane* case or has added so many other exceptions to the three that were stated by Lord Greene M.R. that it no longer operates as a curb on the power of the Court of Appeal to disregard any previous decision of its own which the majority of those members who happen to be selected to sit on a particular appeal think is wrong. Such, however, has not been the view of the other two members of the Court of Appeal who were sitting with the Master of the Rolls in any of those cases to which he refers. Where they felt able to disregard a previous decision of the Court of Appeal this was only because, in their opinion, it fell within the first or second exception stated in the *Bristol Aeroplane* case.

. . . . . .

The reasons why his colleagues had not agreed to follow him are plain enough. In an appellate court of last resort a balance must be struck between the need on the one side for the legal certainty resulting from the binding effort of previous decisions, and, on the other side the avoidance of undue restriction on the proper development of the law. In the case of an intermediate appellate court, however, the second desideratum can be taken care of by appeal to a superior appellate court, if reasonable means of access to it are available; while the risk to the first desideratum, legal certainty, if the court is not bound by its own previous decisions grows ever greater with increasing membership and the number of three-judge divisions in which it sits—as the arithmetic which I have earlier mentioned shows. So the balance does not lie in the same place as in the case of a court of last resort. That is why the Lord Chancellor's announcement about the future attitude towards precedent of the House of Lords in its judicial capacity concluded with the words: "This announcement is not intended to affect the use of precedent elsewhere than in this House." . . . . . .

In the instant case Lord Denning M.R. in effect reiterated his opinion that the Court of Appeal in relation to its own previous decisions should adopt the same rule as that which the House of Lords since the announcement in 1966 has applied in relation to its previous decisions. Sir George Baker P., on the other hand, preferred to deal with the problem of *stare decisis* by adding a new exception to the rule in the *Bristol Aeroplane* case (1944), which he formulated as follows (1978):

"The court is not bound to follow a previous decision of its own if satisfied that that decision was clearly wrong and cannot stand in the face of the will and intention of Parliament expressed in simple language in a recent statute passed to remedy a serious mischief or abuse, and further adherence to the previous decision must lead to injustice in the particular case and unduly restrict proper development of the law with injustice to others."

Shaw L.J. phrased the exception rather differently. He said:

"It would be in some such terms as that the principle of stare decisis should be relaxed where its application would have the effect of depriving actual and potential victims of violence of a vital protection which an Act of Parliament was plainly designed to afford to them, especially where, as in the context of domestic violence, that deprivation must inevitably give rise to an irremediable detriment to such victims and create in regard to them an injustice irreversible by a later decision of the House of Lords."

My Lords, the exception as stated by Sir George Baker P. would seem wide enough to cover any previous decision on the construction of a statute which the majority of the court thought was wrong and would have consequences that were regrettable, at any rate if they felt sufficiently strongly about it. As stated by Shaw L.J. the exception would appear to be what might be termed a "one-off" exception. It is difficult to think of any other statute to which it would apply.

In my opinion, this House should take this occasion to reaffirm expressly, unequivocally and unanimously that the rule laid down in the *Bristol Aeroplane* case (1944) as to *stare decisis* is still binding on the Court of Appeal.

Question

Is the Court of Appeal bound by what the House of Lords said in *Davis* v. *Johnson* in so far as it relates to the operation of the doctrine of precedent in the Court of Appeal?

Williams v. Fawcett

[1985] 1 All E.R. 787 (C.A.)

[The respondent was allegedly in breach of a court order not to molest the applicant and the applicant sought an order committing him for contempt. The respondent appealed on the grounds that the order did not specify the alleged breaches and was not signed by a "proper officer" of the court. The appeal was allowed on the first ground but the Court of Appeal held that notwithstanding decisions of its own to the contrary there was no requirement that the order be signed by a proper officer of the court.]

Sir John Donaldson M.R. If we are bound by these decisions, and we are unless they can be treated as having been reached *per incuriam*, they represent a very considerable change in the law for which, so far as I can see, there is absolutely no warrant. The change to which I refer is, of course, a requirement that these notices shall be signed by the proper officer. The rule of *stare decisis* is of the very greatest importance, particularly in an appellate court, such as this, which sits in six or seven divisions simultaneously. But for this rule, the law would not only bifurcate; it would branch off in six or seven different directions.

That of course has been stressed over and over again. It was emphasised in the classic case of *Young* v. *Bristol Aeroplane Co. Ltd.* (1944) and in *Morelle Ltd.* v. *Wakeling* (1955) which considered *Young's* case. But in each of those cases, as I will demonstrate briefly, the court retained the power in an exceptional case to depart from its previous decisions. Thus in *Young's* case (1944) Lord Greene M.R. said:

"Where the court has construed a statute or a rule having the force of a statute, its decision stands on the same footing as any other decision on a question of law. But where the court is satisfied that an earlier decision was given in ignorance of the terms of a statute or a rule having the force of a statute the position is very different. It cannot, in our opinion, be right to say that in such a case the court is entitled to disregard the statutory provision and is bound to follow a decision of its own given when that provision was not present to its mind. Cases of this description are examples of decisions given *per incuriam*. We do not think that it would be right to say that there may not be other cases of decisions given *per incuriam* in which this court might properly consider itself entitled not to follow an earlier decision of its own. Such cases would obviously be of the rarest occurrence and must be dealt with in accordance with their special facts."

Morelle's case was a five-judge Court of Appeal, although I hasten to add that it is now well-established that a five-judge Court of Appeal has no more authority than a three-judge Court of Appeal. It consisted of Evershed M.R, Denning, Jenkins, Morris and Romer L.JJ. I read from the judgment:

"As a general rule the only cases in which decisions should be held to have been given per incuriam are those of decisions given in ignorance or forgetfulness of some inconsistent statutory provision or of some authority binding on the court concerned; so that in such cases some part of the decision or some step in the reasoning on which it is based is found, on that account, to be demonstrably wrong. This definition is not necessarily exhaustive, but cases not strictly within it which can properly be held to have been decided per incuriam must, in our judgment, consistently with the stare decisis rule which is an essential feature of our law, be, in the language of Lord Greene M.R., of the rarest occurrence. In the present case, it is not shown that any statutory provision or binding authority was overlooked... As we have already said, it is, in our judgment, impossible to fasten on any part of the decision under consideration, or on any step in the reasoning on which the judgments were based, and to say of it: 'Here was a manifest slip or error.' "

In my judgment, one *can* say that in so far as the authorities which I have cited decide that a notice to show cause must be signed by the "proper officer" there was a manifest slip or error. There is no warrant for that proposition whatsoever either in the rules or in the statute. So I ask myself: is this case exceptional? I remind myself of the dangers of treating a decision as given *per incuriam* simply on the ground that it can be demonstrated to be wrong, even if the error is fairly clear on an examination of the authorities. However, for my part I think there are very exceptional features about the four decisions of this court to which I have referred and they are these.

There is, first of all, the clearness with which the growth of the error can be detected if the decisions are read consecutively. Second, these cases are all concerned with the liberty of the subject. It is true that if we were to leave the law as it has been declared to be, namely that these notices have to be signed by the proper officer, there are a number of subjects who would have to be released forthwith, because it is almost unknown for any notice to show cause to be signed by the proper officer. The change would, therefore, be beneficial to some subjects. But the other side of the coin is that these cases are also concerned with the maintenance of the authority of the courts to insist on obedience to their orders. They are therefore in a very special category. They are also, as I have said, cases which appear to be by no means unusual. Unfortunately there are a number of committals for contempt, particularly in the field of domestic violence. They are cases which are most unlikely to reach the House of Lords, which, if we do not act, is alone able to correct the error which has crept into the law.

I say that such a case is unlikely to reach the House of Lords because if the law is to be left as it has evolved, then this court would quash the committal order and it would be for the respondent to take the case to the House of Lords. I doubt whether any respondents would take that course, bearing in mind that there would be a substantial delay before the appeal to the House of Lords was heard and that he or she would, probably rightly, consider it unlikely that the House of Lords would require the contemnor to return to prison to complete his sentence.

Rickards v. Rickards

[1989] 3 All E.R. 193 (C.A.)

[In matrimonial proceedings an order was made against the husband with leave to appeal within five days. He failed to appeal within the allotted time and sought an extension but this was refused by the county court judge. He appealed to the Court of Appeal. In *Podbery* v. *Peak* ([1981] 1 All E.R. 699) the Court of Appeal had decided that it had no jurisdiction to hear an appeal from a county court judge's refusal to extend the time for appealing notwithstanding that the relevant provision in the County Courts Act (reading: "if any party to any proceedings in a county court is dissatisfied with the determination of the judge ... he may appeal from it to the Court of

Appeal") appeared not to place any such limitation on the jurisdiction of the Court of Appeal.]

Lord Donaldson M.R. ...

I am satisfied that this court erred in *Podbery* v. *Peak* in holding that *Lane* v. *Esdaile* applied to applications for an extension of time for appealing. Accordingly, I am confronted with the question of whether we are bound to, or should, follow it and thereby decline to exercise an appellate jurisdiction which I have no doubt that we have.

The importance of the rule of stare decisis in relation to the Court of Appeal's own decisions can hardly be overstated. We now sometimes sit in eight divisions and, in the absence of such a rule, the law would quickly become wholly uncertain. However, the rule is not without exceptions, albeit very limited. These exceptions were considered in *Young* v. *Bristol Aeroplane Co. Ltd.* [1944] 2 All E.R. 293, [1944] K.B. 718, *Morelle Ltd.* v. *Wakeling* [1955] 1 All E.R. 708, [1955] 2 Q.B. 379 and, more recently, in *Williams* v. *Fawcett* [1985] 1 All E.R. 787 at 794–795, [1986] Q.B. 604 at 615–616, where relevant extracts from the two earlier decisions are set out. These decisions show that this court is justified in refusing to follow one of its own previous decisions not only where that decision is given in ignorance or forgetfulness of some inconsistent statutory provision or some authority binding on it, but also, in rare and exceptional cases, if it is satisfied that the decision involved a manifest slip or error.

In previous cases the judges of this court have always refrained from defining this exceptional category and I have no intention of departing from that approach save to echo the words of Lord Greene M.R. (in *Young*'s case [1944] 2 All E.R. 293 at 300, [1944] 1 K.B. 718 at 729) and Evershed M.R. (in *Morelle*'s case [1955] 1 All E.R. 708 at 718, [1955] 2 Q.B. 379 at 406) and to say that they will be of the rarest occurrence. Nevertheless, some general considerations are relevant. First, the preferred course must always be to follow the previous decision, but to give leave to appeal in order that the House of Lords may remedy the error. This was attempted in *Bokhari* v. *Mahmood*, but failed because of the understandable reluctance of the defendant to prosecute the appeal. Second, certainty in relation to substantive law is usually to be preferred to correctness, since this at least enables the public to order their affairs with confidence. Erroneous decisions as to procedural rules affect only the parties engaged in the relevant litigation. This is a much less extensive group and, accordingly, a departure from established practice is to that extent less undesirable. Third, an erroneous decision which involves the jurisdiction of the court is particularly objectionable, either because it will involve an abuse of power if the true view is that the court has no jurisdiction or a breach of the court's statutory duty if the true view is that the court is wrongly declining jurisdiction. Such a decision, of which this case provides an example, is thus in a special category. Nevertheless, this court must have very strong reasons if any departure from its own previous decisions is to be justifiable. Indeed, it has only done so on one previous occasion of which I am aware (see *Williams* v. *Fawcett*).

In the instant case, I am fully satisfied that we are justified in treating *Podbery* v. *Peak* as a decision given per incuriam. It involves a wrongful rejection of the jurisdiction of this court and, if we follow it, there is no possibility of an appeal to the House of Lords in the instant case. In the light of our decision on the merits of the husband's appeal, he has no incentive to appeal and the wife, having succeeded, cannot do so. The decision in *Podbery* v. *Peak* is likely to affect a large number of decisions in matrimonial causes which, although of vital importance to the parties, arise in circumstances in which neither party can be expected to pursue the matter to the House of Lords because of the cost which, in the case of legally aided appeals, may still ultimately fall on the parties because of the legal aid funds' charge. It is therefore unlikely to be considered by the House of Lords in any other case and mean while we should be in continuing breach of our statutory duty.

I would therefore hold that we have jurisdiction to entertain the husband's appeal.

3.   COURT OF APPEAL (CRIMINAL DIVISION)

R. v. Gould

[1968] 2 Q.B. 65 (C.A.)

Diplock L.J.   The question of law in this appeal is whether, on a charge of bigamy under section 57 of the Offences against the Person Act 1861, a defendant's honest belief upon reasonable grounds that at the time of his second marriage his former marriage had been dissolved is a good defence to the charge. In *R.* v. *Wheat* (1921) the Court of Criminal Appeal decided that it was not. The deputy chairman rightly regarded himself as bound by that decision. But we are not.

In its criminal jurisdiction, which it has inherited from the Court of Criminal Appeal, the Court of Appeal does not apply the doctrine of *stare decisis* with the same rigidity as in its civil jurisdiction. If upon due consideration we were to be of opinion that the law had been either misapplied or misunderstood in an earlier decision of this court or its predecessor, the Court of Criminal Appeal, we should be entitled to depart from the view as to the law expressed in the earlier decision notwithstanding that the case could not be brought within any of the exceptions laid down in *Young* v. *Bristol Aeroplane Co. Ltd.* (1944) as justifying the Court of Appeal in refusing to follow one of its own decisions in a civil case (*Rex* v. *Taylor*) (1950). *A fortiori*, we are bound to give effect to the law as we think it is if the previous decision to the contrary effect is one of which the *ratio decidendi* conflicts with that of other decisions of this court or its predecessors of co-ordinate jurisdiction.

Questions

1. Why should the rules relating to the precedent differ according to whether the Court of Appeal is exercising civil or criminal jurisdiction?
2. Why should the House of Lords recognise (see *Practice Statement* above, p. 30) the especial need for certainty in the criminal law which the Court of Appeal does not apparently recognise?

Note

It appears that the Criminal Division will overrule a previous decision only where the liberty of the subject is involved; it will accordingly treat as binding a previous decision that is *favourable* to the defendant.

4. DIVISIONAL COURTS

Police Authority for Huddersfield v. Watson

[1947] K.B. 842 (D.C.)

Lord Goddard C.J. Mr. Streatfeild has argued that it is open to us to depart from *Garvin's* case (1944) if we think it was wrongly decided. As we have not heard his full argument, I prefer only to say this: Nothing that I have heard in this case, as far as the argument has gone, satisfies me that *Garvin's* case was wrongly decided; but whether it was rightly decided or not I am clearly of opinion that we ought to follow it. This court is made a final court of appeal in these matters, and I can imagine nothing more disastrous than that where the court has given a decision upon the construction or application of this Act another court should give a decision contrary to the decision already given, because there then would be two conflicting cases. You might get a court consisting perhaps of different judges choosing one of those decisions, and another court choosing the other decision, and there would be no finality in the matter at all. For myself, I think we ought to hold that we are bound by this decision, and I say so for this reason: The Court of Appeal in *Young* v. *Bristol Aeroplane Co. Ltd.* (1944), held, after argument before the full court of six judges, that the Court of Appeal was bound by its own decisions, with certain welldefined exceptions. [His Lordship referred to the *Young* exceptions and continued:]

If that is the rule which is applicable in the Court of Appeal—it is to be remembered that Court of Appeal judgments are reviewable in the House of Lords, at any rate by leave—and the Master of the Rolls pointed out in the course of his judgment that in some cases Court of Appeal judgments are final, as in bankruptcy, and in others are reviewable by the House of Lords, and yet he draws no distinction—and if, therefore, in a court most of whose decisions are reviewable, although it may be only by leave, in the House of Lords, those decisions are binding on the court, how much more important is it that this court, which is a final court, should follow its own decisions and consider that it ought to give full force and effect to them. Otherwise, as I have said, a great deal of uncertainty would be introduced into the law.

I know that in the writings of various eminent people the doctrine of *stare decisis* has been canvassed from time to time. In my opinion, if one thing is certain it is that *stare decisis* is part of the law of England, and in a system of law such as ours, where the common law, and equity largely, are based on decisions, it seems to me it would be very unfortunate if a court of final appeal has given a decision and has laid down a definite principle and it cannot be said the court has been misled in any way by not being referred to authorities, statutory or judicial, which bear on the question, that it should then be said that that decision was not to be a binding authority.

Watson's case concerned a matter of civil law but in *Younghusband* v. *Luftig* (1949) it was said that the position was the same in relation to criminal cases.

But in R. v. *Greater Manchester Coroner, ex p. Tal* [1984] 3 All E.R. 240, the view was expressed that in relation to criminal cases the Divisional Court should adopt the more flexible approach of the Criminal Division of the Court of Appeal.

5.   OTHER COURTS

Judges of the High Court are not bound by the decisions of their fellow judges in the High Court. It has been assumed, though not authoritatively established, that circuit judges and magistrates are bound by decisions of the High Court.

Chapter 3

The Legal System in Operation

1. POLICE POWERS: GENERAL

R. v. Dytham

[1979] Q.B. 722 (C.A.)

Lord Widgery C.J....

The appellant was a police constable in Lancashire. On March 17, 1977, at about 1 a.m. he was on duty in uniform and was standing by a hot dog stall in Duke Street, St. Helens. A Mr. Wincke was inside the stall and a Mr. Sothern was by it. Some 30 yards away was the entrance to Cindy's Club. A man named Stubbs was ejected from the club by a bouncer. A fight ensued in which a number of men joined. There arose cries and screams and other indications of great violence. Mr. Stubbs became the object of a murderous assault. He was beaten and kicked to death in the gutter outside the club. All this was audible and visible to the three men at the hot dog stall. At no stage did the appellant make any move to intervene or any attempt to quell the disturbance or to stop the attack on the victim. When the hubbub had died down he adjusted his helmet and drove away. According to the other two at the hot dog stall, he said that he was due off and was going off.

His conduct was brought to the notice of the police authority. As a result he appeared on October 10, 1978, at the Crown Court at Liverpool to answer an indictment which was in these terms:

"The charge against you is one of misconduct of an officer of justice, in that you...misconducted yourself whilst acting as an officer of justice in that you being present and a witness to a criminal offence namely a violent assault upon one...Stubbs by three others deliberately failed to carry out your duty as a police constable by wilfully

46

omitting to take any steps to preserve the Queen's peace or to protect the person of the said ... Stubbs or to arrest or otherwise bring to justice [his] assailants."

On arrangement the appellant pleaded not guilty and the trial was adjourned to November 7. On that day, before the jury was empanelled, counsel for the appellant took an objection to the indictment by way of demurrer. The burden of that objection was that the indictment as laid disclosed no offence known to the law. Neill J. ruled against the objection and the trial proceeded. The defence on the facts was that the appellant had observed nothing more than that a man was turned out of the club. It was common ground that in that situation his duty would not have required him to take any action. The jury were directed that the crucial question for their consideration was whether the defendant had seen the attack on the victim. If he had they could find him guilty of the offence charged in the indictment. The jury did return a verdict of guilty. Hence this appeal which is confined to the matters of law raised by the demurrer pleaded at the court of trial.

At the outset of his submissions in this court counsel for the appellant conceded two matters. The first was that a police constable is a public officer. The second was that there does exist at common law an offence of misconduct in a public office.

From that point the argument was within narrow limits though it ran deep into constitutional and jurisprudential history. The effect of it was that not every failure to discharge a duty which devolved on a person as the holder of a public office gave rise to the common law offence of misconduct in that office. As counsel for the appellant put it, non-feasance was not enough. There must be a malfeasance or at least a misfeasance involving an element of corruption. In support of this contention a number of cases were cited from the eighteenth and nineteenth century reports. It is the fact that in nearly all of them the misconduct asserted involved some corrupt taint; but this appears to have been an accident of circumstance and not a necessary incident of the offence. Misconduct in a public office is more vividly exhibited where dishonesty is revealed as part of the dereliction of duty. Indeed in some cases the conduct impugned cannot be shown to have been misconduct unless it was done with a corrupt or oblique motive. This was the position for example in *Rex* v. *Bembridge* (1783) 3 Doug.K.B. 327; and also in the modern case of *Reg.* v. *Llewellyn-Jones* [1968] 1 Q.B. 429. There the registrar of a county court was charged in a count which alleged that he had made an order in relation to funds under his control "in the expectation that he would gain personal advantage from the making of such order."

On a motion to quash the count as disclosing no offence known to the law I, as trial judge in the course of my ruling, made the following pronouncement, (1966) 51 Cr.App.R. 4, 6:

"The authorities to which I have been referred show that there is a variety of ways in which the holder of a public office may be indicted under this principle for misconduct or misbehaviour. It is clear that a culpable failure to exercise a public duty may, because the duty is a public one, lay the defaulter open to indictment for criminal offences, whereas, had he been working for a private employer, his default would have been no more than a civil liability. Even so, it is not easy to lay down with precision the exact limits of the kind of misconduct or misbehaviour which can result in an indictment under this rule. I have formed a clear view, but stated in hypothetical terms, that if the registrar of a county court when exercising his power to order payment out of court of money held on behalf of a beneficiary were to make an order in expectation of some personal benefit which he hoped to obtain and in circumstances where, had it not been for the personal benefit, he would not have made the order, that would be an example of misconduct in a public duty sufficient to come within this rule. The reason why I feel that that would come within the rule is because in that hypothetical case a public officer would be distorting the course of justice to meet his own personal ends and, in my opinion, it would be sufficient to justify a conviction if it could be shown that he had made such an order with intent to obtain personal benefit for himself and in circumstances in which there were no grounds for supposing that he would not have made the order but for his personal interest and expectation. On the other hand, I have reached an equally clear view that it is not enough to bring a county court registrar within the principle merely to show that, when making an order which was within his powers and which he could make for perfectly proper motives, he knew that by a side wind, as it were, he was going to gain some personal benefit. The mere fact that he knows of his personal interest is, in my view, a very good ground for his declining to exercise jurisdiction and for his arranging for someone else, such as the judge, to make an order for him. Everyone in judicial office knows how unwise it is to deal with a case in which personal interests are raised, but I would not be prepared to say that it would be misconduct for this purpose for a registrar to make a decision which did affect his personal interests, merely because he knew that his interests were so involved, if the decision was made honestly and in a genuine belief that it was a proper exercise of his jurisdiction so far as the beneficiaries and other persons concerned came into it.

When one looks at the terms of count 1 as it now stands, it seems to me that it alleges no more than knowledge on the part of the defendant that his personal interest was involved. For the reasons I have given, it is not enough to disclose an offence known to the law and, if the matter rested there, that count and others to which similar considerations apply would have to be quashed. On the other hand, it is not difficult to amend count 1 so as to introduce the vital element to which I have already referred and I am satisfied that such an amendment can be made without injustice in the circumstances of this case."

So also in *Reg.* v. *Wyat* (1705) 1 Salk. 380 it was held that "where an officer" (in that case a constable) "neglects a duty incumbent on him, either by common law or statute, he is for his default indictable." Counsel for the appellant contended that this was too wide a statement of principle since it omitted any reference to corruption or fraud; but in *Stephen's Digest of the Criminal Law*, 9th ed. (1950), p. 114, art. 145 are to be found these words:

"Every public officer commits a misdemeanour who wilfully neglects to perform any duty which he is bound either by common law or by statute to perform provided that the discharge of such duty is not attended with greater danger than a man of ordinary firmness and activity may be expected to encounter."

In support of this proposition *Reg.* v. *Wyat* is cited as well as *Rex* v. *Bembridge*, 3 Doug.K.B. 32, a judgment of Lord Mansfield. The neglect must be wilful and not merely inadvertent; and it must be culpable in the sense that it is without reasonable excuse or justification.

In the present case it was not suggested that the appellant could not have summoned or sought assistance to help the victim or to arrest his assailants. The charge as framed left this answer open to him. Not surprisingly he did not seek to avail himself of it, for the facts spoke strongly against any such answer. The allegation made was not of mere non-feasance but of deliberate failure and wilful neglect.

This involves an element of culpability which is not restricted to corruption or dishonesty but which must be of such a degree that the misconduct impugned is calculated to injure the public interest so as to call for condemnation and punishment. Whether such a situation is revealed by the evidence is a matter that a jury has to decide. It puts no heavier burden upon them than when in more familiar contexts they are called upon to consider whether driving is dangerous or a publication is obscene or a place of public resort is a disorderly house: see *Reg.* v. *Quinn* [1952] 2 Q.B. 245.

The judge's ruling was correct. The appeal is dismissed.

Appeal dismissed.

Questions

1. Suppose Dytham had been taking his annual holiday in St. Helens when he had witnessed the attack. Would he still have been liable for taking no action?

2. Lord Widgery says that to commit this offence the police officer's conduct must involve an element of culpability of such a degree that the misconduct impugned is calculated to injure the public interest so as to call for condemnation and punishment. Is this a helpful test for the jury to apply?

3. A police officer has a discretion in the enforcement of the criminal law and may in many situations properly give a friendly warning rather than institute criminal proceedings. Suppose a police officer decides to give a friendly warning to (i) a motorist who is driving at 100 m.p.h. along the M1; (ii) his chief constable who is also driving along the M1 at 100 m.p.h; (iii) boys of 14 and 15, whom he has apprehended stealing in a supermarket; and (iv) a pensioner who, at his wife's request and in order to end a pain-filled existence, had given her an overdose of drugs to end her life. Which, if any, of these actions would injure the public interest so as to call for condemnation and punishment?

2.   POLICE POWERS: INTERROGATION

The framework for interrogation is set by provisions of the Police & Criminal Evidence Act (PACE) and the Codes of Practice made thereunder. Part V of PACE (sections 34–52) deals with the timescale for detention and the duties of custody and review officers. These provisions are prolix and are not reproduced here; they are summarised in H.S.B. at pp. 110–112. So far as the conduct of interrogations is concerned two important provisions of PACE are sections 76 and 78.

76.—(1) In any proceedings a confession made by an accused person may be given in evidence against him so far as it is relevant to any matter in issue in the proceedings and is not excluded by the court in pursuance of this section.

(2) If, in any proceedings where the prosecution proposes to give in evidence a confession made by an accused person, it is represented to the court that the confession was or may have been obtained—

   (*a*)   by oppression of the person who made it; or

(*b*) in consequence of anything said or done which was likely, in the circumstances existing at the time, to render unreliable any confession which might be made by him in consequence thereof,

the court shall not allow the confession to be given in evidence against him except in so far as the prosecution proves to the court beyond reasonable doubt that the confession (notwithstanding that it may be true) was not obtained as aforesaid.

(3) In any proceedings where the prosecution proposes to give in evidence a confession made by an accused person, the court may of its own motion require the prosecution, as a condition of allowing it to do so, to prove that the confession was not obtained as mentioned in subsection (2) above.

(4) The fact that a confession is wholly or partly excluded in pursuance of this section shall not affect the admissibility in evidence—

(*a*) of any facts discovered as a result of the confession; or
(*b*) where the confession is relevant as showing that the accused speaks, writes or expresses himself in a particular way, of so much of the confession as is necessary to show that he does so.

(5) Evidence that a fact to which this subsection applies was discovered as a result of a statement made by an accused person shall not be admissible unless evidence of how it was discovered is given by him or on his behalf.

(6) Subsection (5) above applies—

(*a*) to any fact discovered as a result of a confession which is wholly excluded in pursuance of this section; and
(*b*) to any fact discovered as a result of a confession which is partly so excluded, if that fact is discovered as a result of the excluded part of the confession.

(7) Nothing in Part VII of this Act shall prejudice the admissibility of a confession made by an accused person.

(8) In this section "oppression" includes torture, inhuman or degrading treatment, and the use or threat of violence (whether or not amounting to torture).

78.—(1) In any proceedings the court may refuse to allow evidence on which the prosecution proposes to rely to be given if it appears to the court that, having regard to all the circumstances, including the circumstances in which the evidence was obtained, the admission of the evidence would have such an adverse effect on the fairness of the proceedings that the court ought not to admit it.

(2) Nothing in this section shall prejudice any rule of law requiring a court to exclude evidence.

The principal provisions of the Codes of Practice governing interrogation are as follows—

10 Cautions

(a) *Where a caution must be given*

10.1 A person whom there are grounds to suspect of an offence must be cautioned before any questions about it (or further questions if it is his answers to previous questions that provide grounds for suspicion) are put to him for the purpose of obtaining evidence which may be given to a court in a prosecution. He therefore need not be cautioned if questions are put for other purposes, for example, to establish his identity, his ownership of, or responsibility for, any vehicle or the need to search him in the exercise of powers of stop and search.

10.2   When a person who is not under arrest is initially cautioned before or during an interview at a police station or other premises, he must at the same time be told that he is not under arrest and is not obliged to remain with the officer.

10.3   A person must be cautioned upon arrest for an offence unless (a) it is impracticable to do so by reason of his condition or behaviour at the time; or (b) he has already been cautioned immediately prior to arrest in accordance with paragraph 10.1 above.

(b)   *Action—general*

10.4   The caution shall be in the following terms: "You do not have to say anything unless you wish to do so, but what you say may be given in evidence." Minor deviations do not constitute a breach of this requirement provided that the sense of the caution is preserved. [See Notes 10C and 10D]

10.5   When there is a break in questioning under caution the interviewing officer must ensure that the person being questioned is aware that he remains under caution. If there is any doubt the caution should be given again in full when the interview resumes. [See Note 10A.]

(c)   *Documentation*

10.6   A record shall be made when a caution is given under this section, either in the officer's pocket book or in the interview record as appropriate.

Notes for guidance

10A   In considering whether or not to caution again after a break, the officer should bear in mind that he may have to satisfy a court that the person understood that he was still under caution when the interview resumed.

10B   It is not necessary to give or repeat a caution when informing a person who is not under arrest that he may be prosecuted for an offence.

10C   If it appears that a person does not understand what the caution means the officer who has given it should go on to explain it in his own words.

10D   In case anyone who is given a caution is unclear about its significance the officer concerned should explain that the caution is given in pursuance of the general principle of English law that a person need not answer any questions or provide any information which might tend to incriminate him, and that no adverse inferences from this silence may be drawn at any trial that takes place. The person should not, however, be left with a false impression that non-co-operation will have no effect on his immediate treatment as, for example, his refusal to provide his name and address when charged with an offence may render him liable to detention.

11 Interviews—general

(a) *Action*

11.1 Following a decision to arrest a suspect he must not be interviewed about the relevant offence except at a police station (or other authorised place of detention) unless the consequent delay would be likely:

(a) to lead to interference with or harm to evidence connected with an offence or interference with or physical harm to other persons; or

(b) to lead to the alerting of other persons suspected of having committed an offence but not yet arrested for it; or

(c) to hinder the recovery of property obtained in consequence of the commission of such an offence.

Interviewing in any of these circumstances should cease once the relevant risk has been averted or the necessary questions have been put in order to attempt to avert that risk. For the definition of an interview see Note 11A.

11.2 Immediately prior to the commencement or re-commencement of any interview at a police station or other authorised place of detention, the interviewing officer should remind the suspect of his entitlement to free legal advice. It is the responsibility of the interviewing officer to ensure that all such reminders are noted in the record of interview.

11.3 No police officer may try to obtain answers to questions or to elicit a statement by the use of oppression or shall indicate, except in answer to a direct question, what action will be taken on the part of the police if the person being interviewed answers questions, makes a statement or refuses to do either. If the person asks the officer directly what action will be taken in the event of his answering questions, making a statement or refusing to do either, then the officer may inform the person what action the police propose to take in that event, provided that that action is itself proper and warranted.

11.4 As soon as a police officer who is making enquiries of any person about an offence believes that a prosecution should be brought against him and that there is sufficient evidence for it to succeed, he should ask the person if he has anything else to say. If the person indicates that he has nothing more to say the officer shall without delay cease to question him. This should not, however, be taken to prevent officers in revenue cases or acting under the confiscation provisions of the Criminal Justice Act 1988 or the Drug Trafficking Offences Act 1986 from inviting suspects to complete a formal question and answer record after the interview is concluded.

(b) *Interview records*

11.5 (a) An accurate record must be made of each interview with a person suspected of an offence, whether or not the interview takes place at a police station.

(b) The record must state the place of the interview, the time it begins and ends, the time the record is made (if different), any breaks in the interview and the names of all those present, and must be made on the forms provided for this purpose or in the officer's pocket-book or in accordance with the code of practice for the tape-recording of police interview with suspects.

(c) The record must be made during the course of the interview, unless in the investigating officer's view this would not be practicable or would interfere with the conduct of the interview, and must constitute either a verbatim record of what has been said or, failing this, an account of the interview which adequately and accurately summarises it.

11.6   The requirement to record the names of all those present at an interview does not apply to police officers interviewing persons detained under the Prevention of Terrorism (Temporary Provisions) Act 1989. Instead the record shall state the warrant number and duty station of such officers.

11.7   If an interview record is not made during the course of the interview it must be made as soon as practicable after its completion.

11.8   Written interview records must be timed and signed by the maker.

11.9   If an interview record is not completed in the course of the interview the reason must be recorded in the officer's pocket-book.

11.10   Unless it is impracticable the person interviewed shall be given the opportunity to read the interview record and to sign it as correct or to indicate the respects in which he considers it inaccurate. If the interview is tape-recorded the arrangements set out in the relevant Code of Practice apply. If the person concerned cannot read or refuses to read the record or to sign it, the senior police officer present shall read it over to him and ask him whether he would like to sign it as correct (or make his mark) or to indicate the respects in which he considers it inaccurate. The police officer shall then certify on the interview record itself what has occurred.

11.11   If the appropriate adult or the person's solicitor is present during the interview, he should also be given an opportunity to read and sign the interview record (or any written statement taken down by a police officer).

11.12   Any refusal by a person to sign an interview record when asked to do so in accordance with the provisions of this Code must itself be recorded.

11.13   A written record should also be made of any comments by a suspected person, including unsolicited comments, which are outside the context of an interview but which might be relevant to the offence. Any such record must be timed and signed by the maker. Where practicable the person shall be given the opportunity to read that record and to sign it as correct or to indicate the respects in which he considers it inaccurate. Any refusal to sign should be recorded.

12   Interviews in police stations

(a)   *Action*

12.1   If a police officer wishes to interview, or conduct enquiries which require the presence of, a detained person the custody officer is responsible for deciding whether to deliver him into his custody.

12.2   In any period of 24 hours a detained person must be allowed a continuous period of at least eight hours for rest, free from questioning, travel or any interruption arising out of the investigation concerned. This period should normally be at night. The period of rest may not be interrupted or delayed unless there are reasonable grounds for believing that it would:

(i)   involve a risk of harm to persons or serious loss of, or damage to, property;

(ii)   delay unnecessarily the person's release from custody; or

(iii)   otherwise prejudice the outcome of the investigation.

If a person is arrested at a police station after going there voluntarily, the period of 24 hours runs from the time of his arrest and not the time of arrival at the police station.

12.3 A detained person may not be supplied with intoxicating liquor except on medical directions. No person who is unfit through drink or drugs to the extent that he is unable to appreciate the significance of questions put to him and his answers may be questioned about an alleged offence in that condition except in accordance with Annex C. [See Note 12B]

12.4 As far as practicable interviews shall take place in interview rooms which must be adequately heated, lit and ventilated.

12.5 Persons being questioned or making statements shall not be required to stand.

12.6 Before the commencement of an interview each interviewing officer shall identify himself and any other officers present by name and rank to the person being interviewed, except in the case of persons detained under the Prevention of Terrorism (Temporary Provisions) Act 1989 when each officer shall identify himself by his warrant number and rank rather than his name.

12.7 Breaks from interviewing shall be made at recognised meal times. Short breaks for refreshment shall also be provided at intervals of approximately two hours, subject to the interviewing officer's discretion to delay a break if there are reasonable grounds for believing that it would:

(i) involve a risk of harm to persons or serious loss of, or damage to, property;

(ii) delay unnecessarily the person's release from custody; or

(iii) otherwise prejudice the outcome of the investigation.

12.8 If in the course of the interview a complaint is made by the person being questioned or on his behalf concerning the provisions of this Code then the interviewing officer shall:

(i) record it in the interview record; and

(ii) inform the custody officer, who is then responsible for dealing with it in accordance with section 9 of this Code.

(b) *Documentation*

12.9 A record must be made of the times at which a detained person is not in the custody of the custody officer, and why; and of the reason for any refusal to deliver him out of that custody.

12.10 A record must be made of any intoxicating liquor supplied to a detained person, in accordance with paragraph 12.3 above.

12.11 Any decision to delay a break in an interview must be recorded, with grounds, in the interview record.

12.12 All written statements made at police stations under caution shall be written on the forms provided for the purpose.

12.13 All written statements made under caution shall be taken in accordance with Annex D to this code.

Notes for guidance

12A If the interview has been contemporaneously recorded and the record signed by the person interviewed in accordance with paragraph 11.10 above, or has been tape recorded, it is normally unnecessary to ask for a written statement. Statements under caution should normally be taken in these circumstances only at the person's express wish. An officer may, however, ask him whether or not he wants to make such a statement.

12B   The police surgeon can give advice about whether or not a person is fit to be interviewed in accordance with paragraph 12.3 above.

3.   POLICE POWERS: DETAINEE'S RIGHTS

Where a person is arrested and is held in police custody, that person is (i) by section 56(1) of PACE entitled, if he so requests, to have one friend or relative or other person who is known to him or who is likely to take an interest in his welfare told, as soon as practicable, that he has been arrested and is being detained; and (ii) by section 58(1) is entitled to consult privately with a solicitor at any time. The police may, however, delay the exercise of these rights up to a maximum of 36 hours from the time when detention commenced. The provisions concerning delay are substantially the same in both sections. The material provisions of section 58 read as follows—

58.—(1)   A person who is in police detention shall be entitled, if he so requests, to consult a solicitor privately at any time.

(2)   Subject to subsection (3) below, a request under subsection (1) above and the time at which it was made shall be recorded in the custody record.

(3)   Such a request need not be recorded in the custody record of a person who makes it at a time while he is at a court after being charged with an offence.

(4)   If a person makes such a request, he must be permitted to consult a solicitor as soon as is practicable except to the extent that delay is permitted by this section.

(5)   In any case he must be permitted to consult a solicitor within 36 hours from the relevant time, as defined in section 41(2) above.

(6)   Delay in compliance with a request is only permitted—

   (a)   in the case of a person who is in police detention for a serious arrestable offence; and
   (b)   if an officer of at least the rank of superintendent authorises it.

(7)   An officer may give an authorisation under subsection (6) above orally or in writing but, if he gives it orally, he shall confirm it in writing as soon as is practicable.

(8)   An officer may only authorise delay where he has reasonable grounds for believing that the exercise of the right conferred by subsection (1) above at the time when the person in police detention desires to exercise it—

   (a)   will lead to interference with or harm to evidence connected with a serious arrestable offence or interference with or physical injury to other persons; or
   (b)   will lead to the alerting of other persons suspected of having committed such an offence but not yet arrested for it; or
   (c)   will hinder the recovery of any property obtained as a result of such an offence.

(9)   If delay is authorised—

   (a)   the person in police detention shall be told the reason for it; and
   (b)   the reason shall be noted on his custody record.

(10)   The duties imposed by subsection (9) above shall be performed as soon as is practicable.

(11) There may be no further delay in permitting the exercise of the right conferred by subsection (1) above once the reason for authorising delay ceases to subsist.

Subsections (12)–(18) are omitted.

What constitutes a "serious arrestable offence" is defined by section 114 of and Schedule 5 to PACE. The provisions are again somewhat prolix but, broadly, an arrestable offence is serious if (i) it is so designated, (*e.g.* treason, murder, manslaughter, rape); or (ii) if it is an arrestable offence which has specified serious consequences, (*e.g.* it has or may lead to serious harm to the security of the state, or the death of any person, or serious injury to any person, or substantial gain or loss to any person).

4. POLICE POWERS: ARREST

The principal, though not the only, statutory powers of arrest are contained in sections 24 and 25 of PACE; in addition there is a common law power to arrest for breach of the peace.

Arrest without warrant for arrestable and other offences

24.—(1) The powers of summary arrest conferred by the following subsections shall apply—

(*a*) to offences for which the sentence is fixed by law;

(*b*) to offences for which a person of 21 years of age or over (not previously convicted) may be sentenced to imprisonment for a term of five years (or might be so sentenced but for the restrictions imposed by section 33 of the Magistrates' Courts Act 1980); and

(*c*) to the offences to which subsection (2) below applies, and in this Act "arrestable offence" means any such offence.

(2) The offences to which this subsection applies are—

(*a*) offences for which a person may be arrested under the customs and excise Acts, as defined in section 1(1) of the Customs and Excise Management Act 1979;

(*b*) offences under the Official Secrets Act 1911 and 1920 that are not arrestable offences by virtue of the term of imprisonment for which a person may be sentenced in respect of them;

(*c*) offences under section 14 (indecent assault on a woman), 22 (causing prostitution of women) or 23 (procuration of girl under 21) of the Sexual Offences Act 1956;

(*d*) offences under section 12(1) (taking motor vehicle or other conveyance without authority, etc.) or 25(1) (going equipped for stealing, etc.) of the Theft Act 1968; and

(*e*) offences under section 1 of the Public Bodies Corrupt Practices Act 1889 (corruption in office) or section 1 of the Prevention of Corruption Act 1906 (corrupt transactions with agents).

(3) Without prejudice to section 2 of the Criminal Attempts Act 1981, the powers of summary arrest conferred by the following subsections shall also apply to the offences of—

(*a*) conspiring to commit any of the offences mentioned in subsection (2) above;

(b) attempting to commit any such offence;

(c) inciting, aiding, abetting, counselling or procuring the commission of any such offence,

and such offences are also arrestable offences for the purposes of this Act.

(4) Any person may arrest without a warrant—

(a) anyone who is in the act of committing an arrestable offence;

(b) anyone whom he has reasonable grounds for suspecting to be committing such an offence.

(5) Where an arrestable offence has been committed, any person may arrest without a warrant—

(a) anyone who is guilty of the offence;

(b) anyone whom he has reasonable grounds for suspecting to be guilty of it.

(6) Where a constable has reasonable grounds for suspecting that an arrestable offence has been committed, he may arrest without a warrant anyone whom he has reasonable grounds for suspecting to be guilty of the offence.

(7) A constable may arrest without a warrant—

(a) anyone who is about to commit an arrestable offence;

(b) anyone whom he has reasonable grounds for suspecting to be about to commit an arrestable offence.

General arrest conditions

25.—(1) Where a constable has reasonable grounds for suspecting that any offence which is not an arrestable offence has been committed or attempted, or is being committed or attempted, he may arrest the relevant person if it appears to him that service of a summons is impracticable or inappropriate because any of the general arrest conditions is satisfied.

(2) In this section, "the relevant person" means any person whom the constable has reasonable grounds to suspect of having committed or having attempted to commit the offence or of being in the course of committing or attempting to commit it.

(3) The general arrest conditions are—

(a) that the name of the relevant person is unknown to, and cannot be readily ascertained by, the constable;

(b) that the constable has reasonable grounds for doubting whether a name furnished by the relevant person as his name is his real name;

(c) that—

(i) the relevant person has failed to furnish a satisfactory address for service; or

(ii) the constable has reasonable grounds for doubting whether an address furnished by the relevant person is a satisfactory address for service;

(d) that the constable has reasonable grounds for believing that arrest is necessary to prevent the relevant person—

(i) causing physical harm to himself or any other person;

(ii) suffering physical injury;

(iii) causing loss of or damage to property;

(iv) committing an offence against public decency; or
(v) causing an unlawful obstruction of the highway;

(e) that the constable has reasonable grounds for believing that arrest is necessary to protect a child or other vulnerable person from the relevant person.

(4) For the purposes of subsection (3) above an address is a satisfactory address for service if it appears to the constable—

(a) that the relevant person will be at it for a sufficiently long period for it to be possible to serve him with a summons; or

(b) that some other person specified by the relevant person will accept service of a summons for the relevant person at it.

(5) Nothing in subsection (3)(d) above authorises the arrest of a person under sub-paragraph (iv) of that paragraph except where members of the public going about their normal business cannot reasonably be expected to avoid the person to be arrested.

(6) This section shall not prejudice any power of arrest conferred apart from this section.

Information to be given on arrest

28.—(1) Subject to subsection (5) below, when a person is arrested otherwise than by being informed that he is under arrest, the arrest is not lawful unless the person arrested is informed that he is under arrest as soon as is practicable after his arrest.

(2) Where a person is arrested by a constable subsection (1) above applies regardless of whether the fact of the arrest is obvious.

(3) Subject to subsection (5) below, no arrest is lawful unless the person arrested is informed of the ground for the arrest at the time of, or as soon as is practicable after, the arrest.

(4) Where a person is arrested by a constable, subsection (3) above applies regardless of whether the ground for the arrest is obvious.

(5) Nothing in this section is to be taken to require a person to be informed—

(a) that he is under arrest; or
(b) of the ground for the arrest,

if it was not reasonably practicable for him to be so informed by reason of his having escaped from arrest before the information could be given.

Nicholas v. D.P.P.

[1987] Crim.L.R. 474 (D.C.)

The appellant was convicted of assaulting a police officer in the execution of his duty, contrary to section 51(1) of the Police Act 1964. He had been warned by the officer about riding his bicycle without his hands on the handlebar and reacted by making an obscene gesture. The officer then asked the appellant for his name as he had been riding his bicycle in a dangerous manner. He refused to give his name. The officer said he had power to arrest him under the Police and Criminal Evidence Act 1984 but the appellant again refused to give his name. The officer told the appellant he was being arrested for failing to give his name and address. A struggle then ensued in the course of which the appellant pulled the officer's hair and put his arm round the officer's throat. The appellant appealed by way of case stated on the ground that the officer was not empowered to arrest the appellant because he had not followed the procedure provided by the Police and Criminal Evidence Act 1984. Counsel submitted:

(1)   that section 25 of the 1984 Act implicitly required an officer to explain why he required a person's name and address, *e.g.* in order to serve a summons;

(2)   the appellant had not been informed of the ground for the arrest at the time of, or as soon as was practicable after it—section 28 of the 1984 Act.

Held, dismissing the appeal, that the appellant was lawfully arrested. The provisions of section 25 are satisfied if the officer asks for the name and address of a person reasonably suspected of having committed an offence and the person refuses to give them. The specific provision in section 28(4) requiring that the person arrested be informed of the ground for the arrest even if it is obvious overrules the third proposition set out by Viscount Simon in *Christie* v. *Leachinsky* [1947] A.C. 573 at p. 587. If there has been no prior indication at any time of the nature of the offence which the constable suspects has been committed, it does not suffice to satisfy section 28(3) to ask for a name and address and then to use a failure to give the name and address as a ground for arrest. As a general principle, at the time of arrest the arresting officer must indicate in some words the offence for which the defendant is being arrested. If he goes on and says that he is arresting the defendant because he has not given his name and address, he has then given all the detail that could possibly be required. "At the time of arrest" comprehends both the precise moment at which the officer lays his hands on the defendant and says he is arresting him and a short but reasonable period of time around the moment of arrest, both before and, as the statute itself specifies, after. Whether words are spoken at the time of arrest or not is a matter of fact for the justices to decide. On the facts found by the justices in the present case the requirements of section 28(3) were satisfied. The officer had given a sufficient indication to the appellant of the offence he was alleged to have been committing.

5. POLICE POWERS: SEARCH AND SEIZURE

The provisions in PACE concerning search and seizure are too extensive to be reproduced here; they are summarised in H.S.B. at pp. 121–125.

6. POLICE POWERS: ILLEGALLY-OBTAINED EVIDENCE

PACE, together with the Codes of Practice, regulates the exercise by the police of their powers in very considerable detail. The aim of the legislation was to give the police, and the public as well, a clear statement of their powers, and to protect the public from any oppressive use of those powers. The improper use by the police of their powers may give rise to a civil action for damages and the police officer may be liable to disciplinary proceedings (see H.S.B. at p. 125). This section is, however, concerned with the effect of breaches of PACE or of the Codes on any subsequent criminal proceedings, in particular on the admissibility of evidence following breaches of the Act or the Codes. It will be appreciated, to take an obvious example, that a confession by the defendant obtained by torturing him would be a flagrant breach of section 76 (above, p. 50) and is inadmissible. At the other extreme, a failure by a police officer to record a five-minute break in an interview to allow the suspect to go to the lavatory, though technically a breach of the Codes (see 12.11 above, p. 55) would not render the suspect's subsequent confession inadmissible. Between these two extremes a line must be drawn somewhere and section 78 (above, p. 51), was intended to afford general guidance as to where that line should be drawn.

In this connection it may be helpful to explain the origins of section 78. It was not part of the original Bill but during the Bill's progress Lord Scarman moved an amendment in the House of Lords, the effect of which would have been to exclude all evidence obtained by illegal, improper or deceptive conduct. This amendment went too far for the Government's liking and section 78 was introduced as an acceptable compromise. Strictly it would seem to render section 76 otiose because confessions excluded under section 76 must inevitably also be excluded under section 78 since the admission of confessions so obtained must adversely affect the fairness of the proceedings. Clearly section 78 may be used to exclude evidence which would not be excluded by virtue of section 76 and it would seem that the precise ambit of section 78 is for the courts to determine.

R. v. Fulling

[1987] 2 All E.R. 66 (C.A.)

F. and others were arrested in connection with an insurance fraud. She initially refused to say anything despite persistent questioning. During a break from questioning she was informed by a police officer that her lover, X, had been having an affair with Y. Y had also been arrested in connection with the fraud and was in the next cell to F. F. claimed that she was so distressed by the news and the presence of Y that she made a confession in order to get away from the police station. The trial judge ruled that the confession had not been obtained by oppression and was admissible. F. was convicted and appealed.

Lord Lane C.J....

Counsel for the appellant submits to us that...the basis of the judge's ruling was wrong, in particular when he held that the word "oppression" means something above and beyond that which is inherently oppressive in police custody and must import some impropriety, some oppression actively applied in an improper manner by the police. It is submitted that that flies in the face of the opinions of their Lordships in *D.P.P.* v. *Ping Lin.*

The point is one of statutory construction. The wording of the 1984 Act does not follow the wording of earlier rules or decisions, nor is it expressed to be a consolidating Act, nor yet to be declaratory of the common law. The title runs as follows:

> "An Act to make further provision in relation to the powers and duties of the police, persons in police detention, criminal evidence, police discipline and complaints against the police; to provide for arrangements for obtaining the views of the community on policing and for a rank of deputy chief constable; to amend the law relating to the Police Federations and Police Forces and Police Cadets in Scotland; and for connected purposes."

It is a codifying Act, and therefore the principles set out in *Bank of England* v. *Vagliano Bros.* [1891] A.C. 107 at 144–145, [1891–94] All E.R. Rep. 93 at 113 apply. Lord Herschell, having pointed out that the Bills of Exchange Act 1882 which was under consideration was intended to be a codifying Act, said:

> "I think the proper course is in the first instance to examine the language of the statute and to ask what is its natural meaning, uninfluenced by any considerations derived from the previous state of the law, and not to start with inquiring how the law previously stood, and then, assuming that it was probably intended to leave it unaltered, to see if the words of the enactment will bear an interpretation in conformity with this view. If a statute, intended to embody in a code a particular branch of the law, is to be treated in

this fashion, it appears to me that its utility will be almost entirely destroyed, and the very object with which it was enacted will be frustrated. The purpose of such a statute surely was that on any point specifically dealt with by it, the law should be ascertained by interpreting the language used instead of, as before, by roaming over a vast number of authorities in order to discover what the law was, extracting it by a minute examination of the prior decisions, dependent upon a knowledge of the exact effect even of an obsolete proceeding such as a demurrer to evidence."

. . .

Section 76(2) of the 1984 Act distinguishes between two different ways in which a confession may be rendered inadmissible: first, where it has been obtained by oppression (para. (*a*)); secondly, where it has been made in consequence of anything said or done which was likely in the circumstances to render unreliable any confession which might be made by the defendant in consequence thereof (para. (*b*)). Paragraph (*b*) is wider than the old formulation, namely that the confession must be shown to be voluntary in the sense that it was not obtained by fear of prejudice or hope of advantage, excited or held out by a person in authority. It is wide enough to cover some of the circumstances which under the earlier rule were embraced by what seems to us to be the artificially wide definition of oppression approved in *R.* v. *Prager* [1972] 1 All E.R. 1114, [1972] 1 W.L.R. 260.

This in turn leads us to believe that "oppression" in section 76(2)(*a*) should be given its ordinary dictionary meaning. The *Oxford English Dictionary* as its third definition of the word runs as follows: "Exercise of authority or power in a burdensome, harsh, or wrongful manner; unjust or cruel treatment of subjects, inferiors, etc.: the imposition of unreasonable or unjust burdens." One of the quotations given under that paragraph runs as follows: "There is not a word in our language which expresses more detestable wickedness than *oppression.*"

We find it hard to envisage any circumstances in which such oppression would not entail some impropriety on the part of the interrogator. We do not think that the judge was wrong in using that test. What however is abundantly clear is that a confession may be invalidated under section 76(2)(*b*) where there is no suspicion of impropriety. No reliance was placed on the words of section 70(2)(*b*) either before the judge at trial or before this court. Even if there had been such reliance, we do not consider that the policeman's remark was likely to make unreliable any confession of the appellant's own criminal activities, and she expressly exonerated (or tried to exonerate) her unfaithful lover.

In those circumstances, in the judgment of this court, the judge was correct to reject the submission made to him under section 76 of the 1984 Act. The appeal is accordingly dismissed.

Appeal dismissed.

R. v. Samuel

[1988] 2 All E.R. 135 (C.A.)

On August 6, 1986 the appellant was arrested on suspicion of robbery and taken to a police station. During the course of that day and the next he was interviewed on four occasions about the robbery and two burglaries but he denied the offences. During the second interview he asked for access to a solicitor. Under para. 1 of Annex B to the Code of Practice for Detention, Treatment and Questioning of Persons by Police Officers issued by the Secretary of State pursuant to section 66 of the Police and Criminal Evidence Act 1984, a police officer of the rank of superintendent or above was entitled to delay a suspect's right of access to a solicitor if the suspect was being detained in connection with a serious arrestable offence, if he had not yet been charged with an offence and if the officer had reasonable grounds for believing, *inter alia*, that the granting of access to a solicitor "will lead" to other suspects being alerted before their arrest. The requirement that the officer should have a reasonable belief that access to a solicitor "will lead" to the alerting of other suspects was laid down by s.58(8)(*b*) of the 1984 Act. The police superintendent to whom the appellant's request was referred decided to refuse him access to a solicitor on the ground that two of the offences being investigated, namely the robbery and one of the burglaries, were serious arrestable offences and there was a likelihood of other suspects involved in the robbery being inadvertently warned. At the fourth interview on the morning of August 7, the appellant confessed to the two offences of burglary and he was charged with those offences at 4.30 p.m. At 4.45 p.m. a solicitor instructed by the appellant's family was informed of the charges but was denied access to the appellant. Shortly thereafter the appellant confessed to the robbery in another interview and was charged with that offence. The solicitor was allowed to see him an hour later. At his trial, the appellant contended that the record of his last interview ought to be excluded under section 78(1) of the 1984 Act, on the ground that it had taken place in the unjustified absence of a solicitor in breach of para. 1 of Annex B to the Code of Practice for Detention because (i) the appellant had already been charged with "an offence," *i.e.* the two burglaries, when his access to a solicitor was denied and (ii) the police superintendent did not have reasonable grounds for believing that the granting of access to a solicitor would lead to other suspects being alerted. The trial judge held that there had been no breach of the code, that the police superintendent's belief was reasonable and that if there had been a breach of the code he would in any event exercise his discretion by allowing the evidence to be admitted. The evidence was admitted, and the appellant was convicted. He appealed.

Held—The appeal would be allowed for the following reasons—

(1) On the plain and natural meaning of para. 1 of Annex B to the Code of Practice for Detention the right of a person being detained by the police to have access to a solicitor could not be delayed after he had been charged with any offence and certainly not after he had been charged with a serious arrestable offence in connection with which he was in police custody. Since the appellant had already been charged with the two burglaries, one of which was a serious arrestable offence, before his fourth interview, at which he had confessed to the robbery, access to a solicitor had been wrongly denied to him.

(2) The right of a person detained by the police to have access to a solicitor was a fundamental right of the citizen and a police officer attempting to justify to the court his decision under section 58 of the 1984 Act to delay access had to do so by reference to the specific circumstances of the case, including evidence as to the person detained or the actual solicitor sought to be consulted. In particular, not only did the officer have to believe that the access "will," and not merely "may," lead to the alerting of the other suspects but he had also to believe that if a solicitor was allowed access to the detained person the solicitor would thereafter commit the criminal offence of alerting other suspects or would be hoodwinked into doing so inadvertently or unwittingly. Either belief could only rarely be genuinely held by the police officer.

(3) In the circumstances the refusal of access to the appellant's solicitor before the last interview took place had been unjustified and the interview should not have taken place. If the trial judge had held that the refusal of access to a solicitor was unjustified and that consequently the final interview was unlawful, he might well have concluded that the admission of evidence of that interview would be so unfair that it ought not to be admitted. It followed therefore that the conviction of robbery would be quashed.

R. v. Mason

[1987] 3 All E.R. 481 (C.A.)

M. was arrested on a charge of arson and questioned. There was no direct evidence connecting M. with the fire but the police falsely told M. and his solicitor that they had found near the scene of the crime a fragment of a bottle which had contained inflammable liquid and that M.'s fingerprint was on the bottle. The solicitor thereupon advised M. to answer police questions and explain his involvement with the incident. His subsequent confession was admitted in evidence and M. was convicted.

Watkins L.J. delivered the judgment of the court...

The appellant did not give evidence at the trial. Before the end of the prosecution case and when the confession (because that is what it amounted to) was sought to be put in evidence by counsel for the Crown, objection to its admissibility was made by counsel for the appellant. The judge heard argument in the absence of the jury and heard some evidence from the police as to how the confession had been obtained. He decided that the confession was, in his discretion, admissible.

He was referred in the course of argument to sections 76 and 78 of the Police and Criminal Evidence Act 1984. He gave a ruling at the conclusion of argument and then said he would allow the prosecution to adduce that evidence. He dealt with what he believed to be the effects of sections 76 and 78, and went on to say, with the provisions of section 78 in mind:

> "I have no doubt that this defendant was well aware of his right to remain silent and could have remained silent, with his solicitor being present, had he so chosen that alternative. But he did not choose that alternative; he chose to give the interview, listen to the questions and decide individually which questions he was going to answer. In fact, he answered all of them. I see nothing in his doing that which adversely affects the fairness of the proceedings."

It is contended here by counsel for the appellant that the judge exercised his discretion wrongly. Counsel for the Crown, who also appeared in the court below, has argued that the judge undoubtedly had a discretion and that in exercising it he took account of all the matters which it was necessary for him to take into account and did not give thought to any impermissible matter in coming to his conclusion. He has also submitted that there is no authority for the proposition that section 78 of the 1984 Act refers to confessions and admissions, seeing that they are especially dealt with in section 76.

Section 76, so far as relevant, states: [His Lordship read section 76]

It is to be observed of those provisions that whilst a confession made by an accused person may generally speaking be given in evidence (subsection (1)), the court is obliged to rule out that confession if it finds to exist any one or more of the circumstances referred to in subsection (2).

Section 78(1) states: [His Lordship read section 78]

It is submitted that, when a comparison is made between the provisions of those two sections and reference made to *R. v. Sang* [1979] 2 All E.R. 1222, [1980] A.C. 402, it was not the intention of Parliament that s.78 be understood as though the word "evidence" includes evidence of confessions and admissions. We see no reason whatsoever to put that in our view extremely strained construction on the plain words used in this section. In our judgment on a proper construction of it the word "evidence" includes all the evidence which may be introduced by the prosecution into a trial. Thus it is that regardless of whether the admissibility of a confession falls to be considered under section 76(2), a trial judge has a discretion to deal with the admissibility of a confession under section 78 which, in our opinion, does no more than to restate the power which judges had at common law before the 1984 Act was passed. That power gave a trial judge a discretion whether solely in the interests of the fairness of a trial he would permit the prosecution to introduce admissible evidence sought to be relied on, especially that of a confession or an admission. That being so, we now return to the circumstances of the present case.

It is obvious from the undisputed evidence that the police practised a deceit not only on the appellant, which is bad enough, but also on the solicitor whose duty it was to advise him. In effect, they hoodwinked both solicitor and client. That was a most reprehensible thing to do. It is not however because we regard as misbehaviour of a serious kind conduct of that nature that we have come to the decision soon to be made plain. This is not the place to discipline the police. That has been made clear here on a number of previous occasions. We are concerned with the application of the proper law. The law is, as I have already said, that a trial judge has a discretion to be exercised, of course on right principles, to reject admissible evidence in the interests of a defendant having a fair trial. The judge in the present case appreciated that, as the quotation from his ruling shows. So the only question to be answered by this court is whether, having regard to the way the police behaved, the judge exercised that discretion correctly. In our judgment he did not. He omitted a vital factor from his consideration, namely the deceit practised on the appellant's solicitor. If he had included that in his consideration of the matter we have not the slightest doubt that he would have been driven to an opposite conclusion, namely that the confession be ruled out and the jury not permitted therefore to hear of it. If that had been done, an acquittal would have followed for there was no other evidence in the possession of the prosecution.

For those reasons we have no alternative but to quash this conviction.

Before parting with this case, despite what I have said about the role of the court in relation to disciplining the police, we think we ought to say that we hope never again to hear of deceit such as this being practised on an accused person, and more particularly possibly on a solicitor whose duty it is to advise him, unfettered by false information from the police.

Appeal allowed.

7.   BAIL

Bail is for the most part governed by the provisions of the Bail Act 1976. The principal provisions are reproduced here.

1.—(1)   In this Act "bail in criminal proceedings" means—

(a)   bail grantable in or in connection with proceedings for an offence to a person who is accused or convicted of the offence, or

(b)   bail grantable in connection with an offence to a person who is under arrest for the offence or for whose arrest for the offence a warrant (endorsed for bail) is being issued.

[*Subsections(2)–(5) omitted*]

(6)   Bail in criminal proceedings shall be granted (and in particular shall be granted unconditionally or conditionally) in accordance with this Act.

3.—(1)   A person granted bail in criminal proceedings shall be under a duty to surrender to custody, and that duty is enforceable in accordance with section 6 of this Act.

(2)   No recognizance for his surrender to custody shall be taken from him.

(3)   Except as provided by this section—

(a)   no security for his surrender to custody shall be taken from him,

(b)   he shall not be required to provide a surety or sureties for his surrender to custody, and

(c)   no other requirement shall be imposed on him as a condition of bail.

(4)   He may be required, before release on bail, to provide a surety or sureties to secure his surrender to custody.

(5)   If it appears that he is unlikely to remain in Great Britain until the time appointed for him to surrender to custody, he may be required, before release on bail, to give security for his surrender to custody.

The security may be given by him or on his behalf.

(6)   He may be required (but only by a court) to comply, before release on bail or later, with such requirements as appear to the court to be necessary to secure that—

(a)   he surrenders to custody,

(b)   he does not commit an offence while on bail,

(c)   he does not interfere with witnesses or otherwise obstruct the course of justice whether in relation to himself or any other person.

(d)   he makes himself available for the purpose of enabling inquiries or a report to be made to assist the court in dealing with him for the offence.

[*Subsections (7)–(9) omitted*]

4.—(1)   A person to whom this section applies shall be granted bail except as provided in Schedule 1 to this Act.

(2) This section applies to a person who is accused of an offence when—

(a) he appears or is brought before a magistrates' court or the Crown Court in the course of or in connection with proceedings for the offence, or

(b) he applies to a court for bail in connection with the proceedings.

This subsection does not apply as respects proceedings on or after a person's conviction of the offence or proceedings against a fugitive offender for the offence.

[*Subsections (3)–(7) omitted*]

5.—(1) Subject to subsection (2) below, where—

(a) a court or constable grants bail in criminal proceedings, or

(b) a court withholds bail in criminal proceedings from a person to whom section 4 of this Act applies, or

(c) a court, officer of a court or constable appoints a time or place or a court or officer of a court appoints a different time or place for a person granted bail in criminal proceedings to surrender to custody, or

(d) a court varies any conditions of bail or imposes conditions in respect of bail in criminal proceedings.

that court, officer or constable shall make a record of the decision in the prescribed manner and containing the prescribed particulars and, if requested to do so by the person in relation to whom the decision was taken, shall cause him to be given a copy of the record of the decision as soon as practicable after the record is made.

(2) Where bail in criminal proceedings is granted by endorsing a warrant of arrest for bail the constable who releases on bail the person arrested shall make the record required by subsection (1) above instead of the judge or justice who issued the warrant.

(3) Where a magistrates' court or the Crown Court—

(a) withholds bail in criminal proceedings, or

(b) imposes conditions in granting bail in criminal proceedings, or

(c) varies any conditions of bail or imposes conditions in respect of bail in criminal proceedings,

and does so in relation to a person to whom section 4 of this Act applies, then the court shall, with a view to enabling him to consider making an application in the matter to another court, give reasons for withholding bail or for imposing or varying the conditions.

[*Subsections (4)–(10) omitted*]

6.—(1) If a person who has been released on bail in criminal proceedings fails without reasonable cause to surrender to custody he shall be guilty of an offence.

(2) If a person who—

(a) has been released on bail in criminal proceedings, and

(b) having reasonable cause therefor, has failed to surrender to custody, fails to surrender to custody at the appointed place as soon after the appointed time as is reasonably practicable he shall be guilty of an offence.

(3)   It shall be for the accused to prove that he had reasonable cause for his failure to surrender to custody.

[Subsections (4)–(9) omitted]

8.—(1)   This section applies where a person is granted bail in criminal proceedings on condition that he provides one or more surety or sureties for the purpose of securing that he surrenders to custody.

(2)   In considering the suitability for that purpose of a proposed surety, regard may be had (amongst other things) to—

   (*a*)   the surety's financial resources;

   (*b*)   his character and any previous convictions of his; and

   (*c*)   his proximity (whether in point of kinship, place of residence or otherwise) to the person for whom he is to be surety.

[Subsections (3)–(7) omitted]

SCHEDULE 1

PERSONS ENTITLED TO BAIL: SUPPLEMENTARY PROVISIONS

PART I

DEFENDANTS ACCUSED OR CONVICTED OF IMPRISONABLE OFFENCES

Defendants to whom Part I applies

1.   Where the offence or one of the offences of which the defendant is accused or convicted in the proceedings is punishable with imprisonment the following provisions of this Part of this Schedule apply.

Exceptions to right to bail

2.   The defendant need not be granted bail if the court is satisfied that there are substantial grounds for believing that the defendant, if released on bail (whether subject to conditions or not) would—

(a) fail to surrender to custody, or

(b) commit an offence while on bail, or

(c) interfere with witnesses or otherwise obstruct the course of justice, whether in relation to himself or any other person.

3. The defendant need not be granted bail if the court is satisfied that the defendant should be kept in custody for his own protection or, if he is a child or young person, for his own welfare.

4. The defendant need not be granted bail if he is in custody in pursuance of the sentence of a court or of any authority acting under any of the Services Acts.

5. The defendant need not be granted bail where the court is satisfied that it has not been practicable to obtain sufficient information for the purpose of taking the decisions required by this Part of this Schedule for want of time since the institution of the proceedings against him.

6. The defendant need not be granted bail if, having been released on bail in or in connection with the proceedings for the offence, he has been arrested in pursuance of section 7 of this Act.

Exception applicable only to defendant whose case is adjourned for inquiries or a report

7. Where his case is adjourned for inquiries or a report, the defendant need not be granted bail if it appears to the court that it would be impracticable to complete the inquiries or make the report without keeping the defendant in custody.

8.—(1) Subject to sub-paragraph (3) below, where the defendant is granted bail, no conditions shall be imposed under subsections (4) to (7) of section 3 of this Act unless it appears to the court that it is necessary to do so for the purpose of preventing the occurrence of any of the events mentioned in paragraph 2 of this Part of this Schedule or, in the case of a condition under subsection 6(d) of that section, that it is necessary to impose it to enable inquiries or a report to be made into the defendant's physical or mental condition.

(2) Sub-paragraph (1) above also applies on any application to the court to vary the conditions of bail or to impose conditions in respect of bail which has been granted unconditionally.

(3) The restriction imposed by sub-paragraph (1) above shall not operate to override the direction in section 26(3) of the Magistrates' Courts Act 1952 to a magistrates' court to impose conditions of bail under section 3(6)(d) of this Act of the description specified in the said section 26(3) in the circumstances so specified.

Decisions under paragraph 2

9. In taking the decisions required by paragraph 2 of this Part of this Schedule, the court shall have regard to such of the following considerations as appear to it to be relevant, that is to say—

(a) the nature and seriousness of the offence or default (and the probable method of dealing with the defendant for it),

(b) the character, antecedents, associations and community ties of the defendant,

(c) the defendant's record as respects the fulfilment of his obligations under previous grants of bail in criminal proceedings,

(d) except in the case of a defendant whose case is adjourned for inquiries or a report, the strength of the evidence of his having committed the offence or having defaulted,

as well as to any others which appear to be relevant.

PART II

DEFENDANTS ACCUSED OR CONVICTED OF NON-IMPRISONABLE OFFENCES

Defendants to whom Part II applies

1. Where the offence or every offence of which the defendant is accused or convicted in the proceedings is one which is not punishable with imprisonment the following provisions of this Part of this Schedule apply.

Exceptions to right to bail

2. The defendant need not be granted bail if—

(a) it appears to the court that, having been previously granted bail in criminal proceedings, he has failed to surrender to custody in accordance with his obligations under the grant of bail; and

(b) the court believes, in view of that failure, that the defendant, if released on bail (whether subject to conditions or not) would fail to surrender to custody.

3. The defendant need not be granted bail if the court is satisfied that the defendant should be kept in custody for his own protection or, if he is a child or young person, for his own welfare.

4. The defendant need not be granted bail if he is in custody in pursuance of the sentence of a court or of any authority acting under any of the Services Acts.

5. The defendant need not be granted bail if, having been released on bail in or in connection with the proceedings for the offence, he has been arrested in pursuance of section 7 of this Act.

By section 153 of the Criminal Justice Act 1988 the court is required to give reasons for the grant of bail where the accused is charged with certain serious offences—

153. The following paragraph shall be inserted after paragraph 9 (decisions as to grant or refusal of bail) of Part I of Schedule 1 to the Bail Act 1976—

"9A.—(1) If—

    (a)   the defendant is charged with an offence to which this paragraph applies; and

    (b)   representations are made as to any of the matters mentioned in paragraph 2 of this Part of this Schedule; and

    (c)   the court decides to grant him bail.

the court shall state the reasons for its decision and shall cause those reasons to be included in the record of the proceedings.

(2) The offences to which this paragraph applies are—

    (a)   murder;

    (b)   manslaughter;

    (c)   rape;

    (d)   attempted murder; and

    (e)   attempted rape."

8. TRIAL BY JURY

The principal Act is the Juries Act 1974, the more important provisions of which are as follows.

Qualification for jury service

1. Subject to the provisions of this Act, every person shall be qualified to serve as a juror in the Crown Court, the High Court and county courts and be liable accordingly to attend for jury service when summoned under this Act, if—

    (*a*)   he is for the time being registered as a parliamentary or local government elector and is not less than eighteen nor more than seventy years of age; and

    (*b*)   he has been ordinarily resident in the United Kingdom, the Channel Islands or the Isle of Man for any period of at least five years since attaining the age of thirteen,

but not if he is for the time being ineligible or disqualified for jury service; and the persons who are ineligible, and those who are disqualified, are those respectively listed in Parts I and II of Schedule 1 to this Act.

Summoning

2.—(1) Subject to the provisions of this Act, the Lord Chancellor shall be responsible for the summoning of jurors to attend for service in the Crown Court, the High Court and county courts and for determining the occasions on which they are to attend when so summoned, and the number to be summoned.

(2) In making arrangements to discharge his duty under subsection (1) above, the Lord Chancellor shall have regard to the convenience of the persons summoned and to their respective places of residence, and in

particular to the desirability of selecting jurors within reasonable daily travelling distance of the place where they are to attend.

[*Subsections (3)–(6) omitted*]

Electoral register as basis of jury selection

3.—(1) Every electoral registration officer under the Representation of the People Act 1949 shall as soon as practicable after the publication of any register of electors for his area deliver to such officer as the Lord Chancellor may designate such number of copies of the register as the designated officer may require for the purpose of summoning jurors, and on each copy there shall be indicated those persons on the register whom the registration officer has ascertained to be, or to have been on a date also indicated on the copy, less than eighteen or more than sixty-five years of age.

[*Subsections (2) and (3) omitted*]

Summoning in exceptional circumstances

6.—(1) If it appears to the court that a jury to try any issue before the court will be, or probably will be, incomplete, the court may, if the court thinks fit, require any persons who are in, or in the vicinity of, the court, to be summoned (without any written notice) for jury service up to the number needed (after allowing for any who may not be qualified under section 1 of this Act, and for refusals and challenges) to make up a full jury.

(2) The names of the persons so summoned shall be added to the panel and the court shall proceed as if those so summoned had been included in the panel in the first instance.

Excusal for certain persons and discretionary excusal

9.—(1) A person summoned under this Act shall be entitled, if he so wishes, to be excused from jury service if he is among the persons listed in Part III of Schedule 1 to this Act but, except as provided by that Part of that Schedule in the case of members of the forces and others, a person shall not by this section be exempt from his obligation to attend if summoned unless he is excused from attending under subsection (2) below.

(2) If any person summoned under this Act shows to the satisfaction of the appropriate officer that there is good reason why he should be excused from attending in pursuance of the summons, the appropriate officer may excuse him from so attending and shall do so if the reason shown is that the person is entitled under subsection (1) above to excusal.

(3) Crown Court rules shall provide a right of appeal to the court (or one of the courts) before which the person is summoned to attend against any refusal of the appropriate officer to excuse him under subsection (2) above.

(4) Without prejudice to the preceding provisions of this section, the court (or any of the courts) before which a person is summoned to attend under this Act may excuse that person from so attending.

Discharge of summons in case of doubt as to capacity to act effectively as a juror

10. Where it appears to the appropriate officer, in the case of a person attending in pursuance of a summons under this Act, that on account of physical disability or insufficient understanding of English there is doubt as to his capacity to act effectively as a juror, the person may be brought before the judge, who shall determine whether or not he should act as a juror and, if not, shall discharge the summons; and for this purpose "the judge" means any judge of the High Court or any Circuit judge or Recorder.

Challenge

12.—(1) In proceedings for the trial of any person for an offence on indictment—

    (a)   that person may challenge ... all or any of the jurors for cause, and

    (b)   any challenge for cause shall be tried by the judge before whom that person is to be tried.

(2) Any party to county court proceedings to be tried by a jury shall have the same right of challenge to all or any of the jurors as he would have in the High Court.

(3) A challenge to a juror in any court shall be made after his name has been drawn by ballot (unless the court, pursuant to section 11(2) of this Act, has dispensed with balloting for him) and before he is sworn.

(4) The fact that a person summoned to serve on a jury is not qualified to serve shall be a ground of challenge for cause; but subject to that, and to the foregoing provisions of this section, nothing in this Act affects the law relating to challenge of jurors.

(5) [*omitted*]

(6) Without prejudice to subsection (4) above, the right of challenge to the array, that is to say the right of challenge on the ground that the person responsible for summoning the jurors in question is biased or has acted improperly, shall continue to be unaffected by the fact that, since the coming into operation of section 31 of the Courts Act 1971 (which is replaced by this Act), the responsibility for summoning jurors for service in the Crown Court, the High Court and county courts has lain with the Lord Chancellor.

Majority verdicts

17.—(1) Subject to subsections (3) and (4) below, the verdict of a jury in proceedings in the Crown Court or the High Court need not be unanimous if—

    (a)   in a case where there are not less than eleven jurors, ten of them agree on the verdict; and

    (b)   in a case where there are ten jurors, nine of them agree on the verdict.

(2) Subject to subsection (4) below, the verdict of a jury (that is to say a complete jury of eight) in proceedings in a county court need not be unanimous if seven of them agree on the verdict.

(3) The Crown Court shall not accept a verdict of guilty by virtue of subsection (1) above unless the foreman of the jury has stated in open court the number of jurors who respectively agreed to and dissented from the verdict.

Schedule 1 to the Juries Act which specifies persons who are ineligible, disqualified or excusable as of right is lengthy and there is no point to be served by reproducing it in full here. In summary—

Persons ineligible   are listed in four groups. Group A includes the judiciary. Group B lists others concerned with the administration of justice, (*e.g.* barristers, solicitors, officers and staff of any court, officers of penal establishments, the police and persons employed by the police). Group C renders ministers of religion ineligible. Group D is concerned with the mentally ill.

Persons disqualified   are specified in Part II of Schedule 1 as amended by the Juries (Disqualification) Act 1984. This provision reads—

"A person who at any time in the last ten years has, in the United Kingdom or the Channel Islands or the Isle of Man—

(a)   served any part of a sentence of imprisonment, youth custody or detention; or

(b)   been detained in a Borstal institution; or

(c)   had passed on him or (as the case may be) made in respect of him a suspended sentence of imprisonment or order for detention; or

(d)   had made in respect of him a community service order.

A person who at any time in the last five years has, in the United Kingdom or the Channel Islands or the Isle of Man, been placed on probation."

Persons excusable as of right   include Members of Parliament, serving members of the armed forces, doctors, dentists, nurses, and persons more than 65 years of age.

The right which the defendant formerly enjoyed of challenging up to three jurors without cause has been abolished by s.118 of the Criminal Justice Act 1988.

Practice Note

[1988] 3 All E.R. 1086

The Attorney General has issued the following guidelines on the exercise by the Crown in England and Wales of its right to stand by. The guidelines are to have effect from 5 January 1989 to coincide with the implementation of s.118 of the Criminal Justice Act 1988, which abolishes the right of peremptory challenge. The Attorney General has also reissued his guidelines on jury checks. These incorporate amendments made in 1986, together with a new amendment to para. 9 whereby the Attorney General's personal authority is required before the right to stand by can be exercised on the basis of information obtained as a result of an authorised check.

ATTORNEY GENERAL'S GUIDELINES ON THE EXERCISE BY THE CROWN OF ITS RIGHT OF STAND BY

1. Although the law has long recognised the right of the Crown to exclude a member of a jury panel from sitting as a juror by the exercise in open court of the right to request a stand by or, if necessary, by challenge for cause, it has been customary for those instructed to prosecute on behalf of the Crown to assert that right only sparingly and in exceptional circumstances. It is generally accepted that the prosecution should not use its right in order to influence the overall composition of a jury or with a view to tactical advantage.

2. The approach outlined above is founded on the principles that (a) the members of a jury should be selected at random from the panel subject to any rule of law as to right of challenge by the defence, and (b) the Juries Act 1974 together with the Juries (Disqualification) Act 1984 identified those classes of persons who alone are disqualified from or ineligible for service on a jury. No other class of person may be treated as disqualified or ineligible.

3. The enactment by Parliament of s.118 of the Criminal Justice Act 1988 abolishing the right of defendants to remove jurors by means of peremptory challenge makes it appropriate that the Crown should assert its right to stand by only on the basis of clearly defined and restrictive criteria. Derogation from the principle that members of a jury should be selected at random should be permitted only where it is essential.

4. Primary responsibility for ensuring that an individual does not serve on a jury if he is not competent to discharge properly the duties of a juror rests with the appropriate court officer and, ultimately, the trial judge. Current legislation provides, in ss.9 and 10 of the Juries Act 1974, fairly wide discretions to excuse or discharge jurors either at the person's own request, where he offers "good reason why he should be excused," or where the judge determines that "on account of physical disability or insufficient understanding of English there is doubt as to his capacity to act effectively as a juror."

5. The circumstances in which it would be proper for the Crown to exercise its rights to stand by a member of a jury panel are: (a) where a jury check authorised in accordance with the Attorney General's Guidelines on Jury Checks (see below) reveals information justifying exercise of the right to stand by in accordance with para. 9 of the guidelines and the Attorney General personally authorises the exercise of the

right to stand by; (b) where a person is about to be sworn as a juror who is manifestly unsuitable and the defence agree that, accordingly, the exercise by the prosecution of the right to stand by would be appropriate. An example of the sort of *exceptional* circumstances which might justify stand by is where it becomes apparent that, despite the provisions mentioned in para. 4 above, a juror selected for service to try a complex case is in fact illiterate.

ATTORNEY GENERAL'S GUIDELINES ON JURY CHECKS

1. The principles which are generally to be observed are (a) that members of a jury should be selected at random from the panel, (b) the Juries Act 1974 together with the Juries (Disqualification) Act 1984 identified those classes of persons who alone are either disqualified from or ineligible for service on a jury; no other class of person may be treated as disqualified or ineligible, and (c) the correct way for the Crown to seek to exclude a member of the panel from sitting as a juror is by the exercise in open court of the right to request a stand by or, if necessary, to challenge for cause.

2. Parliament has provided safeguards against jurors who may be corrupt or biased. In addition to the provision for majority verdicts, there is the sanction of a criminal offence for a disqualified person to serve on a jury. The omission of a disqualified person from the panel is a matter for court officials but any search of criminal records for the purpose of ascertaining whether or not a jury panel includes any disqualified person is a matter for the police as the only authority able to carry out such a search and as part of their usual function of preventing the commission of offences. The recommendations of the Association of Chief Police Officers respecting checks on criminal records for disqualified persons are annexed to these guidelines.

3. There are, however, certain exceptional types of case of public importance for which the provisions as to majority verdicts and the disqualification of jurors may not be sufficient to ensure the proper administration of justice. In such cases it is in the interests of both justice and the public that there should be further safeguards against the possibility of bias and in such cases checks which go beyond the investigation of criminal records may be necessary.

4. These classes of case may be defined broadly as (a) cases in which national security is involved and part of the evidence is likely to be heard *in camera*, and (b) terrorist cases.

5. The particular aspects of these cases which may make it desirable to seek extra precautions are (a) in security cases a

danger that a juror, either voluntarily or under pressure, may make an improper use of evidence which, because of its sensitivity, has been given *in camera*, (b) in both security and terrorist cases the danger that a juror's political beliefs are so biased as to go beyond normally reflecting the broad spectrum of views and interests in the community to reflect the extreme views of sectarian interest or pressure group to a degree which might interfere with his fair assessment of the facts of the case or lead him to exert improper pressure on his fellow jurors.

6. In order to ascertain whether in exceptional circumstances of the above nature either of these factors might seriously influence a potential juror's impartial performance of his duties or his respecting the secrecy of evidence given *in camera*, it may be necessary to conduct a limited investigation of the panel. In general, such further investigation beyond one of criminal records made for disqualifications may only be made with the records of police Special Branches. However, in cases falling under para. 4(a) above (security cases), the investigation may, additionally, involve the security services. No checks other than on these sources and no general inquiries are to be made save to the limited extent that they may be needed to confirm the identity of a juror about whom the initial check has raised serious doubts.

7. No further investigation, as described in para. 6 above, should be made save with the personal authority of the Attorney General on the application of the Director of Public Prosecutions and such checks are hereafter referred to as "authorised checks." When a chief officer of police has reason to believe that it is likely that an authorised check may be desirable and proper in accordance with these guidelines he should refer the matter to the Director of Public Prosecutions with a view to his having the conduct of the prosecution from an early stage. The Director will make any appropriate application to the Attorney General.

8. The result of any authorised check will be sent to the Director of Public Prosecutions. The Director will then decide, having regard to the matters set out in para. 5 above, what information ought to be brought to the attention of prosecuting counsel.

9. No right of stand by should be exercised by counsel for the Crown on the basis of information obtained as a result of an authorised check save with the personal authority of the Attorney General and unless the information is such as, having regard to the facts of the case and the offences charged, to afford strong reason for believing that a particular juror might be a security risk, be susceptible to improper

approaches or be influenced in arriving at a verdict for the reason given above.

10. Where a potential juror is asked to stand by for the Crown, there is no duty to disclose to the defence the information on which it was founded; but counsel may use his discretion to disclose it if its nature and source permit it.

11. When information revealed in the course of an authorised check is not such as to cause counsel for the Crown to ask for a juror to stand by but does give reason to believe that he may be biased against the accused, the defence should be given, at least, an indication of why that potential juror may be inimical to their interests; but because of its nature and source it may not be possible to give the defence more than a general indication.

12. A record is to be kept by the Director of Public Prosecutions of the use made by counsel of the information passed to him and of the jurors stood by or challenged by the parties to the proceedings. A copy of this record is to be forwarded to the Attorney General for the sole purpose of enabling him to monitor the operation of these guidelines.

13. No use of the information obtained as a result of an authorised check is to be made except as may be necessary in direct relation to or arising out of the trial for which the check was authorised.

ANNEX TO THE ATTORNEY GENERAL'S GUIDELINES ON JURY CHECKS
RECOMMENDATIONS OF THE ASSOCIATION OF CHIEF POLICE OFFICERS

1. The Association of Chief Police Officers recommends that in the light of observations made in *R.* v. *Mason* [1980] 3 All E.R. 777, [1981] Q.B. 881 the police should undertake a check of the names of potential jurors against records of previous convictions in any case when the Director of Public Prosecutions or a chief constable considers that in all the circumstances it would be in the interests of justice so to do, namely (i) in any case in which there is reason to believe that attempts are being made to circumvent the statutory provisions excluding disqualified persons from service on a jury, including any case when there is reason to believe that a particular juror may be disqualified, (ii) in any case in which it is believed that in a previous related abortive trial an attempt was made to interfere with a juror or jurors, and (iii) in any other case in which in the opinion of the Director of Public Prosecutions or the chief constable it is particularly important to ensure that no disqualified person serves on the jury.

2. The association also recommends that no further checks should be made unless authorised by the Attorney General

under his guidelines and no inquiries carried out save to the limited extent that they may be needed to confirm the identity of a juror about whom the initial check has raised serious doubts.

3. The association further recommends that chief constables should agree to undertake checks of jurors on behalf of the defence only if requested to do so by the Director of Public Prosecutions acting on behalf of the Attorney General. Accordingly if the police are approached directly with such a request they will refer it to the Director.

4. When, as a result of any checks of criminal records, information is obtained which suggests that, although not disqualified under the terms of the Juries Act 1974, a person may be unsuitable to sit as a member of a particular jury the police or the Director may pass the relevant information to prosecuting counsel, who will decide what use to make of it.

R. v. Ford

[1989] 3 All E.R. 445 (C.A.)

Lord Lane C.J. . . .

The points taken by counsel for the appellant are these. First of all he submits that the trial judge was wrong in declining to accede to an application for a multiracial jury. . . .

We deal first of all with the fact that the judge refused the application for a multiracial jury.

This is a problem which has arisen more than once in recent months, and it is likely to be a problem that will arise again. Consequently it seems to us that it is necessary to give careful thought to the way in which a judge should approach the problem.

At common law a judge has a residual discretion to discharge a particular juror who ought not to be serving on the jury. This is part of the judge's duty to ensure that there is a fair trial. It is based on a duty of the judge expressed by Lord Campbell C.J. in *Mansell* v. *R.* (1857) 8 E. & B. 54 at 81, 120 E.R. 20 at 30, and he expressed it as a duty "to prevent the scandal and the perversion of justice". A judge must achieve that by, for example, preventing a juryman from serving who is completely deaf or blind or otherwise incompetent to give a verdict.

It is important to stress, however, that that is to be exercised to prevent individual jurors who are not competent from serving. It has never been held to include a discretion to discharge a competent juror or jurors in an attempt to secure a jury drawn from particular sections of the community, or otherwise to influence the overall composition of the jury. For this latter purpose the law provides that "fairness" is achieved by the principle of random selection.

The way in which random selection should take place is a matter not for the judge but for the Lord Chancellor, as we endeavoured to point out in the course of argument to counsel for the appellant by citing the relevant portion of the Juries Act 1974, which is s.5(1). That reads as follows:

> "The arrangements to be made by the Lord Chancellor under this Act shall include the preparation of lists (called panels) of persons summoned as jurors, and the information to be included in panels, the court sittings for which they are prepared, their division into parts or sets (whether according to the day of first attendance or otherwise), their enlargement or amendment, and all other matters relating to the contents and form of the panels shall be such as the Lord Chancellor may from time to time direct."

There are several cases which give examples of this residual discretion. It may be exercised even in the absence of any objection by any of the parties. The basic position is that a juror may be discharged on grounds that would found a challenge for cause. In addition jurors who are not likely to be willing or able properly to perform their duties may also be discharged.

Those grounds are again set out in the judgment of Lord Campbell C.J. in *Mansell* v. *R.* (1857) 8 E. & B. 54 at 80–81, 120 E.R. 20 at 30 when he said:

> "... if a juryman were completely deaf, or blind, or afflicted with bodily disease which rendered it impossible to continue in the jury box without danger to his life, or were insane, or drunk, or with his mind so occupied by the impending death of a near relative that he could not duly attend to the evidence ..."

That was repeated in different words by Lawton L.J. in *R.* v. *Mason* [1980] 3 All E.R. 777 at 781, [1981] Q.B. 881 at 887. Lawton L.J. gave as an example of common judicial intervention exclusion from the jury of a member of the panel who is infirm, has difficulty in hearing or for whom taking part in a long trial would be unusually burdensome.

That discretion has now been confirmed by express statutory provision in the Juries Act 1974, s.10; and *Practice Note* [1988] 3 All E.R. 177, [1988] 1 W.L.R. 1161 expressly provides for excusal of jurors at the court's discretion on grounds of "personal hardship or conscientious objection to jury service". It does not however envisage excusal on more general grounds such as race, religion or political beliefs.

On occasion however, as counsel for the appellant has pointed out to us by citing certain cases, in particular *R. v. Binns* [1982] Crim.L.R. 522, trail judges have been invited to exercise their discretion not merely to remove an individual juror, but to go further and use the power of discretionary discharge to alter the composition of the panel or of a particular jury.

The most common cases in which this question has arisen have involved questions of ethnic groups where it has been suggested that the jury should consist partly or wholly of member of that same ethnic group. Those applications provide particular difficulty for the judge and the present case is a very good example. They arise without warning and are usually argued without any reference to authority, as indeed was very largely the case in the present instance.

There have been occasions on which it has been accepted that such a discretion exists, most notably *R. v. Thomas* (1989) 88 Cr.App.R. 370, where the prosecution conceded, and the judge accepted, that such a discretion did exist, albeit, it was added, that it was only to be exercised sparingly and in very exceptional circumstances.

In the judgment of this court that concession made in *R. v. Thomas* was not correct. The trial judge had no discretion to interfere in that way with the composition of the panel or of an individual jury.

It is important to note the nature of the objection to the juries in question, and of the discretion that is supposed to meet that objection.

The racial composition of a particular panel or part panel would not be grounds for challenge to the array. A challenge to the array is a challenge to the whole panel on the ground of some irregularity in their summoning by the officer responsible.

In *R. v. Danvers* [1982] Crim.L.R. 680 an application was made to challenge the array at the trial of a defendant of West Indian origin, when all members of the jury panel were found to be white. The appliction was made on the ground that the jury panel did not reflect the ethnic composition of the community, and on the further ground that an all-white jury could not understand the mental and emotional atmosphere in which black families live, so that a black defendant could not have unreserved confidence in an all-white jury. Not surprisingly, due to the fact that the challenge contained no allegation that the all-white jury panel was the result of bias or improper conduct on the part of the summoning officer, the challenge failed. It was held that there is no requirement in law that there should be a black member on a jury or jury panel.

It has never been suggested that the judge has a discretion to discharge a whole panel or part panel on grounds that would not found a valid challenge. Similarly, in the absence of evidence of specific bias, ethnic origins could not found a valid ground for challenge to an individual juror. The alleged discretion of the judge to intervene in the selection of the jury does not therefore fall within any acknowledged catetgory of judicial power or discretion.

There are, moreover, strong reasons why such a discretion should not be recognised. the whole essence of the jury system is random selection, as the passage from Lord Denning M.R.'s judgment in *R.* v. *Crown Court at Sheffield, ex p. Brownlow* [1980] 2 All E.R. 444 at 452–453, [1980] Q.B. 530 at 541, cited in the course of argument, shows. He said:

> "Our philosophy is that the jury should be selected at random, from a panel of persons who are nominated at random. We believe that 12 persons selected at random are likely to be a cross-section of the people as a whole and thus represent the views of the common man ... The parties must take them as they come."

The judgment was supported by Shaw L.J., who was sitting with Lord Denning M.R. in that case.

Secondly, it is worth noting that on occasions in the past when it has been thought desirable that the court should have a power of this kind it has been expressly granted by statute and equally subsequently abolished by statute.

Thirdly, such an application is in effect a request to the judge either to give directions as to the constitution of the panel or to order some individual jurors to be replaced without assigning a cause, that is peremptorily. It is true that in *R.* v. *Bansal* [1985] Crim.L.R. 151, in response to an application of this type, Woolf J. did give directions that the jury panel should be selected from a particular area known to contain members of the Asian community, but the judge does not appear to have had the benefit of full argument on the point.

Responsibility for the summoning of jurors to attend for service in the Crown Court and the High Court is by statute clearly laid on the Lord Chancellor. That is clear from s.2 of the Juries Act 1974 and from s.5, which I have already set out in this judgment. It is not the function of the judge to alter the composition of the panel or to give any directions about the district from which it is to be drawn. The summoning of panels is not a judicial function, but it is specifically conferred by statute on an administrative officer. That fact may not have been drawn to the attention of the court in the cases we have cited and others which have suggested that the judge has power to give directions as to the composition of the panel of juries.

It should also be remembered that the mere fact that a juryman is, for instance, of a particular race or holds a particular religious belief cannot be made the basis for a challenge for cause on the grounds of bias or on any other grounds. If therefore a judge were to exercise his discretion to remove a juror on either of these grounds, he would be assuming bias where none was proved. Such a course is not only unjustified in law, but also indeed might be thought to be seriously derogatory of the particular juryman himself. Further, any attempt to influence the composition of the jury on these grounds would conflict with the requirement that the jury to try an issue before a court shall be selected by ballot in open court from the panel as summoned (see the Juries Act 1974, s.11).

In *R. v. Chandler* [1964] 1 All E.R. 761 at 766, [1964] 2 Q.B. 322 at 337 Lord Parker C.J. held that earlier authorities that had been cited did not establish that the defendant in the particular case of a trial for misdemeanour had a right comparable to that of the Crown to ask a juror to stand by, but he did add:

"That ... is not to say that, in an exceptional case, whether felony or misdemeanour, a judge cannot in his discretion himself stand by a juror or allow a prisoner to do so."

That was either a slip of the tongue or else it may be that Lord Parker C.J. had in mind what was stated in *Mansell* v. *R.* in relation to individual incompetent jurors, because *Mansell* v. *R.* (and the judgment of Lord Campbell C.J.) was cited to the court in that case.

We have been referred among other cases to *R. v. Binns* [1982] Crim.L.R. 522. It is important to recollect and to note that in *R. v. Binns* the original report in the Criminal Law Review was supplemented by a corrigendum which puts the case in a very different light (see [1982] Crim.L.R. 823). In so far as *R. v. Binns* conflicts with the principles which we have endeavoured already to state in this judgment, the opinion expressed in *R. v. Binns* must be said to have been wrong.

The conclusion is that, however well intentioned the judge's motive might be, the judge has no power to influence the composition of the jury, and that it is wrong for him to attempt to do so. If it should ever become desirable that the principle of random selection should be altered, that will have to be done by way of statute and cannot be done by any judicial decision.

We wish to make two final further points. It appears to have been suggested in some of the cases that there is a "principle" that a jury should be racially balanced. One of those cases to which counsel for the appellant has referred us is *R. v. Frazer* [1987] Crim.L.R. 418. There was a similar suggestion in *R. v. Bansal*. The existence of any such principle however was denied in a case which escaped the attention of counsel for the appellant, *R. v. McCalla* [1986] Crim.L.R. 335. No authority is cited by those who have argued for the existence of the principle. In our judgment such a principle cannot be correct, for it would depend on an underlying premise that jurors of a particular racial origin or holding particular religious beliefs are incapable of giving an impartial verdict in accordance with the evidence.

Secondly, the principles we have already set out apply not only where it is argued that a jury of a particular composition ought to be empanelled because of the nature of the particular case or particular defendants, but also where complaint is made that the panel was not truly "random", for instance that the population of a particular area contained 20% of persons of West Indian origin but that only a much lower percentage of such persons was to be found on the panel. For the judge to entertain any such application would equally involve his seeking to investigate the composition of the panel in a manner which, for reasons already indicated, lies outside his jurisdiction, and lies within the jurisdiction of the Lord Chancellor.

So far as the mode of summoning the panel is concerned, the judge is limited, we repeat, to considering, in a challenge for cause, whether the summoning officer has displayed bias or other impropriety. If that cannot be established, the judge has no power to review or take action in respect of any procedures that are alleged to have led to the panel not being in fact "random". Any such complaint would be a complaint of administrative error and has to be tackled by means other than the judge's action. If the officer concerned is in fact not performing his duties properly, in circumstances that fall short of his displaying bias or impropriety, he must be corrected, in other words, by administrative means.

As emphasised above, action could certainly not take the form of directions by the judge as to how the task of selection should in fact be performed. That being the case, in the present instance, although the judge was not given the opportunity of argument on this point to any extent, he was right in the upshot to come to the conclusion that he should not order a multiracial jury to be empanelled, because he had no power so to do. . . .

Chapter 4

The Legal System and The European Dimension

See *Bulmer Ltd.* v. *Bollinger S.A.*, above, p. 22.

The EEC Treaty, Article 177

The Court of Justice shall have jurisdiction to give preliminary rulings concerning:

    (*a*)   the interpretation of this Treaty;

    (*b*)   the validity and interpretation of acts of the institutions of the Community;

    (*c*)   the interpretation of the statutes of bodies established by an act of the Council, where those statutes so provide.

Where such a question is raised before any court or tribunal of a Member State, that court or tribunal may, if it considers that a decision on the question is necessary to enable it to give judgment, request the Court of Justice to give a ruling thereon.

Where any such question is raised in a case pending before a court or tribunal of a Member State, against whose decisions there is no judicial remedy under national law, that court or tribunal shall bring the matter before the Court of Justice.

Macarthys Ltd. v. Smith

[1981] 1 All E.R. 111 (C.A.)

Lord Denning M.R. Although this application is only about costs, I will say a word about it; because it is of public importance.

The applicant, Mrs. Wendy Smith, was employed by wholesale dealers in pharmaceutical products. She was paid a salary of £50 a week. She discovered that a man (who had left) had previously been performing her task. He had been paid £60 a week. She took proceedings under our English statute, the Equal Pay Act 1970 (as amended by the Sex Discrimination Act 1975). She claimed that her pay should be equal to his. An objection was taken that her application was bad in point of law, because our English statute did not apply in the case of successive employment, and is only applied when the man and the woman were employed together at the same time contemporaneously.

That point was argued before this court. The majority of the court held that the objection was well founded. They interpreted it as meaning that the equal pay provisions only applied when the man and the woman were employed at the same time contemporaneously. But then the point arose: what was the position under Community law? We were referred to Art. 119 of the EEC Treaty. The Court of Justice of the European Communities sitting at Luxembourg had decided that Art. 119 of the treaty was directly applicable in the national courts of each country. It was submitted that under Art. 119 there was no requirement that the man and the woman should be employed contemporaneously at the same time, and that, under that Article, the woman was entitled to equal pay even though the man had left before she joined and the woman had taken his job afterwards.

The majority of this court felt that Art. 119 was uncertain. So this court referred the problem to the European Court at Luxembourg. We have now been provided with the decision of that court. It is important now to declare, and it must be made plain, that the provisions of Art. 119 of the EEC Treaty take priority over anything in our English statute on equal pay which is inconsistent with Art. 119. Community law is now part of our law; and, whenever there is any inconsistency, Community law has priority. It is not supplanting English law. It is part of our law which overrides any other part which is inconsistent with it. I turn therefore to the decision given by the European Court. The answer they gave was that the man and the woman need not be employed at the same time. The woman is entitled to equal pay for equal work, even when the woman is employed after the man has left. That interpretation must now be given by all the courts in England. It will apply in this case and in any such case hereafter.

Applying it in this case, the applicant was right. Although she was employed subsequently to the man, she was entitled to be paid the same as the man. She was entitled to be paid not £50, but £60. That is the result of the Community law as applied to our present law. So that must be the decision.

The appeal that the employers brought to this court must therefore be dismissed.

The argument before us today was as to costs. It was argued before us that at the hearing before the tribunals, and indeed before this court, the employers were entitled to look solely to our English statute on equal pay. It was said that, in that statute, our parliamentary draftsmen thought they were carrying out, and intended to carry out, the provisions of the EEC Treaty. So much so that, before the European Court at Luxembourg the United Kingdom government argued that, in order for the woman to be entitled to equal pay, her employment had to be contemporaneous. Accordingly the employers said that they were entitled to go by the English statute, and not the EEC Treaty, and so the costs should not fall on them of the appeal to this court.

The answer is this: the employers had no right to look at our English statute alone. They ought throughout to have looked at the EEC Treaty as well. Community law is part of our law by our own statute, the European Communities Act 1972. In applying it, we should regard it in the same way as if we found an inconsistency between two English Acts of Parliament; and the court had to decide which had to be given priority. In such a case the party who loses has to pay the costs. So it seems to me that the employers should pay all the costs of the appeal to this court.

I may say that the applicant, or those behind her, do not ask for the costs of the reference to Luxembourg. That is a special arrangement which applies in this particular case, although it may not apply in other cases. All we are concerned with today are the costs in this court. In my judgment, the appeal should be dismissed with the costs in this court to be paid by the unsuccessful appellants, the employers.

THE EUROPEAN CONVENTION ON HUMAN RIGHTS

ARTICLE 1

The High Contracting Parties shall secure to everyone within their jurisdiction the rights and freedoms in Section 1 of this Convention [Articles 2 to 18].

ARTICLE 2

1. Everyone's right to life shall be protected by law. No one shall be deprived of his life intentionally save in the execution of a sentence of a court following his conviction of a crime for which this penalty is provided by law.
2. Deprivation of life shall not be regarded as inflicted in contravention of this Article when it results from the use of force which is no more than absolutely necessary:

(a)   in defence of any person from unlawful violence:

(b)   in order to effect a lawful arrest or to prevent the escape of a person lawfully detained;

(c)   in action lawfully taken for the purpose of quelling a riot or insurrection.

ARTICLE 3

No one shall be subjected to torture or to inhuman or degrading treatment or punishment.

ARTICLE 4

1.   No one shall be held in slavery or servitude.

2.   No one shall be required to perform forced or compulsory labour.

3.   For the purpose of this Article the term "forced or compulsory labour" shall not include:

(a)   any work required to be done in the ordinary course of detention imposed according to the provisions of Article 5 of this Convention or during conditional release from such detention:

(b)   any service of a military character or, in case of conscientious objectors in countries where they are recognised, service exacted instead of compulsory military service;

(c)   any service exacted in case of an emergency or calamity threatening the life or well-being of the community;

(d)   any work or service which forms part of normal civic obligations.

ARTICLE 5

1.   Everyone has the right to liberty and security of person. No one shall be deprived of his liberty save in the following cases and in accordance with a procedure prescribed by law:

(a)   the lawful detention of a person after conviction by a competent court;

(b)   the lawful arrest or detention of a person for noncompliance with the lawful order of a court or in order to secure the fulfilment of any obligation prescribed by law;

(c)   the lawful arrest or detention of a person effected for the purpose of bringing him before the competent legal authority on reasonable suspicion of having committed an offence or when it is reasonably considered necessary to prevent his committing an offence or fleeing after having done so;

(d)   the detention of a minor by lawful order for the purpose of educational supervision or his lawful detention for the purpose of bringing him before the competent legal authority;

(e)   the lawful detention of persons for the prevention of the spreading of infectious diseases, of persons of unsound mind, alcoholics or drug addicts or vagrants;

(f)   the lawful arrest or detention of a person to prevent his effecting an unauthorised entry into the country or of a person against whom action is being taken with a view to deportation or extradition.

2.   Everyone who is arrested shall be informed promptly, in a language which he understands, of the reasons for his arrest and of any charge against him.

3.   Everyone arrested or detained in accordance with the provisions of paragraph 1(c) of this Article shall be brought promptly before a judge or other officer authorised by law to exercise judicial power and shall be entitled to trial within a reasonable time or to release pending trial. Release may be conditioned by guarantees to appear for trial.

4.   Everyone who is deprived of his liberty by arrest or detention shall be entitled to take proceedings by which the lawfulness of his detention shall be decided speedily by a court and his release ordered if the detention is not lawful.

5.   Everyone who has been the victim of arrest or detention in contravention of the provisions of this Article shall have an enforceable right to compensation.

ARTICLE 6

1.   In the determination of his civil rights and obligations or of any criminal charge against him, everyone is entitled to a fair and public hearing within a reasonable time by an independent and impartial tribunal established by law. Judgment shall be pronounced publicly but the press and public may be excluded from all or part of the trial in the interest of morals, public order or national security in a democratic society, where the interests of juveniles or the protection of the private life of the parties so require, or to the extent strictly necessary in the opinion of the court in special circumstances where publicity would prejudice the interests of justice.

2.   Everyone charged with a criminal offence shall be presumed innocent until proved guilty according to law.

3.   Everyone charged with a criminal offence has the following minimum rights:

(a)   to be informed promptly, in a language which he understands and in detail, of the nature and cause of the accusation against him;

(b)   to have adequate time and facilities for the preparation of his defence;

(c)   to defend himself in person or through legal assistance of his own choosing or, if he has not sufficient means to pay for legal assistance, to be given it free when the interests of justice so require;

(d)   to examine or have examined witnesses against him and to obtain the attendance and examination of witnesses on his behalf under the same conditions as witnesses against him;

(e)   to have the free assistance of an interpreter if he cannot understand or speak the language used in court.

ARTICLE 7

1.   No one shall be held guilty of any criminal offence on account of any act or omission which did not constitute a criminal offence under national or international law at the time when it was committed. Nor shall a heavier penalty be imposed than the one that was applicable at the time the criminal offence was committed.

2. This Article shall not prejudice the trial and punishment of any person for any act or omission which, at the time when it was committed, was criminal according to the general principles of law recognised by civilised nations.

ARTICLE 8

1. Everyone has the right to respect for his private and family life, his home and his correspondence.

2. There shall be no interference by a public authority with the exercise of this right except such as is in accordance with the law and is necessary in a democratic society in the interests of national security, public safety or the economic well-being of the country, for the prevention of disorder or crime, for the protection of health or morals, or for the protection of the rights and freedom of others.

ARTICLE 9

1. Everyone has the right to freedom of thought, conscience and religion; this right includes freedom to change his religion or belief and freedom, either alone or in community with others and in public or private, to manifest his religion or belief, in worship, teaching, practice and observance.

2. Freedom to manifest one's religion or beliefs shall be subject only to such limitations as are prescribed by law and are necessary in a democratic society in the interests of public safety, for the protection of public order, health or morals, or for the protection of the rights and freedoms of others.

ARTICLE 10

1. Everyone has the right to freedom of expression. This right shall include freedom to hold opinions and to receive and impart information and ideas without interference by public authority and regardless of frontiers. This Article shall not prevent States from requiring the licensing of broadcasting, television or cinema enterprises.

2. The exercise of these freedoms, since it carries with it duties and responsibilities, may be subject to such formalities, conditions, restrictions or penalties as are prescribed by law and are necessary in a democratic society, in the interests of national security, territorial integrity or public safety, for the prevention of disorder or crime, for the protection of health or morals, for the protection of the reputation or rights of others, for preventing the disclosure of information received in confidence, or for maintaining the authority and impartiality of the judiciary.

ARTICLE 11

1. Everyone has the right to freedom of peaceful assembly and to freedom of association with others, including the right to form and to join trade unions for the protection of his interests.

2. No restrictions shall be placed on the exercise of these rights other than such as are prescribed by law and are necessary in a democratic society in the

interests of national security or public safety, for the prevention of disorder or crime, for the protection of health or morals or for the protection of the rights and freedoms of others. This Article shall not prevent the imposition of lawful restrictions on the exercise of these rights by members of the armed forces, of the police or of the administration of the State.

ARTICLE 12

Men and women of marriageable age have the right to marry and to found a family, according to the national laws governing the exercise of this right.

ARTICLE 13

Everyone whose rights and freedoms as set forth in this Convention are violated shall have an effective remedy before a national authority notwithstanding that the violation has been committed by persons acting in an official capacity.

ARTICLE 14

The enjoyment of the rights and freedoms set forth in this Convention shall be secured without discrimination on any ground such as sex, race, colour, language, religion, political or other opinion, national or social origin, association with a national minority, property, birth or other status.

ARTICLE 15

1. In time of war or other public emergency threatening the life of the nation any High Contracting Party may take measures derogating from its obligations under this Convention to the extent strictly required by the exigencies of the situation, provided that such measures are not inconsistent with its other obligations under international law.
2. No derogation from Article 2, except in respect of deaths resulting from lawful acts of war, or from Articles 3, 4 (paragraph 1) and 7 shall be made under this provision.
3. Any High Contracting Party availing itself of this right of derogation shall keep the Secretary-General of the Council of Europe fully informed of the measures which it has taken and the reasons therefor. It shall also inform the Secretary-General of the Council of Europe when such measures have ceased to operate and the provisions of the Convention are again fully executed.

ARTICLE 16

Nothing in Articles 10, 11 and 14 shall be regarded as preventing the High Contracting Parties from imposing restrictions on the political activity of aliens.

ARTICLE 17

Nothing in this Convention may be interpreted as implying for any State, group or person any right to engage in any activity or perform any act aimed at the destruction of any of the rights and freedoms set forth herein or at their limitation to a greater extent than is provided for in the Convention.

ARTICLE **18**

The restrictions permitted under this Convention to the said rights and freedoms shall not be applied for any purpose other than those for which they have been prescribed.

The Malone Case

European Court, Series A, Vol. 82 (1984)

For the English background to this case see H.S.B. at pp. 107 and 169.

Judgment of the Court...

69. Whilst the exact legal basis of the executive's power in this respect was the subject of some dispute, it was common ground that the settled practice of intercepting communications on behalf of the police in pursuance of a warrant issued by the Secretary of State for the purposes of detecting and preventing crime, and hence the admitted interception of one of the applicant's telephone conversations, were lawful under the law of England and Wales. The legality of this power to intercept was established in relation to telephone communications in the judgment of Sir Robert Megarry dismissing the applicant's civil action and, as shown by the independent findings of the Birkett report, is generally recognised for postal communications.

70. The issue to be determined is therefore whether, under domestic law, the essential elements of the power to intercept communications were laid down with reasonable precision in accessible legal rules that sufficiently indicated the scope and manner of exercise of the discretion conferred on the relevant authorities...

[The court considered English law on the interception of communications.]

79. The foregoing considerations disclose that, at the very least, in its present state the law in England and Wales governing interception of communications for police purposes is somewhat obscure and open to differing interpretations. The court would be usurping the function of the national courts were it to attempt to make an authoritative statement on such issues of domestic law.... The court is, however, required under the Convention to determine whether, for the purposes of paragraph 2 of Article 8, the relevant law lays down with reasonable clarity the essential elements of the authorities' powers in this domain.

Detailed procedures concerning interception of communications on behalf of the police in England and Wales do exist.... What is more, published statistics show the efficacy of those procedures in keeping the number of warrants granted relatively low, especially when compared with the rising number of indictable crimes committed and telephones installed.... The public have been made aware of the applicable arrangements and principles through publication of the Birkett report and the White Paper and through statements by responsible Ministers in Parliament....

Nonetheless, on the evidence before the court, it cannot be said with any reasonable certainty what elements of the powers to intercept are incorporated in legal rules and what elements remain within the discretion of the executive. In view of the attendant obscurity and uncertainty as to the state of the law in this essential respect, the court cannot but reach a similar conclusion to that of the Commission. In the opinion of the court, the law of England and Wales does not indicate with reasonable clarity the scope and manner of exercise of the relevant discretion conferred on the public authorities. To that extent, the minimum degree of legal protection to which citizens are entitled under the rule of law in a democratic society is lacking....

82. ...In view of its foregoing conclusion that the interferences found were not "in accordance with the law," the court considers that it does not have to examine further the content of the other guarantees required by paragraph 2 of Article 8 and whether the system complained of furnished those guarantees in the particular circumstances.

83. The process known as "metering" involves the use of a device...which registers the numbers dialled on a particular telephone and the time and duration of each call....

84. As the Government rightly suggested, a meter check printer registers information that a supplier of a telephone service may in principle legitimately obtain, notably in order to ensure that the subscriber is correctly charged or to investigate complaints or possible abuses of the service. By its very nature, metering is therefore to be distinguished from interception of communications, which is undesirable and illegitimate in a democratic society unless justified. The court does not accept, however, that the use of data obtained from metering, whatever the circumstances and purposes, cannot give rise to an issue under Article 8. The records of metering contain information, in particular the numbers dialled, which is an integral element in the communications made by telephone. Consequently, release of that information to the police without the consent of the subscriber also amounts, in

the opinion of the court, to an interference with a right guaranteed by Article 8. . . .

87.   Section 80 of the Post Office Act 1969 has never been applied so as to "require" the Post Office, pursuant to a warrant of the Secretary of State, to make available to the police in connection with the investigation of crime information obtained from metering. On the other hand, no rule of domestic law makes it unlawful for the Post Office voluntarily to comply with a request from the police to make and supply records of metering. . . . The practice described above, including the limitative conditions as to when the information may be provided, has been made public in answer to parliamentary questions. . . . However, on the evidence adduced before the court, apart from the simple absence of prohibition, there would appear to be no legal rules concerning the scope and manner of exercise of the discretion enjoyed by the public authorities. Consequently, although lawful in terms of domestic law, the interference resulting from the existence of the practice in question was not "in accordance with the law," within the meaning of paragraph 2 of Article 8. . . .

88.   This conclusion removes the need for the court to determine whether the interference found was "necessary in a democratic society" for one of the aims enumerated in paragraph 2 of Article 8. . . .

FOR THESE REASONS, THE COURT

1.   *Holds* unanimously that there has been a breach of Article 8 of the Convention; . . .

PART TWO

CRIMINAL LAW

Chapter 1

Actus Reus and Mens Rea: The Ingredients of a Crime

1. ACTUS REUS

A. All Elements of the Actus Reus Must be Proved

R. v. Dyson

[1908] 2 K.B. 454 (C.C.A.)

[D. was charged with the manslaughter of his child. There was evidence that he had inflicted injuries upon the child in November 1906 and again in December 1907. The child died on March 5, 1908. At the trial the judge told the jury that they were entitled to convict D. even if they thought that the death was wholly caused by the injuries inflicted in November 1906. On appeal against conviction:]

Lord Alverstone C.J. The jury convicted the prisoner, who appeals against that conviction upon the ground that the judge misdirected the jury in that he left it to them to find the prisoner guilty if they considered the death to have been caused by the injuries inflicted in 1906. That was clearly not a proper direction, for, whatever one may think of the merits of such a rule of law, it is still undoubtedly the law of the land that no person can be convicted of manslaughter where the death does not occur within a year and a day after the injury was inflicted, for in that event it must be attributed to some other cause. Under these circumstances, there having been a misdirection, the question arises whether the Court can nevertheless dismiss the appeal under s.4, sub-s.1, of the Criminal Appeal Act, 1907, upon the ground that no substantial miscarriage of justice has actually occurred by reason of the conviction. The proper question to have been submitted to the jury was whether the prisoner accelerated the child's death by the injuries which he inflicted in December, 1907. For if he did, the fact that the child was already suffering from meningitis, from which it would in any event have died before long, would afford no answer to the charge of causing its death: *Rex* v. *Martin* (1832). And if that question had been left to the jury, they would in all probability have found the prisoner guilty on that ground; indeed it was the only ground upon which counsel for the prosecution invited them to convict. But it is one thing to say that the jury on a proper direction would probably have so convicted; it is another to say positively that there has been no substantial miscarriage of justice. We feel that we cannot act upon the proviso in subs.1 of s.4, for it is in our judgment plain that we cannot substitute ourselves for the jury and find the facts which are necessary to support the conviction. The proviso is intended to apply to a case in which the evidence is such that the jury must have found the prisoner guilty if they had been properly directed. It does not apply where the evidence leaves it in doubt whether they would have so found; and here the medical evidence established that there were no external marks of recent injury, a fact which might have induced the jury to find that the assault committed in December, 1907, did not accelerate the death.... It is to be regretted that the Legislature when passing the Criminal Appeal Act did not empower the Court to order a new trial, for the present is a case in which it is eminently desirable that such a power should exist. But they did not think fit to do so, and we have no choice but allow the appeal.

Conviction quashed.

Questions

1. The "year and a day rule" is still a part of the *actus reus* of murder and manslaughter today. What purpose does it serve? Is it still needed today? (See 14th Report of the Criminal Law Revision Committee, *Offences Against the Person*, para. 39 (Cmnd. 7844, 1980).

2. Section 4(1) of the Criminal Appeal Act 1907 became section 2(1) of the Criminal Appeal Act 1968. There is now a general power in the Court of Appeal (Criminal Division) to order a retrial; section 43 Criminal Justice Act 1988.

Note

Further illustrations of the need to establish the *actus reus* can be found in *Deller* (1952). But *cf. Dadson* (1850) (See H.S.B., p. 175.)

B. The Need for Voluntary Conduct

A.G.'s Reference (No. 2 of 1992)

(1993) 97 Cr.App.R. 429 (C.A.)

D was a professional lorry driver who had been driving six hours out of the preceding 12 when he was involved in an accident. Throughout the day he had taken appropriate breaks from driving in order to comply with the regulations. After his last stop he drove a further 22 miles down the M6 to a point where the road narrows from three lanes into two. He then appeared deliberately to drive along the hard shoulder off the road for a distance of approximately 700 metres at which point he crashed into the rear of a stationary van which had its hazard lights flashing. In front of the van was a recovery vehicle which had its yellow warning light rotating. The drivers of the two vehicles, who were standing between the vehicles were crushed and killed. The defendant was charged with the offence of causing death by reckless driving (this offence has now been abolished and replaced by causing death by dangerous driving under section 1 Road Traffic Act 1991).

Lord Taylor C.J. The point is defined in the reference as follows:

"Whether the state described as 'driving without awareness' should, as a matter of law, be capable of founding a defence of automatism."

This formulation relates to expert evidence given in the particular case. However, we take the point more generally to raise the question: "What are the requirements and limits of the defence of automatism?"

. . .

Professor Brown said that "driving without awareness" is not a scientific term but a provisional, or interim, descriptive phrase coined at a conference he had attended. He said that there are two essential components to the act of driving: collision avoidance and steering within highway lanes. In a state of "driving without awareness," the driver's capacity to avoid a collision ceases to exist. This is because repetitive visual stimuli experienced on long journeys on straight, flat, featureless motorways can induce a trance-like state in which the focal point of forward vision gradually comes nearer and nearer until the driver is focusing just ahead of his windscreen. He therefore fails to see further ahead in the central field of vision. However, peripheral vision continues to send signals which are dealt with subconsciously and enable the driver to steer within highway lanes.

Professor Brown said this condition can occur insidiously without the driver being aware it is happening. However, he also said that usually a driver would "snap out" of the condition in response to major stimuli appearing in front of him. Thus flashing lights would usually cause him to regain full awareness. Professor Brown was unable to explain why that had not happened in the present case. In fact, the respondent told the police when interviewed that he had seen the flashing lights some quarter of a mile before reaching them. Professor Brown was also unable to explain why the respondent should have steered, apparently deliberately, on to the hard shoulder.

Despite his phrase "driving without awareness," Professor Brown agreed that the driver's body would still be controlling the vehicle, that there would be subconscious motivation to his steering and that although "largely unaware of what was happening ahead" and "largely unaware of steering either" the unawareness was not total. Asked if nothing intrudes into the driver's consciousness when he is in this state, the Professor said: "I would not go so far as to say nothing, but very little." There must, as a matter of common sense, be some awareness if, as Professor Brown accepted, the driver will usually be caused to "snap out" of the condition by strong stimuli noticed by his eyes.

Against this evidential background, the learned recorder directed the jury as follows:

"Professor Brown ... has told you that in his opinion [the respondent] was driving in a state which he describes as 'driving without awareness' in which he moved on to the hard shoulder, mistaking it for the nearside lane, and then continued steering subconsciously until a fraction of a second before the collision. Indeed, Professor Brown's view was that that state of driving without awareness had persisted for quite a long time and had included not only that last half mile, but had included the manoeuvre at junction 6 illustrated in the photograph some miles before.

As a matter of law I direct you that if, because of this state of driving without awareness, [the respondent's] consciousness was, or may have been, so impaired that his mind did not control his actions, he is not guilty of the offence and it is for the prosecution to make you sure that that was not his condition."

The contention on behalf of the Attorney-General is that on the evidence given by Professor Brown, even taken at its highest, there was no basis for leaving the defence of automatism to the jury.

Mr. Jones submits that automatism as a defence in a driving case arises only where there is such total destruction of voluntary control that the defendant cannot be said to be driving at all. He cited *Hill* v. *Baxter* (1958) 42 Cr.App.R. 51, [1958] 1 Q.B. 277, in which Lord Goddard C.J. said, at pp. 56 and 283 respectively:

"I agree that there may be cases where the circumstances are such that the accused could not really be said to be driving at all. Suppose he had a stroke or an epileptic fit, both instances of what may properly be called Acts of God; he might well be in the driver's seat even with his hands on the wheel, but in such a state of unconsciousness that he could not be said to be driving."

Pearson J., at pp. 61 and 286 respectively, gave as examples an epileptic fit, a coma, a blow on the head from a stone thrown up from the road-way and an attack by a swarm of bees so that the driver is:

"prevented from exercising any directional control over the vehicle and any movement of his arms and legs are solely caused by the action of the bees.

In each of these cases it can be said that at the material time he is not driving and therefore not driving dangerously. Then suppose that the man in the driving seat falls asleep. After he has fallen asleep he is no longer driving, but there was an earlier time at which he was falling asleep and therefore failing to perform the driver's elementary and essential duty of keeping himself awake and therefore he was driving dangerously."

In *Bratty* v. *Attorney-General for Northern Ireland* (1961) 46 Cr.App.R. 1, [1963] A.C. 386, a defence of automatism due to an attack of psychomotor epilepsy was raised. Lord Denning at pp. 16 and 409 respectively said of the *actus reus*:

"No act is punishable if it is done involuntarily; and an involuntary act in this context—some people nowadays prefer to speak of it as 'automatism'—means an act which is done by the muscles without any control by the mind, such as a spasm, a reflex action or a convulsion; or an act done by a person who is not conscious of what he is doing, such as an act whilst suffering from concussion or whilst sleepwalking."

The extent of the loss of control is crucial in the present case. Mr. Jones referred to three other authorities in support of his proposition that automatism requires there to be total destruction of voluntary control and that impairment or reduction of voluntary control is insufficient.

Watmore v. *Jenkins* [1962] 2 Q.B. 572 was a decision by a Court of five judges in a case where the defendant was a diabetic and sought to raise automatism due to hypoglycaemia as a defence to driving charges. Giving the judgment of the Court, Winn J. said at p. 586:

"it is ... a question of law what constitutes a state of automatism. It is salutary to recall that this expression is no more than the modern catchphrase which the courts have not accepted as connoting any wider or looser concept than involuntary movement of the body or limbs of a person."

Later, at page 587, he referred to the need for:

"such a complete destruction of voluntary control as could constitute in law automatism."

Secondly, Mr. Jones relies on *Roberts and Others* v. *Ramsbottom* [1980] 1 W.L.R. 823, [1980] 1 All E.R. 7, a civil case in which the defendant driver sought to rely on automatism due to a stroke. At pp. 831 and 14 Neill J. said:

"I am not concerned with the total loss of consciousness but with a clouding or impairment of consciousness."

He then referred *inter alia* to *Watmore* v. *Jenkins* and *Hill* v. *Baxter* and at pp. 832 and 15 concluded:

"I am satisfied that in a civil action a similar approach should be adopted. The driver will be able to escape liability if his actions at the relevant time were wholly beyond his control. The most obvious case is sudden unconsciousness. But if he retained some control, albeit imperfect control, and his driving, judged objectively, was below the required standard, he remains liable. His position is the same as a driver who is old or infirm. In my judgment, unless the facts establish what the law recognises as automatism the driver cannot avoid liability on the basis that owing to some malfunction of the brain, his consciousness was impaired. Counsel put the matter accurately, as I see it, when he said: 'One cannot accept as exculpation any thing less than total loss of consciousness'."

The third case relied upon by Mr. Jones is *Broome* v. *Perkins* (1987) 85 Cr.App.R. 321, where again a driver charged with careless driving relied on an attack of hypoglycaemia as creating automatism. Glidewell L.J. referred to *Bratty's* case and to *Watmore* v. *Jenkins*. At p. 332, he said:

"The question which is posed in the case can be re-phrased to ask: 'On the evidence, could the justices properly conclude that the defendant was not conscious of what he was doing and that his actions were involuntary and automatic throughout the whole of the five mile journey over which the erratic driving was observed?" If, during a part or parts of that journey they were satisfied his actions were voluntary and not automatic, at those times he was driving ... When driving a motor vehicle, the driver's conscious mind receives signals from eyes and ears, decides on the appropriate course of action as a result of those signals, and gives directions to the limbs to control the vehicle. When a person's actions are involuntary and automatic his mind is not controlling or directing his limbs."

Mr. Pert, Q.C., concedes that he can find no authority which runs counter to the principle illustrated by those three cases. Moreover, he conceded that despite Professor Brown's phrase "driving without awareness," the Professor's description of the condition shows that it amounts only to reduced or imperfect awareness. There remains the ability to steer the vehicle straight. There is also usually a capacity to react to stimuli appearing in the road ahead. In the present case the respondent admitted he had actually seen the flashing lights a quarter of a mile from the scene.

Mr. Pert confined his argument to the question whether Professor Brown's evidence properly raised the issue of automatism, which is the sole point of the reference. However, he wished to reserve the question whether the Professor's evidence might have been relevant to refute recklessness (see *Toner* (1991) 93 Cr.App.R. 382).

We were referred to a number of decisions drawing a distinction between insane automatism and non-insane automatism. *Quick* (1973) 57 Cr.App.R. 722, [1973] Q.B. 910; *R.* v. *Sullivan* (1983) 77 Cr.App.R. 176, [1984] A.C. 156; *Hennessy* (1989) 89 Cr.App. R. 10, and *Burgess* (1991) 93 Cr.App.R. 41, [1991] 2 Q.B. 92. The effect of those decisions is that if the defence of automatism is said to arise from internal causes so as to bring the defendant within the *M'Naghten* Rules [see *M'Naghten's* case (1843) 10 Cl. & Fin. 200], then, if it succeeds, the verdict should be one of not guilty by reason of insanity. An epileptic seizure (in *Sullivan*), a stress disorder, prone to recur and lacking the features of novelty or accident (in *Hennessy*) and sleep-walking (in *Burgess*) were all regarded as internal causes. If, however, automatism is said to arise from an external cause, for example a stone hitting the driver on the head, then a successful defendant is entitled to be acquitted.

Here, Mr. Pert argues that the precipitating cause of the condition described by Professor Brown was the external factor of motorway conditions. However that may be, the proper approach is that prescribed by Lord Lane C.J. in *Burgess* at pages 43 and 96C as follows:

"Where the defence of automatism is raised by a defendant, two questions fall to be decided by the judge before the defence can be left to the jury. The first is whether a proper evidential foundation for the defence of automatism has been laid. The second is whether the evidence shows the case to be one of insane automatism, that is to say a case which falls within the *M'Naghten* Rules, or one of non-insane automatism."

The first of those questions is the one raised by this reference. In our judgment, the "proper evidential foundation" was not laid in this case by Professor Brown's evidence of "driving without awareness." As the authorities cited above show, the defence of automatism requires that there was a total destruction of voluntary control on the defendant's part. Impaired, reduced or partial control is not enough. Professor Brown accepted that someone "driving without awareness" within his description, retains some control. He would be able to steer the vehicle and usually to react and return to full awareness when confronted by significant stimuli.

Accordingly, in our judgment, the learned recorder ought not to have left the issue of automatism to the jury in this case and the answer to the point of law as formulated is: no.

Opinion accordingly.

Note

Questions of automatism are often bound up with the defence of insanity (see below, p. 213). What are the practical differences between the defences of noninsane automatism on the one hand and insanity or insane automatism on the other? Similarly issues of automatism and drunkenness may arise together (see below, p. 236).

C. Liability for a State of Affairs

Winzar v. Chief Constable of Kent

The Times, March 28, 1983 (D.C.)

Robert Goff L.J. The appellant had been charged with an offence under Section 12 of the Licensing Act 1872, *viz.* that he had been found drunk in a highway called Westcliff Road, contrary to that Section. The Ramsgate Justices heard the charge on the 6th October 1981 and they convicted him and imposed a fine of £15. The appeal came before the Crown Court, and Judge Edie and the two magistrates dismissed the appeal against conviction and sentence.

The facts found by the Crown Court are as follows: "(1) At 11.50 p.m. on the 24th August 1981 the Appellant was brought in on a stretcher to Ramsgate General Hospital. Dr. Sparkes examined him, and though the Appellant was able to give an account of himself, and mentioned that he suffered from a low sugar condition, Dr. Sparkes formed the opinion that he was drunk, that he was fit to leave the hospital, and thereupon asked him to do so. Dr. Sparkes later saw him slumped on a seat in the corridor and the police were called. (2) W.P.C. Washer arrived at the hospital at 1.15 a.m., saw the Appellant being carried into Westcliff Road, she then spoke to him, he was not able to answer, and she formed the opinion he was drunk. (3) The Appellant was placed in a police car stationed on the hospital forecourt in Westcliff Road, and taken to Ramsgate Police station where he was charged with being found drunk in the highway called Westcliff Road, Ramsgate, cautioned and made no reply."

It appears that the Appellant advanced the following argument before the Crown Court. First, his condition was not brought on by drink; secondly, he was not found on a highway as he had been carried to a police car which was stationed in the hospital forecourt; thirdly, his presence on the highway was momentary; and, fourthly, he was not there of his own volition but only for the purpose of being transported from the hospital to the police car.

The conclusion of the Crown Court was that the Appellant had been drunk and that he had been found on the highway known as Westcliff Road, Ramsgate, even though his presence on the highway was momentary and not of his own volition.

The question posed for the decision of the court is as follows: "Would a drunken person, lawfully ejected from premises after a request to leave, and consequently ascertained to be on the highway, even though momentarily and not of his volition, nevertheless be found on a highway within the meaning of Section 12 of the Licensing Act 1872?" . . .

We turn then to the question which was raised by the Crown Court, which was in effect: Does the fact that the Appellant was only momentarily on the highway and not there of his own volition, prevent his conviction of the offence of being found drunk in a highway?

We were referred to an Australian case, which was the only case found by counsel of direct relevance to the point we have to consider. That is the case of *Sheehan* v. *Piddington* (1955). In that case Mr. Piddington was found drunk in a public place, Marshall Street, Goondiwindi. The evidence showed that the Appellant entered a house in Goondiwindi and woke up a lodger, who was a friend of his. He began to converse with his friend in a manner which led the latter to form the opinion that the Appellant was drunk. A police constable called at the house, and the Apellant was asked to leave several times. He refused, and was finally removed by the police constable on to the footpath of Marshall Street. The police officer advised the Appellant to go home. However, he would not do so. He staggered three or four paces away and then turned round and lurched back towards the gate of the house from which he had already been removed. The police constable decided that he had had enough, and that the man had become a drunken nuisance. Accordingly, he arrested him.

On those facts, it was the conclusion of the full court,—the judgment being given by Macrossan C.J., that the offence of being found drunk in a public place had been proved. It was held that the mere fact that the man had been removed into the public place by force, and had not gone there of his own volition, did not prevent him from being found guilty of the crime for which he had been charged.

It is right to point out that on page 583 of the report, the Chief Justice said: "It is unnecessary to consider in this case what would have been the position had the Appellant been merely ejected by Constable Sheehan from his residence and without any interval of time arrested in Marshal Street." Plainly, that point was reserved by the Chief Justice because it did not arise on the facts of the case before him. On the evidence in that case, the Appellant had been given a chance to go home. He had then tried to get back into the house again and after that, not surprisingly, the police officer arrested him.

That case is persuasive authority for the view that it makes no difference in a case of this kind whether the person charged with the offence has gone into the highway or public place of his own volition or not.

In my judgment, looking at the purpose of this particular offence, it is designed, as Mr. Goymer has submitted, to deal with the nuisance which can be caused by persons who are drunk in a public place. This kind of offence is caused quite simply when a person is found drunk in a public place or in a highway.

Mr. Goymer gave an example which illustrates how sensible that conclusion is. Suppose a person was found as being drunk in a restaurant or a place of that kind and was asked to leave. If he was asked to leave, he would walk out of the door of the restaurant and would be in a public place or in a highway of his own volition. He would be there of his own volition because he had responded to a request. However, if a man in a restaurant made a thorough nuisance of himself, was asked to leave, objected and was ejected, in those circumstances, he would not be in a public place of his own volition because he would have been put there either by a gentleman on the door of the restaurant, or by a police officer, who might have been called to deal with the man in question. It would be nonsense if one were to say that the man who responded to the plea to leave could be said to be found drunk in a public place or in a highway, whereas the man who had been compelled to leave could not.

This leads me to the conclusion that a person is "found to be drunk in a public place or in a highway," within the meaning of those words as used in the section, when he is perceived to be drunk in a public place. It is enough for the commission of the offence if (1) a person is in a public place or a highway, (2) he is drunk, and (3) in those circumstances he is perceived to be there and to be drunk. Once those criteria have been fulfilled, he is liable to be convicted of the offence of being found drunk in a highway.

Appeal dismissed.

Note

See also *R*. v. *Larsonneur* (1933) (HSB, p. 181).

Questions

1. Would it be nonsense to say that "the man who responded to the plea to leave the restaurant could be said to be found drunk in a public place or in a highway, whereas the man who had been compelled to leave could not."?

2. What does this case say about the meaning of the phrase "be found."?

3.　Would it have made any difference had the eviction from the hospital been unlawful?

D.　Liability for Failure to Act

R. v. Gibbins and Proctor

(1918) 82 J.P. 287 (C.C.A.)

[G. and his mistress P. were charged with the murder by starvation of Nelly, G.'s seven year old daughter. The prosecution alleged that G. gave P. enough money to maintain all the family in good health, but that she so hated Nelly that she starved her to death, and did so with the full knowledge of G.]

Darling, J.　It has been said that there ought not to have been a finding of guilty of murder against Gibbins. The court agrees that the evidence was less against Gibbins than Proctor; Gibbins gave her money, and, as far as we can see, it was sufficient to provide for the wants of themselves and all the children. But he lived in the house, and the child was his own, a little girl of seven, and he grossly neglected the child. He must have known what her condition was if he saw her, for she was little more than a skeleton. He is in this dilemma: if he did not see her the jury might well infer that he did not care if she died; if he did he must have known what was going on. The question is whether there was evidence that he so conducted himself as to show that he desired that grievous bodily injury should be done to the child. He cannot pretend that he showed any solicitude for her. He knew that Proctor hated her, knew that she was ill, and that no doctor had been called in, and the jury may have come to the conclusion that he was so infatuated with Proctor, and so afraid of offending her, that he preferred that the child should starve to death rather than that he should be exposed to any injury or unpleasantness from Proctor. It is unnecessary to say more than that there was evidence that Gibbins did desire that grievous bodily harm should be done to the child; he did not interfere in what was being done, and he comes within the definition which I have read, and is therefore guilty of murder.

The case of Proctor is plainer. She had charge of the child. She was under no obligation to do so or to live with Gibbins, but she did so, and receiving money, as it is admitted she did, for the purpose of supplying food, her duty was to see that the child was properly fed and looked after, and to see that she had medical attention if necessary. We agree with what Lord Coleridge, C.J. said in *R. v. Instan* (1893), "There is no case directly in point, but it would be a slur upon, and a discredit to the administration of, justice in this country if there were any doubt as to the legal principle, or as to the present case being within it. The prisoner was under a moral obligation to the deceased from which arose a legal duty towards her; that legal duty the prisoner has wilfully and deliberately left unperformed, with the consequence that there has been an acceleration of the death of the deceased owing to the non-perforance of that legal duty." Here Proctor took upon herself the moral obligation of looking after the children; she was *de facto*, though not *de jure*, the wife of Gibbins, and had excluded the child's own mother. She neglected the child undoubtedly, and the evidence shows that as a result the child died. So a verdict of manslaughter was inevitable.

But it is necessary to go further and see whether it was murder. The evidence is that she had plenty of money; that she kept the child upstairs insufficiently supplied with food; that she hated the child and hit her. There is also evidence that when the child died of starvation both appellants took part in hiding the body and preventing the death from being known. They concocted a story that she had been sent away and was still alive. There is evidence that Proctor told Gibbins to bury the child out of sight, and that he did so in the brickyard where he worked. The jury came to the conclusion that she had done more than wickedly neglect the child; she had deliberately withheld food from it, and therefore we come to the conclusion that there was evidence which justified the jury in returning a verdict against her, not merely of manslaughter, but of murder. The appeals are therefore dismissed.

Appeals dismissed.

Airedale National Health Service Trust v. Bland

[1993] 1 All E.R. 821 (H.L.)

T.B. had been crushed along with many other football supporters in the Hillsborough Stadium disaster. He suffered irreversible brain damage and was classified as being in a persistent vegative state (PVS). He was being fed through a naso-gastric tube and there was general agreement that he had no hope of recovery. The Hospital, with the support of his parents, sought a declaration that it could discontinue all life-saving treatment and also all medical treatment so that he could die with dignity and as little distress as possible.

Lord Goff. I must however stress, at this point, that the law draws a crucial distinction between cases in which a doctor decides not to provide, or to continue to provide, for his patient treatment or care which could or might prolong his life and those in which he decides, for example by administering a lethal drug, actively to bring his patient's life to an end. As I have already indicated, the former may be lawful, either because the doctor is giving effect to his patient's wishes by withholding the treatment or care, or even in certain circumstances in which (on principles which I shall describe) the patient is incapacitated from stating whether or not he gives his consent. But it is not lawful for a doctor to administer a drug to his patient to bring about his death, even though that course is prompted by a humanitarian desire to end his suffering, however great that suffering may be: see *R v. Cox* (September 8, 1992, unreported) per Ognall J in the Crown Court at Winchester. So to act is to cross the Rubicon which runs between on the one hand the care of the living patient and on the other hand euthanasia—actively causing his death to avoid or to end his suffering. Euthanasia is not lawful at common law. It is of course well known that there are many responsible members of our society who believe that euthanasia should be made lawful; but that result could, I believe, only be achieved by legislation which expresses the democratic will that so fundamental a change should be made in our law, and can, if enacted, ensure that such legalised killing can only be carried out subject to appropriate supervision and control. It is true that the drawing of this distinction may lead to a charge of hypocrisy, because it can be asked why, if the doctor, by discontinuing treatment, is entitled in consequence to let his patient die, it should not be lawful to put him out of his misery straight away, in a more humane manner, by a lethal injection, rather than let him linger on in pain until he dies. But the law does not feel able to authorise euthanasia, even in circumstances such as these, for, once euthanasia is recognised as lawful in these circumstances, it is difficult to see any logical basis for excluding it in others.

At the heart of this distinction lies a theoretical question. Why is it that the doctor who gives his patient a lethal injection which kills him commits an unlawful act and indeed is guilty of murder, whereas a doctor who, by discontinuing life support, allows his patient to die may not act unlawfully and will not do so if he commits no breach of duty to his patient? Professor Glanville Williams has suggested (see *Textbook of Criminal Law* (2nd Ed., 1983), p. 282) that the reason is that what the doctor does when he switches off a life support machine 'is in substance not an act but an omission to struggle' and that 'the omission is not a breach of duty by the doctor, because he is not obliged to continue in a hopeless case'.

I agree that the doctor's conduct in discontinuing life support can properly be categorised as an omission. It is true that it may be difficult to describe what the doctor actually does as an omission, for example where he takes some positive step to bring the life support to an end. But discontinuation of life support is, for present purposes, no different from not initiating life support in the first place. In each case, the doctor is simply allowing his patient to die in the sense that he is desisting from taking a step which might, in certain circumstances, prevent his patient from dying as a result of his pre-existing condition; and as a matter of general principle an omission such as this will not be unlawful unless it constitutes a breach of duty to the patient. I also agree that the doctor's conduct is to be differentiated from that of, for example, an interloper who maliciously switches off a life support machine because, although the interloper may perform exactly the same act as the doctor who discontinues life support, his doing so constitutes interference with the life-prolonging treatment then being administered by the doctor. Accordingly, whereas the doctor, in discontinuing life support, is simply allowing his patient to die of his pre-existing condition, the interloper is actively intervening to stop the doctor from prolonging the patient's life, and such conduct cannot possibly be categorised as an omission.

The distinction appears, therefore, to be useful in the present context in that it can be invoked to explain how discontinuance of life support can be differentiated from ending a patient's life by a lethal injection. But in the end the reason for that difference is that, whereas the law considers that discontinuance of life support may be consistent with the doctor's duty to care for his patient, it does not, for reasons of policy, consider that it forms any part of his duty to give his patient a lethal injection to put him out of his agony.

. . .

It is of course the development of modern medical technology, and in particular the development of life support systems, which has rendered cases such as the present so much more relevant than in the past. Even so, where, for example, a patient is brought into hospital in such a condition that, without the benefit of a life support system, he will not continue to live, the decision has to be made whether or not to give him that benefit, if available. That decision can only be made in the best interests of the patient. No doubt, his best interests will ordinarily require that he should be placed on a life support system as soon as necessary, if only to make an accurate assessment of his condition and a prognosis for the future. But, if he neither recovers sufficiently to be taken off it nor dies, the question will ultimately arise whether he should be kept on it indefinitely. As I see it, that question (assuming the continued availability of the system) can only be answered by reference to the best interests of the patient himself, having regard to established medical practice. Indeed, if the justification for treating a patient who lacks the capacity to consent lies in the fact that the treatment is provided in his best interests, it must follow that the treatment may, and indeed ultimately should, be discontinued where it is no longer in his best interests to provide it. The question which lies at the heart of the present case is, as I see it, whether on that principle the doctors responsible for the treatment and care of Anthony Bland can justifiably discontinue the process of artificial feeding upon which the prolongation of his life depends.

It is crucial for the understanding of this question that the question itself should be correctly formulated. The question is not whether the doctor should take a course which will kill his patient, or even take a course which has the effect of accelerating his death. The question is whether the doctor should or should not continue to provide his patient with medical treatment or care which, if continued, will prolong his patient's life. The question is sometimes put in striking or emotional terms, which can be misleading. For example, in the case of a life support system, it is sometimes asked: should a doctor be entitled to switch it off, or to pull the plug? And then it is asked: can it be in the best interests of the patient that a doctor should be able to switch the life support system off, when this will inevitably result in the patient's death? Such an approach has rightly been criticised as misleading, for example by Professor Ian Kennedy (in his paper in *Treat Me Right, Essays in Medical Law and Ethics* (1988)), and by Thomas J in *Auckland Area Health Board* v. *A.-G.* [1993] 1 N.Z.L.R. 235 at 247. This is because the question is not whether it is in the best interests of the patient that he should die. The question is whether it is in the best interests of the patient that his life should be prolonged by the continuance of this form of medical treatment or care.

The correct formulation of the question is of particular importance in a case such as the present, where the patient is totally unconscious and where there is no hope whatsoever of any amelioration of his condition. In circumstances such as these, it may be difficult to say that it is in his best interests that the treatment should be ended. But, if the question is asked, as in my opinion it should be, whether it is in his best interests that treatment which has the effect of artificially prolonging his life should be continued, that question can sensibly be answered to the effect that it is not in his best interests to do so.

Questions

1. Do you agree that this is a case of omission?
2. Does it make any sense for the law to permit the hospital staff to allow T.B. to die slowly when an injection could have terminated everyone's grief quickly and painlessly? See also Gunn and Smith, "Arthur's Case and the Right to Life of a Down's Syndrome Child" [1985] Crim.L.R. 705.

Note

Where the prosecution is seeking to rely on a failure to act as the basis for liability, the court will have to be satisfied that

(i) the crime is one where, in law, liability may be incurred by an omission (see for example *Firth* (1990) where the court held that the word "deceive in section 2(1) Theft Act 1978 could be interpreted to cover a situation in which a doctor had failed to supply relevant information);

(ii) the defendant was under a legal duty to act. A duty to act may be imposed:

(a) expressly by statute
(b) because of status. Gibbins (above) was under a legal obligation to maintain his child. Doctors are under a duty to look after the welfare of their patients; *Airedale National Health Service Trust* (above).
(c) by contractual undertaking (*Pittwood* (1902); HSB ... p. 184).
(d) by voluntary assumption of the duty (Proctor had assumed responsibility for the child (above)).
(e) by conduct (see *Miller* below).

R. v. Miller

[1983] A.C. 161 (H.L.)

[M. had returned from the pub at closing time to the house where he was squatting. He lay on his mattress and lit a cigarette. He fell asleep and awoke to find his mattress on fire. Not having anything with which to extinguish the fire he simply moved to another room and went back to sleep. The house was badly damaged by the fire he had started. He was charged with arson contrary to section 1(1) and (3) of the Criminal Damage Act 1971. (See below, p. 401 for the provisions of the Act.)]

Lord Diplock. The first question to be answered where a completed crime of arson is charged is: "Did a physical act of the accused start the fire which spread and damaged property belonging to another (or did his act cause an existing fire, which he had not started but which would otherwise have burnt itself out harmlessly, to spread and damage property belonging to another)?" I have added the words in brackets for completeness. They do not arise in the instant case; in cases where they do, the accused, for the purposes of the analysis which follows, may be regarded as having started a fresh fire.

The first question is a pure question of causation; it is one of fact to be decided by the jury in a trial upon indictment. It should be answered "No" if, in relation to the fire during the period starting immediately before its ignition and ending with its extinction, the role of the accused was at no time more than that of a passive bystander. In such a case the subsequent questions to which I shall be turning would not arise. The conduct of the parabolical priest and Levite on the road to Jericho may have been indeed deplorable, but English law has not so far developed to the stage of treating it as criminal; and if it ever were to do so there would be difficulties in defining what should be the limits of the offence.

If on the other hand the question, which I now confine to: "Did a physical act of the accused start the fire which spread and damaged property belonging to another?" is answered "Yes," as it was by the jury in the instant case, then for the purpose of the further questions the answers to which are determinative of his guilt of the offence of arson, the conduct of the accused, throughout the period from immediately before the moment of ignition to the completion of the damage to the property by the fire, is relevant; so is his state of mind throughout that period.

Since arson is a result-crime the period may be considerable, and during it the conduct of the accused that is causative of the result may consist not only of his doing physical acts which cause the fire to start or spread but also of his failing to take measures that lie within his power to counteract the danger that he has himself created. And if his conduct, active or passive, varies in the course of the period, so may his state of mind at the time of each piece of conduct. If at the time of any particular piece of conduct by the accused that is causative of the result, the state of mind that actuates his conduct falls within the description of one or other of the states of mind that are made a necessary ingredient of the offence of arson by section 1(1) of the Criminal Damage Act 1971, (*i.e.* intending to damage property belonging to another or being reckless as to whether such property would be damaged) I know of no principle of English criminal law that would prevent his being guilty of the offence created by that subsection. Likewise I see no rational ground for excluding from conduct capable of giving rise to criminal liability, conduct which consists of failing to take measures that lie within one's power to counteract a danger that one has oneself created, if at the time of such conduct one's state of mind is such as constitutes a necessary ingredient of the offence. I venture to think that the habit of lawyers to talk of "*actus reus,*" suggestive as it is of action rather than inaction, is responsible for any erroneous notion that failure to act cannot give rise to criminal liability in English law.

No one has been bold enough to suggest that if, in the instant case, the accused had been aware at the time that he dropped the cigarette that it would probably set fire to his mattress and yet had taken no steps to extinguish it he would not have been guilty of the offence of arson, since he would have damaged property of another being reckless as to whether any such property would be damaged.

I cannot see any good reason why, so far as liability under criminal law is concerned, it should matter at what point of time before the resultant damage is complete a person becomes aware that he has done a physical act which, whether or not he appreciated that it would at the time when he did it, does in fact create a risk that property of another will be damaged; provided that, at the moment of awareness, it lies within his power to take steps, either himself or by calling for the assistance of the fire brigade if this be necessary, to prevent or minimise the damage to the property at risk.

The recorder, in his lucid summing up to the jury (they took 22 minutes only to reach their verdict) told them that the accused having by his own act started a fire in the mattress which, when he became aware of its existence, presented an obvious risk of damaging the house, became under a duty to take some action to put it out. The Court of Appeal upheld the conviction, but their ratio decidendi appears to be somewhat different from that of the recorder. As I understand the judgment, in effect it treats the whole course of conduct of the accused, from the moment at which he fell asleep and dropped the cigarette on to the mattress until the time the damage to the house by fire was complete, as a continuous act of the accused, and holds that it is sufficient to constitute the statutory offence of arson if at any stage in that course of conduct the state of mind of the accused, when he fails to try to prevent or minimise the damage which will result from his initial act, although it lies within his power to do so, is that of being reckless as to whether property belonging to another would be damaged.

My Lords, these alternative ways of analysing the legal theory that justifies a decision which has received nothing but commendation for its accord with commonsense and justice, have, since the publication of the judgment of the Court of Appeal in the instant case, provoked academic controversy. Each theory has distinguished support. Professor J. C. Smith espouses the "duty theory"; Professor Glanville Williams who, after the decision of the Divisional Court in *Fagan v. Metropolitan Police Commissioner* (1969) appears to have been attracted by the duty theory, now prefers that of the continuous act. When applied to cases where a person has unknowingly done an act which sets in train events that, when he becomes aware of them, present an obvious risk that property belonging to another will be damaged, both theories lead to an identical result; and since what your Lordships are concerned with is to give guidance to trial judges in their task of summing up to juries, I would for this purpose adopt the duty theory as being the easier to explain to a jury; though I would commend the use of the word "responsibility," rather than "duty" which is more appropriate to civil than to criminal law, since it suggests an obligation owed to another person, *i.e.* the person to whom the endangered property belongs, whereas a criminal statute defines combinations of conduct and state of mind which render a person liable to punishment by the state itself.

Note

See below, p. 139 for an appropriate direction on the *mens rea* requirement in such a case.

E. Causation

(1) *The accused's conduct must amount to a factual cause of the prohibited conduct*

The principles of causation apply to any crime in which the prosecution must prove that the accused caused a prohibited result, *e.g.* damage to property, but they are nearly always seen in the context of causing death.

Note

See *Dalloway* (1847); H.S.B., p. 186.

(2) *The accused's conduct must be capable of amounting to a legal cause of the prohibited result*

R. v. Cheshire

[1991] 3 All E.R. 670 (C.A.)

The accused had shot the victim causing serious injuries. These injuries responded to hospital treatment and it appeared that he would make a full recovery. Unfortunately he had suffered breathing problems, and a tube had been inserted into his windpipe to enable him to breathe freely. The surgeons failed to notice that his windpipe was becoming blocked as a result of narrowing near the site of the tracheotomy scar and he eventually suffocated. Cheshire was charged with murder. At his trial, evidence indicated that this medical condition was a rare but not unknown complication. A witness testified that at the time of death the gunshot wounds were no longer life threatening, but that death had been due to a failure to recognise the problems with the breathing tube. In other words he had been killed by the negligence of the hospital staff who should have recognised the problem.

On appeal it was argued that the trial judge had misdirected the jury on the issue of causation. The trial judge had said

"My direction to you is this, and I have to take the responsibility and you have to observe my direction: if the treatment could have been better, if it is no more than that, then the bullets caused the death, even if the treatment was incompetent, negligent. The bullets caused the death. For you to find that the chain was broken, the medical treatment or lack of medical treatment must be reckless. Mr. Boal when opening used the words "gross negligence". Mr. Eadie observed to you that gross negligence he regarded as the same as recklessness, and he is right, and I am using the word "recklessness", which is a strong word. Mere carelessness or mere negligence are not recklessness.

Reckless conduct is where somebody could not care less. He acts or he fails to act careless of the consequences, careless of the comfort and safety of another person. It is that which you are looking for when you examine the medical evidence. The question is: Do you see it, because nothing less alters the situation. In closing speeches Mr. Boal spoke of a high degree of negligence. Mr. Stewart when cross-examining the witnesses spotted and high-lighted acts which he said were not just inexperience, but negligence, and you may agree with him. But the direction I give you is what I have spoken. You are looking for recklessness."

Beldam L.J. Since the apportionment of responsibility for damage has become commonplace in the civil law, judges have sought to distinguish the blameworthiness of conduct from its causative effect. Epithets suggestive of degrees of blameworthiness may be of little help in deciding how potent the conduct was in causing the result. A momentary lapse of concentration may lead to more serious consequences than a more glaring neglect of duty. In the criminal law the jury considering the factual question, did the accused's act cause the deceased's death, will we think derive little assistance from figures of speech more appropriate for conveying degrees of fault or blame in questions of apportionment. Unless authority suggests otherwise, we think such figures of speech are to be avoided in giving guidance to a jury on the question of causation. Whilst medical treatment unsuccess-fully given to prevent the death of a victim with the care and skill of a competent medical practitioner will not amount to an intervening cause, it does not follow that treatment which falls below that standard of care and skill will amount to such a cause. As Professors Hart and Honoré comment, treatment which falls short of the standard expected of the competent medical practitioner is unfortunately only too frequent in human experience for it to be considered abnormal in the sense of extraordinary. Acts or omissions of a doctor treating the victim for injuries he has received at the hands of an accused may conceivably be so extraordinary as to be capable of being regarded as acts independent of the conduct of the accused but it is most unlikely that they will be.

We have not been referred to any English authority in which the terms of the direction which should be given to a jury in such a case have been considered. We were referred to *R. v. Jordan* (1956) 40 Cr.App.R. 152 in which the appellant, who had been convicted of murder, sought leave to call further evidence about the cause of the victim's death. The application was granted and evidence was received by the court that the stab wound from which the victim died eight days later was not the cause of the victim's death. The deceased had died from the effects of sensitivity to Terramycin which had been given to him after his intolerance to it was established and in abnormal quantity. The court considered that the introduction into the system of the victim of a substance shown to be poisonous to him and in quantities which were so great as to result in pulmonary oedema leading to pneumonia were factors which ought to have been before the jury and which in all probability would have affected their decision.

R. v. Jordan was described in the later cause of *R. v. Smith* [1959] 2 All E.R. 193, [1959] 2 Q.B. 35 as a very particular case dependent upon its exact facts. The appellant in *R. v. Smith* had been convicted at court-martial of the murder of another soldier by stabbing him. The victim had been dropped twice while being taken to the medical reception station and was subsequently given treatment which was said to be incorrect and harmful. Lord Parket C.J., giving the judgment of the Court-Martial Appeal Court, rejected a contention that his death did not result from the stab wound. He said [1959] 2 All E.R. 193 at 198, [1959] 2 Q.B. 35 at 42–43):

"It seems to the court that, if at the time of death the original wound is still an operating cause and a substantial cause, then the death can properly be said to be the result of the wound, albeit that some other cause of death is also operating. Only if it can be said that the original wounding is merely the setting in which another cause operates can it be said that the death does not result from the wound. Putting it in another way, only if the second cause is so overwhelming as to make the original wound merely part of the history can it be said that the death does not flow from the wound."

Both these cases were considered by this court in *R. v. Malcherek, R. v. Steel* [1981] 2 All E.R. 422, [1981] 1 W.L.R. 690 in which it had been argued that the act of a doctor in disconnecting a life support machine had intervened to cause the death of the victim to the exclusion of injuries inflicted by the appellants. In rejecting this submission Lord Lane C.J., after considering *R. v. Jordan* and *R. v. Smith*, said: ([1981] 2 All E.R. 422 at 428, [1981] 1 W.L.R 690 at 696):

"In the view of this court, if a choice has to be made between the decision in *R. v. Jordan* and that in *R. v. Smith*, which we do not believe it does (*R. v. Jordan* being a very exceptional case), then the decision in *R. v. Smith* is to be preferred."

Later in the same judgment Lord Lane C.J. said ([1981] 2 All E.R. 422 at 428–429, [1981] 1 W.L.R. 690 at 696–697):

"There may be occasions, although they will be rare, when the original injury has ceased to operate as a cause at all, but in the ordinary case if the treatment is given bona fide by competent and careful medical practitioners, then evidence will not be admissible to show that the treatment would not have been administered in the same way by other medical practitioners. In other words, the fact that the victim has died, despite or because of medical treatment for the initial injury given by careful and skilled medical practitioners, will not exonerate the original assailant from responsibility for the death."

In those two cases it was not suggested that the actions of the doctors in disconnecting the life support machines were other than competent and careful. The court did not have to consider the effect of medical treatment which fell short of the standard of care to be expected of competent medical practitioners.

A case in which the facts bear a close similarity to the case with which we are concerned is *R. v. Evans and Gardiner (No. 2)* [1976] V.R. 523. In that case the deceased was stabbed in the stomach by the two applicants in April 1974. After operation the victim resumed an apparently healthy life but nearly a year later, after suffering abdominal pain and vomiting and undergoing further medical treatment, he died. The cause of death was a stricture of the small bowel, a not uncommon sequal to the operation carried out to deal with the stab wound inflicted by the applicants. It was contended that the doctors treating the victim for the later symptoms ought to have diagnosed the presence of the stricture, that they had been negligent not to do so and that timely operative treatment would have saved the victim's life.

The Supreme Court of Victoria held that the test to be applied in determining whether a felonious act has caused a death which follows, in spite of an intervening act, is whether the felonious act is still an operating and substantial cause of the death.

The summing up to the jury had been based on the passage already quoted from Lord Parker C.J.'s judgment in *R. v. Smith* and the Supreme Court indorsed a direction in those terms. It commented upon the limitations of *R. v. Jordan* and made observations on the difference between the failure to diagnose the consequence of the original injury and cases in which medical treatment has been given which has a positive adverse effect on the victim. It concluded (at 529):

"But in the long run the difference between a positive act of commission and an omission to do some particular act is for these purposes ultimately a question of degree. As an event intervening between an act alleged to be felonious and to have resulted in death, and the actual death, a positive act of commission or an act of omission will serve to break the chain of causation only if it can be shown that the act or omission accelerated the death, so that it can be said to have caused the death and thus to have prevented the felonious act which would have caused death from actually doing so."

Later in the judgment the court said (at 534):

"In these circumstances we agree with the view of the learned trial Judge expressed in his report to this Court that there was a case to go to the jury. The failure of the medical practitioners to diagnose correctly the victim's condition, however inept or unskilful, was not the cause of death. It was the blockage of the bowel which caused death and the real question for the jury was whether that blockage was due to the stabbing. There was plenty of medical evidence to support such a finding, if the jury chose to accept it."

It seems to us that these two passages demonstrate the difficulties in formulating and explaining a general concept of causation but what we think does emerge from this and the other cases is that when the victim of a criminal attack is treated for wounds or injuries by doctors or other medical staff attempting to repair the harm done, it will only be in the most extraordinary and unusual case that such treatment can be said to be so independent of the acts of the accused that it could be regarded in law as the cause of the victim's death to the exclusion of the accused's acts.

Where the law requires proof of the relationship between an act and its consequences as an element of responsibility, a simple and sufficient explanation of the basis of such relationship has proved notoriously elusive.

In a case in which the jury have to consider whether negligence in the treatment of injuries inflicted by the accused was the cause of death we think it is sufficient for the judge to tell the jury that they must be satisfied that the Crown have proved that the acts of the accused caused the death of the deceased, adding that the accused's acts need not be the sole cause or even the main cause of death, it being sufficient that his acts contributed significantly to that result. Even though negligence in the treatment of the victim was the immediate cause of his death, the jury should not regard it as excluding the responsibility of the accused unless the negligent treatment was so independent of his acts, and in itself so potent in causing death, that they regard the contribution made by his acts as insignificant.

It is not the function of the jury to evaluate competing causes or to choose which is dominant provided they are satisfied that the accused's acts can fairly be said to have made a significant contribution to the victim's death. We think the word 'significant' conveys the necessary substance of a contribution made to the death which is more than negligible.

In the present case the passage in the summing up complained of has to be set in the context of the remainder of the direction given by the judge on the issue of causation. He directed the jury that they had to decide whether the two bullets fired into the deceased on December 10 caused his death on February 15 following. Or, he said, put in another way, did the injuries caused cease to operate as a cause of death because something else intervened? He told them that the prosecution did not have to prove that the bullets were the only cause of death but they had to prove that they were one operative and substantial cause of death. He was thus following the words used in *R. v. Smith*.

The judge then gave several examples for the jury to consider before reverting to a paraphrase of the alternative formulation used by Lord Parker C.J. in *R. v. Smith*. Finally, he reminded the jury of the evidence which they had heard on this issue. We would remark that on several occasions during this evidence the jury had passed notes to the judge asking for clarification of expressions used by the medical witnesses, which showed that they were following closely the factual issues they had to consider. If the passage to which exception has been taken had not been included, no possible criticism could have been levelled at the summing up. Although for reasons we have stated we think that the judge erred when he invited the jury to consider the degree of fault in the medical treatment rather than its consequences, we consider that no miscarriage of justice has actually occurred. Even if more experienced doctors than those who attended the deceased would have recognised the rare complication in time to have prevented the deceased's death, that complication was a direct consequence of the appellant's acts, which remained a significant cause of his death. We cannot conceive that, on the evidence given, any jury would have found otherwise.

Accordingly, we dismiss the appeal.

Appeal dismissed.

(3) Can the victim's own conduct break the chain of causation?

R. v. Blaue

(1975) 61 Cr.App.R. 271 (C.A.)

[B. had stabbed and seriously wounded a girl of 18. She refused a blood transfusion on the ground she was a Jehovah's Witness, and later died. It seems fairly clear that the blood transfusion would have given her the chance to undergo surgery which would have had a high chance of success.]

Lawton L.J. In *R. v. Holland* (1841) the defendant, in the course of a violent assault, had injured one of his victim's fingers. A surgeon had advised amputation because of danger to life through complications developing. The advice was rejected. A fortnight later the victim died of lockjaw: "... the real question is", said Maule J, "whether in the end the wound inflicted by the prisoner was the cause of death?" That distinguished judge left the jury to decide that question as did the judge in this case. They had to decide it as juries always do, by pooling their experience of life and using their common sense. They would not have been handicapped by a lack of training in dialectics or moral theology.

Maule J's direction to the jury reflected the common law's answer to the problem. He who inflicted an injury which resulted in death could not excuse himself by pleading that his victim could have avoided death by taking greater care of himself.... The common law in Sir Matthew Hale's time probably was in line with contemporary concepts of ethics. A man who did a wrongful act was deemed *morally* responsible for the natural and probable consequences of that act. Counsel for the appellant asked us to remember that since Sir Matthew Hale's day the rigour of the law relating to homicide has been eased in favour of the accused. It has been—but this has come about through the development of the concept of intent, not by reason of a different view of causation....

The physical cause of death in this case was the bleeding into the pleural cavity arising from the penetration of the lung. This had not been brought about by any decision made by the deceased girl but by the stab wound.

Counsel for the appellant tried to overcome this line of reasoning by submitting that the jury should have been directed that if they thought the girl's decision not to have a blood transfusion was an unreasonable one, then the chain of causation would have been broken. At once the question arises—reasonable by whose standards? Those of Jehovah's Witnesses? Humanists? Roman Catholics? Protestants of AngloSaxon descent? The man on the Clapham omnibus? But he might well be an admirer of Eleazar who suffered death rather than eat the flesh of swine; or of Sir Thomas Moore who, unlike nearly all his contemporaries, was unwilling to accept Henry VIII as Head of the Church of England. Those brought up in the Hebraic and Christian traditions would probably be reluctant to accept that these martyrs caused their own deaths.

As was pointed out to counsel for the appellant in the course of argument, two cases, each raising the same issue of reasonableness because of religious beliefs, could produce different verdicts depending on where the cases were tried. A jury drawn from Preston, sometimes said to be the most Catholic town in England, might have different views about martyrdom to one drawn from the inner suburbs of London. Counsel for the appellant accepted that this might be so; it was, he said, inherent in trial by jury. It is not inherent in the common law as expounded by Sir Matthew Hale and Maule J. It has long been the policy of the law that those who use violence on other people must take their victims as they find them. This in our judgment means the whole man, not just the physical man. It does not lie in the mouth of the assailant to say that his victim's religious beliefs which inhibited him from accepting certain kinds of treatment were unreasonable. The question for decision is what caused her death. The answer is the stab wound. The fact that the victim refused to stop this end coming about did not break the causal connection between the act and death.

Questions

Is this case authority for the proposition that failure by a victim to take proper care of himself can never excuse the initial assailant from responsibility? Does it make any difference whether the initial wound was trivial or serious? Would it support a conclusion that a rapist should be held responsible for the subsequent suicide of his distraught victim?

R. v. Pagett

(1983) 76 Cr.App.R. 279 (C.A.)

[P. had forcibly abducted a young girl. Armed police had surrounded the house where he was holding the girl and he threatened to shoot her. He later tried to leave the house holding the girl in front of him as a shield. He fired shots at the police who instinctively fired back. Police bullets struck and killed the girl.]

Goff L.J. In our judgment, the question whether an accused person can be held guilty of homicide, either murder or manslaughter, of a victim the immediate cause of whose death is the act of another person must be determined on the ordinary principles of causation, uninhibited by any such rule of policy as that for which Lord Gifford has contended. We therefore reject the second ground of appeal.

We turn to the first ground of appeal, which is that the learned judge erred in directing the jury that it was for him to decide *as a matter of law* whether by his unlawful and deliberate acts the appellant caused or was a cause of Gail Kinchen's death. It is right to observe that this direction of the learned judge followed upon a discussion with counsel, in the absence of the jury; though the appellant, having dismissed his own counsel, was for this purpose without legal representation. In the course of this discussion, counsel for the prosecution referred the learned judge to a passage in Professor Smith and Professor Hogan's *Criminal Law* (4th ed. (1978), p. 272), which reads as follows: "Causation is a question of both fact and law. D's act cannot be held to be the cause of an event if the event would have occurred without it. The act, that is, must be a *sine qua non* of the event and whether it is so is a question of fact. But there are many acts which are *sine qua non* of a homicide and yet are not either in law, or in ordinary parlance, the cause of it. If I invite P to dinner and he is run over and killed on the way, my invitation may be a *sine qua non* of his death, but no one would say I killed him and I have not caused his death in law. Whether a particular act which is a *sine qua non* of an alleged *actus reus* is also a cause of it is a question of law. Where the facts are admitted the judge may direct the jury that a particular act did, or did not, cause a particular result." There follows a reference to *Jordan* (1956).

For the appellant, Lord Gifford criticised the statement of the learned authors that "Whether a particular act which is a *sine qua non* of an alleged *actus reus* is also a cause of it is a question of law." He submitted that that question had to be answered by the jury as a question of fact. In our view, with all respect, both the passage in Smith and Hogan's *Criminal Law*, and Lord Gifford's criticism of it, are over-simplifications of a complex matter. . . .

Now the whole subject of causation in the law has been the subject of a well-known and most distinguished treatise by Professors Hart and Honoré, *Causation in the Law*. Passages from this book were cited to the learned judge, and were plainly relied upon by him; we, too, wish to express our indebtedness to it. It would be quite wrong for us to consider in this judgment the wider issues discussed in that work. But, for present purposes, the passage which is of most immediate relevance is to be found in Chapter XII, in which the learned authors consider the circumstances in which the intervention of a third person, not acting in concert with the accused, may have the effect of relieving the accused of criminal responsibility. The criterion which they suggest should be applied in such circumstances is whether the intervention is voluntary, *i.e.* whether it is "free, deliberate and informed." We resist the temptation of expressing the judicial opinion whether we find ourselves in complete agreement with that definition; though we certainly consider it to be broadly correct and supported by authority. Among the examples which the authors give of non-voluntary conduct, which is not effective to relieve the accused of responsibility, are two which are germane to the present case, *viz.* a reasonable act performed for the purpose of self-preservation, and an act done in performance of a legal duty.

There can, we consider, be no doubt that a reasonable act performed for the purpose of self-preservation, being of course itself an act caused by the accused's own act, does not operate as a *novus actus interveniens*. If authority is needed for this almost self-evident proposition, it is to be found in such cases as *Pitts* (1842) and *Curley* (1909). In both these cases, the act performed for the purpose of self-preservation consisted of an act by the victim in attempting to escape from the violence of the accused, which in fact resulted in the victim's death. In each case it was held as a matter of law that, if the victim acted in a reasonable attempt to escape the violence of the accused, the death of the victim was caused by the act of the accused. Now one form of self-preservation is self-defence; for present purposes, we can see no distinction in principle between an attempt to escape the consequences of the accused's act, and a response which takes the form of self-defence. Furthermore, in our judgment, if a reasonable act of self-defence against the act of the accused causes the death of a third party, we can see no reason in principle why the act of self-defence, being an involuntary act caused by the act of the accused, should relieve the accused from criminal responsibility for the death of the third party. Of course, it does not necessarily follow that the accused will be guilty of the murder, or even of the manslaughter, of the third party; though in the majority of cases he is likely to be guilty at least of manslaughter. Whether he is guilty of murder or manslaughter will depend upon the question whether all the ingredients of the relevant offence have been proved; in particular, on a charge of murder, it will be necessary that the accused had the necessary intent.

There is however one further aspect of the present case to which we must advert. On the evidence, Gail Kinchen was not just an innocent bystander killed by a shot fired from the gun of a police officer who, acting in reasonable self-defence, fired his gun in response to a lethal attack by the appellant: though on those facts alone it would, in our opinion, have been open to the jury to convict the appellant of murder or manslaughter. But if, as the jury must have found to have occurred in the present case, the appellant used Gail Kinchen by force and against her will as a shield to protect him from any shots fired by the police, the effect is that he committed not one but two unlawful acts, both of which were dangerous—the act of firing at the police, and the act of holding Gail Kinchen as a shield in front of him when the police might well fire shots in his direction in self-defence. Either act could in our judgment, if on the principles we have stated it was held to cause the death of Gail Kinchen, constitute the *actus reus* of the manslaughter or, if the necessary intent were established, murder of Gail Kinchen by the appellant, even though the shot which killed her was fired not by the appellant but by a police officer.

2. MENS REA

A. Degrees of Culpability

(i) Intention and Knowledge

In most crimes liability can be established by proof of intention or recklessness; and so a precise definition of intention does not have to be attempted. In some crimes, intention only will suffice (in respect of at least one element of the *actus reus*); in these crimes it is necessary to know what constitutes intention.

Cunliffe v. Goodman

[1950] 2 K.B. 237 (C.A.)

Asquith L.J. An "intention" to my mind connotes a state of affairs which the party intending; I will call him X—does more than merely contemplate: it connotes a state of affairs which, on the contrary, he decides, so far as in him lies, to bring about, and which in point of possibility, he has a reasonable prospect of being able to bring about by his own act of volition.

Note

See further *R.* v. *Moloney* (below, p. 301); *R.* v. *Hancock and Shankland* (below, p. 307); *R* v. *Nedrick* (below, p. 316).

Question

X plants a bomb in a local public house which he desires to destroy. He gives the landlord 60 seconds' warning knowing that this is almost certainly not enough time to evacuate the premises. Five people are seriously wounded. Can he be convicted of unlawfully and maliciously wounding these people with intent to cause them grievous bodily harm?

(ii)   Recklessness

As a result of recent decisions it can be said that recklessness involves the taking of an unjustified risk either deliberately or without adverting to the existence of the risk.

(1)   *Deliberate risk taking*

R. v. Cunningham

[1957] 2 Q.B. 396 (C.C.A.)

[C. had wrenched a gas meter off the wall in a cellar in order to steal its contents. As a result escaping gas seeped through a wall of loose stone rubble which divided the cellar of the house from the cellar of the adjoining house. The escaping gas partially asphyxiated a woman occupant in the adjoining house. He was charged with unlawfully and maliciously causing a certain noxious thing to be taken by the victim so as thereby to endanger her life (Offences Against the Person Act 1861, s.23). The trial judge directed the jury that " 'Malicious' for this purpose means wicked—some thing which he has no business to do and perfectly well knows it." On appeal against conviction:]

Byrne J. With the utmost respect to the learned judge, we think it is incorrect to say that the word "malicious" in a statutory offence merely means wicked. We think the judge was, in effect, telling the jury that if they were satisfied that the appellant acted wickedly—and he had clearly acted wickedly in stealing the gas meter and its contents—they ought to find that he had acted maliciously in causing the gas to be taken by Mrs. Wade so as thereby to endanger her life.

In our view it should have been left to the jury to decide whether, even if the appellant did not intend the injury to Mrs. Wade, he foresaw that the removal of the gas meter might cause injury to someone but nevertheless removed it. We are unable to say that a reasonable jury, properly directed as to the meaning of the word "maliciously" in the context of section 23, would without doubt have convicted.

In these circumstances this court has no alternative but to allow the appeal and quash the conviction.

Appeal allowed.

(2) *Inadvertent risk taking*

R. v. Caldwell

[1982] A.C. 341 (H.L.)

[C. set fire to a hotel where 10 guests were in residence, believing he had a grievance against the proprietor. No great damage was caused. He was charged under section 1 of the Criminal Damage Act 1971 which is set out in Chapter 10. In the indictment count 2 contained a charge under section 1(1) of the Act which is the basic offence of criminal damage; to this he pleaded guilty. In another count he was charged with an offence under section 1(2) which involves intentionally or recklessly endangering life to which he pleaded not guilty. The House was mainly concerned with the question of whether self-induced intoxication could provide a defence to this second

charge, but in the course of the speeches attention was given to the meaning
of the word "reckless."]

Lord Diplock. My Lords, the Criminal Damage Act 1971
replaced almost in their entirety the many and detailed
provisions of the Malicious Damage Act 1861. Its purpose, as
stated in its long title, was to *revise* the law of England and
Wales as to offences of damage to property. As the brevity of
the Act suggests, it must have been hoped that it would also
simplify the law.

In the Act of 1861, the word consistently used to describe
the *mens rea* that was a necessary element in the multifarious
offences that the Act created was "maliciously"—a technical
expression, not readily intelligible to juries, which became the
subject of considerable judicial exegesis. This culminated in a
judgment of the Court of Criminal Appeal in *Reg.* v.
Cunningham (1957) (above) which approved, as an accurate
statement of the law, what had been said by Professor Kenny
in the first edition of his *Outlines of Criminal Law* published in
1902:

"In any statutory definition of a crime, malice must be
taken... as requiring either (1) an actual intention to do the
particular kind of harm that in fact was done; or (2)
recklessness as to whether such harm should occur or not
(*i.e.*, the accused has foreseen that the particular kind of
harm might be done and yet has gone on to take the risk of
it)."

My Lords, in this passage Professor Kenny was engaged in
defining for the benefit of students the meaning of "malice"
as a term of art in criminal law. To do so he used ordinary
English words in their popular meaning. Among the words
he used was "recklessness," the noun derived from the
adjective "reckless," of which the popular or dictionary
meaning is: careless, regardless, or heedless, of the possible
harmful consequences of one's acts. It presupposes that if
thought were given to the matter by the doer before the act
was done, it would have been apparent to him that there was
a real risk of its having the relevant harmful consequences;
but, granted this, recklessness covers a whole range of states
of mind from failing to give any thought at all to whether or
not there is any risk of those harmful consequences, to
recognising the existence of the risk and nevertheless deciding
to ignore it. Conscious of this imprecision in the popular
meaning of recklessness as descriptive of a state of mind,
Professor Kenny, in the passage quoted, was, as it seems to

me, at pains to indicate by the words in brackets the particular species within the genus reckless states of mind that constituted "malice" in criminal law. This parenthetical restriction on the natural meaning of recklessness was necessary to an explanation of the meaning of the adverb "maliciously" when used as a term of art in the description of an offence under the Malicious Damage Act 1861 (which was the matter in point in *Reg.* v. *Cunningham* (1957); but it was not directed to and consequently has no bearing on the meaning of the adjective "reckless" in section 1 of the Criminal Damage Act 1971. To use it for that purpose can, in my view, only be misleading.

My Lords, the restricted meaning that the Court of Appeal in *Reg.* v. *Cunningham* had placed upon the adverb "maliciously" in the Malicious Damage Act 1861 in cases where the prosecution did not rely upon an actual intention of the accused to cause the damage that was in fact done, called for a meticulous analysis by the jury of the thoughts that passed through the mind of the accused at or before the time he did the act that caused the damage, in order to see on which side of a narrow dividing line they fell. If it had crossed his mind that there was a risk that someone's property might be damaged but, because his mind was affected by rage or excitement or confused by drink, he did not appreciate the seriousness of the risk or trusted that good luck would prevent its happening, this state of mind would amount to malice in the restricted meaning placed upon that term by the Court of Appeal; whereas if, for any of these reasons, he did not even trouble to give his mind to the question whether there was any risk of damaging the property, this state of mind would not suffice to make him guilty of an offence under the Malicious Damage Act 1861.

Neither state of mind seems to me to be less blameworthy than the other; but if the difference between the two constituted the distinction between what does and what does not in legal theory amount to a guilty state of mind for the purposes of a statutory offence of damage to property, it would not be a practicable distinction for use in a trial by jury. The only person who knows what the accused's mental processes were is the accused himself—and probably not even he can recall them accurately when the rage or excitement under which he acted has passed, or he has sobered up if he were under the influence of drink at the relevant time. If the accused gives evidence that because of his rage, excitement or drunkenness the risk of particular harmful consequences of his acts simply did not occur to him, a jury would find it hard to be satisfied beyond reasonable doubt that his true mental process was not that, but was the slightly different mental process required if one applies the restricted meaning of "being reckless as to whether" something would happen, adopted by the Court of Appeal in *Reg.* v. *Cunningham.*

My Lords, I can see no reason why Parliament when it decided to revise the law as to offences of damage to property should go out of its way to perpetuate fine and impracticable distinctions such as these, between one mental state and another. One would think that the sooner they were got rid of, the better.

When cases under section 1(1) of the new Act, in which the prosecution's case was based upon the accused having been "reckless as to whether... property would be destroyed or damaged," first came before the Court of Appeal, the question as to the meaning of the expression "reckless" in the context of that subsection appears to have been treated as soluble simply by posing and answering what had by then, unfortunately, become an obsessive question among English lawyers: Is the test of recklessness "subjective" or "objective"? The first two reported cases, in both of which judgments were given off the cuff, are first *Reg.* v. *Briggs (Note)* (1977) which is reported in a footnote to the second, *Reg.* v. *Daryl Parker* (1977). Both classified the test of recklessness as "subjective." This led the court in *Reg.* v. *Briggs (Note)* (1977) to say: "A man is reckless in the sense required when he carries out a deliberate act knowing that there is some risk of damage resulting from that act but nevertheless continues in the performance of that act." This leaves over the question whether the risk of damage may not be so slight that even the most prudent of men would feel justified in taking it, but it excludes that kind of recklessness that consists of acting without giving any thought at all to whether or not there is any risk of harmful consequences of one's act; even though the risk is great and would be obvious if any thought were given to the matter by the doer of the act. *Reg.* v. *Daryl Parker* (1977), however, opened the door a chink by adding as an alternative to the actual knowledge of the accused that there is some risk of damage resulting from his act and his going on to take it, a mental state described as "closing his mind to the obvious fact" that there is such a risk.

Reg. v. *Stephenson* (1979), the first case in which there was full argument, though only on one side, and a reserved judgment, slammed the door again upon any less restricted interpretation of "reckless" as to whether particular consequences will occur than that originally approved in *Reg.* v. *Briggs (Note)* (1977). The appellant, a tramp, intending to pass the night in a hollow in the side of a haystack, had lit a fire to keep himself warm; as a result of this the stack itself caught fire. At his trial he was not himself called as a witness but a psychiatrist gave evidence on his behalf that he was schizophrenic and might not have had the same ability to foresee or appreciate risk as a mentally normal person. The judge had given to the jury the direction on the meaning of reckless that had been approved in *Reg.* v. *Daryl Parker* (1977). The argument for the appellant on the appeal was that this let in an "objective" test whereas the test should be entirely "subjective." It was buttressed by copious citation from previous judgments in civil and criminal cases where the expressions "reckless" or "recklessness" had been used by judges in various contexts. Counsel for the Crown expressed his agreement with the submissions for the appellant. The judgment of the court contains an analysis of a number of the cited cases, mainly in the field of civil law. These cases do not disclose a uniform judicial use of the terms; and as respects judicial statements made before the current vogue for classifying all tests of legal liability as either "objective" or "subjective" they are not easily assignable to one of those categories rather than the other. The court, however, reached its final conclusion by a different route. It made the assumption that although Parliament in replacing the Act of 1861 by the Act of 1971 had discarded the word "maliciously" as descriptive of the *mens rea* of the offences of which the *actus reus* is damaging property, in favour of the more explicit phrase "intending to destroy or damage any such property or being reckless as to whether any such property would be destroyed," it nevertheless intended the words to be interpreted in precisely the same sense as that in which the single adverb "maliciously" had been construed by Professor Kenny in the passage that received the subsequent approval of the Court of Appeal in *Reg.* v. *Cunningham* (1957).

My Lords, I see no warrant for making any such assumption in an Act whose declared purpose is to revise the then existing law as to offences of damage to property, not to perpetuate it. "Reckless" as used in the new statutory definition of the *mens rea* of these offences is an ordinary English word. It had not by 1971 become a term of legal art with some more limited esoteric meaning than that which it bore in ordinary speech—a meaning which surely includes not only deciding to ignore a risk of harmful consequences resulting from one's acts that one has recognised as existing, but also failing to give any thought to whether or not there is any such risk in circumstances where, if any thought were given to the matter, it would be obvious that there was.

If one is attaching labels, the latter state of mind is neither more nor less "subjective" than the first. But the label solves nothing. It is a statement of the obvious; *mens rea* is, by definition, a state of mind of the accused himself at the time he did the physical act that constitutes the *actus reus* of the offence; it cannot be the mental state of some non-existent, hypothetical person.

Nevertheless, to decide whether someone has been "reckless" as to whether harmful consequences of a particular kind will result from his act, as distinguished from his actually intending such harmful consequences to follow, does call for some consideration of how the mind of the ordinary prudent individual would have reacted to a similar situation. If there were nothing in the circumstances that ought to have drawn the attention of an ordinary prudent individual to the possibility of that kind of harmful consequence, the accused would not be described as "reckless" in the natural meaning of that word for failing to address his mind to the possibility; nor, if the risk of the harmful consequences was so slight that the ordinary prudent individual upon due consideration of the risk would not be deterred from treating it as negligible, could the accused be described as "reckless" in its ordinary sense if, having considered the risk, he decided to ignore it. (In this connection the gravity of the possible harmful consequences would be an important factor. To endanger life must be one of the most grave.) So to this extent, even if one ascribes to "reckless" only the restricted meaning, adopted by the Court of Appeal in *Reg.* v. *Stephenson* (1979) and *Reg.* v. *Briggs (Note)* (1977) of foreseeing that a particular kind of harm might happen and yet going on to take the risk of it, it involves a test that would be described in part as "objective" in current legal jargon. Questions of criminal liability are seldom solved by simply asking whether the test is subjective or objective.

In my opinion, a person charged with an offence under section 1(1) of the Criminal Damage Act 1971 is "reckless as to whether any such property would be destroyed or damaged" if (1) he does an act which in fact creates an obvious risk that property will be destroyed or damaged and (2) when he does the act he either has not given any thought to the possibility of there being any such risk or has recognised that there was some risk involved and has nonetheless gone on to do it. That would be a proper direction to the jury; cases in the Court of Appeal which held otherwise should be regarded as overruled.

Where the charge is under section 1(2) the question of the state of mind of the accused must be approached in stages, corresponding to paragraphs (*a*) and (*b*). The jury must be satisfied that what the accused did amounted to an offence under section 1(1), either because he actually intended to destroy or damage the property or because he was reckless (in the sense that I have described) as to whether it might be destroyed or damaged. Only if they are so satisfied must the jury go on to consider whether the accused also either actually intended that the destruction or damage of the property should endanger someone's life or was reckless (in a similar sense) as to whether a human life might be endangered.

Appeal dismissed.

Notes

1. See further *Reid* (below, p. 344).
2. The question of self-induced intoxication is considered below, p. 227.
3. Where the prosecution are relying on recklessness in a case where liability is based upon a failure to act (see above, p. 117) Lord Diplock said that a modified direction to the jury would be necessary.

R. v. Miller

[1983] A.C. 161 (H.L.)

Lord Diplock. While in the general run of cases of destruction or damage to property belonging to another by fire (or other means) where the prosecution relies upon the recklessness of the accused, the direction recommended by this House in *Reg.* v. *Caldwell* (1982) is appropriate, in the exceptional case, (which is most likely to be one of arson and of which the instant appeal affords a striking example) where the accused is initially unaware that he has done an act that in fact sets in train events which, by the time the accused becomes aware of them, would make it obvious to anyone who troubled to give his mind to them that they present a risk that property belonging to another would be damaged, a suitable direction to the jury would be: that the accused is guilty of the offence under section 1(1) of the Criminal Damage Act 1971 if, when he does become aware that the events in question have happened as a result of his own act, he does not try to prevent or reduce the risk of damage by his own efforts or if necessary by sending for help from the fire brigade, and the reason why he does not is either because he has not given any thought to the possibility of there being any such risk or because, having recognised that there was some risk involved, he has decided not to try to prevent or reduce it.

Question

Lord Diplock talks of recklessness as involving, *inter alia*, the creation of an "obvious risk." What does he mean by this? To whom must the risk be obvious

   (i)   to the accused;
   (ii) to a reasonable person;
   (iii) to a reasonable person of the accused's age with such of his characteristics as would affect his appreciation of the risk?

R. v. Sangha

(1988) 87 Cr.App.R. 88 (C.A.)

The question for the court to decide was whether by setting fire to two armchairs the accused had created an obvious and serious risk to property thereby endangering life. The issue was obscured by the fact that building experts would know that the construction of this particular building made it highly unlikely that the fire could spread and endanger life.

Croom Johnson L.J.   In our judgment, when consideration is given as to whether an act of setting fire to something creates an obvious and serious risk of damaging property and thereby endangering the life of another, the test to be applied is this: Is it proved that an ordinary prudent bystander would have perceived an obvious risk that property would be damaged and that life would thereby be endangered? The ordinary prudent bystander is not deemed to be invested with expert knowledge relating to the construction of the property, nor to have the benefit of hindsight. The time at which his perception is material is the time when the fire is started.

The section used the word "would" in the context of recklessness as to whether property would be destroyed or damaged, or as to whether the life of another would be thereby endangered. We interpret this word "would" as going to the expectations of the normal prudent bystander.

Applying this test to the facts of the case before us, it is clear that in setting fire to these armchairs (as the jury found the appellant did), he created a risk which was obvious and serious that property would be damaged and that the life of another would thereby be endangered. The fact that there were special features here which prevented that risk from materialising is irrelevant.

Question

Is there a loophole in the Caldwell definition of recklessness?

R. v. Reid

[1992] 3 All E.R. 673

Lord Goff. It has been pointed out that, although Lord Diplock's two categories of recklessness taken together have the effect that, in most cases where the defendant is driving dangerously in the sense I have described [that is he has by his driving created an obvious and serious risk of causing physical harm to other road users or substantial damage to property], he will in fact be driving recklessly, nevertheless there are cases in which this is not so. This may occur where the defendant considers the possibility of risk but nevertheless concludes that there is none. But we have to remember that, ex hypothesi, the defendant is driving dangerously in the sense I have described; and in practice his evidence that in such circumstances he thought that there was no risk is only likely to carry weight if he can point to some specific fact as to which he was mistaken and which, if true, would have excluded the possibility of risk which might occur if, for example, as my noble and learned friend Lord Ackner has pointed out, he misunderstood in good faith some direction or instruction, or if he drove the wrong way down a one-way street at a normal speed in the mistaken belief that it was a two-way street. If that was indeed the case, his driving might well not be described as reckless, though such cases are likely to be rare. It has been suggested that there is therefore a "loophole" or "lacuna" in Lord Diplock's definition of recklessness. I feel bound to say that I myself regard these expressions as misleading. The simple fact is that Lord Diplock was concerned to define driving recklessly, not dangerous driving; and it is not in every case where the defendant is in fact driving dangerously that he should be held to be driving recklessly, although in most cases the two will coincide. Another example where they may not coincide could occur where a driver who, while driving, is afflicted by illness or shock which impairs his capacity to address his mind to the possibility of risk; it may well not be right to describe him as driving recklessly in such circumstances. Likewise (as my noble and learned friend has pointed out), if a driver takes evasive action in an emergency, his action may involve the taking of a risk which is regarded as justified in the special circumstances, so that he cannot be described as driving recklessly. Such cases, which again are likely to be rare, can be dealt with if and when they arise. It is however unnecessary to consider any such case on the present appeal.

Note

See also *Chief Constable of Avon and Somerset Constabulary* v. *Shimmen* (1987) 84 Cr.App.R. 7 (D.L.)

Is this decision in *Elliot* v. *C* (below) reconcilable with Lord Goff's example above of the "driver, who while driving, is afflicted by illness or shock which impairs his ability to address his mind to the possibility of risk"?

R. v. Stephen Malcolm R.

(1984) 149 J.P. 89 (C.A.)

R. was convicted, at the age of 15, of several offences, one of which was arson with intent to endanger life (or being reckless as to whether the life of another would be endangered), contrary to section 1(2) and 1(3) of the Criminal Damage Act 1971. He had pleaded guilty when the trial judge rejected a submission by his counsel to the effect that R. was reckless in the *Caldwell* sense only if he had created a risk which would have been obvious to someone of his age and with any of his characteristics which might affect his appreciation of the risk.

The Divisional Court considered these principles recently in the case of *Elliott* v. *C.* (1983). That was an appeal by the prosecution by way of case stated from the justices of the petty sessional division of Canterbury, who on September 28, 1982 found that the respondent C., who was a minor, was not guilty of a charge and dismissed an information which alleged that she on June 16, 1982 without lawful excuse had destroyed by fire a shed and its contents intending to destroy such property or being reckless whether such property would be destroyed contrary to the same section in the Criminal Damage Act 1971 as that with which we are concerned. She was a schoolgirl who had reached the age of 14 years in May 1982. She lived with her foster mother and was in a remedial class at school. On the evening of June 15, 1982 she went out with an older schoolfriend. She hoped to stay the night at the friend's home, but was unable to do so. She did not return to her own home, but stayed out all night, not sleeping for the whole of the night. At about 5 am on June 16, 1982 she entered Mr. Davies's garden shed. She found white spirit in a plastic container. She poured this on to the carpet on the floor of the shed, threw two lighted matches on to the spirit, the second of which ignited. The fire immediately flared up out of control and the girl left the shed. In due course proceedings were taken against her.

The magistrates found that while she had realised that the contents of the bottle which contained the white spirit were possibly inflammable, she had not handled it before and had not appreciated how explosively it would burn and immediately become out of her control, thus destroying the shed and its contents, placing her own life at risk. She had not given thought at the time that she started the fire to the possibility of there being a risk that the shed and its contents would be destroyed by her actions. In the circumstances the risk would not have been obvious to her or been appreciated by her if she had given thought to it. In reaching their findings the magistrates said that they had paid due regard to the girl's age and understanding, her lack of experience in dealing with inflammable spirit and the fact that she must have been tired and exhausted at the time. They had had the case of *Caldwell* drawn to their attention and they said that they found it implicit in the decision that a defendant should only be held to have acted recklessly by virtue of his failure to give any thought to an obvious risk that property would be destroyed or damaged where such risk would be obvious to him if he had given any thought to the matter. They therefore dismissed the information.

[Ackner L.J. said that in the Divisional Court, Glidewell J. had felt that the correct interpretation of the three House of Lords authorities compelled him to hold that the prosecuting counsel was right in his submission that the risk had to be obvious to a reasonable prudent man, not necessarily to the particular defendant if he or she had given thought to it.]

Robert Goff L.J., in his judgment—and we should perhaps emphasise that both judgments were reserved—expressed his unhappiness at having to reach the same conclusion, but held compelled by the authorities, to which we have referred, to do so. He referred to certain articles written by jurists which were critical of Lord Diplock's statement of principle, unless that principle was to be taken as qualified to the extent that the defendant should be regarded as having acted recklessly by virtue of his failure to give any thoughts to an obvious risk that property would be destroyed or damaged (or for that matter the life of another would be endangered) only where such risk would have been obvious to him if he had given any thought to the matter. However, for the reasons given by Robert Goff L.J., in his characteristically careful analysis of the matter, such a qualification, in his judgment, had been clearly rejected by Lord Diplock and by the majority of the court in *Caldwell's* case. . . .

In the face of that difficult situation, Mr. Timms sought to induce us to adopt a via media. He said he accepted it would be wrong to ask the question whether the defendant himself was aware of the risk, but it would be right to inquire whether a person of the age of the defendant and with his characteristics which might be relevant to his ability to foresee the risk, would have appreciated it. He drew our attention in particular to the submission made by the prosecution before the magistrates in *Elliott's* case . . . "that in relation to the defendant aged 14 years, the proper approach was whether such risk would have been obvious to a normal 14 year old child." Therefore he said he was not seeking to relate the test to the particular defendant, but merely, so to speak, to a class of which he is a member. This, he says, provides him with the same logical basis of approach to the reasonable man or the reasonably prudent person as *Camplin* had suggested. We do not think that that via media was for one moment in the mind of Lord Diplock. The opportunity so to ingraft this important modification on the principle which he had enunciated had arisen in the subsequent cases and would have been just the sort of point (if it was a valid one) which we would have expected the House of Lords to have desired to have dealt with, thus clearing up the position, when they had the opportunity to do so when considering whether or not to give leave in *Elliott's* case. If they had desired to say, for instance, that the age of the defendant was a factor to which particular regard must be had in applying the test, then *Elliott* was just the sort of case to do that, excising, if appropriate, any reference to any other ephemeral characteristics such as exhaustion from which the girl was said to be suffering. But they did not take that opportunity. We do not think that we should seek by this subtlety to avoid applying principles which we also have difficulty in accepting. We respectfully share the regrets voiced by Robert Goff L.J. that in essence "recklessness" has now been construed synonymously with "carelessness."

. . .
We therefore dismiss the appeal against conviction. Although we would have preferred that the judge should have at least been entitled in law to have left the jury the question, would a boy of the defendant's age have appreciated that to have thrown petrol bombs very close to the windows of this dwelling house was a danger to the life of the occupants of that house, we have little doubt that on the facts of this case the answer would have been clearly in the affirmative. As we have already stressed, this was a ground floor flat and the petrol bombs were thrown so close to the window where the girl whom it was sought, so it was said, to frighten her, had her bedroom, that one landed within 18 inches of that window.

Note

See also *W. (A Minor)* v. *Dolbey* (1989) 88 Cr.App.R. 1 (H.S.B. p. 183).

Questions

1. To what crimes will the *Caldwell* definition apply? (See Lord Diplock in *Lawrence* (1982).)
Lord Roskill in *Seymour* (1983) speaking of the statutory offence of causing death by reckless driving and the common law offence of "motor" manslaughter said:

> "My Lords, I would accept the submission of counsel for the Crown that once it is shown that the two offences co-exist it would be quite wrong to give the adjective 'reckless' or the adverb 'recklessly' a different meaning according to whether the statutory or the common law offence is charged. 'Reckless' should today be given the same meaning in relation to all offences which involve 'recklessness' as one of the elements unless Parliament has otherwise ordained."

2. Does the *Caldwell* test apply to "recklessness" in the definition of rape? (See the Sexual Offences Amendment Act 1976, s.1, below, p. 402; see also next case.)

R. v. Satnam and Kewal

(1984) 78 Cr.App.R. 149 (C.A.)

Bristow J. We think that in enacting [section 1 of the Sexual Offences Amendment Act 1976] Parliament must have accepted the recommendations of the Heilbron Committee, so that the provisions are declaratory of the existing law as stated in *D.P.P.* v. *Morgan* [below, p. 157].

Any direction as to the definition of rape should therefore be based upon section 1 of the 1976 Act and upon *D.P.P.* v. *Morgan*, without regard to *R.* v. *Caldwell* or *R.* v. *Lawrence*, which were concerned with recklessness in a different context and under a different statute.

The word "reckless" in relation to rape involves a different concept to its use in relation to malicious damage or, indeed, in relation to offences against the person. In the latter cases the foreseeability, or possible foreseeability, is as to the consequences of the criminal act. In the case of rape the foreseeability is as to the state of mind of the victim.

. . . . . .

In summing up a case of rape which involves the issue of consent, the judge should, in dealing with the state of mind of the defendant, first of all direct the jury that before they could convict of rape the Crown has to prove either that the defendant knew the woman did not want to have sexual intercourse, or was reckless as to whether she wanted to or not. If they were sure he knew she did not want to they should find him guilty of rape knowing there to be no consent. If they were not sure about that, then they would find him not guilty of such rape and should go on to consider reckless rape. If they thought he might genuinely have believed that she did want to, even though he was mistaken in his belief, they would find him not guilty. In considering whether his belief was genuine, they should take into account all the relevant circumstances (which could at that point be summarised) and ask themselves whether, in the light of those circumstances, he had reasonable grounds for such a belief. If, after considering those circumstances, they were sure he had no genuine belief that she wanted to, they would find him guilty. If they came to the conclusion that he could not care less whether she wanted to or not, but pressed on regardless, then he would have been reckless and could not have believed that she wanted to, and they would find him guilty of reckless rape.

1. What meaning should be given to the word "reckless" in section 15(4) of the Theft Act 1968 (below, p. 399)?

2. Does the *Caldwell* definition of recklessness apply to (i) unlawfully and maliciously wounding or inflicting grievous bodily harm; (ii) assault occasioning actual bodily harm; (iii) common assault? See *Savage and Parmenter* ((1991) below, p. 389).

3. Does the *Caldwell* definition of recklessness apply to involuntary manslaughter? See below, p. 334.

(iii)   Negligence

Blyth v. Birmingham Waterworks Co.

(1856) 11 Exch. 781

Alderson B. Negligence is the omission to do something which a reasonable man, guided upon those considerations which ordinarily regulate the conduct of human affairs, would do, or doing something which a prudent and reasonable man would not do.

This is a definition of negligence in a civil law case.

Questions

1. In which crimes does negligence form the basis for liability? (See section 3 Road Traffic Act 1988, formerly section 3 Road Traffic Act 1972 (H.S.B. 198); *Morgan* (below, p. 157); manslaughter (below, p. 334).) Although negligence is rarely the direct basis for criminal liability it may arise indirectly (for example as a defence to strict liability offences). (See H.S.B., p. 198 and p. 228.)

2. How does negligence, as defined by Alderson B., differ from recklessness as defined by Lord Diplock in *Caldwell* (above, p. 133; see also H.S.B. p. 204)?

(iv)   Blameless Inadvertence

In the states of mind so far considered there can be detected at least some element of culpability. Where the accused cannot be said to be at fault in his failure to perceive some element of the *actus reus*, it is sometimes said that he is, in respect of that element, blamelessly inadvertent. Does it therefore follow that he cannot be convicted of the offence in question?

R. v. Prince

(1875) L.R. 2 C.C.R. 154 (Court for Crown Cases Reserved)

[P. was charged under the then equivalent of section 20 of the Sexual Offences Act 1956 which provides:

"It is an offence for a person acting without lawful authority or excuse to take an unmarried girl under the age of 16 out of the possession of her parent or guardian against his will."

He knew full well that her father would not consent and that he had no right to take her out of her father's possession. However he honestly and, in the eyes of the jury, reasonably believed that she was 18 years old. So as far as that aspect of the *actus reus* was concerned he might be said to lack *mens rea*.]

Bramwell B.   read a judgment to which *Kelly C.B.*, *Cleasby B.*, *Grove J.*, *Pollock B.*, and *Amphlett B.* assented.

... It is impossible to suppose that a person taking a girl out of her father's possession against his will is guilty of no offence within the statute unless he, the taker, knows she is under 16— that he would not be guilty if the jury were of opinion he knew neither one way nor the other. Let it be then that the question is whether he is guilty where he knows, as he thinks, that she is over 16. This introduces the necessity for reading the statute with some strange words introduced; as thus: "Who-so-ever shall take any unmarried girl being under the age of sixteen, and not believing her to be over the age of sixteen, out of the possession," etc. Those words are not there, and the question is whether we are bound to construe the statute as though they were, on account of the rule that *mens rea* is necessary to make an act a crime.

I am of opinion that we are not, nor as though the word "knowingly" was there, and for the following reasons. The act forbidden is wrong in itself, if without lawful cause. I do not say illegal, but wrong. I have not lost sight of this, that though the statute probably principally aims at seduction for carnal purposes, the taking may be by a female, with a good motive. Nevertheless, though there may be cases which are not immoral in one sense, I say that the act forbidden is wrong. Let us remember what is the case supposed by the statute. It supposes that there is a girl—it does not say a woman, but a girl something between a child and a woman—it supposes she is in the possession of her father or mother, or other person having lawful care and charge of her, and it supposes there is a taking, and that that taking is against the will of the person in whose possession she is. It is, then, a taking of a girl in the possession of someone, against his will. I say that done without lawful cause is wrong, and that the legislature meant it should be at the risk of the taker, whether or not the girl was under 16. I do not say that taking a woman of 50 from her brother's or even father's house is wrong. She is at an age when she has a right to choose for herself; she is not a girl, nor of such tender age that she can be said to be in possession of or under the care or in the charge of anyone. If I am asked where I draw the line, I answer at when the female is no longer a girl in anyone's possession. But what the statute contemplates, and what I say is wrong, is the taking of a female of such tender years that she is properly called a girl, and can be said to be in another's possession, and in that other's care of charge. No argument is necessary to prove this; it is enough to state the case. The legislature has enacted that if anyone does this wrong act he does it at the risk of the girl turning out to be under 16. This opinion gives full scope to the doctrine of *mens rea*. If the taker believed he had the father's consent, though wrongly, he would have no *mens rea*. So if he did not know she was in anyone's possession, nor in the care or charge of anyone. In those cases he would not know he was doing the act forbidden by the statute, an act which, if he knew she was in the possession and care or charge of anyone, he would know was a crime or not according as she was under 16 or not. He would know he was doing an act wrong itself, whatever was his intention, if done without lawful cause. In addition to these considerations one may add that the statute does use the word "unlawfully," and does not use the words "knowingly or not believing to the contrary." If the question was whether his act was unlawful there would be no difficulty as it clearly was not lawful. . . .

Blackburn J. read the following judgment to which *Cockburn C.J., Mellor, Quain, Lush, Archibald, Field* and *Lindley JJ.* assented. . . . The question, therefore is reduced to whether the words in s.55 of the Offences against the Person Act 1861, that whosoever shall unlawfully take "any unmarried girl being under the age of sixteen, out of the possession of her father" are to be read as if they were "being under the age of sixteen, and he knowing she was under that age." No such words are contained in the statute, nor is there the word "maliciously," "knowingly," or any other word used that can be said to involve a similar meaning. The argument in favour of the prisoner must, therefore, entirely proceed on the ground that in general a guilty mind is an essential ingredient in a crime, and that where a statute creates a crime the intention of the legislature should be presumed to be to include "knowingly" in the definition of the crime, and the statute should read as if that word were inserted, unless the contrary intention appears. We need not inquire at present whether the canon of construction goes quite so far as above stated, for we are of opinion that the intention of the legislature sufficiently appears to have been to punish the abductor unless the girl, in fact, was of such an age as to make her consent an excuse irrespective of whether he knew her to be too young to give an effectual consent, and to fix that age at 16.

The section in question is one of a series of enactments beginning with s.50 forming a code for the protection of women and the guardians of young women. These enactments are taken with scarcely any alteration from the repealed statute, the Offences against the Person Act 1828, which had collected them into a code from a variety of old statutes all repealed by it. Section 50 enacts that:

> "Whosoever shall unlawfuly and carnally know and abuse any girl under the age of ten years, shall be guilty of felony."

By s.51:

> "Whosoever shall unlawfully and carnally know and abuse any girl being above the age of ten years and under the age of twelve years, shall be guilty of a misdemeanour."

It seems impossible to suppose that the intention of the legislature in those two sections could have been to make the crime depend upon the knowledge of the prisoner of the girl's actual age. It would produce the monstrous result that a man who had carnal connection with a girl in reality not quite ten years old, but whom he, on reasonable grounds, believed to be a little more than ten, was to escape altogether. He could not, in that view of the statute, be convicted of the felony, for he did not know her to be under ten. He could not be convicted of the misdemeanour because she was, in fact, not above the age of ten. It seems to us that the intention of the legislature was to punish those who had connection with young girls, though with their consent, unless the girl was, in fact, old enough to give valid consent. The man who has connection with a child relying on her consent does it at his peril if she is below the statutable age.

Section 55, on which the present case arises, uses precisely the same words as those in ss.50 and 51, and must be construed in the same way, and if we refer to the repealed statute 4 & 5 Phil. & Mary, c. 8 (Abduction Act 1557), from s.3 of which the words in s.55 are taken with very little alteration, it strengthens the inference that such was the intention of the legislature. The preamble states as the mischief aimed at, that female children, heiresses, and others having expectations, were, unawares of their friends, brought to contract marriages of disparagement "to the great heaviness of their friends," and then to remedy this enacts by the first section that it shall not be lawful for anyone to take an unmarried girl being under 16 out of the custody of her father or the person to whom he either, by will or by act in his lifetime, gives the custody, unless it be bona fide done by or for the master or mistress of such child, or the guardian in chivalry or in socage of such child. This recognises a legal right to the possession of the child depending on the real age of the child, and not on what appears. The object of the legislature, being as it appears by the preamble to protect this legal right to the possession, would be baffled if it was an excuse that the person guilty of the taking thought the child above sixteen. The words "unlawfully take" as used in s.3 of 4 & 5 Phil. & Mary, c. 8 (Abduction Act 1557), mean without the authority of the master, or mistress, or guardian mentioned in the immediately preceding section. . . .

Note

This case is one of the leading authorities in what is known as strict (or absolute) liability. See further *Hibbert* (1869) for an interesting comparison (see H.S.B., p. 219). Strict liability will be considered further in Chapter 2; see below, p. 167.

Question

The imposition of liability without fault certainly makes the task of the prosecutor more straightforward. Should all crimes be dealt with in this way, leaving the issue of culpability as a matter of relevance only to the sentence? What sentence would you deem appropriate for *Prince*? He received six months' imprisonment.

B.   Coincidence of Actus Reus and Mens Rea

R. v. Le Brun

[1991] 4 All E.R. 673 (C.A.)

After spending the evening at the house of some friends who lived nearby the appellant and his wife left at about 2 a.m. to walk home. While they were walking home they got into a heated argument in the course of which the appellant hit his wife on the jaw knocking her down unconscious. The appellant attempted to lift or drag the body of his unconscious wife away from the scene but she slipped from his grasp and her head hit the pavement causing a fracture to the skull from which she died. The appellant was charged with murder.

Lord Lane C.J.   The main thrust of his argument is to be found in ground 3 of the notice of appeal, which I will now read:

"The learned judge erred in law in directing the jury that they could convict the appellant of murder or manslaughter (depending on the intention with which he had previously assaulted the victim) if they were sure that, having committed the assault with no serious injury resulting, the appellant had accidentally dropped the victim causing her death whilst either: (a) attempting to move her to her home against her wishes, including any wishes she may have expressed prior to the previous assault, and/or (b) attempting to dispose of her body or otherwise cover up the previous assault."

Problems of causation and remoteness of damage are never easy of solution. We have had helpful arguments from both counsel on this point, the point in the present case being, to put it in summary before coming to deal with it in more detail, that the intention of the appellant to harm his wife one way or another may have been separated by a period of time from the act which in fact caused the death, namely the fact of her falling to the ground and fracturing her skull. That second incident may have taken place without any guilty mind on the part of the appellant.

The learned editors of Smith and Hogan *Criminal Law* (6th Ed., 1988), p. 320 say:

"An intervening act by the original actor will not break the chain of causation so as to excuse him, where the intervening act is part of the same transaction; but it is otherwise if the act which causes the *actus reus* is part of a completely different transaction. For example, D, having wounded P, visits him in hospital and accidentally infects him with smallpox of which he dies."

The problem in the instant case can be expressed in a number of different ways, of which causation is one. Causation on the facts as the jury in this case must have found them—I say at the best from the point of view of the appellant—is in one sense clear. Death was caused by the victim's head hitting the ground as she was being dragged away by the appellant. The only remoteness was that between the initial unlawful blow and the later moment when the skull was fractured causing death.

The question can be perhaps framed in this way. There was here an initial unlawful blow to the chin delivered by the appellant. That, again on what must have been the jury's finding, was not delivered with the intention of doing really serious harm to the wife. The guilty intent accompanying that blow was sufficient to have rendered the appellant guilty of manslaughter, but not murder, had it caused death. But it did not cause death. What caused death was the later impact when the wife's head hit the pavement. At the moment of impact the appellant's intention was to remove her, probably unconscious, body to avoid detection. To that extent the impact may have been pro tanto accidental. May the earlier guilty intent by joined with the later non-guilty blow which caused death to produce in the conglomerate a proper verdict of manslaughter?

It has usually been in the context of murder that the problem has arisen in the previous decisions. We have had our attention directed to a Privy Council case, *Thabo Meli* v. *R.* [1954] 1 All E.R. 373, [1954] 1 W.L.R. 228. It is to be observed that two members of the Judicial Committee on that occasion were Lord Goddard C.J. and Lord Reid. The facts of the case were these. The appellants, all in accordance with their preconceived plan, took a man to a hut, gave him beer so that he was partially intoxicated and then struck him over the head. They thought he was dead. They took what they thought was his lifeless body, rolled it over a cliff and then dressed up the scene as though the whole affair was an accident. In fact the man was not dead. It was established from medical evidence that the final cause of his death was exposure. He had been left at the bottom of the cliff over which he had been rolled.

At their trial for murder the appellants contended that the two acts were separate acts and that, while the first act was accompanied by a guilty mind, it was not the cause of death. The second act, while it was the cause of death, was not accompanied by the guilty mind. Therefore they were not guilty of murder, a similar situation to that which exists in the present case.

Lord Reid delivering the judgment of the Board said [1954] 1 All E.R. 373 at 374, [1954] 1 W.L.R. 228 at 230):

"It appears to their Lordships impossible to divide up what was really one series of acts in this way. There is no doubt that the accused set out to do all these acts in order to achieve their plan, and as parts of their plan; and it is much too refined a ground of judgment to say that, because they were under a misapprehension at one stage and thought that their guilty purpose had been achieved before, in fact, it was achieved, therefore they are to escape the penalties of the law."

That decision of course is not binding upon us. It is of very persuasive authority and it was adopted by another division of this court in R. v. *Moore and Dorn* [1975] Crim.L.R. 229.

However, it will be observed that the present case is different from the facts of those two cases in that death here was not the result of a preconceived plan which went wrong, as was the case in those two decisions which we have cited. Here the death, again assuming the jury's finding to be such as it must have been, was the result of an initial unlawful blow, not intended to cause serious harm, in its turn causing the appellant to take steps possibly to evade the consequences of his unlawful act. During the taking of those steps he commits the *actus reus* but without the *mens rea* necessary for murder or manslaughter. Therefore the *mens rea* is contained in the initial unlawful assault, but the *actus reus* is the eventual dropping of the head on the ground.

Normally the *actus reus* and the *mens rea* coincide in point of time. What is the situation when they do not? Is it permissible, as the Crown contends here, to combine them to produce a conviction for manslaughter?

The answer is perhaps to be found in the next case to which we were referred, and that was R. v. *Church* [1965] 2 All E.R. 72, [1966] 1 Q.B. 59. In that case the defendant was charged with the murder of a woman whose body was found in a river. The cause of death was drowning. The defendant had it seemed attacked the woman and rendered her semi-conscious. He thought she was dead and in his panic he threw her into the river. He was acquitted of murder but convicted of manslaughter. Edmund Davies J., giving the judgment of the court, said [1965] 2 All E.R. 72 at 76, [1966] 1 Q.B. 59 at 70):

> "We adopt as sound Dr. Glanville Williams' view in [*Criminal Law: The General Part* (2nd. Ed., 1961), p. 174] that, "If a killing by the first act would have been manslaughter, a later destruction of the supposed corpse should also be manslaughter." Had Mrs. Nott [the victim] died of her initial injuries, a manslaughter verdict might quite conceivably have been returned on the basis that the appellant inflicted them under the influence of provocation or that the jury were not convinced that they were inflicted with murderous intent. All that was lacking in the direction given in this was that, when the judge turned to consider manslaughter, he did not again tell the jury that they were

entitled (if they thought fit) to regard the conduct of the appellant in relation to Mrs. Nott as constituting throughout a series of acts which culminated in her death, and that, if that was how they regarded the appellant's behaviour, it mattered not whether he believed her to be alive or dead when he threw her in the river."

It seems to us that where the unlawful application of force and the eventual act causing death are parts of the same sequence of events, the same transaction, the fact that there is an appreciable interval of time between the two does not serve to exonerate the defendant from liability. That is certainly so where the appellant's subsequent actions which caused death, after the initial unlawful blow, are designed to conceal his commission of the original unlawful assault.

It would be possible to express the problem as one of causation. The original unlawful blow to the chin was *a causa sine qua non* of the later *actus reus*. It was the opening event in a series which was to culminate in death: the first link in the chain of causation, to use another metaphor. It cannot be said that the actions of the appellant in dragging the victim away with the intention of evading liability broke the chain which linked the initial blow with the death.

In short, in circumstances such as the present, which is the only concern of this court, the act which causes death and the necessary mental state to constitute manslaughter need not coincide in point of time.

[Lord Lane referred to several passages from the trial judge's summing up and then continued:]

The complaint made by Mr. Wilson-Smith is primarily directed at the portion of that passage which we have read, namely the passage which runs: 'if he was doing that because he was determined to make her come home even though she had refused to do so . . . '

The argument advanced on behalf of the appellant is this. There has to be shown by the Crown in order to succeed a continuing transaction, or an unbroken chain of causation between the act which proved the *mens rea* and the final incident which resulted in death before it can be said that there is a sufficient connection between the *mens rea* and the *actus reus*. The mere fact that this man attempts to get his wife home when she is unconscious, it is argued, coupled with her earlier unwillingness to go home, is not enough to show a continuing transaction of an unbroken chain as has to be shown.

In every case, and this is no exception, the summing up has to be read against the background of fact which lies behind the whole of the case. Part of the background is, as we have already indicated when trying to set out the facts of the case, that the dispute between the two was certainly in part, and probably very largely, about whether she was going to go home or not.

. . .

The judge was drawing a sharp distinction between actions by the appellant which were designed to help his wife and actions which were not so designed: on the one hand that would be a way in which the prosecution could establish the connection if he was not trying to assist his wife; on the other hand if he was trying to assist his wife, the chain of causation would have been broken and the nexus between the two halves of the prosecution case would not exist.

Having said that, we conclude that the direction of the judge taken as a whole was satisfactory. It was satisfactory in so far, and only in so far, as the directions related to manslaughter. In that respect, in our judgment, they comply with the view of the law which we have endeavoured to set out by reference to the authorities. In short the criticisms of the judge's treatment of submissions and the criticisms of the summing up are not justified. In our judgment accordingly the appeal fails and must be dismissed.

Appeal dismissed.

Note

See also *Att.-Gen.'s Reference (No. 4 of 1980)* (1981) (H.S.B., p. 208).

C.   Transferred Malice

R. v. Latimer

(1886) 17 Q.B.D. 359

[L. who had argued with X in a public house aimed a blow at him with a belt. The belt lightly struck X, but glanced off severely cutting Y's face. He was charged, *inter alia*, with unlawfuly and maliciously wounding Y.]

Lord Coleridge C.J.   We are of opinion that this conviction must be sustained. It is common knowledge that a man who has an unlawful and malicious intent against another, and, in attempting to carry it out, injures a third person, is guilty of what the law deems malice against the person injured;

because the offender is doing an unlawful act, and has that which the judges call general malice, and that is enough. Such would be the case if the matter were *res integra*, and it is not so, for *R. v. Hunt* is an express authority on the point. There a man intended to injure *A*, and said so, and, in the course of doing it, stabbed the wrong man, and had clearly malice in fact, but no intention of injuring the man who was stabbed.... The indictment in *R. v. Pembliton* (1874) was on the Act making unlawful and malicious injury to property a statutory offence; and the jury expressly negatived, and the facts expressly negatived, any intention to do injury to property; and the court held that under the Act making it an offence to injure any property there must be an intent to injure property. *R. v. Pembliton*, therefore, does not govern the present case; and on no other ground is there anything to be said for the prisoner.

Questions

1. In *Pembliton* (1874) the accused was involved in a fight outside a public house. He picked up a large stone and threw it at the people he had been fighting. It flew over the heads of the intended victims and smashed a large plate glass window behind them. P. was charged with the then equivalent of criminal damage (see below, p. 401). Could he have been convicted of such an offence? What other offences may he have committed? Why was his conviction quashed?

2. In *Latimer* it would seem that L. would be guilty whether or not he foresaw the harm to Y—or was not even negligent in respect of such harm. Is there a case for saying that liability in these cases should depend on at least the existence of negligence?

D. Mistake

Question

X has been charged with abducting Y, a 15-year-old girl. Would he have any defence if he believed:

  (1) abducting 15-year-old girls was no criminal offence? (See *Esop* (1836) H.S.B., p. 210);
  (2) that Y was in fact 16 years old (see *Prince* above, p. 147);
  (3) that Y was a common prostitute? (see *Hibbert* (1869) H.S.B., p. 219).

D.P.P. v. Morgan

[1976] A.C. 182 (H.L.)

[M. invited some friends to his house to have intercourse with his wife. He told them to ignore any signs of resistance as this would just be his wife's way of increasing her enjoyment. M. and his friends were charged with rape. The friends pleaded not guilty on the ground that they believed that the wife had consented to intercourse. The trial judge directed the jury that such a belief would afford a defence only if it had been based on reasonable grounds. It would not suffice that the accused honestly believed she had consented. Their appeals against conviction were dismissed by the Court of Appeal, but leave was granted to appeal to the House of Lords.]

Lord Cross.... Secondly, I would say something as to how far—if at all—the decision in *Reg.* v. *Tolson*, (1889), which was, of course, a case of bigamy, has a bearing on this case. The statute there provided that "Whosoever, being married, shall marry any other person during the life of the former husband or wife, ... shall be guilty of felony," with a proviso that

> "nothing in this section contained shall extend ... to any person marrying a second time whose husband or wife shall have been continually absent from such person for the space of seven years then last past, and shall not have been known by such person to be living within that time...."

The defendant who was found by the jury to have had reasonable grounds for believing that her husband was then dead—though in fact he was not—went through a ceremony of marriage with another man within seven years of the time when she last knew of his being alive. She therefore fell within the very words of the statute. Nevertheless, the majority of the Court of Crown Cases Reserved held that she was entitled to be acquitted because on general principles of criminal liability, having no particular relation to the crime of bigamy, a mistaken belief based on reasonable grounds in the existence of facts, which, if true, would have made the act charged against her innocent, afforded her a defence since it was not to be supposed that Parliament intended bigamy to be an "absolute" offence to the commission of which the state of mind of the defendant was wholly irrelevant. The minority of the judges, on the other hand, thought that the existence of the proviso which gave an express exemption from liability in certain circumstances made it impossible to imply an exemption from liability in other circumstances not covered by it. If the Sexual Offences Act 1956 had provided that it was an offence for a man to have sexual intercourse with a woman who did not consent to it then the case of *Reg.* v. *Tolson* would undoubtedly have been in point; but what the Act says is that it is an offence for a man to "rape" a woman and, as I see it, one cannot say that *Reg.* v. *Tolson* applies to rape unless one reads the words "rape a woman" as equivalent to

"have intercourse with a woman who is not consenting to it."
Counsel for the Director says, of course, that they are
equivalent but the question remains whether he is right.

Finally, I must refer to an alternative submission, made by
counsel for the appellant—namely, that in *Reg.* v. *Tolson* the
court was wrong in saying that to afford a defence to a charge
of bigamy the mistaken belief of the defendant had to be
based on reasonable grounds. It is, of course, true that the
question whether a mistaken belief honestly held but based
on no reasonable grounds would have afforded a defence was
not argued in that case. There had been several conflicting
decisions by judges on assize—one saying that an honest
belief would be a defence, others that a belief on reasonable
grounds wuld be a defence, and yet others that not even a
belief on reasonable grounds would be a defence. In *Reg.* v.
Tolson Stephen J. asked the jury whether they thought that
the defendant in good faith and on reasonable grounds
believed her husband to be dead at the date of her second
marriage. Having obtained an affirmative answer he then, in
order to get the point settled by the Court of Crown Cases
Reserved, directed the jury—contrary to his own opinion—that such a belief would not be a defence and, after
they had duly convicted Mrs. Tolson, sentenced her to one
day's imprisonment. On her appeal against her conviction,
her counsel was not, of course, concerned to dispute the view
that a mistaken belief had to be based on reasonable grounds,
since the jury had held that his client had had reasonable
grounds for her belief, and the question whether an honest
belief would have been enough was never argued. If it had
been argued, it is possible that some of the judges who were
in the majority— though having regard to the way in which
he framed his question, I do not think that Stephen J. would
have been one of them—might have held that a mistaken
belief honestly but unreasonably held was enough. But *Reg.*
v. *Tolson* was decided over 80 years ago. It is accepted as a
leading authority in the law of bigamy not only in this
country . . . but also in Australia. . . . Moreover, the phrase "an
honest and reasonable belief entertained by the accused of the
existence of facts, which, if true, would make the act charged
against him innocent" has been adopted on several occasions
as a definition of *mens rea* generally applicable to cases where
the offence is not an absolute one but the words defining it
do not expressly or impliedly indicate that some particular
mens rea is required to establish it. . . . Counsel did not refer
us to any case in which the propriety of the inclusion of the
element of "reasonableness" has been doubted; and its

inclusion was, in fact, approved in *Reg.* v. *King* (1964) and by
Lord Diplock in *Sweet* v. *Parsley* [below, p. 167]. So, even if I
had been myself inclined to think that the inclusion of the
element of reasonableness was wrong, I would not have
thought it right for us to call it in question in this case. In
fact, however, I can see no objection to the inclusion of the
element of reasonableness in what I may call a *"Tolson"* case.
If the words defining an offence provide either expressly or
impliedly that a man is not to be guilty of it if he believes
something to be true, then he cannot be found guilty if the
jury think that he may have believed it to be true, however
inadequate were his reasons for doing so. But, if the
definition of the offence is on the face of it "absolute" and the
defendant is seeking to escape his prima facie liability by a
defence of mistaken belief, I can see no hardship to him in
requiring the mistake—if it is to afford him a defence—to be
based on reasonable grounds. As Lord Diplock said in *Sweet*
v. *Parsley* (1970), there is nothing unreasonable in the law
requiring a citizen to take reasonable care to ascertain the facts
relevant to his avoiding doing a prohibited act. To have
intercourse with a woman who is not your wife is, even
today, not generally considered to be a course of conduct
which the law ought positively to encourage and it can be
argued with force that it is only fair to the woman and not in
the least unfair to the man that he should be under a duty to
take reasonable care to ascertain that she is consenting to the
intercourse and be at the risk of a prosecution if he fails to
take such care. So if the Sexual Offences Act 1956 had made it
an offence to have intercourse with a woman who was not
consenting to it, so that the defendant could only escape
liability by the application of the *"Tolson"* principle, I would
not have thought the law unjust.

But, as I have said, section 1 of the Act of 1956 does not say
that a man who has sexual intercourse with a woman who
does not consent to it commits an offence; it says that a man
who rapes a woman commits an offence. Rape is not a word
in the use of which lawyers have a monopoly and the first
question to be answered in this case, as I see it, is whether
according to the ordinary use of the English language a man
can be said to have committed rape if he believed that the
woman was consenting to the intercourse and would not have
attempted to have it but for this belief, whatever his grounds
for so believing. I do not think that he can. Rape, to my
mind, imports at least indifference as to the woman's consent.
I think, moreover, that in this connection the ordinary man
would distinguish between rape and bigamy. To the question

whether a man who goes through a ceremony of marriage with a woman believing his wife to be dead, though she is not, commits bigamy, I think that he would reply "Yes,—but I suppose that the law contains an escape clause for bigamists who are not really to blame." On the other hand, to the question whether a man, who has intercourse with a woman believing that she is consenting to it, though she is not, commits rape, I think that he would reply "No. If he was grossly careless then he may deserve to be punished but not for rape." That being my view as to the meaning of the word "rape" in ordinary parlance, I next ask myself whether the law gives it a different meaning. There is very little English authority on the point but what there is—namely, the reported directions of several common law judges in the early and the middle years of the last century—accords with what I take to be the ordinary meaning of the word. The question has been canvassed in a number of recent cases in New South Wales and Victoria but there is only one of them—*Reg.* v. *Daly* (1968)— that I find of much assistance. In none of the others do the judges advert to the fact that to include an intention to have intercourse whether or not the woman consents in the definition of rape and to say that a reasonable mistake with regard to consent is an available defence to a charge of rape are two incompatible alternatives which cannot be combined in a single direction to a jury—as, incidentally, the judge combined them in one passage in his summing up in this case. In *Reg.* v. *Daly* the court, as well as drawing that distinction which I regard as fundamental, indicated pretty clearly that it thought—as I do— that the former approach to the problem was the right one. For these reasons, I think that the summing up contained a misdirection.

Proviso applied.

Questions

1. Why does a belief that one is free to marry have to be reasonable on a charge of bigamy, yet a belief that an alleged rape victim was consenting need only to be genuine?

The speeches in *Morgan* led to the establishment of a Committee under Heilbron J. (Cmnd. 6352 (1975)) and subsequently to the Sexual Offences (Amendment) Act 1976 (below, p. 402).

2. In the crime of assault the accused may have a defence if the prosecution fails to prove he acted unlawfully. The touching of another may be lawful if: (a) the person consents to be touched; (b) the accused was acting reasonably in self-defence or to prevent the commission of a crime. Where the accused mistakenly believes the other consented or that his action is necessary, *e.g.* to prevent a crime, is it sufficient that he genuinely holds that belief or must it be based upon reasonable grounds?

Beckford v. R.

(1987) 85 Cr.App.R. 378 (P.C.)

Beckford, a police officer, was charged with murder. He pleaded self-defence, but was convicted. The question for the prosecution was whether the prosecution had proved that Beckford had not acted in self-defence.

Lord Griffiths.   At the conclusion of the defence case the only live issue for the jury was whether the prosecution had proved that the appellant had not killed in self-defence. The first ground of appeal before the Court of Appeal in Jamaica, and the only ground with which their Lordships are concerned, was that the trial judge had misdirected the jury on the issue of self-defence. . . .

It is accepted by the prosecution that there is no difference in the law of self-defence between the law of Jamaica and the English common law and it therefore falls to be decided whether it was correctly decided by the Court of Appeal in *Gladstone Williams* (1984) 78 Cr.App.R. 276 that the defence of self-defence depends upon what the accused "honestly" believed the circumstances to be and not upon the reason-ableness of that belief—what the Court of Appeal in Jamaica referred to as the "honest belief" and "reasonable belief" schools of thought.

There can be no doubt that prior to the decision of the House of Lords in *D.P.P.* v. *Morgan* (1976) 61 Cr.App.R. 136, [1976] A.C. 182 the whole weight of authority supported the view that it was an essential element of self-defence not only that the accused believed that he was being attacked or in imminent danger of being attacked but also that such belief was based on reasonable grounds. . . .

The question then is whether the present Lord Chief Justice, Lord Lane, in *Williams (Gladstone) (supra)* was right to depart from the law as declared by his predecessors in the light of the decision of the House of Lords in *D.P.P.* v. *Morgan.*

Morgan was a case of rape and counsel for the prosecution has submitted that the decision of the majority turns solely upon their view of the specific intention required for the commission of that crime and accordingly had no relevance to the law of self-defence. It was further submitted that the question now before their Lordships was settled by an earlier decision of the Privy Council in *Palmer* v. *R.* (1971) 55 Cr.App.R. 223, [1971] A.C. 814. This submission is founded upon the fact that Lord Morris in giving the judgment of the Board set out a very lengthy passage from the summing up of the judge and commented at p. 231 and p. 824 respectively:

"Their Lordships conclude that there is no room for criticism of the summing up or of the conduct of the trial unless there is a rule that in every case where the issue of self-defence is left to the jury they must be directed that if they consider that excessive force was used in defence then they should return a verdict of guilty of manslaughter. For the reasons which they will set out their Lordships consider there is no such rule."

The only question raised for the determination of the Board was that stated by Lord Morris. It is true that, in the passage quoted from the summing up the judge had stated the ingredients of self-defence in the then conventional form of reasonable belief; but it was not this part of his summing up that was under attack nor did it receive any particular consideration by the Board. Their Lordships are unable to attach greater weight to the approval of the summing up than as indicating that it was in conformity with the practice of directing juries that the accused must have reasonable grounds for believing that self-defence was necessary.

In *D.P.P.* v. *Morgan* (1975) 61 Cr.App.R. 136 [1976] A.C. 182, each member of the House of Lords held that the *mens rea* required to commit rape is the knowledge that the woman is not consenting or recklessness as to whether she is consenting or not. From this premise the majority held that unless the prosecution proved that the man did not believe the woman was consenting or was at least reckless as to her consent they had failed to prove the necessary *mens rea* which is an essential ingredient of the crime. Lord Edmund-Davies in his dissent referred to the large body of distinguished academic support for the view that it is morally indefensible to convict a person of a crime when owing to a genuine mistake as to the facts he believes that he is acting lawfully and has no intention to commit the crime and therefore has no guilty mind. He expressed his preference for this moral approach but felt constrained by the weight of authority, including the cases on self-defence, to hold that the law required the accused's belief should not only be genuine but also based upon reasonable grounds.

In *Kimber* (1983) 77 Cr.App.R. 225 the Court of Appeal applied the decision in *Morgan* to a case of indecent assault and held that a failure to direct the jury that the prosecution had to make them sure that the accused had never believed that the woman was consenting was a misdirection. Lawton

L.J. in the course of his judgment rejected the submission that the decision in *Morgan* was confined to rape and clearly regarded it as of far wider significance. . . .

In *D.P.P.* v. *Williams (Gladstone)* (*supra*) the decision in *Morgan* was carried a step further and in their Lordships' view to its logical conclusion.

[In *Williams* the defendant (W.) was charged with assaulting M. W. claimed that he believed M. was unlawfully assaulting a youth and that he had merely tried to intervene to stop M. The Court of Appeal held that W.'s conviction should be quashed because he should have been judged upon what he actually believed the situation to be and not upon whether the belief had been reasonably held].

In the course of his judgment the Lord Chief Justice, Lord Lane, discussing the offence of assault said at p. 280:

"The mental element necessary to constitute guilt is the intent to apply unlawful force to the victim. We do not believe that the mental element can be substantiated by simply showing an intent to apply force and no more."

And later in the judgment at p. 281 he expressly disapproved the decision of the Divisional Court in *Albert* v. *Lavin* (1981) 72 Cr.App.R. 178 in which it was said that the word "unlawful" was tautologous and not part of the definitional element of assaulting a police officer in the course of his duty. In so doing Lord Lane was expressing the same view of *Albert* v. *Lavin* that had been previously expressed by Lawton L.J. in *Kimber* (*supra*).

The common law recognises that there are many circumstances in which one person may inflict violence upon another without committing a crime, as for instance, in sporting contests, surgical operations or in the most extreme example, judicial execution. The common law has always recognised as one of these circumstances the right of a person to protect himself from attack and to act in the defence of others and if necessary to inflict violence on another in so doing. If no more force is used than is reasonable to repel the attack such force is not unlawful and no crime is committed. Furthermore a man about to be attacked does not have to wait for his assailant to strike the first blow or fire the first shot; circumstances may justify a pre-emptive strike.

It is because it is an essential element of all crimes of violence that the violence or the threat of violence should be unlawful that self-defence, if raised as an issue in a criminal trial, must be disproved by the prosecution. If the prosecution fail to do so the accused is entitled to be acquitted because the prosecution will have failed to prove an essential element of the crime namely that the violence used by the accused was unlawful.

If then a genuine belief, albeit without reasonable grounds, is a defence to rape because it negatives the necessary intention, so also must a genuine belief in facts which if true would justify self-defence be a defence to a crime of personal violence because the belief negatives the intent to act unlawfully. Their Lordships therefore approve the following passage from the judgment of Lord Lane in *Williams (Gladstone)* at p. 281 as correctly stating the law of self-defence:

"The reasonableness or unreasonableness of the defendant's belief is material to the question of whether the belief was held by the defendant at all. If the belief was in fact held, its unreasonableness, so far as guilt or innocence is concerned, is neither here nor there. It is irrelevant. Were it otherwise, the defendant would be convicted because he was negligent in failing to recognise that the victim was not consenting or that a crime was not being committed and so on. In other words the jury should be directed first of all that the prosecution have the burden or duty of proving the unlawfulness of the defendant's actions; secondly, if the defendant may have been labouring under a mistake as to the facts, he must be judged according to this mistaken view of the facts; thirdly, that is so whether the mistake was, on an objective view, a reasonable mistake or not. In a case of self-defence, where self-defence or the prevention of crime is concerned, if the jury came to the conclusion that the defendant believed, or may have believed, that he was being attacked or that a crime was being committed, and that force was necessary to protect himself or to prevent the crime, then the prosecution have not proved their case. If however the defendant's alleged belief was mistaken and if the mistake was an unreasonable one, that may be a powerful reason for coming to the conclusion that the belief was not honestly held and should be rejected. Even if the jury come to the conclusion that the mistake was an unreasonable one, if the defendant may genuinely have been labouring under it, he is entitled to rely upon it."

Looking back, *D.P.P.* v. *Morgan* can now be seen as a landmark decision in the development of the common law returning the law to the path upon which it might have developed but for the inability of an accused to give evidence on his own behalf. Their Lordships note that not only has this development the approval of such distinguished criminal lawyers as Professor Glanville Williams and Professor Smith (see *Textbook of Criminal Law* (2nd ed.), pp. 137–138 and Smith and Hogan, *Criminal Law* (5th ed.), pp. 329–330) but it also has the support of the Criminal Law Revision Committee: see 14th Report on Offences against the Person (1980) Cmnd. 7844; and of the Law Commission: see the Law Commission Report (1985) No. 143, *Codification of the Criminal law*.

There may be a fear that the abandonment of the objective standard demanded by the existence of reasonable grounds for belief will result in the success of too many spurious claims of self-defence. The English experience has not shown this to be the case. The Judicial Studies Board with the approval of the Lord Chief Justice has produced a model direction on selfdefence which is now widely used by judges when summing up to juries. The direction contains the following guidance:

"Whether the plea is self-defence or defence of another, if the defendant may have been labouring under a mistake as to the facts, he must be judged according to his mistaken belief of the facts: that is so whether the mistake was, on an objective view, a reasonable mistake or not."

Their Lordships have heard no suggestion that this form of summing up has resulted in a disquieting number of acquittals. This is hardly surprising for no jury is going to accept a man's assertion that he believed that he was about to be attacked without testing it against all the surrounding circumstances. In assisting the jury to determine whether or not the accused had a genuine belief the judge will of course direct their attention to those features of the evidence that make such a belief more or less probable. Where there are no reasonable grounds to hold a belief it will surely only be in exceptional circumstances that a jury will conclude that such a belief was or might have been held.

Their Lordships therefore conclude that the summing up in this case contained a material misdirection and answer that the test to be applied for self-defence is that a person may use such force as is reasonable in the circumstances as he honestly believes them to be in the defence of himself or another.

Note

See further *Scarlett* (below, p. 268).

Chapter 2

Strict Liability

1. DEFINITION

Where blameless inadvertence suffices as to an element of the *actus reus*, the crime is said to be an offence of strict liability (see above, p. 147).

2. HOW CAN YOU RECOGNISE CRIMES OF STRICT LIABILITY?

Sweet v. Parsley

[1970] A.C. 132 (H.L.)

[The appellant who had leased a farm to tenants was charged with being concerned in the management of premises which were used for the purpose of smoking cannabis contrary to section 5(*b*) of the Dangerous Drugs Act 1965. The magistrates convicted her even though they found she had no knowledge that her tenants were smoking drugs. Her appeal was dismissed by the Divisional Court and she appealed to the House of Lords.]

Lord Reid. My Lords, a Divisional Court dismissed her appeal, holding that she had been concerned in the management of those premises. The reasons given for holding that she was managing the property were that she was in a position to choose her tenants: that she could put them under as long or as short a tenancy as she desired: and that she could make it a term of any letting that smoking of cannabis was not to take place. All these reasons would apply to every occupier who lets out parts of his house or takes in lodgers or paying guests. But this was held to be an absolute offence, following the earlier decision in *Yeandel* v. *Fisher* (1966).

How has it come about that the Divisional Court has felt bound to reach such an obviously unjust result? It has in effect held that it was carrying out the will of Parliament because Parliament has chosen to make this an absolute offence. And, of course, if Parliament has so chosen the courts must carry out its will, and they cannot be blamed for any unjust consequences. But has Parliament so chosen?

I dealt with this matter at some length in *Warner's* case (1969). On reconsideration I see no reason to alter anything which I there said. But I think that some amplification is necessary. Our first duty is to consider the words of the Act: if they show a clear intention to create an absolute offence that is an end of the matter. But such cases are very rare. Sometimes the words of the section which creates a particular offence make it clear that *mens rea* is required in one form or another. Such cases are quite frequent. But in a very large number of cases there is no clear indication either way. In such cases there has for centuries been a presumption that Parliament did not intend to make criminals of persons who were in no way blameworthy in what they did. That means that whenever a section is silent as to *mens rea* there is a presumption that, in order to give effect to the will of Parliament, we must read in words appropriate to require *mens rea*.

Where it is contended that an absolute offence has been created, the words of Alderson B. in *Attorney-General* v. *Lockwood* (1842) have often been quoted:

"The rule of law, I take it, upon the construction of all statutes, and therefore applicable to the construction of this is, whether they be penal or remedial, to construe them according to the plain, literal, and grammatical meaning of the words in which they are expressed, unless that construction leads to a plain and clear contradiction of the apparent purpose of the Act, or to some palpable and evident absurdity."

That is perfectly right as a general rule and where there is no legal presumption. But what about the multitude of criminal enactments where the words of the Act simply make it an offence to do certain things but where everyone agrees that there cannot be a conviction without proof of *mens rea* in some form? This passage, if applied to the present problem, would mean that there is no need to prove *mens rea* unless it would be "a plain and clear contradiction of the apparent purpose of the Act" to convict without proof of *mens rea*. But that would be putting the presumption the wrong way round: for it is firmly established by a host of authorities that *mens rea* is an essential ingredient of every offence unless some reason can be found for holding that that is not necessary.

It is also firmly established that the fact that other sections of the Act expressly require *mens rea*, for example because they contain the word "knowingly," is not in itself sufficient to justify a decision that a section which is silent as to *mens rea* creates an absolute offence. In the absence of a clear indication in the Act that an offence is intended to be an absolute offence, it is necessary to go outside the Act and examine all relevant circumstances in order to establish that this must have been the intention of Parliament. I say "must have been" because it is a universal principle that if a penal provision is reasonably capable of two interpretations, that interpretation which is most favourable to the accused must be adopted.

What, then, are the circumstances which it is proper to take into account? In the well-known case of *Sherras* v. *De Rutzen* (1895) Wright J. only mentioned the subject-matter with which the Act deals. But he was there dealing with something which was one of a class of acts which "are not criminal in any real sense, but are acts which in the public interest are prohibited under a penalty." It does not in the least follow that when one is dealing with a truly criminal act it is sufficient merely to have regard to the subject-matter of the enactment. One must put oneself in the position of a legislator. It has long been the practice to recognise absolute offences in this class of quasicriminal acts, and one can safely assume that, when Parliament is passing new legislation dealing with this class of offences, its silence as to *mens rea* means that the old practice is to apply. But when one comes to acts of a truly criminal character, it appears to me that there are at least two other factors which any reasonable legislator would have in mind. In the first place a stigma still attaches to any person convicted of a truly criminal offence, and the more serious or more disgraceful the offence the greater the stigma. So he would have to consider whether, in a case of this gravity, the public interest really requires that an innocent person should be prevented from proving his innocence in order that fewer guilty men may escape. And equally important is the fact that fortunately the Press in this country are vigilant to expose injustice and every manifestly unjust conviction made known to the public tends to injure the body politic by undermining public confidence in the justice of the law and of its administration. But I regret to observe that, in some recent cases where serious offences have been held to be absolute offences, the court has taken into account no more than the wording of the Act and the character and seriousness of the mischief which constitutes the offence.

The choice would be much more difficult if there were no other way open than either *mens rea* in the full sense or an absolute offence; for there are many kinds of case where putting on the prosecutor the full burden of proving *mens rea* creates great difficulties and may lead to many unjust acquittals. But there are at least two other possibilities. Parliament has not infrequently transferred the onus as regards *mens rea* to the accused, so that, once the necessary facts are proved, he must convince the jury that on balance of probabilities he is innocent of any criminal intention. I find it a little surprising that more use has not been made of this method: but one of the bad effects of the decision of this House in *Woolmington* v. *Director of Public Prosecutions* (1935) (below, p. 208) may have been to discourage its use. The other method would be in effect to substitute in appropriate classes of cases gross negligence for *mens rea* in the full sense as the mental element necessary to constitute the crime. It would often be much easier to infer that Parliament must have meant that gross negligence should be the necessary mental element than to infer that Parliament intended to create an absolute offence. A variant of this would be to accept the view of Cave J. in *Reg.* v. *Tolson* (1889). This appears to have been done in Australia where authority appears to support what Dixon J. said in *Proudman* v. *Dayman* (1941):

> "As a general rule an honest and reasonable belief in a state of facts which, if they existed, would make the defendant's act innocent affords an excuse for doing what would otherwise be an offence."

It may be that none of these methods is wholly satisfactory but at least the public scandal of convicting on a serious charge persons who are in no way blameworthy would be avoided.

If this section means what the Divisional Court have held that it means, then hundreds of thousands of people who sublet part of their premises or take in lodgers or are concerned in the management of residential premises or institutions are daily incurring a risk of being convicted of a serious offence in circumstances where they are in no way to blame. For the greatest vigilance cannot prevent tenants, lodgers or inmates or guests whom they bring in from smoking cannabis cigarettes in their own rooms. It was suggested in argument that this appellant brought this conviction on herself because it is found as a fact that when the police searched the premises there were people there of the "beatnik fraternity." But surely it would be going a very long way to say that persons managing premises of any kind ought to safeguard themselves by refusing accommodation to all who are of slovenly or exotic appearance, or who bring in guests of that kind. And unfortunately drug taking is by no means confined to those of unusual appearance.

Speaking from a rather long experience of membership of both Houses, I assert with confidence that no Parliament within my recollection would have agreed to make an offence of this kind an absolute offence if the matter had been fully explained to it. So, if the court ought only to hold an offence to be an absolute offence where it appears that that must have been the intention of Parliament, offences of this kind are very far removed from those which it is proper to hold to be absolute offences.

I must now turn to the question what is the true meaning of section 5 of the 1965 Act. It provides:

> "If a person—(a) being the occupier of any premises, permits those premises to be used for the purpose of smoking cannabis or cannabis resin or of dealing in cannabis or cannabis resin (whether by sale or otherwise); or (b) is concerned in the management of any premises used for any such purpose as aforesaid; he shall be guilty of an offence against this Act."

We are particularly concerned with paragraph (b), and the first question is what is meant by "used for any such purpose." Is the "purpose" the purpose of the smoker or the purpose of the management? When in *Warner's* case (1969) I dealt briefly with *Yeandel's* case (1966), I thought it was the purpose of the smoker, but fuller argument in the present case brought out that an identical provision occurs in section 8(d) which deals with opium. This latter provision has been carried on from the Dangerous Drugs Act 1920, and has obviously been copied into the later legislation relating to cannabis. It would require strong reasons—and there are none—to justify giving this provision a new meaning in section 5 different from that which it had in the 1920 Act and now has in section 8 of the 1965 Act. I think that in section 8 it is clear that the purpose is the purpose of the management. The first purpose mentioned is the purpose of the preparation of opium for smoking which can only be a purpose of the management. I believe that opium cannot be smoked casually anywhere at any time as can a cannabis cigarette. The section is dealing with "opium dens" and the like when the use of opium is the main purpose for which the premises are used. But it is a somewhat strained use of language to say that an ordinary room in a house is "used for the purpose" of smoking cannabis when all that happens is that some visitor lights a cannabis cigarette there. Looking to the origin and context of this provision, I have come to the conclusion that it cannot be given this wide meaning. No doubt this greatly reduces the scope of this provision when applied to the use of cannabis. But that is apt to happen when a draftsman simply copies an existing provision without regard to the different circumstances in which it is to operate. So, if the purpose is the purpose of the management, the question whether the offence with regard to opium in 1920, and now with regard to cannabis, is absolute can hardly arise. It could only arise if, although the manager not only knew about cannabis smoking and conducted the premises for that purpose, some person concerned in the management had no knowledge of that. One would first have to decide whether a person who is not actually assisting in the management can be regarded as being "concerned in the management," although ignorant of the purpose for which the manager was using the premises. Even if such a person could be regarded as "concerned in the management," I am of opinion that, for the reasons which I have given, he could not be convicted without proof of *mens rea*.

I would allow the appeal and quash the appellant's conviction.

Lord Diplock. Where the crime consists of doing an act which is prohibited by statute the proposition as to the state of mind of the doer which is contained in the full definition of the crime must be ascertained from the words and subject-matter of the statute. The proposition, as Stephen J. pointed out, may be stated explicitly by the use of such qualifying adverbs as "maliciously," "fraudulently," "negligently" or "knowingly"—expressions which in relation to different kinds of conduct may call for judicial exegesis. And even without such adverbs the words descriptive of the prohibited act may themselves connote the presence of a particular mental element. Thus where the prohibited conduct consists in permitting a particular thing to be done the word "permit" connotes at least knowledge or reasonable grounds for suspicion on the part of the permittor that the thing will be done and an unwillingness to use means available to him to prevent it and, to take a recent example, to have in one's "possession" a prohibited substance connotes some degree of awareness of that which was within the possessor's physical control: *Reg.* v. *Warner* (1969).

But only too frequently the actual words used by Parliament to define the prohibited conduct are in themselves descriptive only of a physical act and bear no connotation as to any particular state of mind on the part of the person who does the act. Nevertheless, the mere fact that Parliament has made the conduct a criminal offence gives rise to *some* implication about the mental element of the conduct proscribed. . . .

This implication stems from the principle that it is contrary to a rational and civilised criminal code, such as Parliament must be presumed to have intended, to penalise one who has performed his duty as a citizen to ascertain what acts are prohibited by law (*ignorantia juris non excusat*) and has taken all proper care to inform himself of any facts which would make his conduct lawful.

Where penal provisions are of general application to the conduct of ordinary citizens in the course of their everyday life the presumption is that the standard of care required of them in informing themselves of facts which would make their conduct unlawful, is that of the familiar common law duty of care. But where the subject-matter of a statute is the regulation of a particular activity involving potential danger to public health, safety or morals in which citizens have a choice as to whether they participate or not, the court may feel driven to infer an intention of Parliament to impose by penal sanctions a higher duty of care on those who choose to participate and to place upon them an obligation to take whatever measures may be necessary to prevent the prohibited act, without regard to those considerations of cost or business practicability which play a part in the determination of what would be required of them in order to fulfil the ordinary common law duty of care. But such an inference is not lightly to be drawn, nor is there any room for it unless there is something that the person on whom the obligation is imposed can do directly or indirectly, by supervision or inspection, by improvement of his business methods or by exhorting those whom he may be expected to influence or control, which will promote the observance of the obligation (see *Lim Chin Aik* v. *The Queen* (1963)).

Gammon (Hong Kong) Ltd. v. Att.-Gen. of Hong Kong

[1984] 3 W.L.R. 347 (P.C.)

Lord Scarman. In their Lordships' opinion, the law relevant to this appeal may be stated in the following propositions (the formulation of which follows closely the written submission of the appellants' counsel, which their Lordships gratefully acknowledge): (1) there is a presumption of law that *mens rea* is required before a person can be held guilty of a criminal offence; (2) the presumption is particularly strong where the offence is "truly criminal" in character; (3) the presumption applies to statutory offences, and can be displaced only if this is clearly or by necessary implication the effect of the statute; (4) the only situation in which the presumption can be displaced is where the statute is concerned with an issue of social concern; public safety is such an issue; (5) even where a statute is concerned with such an issue, the presumption of *mens rea* stands unless it can also be shown that the creation of strict liability will be effective to promote the objects of the statute by encouraging greater vigilance to prevent the commission of the prohibited act.

Notes

Since strict liability occurs almost exclusively in statutory offences, identification is largely a matter of statutory interpretation. The starting point is the presumption that *actus non facit reum nisi mens sit rea*. This presumption is, however, rebuttable. The following factors have been held to be matters to be taken into consideration.

(i) The presumption is more readily rebuttable in crimes which are regarded as not truly criminal in nature "but are acts which in the public interest are prohibited under a penalty." See, *e.g. Alphacell* v. *Woodward* (1972). (See H.S.B., pp. 221, 226.)

(ii) Certain words may indicate the requirement or otherwise of *mens rea*.
permit and *allow* generally indicate the need to prove *mens rea*;
cause and *use* generally indicate strict liability;
possess indicates a partial requirement of *mens rea*;
knowingly normally indicates the need for *mens rea*, but occasionally may be used indirectly to impose strict liability. This may occur when section (A) of an Act contains the word "knowingly" but section (B) does not. The courts may conclude that the absence of the word in section (B) means Parliament intended that section to impose strict liability.
(See further H.S.B., p. 224.)

(iii) Strict liability can be said to be more frequently found in certain factual situations, *e.g.* legislation regulating sale of food and drink, control of pollution, and road traffic offences. (See H.S.B., pp. 226–227).

(iv) It was said that strict liability is normally restricted to offences bearing only a small penalty. This, however, should not be regarded as a reliable guideline in view of Lord Scarman's remarks in *Gammon (Hong Kong) Ltd.* v. *Att.-Gen. of Hong Kong* (1984).

"The severity of the maximum penalties is a more formidable point. But it has to be considered in the light of the ordinance read as a whole. For reasons which their Lordships have already developed, there is nothing inconsistent with the purpose of the ordinance in imposing severe penalties for offences of strict liability. The legislature could reasonably have intended severity to be a significant deterrent, bearing in mind the risks to public safety arising from some contraventions of the ordinance. Their Lordships agree with the view on this point of the Court of Appeal.

It must be crucially important that those who participate in or bear responsibility for the carrying out of works in a manner which complies with the requirements of the ordinance should know that severe penalties await them in the event of any contravention or non-compliance with the ordinance by themselves or by anyone over whom they are required to exercise supervision or control."

3. DEFENCES

Statutes are now providing defences to offences of strict liability. Such defences may take the form of providing the accused with a defence if he can prove that he was not negligent, and they may require that he proves that a third party was, in reality, responsible for the prohibited act. The following are two examples of such legislation.

Section 28 of the Misuse of Drugs Act 1971 provides a defence, *inter alia*, for persons charged with possession of controlled drugs.

"(2) Subject to subsection (3) below, in any proceedings for an offence to which this section applies it shall be a defence for the accused to prove that he neither knew nor suspected nor had reason to suspect the existence of some fact alleged by the prosecution which it is necessary for the prosecution to prove if he is to be convicted of the offence charged."

Section 100 of the Food Act 1984 provides a good illustration of what is known of as the third-party defence.

(1) A person against whom proceedings are brought under this Act shall —

(*a*) upon information duly laid by him, and
(*b*) on giving to the prosecution not less than three clear days' notice of his intention,

be entitled to have any person to whose act or default he alleges that the contravention of the provisions in question was due brought before the court in the proceedings; and —

(i) if, after the contravention has been proved, the original defendant proves that the contravention was due to the act or default of that other person, that other person may be convicted of the offence; and
(ii) if the original defendant further proves that he has used all due diligence to secure that the provisions in question were complied with, he shall be acquitted of the offence.

See further H.S.B., p. 228.

Chapter 3

Parties to Criminal Conduct

1. PRINCIPAL OR PERPETRATOR

The principal or perpetrator is one who, with the relevant *mens rea*, by his own act or omission immediately brings about the *actus reus*. For example, in murder the one who fires the gun, in criminal damage the one who breaks the window, in burglary the one who enters the building. His identification is normally straightforward but not always, (H.S.B. p. 283). The rule that a husband could not be charged as the principal offender in the rape of his wife unless he came within certain limited exceptions was declared no longer to be the law by the House of Lords in R. v. R. (1991). The rule that a boy under the age of 14 could not be the principal offender in any crime which required him to have sexual intercourse is abolished by the Sexual Offences Act 1993.

2. SECONDARY PARTIES

Callow v. Tillstone

(1900) 83 L.T. 411 (D.C.)

[G., a butcher, was convicted of the offence of exposing for sale meat which was unsound and unfit for human consumption. The meat in question was from a heifer which had been destroyed after becoming ill from eating yew leaves. C., a veterinary surgeon, had negligently carried out an examination of the dead beast and had pronounced it sound and healthy. C. was now charged with aiding and abetting G., the principal offender, who had been convicted despite being blameless—see above.]

Lawrance J. In this case we have no doubt that the justices came to a wrong conclusion in finding that the appellant Callow was guilty of the offence charged against him. What they had found him guilty of was only negligence, and the question now arises upon that finding whether Callow, who was the veterinary surgeon called in in the case, can be found guilty of aiding and abetting the exposing for sale of this unsound meat, when all that the justices find against him is negligence. The justices found that Callow had been guilty of negligence and thereby abetted Grey, and upon that they convicted him. We think that is not sufficient, and the case of *Benfield* v. *Simms* (1898) is very strong to show that it is not sufficient. In that case, where there was a conviction, the defendant, a veterinary surgeon, had— according to the finding of the justices—knowingly counselled the owner of a horse to cause the act of cruelty in question and Chennell J. says at the end of his judgment, that the decision of the court in that case "afforded no ground whatever for supposing that a veterinary surgeon who gives a wrong opinion and commits an error in judgment is liable to be convicted of cruelty if the effect of his opinion being followed is that the act of cruelty does in fact result." I think, therefore, the appeal must be allowed.

Kennedy J. I am entirely of the same opinion. It seems to me that all that is found by the justices against the appellant is negligence, and to my mind a person cannot be convicted of aiding and abetting the commission of this offence upon such a finding. In this case the appellant gave his certificate, one is bound to assume, quite honestly, and therefore it seems to me he ought not to be convicted under s.5 of the aiding and abetting the exposing of the meat for sale.

Appeal allowed. Conviction quashed.

Att.-Gen.'s Reference (No. 1 of 1975)

[1975] Q.B. 773 (C.A.)

Lord Widgery C.J. gave the following opinion of the court. This case comes before the court on a reference from the Attorney-General, under section 36 of the Criminal Justice Act 1972, and by his reference he asks the following question:

"Whether an accused, who surreptitiously laced a friend's drinks with double measures of spirits when he knew that his friend would shortly be driving his car home, and in consequence his friend drove with an excess quantity of alcohol in his body and was convicted of the offence under section 6(1) of the Road Traffic Act 1972, is entitled to a ruling of no case to answer on being later charged as an aider and abettor counsellor and procurer, on the ground that there was no shared intention between the two, that the accused did not by accompanying him or otherwise positively encourage the friend to drive, or on any other ground."

. . . . . .

The language in the section which determines whether a "secondary party," as he is sometimes called, is guilty of a criminal offence committed by another embraces the four words "aid, abet, counsel or procure." The origin of those words is to be found in section 8 of the Accessories and Abettors Act 1861, which provides:

"Whosoever shall aid, abet, counsel or procure the commission of any misdemeanor, whether the same be a misdemeanor at common law or by virtue of any Act passed or to be passed, shall be liable to be tried, indicted and punished as a principal offender."

Thus, in the past, when the distinction was still drawn between felony and misdemeanour, it was sufficient to make a person guilty of a misdemeanour if he aided, abetted, counselled or procured the offence of another. When the difference between felonies and misdemeanours was abolished in 1967, section 1 of the Criminal Law Act 1967 in effect provided that the same test should apply to make a secondary party guilty either of treason or felony.

Of course it is the fact that in the great majority of instances where a secondary party is sought to be convicted of an offence there has been a contact between the principal offender and the secondary party. Aiding and abetting almost inevitably involves a situation in which the secondary party and the main offender are together at some stage discussing the plans which they may be making in respect of the alleged offence, and are in contact so that each knows what is passing through the mind of the other.

In the same way it seems to us that a person, who counsels the commission of a crime by another, almost inevitably comes to a moment when he is in contact with that other, when he is discussing the offence with that other and when, to use the words of the statute, he counsels the other to commit the offence.

The fact that so often the relationship between the secondary party and the principal will be such that there is a meeting of minds between them caused the trial judge in the case from which this reference is derived to think that this was really an essential feature of proving or establishing the guilt of the secondary party and, as we understand his judgment, he took the view that in the absence of some sort of meeting of minds, some sort of mental link between the secondary party and the principal, there could be no aiding, abetting or counselling of the offence within the meaning of the section.

So far as aiding, abetting and counselling is concerned we would go a long way with that conclusion. It may very well be as I said a moment ago, difficult to think of a case of aiding, abetting or counselling when the parties have not met and have not discussed in some respects the terms of the offence which they have in mind. But we do not see why a similar principle should apply to procuring. We approach section 8 of the Act of 1861 on the basis that the words should be given their ordinary meaning, if possible. We approach the section on the basis also that if four words are employed here, "aid, abet, counsel or procure," the probability is that there is a difference between each of those four words and the other three, because, if there were no such difference, then Parliament would be wasting time in using four words where two or three would do. Thus, in deciding whether that which is assumed to be done under our reference was a criminal offence we approach the section on the footing that each word must be given its ordinary meaning.

To procure means to produce by endeavour. You procure a thing by setting out to see that it happens and taking the appropriate steps to produce that happening. We think that there are plenty of instances in which a person may be said to procure the commission of a crime by another even though there is no sort of conspiracy between the two, even though there is no attempt at agreement or discussion as to the form which the offence should take. In our judgment the offence described in this reference is such a case.

If one looks back at the facts of the reference: the accused surreptitiously laced his friend's drink. This is an important element and, although we are not going to decide today anything other than the problem posed to us, it may well be that, in similar cases where the lacing of the drink or the introduction of the extra alcohol is known to the driver, quite different considerations may apply. We say that because, where the driver has no knowledge of what is happening, in most instances he would have no means of preventing the offence from being committed. If the driver is unaware of what has happened, he will not be taking precautions. He will get into his car seat, switch on the ignition and drive home and, consequently, the conception of another procuring the commission of the offence by the driver is very much stronger where the driver is innocent of all knowledge of what is happening, as in the present case where the lacing of the drink was surreptitious.

The second thing which is important in the facts set out in our reference is that, following and in consequence of the introduction of the extra alcohol, the friend drove with an excess quantity of alcohol in his blood. Causation here is important. You cannot procure an offence unless there is a causal link between what you do and the commission of the offence, and here we are told that in consequence of the addition of this alcohol the driver, when he drove home, drove with an excess quantity of alcohol in his body.

Giving the words their ordinary meaning in English, and asking oneself whether in those circumstances the offence has been procured, we are in no doubt that the answer is that it has. It has been procured because, unknown to the driver and without his collaboration, he has been put in a position in which in fact he has committed an offence which he never would have committed otherwise. We think that there was a case to answer and that the trial judge should have directed the jury that an offence is committed if it is shown beyond reasonable doubt that the defendant knew that his friend was going to drive, and also knew that the ordinary and natural result of the additional alcohol added to the friend's drink would be to bring him above the recognised limit of 80 milligrammes per 100 millilitres of blood.

It was suggested to us that, if we held that there may be a procuring on the facts of the present case, it would be but a short step to a similar finding for the generous host, with somewhat bibulous friends, when at the end of the day his friends leave him to go to their own homes in circumstances in which they are not fit to drive and in circumstances in which an offence under the Road Traffic Act 1972 is committed. The suggestion has been made that the host may in those circumstances be guilty with his guests on the basis that he has either aided, abetted, counselled or procured the offence.

The first point to notice in regard to the generous host is that that is not a case in which the alcohol is being put surreptitiously into the glass of the driver. That is a case in which the driver knows perfectly well how much he has to drink and where to a large extent it is perfectly right and proper to leave him to make his own decision.

Furthermore, we would say that, if such a case arises, the basis on which the case will be put against the host is, we think, bound to be on the footing that he has supplied the tool with which the offence is committed. This, of course, is a reference back to such cases as those where oxy-acetylene equipment was bought by a man knowing it was to be used by another for a criminal offence: see *Reg.* v. *Bainbridge* (1960). There is ample and clear authority as to the extent to which supplying the tools for the commission of an offence may amount to aiding and abetting for present purposes.

Accordingly, so far as the generous host type of case is concerned, we are not concerned at the possibility that difficulties will be created, as long as it is borne in mind that in those circumstances the matter must be approached in accordance with well-known authority governing the provision of the tools for the commission of an offence, and never forgetting that the introduction of the alcohol is not there surreptitious, and that consequently the case for saying that the offence was procured by the supplier of the alcohol is very much more difficult.

Our decision on the reference is that the question posed by the Attorney-General should be answered in the negative.

See also *Blakely and Sutton* v. *D.P.P.* ((1991); H.S.B., p. 237 and 245).

A. The Actus Reus of Secondary Participation

R. v. Clarkson

[1971] 3 All E.R. 344 (C.M.A.C.)

[A girl was subjected to a brutal multiple rape in military barracks in Germany. The accused in question had been drinking and had entered the room where the rapes occurred and stood watching.]

Megaw L.J. As has been said, there was no evidence on which the prosecution sought to rely that either the appellant Clarkson or the appellant Carroll had done any physical act or uttered any word which involved direct physical participation or verbal encouragement. There was no evidence that they had touched the girl, helped to hold her down, done anything to her, done anything to prevent others from assisting her or to prevent her from escaping, or from trying to ward off her attackers, or that they had said anything which gave encouragement to the others to commit crime or to participate in committing crime. Therefore, if there was here aiding and abetting by the appellants Clarkson or Carroll it could only have been on the basis of inferences to be drawn that by their very presence they, each of them separately as concerns himself, encouraged those who were committing rape. Let it be accepted, and there was evidence to justify this assumption, that the presence of those two appellants in the room where the offence was taking place was not accidental in any sense and that it was not by chance, unconnected with the crime, that they were there. Let it be accepted that they entered the room when the crime was committed because of what they had heard, which indicated that a woman was being raped, and they remained there.

R. v. *Coney* (1882) decided that non-accidental presence at the scene of the crime is not conclusive of aiding and abetting. The jury has to be told by the judge, or as in this case the court-martial has to be told by the judge-advocate, in clear terms what it is that has to be proved before they can convict of aiding and abetting; what it is of which the jury or the courtmartial, as the case may be, must be sure as matters of inference before they can convict of aiding and abetting in such a case where the evidence adduced by the prosecution is limited to non-accidental presence. What has to be proved is stated by Hawkins J. in a well-known passage in his judgment in R. v. *Coney* where he said:

"In my opinion, to constitute an aider and abettor some active steps must be taken by word, or action, with the intent to instigate the principal or principals. Encouragement does not of necessity amount to aiding and abetting, it may be intentional or unintentional, a man may unwittingly encourage another in fact by his presence, by misinterpreted words, or gestures, or by his silence, or noninterference, or he may encourage intentionally by expressions, gestures, or actions intended to signify approval. In the latter case he aids and abets, in the former he does not. It is no criminal offence to stand by, a mere passive spectator of a crime, even of a murder. Non-interference to prevent a crime is not itself a crime. But the fact that a person was voluntarily and purposely present witnessing the commission of a crime, and offered no opposition to it, though he might reasonably be expected to prevent and had the power to do so, or at least to express his dissent, might under some circumstances, afford cogent evidence upon which a jury would be justified in finding that he wilfully encouraged and so aided and abetted. But it would be purely a question for the jury whether he did so or not."

It is not enough, then, that the presence of the accused has, in fact, given encouragement. It must be proved that the accused intended to give encouragement; that he *wilfully* encouraged. In a case such as the present, more than in many other cases where aiding and abetting is alleged, it was essential that the element should be stressed; for there was here at least the possibility that a drunken man with his self-discipline loosened by drink, being aware that a woman was being raped, might be attracted to the scene and might stay on the scene in the capacity of what is known as a voyeur; and, while his presence should offer encouragement to rapers and would-be rapers or discouragement to the victim, he might not realise that he was giving encouragement; so that, while encouragement there might be it would not be a case in which, to use the words of Hawkins J., the accused person "wilfully encouraged."

A further point is emphasised in passages in the judgment of the Court of Criminal Appeal in *R.* v. *Allan* (1965). That was a case concerned with participation in an affray. Edmund Davies J., giving the judgment of the court, said:

"In effect, it amounts to this: that the learned judge thereby directed the jury that they were in duty bound to convict an accused who was proved to have been present and witnessing an affray if it was also proved that he nursed an intention to join in if help was needed by the side which he favoured, and this notwithstanding that he did nothing by words or deeds to evince his intention and outwardly played the rôle of a purely passive spectator. It was said that, if that direction is right, where A and B behave themselves to all outward appearances in an exactly similar manner, but it be proved that A had the intention to participate if needs be, whereas B had no such intention, then A must be convicted of being a principal in the second degree to the affray, whereas B should be acquitted. To do that, it is objected, would be to convict A on his thoughts, even though they found no reflection in his actions."

The other passage in the judgment is this:

"In our judgment, before a jury can properly convict an accused person of being a principal in the second degree to an affray, they must be convinced by the evidence that, at the very least, he by some means or other encouraged the participants. To hold otherwise would be, in effect, as counsel for the appellants rightly expressed it, to convict a man on his thoughts, unaccompanied by any physical act other than the fact of his mere presence."

From that it follows that mere intention is not in itself enough. There must be an intention to encourage; and there must also be encouragement in fact, in cases such as the present case.

Question

Can a defendant be liable as a secondary party by failing to act?

Du Cros v. Lambourne

[1907] 1 K.B. 40 (D.C.)

[The accused had been charged with driving a car at a speed dangerous to the public. It appeared that though the car was his, it had been driven by another. (It is generally accepted that an indictment need not specify whether the accused was the principal or secondary party—so long as the crime was perpetrated by someone and the accused was a party to it.)]

Lord Alverstone C.J. It has been contended on his behalf that there was no evidence, and reliance was placed on certain of the judgments in *Reg.* v. *Coney* in support of this contention. *Reg.* v. *Coney* was a case of spectators at a prize-fight, and I do not think that the general language used in the judgments was intended to be, or can be, treated as applying to every kind of case. We have to consider the facts found in this case. The case states that the appellant must have known that the speed of the car was dangerous; that if Miss Godwin was driving, she was doing so with the consent and approval of the appellant, who was in control of the car, and that he could, and ought to, have prevented her from driving at this excessive and dangerous speed, but that he allowed her to do so and did not interfere in any way. I will not attempt to lay down any general rule or principle, but having regard to these findings of fact, it is, in my opinion, impossible to say that there was in this case no evidence of aiding and abetting on the part of the appellant. The case further states that, having regard to the above facts, the court of quarter sessions dismissed the appeal, holding that it was not necessary to decide whether the appellant was himself driving or not. This can only mean that the mind of the court had been addressed to the question of aiding and abetting, and it being in my opinion impossible to say that there was no evidence on which the appellant could be convicted of aiding and abetting, this appeal must be dismissed.

Question

Suppose a group of people are sharing a flat together and A discovers that B has possession of a controlled drug. If A continues to live in the flat, will A be in danger of being held to have given passive encouragement to B's offence? See *Bland* (1987).

B. Mens Rea of Secondary Participation

R. v. Bainbridge

[1959] 3 All E.R. 200 (C.C.A.)

[B. purchased some oxygen cutting equipment for some men who six weeks later used it for breaking into the Midland Bank at Stoke Newington: B. said that he thought the equipment was probably going to be used for an illegal purpose—possibly breaking up stolen goods, but he had no idea that it was to be used for breaking into a bank. On appeal against conviction of B. as a secondary part to the break-in]:

Lord Parker C.J. Counsel for the appellant, who argued this case very well, contended that that direction was wrong. As he put it, in order that a person should be convicted of being accessory before the fact, it must be shown that, at the time when he bought the equipment in a case such as this, he knew that a particular crime was going to be committed; and by "a particular crime" counsel meant that the premises in this case which were going to be broken into were known to the appellant and contemplated by him, and not only the premises in question but the date when the crime was going to occur; in other words, that he must have known that on a particular date the Stoke Newington branch of the Midland Bank was intended to be broken into.

The court fully appreciates that it is not enough that it should be shown that a person knew that some illegal venture was intended. To take this case, it would not be enough if the appellant knew—he says that he only suspected—that the equipment was going to be used to dispose of stolen property. That would not be enough. Equally, this court is quite satisfied that it is unnecesssary that knowledge of the intention to commit the particular crime which was in fact committed should be shown, and by "particular crime" I am using the words in the same way as that in which counsel for the appellant used them, namely, on a particular date and particular premises.

It is not altogether easy to lay down a precise form of words which will cover every case that can be contemplated, but, having considered the cases and the law, this court is quite clear that the direction of Judge Aarvold in this case cannot be criticised. Indeed, it might well have been made with the passage in *Foster's Crown Cases* (3rd edn.) (1792) at p. 369 in mind, because there the learned author says:

> "If the principal totally and substantially varieth, if being solicited to commit a felony of one kind he *wilfully and knowingly* committeth a felony of another, *he* will stand single in that offence, and the person soliciting will not be involved in his guilt. For on *his* part it was no more than a fruitless ineffectual temptation."

The converse of course is that, if the principal does not totally and substantially vary the advice or the help and does not wilfully and knowingly commit a different form of felony altogether, the man who has advised or helped, aided or abetted, will be guilty as an accessory before the fact.

Judge Aarvold in this case, in the passages to which I have referred, makes it clear that there must be not merely suspicion but knowledge that a crime of the type in question was intended, and that the equipment was bought with that in view. In his reference to the felony of the type intended it was, as he states, the felony of breaking and entering premises and the stealing of property from those premises. The court can see nothing wrong in that direction.

Appeal dismissed.

D.P.P. for Northern Ireland v. Maxwell

[1978] 1 W.L.R. 1350

[M. was a member of the Ulster Volunteer Force, a unit proscribed in Northern Ireland. On the night in question he guided some terrorists to a public house where they planted a bomb. It was found at first instance that he knew that what was planned would be violent, involving danger to persons or premises. He did not, however, know exactly what offence would be committed. He appealed against his conviction for secondary participation. The judgment of the Court of Criminal Appeal in Northern Ireland was delivered by Lord Lowry C.J. A further appeal by Maxwell was dismissed by the House of Lords. Their Lordships strongly approved the judgment of Lord Lowry C.J.]

Lord Lowry C.J. Once the "particular crime" theory of guilty knowledge is rejected in favour of the *Bainbridge* principle, the question arises how far that principle goes. In a practical sense the question is whether the principle applies to the facts proved in this case.

Suppose the intending principal offender (whom I shall call "the principal") tells the intended accomplice (whom I shall call "the accomplice") that he means to shoot A or else leave a bomb at A's house and the accomplice agrees to drive the principal to A's house and keep watch while there, it seems clear that the accomplice would be guilty of aiding and abetting whichever crime the principal committed, because he would know that one of two crimes was to be committed, he would have assisted the principal and he would have intended to assist him. Again, let us suppose that the principal tells the accomplice that the intention is to murder A at one house but, if he cannot be found or the house is guarded, the alternative plan is to go to B's house and leave a bomb there or thirdly to rob a particular bank (or indeed murder somebody, or bomb somebody's house or rob any bank, as to which see *R. v. Bainbridge*) and requests the accomplice to make a reconnaissance of a number of places and report on the best way of gaining access to the target. The accomplice agrees and makes all the reconnaissances and reports, and the principal then without a further communication, selects a target and commits the crime. It seems clear that, whichever crime the principal commits, all the ingredients of the accomplice's guilt are present. In each of these examples the accomplice knows exactly what is contemplated and the only thing he does not know is to which particular crime he will became an accessory when it is committed. His guilt springs from the fact that he contemplates the commission of one (or more) of a number of crimes by the principal and he intentionally lends his assistance in order that such a crime will be committed. In other words, he knows that the principal is committing or about to commit one of a number of specified illegal acts and with that knowledge he helps him to do so.

The situation has something in common with that of two persons who agree to rob a bank on the understanding, either express or implied from conduct (such as the carrying of a loaded gun by one person with the knowledge of the other), that violence *may* be resorted to. The accomplice knows, not that the principal *will* shoot the cashier, but that he may do so; and, if the principal does shoot him, the accomplice will be guilty of murder. A different case is where the accomplice has only offence A in contemplation and the principal commits offence B. Here the accomplice, although morally culpable (and perhaps guilty of conspiring to commit offence A), is not guilty of aiding and abetting offence B. The principle with which we are dealing does not seem to us to provide a warrant, on the basis of combatting lawlessness generally, for convicting an alleged accomplice of *any* offence which, helped by his preliminary acts, a principal may commit. The relevant crime must be within the contemplation of the accomplice and only exceptionally would evidence be found to support the allegation that the accomplice had given the principal a completely blank cheque.

Interesting hypothetical problems can be posed, if, for example, one person supplies to another house-breaking implements or weapons which are used, and perhaps used repeatedly, by the person supplied or by a third person, either immediately or months or years later. Such questions must, we think, be solved by asking whether the crime actually committed is fairly described as the crime or one of a number of crimes within the contemplation of the accomplice. They are typical of the kind of problem which may be encountered in the application of any principle of the common law which, while requiring to be soundly based, can only proceed from one instance to another. But those questions do not arise in the present case.

The facts found here show that the appellant, as a member of an organisation which habitually perpetrates sectarian acts of violence with firearms and explosives, must, as soon as he was briefed for his role, have contemplated the bombing of the Crosskeys Inn as not the only possibility but one of the most obvious possibilities among the jobs which the principals were likely to be undertaking and in the commission of which he was intentionally assisting. He was therefore in just the same situation, so far as guilty knowledge is concerned, as a man who had been given a list of jobs and told that one of them would be carried out. And so he is guilty of the offence alleged against him in count 1.

[Lord Dilhorne and Lord Edmund Davies said though the indictment could not technically be challenged, where the accused was not being charged as a principal offender, it would be better if the particulars of the offence could indicate the exact nature of the allegations against the accused.]

National Coal Board v. Gamble

[1959] 1 Q.B. 11 (D.C.)

[The N.C.B. supplied X with coal. One of X's drivers would load his lorry with coal and would then proceed to have his lorry weighed. If the weight was correct an employee of the N.C.B. would issue the driver with a ticket and the driver would then drive out on to the public roads. On the occasion in question the weighbridge operator noticed that the lorry was overloaded. It is a criminal offence to drive a lorry on a public road where the load exceeds a certain weight. The driver said he would take the risk and the weighbridge operator issued a ticket. The driver committed the offence as a principal offender as soon as he drove on to the road. The question for the court was whether the weighbridge operator was a secondary party and further whether the N.C.B. was liable for the acts of its employee.]

Devlin J. A person who supplies the instrument for a crime or anything essential to its commission aids in the commission of it; and if he does so knowingly and with intent to aid, he abets it as well and is therefore guilty of aiding and abetting. I use the word "supplies" to comprehend giving, lending, selling or any other transfer of the right of property. In a sense a man who gives up to a criminal a weapon which the latter has a right to demand from him aids in the commission of the crime as much as if he sold or lent the article. But this has never been held to be aiding in law.... The reason, I think, is that in the former case there is in law a positive act and in the latter only a negative one. In the transfer of property there must be either a physical delivery or a positive act of assent to a taking. But a man who hands over to another his own property on demand, although he may physically be performing a positive act, in law is only refraining from detinue. Thus in law the former act is one of the assistance voluntarily given and the latter is only a failure to prevent the commission of the crime by means of a forcible detention, which would not even be justified except in the case of felony. Another way of putting the point is to say that aiding and abetting is a crime that requires proof of *mens rea*, that is to say of intention to aid as well of knowledge of the circumstances, and that proof of the intent involves proof of a positive act of assistance voluntarily done.

These considerations make it necessary to determine at what point the property in the coal passed from the board and what the board's state of knowledge was at that time. If the property had passed before the board knew of the proposed crime, there was nothing they could legally do to prevent the driver of the lorry from taking the overloaded lorry out on to the road. If it had not, then they sold the coal with knowledge that an offence was going to be committed.

[It was found, by the justices at the trial, that the weighbridge operator could have refused to transfer the property after he had discovered the excess weight].

This is the conclusion to which the justices came. Mr. Thompson submits on behalf of the board that it does not justify a verdict of guilty of aiding and abetting. He submits, first, that even if knowledge of the illegal purpose had been acquired before delivery began, it would not be sufficient for the verdict; and secondly, that if he is wrong about that, the knowledge was acquired too late, and the board was not guilty of aiding and abetting simply because Haslam failed to stop the process of delivery after it had been initiated.

On his first point Mr. Thompson submits that the furnishing of an article essential to the crime with knowledge of the use to which it is to be put does not of itself constitute aiding and abetting; there must be proved in addition a purpose or motive of the defendant to further the crime or encourage the criminal. Otherwise, he submits, there is no *mens rea*.

I have already said that in my judgment there must be proof of intent to aid. . . . I would agree that proof that the article was knowingly supplied is not conclusive evidence of intent to aid. *Rex* v. *Steane* (1947), in which the defendant was charged with having acted during the war with intent to assist the enemy contrary to the Defence Regulations then in force, makes the same point. But prima facie—and *Rex* v. *Steane* makes this clear also—a man is presumed to intend the natural and probable consequences of his acts, and the consequence of supplying essential material is that assistance is given to the criminal. It is always open to the defendant, as in *Rex* v. *Steane*, to give evidence of his real intention. But in this case the defence called no evidence. The prima facie presumption is therefore enough to justify the verdict, unless it is the law that some other mental element besides intent is necessary to the offence.

This is what Mr. Thompson argues, and he describes the additional element as the purpose or motive of encouraging the crime. No doubt evidence of an interest in the crime or of an express purpose to assist it will greatly strengthen the case for the prosecution. But an indifference to the result of the crime does not of itself negative abetting. If one man deliberately sells to another a gun to be used of murdering a third, he may be indifferent about whether the third man lives or dies and interested only in the cash profit to be made out of the sale, but he can still be an aider and abettor. To hold otherwise would be to negative the rule that *mens rea* is a matter of intent only and does not depend on desire or motive.

The authorities, I think, support this conclusion, though none has been cited to us in which the point has been specifically argued and decided.... The same principle has been applied in civil cases where the seller has sued upon a contract for the supply of goods which he knew were to be used for an illegal purpose....

The case chiefly relied on by Mr. Thompson was *Reg.* v. *Coney* (1882). In that case the defendants were charged with aiding and abetting an illegal prize fight at which they had been present. The judgments all refer to "encouragement," but it would be wrong to conclude from that that proof of encouragement is necessary to every form of aiding and abetting. Presence on the scene of the crime without encouragement or assistance is no aid to the criminal; the supply of essential material is. Moreover, the decision makes it clear that encouragement can be inferred from mere presence. Cave J., who gave the leading judgment, said of the summing-up: "It may mean either that mere presence unexplained is evidence of encouragement, and so of guilt, or that mere presence unexplained is conclusive proof of encouragement, and so of guilt. If the former is the correct meaning I concur in the law so laid down; if the latter, I am unable to do so." This dictum seems to me to support the view I have expressed. If voluntary presence is prima facie evidence of encouragement and therefore of aiding and abetting, it appears to me to be *a fortiori* that the intentional supply of an essential article must be prima facie evidence of aiding and abetting.

As to Mr. Thompson's alternative point, I have already expressed the view that the facts show an act of assent made by Haslam after knowledge of the proposed illegality and without which the property would not have passed. If some positive act to complete delivery is committed after knowledge of the illegality, the position in law must, I think, be just the same as if the knowledge had been obtained before the delivery had been begun. Of course, it is quite likely that Haslam was confused about the legal position and thought that he was not entitled to withhold the weighbridge ticket. There is no *mens rea* if the defendant is shown to have a genuine belief in the existence of circumstances which, if true, would negative an intention to aid; see *Wilson* v. *Inyang* (1951). But this argument, which might have been the most cogent available to the defence, cannot now be relied upon, because Haslam was not called to give evidence about what he thought or believed.

The fact that no evidence was called for the defence makes this case a peculiar one. We were told that the board desired to obtain a decision on principle which would enable them to regulate their practice in the future. They therefore accepted responsibility for Haslam's act without going into any questions of vicarious liability; and they called no evidence in order, we were told, that the decision might be given on facts put against them as strongly as might be. What they wished to establish was that responsibility for overloaded lorries rested solely with the carrier and that the sale and delivery of the coal could not, if that was all that could be proved, involve them in a breach of the criminal law. For the reasons I have given I think that the law cannot be so stated and that the appeal should be dismissed.

Note

For requirements of vicarious liability see H.S.B., pp. 250 *et seq.*

Question

Would it make any difference that the accused hoped the criminal offence would not be committed, and had even tried to persuade the would-be principal offender against it?

Lynch v. D.P.P. for Northern Ireland

[1975] A.C. 653 (H.L.)

[The defendant had driven two men to the place where they killed another. The majority of the speeches are concerned with the defence of duress. The above question was however considered.]

Lord Morris of Borth-y-Gest. If in the present case the jury were satisfied that the car was driven towards the garage in pursuance of a murderous plan and that the appellant knew that that was the plan and intentionally drove the car in execution of that plan, he could be held to have aided and abetted even though he regretted the plan or indeed was horrified by it. However great his reluctance, he would have intended to aid and abet.

C. Liability for Unforeseen Consequences

Questions

1. A provides B with a gun to kill C. B aims at C but misses and accidentally hits D, killing him. Is A a secondary party to the killing?
2. A and B plan a burglary. A will drive the getaway car while B will enter the house to steal money. It is agreed B should carry a cosh to protect himself against the occupiers should they be aroused. C, the occupier, is awakened and comes down to investigate. B coshes him, causing him serious injury. Is A a secondary party to the attack on C? Would it make any difference if B had, unknown to A, taken a gun which he used to kill C?

Davies v. D.P.P.

[1954] A.C. 378 (H.L.)

[A fight between two rival gangs had broken out on Clapham Common during the course of which it was alleged that D. had knifed and killed a member of the rival gang. The prosecution called Lawson, a member of D.'s gang, to give evidence against D. Under the rules of evidence if the jury found L. to be an accomplice in the killing, his evidence could only be relied upon if the trial judge had warned the jury of the dangers of acting upon the uncorroborated evidence of an accomplice. No such warning was given and the House of Lords had to determine whether there was any evidence upon which the jury could have held L. to be an accomplice in the killing.]

Lord Simonds L.C. In particular, I can see no reason why, if half a dozen boys fight another crowd, and one of them produces a knife and stabs one of the opponents to death, all the rest of his group should be treated as accomplices in the use of a knife and the infliction of mortal injury by that means, unless there is evidence that the rest intended or concerted or at least contemplated an attack with a knife by one of their number, as opposed to a common assault. If all that was designed or envisaged was in fact a common assault, and there was no evidence that Lawson, a party to the common assault, knew that any of his companions had a knife, then Lawson was not an accomplice in the crime consisting in its felonious use.

Note

See also R. v. *Anderson and Morris* (1966; H.S.B., p. 242).

Hui Chi-ming v. R.

[1991] 3 All E.R. 897 (PC)

Ah Po (P), the boyfriend of a girl who claimed to have been intimidated by a man, persuaded a group of friends to go with him to find the man, saying that they were going to find someone to hit. Hui Ching-ming (H), one of the group was aware that P was carrying a length of metal pipe. They found a man whom they believed to be the one who had intimidated P's girlfriend and P struck him with the metal pipe; the victim later died of the injuries sustained. P was convicted of manslaughter. Two years later H was indicted for murder, though it was not suggested that he had actually hit the victim. He appealed against his conviction on the ground that the judge had been wrong to direct the jury that they should convict H of murder if they were satisfied that he had contemplated that P might use the pipe to cause really serious bodily injury.

Lord Lowry. Mr. Thomas Q.C., who appeared for the appellant before the Board, made two further points. The first, which stemmed from the appellant's basic proposition, was that the judge should have told the jury that, for the appellant to be guilty of murder, it was necessary that Ah Po contemplated the possibility of at least grievious bodily harm being caused when the unlawful agreement to assualt Ah Hung was made; otherwise his severe attack on the victim, though intended when it was made, would have gone beyond what was authorised by the agreement. The second point was that Sir Robin Cooke's equation in *Chan Wing-Siu* v. R. (1984) of contemplation with authorisation meant that an accomplice who merely *foresees* the further and additional act of the principal is not thereby rendered liable for that act. Neither point poses any problem on the assumed basis that the jury found the unlawful joint enterprise to be one of the first type, which was covered by paragraphs 8 and 9 of the judge's directions ("type 1"). Both points were directed to the question of guilty intent on the part of the accomplice in relation to an unlawful joint enterprise of the second type (as their Lordships for the purposes of argument will assume the crime to have been), which was dealt with in paragraphs 10 and 13 of the directions ("type 2"). Paragraph 10 clearly recalls Sir Robin Cooke's reference in *Chan* to the accomplice's "contemplation" of "a crime forseen as a possible incident of the common unlawful enterprise," which tends to indicate, not surprisingly, that the judge's directions were based on *Chan*. The principle enunciated in *Chan* has since been clearly stated by Lord Lane C.J. in the Court of Appeal (Criminal Division) in *Ward* (1987) 85 Cr.App.R. 71 and *Slack* (1989) 89 Cr.App.R. 252, [1989] Q.B. 775, in both of which *Chan* was expressly approved and applied, and most recently in *Hyde* (1991) 92 Cr.App.R. 131, [1991] 1 Q.B. 134, which also applied *Chan*. Having referred to *Slack* Lord Lane C.J. said (at p. 135 and p. 138 respectively):

"There are, broadly speaking, two main types of joint enterprise cases where death results to the victim. The first is where the primary object of the participants is to do some kind of physical injury to the victim. The second is where the primary object is not to cause physical injury to any victim but, for example, to commit burglary. The victim is assaulted and killed as a possibly unwelcome incident of the burglary. The latter type of case may pose more complicated questions than the former, but the principle in each is the same. A must be proved to have intended to kill or to do serious bodily harm at the time he killed. As was pointed out in *Slack* (1989) 89 Cr.App.R. 252, [1989] Q.B. 775, 781, B, to be guilty, must be proved to have lent himself to a criminal enterprise involving the infliction of serious harm or death, or to have had an express or tacit understanding with A that such harm or death should, if necessary, be inflicted.

We were there endeavouring, respectfully, to follow the principles enunciated by Sir Robin Cooke in *Chan Wing-Siu* v. *R.* (1985) 80 Cr.App.R. 117, 121, [1985] A.C. 168, 175: 'The case must depend rather on the wider principle whereby a secondary party is criminally liable for acts by the primary offender of a type which the former forsees but does not necessarily intend. That there is such a principle is not in doubt. It turns on contemplation or, putting the same idea in other words, authorisation, which may be express but is more usually implied. It meets the case of a crime foreseen as a possible incident of the common unlawful enterprise. The criminal culpability lies in participating in the venture with the foresight. It has been pointed out by Professor J.C. Smith, in his commentary on *Wakely* [1990] Crim.L.R. 119, 120–121, that in the judgments in *Slack* and also in *Wakely* itself, to both of which I was a party, insufficient attention was paid by the Court to the distinction between on the one hand tacit agreement by B that A should use violence, and on the other hand a realisation by B that A, the principal party, may use violence despite B's refusal to authorise or agree to its use. Indeed in *Wakely* we went so far as to say: 'The suggestion that a mere foresight of the real or definite possibility of violence being used is sufficient to constitute the mental element of murder is prima facie, academically speaking at least, not sufficient.' On reconsideration, that passage is not in accordance with the principles set out by Sir Robin Cooke which we were endeavouring to follow and was wrong, or at least misleading. If B realises (without agreeing to such conduct being used) that A may kill or intentionally inflict serious injury, but nevertheless continues to partici- pate with A in the venture, that will amount to a sufficient mental element for B to be guilty of murder if A, with the requisite intent, kills in the course of the venture. As Professor Smith points out, B has in those circumstances lent himself to the enterprise and by so doing he has given assistance and encouragement to A in carrying out an enterprise which B realises may involve murder.

That being the case it seems to us that the judge was correct when he directed the jury in the terms of those passages of the summing up which we have already quoted. It may be that a simple direction on the basis of *Anderson and Morris* (1966) 50 Cr.App.R. 216, [1966] 2 Q.B. 110 would, in the circumstances of this case, have been enough, but the direction given was sufficiently clear and the outcome scarcely surprising. That ground of appeal, which was in the forefront of the arguments of each of the appellants, therefore fails."

That passage from the judgment in Hyde (*supra*) correctly states, in their Lordships' opinion, the law applicable to a joint enterprise of the kind described, which results in the commission of murder by the principal as an incident of the joint enterprise. Against that background their Lordships consider the two arguments set out above. The first can be readily disposed of on the facts by pointing out that Ah Po's arming himself with the waterpipe before setting out showed unequivocally what he *did* contemplate at that stage, since the connection between the argument and the facts to which it was directed was tenuous, to say the least.

Counsel's submission, however, was based on the passage already cited from *Johns* v. *R.* (1980) 143 C.L.R. 108, 130–131. The issue in that case was whether an accessory before the fact is, like a principal in the second degree, responsible for an act constituting the offence charged if such act was contemplated as a *possible* incident of the common purpose, or whether it has to be established as a *likely or probable* consequence of the way in which the crime was to be committed. The court unanimously accepted the former alternative. But, in the course if their judgment, Mason, Murphy and Wilson JJ. stated the law in the manner already quoted, requiring the act to have been within the contemplation of *both the principal and the accessory* as an act which might be done in the course of carrying out the primary criminal intention. It is on the basis of that passage that the appellant contends that the secondary party cannot be liable unless the relevant act was within the contemplation of both the principal and the secondary party.

Johns v. *R.* is a leading case on the law relating to accessories. It was specifically relied on by Sir Robin Cooke in *Chan*, in which the same central issue fell to be considered. It is, however, plain that, in the passage upon which the appellant relies, attention was being concentrated on those cases in which the question is whether the act of the principal falls within the common purpose of the parties. This appears from the immediately succeeding sentence in the judgment of Mason, Murphy and Wilson JJ. (not quoted in the written case for the appellant), which reads as follows: (143 C.L.R. 108, 131):

> "Such an act is one which falls within the parties' own purpose and design precisely because it is within their contemplation and is foreseen as a possible incident of the execution of their planned enterprise."

In such a case the contemplation of both parties will be relevant. But, as appears from Sir Robin Cooke's judgment in *Chan* (and as was recognised by Lord Lane C.J. in *Hyde*, departing in this respect from some of the observations contained in the earlier judgments in *Slack* and *Wakely*), the secondary party may be liable simply by reason of his participating in the joint enterprise with foresight that the principal may commit the relevant act as part of the joint enterprise. We therefore find Sir Robin Cooke focussing upon the contemplation of the secondary party alone, as in the following passage ((1985) 80 Cr.App.R. 117, 123, [1985] A.C. 168, 178):

> "In some cases in this field it is enough to direct the jury by adapting to the circumstances the simple formula common in a number of jurisdictions. For instance, did the particular accused contemplate that in carrying out a common unlawful purpose one of his partners in the enterprise might use a knife or a loaded gun with the intention of causing really serious bodily harm?"

In practice, of course, in most cases the contemplation of both the primary and the secondary party is likely to be the same; if there is an alleged difference, it will arise where the secondary party asserts in his defence that he did not have in contemplation the act which was in the contemplation of the principal. But their Lordships are unable to accept that in every case the relevant act must be shown to have been in the contemplation of *both* parties before the secondary party can be proved guilty.

Let it be supposed that two men embark on a robbery. One (the principal) to the knowledge of the other (the accessory) is carrying a gun. The accessory contemplates that the principal may use the gun to wound or kill if resistance is met with or the pair are detected at their work but, although the gun is loaded, the only use initially contemplated by the principal is for the purpose of causing fear, by pointing the gun or even by discharging it, with a view to overcoming resistance or evading capture. Then at the scene the principal changes his mind, perhaps through panic or because to fire for effect offers the only chance of escape, and shoots the victim dead. His act is clearly an incident of the unlawful enterprise and the possibility of its occurrence as such was contemplated by the accomplice. According to what was said in *Chan* the accomplice, as well as the principal, would be guilty of murder. Their Lordships have to say that, having regard to what is said in *Chan* and the cases which applied it, they do not consider the prior contemplation of the principal to be a necessary additional ingredient. In their opinion the judge had no duty to direct the jury to that effect in paragraphs 10 and 13 of the relevant passage in his summing up.

In none of the cases reviewed, including the case under appeal, was the prior contemplation of the principal a live issue. But is must be recognised that to hold the accomplice to be guilty in the example their Lordships have posed is consistent with *Chan* and *Hyde*.

Their Lordships appreciate that the hypothetical example they have given is largely theoretical. Rarely, if ever, will a case arise in which the accessory, but not the principal, contemplates the possibility of a further relevant offence and, if the facts appeared to support such a hypothesis, the defence would no doubt seize the opportunity to contend that the accomplice himself had not been proved to have contemplated something which was not in the mind of the principal. Alternatively, he might contend that the principal's further act had gone beyond the contemplated area of guilty conduct, with the result that the accessory to the planned offence was not criminally liable for the new offence. In truth, the point taken by the appellant was academic; but for the reasons they have given, their Lordships reject it as unsound.

The appellant's second point relies on Sir Robin Cooke's use of the word "authorisation" as a synonym for contemplation in the passage already cited from his judgment. Their Lordships consider that Sir Robin used this word—and in that regard they do not differ from counsel—to emphasise the fact that mere foresight is not enough: the accessory, in order to be guilty, must have foreseen the relevant offence which the principal may commit *as a possible incident of the common unlawful enterprise* and must, with such foresight, still have participated in the enterprise. The word "authorisation" explains what is meant by contemplation, but does not add a new ingredient. That this is so is manifest from Sir Robin's pithy conclusion to the passage cited: "The criminal culpability lies in participating in the venture with that foresight."

Their Lordships are satisfied that the trial judge accurately conveyed that idea to the jury by paragraph 10 of his directions.

This was a strong case of at least tacit agreement that Ah Hung should be attacked accompanied by foresight, as admitted by the appellant, that a very serious assault might occur, even if that very serious assault had not been planned from the beginning. It is, moreover, easier to prove against an accomplice that he contemplated and by his participation accepted the use of extra force in the execution of the planned assault than it normally would be to show contemplation and acceptance of a new offence, such as murder added to burglary.

Their Lordships therefore reject all the criticisms of the judge's directions to the jury on joint enterprise.

Question

Can a contemplated eventuality ever be too remote; if, for example, a secondary party saw the use of force as a million to one chance? See *Roberts* [1993].

Note

Rook [1993] confirms the view that the legal requirements of secondary party liability—aiding, abetting, counselling or procuring—are the same whether or not the defendant is present at the scene of the crime. The principles enunciated in *Hui Chi-ming* are equally applicable to the person who supplied the tools for a burglary as they are to the persons who actually break into the house.

D.   No Conviction of Principal Offender

Question

Is it possible to convict the defendant as an accomplice to an offence in the absence of a conviction of the principal offender?

(i)   There is no objection to convicting A as a secondary party where the principal is not convicted.

        (a)   because he has not been apprehended;

        (b)   because he has a defence not available to A;

        (c)   because evidence admissible against A is not available against the principal.

(ii)   Where the evidence against A, the accomplice and B, the principal, is substantially the same then it will normally be wrong to acquit B yet convict A.

(iii) There must, however, be a crime to which A can be a secondary party.

Thornton v. Mitchell

[1940] 1 All E.R. 339 (D.C.)

[A bus conductor was helping his driver to reverse their bus by ringing the bell to indicate that there were no persons behind the bus. He negligently rang the bell when two pedestrians were behind the bus. The driver reversed injuring both, one fatally. The charge against the driver of driving without due care and attention was dismissed, but the magistrates convicted the conductor of aiding and abetting that offence.]

Lord Hewart C.J.   [The magistrates say:]

"We, being of opinion that the conductor [had been very negligent], held that he was guilty of aiding and abetting, counselling and procuring the said Hollinrake to drive without due care and attention, and accordingly we inflicted a fine."

In my opinion, this case is *a fortiori* upon *Morris* v. *Tolman* (1923), to which our attention has been directed. I will read one sentence from the judgment of Avory J.:

" . . . in order to convict, it would be necessary to show that the respondent was aiding the principal, but a person cannot aid another in doing something which that other has not done."

That, I think, is the very thing which these justices have decided that this bus conductor did. In one breath they say that the principal did nothing which he should not have done, and in the next breath they hold that the bus conductor aided and abetted the driver in doing something which had not been done or in not doing something which he ought to have done. I really think that, with all respect to the ingenuity of counsel for the respondent, the case is too plain for argument, and his appeal must be allowed and the conviction quashed.

Question

Was there a charge which might successfully have been brought against the conductor?

R. v. Cogan and Leak

[1976] Q.B. 217 (C.A.)

[L. had invited C. to have sexual intercourse with his (L.'s) wife. It is clear that she did not consent to the intercourse but did so because she was afraid of her husband. The jury found that C. honestly believed she was consenting, but that he had no reasonable grounds for such a belief. In the light of the decision of the House of Lords in *Morgan* (above, p. 157) C.'s conviction for rape was quashed. L., however, had no such belief that his wife was consenting, but at the time of this case a man could not, subject to certain exceptions, be held liable as the principal offender in the rape of his wife. Under those circumstances the question for the Court of Appeal was whether, following the C.'s acquittal, L.'s conviction for aiding and abetting the rape of his wife could still be upheld. The marital exemption which prevented the prosecution of a husband for the rape of his wife no longer exists (see above, p. 176). The case is still of value for its discussion of secondary party liability where the principal offender is acquitted. The question for the Court of Appeal was whether, following C.'s acquittal, L.'s conviction for aiding and abetting the rape of his wife could still be upheld.]

Lawton L.J. The only case which Mr. Herrod submitted had a direct bearing upon the problem of Leak's guilt was *Walters* v. *Lunt* (1951). In that case the respondents had been charged, under section 33(1) of the Larceny Act 1916, with receiving from a child aged seven years, certain articles knowing them to have been stolen. In 1951, a child under eight years was deemed in law to be incapable of committing a crime: it followed that at the time of receipt by the respondents the articles had not been stolen and that the charge had not been proved. That case is very different from this because here one fact is clear—the wife had been raped. Cogan had had sexual intercourse with her without her consent. The fact that Cogan was innocent of rape because he believed that she was consenting does not affect the position that she was raped.

Her ravishment had come about because Leak had wanted it to happen and had taken action to see that it did by persuading Cogan to use his body as the instrument for the necessary physical act. In the language of the law the act of sexual intercourse without the wife's consent was the *actus reus*: it had been procured by Leak who had the appropriate *mens rea*, namely, his intention that Cogan should have sexual intercourse with her without her consent. In our judgment it is irrelevant that the man whom Leak had procured to do the physical act himself did not intend to have sexual intercourse with the wife without her consent. Leak was using him as a means to procure a criminal purpose.

Before 1861 a case such as this, pleaded as it was in the indictment, might have presented a court with problems arising from the old distinctions between principals and accessories in felony. Most of the old law was swept away by section 8 of the Accessories and Abettors Act 1861 and what remained by section 1 of the Criminal Law Act 1967. The modern law allowed Leak to be tried and punished as a principal offender. In our judgment he could have been indicted as a principal offender. It would have been no defence for him to submit that if Cogan was an "innocent" agent, he was necessarily in the old terminology of the law a principal in the first degree, which was a legal impossibility as a man cannot rape his own wife during cohabitation. The law no longer concerns itself with the niceties of degrees in participation in crime; but even if it did Leak would still be guilty. The reason a man cannot by his own physical act rape his wife during cohabitation is because the law presumes consent from the marriage ceremony: see *Hale, Pleas of the Crown* (1778), vol. 1, p. 629. There is no such presumption when a man procures a drunken friend to do the physical act for him. Hale C.J. put this case in one sentence, at p. 629:

" . . . tho in marriage she hath given up her body to her husband, she is not to be by him prostituted to another."

Had Leak been indicted as a principal offender, the case against him would have been clear beyond argument. Should he be allowed to go free because he was charged with "being aider and abettor to the same offence"? If we are right in our opinion that the wife had been raped (and no one outside a court of law would say that she had not been), then the particulars of offence accurately stated what Leak had done, namely, he had procured Cogan to commit the offence.

Notes

1. See also *Bourne* (1952).
2. There was at one time thought to be a general principle that a secondary party's liability could not exceed that of the principal. The House of Lords in *Howe* (1987) (see below, p. 254), overruling the case of *Richards* (1974), have now made it clear that there is no such restriction. This means, for example, that a secondary party might still face a charge of murder where the principal offender, because he lacked sufficient *mens rea*, was only guilty of manslaughter.

E. Repentance by Secondary Party

R. v. Becerra

[1976] 62 Cr.App.R. 212 (C.A.)

[B. together with C. and G. went to burgle a flat. During the burglary they were disturbed by L., the tenant. B. called out, "let's go" and climbed out of a window, followed by G. C., who had been handed a knife by B., stabbed and killed L. B. and C. were charged with murder. On appeal against conviction B. argued that even if there were a joint plan between himself and C. to meet resistance with serious violence or even death, he had effectively withdrawn from the common venture before it was put into effect.]

Roskill L.J. Mr. Owen says that ... the learned judge in effect, though perhaps not in so many words, withdrew the defence of "withdrawal" from the jury, because the learned judge was saying to the jury that the only evidence of Becerra's suggested "withdrawal" was the remark, if it were made, "Come on let's go," coupled with the fact of course that Becerra then went out through the window and ran away and that that could not in those circumstances amount to "with– drawal" and therefore was not available as a defence, even if they decided the issue of common design against Becerra. It is upon that passage in the summing-up that Mr. Owen has principally focused his criticism.

It is necessary, before dealing with that argument in more detail, to say a word or two about the relevant law. It is a curious fact, considering the number of times in which this point arises where two or more people are charged with criminal offences, particularly murder or manslaughter, how relatively little authority there is in this country upon the point. But the principle is undoubtedly of long standing.

Perhaps it is best first stated in *Saunders and Archer* (1577) (in the eighteenth year of the first Queen Elizabeth) at p. 476 in a note by *Plowden*, thus: " ... for if I command one to kill

J.S. and before the Fact done I go to him and tell him that I have repented, and expressly charge him not to kill J.S. and he afterwards kills him, there I shall not be Accessory to this Murder, because I have countermanded my first Command, which in all Reason shall discharge me, for the malicious Mind of the Accessory ought to continue to do ill until the Time of the Act done, or else he shall not be charged; but if he had killed J.S. before the Time of my Discharge or Countermand given, I should have been Accessory to the Death, notwithstanding my private Repentance."

The next case to which I may usefully refer is some 250 years later, but over 150 years ago: *Edmeads and Others* (1828), where there is a ruling of Vaughan B. at a trial at Berkshire Assizes, upon an indictment charging Edmeads and others with unlawfully shooting at gamekeepers. At the end of his ruling the learned Baron said on the question of common intent, "that is rather a question for the jury; but still, on this evidence, it is quite clear what the common purpose was. They all draw up in lines, and point their guns at the gamekeepers, and they are all giving their countenance and assistance to the one of them who actually fires the gun. If it could be shown that either of them separated himself from the rest, and showed distinctly that he would have no hand in what they were doing, the objection would have much weight in it"

I can go forward over 100 years. Mr. Owen (to whose juniors we are indebted for their research into the relevant Canadian and United States cases) referred us to several Canadian cases, to only one of which is it necessary to refer in detail, a decision of the Court of Appeal of British Columbia in *Whitehouse (alias Savage)* (1941). I need not read the headnote. The Court of Appeal held that the trial judge concerned in that case, which was one of murder, had been guity of misdirection in his direction to the jury on this question of "withdrawal." The matter is, if I may most respectfully say so, so well put in the leading judgment of Sloan J.A., that I read the whole of the passage: "Can it be said on the facts of this case that a mere change of mental intention and a quitting of the scene of the crime just immediately prior to the striking of the fatal blow will absolve those who participate in the commission of the crime by overt acts up to that moment from all the consequences of its accomplishment by the one who strikes in ignorance of his companions' change of heart? I think not. After a crime has been committed and before a prior abandonment of the common enterprise may be found by a jury there must be, in my view, in the absence of exceptional circumstances, something more than a mere mental change of intention and physical change of place by those associates who wish to dissociate themselves from the consequences attendant upon their willing assistance up to the moment of the actual commission of that crime. I would not attempt to define too closely what must be done in criminal matters involving participation in a common unlawful purpose to break the chain of causation and responsibility. That must depend upon the circumstances of each case but it seems to me that one essential element ought to be established in a case of this kind: Where practicable and reasonable there must be timely communication of the intention to abandon the common purpose from those who wish to dissociate themselves from the contemplated crime to those who desire to continue in it. What is "timely communication" must be determined by the facts of each case but where practicable and reasonable it ought to be such communication, verbal or otherwise, that will serve unequivocal notice upon the other party to the common unlawful cause that if he proceeds upon it he does so without the further aid and assistance of those who withdraw. The unlawful purpose of him who continues alone is then his own and not one in common with those who are no longer parties to it nor liable to its full and final consequences." The learned judge then went on to cite a passage from 1 Hale's *Pleas of the Crown* 618 and the passage from *Saunders and Archer* (*supra*) to which I have already referred.

In the view of each member of this court, that passage, if we may respectfully say so, could not be improved upon and we venture to adopt it in its entirety as a correct statement of the law which is to be applied in this case.

The last case, an English one, is *Croft* (1944), a well-known case of a suicide pact where, under the old law, the survivor of a suicide pact was charged with and convicted of murder. It was sought to argue that he had withdrawn from the pact in time to avoid liability (as the law then was) for conviction for murder.

The Court of Criminal Appeal, comprising Lawrence J. (as he then was), Lewis and Wrottesley JJ. dismissed the appeal and upheld the direction given by Humphreys J. to the jury at the trial. Towards the end of the judgment Lawrence J. said: " . . . counsel for the appellant complains—although I do not understand that the point had ever been taken in the court below—that the summing-up does not contain any reference to the possibility of the agreement to commit suicide having been determined or countermanded. It is true that the learned judge does not deal expressly with that matter except in a passage where he says: 'Even if you accept his statement in the witnessbox that the vital and second shot was fired when he had gone through that window, he would still be guilty of murder if she was then committing suicide as the result of an agreement which they had mutually arrived at that that should be the fate of both of them, and it is no answer for him that he altered his mind after she was dead and did not commit suicide himself' ... the authorities, such as they are, show in our opinion, that where a person has acted as an accessory before the fact, in order that he should not be held guilty as an accessory before the fact, he must give express and actual countermand or revocation of the advising, counselling, procuring, or abetting which he had given before."

It seems to us that those authorities make plain what the law is which has to be applied in the present case.

We therefore turn back to consider the direction which the learned judge gave in the present case to the jury and what was the suggested evidence that Becerra had withdrawn from the common agreement. The suggested evidence is the use by Becerra of the words "Come on let's go," coupled, as I said a few moments ago, with his act in going out through the window. The evidence, as the judge pointed out, was that Cooper never heard that nor did the third man. But let it be supposed that that was said and the jury took the view that it was said.

On the facts of this case, in the circumstances then prevailing, the knife having already been used and being contemplated for further use when it was handed over by Becerra to Cooper for the purpose of avoiding (if necessary) by violent means the hazards of identification, if Becerra wanted to withdraw at that stage, he would have to "countermand," to use the word that is used in some of the cases or "repent" to use another word so used in some manner vastly different and vastly more effective than merely to say "Come on, let's go" and go out through the window.

It is not necessary, on this application, to decide whether the point of time had arrived at which the only way in which he could effectively withdraw, so as to free himself from joint responsibility for any act Cooper thereafter did in furtherance of the common design, would be physically to intervene so as to stop Cooper attacking Lewis, as the judge suggested, by interposing his own body between them or somehow getting in between them or whether some other action might suffice. That does not arise for decision here. Nor is it necessary to decide whether or not the learned judge was right or wrong, on the facts of this case, in that passage ... which Mr. Owen criticised: "and at least take all reasonable steps to prevent the commission of the crime which he had agreed the others should commit." It is enough for the purposes of deciding this application to say that under the law of this country as it stands, and on the facts (taking them at their highest in favour of Becerra), that which was urged as amounting to withdrawal from the common design was not capable of amounting to such withdrawal. Accordingly Becerra remains responsible, in the eyes of the law, for everything that Cooper did and continued to do after Becerra's disappearance through the window as much as if he had done them himself.

Appeal dismissed.

Note

See also *Rook* [1993].

Chapter 4

Defences

1. INTRODUCTION

In a criminal case it is the duty of the prosecution to establish the accused's guilt. What exactly does that mean?

Woolmington v. D.P.P.

[1935] A.C. 462 (H.L.)

[W.'s wife had left him and had returned to live with her mother. W. went to try to persuade her to return. While at his mother-in-law's house his wife was killed by a shot from a gun he was carrying. His story was that he had taken the gun to frighten her by saying he would kill himself if she did not return, and that it had gone off accidentally.

In directing the jury Swift J. said:]

"If you come to the conclusion that she died in consequence of injuries from the gun which he was carrying, you are put by the law of this country into this position: The killing of a human being is homicide, however he may be killed, and all homicide is presumed to be malicious and murder, unless the contrary appears from circumstances of alleviation, excuse, or justification. 'In every charge of murder, the fact of killing being first proved, all the circumstances of accident, necessity, or infirmity are to be satisfactorily proved by the prisoner, unless they arise out of the evidence produced against him: for the law will presume the fact to have been founded in malice until the contrary appeareth.' That has been the law of this country for all time since we had law. Once it is shown to a jury that somebody has died through the act of another, that is presumed to be murder, unless the person who has been guilty of the act which causes the death can satisfy a jury that what happened was something less, something which might be alleviated, something which might be reduced to a charge of manslaughter, or was something which was accidental, or was something which could be justified."

[W. was convicted of murder. His appeal against conviction finally reached the House of Lords. Viscount Sankey L.C., having reviewed the various authorities concluded:]

Viscount Sankey L.C. If at any period of a trial it was permissible for the judge to rule that the prosecution had established its case and that the onus was shifted on to the prisoner to prove that he was not guilty and that unless he discharged that onus the prosecution was entitled to succeed, would be enabling the judge in such a case to say that the jury must in law find the prisoner guilty and so make the judge decide the case and not the jury, which is not the common law. It would be an entirely different case from those exceptional instances of special verdicts where a judge asks the jury to find certain facts and directs them that on such facts the prosecution is entitled to succeed. Indeed, a consideration of such special verdicts shows that it is not till the end of the evidence that a verdict can properly be found and that at the end of the evidence it is not for the prisoner to establish his innocence, but for the prosecution to establish his guilt. Just as there is evidence on behalf of the prosecution so there may be evidence on behalf of the prisoner which may cause a doubt as to his guilt. In either case, he is entitled to the benefit of the doubt. But while the prosecution must prove the guilt of the prisoner, there is no such burden laid on the prisoner to prove his innocence and it is sufficient for him to raise a doubt as to his guilt; he is not bound to satisfy the jury of his innocence. . . .

This is the real result of the perplexing case of *Rex* v. *Abramovitch* (1914), which lays down the same proposition, although perhaps in somewhat involved language. Juries are always told that, if conviction there is to be, the prosecution must prove the case beyond reasonable doubt. This statement cannot mean that in order to be acquitted the prisoner must "satisfy" the jury. This is the law as laid down in the Court of Criminal Appeal in *Rex* v. *Davies* (1913), the headnote of which correctly states that where intent is an ingredient of a crime there is no onus on the defendant to prove that the act alleged was accidental. Throughout the web of the English Criminal Law one golden thread is always to be seen, that it is the duty of the prosecution to prove the prisoner's guilt subject to what I have already said as to the defence of insanity and subject also to any statutory exception. If, at the end of and on the whole of the case, there is a reasonable doubt, created by the evidence given by either the prosecution or the prisoner, as to whether the prisoner killed the deceased with a malicious intention, the prosecution has not made out the case and the prisoner is entitled to an acquittal. No matter what the charge or where the trial, the principle that the prosecution must prove the guilt of the prisoner is part of the common law of England and no attempt to whittle it down can be entertained.

Note

The standard of proof required is proof beyond reasonable doubt.

Question

If X is charged with murder what is the position if:

  (i)   he claims it was an accident;
  (ii) he claims he was acting in self-defence;
  (iii) he claims he was acting in a state of automatism;
  (iv) he claims he was insane at the time he committed the offence;
  (v)   he claims he was suffering from diminished responsibility?

(See H.S.B., p. 256.)

2.   MENTAL ABNORMALITY

A.   *Insanity*

R. v. M'Naghten

(1843) 10 C. & Fin. 200

[M. had killed the secretary to Sir Robert Peel by shooting him in the back. His acquittal on the ground of insanity attracted a good deal of controversey. The House of Lords debated the matter and summoned the judges to answer certain questions which were put.]

Tindal L.C.J.   The first question proposed by your Lordships is this: "What is the law respecting alleged crimes committed by persons afflicted with insane delusion in respect of one or more particular subjects or persons; as, for instance, where, at the time of the commission of the alleged crime, the accused knew he was acting contrary to law, but did the act complained of with a view, under the influence of insane delusion, of redressing or revenging some supposed grievance or injury, or of producing some supposed public benefit?"

In answer to which question, assuming that your Lordships' inquiries are confirmed [*sic*] to those persons who labour under such partial delusions only, and are not in other respects insane, we are of opinion that (notwithstanding the party accused did the act complained of with a view, under the influence of insane delusion, of redressing or revenging some supposed grievance or injury, or of producing som public benefit) he is nevertheless punishable, according to the nature of the crime committed, if he knew, at the time of committing such crime, that he was acting contrary to law; by which expression we understand your Lordships to mean the law of the land.

Your Lordships are pleased to inquire of us, secondly: "What are the proper questions to be submitted to the jury, where a person alleged to be afflicted with insane delusion respecting one or more particular subjects or persons is charged with the commission of a crime (murder, for example), and insanity is set up as a defence?" And, thirdly: "In what terms ought the question to be left to the jury as to the prisoner's state of mind at the time when the act was committed?" And as these two questions appear to us to be more conveniently answered together, we have to submit our opinion to be that *the jury ought to be told in all cases that every man is to be presumed to be sane, and to possess a sufficient degree of reason to be responsible for his crimes, until the contrary be proved to their satisfaction; and that, to establish a defence on the ground of insanity, it must be clearly proved that, at the time of the committing of the act, the party accused was labouring under such a defect of reason, from disease of the mind, as not to know the nature and quality of the act he was doing; or, if he did know it, that he did not know he was doing what was wrong.* [Author's italics.] The mode of putting the latter part of the question to the jury on these occasions has generally been whether the accused at the time of doing the act knew the difference between right and wrong; which mode, though rarely, if ever, leading to any mistake with the jury, is not, as we conceive, so accurate when put generally, and in the abstract, as when put with reference to the party's knowledge of right and wrong in respect to the very act with which he is charged. If the question were to be put as to the knowledge of the accused, solely and exclusively with reference to the law of the land, it might tend to confound the jury, by inducing them to believe that an actual knowledge of the law of the land was essential in order to lead to a conviction; whereas the law is administered upon the principle that every one must be taken conclusively to know it, without proof that he does know it. If the accused was conscious that the act was one which he ought not to do, and if that act was at the same time contrary to the law of the land, he is punishable. The usual course, therefore, has been to leave the question to the jury, whether the party accused had a sufficient degree of reason to know that he was doing an act that was wrong; and this course we think is correct, accompanied with such observations and explanations as the circumstances of each particular case may require.

The fourth question which your Lordships have proposed to us is this: "If a person under an insane delusion as to existing facts commits an offence in consequence thereof, is he thereby excused?" To which question the answer must of course depend on the nature of the delusion; but, making the same assumption as we did before, namely, that he labours under such partial delusion only, and is not in other respects insane, we think he must be considered in the same situation as to responsibility as if the facts with respect to which the delusion exists were real. For example, if, under the influence of his delusion, he supposes another man to be in the act of attempting to take away his life and he kills that man, as he supposes, in self-defence, he would be exempt from punishment. If his delusion was that the deceased had inflicted a serious injury to his character and fortune, and he killed him in revenge for such supposed injury, he would be liable to punishment.

The question lastly proposed by your Lordships is: "Can a medical man, conversant with the disease of insanity, who never saw the prisoner previously to the trial, but who was present during the whole trial and the examination of all the witnesses, be asked his opinion as to the state of the prisoner's mind at the time of the commission of the alleged crime, or his opinion whether the prisoner was conscious at the time of doing the act that he was acting contrary to law, or whether he was labouring under any and what delusion at the time?" In answer thereto, we state to your Lordships that we think the medical man, under the circumstances supposed, cannot in strictness be asked his opinion in the terms above stated, because each of those questions involves the determination of the truth of the facts deposed to, which it is for the jury to decide, and the questions are not mere questions upon a matter of science, in which case such evidence is admissible. But, where the facts are admitted, or not disputed, and the question becomes substantially one of science only, it may be convenient to allow the question to be put in the general form, though the same cannot be insisted on as a matter of right.

Questions

1. In the italicised passage what is meant by "not to know the nature and quality of the act he was doing?"
2. In the passage "that he did not know he was doing what was wrong" what is meant by "wrong"?
3. Is there a recognised medical concept known as insanity?
4. What is a disease of the mind?

Note

The Criminal Procedure (Insanity and Unfitness to Plead) Act 1991 makes important changes in the procedures relating to both Insanity and Unfitness to Plead: see H.S.B., p. 258.

R. v. Hennessey

[1989] 2 All E.R. [C.A.]

H. was charged with taking a car and driving while disqualified. He pleaded automatism. To support his plea he adduced evidence that at the relevant time he was suffering from stress, anxiety and depression and as a result, he had not taken his proper dose of insulin. This led to a state of hyperglycaemia. The judge ruled that this was evidence of insanity and not non-insane automatism. As a result H. changed his plea to guilty and appealed to the Court of Appeal. H. contended that the trial judge was wrong to reject his submission that the automatism had not been caused solely by a disease of the mind, but had to a large extent been caused by the external factors of stress and anxiety.

Lord Lane C.J. The defence to these charges accordingly was that the appellant had failed to take his proper twice a day dose of insulin for two or three days and at the time the events in question took place he was in a state of automatism and did not know what he was doing. Therefore it is submitted that the guilty mind, which is necessary to be proved by the prosecution, was not proved, and accordingly that he was entitled to be acquitted.

The judge took the view, rightly in our view, that the appellant, having put his state of mind in issue, the preliminary question which he had to decide was whether this was truly a case of automatism or whether it was a case of legal "insanity" within the M'Naghten rules (see *M'Naghten's Case* (1843) 10 Cl. & Fin. 200, [1843–60] All E.R.

Rep. 229). He concluded that it was the latter, and he so ruled, whereupon the appellant changed his plea to guilty and was sentenced to the terms of imprisonment suspended which we have already mentioned. The judge then certified the case fit for appeal in the terms which I have already described.

The M'Naghten rules in the earlier part of the last century have in many ways lost their importance; they certainly have lost the importance they once had, but they are still relevant in so far as they may affect the defence of automatism. Although the rules deal with what they describe as insanity, it is insanity in the legal sense and not in the medical or psychological sense. The rules were, as is well known, embodied in replies given by the judges of the day to certain abstract questions which were placed before them. The historical reasons for the questions being posed it is not necessary for us to describe, interesting though they are. [Lord Lane then outlined the *M'Naghten Rules* see above, p. 210].

The importance of the rules in the present context, namely the context of automatism, is this. If the defendant did not know the nature and quality of his act because of something which *did not* amount to defect of reason from disease of the mind then he will probably be entitled to be acquitted on the basis that the necessary criminal intent which the prosecution has to prove is not proved. But, if, on the other hand, his failure to realise the nature and quality of his act was due to a defect of reason from disease of the mind, then in the eyes of the law he is suffering from insanity, albeit M'Naghten insanity.

It should perhaps be added, in order to complete the picture, though it is not relevant to the present situation, that where a defendant's failure to appreciate what he was doing was wrong (that is the second part of the second of the M'Naghten rules) where that failure is due to some reason other than a defect of reason from disease of the mind he will generally have no valid defence at all.

If one wants any confirmation, it is to be found, if we may respectfully say so, in Smith and Hogan *Criminal Law* (6th ed., 1988) p. 186, where these matters are very helpfully and clearly set out. If we may just cite the passage from that page, it runs as follows:

> "When a defendant puts his state of mind in issue, the question whether he has raised the defence of insanity is one of law for the judge. Whether D, or indeed his medical witnesses, would call the condition on which he relies

"insanity" is immaterial. The expert witnesses may testify as to the factual nature of the condition but it is for the judge to say whether that is evidence of 'a defect of reason, from disease of the mind,' because, as will appear, these are legal, not medical, concepts."

In the present case, therefore, what had to be decided was whether the defendant's condition was properly described as a disease of the mind. That does not mean any disease of the brain. It means a disease which affects the proper functioning of the mind. There have been a series of authorities on that particular subject. One such instance is R. v. *Kemp* [1956] 3 All E.R. 249, [1957] 1 Q.B. 399 and the judgment of Devlin J. therein.

The question in many cases, and this is one such case, is whether the function of the mind was disturbed on the one hand by disease or on the other hand by some external factor. The matter was discussed, as counsel for the appellant has helpfully pointed out to us, by the House of Lords in R. v. *Sullivan* [1983] 2 All E.R. 673 at 677–678, [1984] A.C. 156 at 172 in the speech of Lord Diplock, which reads as follows:

"I agree with what was said by Devlin J. in R. v. *Kemp* [1956] 3 All E.R. 249 at 253, [1957] 1 Q.B. 399 at 407 that 'mind' in the M'Naghten Rules is used in the ordinary sense of the mental faculties of reason, memory and understanding. If the effect of a disease is to impair these faculties so severely as to have either of the consequences referred to in the latter part of the rules, it matters not whether the aetiology of the impairment is organic, as in epilepsy, or functional, or whether the impairment itself is permanent or is transient and intermittent, provided that it subsisted at the time of commission of the act. The purpose of the legislation relating to the defence of insanity, ever since its origin in 1880, has been to protect society against recurrence of the dangerous conduct. The duration of a temporary suspension of the mental faculties of reason, memory and understanding, particularly if, as in the appellant's case, it is recurrent, cannot on any rational ground be relevant to the application by the courts of the M'Naghten Rules, though it may be relevant to the course adopted by the Secretary of State, to whom the responsibility for how the defendant is to be dealt with passes after the return of the special verdict of not guilty by reason of insanity."

The point was neatly raised in R. v. *Quick*, R. v. *Paddison* [1973] 3 All E.R. 347, [1973] Q.B. 910, also referred to us by counsel for the appellant, in which Lawton L.J. reviewed the authorities. It might perhaps help if I read a short passage from the headnote ([1973] Q.B. 910):

"The defendants, Q. and P., nurses at a mental hospital, were jointly and severally charged with assaulting a patient occasioning actual bodily harm. Both pleaded not guilty. Q., a diabetic, relied on the defence of automatism. He gave evidence that he had taken insulin as prescribed on the morning of the assault, had drunk a quantity of spirits and eaten little food thereafter and had no recollection of the assault. He called medical evidence to the effect that his condition at the material time was consistent with that of hypoglycaemia. The judge ruled that that evidence could only support a defence of insanity, not automatism. Q. then pleaded guilty and P. was convicted of aiding and abetting Q. by encouragement. The defendants appealed against conviction."

I turn to the passage in the judgment where Lawton L.J. said ([1973] 3 All E.R. 347 at 356, [1973] Q.B 910 at 922–923):

"A malfunctioning of the mind of transitory effect caused by the application to the body of some external factor such as violence, drugs, including anaesthetics, alcohol and hypnotic influences cannot fairly be said to be due to disease. Such malfunctioning, unlike that caused by a defect of reason from disease of the mind, will not always relieve an accused from criminal responsibility... In this case Quick's alleged mental condition, if it ever existed, was not caused by his diabetes but by his use of the insulin prescribed by his doctor. Such malfunctioning of his mind as there was, was caused by an external factor and not by a bodily disorder in the nature of a disease which disturbed the working of his mind. It follows in our judgment that Quick was entitled to have his defence of automatism left to the jury and that Bridge J.'s ruling as to the effect of the medical evidence called by him was wrong."

Thus in *R. v. Quick* the fact that his condition was, or may have been, due to the injections of insulin meant that the malfunction was due to an external factor and not to the disease. The drug it was that caused the hypoglycaemia, the low blood sugar. As suggested in another passage of the judgment of Lawton L.J., hyperglycaemia, high blood sugar, caused by an inherent defect and not corrected by insulin is a disease, and if, as the defendant was asserting here, it does cause a malfunction of the mind, then the case may fall within the M'Naghten rules.

The burden of the argument of counsel for the appellant to us is this. It is that the appellant's depression and marital troubles were a sufficiently potent external factor in his condition to override, so to speak, the effect of the diabetic shortage of insulin on him. He refers us not only to the passage which I have already cited in *R.* v. *Quick*, but also to a further passage in *Hill* v. *Baxter* [1958] 1 All E.R. 193 at 197, [1958] 1 Q.B. 277 at 285 which is part of the judgment of Devlin J., sitting with Lord Goddard C.J. and Pearson J., in the Divisional Court of Queen's Bench Division. It reads as follows:

> "I have drawn attention to the fact that the accused did not set up a defence of insanity. For the purposes of the criminal law there are two categories of mental irresponsibility, one where the disorder is due to disease and the other where it is not. The distinction is not an arbitrary one. If disease is not the cause, if there is some temporary loss of consciousness arising accidentally, it is reasonable to hope that it will not be repeated and that it is safe to let an acquitted man go entirely free. If, however, disease is present, the same thing may happen again and therefore since 1800 the law has provided that persons acquitted on this ground should be subject to restraint."

That is the submission made by counsel as a basis for saying the judge's decision was wrong and that this was a matter which should have been decided by the jury.

In our judgment, stress, anxiety and depression can no doubt be the result of the operation of external factors, but they are not, it seems to us, in themselves separately or together external factors of the kind capable in law of causing or contributing to a state of automatism. They constitute a state of mind which is prone to recur. They lack the feature of novelty or accident, which is the basis of the distinction drawn by Lord Diplock in *R.* v. *Sullivan*. It is contrary to the observations of Devlin J., to which we have just referred in *Hill* v. *Baxter*. It does not, in our judgment, come within the scope of the exception "some external physical factor such as a blow on the head ... or the administration of an anaesthetic..." (see *R.* v. *Sullivan* [1983] 2 All E.R. 673 at 678, [1984] A.C. 156 at 172).

For those reasons we reject the arguments, able though they were, of counsel for the appellant. It is not in those circumstances necessary for us to consider the further arguments which he addressed to us based on the decision in *R.* v. *Bailey* [1983] 2 All E.R. 503, [1983] 1 W.L.R. 760. In our judgment the reasoning and judgment of the circuit judge were correct.

Accordingly this appeal must be dismissed.

Appeal dismissed.

R. v. Burgess

(1991) 93 Cr.App.R. 41 (C.A.)

The appellant, a single man of 32, and a neighbour, a female friend, spent the evening at her flat watching video tapes during which the neighbour fell asleep on a sofa. While she was asleep the appellant hit her over the head with a bottle and the video recorder and then grasped her round the throat. When she cried out he appeared to come to his senses and showed great anxiety over what he had done. He called for an ambulance for the victim, who had been severely cut on the head, and then ran away from the scene. The appellant was charged with wounding with intent. At his trial his defence was that he lacked the *mens rea* necessary to make him guilty of the offence because he was sleepwalking when he attacked the victim and was in a state of non-insane automatism. The judge ruled that, assuming the appellant was not conscious at the time of what he was doing, the medical evidence amounted to evidence of insanity within the M'Naghten Rules and not merely evidence of non-insane automatism. The appellant was found not guilty by reason of insanity and ordered to be detained in a secure hospital. He appealed on the ground that the judge's ruling was wrong.

Lord Lane C.J. On July 20, 1989, in the Crown Court at Bristol before Judge Sir Ian Lewis and a jury, the appellant was found not guilty by reason of insanity on a charge of wounding with intent. He was ordered to be admitted and detained in such hospital as the Secretary of State should direct. He now appeals against that verdict by certificate of the trial judge under section 1(2) of the Criminal Appeal Act 1968. The appellant did not dispute the fact that in the early hours of June 2, 1988, he had attacked Katrina Curtis by hitting her on the head first with a bottle when she was asleep, then with a video recorder and finally grasping her round the throat. She suffered a gaping three centimetre laceration to her scalp requiring sutures. His case was that he lacked the *mens rea* necessary to make him guilty of the offence, because he was "sleepwalking" when he attacked Miss Curtis. He was, it was alleged, suffering from "non-insane" automatism and he called medical evidence, in particular from Dr. D'Orban and Dr. Eames to support that contention. The prosecution on the other hand contended that this was not a case of automatism at all, but that the appellant was conscious of what he was doing. If, contrary to that contention, he was not conscious of what he was doing, then the case fell within the M'Naghten Rules, and accordingly the verdict should be not guilty by reason of insanity. The prosecution called an equally eminent expert in the shape of Dr. Fenwick.

Where the defence of automatism is raised by a defendant, two questions fall to be decided by the judge before the defence can be left to the jury. The first is whether a proper evidential foundation for the defence of automatism has been laid. The second is whether the evidence shows the case to be one of insane automatism, that is to say a case which falls within the M'Naghten Rules, or one of non-insane automatism. The judge in the present case undertook that task and on the second question came to the conclusion that (assuming the appellant was not conscious at the time of what he was doing), on any view of the medical evidence so far as automatism was concerned, it amounted to evidence of insanity within the M'Naghten Rules and not merely to evidence of non-insane automatism. The sole ground of appeal is that that ruling was wrong.

. . .

The appellant plainly suffered from a defect from some sort of failure (for lack of a better term) of the mind causing him to act as he did without conscious motivation. His mind was to some extent controlling his actions which were purposive rather than the result simply of muscular spasm, but without his being consciously aware of what he was doing. Can it be said that "failure" was a *disease* of the mind rather than a defect or failure of the mind not due to disease? That is the distinction, by no means always easy to draw, upon which this case depends, as others have depended in the past. One can perhaps narrow the field of enquiry still further by eliminating what are sometimes called the "external factors" such as concussion caused by a blow on the head. There were no such factors here. Whatever the cause may have been, it was an "internal" cause.

What help does one derive from the authorities as to the meaning of "disease" in this context? Lord Denning in *Bratty v. Attorney-General for Northern Ireland* (1961) 46 Cr.App.R. 1, 20, [1963] A.C. 386, 412 said this:

"Upon the other point discussed by Devlin J., namely, what is a 'diseases of the mind' within the M'Naghten Rules. I would agree with him that this is a question for the judge. The major mental diseases, which the doctors call psychoses, such as schizophrenia, are clearly diseases of the mind. But in *Charlson's* case [1955] 39 Cr.App.R. 37, [1055] 1

W.L.R. 317, Barry J. seems to have assumed that other diseases such as epilepsy or cerebral tumour are not diseases of the mind, even when they are such as to manifest themselves in violence. I do not agree with this. It seems to me that any mental disorder which has manifested itself in violence and is prone to recur is a disease of the mind. At any rate it is the sort of disease for which a person should be detained in hospital rather than be given an unqualified acquittal."

It seems to us that if there is a danger of recurrence that may be an added reason for categorising the condition as a disease of the mind. On the other hand, the absence of the danger of recurrence is not a reason for saying that it cannot be a disease of the mind. Subject to that possible qualification, we respectfully adopt Lord Denning's suggested definition.

There have been several occasions during the course of judgments in the Court of Appeal and the House of Lords where observations have been made, *obiter*, about the criminal responsibility of sleepwalkers, where sleepwalking has been used as a self-evident illustration of non-insane automatism. For example in the speech of Lord Denning, from which we have already cited an extract, appears this passage at p. 16 and p. 409;

> "No act is punishable if it is done involuntarily: and an involuntary act in this context—some people nowdays prefer to speak of it as 'automatism'—means an act which is done by the muscles without any control by the mind, such as a spasm, a reflex action or a convulsion; or an act done be a person who is not conscious of what he is doing, such as an act done whilst suffering from concussion or whilst sleep-walking. The point was well put by Stephen J. in 1889: 'Can anyone doubt that a man who, though he might be perfectly sane, committed what would otherwise be a crime in a state of somnambulism, would be entitled to be acquitted? Any why is this? Simply because he would not know what he was doing.' [See *Tolson* (1889) 23 Q.B.D. 168, 187]".

We have also been referred to a Canadian decision, *Parks* (1990) 56 C.C.C. (3d) 449. In that case the defendant was charged with murder. The undisputed facts were that he had, whilst according to him he was asleep, at night driven his motor car some 23 kilometres to the house of his wife's parents where he had stabbed and beaten both his mother-in-law and his father-in-law. His mother-in-law died as a result and his father-in-law sustained serious injuries. A number of defence witnesses, including experts in sleep disorders, gave evidence to the effect that sleepwalking is not regarded as a disease of the mind, mental illness or mental disorder, and the trial judge directed the jury that if the accused was in a state of somnambulism at the time of the killing, then he was entitled to be acquitted on the basis of non-insane automatism. The defendant was acquitted of the murder of his mother-in-law and subsequently acquitted of the attempted murder of his father-in-law. The Crown appealed from the accused's acquittal and it was held by the Ontario Court of Appeal that the appeal should be dismissed. The Court concluded that sleep is a normal condition and "the impairment of the respondent's faculties of reason, memory and understanding was caused not by any disorder or abnormal condition but by a natural normal condition—sleep." We accept of course that sleep is a normal condition, but the evidence in the instant case indicates that sleepwalking and particularly violence in sleep, is not normal. We were told that the case of *Parks* is to be taken to the Supreme Court of Canada. That case apart, in none of the other cases where sleepwalking has been mentioned, so far as we can discover, has the court had the advantage of the sort of expert medical evidence which was available to the judge here. One turns then to examine the evidence upon which the judge had to base his decision and for this purpose the two medical experts called by the defence are the obvious principal sources. Dr. D'Orban in examination in chief said:

"On the evidence available to me, and subject to the results of the tests when they became available, I came to the same conclusion as Dr. Nicholas and Dr. Eames whose reports I had read, and that was that Mr Burgess's actions had occurred during the course of a sleep disorder."

He was asked, "Assuming this is a sleep associated automatism, is it an internal or external factor?" Answer: "In this particular case, I think that one would have to see it as an internal factor."

Then in cross-examination: Question: "Would you go as far as to say that it was liable to recur?" Answer: "It is possible for it to recur, yes." Finally, in answer to a question from the judge, namely, "Is this a case of automatism associated with a pathological condition or not?" Answer: "I think the answer would have to be yes, because it is an abnormality of the brain function, so it would be regarded as a pathological condition."

Dr Eames in cross-examination agreed with Dr. D'Orban as to the internal rather than the external factor. He accepted that there is a liability to recurrence of sleepwalking. He could not go as far as to say that there is no liability of serious violence but he agreed with the other medical witnesses that there is no recorded case of violence of this sort recurring.

The prosecution, as already indicated, called Dr. Fenwick, whose opinion was that this was not a sleepwalking episode at all. If it was a case where the appellant was unconscious of what he was doing, the most likely explanation was that he was in what is described as an hysterical dissociative state. That is a state in which, for psychological reasons, such as being overwhelmed by his emotions, the person's brain works in a different way. He carries out acts of which he has no knowledge and for which he has no memory. It is quite different from sleepwalking.

He then went on to describe features of sleepwalking. This is what he said:

> "Firstly, violent acts in sleepwalking are very common. In just an exposure of one day to a sleepwalking clinic, you will hear of how people are kicked in bed, hit in bed, partially strangled—it is usually just arms round the neck, in bed, which is very common. Serious violence fortunately is rare. Serious violence does recur, or certainly the propensity for it to recur is there, although there are very few cases in the literature—in fact I know of none—in which somebody has come to court twice for a sleepwalking offence. This does not mean that sleepwalking violence does not recur; what is does mean is that those who are associated with the sleeper take the necessary precautions.
>
> "Finally, should a person be detained in hospital? The answer to that is: Yes, because sleepwalking is treatable. Violent night terrors are treatable. There is a lot which can be done for the sleepwalker, so sending them to hospital after a violent act to have their sleepwalking sorted out, makes good sense."

Dr. Fenwick was also of the view that in certain circumstances hysterical dissociative states are also subject to treatment. It seems to us that on this evidence the judge was right to conclude that this was an abnormality or disorder, albeit transitory, due to an internal factor, whether functional or organic, which had manifested itself in violence. It was a disorder or abnormality which might recur, though the possibility of it recurring in the form of serious violence was unlikely. Therefore since this was a legal problem to be decided on legal principles, it seems to us that on those principles the answer was as the judge found it to be. It does however go further than that. Dr. D'Orban, as already described, states it as his view that the condition would be regarded as pathological. Pathology is the science of diseases. It seems therefore that in this respect at least there is some similarity between the law and medicine. The learned judge was alive to the apparent incongruity of labelling this sort of disability as insanity. He drew attention, as we would also wish to do, to the passage of the speech of Lord Diplock in *Sullivan* at p. 183 and p. 173, where he said this:

"... it is natural to feel reluctant to attach the label of insanity to a sufferer from psychomotor epilepsy of the kind to which Mr. Sullivan was subject, even though the expression in the context of a special verdict of 'not guilty be reason of insanity' is a technical one which includes a purely temporary and intermittent suspension of the mental faculties of reason, memory and understanding resulting from the occurrence of an epileptic fit. But the label is contained in the current statute, it has appeared in this statute's predecessors ever since 1800. It does not lie within the power of the courts to alter it. Only Parliament can do that. It has done so twice; it could do so once again."

Appeal dismissed

(See also *Bailey* (1983) below, p. 236).

B. Diminished Responsibility

See Homicide Act 1957, s.2 (below, p. 395).

R. v. Byrne

[1960] 2 Q.B. 396 (C.A.)

[B. killed a girl and then perpetrated horrifying mutilations on her body. The only defence was that the accused was suffering from diminished responsibility. It was accepted that he was a sexual psychopath and that as such he suffered from violent perverted sexual desires which he found difficult or impossible to control. The trial judge gave the jury a direction which, in effect, told the jury that B.'s condition did not constitute diminished responsibility. On appeal against conviction:]

Lord Parker C.J. [His Lordship reviewed the defence of insanity and continued:] The ability of the accused to control his physical acts by exercise of his will was relevant before the passing of the Homicide Act 1957 in one case only: that of provocation. Loss of self-control on the part of the accused so as to make him for the moment not master of his mind had the effect of reducing murder to manslaughter if: (i) it was induced by an act or series of acts done by the deceased to the accused, and (ii) such act or series of acts would have induced a reasonable man to lose his self-control and act in the same manner as the accused acted. . . .

Whether loss of self-control induced by provocation negatived the ordinary presumption that a man intends the natural ordinary consequences of his physical acts so that, in such a case, the prosecution had failed to prove the essential mental element in murder (namely, that the accused intended to kill or to inflict grievous bodily harm) is academic for the purposes of our consideration. What is relevant is that loss of self-control has always been recognised as capable of reducing murder to manslaughter, but that the criterion has always been the degree of self-control which would be exercised by a reasonable man, that is to say, a man with a normal mind.

It is against that background of the existing law that section 2(1) of the Homicide Act 1957 falls to be construed. To satisfy the requirements of the subsection the accused must show: (a) that he was suffering from an abnormality of mind, and (b) that such abnormality of mind (i) arose from a condition of arrested or retarded development of mind or any inherent causes, or was induced by disease or injury and (ii) was such as substantially impaired his mental responsibility for his acts in doing or being a party to the killing.

"Abnormality of mind," which has to be contrasted with the time-honoured expression in the M'Naghten Rules "defect of reason," means a state of mind so different from that of ordinary human beings that the reasonable man would term it abnormal. It appears to us to be wide enough to cover the mind's activities in all its aspects, not only the perception of physical acts and matters, and the ability to form a rational judgment as to whether an act is right or wrong, but also the ability to exercise will power to control physical acts in accordance with that rational judgment. The expression "mental responsibility for his acts" points to a consideration of the extent to which the accused's mind is answerable for his physical acts which must include a consideration of the extent of his ability to exercise will power to control his physical acts.

Whether the accused was at the time of the killing suffering from any "abnormality of mind" in the broad sense which we have indicated above is a question for the jury. On this question medical evidence is no doubt of importance, but the jury are entitled to take into consideration all the evidence, including the acts or statements of the accused and his demeanour. They are not bound to accept the medical evidence if there is other material before them which, in their good judgment, conflicts with it and outweighs it.

The aetiology of the abnormality of mind (namely, whether it arose from a condition of arrested or retarded development of mind or any inherent causes, or was induced by disease of injury) does, however, seem to be a matter to be determined on expert evidence.

Assuming that the jury are satisfied on the balance of probabilities that the accused was suffering from "abnormality of mind" from one of the causes specified in the parenthesis of the subsection, the crucial question nevertheless arises: was the abnormality such as substantially impaired his mental responsibility for his acts in doing or being a party to the killing? This is a question of degree and essentially one for the jury. Medical evidence is, of course, relevant, but the question involves a decision not merely as to whether there was some impairment of the mental responsibility of the accused for his acts but whether such impairment can properly be called "substantial," a matter upon which juries may quite legitimately differ from doctors.

Furthermore, in a case where the abnormality of mind is one which affects the accused's self-control the step between "he did not resist his impulse" and "he could not resist his impulse" is, as the evidence in this case shows, one which is incapable of scientific proof. A *fortiori* there is no scientific measurement of the degree of difficulty which an abnormal person finds in controlling his impulses. These problems which in the present state of medical knowledge are scientifically insoluble, the jury can only approach in a broad, common-sense way. This court has repeatedly approved directions to the jury which have followed directions given in Scots cases where the doctrine of diminished responsibility forms part of the common law. We need not repeat them. They are quoted in *Reg.* v. *Spriggs* (1958). They indicate that such abnormality as "substantially impairs his mental responsibility" involves a mental state which in popular language (not that of the M'Naghten Rules) a jury would regard as amounting to partial insanity or being on the border-line of insanity.

It appears to us that the judge's direction to the jury . . . amounted to a direction that difficulty or even inability of an accused person to exercise will power to control his physical acts could not amount to such abnormality of mind as substantially impairs his mental responsibility. For the reasons which we have already expressed we think that this construction of the Act is wrong. Inability to exercise will power to control physical acts, provided that it is due to abnormality of the mind from one of the causes specified in the parenthesis in the subsection is, in our view, sufficient to entitle the accused to the benefit of the section; difficulty in controlling his physical acts depending on the degree of difficulty, may be. It is for the jury to decide on the whole of the evidence whether such inability or difficulty has, not as a matter of scientific certainty but on the balance of probabilities, been established, and in the case of difficulty whether the difficulty is so great as to amount in their view to a substantial impairment of the accused's mental responsibility for his acts. The direction in the present case thus withdrew from the jury the essential determination of fact which it was their province to decide.

As already indicated, the medical evidence as to the appellant's ability to control his physical acts at the time of the killing was all one way. The evidence of the revolting circumstances of the killing and the subsequent mutilations as of the previous sexual history of the appellant pointed, we think plainly, to the conclusion that the accused was what would be described in ordinary language as on the border-line of insanity or partially insane. Properly directed, we do not think that the jury could have come to any other conclusion than that the defence under section 2 of the Homicide Act was made out.

The appeal will be allowed and a verdict of manslaughter substituted for the verdict of murder. The only possible sentence having regard to the tendencies of the accused is imprisonment for life. The sentence will, accordingly, not be disturbed.

Appeal allowed.

R. v. Tandy

(1988) 87 Cr.App.R. 45 (C.A.)

T. was convicted of murdering her 11-year-old daughter. She pleaded diminished responsibility caused by alcoholism. During the day in question T. had consumed 9/10 of a bottle of vodka. As to whether diminished responsibility can be pleaded when it arises from alcoholism,

Watkins L.J. So in this case it was for the appellant to show: (1) that she was suffering from an abnormality of mind at the time of the act of strangulation; (2) that that abnormality of mind was induced by disease, namely the disease of alcoholism; and (3) that the abnormality of mind induced by the disease of alcoholism was such as substantially impaired her mental responsibility for her act of strangling her daughter.

The principles involved in seeking answers to these questions are, in our view, as follows.

The appellant would not establish the second element of the defence unless the evidence showed that the abnormality of mind at the time of the killing was due to the fact that she was a chronic alcoholic. If the alcoholism had reached the level at which her brain had been injured by the repeated insult from intoxicants so that there was gross impairment of her judgment and emotional responses, then the defence of diminished responsibility was available to her, provided that she satisfied the jury that the third element of the defence existed. Further, if the appellant were able to establish that the alcoholism had reached the level where although the brain had not been damaged to the extent just stated, the appellant's drinking had become involuntary, that is to say she was no longer able to resist the impulse to drink, then the defence of diminished responsibility would be available to her, subject to her establishing the first and third elements, because if her drinking was involuntary, then her abnormality of mind at the time of the act of strangulation was induced by her condition of alcoholism.

On the other hand, if the appellant had simply not resisted an impulse to drink and it was the drink taken on the Wednesday which brought about the impairment of judgment and emotional response, then the defence of diminished responsibility was not available to the defendant.

3. INTOXICATION

R. v. Majewski

[1977] A.C. 433 (H.L.)

[M. was charged with various assaults occasioning actual bodily harm and assaults on a police constable in the execution of his duty. His defence was that voluntary consumption of alcohol and drugs had so affected him that he could recall nothing of the alleged incidents. The trial judge told the jury that they could ignore the subject of drink and drugs as being in any way a defence to any of the charges against the accused. This was because these offences were offences of basic intent; self-induced intoxication could only be a defence to a crime requiring specific intent. His appeal against conviction was dismissed by the court of Appeal but that Court certified that the following point of law of general public importance was involved:

> "Whether a defendant may properly be convicted of assault notwithstanding that, by reason of his self-induced intoxication, he did not intend to do the act alleged to constitute the assault."]

Lord Elwyn-Jones L.C. The appeal raises issues of considerable public importance. In giving the judgment of the Court of Appeal, Lawton L.J. rightly observed that:

> "The facts are commonplace—indeed so commonplace that their very nature reveals how serious from a social and public standpoint the consequences would be if men could behave as the [appellant] did and then claim that they were not guilty of any offence."

. . . [T]he crux of the case for the Crown was that, illogical as the outcome may be said to be, the judges have evolved for the purpose of protecting the community a substantive rule of law that, in crimes of basic intent as distinct from crimes of specific intent, self-induced intoxication provides no defence and is irrelevant to offences of basic intent, such as assault.

What then is the mental element required in our law to be established in assault? This question has been most helpfully answered in the speech of Lord Simon of Glaisdale in *Reg.* v. *Morgan* (1976):

> "By 'crimes of basic intent' I mean those crimes whose definition expresses (or, more often, implies) a *mens rea* which does not go beyond the *actus reus*. The *actus reus* generally consists of an act and some consequence. The consequence may be very closely connected with the act or more remotely connected with it: but with a crime of basic intent the *mens rea* does not extend beyond the act and its consequence, however remote, as defined in the *actus reus*. I take assault as an example of a crime of basic intent where the consequence is very closely connected with the act. The *actus reus* of assault is an act which causes another person to apprehend immediate and unlawful violence. The *mens rea* corresponds exactly. The prosecution must prove that the accused foresaw that his act would probably cause another person to have apprehension of immediate and

unlawful violence, or would possibly have that consequence, such being the purpose of the act, or that he was
reckless as to whether or not his act caused Buch
apprehension. This foresight (the term of art is 'intention')
or recklessness is the *mens rea* in assault. For an example of
a crime of basic intent where the consequence of the act
involved in the *actus reus* as defined in the crime is less
immediate, I take the crime of unlawful wounding. The act
is, say, the squeezing of a trigger. A number of
consequences (mechanical, chemical, ballistic and
physiological) intervene before the final consequence involved in the defined *actus reus*—namely, the wounding of
another person in circumstances unjustified by law. But
again here the *mens rea* corresponds closely to the *actus reus*.
The prosecution must prove that the accused foresaw that
some physical harm would ensue to another person in
circumstances unjustified by law as a probable (or possible
and desired) consequence of his act, or that he was reckless
as to whether or not such consequence ensued."

How does the fact of self-induced intoxication fit into that
analysis? If a man consciously and deliberately takes alcohol
and drugs not on medical prescription, but in order to escape
from reality, to go "on a trip," to become hallucinated,
whatever the description may be and thereby disables himself
from taking the care he might otherwise take and as a result
by his subsequent actions causes injury to another—does our
criminal law enable him to say that because he did not know
what he was doing he lacked both intention and recklessness
and accordingly is entitled to an acquittal?

[Lord Elwyn-Jones reviewed the authorities, especially *D.P.P.* v. *Beard*
(1920) in which Lord Birkenhead L.C. concluded that (except in cases where
insanity is pleaded) the decisions "establish that where a specific intent is an
essential element in the offence, evidence of a state of drunkenness rendering
the accused incapable of forming such an intent should be taken into
consideration in order to determine whether he had in fact formed the intent
necessary to constitute the particular crime. If he was so drunk that he was
incapable of forming the intent required he could not be convicted of a crime
which was committed only if the intent was proved.... In a charge of
murder based upon intention to kill or to do grievous bodily harm, if the jury
are satisfied that the accused was, by reason of his drunken condition,
incapable of forming the intent to kill or to do grievous bodily harm...he
cannot be convicted of murder. But nevertheless unlawful homicide has been
committed by the accused, and consequently he is guilty of unlawful
homicide without malice aforethought, and that is manslaughter: *per* Stephen
J. in *Reg.* v. *Doherty* (1887)."
The passage concludes: "the law is plain beyond all question that in cases
falling short of insanity a condition of drunkenness at the time of committing
an offence causing death can only, when it is available at all, have the effect

of reducing the crime from murder to manslaughter." Lord Elwyn-Jones
continued:]

From this it seemed clear—and this is the interpretation
which the judges have placed upon the decision during the
ensuing half century—that it is only in the limited class of
cases requiring proof of specific intent that drunkenness can
exculpate. Otherwise in no case can it exempt completely
from criminal liability.

[Lord Elwyn-Jones concluded his review of the authorities by noting that
this principle had never been overruled by the House of Lords and it
remained to determine whether it should be. He continued:]

I do not for my part regard that general principle as either
unethical or contrary to the principles of natural justice. If a
man of his own volition takes a substance which causes him
to cast off the restraints of reason and conscience, no wrong is
done to him by holding him answerable criminally for any
injury he may do while in that condition. His course of
conduct in reducing himself by drugs and drink to that
condition in my view supplies the evidence of *mens rea*, of
guilty mind certainly sufficient for crimes of basic intent. It is
a reckless course of conduct and recklessness is enough to
constitute the necessary *mens rea* in assault cases: see *Reg.* v.
Venna (1976). The drunkenness is itself an intrinsic, an
integral part of the crime, the other part being the evidence of
the unlawful use of force against the victim. Together they
add up to criminal recklessness. On this I adopt the
conclusion of Stroud in (1920) 36 L.Q.R. 273 that:

"... it would be contrary to all principle and authority to
suppose that drunkenness" (and what is true of drunkenness is equally true of intoxication by drugs) "can be a
defence for crime in general on the ground that 'a person
cannot be convicted of a crime unless the *mens* was *rea*.' By
allowing himself to get drunk, and thereby putting himself
in such a condition as to be no longer amenable to the law's
commands, a man shows such regardlessness as amounts
to *mens rea* for the purpose of all ordinary crimes."

This approach is in line with the American Model Penal
Code (s.208(2)):

"When recklessness establishes an element of the offence, if
the actor, due to self-induced intoxication, is unaware of a
risk of which he would have been aware had he been
sober, such unawareness is immaterial."

The final question that arises is whether section 8 of the Act
of 1967 [see below, p. 396] has had the result of abrogating or

qualifying the common law rule. That section emanated from the consideration the Law Commission gave to the decision of the House in *Director of Public Prosecutions* v. *Smith* (1961). Its purpose and effect was to alter the law of evidence about the presumption of intention to produce the reasonable and probable consequences of one's acts. It was not intended to change the common law rule. In referring to "all the evidence" it meant all the *relevant* evidence. But if there is a substantive rule of law that in crimes of basic intent, the factor of intoxication is irrelevant (and such I hold to be the substantive law), evidence with regard to it is quite irrelevant. Section 8 does not abrogate the substantive rule and it cannot properly be said that the continued application of that rule contravenes the section. For these reasons, my conclusion is that the certified question should be answered "Yes," that there was no misdirection in this case and that the appeal should be dismissed.

My noble and learned friends and I think it may be helpful if we give the following indication of the general lines on which in our view the jury should be directed as to the effect upon the criminal responsibility of the accused of drink or drugs or both, whenever death or physical injury to another person results from something done by the accused for which there is no legal justification and the offence with which the accused is charged is manslaughter or assault at common law or the statutory offence of unlawful wounding under section 20, or of assault occasioning actual bodily harm under section 47 of the Offences against the Person Act 1861.

In the case of these offences it is no excuse in law that, because of drink or drugs which the accused himself had taken knowingly and willingly, he had deprived himself of the ability to exercise self-control to realise the possible consequences of what he was doing, or even to be conscious that he was doing it. As in the instant case, the jury may be properly instructed that they "can ignore the subject of drink or drugs as being in any way a defence" to charges of this character.

R. v. O'Grady

(1987) 85 Cr.App.R. 315 (C.A.)

O. and a friend had been drinking heavily. During the course of the evening they had a fight. The following morning O. discovered the dead body of his friend. He went to the police station and reported a murder. He told the police that if he had not hit his friend, he himself would now be dead. O'Grady having been charged with murder was convicted of manslaughter.

Lord Lane C.J. The judge gave an impeccable direction on the ingredients of murder and upon the way in which intoxication may affect proof of intent to kill or to do serious bodily harm. Likewise impeccable was his direction on provocation, including the correct observation that, when considering whether a reasonable man would have been caused to lose his self-control, questions of drink are irrelevant.

Finally he gave the classic direction on self-defence. He made no mention of the possibility that the appellant might by reason of intoxication have been mistaken as to the threat posed to him by McCloskey's action. This was no doubt because no one had taken the point.

Counsel for the prosecution towards the close of the judge's directions saw fit to invite the judge to remedy what he plainly regarded as this lacuna in the charge to the jury. Counsel for the appellant wisely held his peace. The judge then gave this further direction:

> "It might be a view that you might take—I know not—that this defendant thought he was under attack from the other man mistakenly and made a mistake in thinking that he was under attack because of the drink that was in him. If he made such a mistake in drink he would nevertheless be entitled to defend himself even though he mistakenly believed that he was under attack. He would be entitled in those circumstances to defend himself. But if in taking defensive measures, then he went beyond what is reasonable either because of his mind being affected by drink or for any other reason, then the defence of self-defence would not avail him because, as I told you earlier on, you are entitled to defend yourself if it is necessary to do so, but the defensive measures that you take must be reasonable ones and not go beyond what is reasonable."

The grounds of appeal advanced by Mr. Wadsworth are as follows: (1) Whilst the judge was correct to refer to mistake induced by drink in connection with self-defence, he was wrong to limit the reference to mistake as to the existence of an attack; he should have included the possibility of mistake as to the severity of an attack which was the most likely possibility on the facts. (2) By leaving the matter to the jury as he did, the judge in effect divorced the reasonableness of the appellant's reaction from the appellant's state of mind at the time. (3) The judge failed when giving his further direction to the jury to remind them that a defendant is never required to judge to a nicety the amount of force which is necessary and that they should give great weight to the view formed by the appellant at the time, even though that view might have been affected by alcohol.

As to the first two grounds, these rquire an examination of the law as to intoxication in relation to mistake.

As the learned single judge pointed out helpfully in his observations for the benefit of the court:

"Given that a man who *mistakenly* believes he is under attack is entitled to use reasonable force to defend himself, it would seem to follow that, if he is under attack and mistakenly believes the attack to be more serious than it is, he is entitled to use reasonable force to defend himself against an attack of the severity he believed it to have. If one allows a mistaken belief induced by drink to bring this principle into operation, an act of gross negligence (viewed objectively) may become lawful even though it results in the death of the innocent victim. The drunken man would be guilty of neither murder nor manslaughter."

How should the jury be invited to approach the problem? One starts with the decision of this court in *Williams (Gladstone)* (1984) 78 Cr.App.R. 276, namely that where the defendant might have been labouring under a mistake as to the facts he must be judged according to that mistaken view, whether the mistake was reasonable or not. It is then for the jury to decide whether the defendant's reaction to the threat (real or imaginary) was a reasonable one. The court was not in that case considering what the situation might be where the mistake was due to voluntary intoxication by alcohol or some other drug.

We have come to the conclusion that where the jury are satisfied that the defendant was mistaken in his belief that any force or the force which he in fact used was necessary to defend himself and are further satisfied that the mistake was caused by voluntarily induced intoxication, the defence must fail. We do not consider that any distinction should be drawn on this aspect of the matter between offences involving what is called specific intent, such as murder, and offences of so-called basic intent, such as manslaughter. Quite apart from the problem of directing a jury in a case such as the present where manslaughter is an alternative verdict to murder, the question of mistake can and ought to be considered separately from the question of intent. A sober man who mistakenly believes he is in danger of immediate death at the hands of an attacker is entitled to be acquitted of both murder and manslaughter if his reaction in killing his supposed assailant was a reasonable one. What his intent may have been seems to us to be irrelevant to the problem of selfdefence or no. Secondly, we respectfully adopt the reasoning of McCullough J. already set out.

This brings us to the question of public order. There are two competing interests. On the one hand the interest of the defendant who has only acted according to what he believed to be necessary to protect himself, and on the other hand that of the public in general and the victim in particular who, probably through no fault of his own, has been injured or perhaps killed because of the defendant's drunken mistake. Reason recoils from the conclusion that in such circumstances a defendant is entitled to leave the court without a stain on his character.

We find support for that view in the decision of the House of Lords in *Director of Public Prosecutions* v. *Majewski* (1976) 62 Cr.App.R. 262, [1977] A.C. 443, and in particular in the speeches of Lord Simon of Glaisdale and Lord Edmund-Davies. We cite a passage from the speech of the former at pp. 272 and 476 respectively as follows:

"(1) One of the prime purposes of the criminal law, with its penal sanctions, is the protection from certain proscribed conduct of persons who are pursuing their lawful lives. Unprovoked violence has, from time immemorial, been a significant part of such proscribed conduct. To accede to the argument on behalf of the appellant would leave the citizen legally unprotected from unprovoked violence where such violence was the consequence of drink or drugs having obliterated the capacity of the perpetrator to know what he was doing or what were its consequences.

(2) Though the problem of violent conduct by intoxicated persons is not new to society, it has been rendered more acute and menacing by the more widespread use of hallucinatory drugs. For example, in *Lipman* [1970] 1 Q.B. 152, the accused committed his act of mortal violence under the hallucination (induced by drugs) that he was wrestling with serpents. He was convicted of manslaughter. But, on the logic of the appellant's argument, he was innocent of any crime."

Lord Edmund-Davies at pp. 284 and 492 says this:

"The criticism by the academics of the law presently administered in this country is of a twofold nature: (1) it is illogical and therefore inconsistent with legal principle to treat a person who of his own volition has taken drink or drugs any differently from a man suffering from some bodily or mental disorder of the kind earlier mentioned or whose beverage had, without his connivance, been 'laced' with intoxicants; (2) it is unethical to convict a man of a crime requiring a guilty state of mind when *ex hypothesi*, he lacked it."

Lord Edmund-Davies then demonstrated the fallacy of those criticisms.

Finally we draw attention to the decision of this court in *Lipman* (1969) 53 Cr.App.R. 600, [1970] 1 Q.B. 152, itself. The defence in that case was put on the grounds that the defendant, because of the hallucinatory drug which he had taken, had not formed the necessary intent to found a conviction for murder, thus resulting in his conviction for manslaughter. If the appellant's contentions here are correct, Lipman could successfully have escaped conviction altogether by raising the issue that he believed he was defending himself legitimately from an attack by serpents. It is significant that no one seems to have considered that possibility.

We have therefore come to the conclusion that a defendant is not entitled to rely, so far as self-defence is concerned, upon a mistake of fact which has been induced by voluntary intoxication.

Appeal dismissed.

July 24. The court, similarly constituted, certified under section 33(2) of the Criminal Appeal Act 1968, that the following point of law of general public importance was involved in its decision, *viz*. "Is a defendant who raises the issue of selfdefence entitled to be judged upon the basis that he mistakenly believed to be the situation when that mistaken belief was brought about by self-induced intoxication by alcohol or other drugs?"

Leave to appeal to the House of Lords was refused.

Notes

1. The Court of Appeal approved O'Grady in *O'Connor* [1991].
2. In *Caldwell* (above, p. 133) Lord Diplock held that where the charge of an offence under section 1(2) of the Criminal Damage Act 1971 is framed so as to charge the defendant only with "*intending* by the destruction or damage [of the property] to endanger the life of another," evidence of self-induced intoxication can be relevant to his defence. If, however, the charge is, or

includes, a reference to his being "reckless as to whether the life of another would thereby be endangered," this is a basic intent offence to which evidence of self-induced intoxication cannot be relevant.

Question

What approach should be taken by the court in a case where the accused has "committed" an offence in a state of automatism induced by a medically prescribed drug? (see *Hennessey*, above, p. 213). Should the answer be different if the symptoms were caused by the accused's failure to observe his doctor's instructions as to diet or consumption of alcohol? Is this another area in which the courts should distinguish between crimes of basic and specific intent?

R. v. Bailey

(1983) 77 Cr.App.R. 76 (C.A.)

[B. was a diabetic who took insulin to control his condition. On the occasion in question he claimed that he assaulted his victim during a period of unconsciousness caused by hypoglycaemia because of his failure to take sufficient food following his last dose of insulin. He was convicted of wounding with intent (Offences Against the Person Act 1861, s.18); the jury were not required to give a verdict on an alternative count of unlawful wounding (Offences Against the Person Act 1861, s.20). He appealed to the Court of Appeal against conviction. Clearly the defence would be available to the charge of wounding with intent; was it, however, available to the basic intent offence of unlawful wounding under s.20 Offences Against the Person Act 1861?]

Griffiths L.J. Automatism resulting from intoxication as a result of a voluntary ingestion of alcohol or dangerous drugs does not negative the *mens rea* necessary for crimes of basic intent, because the conduct of the accused is reckless and recklessness is enough to constitute the necessary *mens rea* in assault cases where no specific intent forms part of the charge. See *D.P.P.* v. *Majewski* (*supra*) in the speech of Lord EdmundDavies where he said: "The law therefore establishes a conclusive presumption against the admission of proof of intoxication for the purpose of disproving *mens rea* in ordinary crimes. Where this presumption applies, it does not make 'drunkenness' itself a crime but the drunkenness is itself an integral part of the crime, as forming, together with the other unlawful conduct charged against the defendant, a complex act of criminal recklessness."

The same considerations apply where the state of automatism is induced by the voluntary taking of dangerous drugs. See *Lipman* (1969) where a conviction for manslaughter was upheld, the appellant having taken L.S.D. and killed his mistress in the course of an hallucinatory trip. It was submitted on behalf of the Crown that a similar rule should be applied as a matter of public policy to all cases of self-induced automatism. But it seems to us that there may be material distinctions between a man who consumes alcohol or takes dangerous drugs and one who fails to take sufficient food after insulin to avert hypoglycaemia.

It is common knowledge that those who take alcohol to excess or certain sorts of drugs may become aggressive or do dangerous or unpredictable things; they may be able to foresee the risks of causing harm to others, but nevertheless persist in their conduct. But the same cannot be said without more of a man who fails to take food after an insulin injection. If he does appreciate the risk that such a failure may lead to aggressive, unpredictable and uncontrollable conduct and he nevertheless deliberately runs the risk or otherwise disregards it, this will amount to recklessness. But we certainly do not think that it is common knowledge, even among diabetics, that such is a consequence of a failure to take food; and there is no evidence that it was known to this appellant. Doubtless he knew that if he failed to take his insulin or proper food after it, he might lose consciousness, but as such he would only be a danger to himself unless he put himself in charge of some machine such as a motor car, which required his continued conscious control.

In our judgment, self-induced automatism, other than that due to intoxication from alcohol or drugs, may provide a defence to crimes of basic intent. The question in each case will be whether the prosecution have proved the necessary element of recklessness. In cases of assault, if the accused knows that his actions or inaction are likely to make him aggressive, unpredictable or uncontrolled with the result that he may cause some injury to others and he persists in the action or takes no remedial action when he knows it is required, it will be open to the jury to find that he was reckless.

. . . . . .

In the present case the recorder never invited the jury to consider what the appellant's knowledge or appreciation was of what would happen if he failed to take food after his insulin or whether he realised that he might become aggressive. Nor were they asked to consider why the appellant had omitted to take food in time. They were given no direction on the elements of recklessness. Accordingly, in our judgment, there was also a misdirection in relation to the second count in the indictment of unlawful wounding.

But we have to consider whether, notwithstanding these misdirections, there has been any miscarriage of justice and whether the jury properly directed could have failed to come to the same conclusion. As Lawton L.J. said in *Quick's* case (1973), referring to the defence of automatism, it is a "quagmire of law, seldom entered nowadays save by those in desperate need of some kind of defence." This case is no exception. We think it very doubtful whether the appellant laid a sufficient basis for the defence to be considered by the jury at all. But even if he did, we are in no doubt that the jury properly directed must have rejected it. Although an episode of sudden transient loss of consciousness or awareness was theoretically possible, it was quite inconsistent with the graphic description that the appellant gave to the police both orally and in his written statement. There was abundant evidence that he had armed himself with the iron bar and gone to Harrison's house for the purpose of attacking him, because he wanted to teach him a lesson, and because he was in the way.

Moreover, the doctor's evidence to which we have referred showed it was extremely unlikely that such an episode could follow some five minutes after taking sugar and water. For these reasons we are satisfied that no miscarriage of justice occurred and the appeal will be dismissed.

Appeal dismissed.
Proviso applied.

Question

The harshness of the above rules can be attributed to the reluctance of the courts to allow the defendant to rely as a defence upon a condition for which he was entirely responsible. What approach should the courts adopt when the defendant pleads that he was not to blame for his intoxicated condition?

R. v. Kingston

[1993] 4 All E.R. 373

P, who held a grudge against K, lured a 15-year-old boy to his flat and gave him a drink laced with sedatives. When the boy became unconscious P laid him on a bed and invited K, a known homosexual paedophile, to sexually abuse the boy. While K abused the boy, P took photographs and a tape recording for the purpose of blackmailing K. The boy was aware of nothing until he awoke the following morning. P and K were charged with indecently assaulting the boy. K pleaded not guilty, saying that he had no recollection of the incident, but that he was fairly sure that he had also been drugged by P. His defence, in effect, was that he would not have assaulted the boy but for the drugs which removed his inhibitions. The trial judge directed the jury that they should acquit if they found that because of the drugs K did not intend to commit an indecent assault on the boy. If, however, they came to the conclusion that he did intend to assault the boy, despite the effect of the drugs, they should convict because a drugged intent was still an intent. He was convicted and appealed.

Lord Taylor C.J.

Involuntary intoxication

Mr. Taylor's submission is that the law recognises that, exceptionally, an accused person may be entitled to be acquitted if there is a possibility that, although his act was intentional, the intent itself arose out of circumstances for which he bears no blame. The principle can be found classically in *Hale's Pleas of the Crown*. Hale begins by contrasting two kinds of offender: those who are demented, whether in their conduct or in their mind alone, of whom he says (1 Hale P.C. 31):

" ... if they are totally depriv'd of the use of reason, they cannot be guilty ordinarily of capital offenses, for they have not the use of understanding, and act not as reasonable creatures, but their actions are in effect in the condition of brutes."

and those who are demented by drunkenness and equally deprived of the use of reason (p. 32):

" ... but by the laws of *England* such a person shall have no privilege by this voluntary contracted madness but shall have the same judgment as if he were in his right senses."

Pausing there, the common law, amplified in places by statute, continues to recognise precisely this distinction: see in particular the M'Naghten Rules and *D.P.P.* v. *Majewski* [1976] 2 All E.R. 142, [1977] A.C. 443. Hale continues:

"But yet there seems to be two allays to be allow'd in this case. 1. That if a person by the unskilfulness of his physician, or by the contrivance of his enemies, eat or drink such a thing as causeth such a temporary or permanent phrenzy ... this puts him into the same condition, in reference to crimes, as any other phrenzy, and equally excuseth him."

It is not necessary to adopt the seventeenth century psychology, still rooted in the medieval theories of the humours, upon which Hale relied, any more than it is to adopt Mr. Taylor's dichotomy between the higher and lower mind, in order to recognise the common justice of Hale's principle. It reappears briefly and vividly in *Pearson's Case* (1835) 2 Lew C.C. 144, 168 E.R. 1108 tried by Park J. at Carlisle Assizes. Pearson's defence to the charge of murder was that he was drunk when he beat his wife to death. Park J. is briefly reported as ruling (2 Lew C.C. 144 at 145, 168 E.R. 1108):

"Voluntary drunkenness is no excuse for crime. If a party be made drunk by stratagem, or the fraud of another, he is not responsible."

It is not apparent from the report whether the accused was claiming that his drunkenness was involuntary or, therefore, whether the second remark is obiter. But, extraordinarily, it is effectively the last word on the subject in the reported authorities. It appears, however, that the American Model Penal Code has adopted this distinction.

The Law Commission, in *Intoxication and Criminal Liability* (consultation Paper No. 127 (1993)), para. 2.28, states, when dealing with the present law:

"Involuntary intoxication is always taken into account in determining the existence of a subjective *mens rea*."

No authority is cited, and there is no further consideration of that proposition or of the questions implicit in it.

We are not concerned in this case with intoxication whether voluntary or involuntary, in relation to specific intent, for in *R.* v. *Culyer* (1992) *The Times*, April 17, this court held, following the decision of the House of Lords in *R.* v. *Court* [1988] 2 All E.R. 221, [1989] A.C. 28, that indecent assault may still require proof only of basic intent if the act is unambiguously indecent.

In Smith and Hogan *Criminal Law* (7th Ed., 1992), p. 220, which differs significantly on this topic from some earlier editions, the authors say:

"Evidence of intoxication negativing *mens rea* is a defence ... to all crimes where the drink or drug was taken involuntarily."

The editors of *Archbold's Evidence and Practice in Criminal Cases* (44th Ed., 1992), p. 2004, para. 17–138 appear to take the same view, as does Professor Glanville Williams in his *Textbook of Criminal Law* (2nd Ed., 1983), p. 482:

"In crimes of basic intent, the House of Lords recognised in *Majewski* that involuntary intoxication negativing *mens rea* would be a defence, even though voluntary intoxication would not."

Any such recognition to be found in *D.P.P.* v. *Majewski* [1976] 2 All E.R. 142, [1977] A.C. 443 can only be implied from the specific confinement of the opinions expressed by their Lordships to voluntary or self-induced intoxication. But we agree that nothing in those opinions is inconsistent with the foregoing views of the law. It is also of interest that section 6 of the Public Order Act 1986 adopts much the same approach, though with a special onus. Subsection (5) provides:

"For the purposes of this section, a person whose awareness is impaired by intoxication shall be taken to be aware of that of which he would be aware if not intoxicated, unless he shows either that his intoxication was not self-induced or that it was caused solely by the taking or administration of a substance in the course of medical treatment."

In *R* v. *Allen* [1988] Crim. L.R. 698 this court held that mere ignorance of the strength of the drink that a person is voluntarily taking does not make his consequent intoxication other than voluntary. We would observe that there may be a difference between a failure to appreciate what might have been appreciated, whether it is the strength of the drink or the fact that the drinker's threshold is lowered by fatigue and so forth, and ignorance that a drink, alcoholic or not, has been deliberately and artifically laced to make it a trap for the unwary. This, however, does not have to be decided at present. We note, however, that in his commentary on *R.* v. *Allen* Professor J.C. Smith says of the accused ([1988] Crim. L.R. 698 at 699):

"It may be that he would not have committed the offences if he had not been drinking, but that is neither here nor there so far as liability to conviction is concerned."

While this comment will be true of voluntary intoxication, which is what *R.* v. *Allen* was about, we do not consider it to be true of involuntary intoxication.

Russell on Crime (12th Ed., 1964) adopts Hale's formulation on involuntary 'dementia' without elaboration.

Smith and Hogan *Criminal Law* (7th Ed., 1992), p. 228 states under the cross-head "Involuntary Intoxication":

"There is little authority on the subject but it is clear that the rule in *Majewski* does not apply and it follows that involuntary intoxication negativing the *mens rea* of the offence charged, whether specific intent or basic intent, is a defence. Where it does not negative *mens rea*, it will not be a defence even though it may well be that D would not have committed the offence had he not been intoxicated; but it will then, of course, be a substantial mitigating factor."

That formulation leaves open the question as to when involuntarily intoxication negatives *mens rea*.

In our judgment, the question can be answered by turning to first principles. The importance of ensuring, under a system of law, that members of the community are safeguarded in their persons and property is obvious and was firmly stated in *D.P.P.* v. *Majewski* [1976] 2 All E.R. 142 at 168, [1977] A.C. 443 at 495 *per* Lord Edmund-Davies, for example. However, the purpose of the criminal law is to inhibit, by proscription and by penal sanction, antisocial acts which individuals may otherwise commit. Its unspoken premise is that people may have tendencies and impulses to do those things which are considered sufficiently objectionable to be forbidden. Having paedophiliac inclinations and desires is not proscribed; putting them into practice is. If the sole reason why the threshold between the two has been crossed is or may have been that the inhibition which the law requires has been removed by the clandestine act of a third party, the purposes of the criminal law are not served by nevertheless holding that the person performing the act is guilty of an offence. A man is not responsible for a condition produced "by stratagem, or the fraud of another." If therefore drink or a drug, surreptitiously administered, causes a person to lose his self-control and for that reason to form an intent which he would not otherwise have formed, it is consistent with the principle that the law should exculpate him because the operative fault is not his. The law permits a finding that the intent formed was not a criminal intent or, in other words, that the involuntary intoxication negatives the *mens rea*. As was pointed out in argument, there is some analogy to be found here in the rationale underlying the defence of duress. While it is not necessary for the decision of this case, it appears to us that, if the principle applies where the offence is one of basic intent, it should apply also where the offence is one of specific intent.

We would add that there must be evidence capable of giving rise to the defence of involuntary intoxication before a judge is obliged to leave the issue to the jury. However, once there is an evidential foundation for the defence, the burden is upon the Crown to prove that the relevant intent was formed and that notwithstanding the evidence relied on by the defence it was a criminal intent.

By answering the first of the questions put to him at the beginning of the trial in the negative, the learned judge may have inhibited a sufficient ventilation of this issue at a later stage. Further, by summing up as he did, the learned judge effectively withdrew the issue from the jury. In our judgment, that amounted to a material misdirection.

In the present case Mr. Lett for the Crown submitted that the evidence negatived the suggestion that involuntary intoxication had any significant effect on the formation or carrying out of the intent. He drew our attention to passages in the transcript of the audio tape in which remarks by the appellant may be interpreted as showing a state of mind not appreciably affected by drugs. He also reminded the court of the medical evidence that the drugs found in Penn's possession would have had a tendency to induce sleep but would not have induced action which the recipient of the drug would not otherwise have carried out. Whilst it is not certain that the issue of involuntary intoxication would have troubled the jury, there was strong evidence that this appellant had been set up for blackmail and we cannot be sure that, given a direction in law along the lines we have indicated, the jury would inevitably have convicted. Accordingly, we would not think it appropriate to apply the proviso and we hold that the conviction must on this first ground be quashed.

Questions

1. Would Kingston have had a defence if

   (a) he had been taking the drugs as part of a course of medical treatment?
   (b) P had forced him to swallow the drugs?
   (c) P had shown him some pictures of naked boys and this had induced him to assault the 15-year-old in P's flat?

2. D has been nursing a desire to kill his wife, but has lacked the courage to do so. One night his friends at the pub lace his drinks with vodka. He arrives home in a very aggressive mood and with the courage to kill his wife. He stabs her to death with the kitchen knife. Does he have a defence?

4. NECESSITY DURESS AND SELF-DEFENCE

Although these defences each possess individual characteristics of their own, they are all based upon a general concept of necessity. (See further—*Justification and Excuse in the Criminal Law* by J. C. Smith (1989).)

A. Necessity

R. v. Dudley and Stephens

(1884) 14 Q.B.D. 273 (Q.B.D.)

[The two accused had been charged with the murder of a cabin boy. D. and S. together with the cabin boy and another had been forced to take to a lifeboat following a storm at sea. After 20 days in the boat, the last eight of which had been without food or water, desperate for survival, they killed the cabin boy and fed off his flesh and blood. Four days later they were picked up. (The jury returned a special verdict.)]

Lord Coleridge C.J. The verdict finds in terms that "if the men had not fed upon the body of the boy they would *probably* not have survived," and that "the boy being in a much weaker condition was *likely* to have died before them." They might possibly have been picked up next day by a passing ship; they might possibly not have been picked up at all; in either case it is obvious that the killing of the boy would have been an unnecessary and profitless act. It is found by the verdict that the boy was incapable of resistance, and, in fact, made none; and it is not even suggested that his death was due to any violence on his part attempted against, or even so much as feared by, those who killed him. Under these circumstances the jury say that they are ignorant whether those who killed him were guilty of murder, and have referred it to this court to determine what is the legal consequence which follows from the facts which they have found.

. . . . . .

Now it is admitted that the deliberate killing of this unoffending and unresisting boy was clearly murder, unless the killing can be justified by some well-recognised excuse admitted by the law. It is further admitted that there was in this case no such excuse, unless the killing was justified by what has been called "necessity." But the temptation to the act which existed here was not what the law has ever called necessity. Nor is this to be regretted. Though law and morality are not the same, and many things may be immoral which are not necessarily illegal, yet the absolute divorce of law from morality would be of fatal consequence; and such divorce would follow if the temptation to murder in this case were to be held by law an absolute defence of it. It is not so. To preserve one's life is generally speaking a duty, but it may be the plainest and the highest duty to sacrifice it. War is full of instances in which it is a man's duty not to live, but to die. The duty, in case of shipwreck, of a captain to his crew, of the crew to the passengers, of soldiers to women and children, as in the noble case of the *Birkenhead*; these duties impose on men the moral necessity, not of the preservation, but of the sacrifice of their lives for others, from which in no country, least of all, it is to be hoped, in England, will men ever shrink, as indeed, they have not shrunk. It is not correct, therefore, to say that there is any absolute or unqualified necessity to preserve one's life. "Necesse est ut eam, non ut vivam," is a saying of a Roman officer quoted by Lord Bacon himself with high eulogy in the very chapter on necessity to which so much reference has been made. It would be a very easy and cheap display of commonplace learning to quote from Greek and Latin authors, from Horace, from Juvenal, from Cicero, from Euripides, passage after passage, in which the duty of dying for others has been laid down in glowing and emphatic language as resulting from the principles of heathen ethics; it is enough in a Christian country to remind ourselves of the Great Example whom we profess to follow. It is not needful to point out the awful danger of admitting the principle which has been contended for. Who is to be the judge of this sort of necessity? By what measure is the comparative value of lives to be measured? Is it to be strength, or intellect, or what? It is plain that the princple leaves to him who is to profit by it to determine the necessity which will justify him in deliberately taking another's life to save his own. In this case the weakest, the youngest, the most unresisting, was chosen. Was it more necessary to kill him than one of the grown men? The answer must be "No"—

"So spake the Fiend, and with necessity,
The tyrant's plea, excused his devilish deeds."

It is not suggested that in this particular case the deeds were "devilish," but it is quite plain that such a principle once admitted might be made the legal cloak for unbridled passion and atrocious crime. There is no safe path for judges to tread but to ascertain the law to the best of their ability and to declare it according to their judgment; and if in any case the law appears to be too severe on individuals, to leave it to the Sovereign to exercise that prerogative of mercy which the Constitution has intrusted to the hands fittest to dispense it.

It must not be supposed that in refusing to admit temptation to be an excuse for crime it is forgotten how terrible the temptation was; how awful the suffering; how hard in such trials to keep the judgment straight and the conduct pure. We are often compelled to set up standards we cannot reach ourselves, and to lay down rules which we could not ourselves satisfy. But a man has no right to declare temptation to be an excuse, though he might himself have yielded to it, nor allow compassion for the criminal to change or weaken in any manner the legal definition of the crime. It is therefore our duty to declare that the prisoners' act in this case was wilful murder, that the facts as stated in the verdict are no legal justification of the homicide; and to say that in our unanimous opinion the prisoners are upon this special verdict guilty of murder.

[The sentence of death was later commuted to six months' imprisonment without hard labour.]

Question

Would or should the court have taken a different line had the cabin boy consented to die or had the crew drawn lots to select the victim?

Note

In a civil action concerning the power of the chief officer of the London Fire Brigade to instruct his drivers that, with care, they might disobey a red traffic sign, Lord Denning M.R. said—in *Buckoke* v. *Greater London Council* (1972):

"During the argument I raised the question: Might not the driver of a fire engine be able to raise the defence of necessity? I put this illustration: A driver of a fire escape with ladders approaches the traffic lights. He sees 200 yards down the road a blazing house with a man at an upstairs window in extreme peril. The road is clear in all directions. At that moment the lights turn red. Is the driver to wait for 60 seconds, or more, for the lights to turn green? If the driver waits for that time, the man's life will be lost. I suggested to both counsel that the driver might be excused in crossing the lights to save the man. He might have the defence of necessity. Both counsel denied it. They would not allow him any defence in law. The circumstances went to mitigation, they said, and did not take away his guilt. If counsel are correct—and I accept that they are—nevertheless such a man should not be prosecuted. He should be congratulated."

But see now *R.* v. *Martin* (below, p. 260).

B.   Duress

(i)   Duress by threats

R. v. Howe et al.

(1987) 85 Cr.App.R. 32 (H.L.)

The case involved two brutal killings and a third incident in which the intended victim escaped. In the first killing H. and B. were secondary parties and in the second they were co-principals. The trial judge left the defence of duress to the jury only in relation to the first killing but ruled that it was not available in respect of the principal offender to murder.

Three questions were certified by the Court of Appeal for consideration by the House of Lords.

"(1) Is duress available as a defence to a person charged with murder as a principal in the first degree (the actual killer)?

(2) Can one who incites or procures by duress another to kill or to be a party to a killing be convicted of murder if that other is acquitted by reason of duress?

(3) Does the defence of duress fail if the prosecution prove that a person of reasonable firmness sharing the characteristics of the defendant would not have given way to the threats as did the defendant?"

Lord Mackay:

Question 1

The question whether duress is available as a defence in law to a person charged with murder as a principle in the first degree (the actual killer) has not been the subject of a previous decision of this House. The matter received consideration in this House in *Lynch* v. *D.P.P. for Northern Ireland* [1975] 1 All E.R. 913, [1975] A.C. 653.

Lynch had driven a motor car containing a group of the IRA in Northern Ireland on an expedition in which they shot and killed a police officer. He was tried along with two other men on a count that he murdered the police constable and was convicted and sentenced to life imprisonment. This House, by a majority of three to two, allowed Lynch's appeal and ordered a new trial pursuant to section 13 of the Criminal Appeal (Northern Ireland) Act 1968. At the new trial Lynch was allowed to plead the defence of duress but this defence was rejected by the jury and Lynch was again convicted.

It was accepted by the majority of the House in *Lynch*'s case that at that time the balance of such judicial authority as existed was against the admission of the defence of duress in cases of first degree murder. The writers were generally agreed in saying that the defence was not available in murder although later writers appear to have said so following Hale. The references are *Hale's Pleas of the Crown* (1 Hale P.C. (1736) 51, 434); *East's Pleas of the Crown* (1 East P.C. (1803) 294); *Blackstone's Commentaries on the Laws of England* (4 Bl.Com. (1809 Ed.) 30); Glanville Williams *Criminal Law: The General*

Part (2nd Ed., 1961), p. 759, para. 247; *Russell on Crime* (12th Ed., 1964), Vol. I, pp. 90–91; Smith and Hogan *Criminal Law* (3rd Ed., 1973), pp. 166–167. Since the fundamental passage is that from Hale, I think it is appropriate to quote it in full:

> "If a man be menaced with death, unless he will commit an act of treason, murder, or robbery, the fear of death doth not excuse him, if he commit the fact; for the law hath provided a sufficient remedy against such fears by applying himself to the courts and officers of justice for a writ or precept *de securitate pacis*. Again, if a man be desperately assaulted, and in peril of death, and cannot otherwise escape, unless to satisfy his assailant's fury he will kill an innocent person then present, the fear and actual force will not acquit him of the crime and punishment of murder, if he commit the fact; for he ought rather to die himself, than kill an innocent: but if he cannot otherwise save his own life, the law permits him in his own defence to kill the assailant; for by the violence of the assault, and the offence committed upon him by the assailant himself, the law of nature and necessity, hath made him his own *protector cum debito moderamine inculpatœ tutelœ*, as shall be farther shewed, when we come to the chapter of homicide *se defendendo*."

Counsel for Burke, Bannister and Howe in his very detailed and careful submission accepted this position as reflecting the law up to the time of *Lynch's* case. Since that time, on this question there has been the decision of the Privy Council in *Abbott* v. *R* [1976] 3 All E.R. 140, [1977] A.C. 755, a majority decision in which the minority consisted of Lord Wilberforce and Lord Edmund-Davies, who, along with Lord Morris, had constituted the majority in *Lynch's* case. Counsel for these appellants submitted that your Lordships should hold that the reasoning of the majority in *Lynch's* should be applied and extended to cover the present cases. He recognised that this would involve a change in the law on this matter but argued that the change was one which your Lordships should properly decide to make as the consequence of the decision of the House in *Lynch's* case.

In a present appeal, as I have said, the reason advanced on behalf of the appellants to allow the defence of duress to persons in the appellant's position as the actual killers is based on the assertion that this House in *Lynch's* case allowed it to a person who was charged with murder as a principal in the second degree otherwise described as an aider and abettor and that there was no relevant distinction between that case and the case of the actual killer. He submitted that the reasoning of the majority in *Lynch's* case when logically applied to the circumstances of the present case led to the result that the defence of duress should have been admitted here and that the appeal should accordingly be allowed.

[Lord Mackay then reviewed Lynch and continued]

In my opinion, it is plain from these quotations that the majority of this House in *Lynch's* case, and particularly Lord Morris, were reaching a decision without committing themselves to the view that the reasoning which they had used would apply to an actual killer. To take one example, it would have been impossible to cite Bray C.J. in support of the proposition that the defence of duress should be allowed in a charge of murder unless this distinction had been taken.

While therefore *Lynch's* case was decided by reasoning which does not extend to the present case, the question remains whether there is potential distinction between this case and *Lynch's* case by which to determine whether or not the defence of duress should be available. I consider that *Smith and Hogan* were perfectly right in the passage cited from that work by Lord Edmund-Davies to which I have already referred. I have not been able to find any writer of authority that is able to give rational support for the view that the distinction between principals in the first degree and those in the second degree is relevant to determine whether or not duress should be available in a particular case of murder. Whatever may have divided Lord Wilberforce and Lord Edmund-Davies on the one hand from Lord Simon and Lord Kilbrandon on the other, it is apparent that all agree that this is not a distinction which should receive practical effect in the law.

I believe that the discussions of this matter have shown that at one extreme, namely that of the person who actually kills by a deliberate assault on a person who is then present, there is a fair body of support for the view either that the defence of duress should not be allowed or that the practical result will be, even if it is allowed, that it will never be established, while there is also strong support for the view that at the other extreme minor participation which the law regards as sufficient to impute criminal guilt should be capable of being excused by the defence of duress. A similar consideration was no doubt present to the mind of Hume, the eminent writer on the Scottish criminal law, where in his work *Commentaries in the Law of Scotland respecting Crimes* (3rd Ed., 1829), p. 53 in relation to the defence in Scotland known as coercion, after a reference to the case of James Graham who claimed that he had been forced by Rob Roy and his gang to take part in an armed robbery, he says:

"But generally, and with relation to the ordinary condition of a well-regulated society, where everyman is under the shield of the law, and has the means of resorting to that protection, this is at least somewhat a difficult plea, and can hardly be serviceable in the case of a trial for any atrocious crime, unless it has the support of these qualifications: an immediate danger of death or great bodily harm; an inability to resist the violence; *a backward and inferior part in the perpetration*; and a disclosure of the fact, as well as restitution of the spoil, on the first safe and convenient occasion." (My emphasis)

So far, I have not found any satisfactory formulation of a distinction which would be sufficiently precise to be given practical effect in law and at the same time differentiate between levels of culpability so as to produce a satisfactory demarcation between those accused of murder who should be entitled to resort to the defence of duress and those who were not.

The House is therefore, in my opinion, faced with the unenviable decision of either departing altogether from the doctrine that duress is not available in murder or departing from the decision of his House in *Lynch's* case. While a variety of minor attacks on the reasoning of the majority were mounted by counsel for the Crown in the present case, I do not find any of these sufficiently important to merit departing from *Lynch's* case on these grounds. I do, however, consider that, having regard to the balance of authority on the question of duress as a defence to murder prior to *Lynch's* case, for this House now to allow the defence of duress generally in response to a charge of murder would be to effect an important and substantial change in the law. In my opinion too, it would involve a departure from the decision in the famous case of *R. v. Dudley and Stephens* (1884) 14 Q.B.D. 273, [1881–5] All E.R. Rep 61. The justification for allowing a defence of duress to a charge or murder is that a defendant should be excused who killed as the only way of avoiding death himself or preventing the death of some close relation such as his own well-loved child. This essentially was the dilemma which Dudley and Stephens faced and in denying their defence the court refused to allow this consideration to be used in a defence to murder. If that refusal was right in the case of Dudley and Stephens it cannot be wrong in the present appeals. Although the result of recognising the defence advanced in that case would be that no crime was committed and in the case with which we are concerned that a murder was committed and a particular individual was not guilty of it (subject to the consideration of the second certified question) that does not distinguish the two cases from the point of view now being considered.

To change the law in the manner suggested by counsel for the appellants in the present case would, in my opinion, introduce uncertainty over a field of considerable importance.

So far I have referred to the defence of duress as if it were a precisely defined concept, but it is apparent from the decisions that it is not so and I cannot do better in this connection than refer to what Lord Simon said on this point in *Lynch's* case [1975] 1 ALl E.R. 913 at 931, [1975] A.C. 653 at 686:

"Before turning to examine these considerations, it is convenient to have a working definition of duress—even though it is actually an extremely vague and elusive juristic concept. I take it for present purposes to denote such [well-grounded] fear, produced by threats, of death or grievous bodily harm [or unjustified imprisonment] if a certain act is not done, as overbears the actor's wish not to perform the act, and is effective, at the time of the act, in constraining him to perform it. I am quite uncertain whether the words which I have put in square brackets should be included in any such definition. It is arguable that the test should be purely subjective, and that it is contrary to principle to require the fear to be a reasonable one. Moreover, I have assumed, on the basis of *R. v. Hudson* [1971] 2 All E.R. 244, [1971] 2 Q.B. 202, that threat of future injury may suffice. although Stephen *Digest of the Criminal Law* (1877) note to art. 10 is to the contrary. Then the law leaves it also quite uncertain whether the fear induced by threats must be of death or grievous bodily harm, or whether threatened loss of liberty suffices: cases of duress in the law of contract suggest that duress may extend to fear of unjustified imprisonment; but the crminal law returns no clear answer. It also leaves entirely unanswered whether, to constitute such a general criminal defence, the threat must be of harm to the person required to perform the act, or extends to the immediate family of the actor (and how immediate?), or to any person. Such questions are not academic, in these days when hostages are so frequently seized."

To say that a defence in respect of which so many questions remain unsettled should be introduced in respect of the whole field of murder is not to promote certainty in the law. In this connection it is worth observing that, when in their Report on Defences of General Application (Law.Com. No. 83) the Law Commission recommended that the defence of duress should be available in murder, they suggested a definition of duress which is, I believe, considerably narrower than that generally thought to be available in the present law in respect of other offences. In particular, they required that the defendant must believe that 'the threat will be carried out immediately, before he can have any real opportunity of seeking official protection' and they suggested that the fact that any official protection which might have been available in the circumstances would or might not have been effective to prevent the harm threatened should be immaterial in this context. It is of interest and importance to notice that this point figured long before in Hale's statement which I have quoted. It is to be noted that it was of this very part of Hale's statement that Lord Wilberforce said in *Lynch's* case [1975] 1 All E.R. 913 at 928, [1975] A.C. 653 at 682:

"Even if this argument was ever realistic, he would surely have recognised that reconsideration of it must be required in troubled times."

I notice that in the Law Commission report dated March 28, 1985 (Law Com. No. 143), which contains a report to the Law Commission in respect of the codification of the criminal law by a team from the Society of Public Teachers of Law, doubt is expressed on the soundness of this recommendation in Law Com. No. 83. This particular matter does not arise in the circumstances of the present case, but the great difficulty that has been found in obtaining a consensus of informed opinion on it is just one illustration of the uncertain nature of what would be introduced into this most important area of the criminal law if the defence of duress were to be available.

Since the decision in *Lynch's* case the Law Commission have published in their report (Law Com. No. 83), to which I have referred, the result of an extensive survey of the law relating to duress and have made recommendations on it which have been laid before Parliament. In my opinion the problems which have been evident in relation to the law of murder and the availability of particular defences is not susceptible of what Lord Reid described as a solution by a policy of make do and mend (see *Myers* v. *D.P.P.* [1964] 2 All E.R. 881 at 886, [1965] A.C. 1001 at 1002). While I appreciate fully the gradual development that has taken place in the law relating to the defence of duress, I question whether the law has reached a sufficiently precise definition of that defence to make it right for us sitting in our judicial capacity to introduce it as a defence for an actual killer for the first time in the law of England. Parliament, in its legislative capacity, although recommended to do so by the report of the Law Commission, has not taken any steps to make the defence of duress available generally to a charge of murder even where it has the power to define with precision the circumstances in which such a defence would be available.

It has also been suggested for consideration whether, if the defence of duress is to be allowed in relation to murder by the actual killer, the defence should have the effect, if sustained, of reducing the crime to that of manslaughter by analogy with the defence of provocation. Provocation itself was introduced into the law by judicial decision in recognition of human frailty, although it is now the subject of a statutory provision (see the Homicide Act 1957, s.3) and it was suggested that the same approach might be taken now with regard to duress.

. . .

In my opinion we would not be justified in the present state of the law in introducing for the first time into our law the concept of duress acting to reduce the charge to one of manslaughter even if there were grounds on which it might be right to do so. On that aspect of the matter the Law Commission took the view that where the defence of duress had been made out it would be unjust to stigmatise the person accused with a conviction and there is clearly much force in that view.

The argument for the appellants essentially is that, *Lynch's* case having been decided as it was and there being no practical distinction available between *Lynch's* case and the present case, this case should be decided in the same way. The opposite point of view is that, since *Lynch's* case was concerned not with the actual killer but with a person who was made guilty of his act by the doctrine of accession, the correct starting point for this matter is the case of the actual killer. In my opinion this latter is the correct approach. The law has extended the liability to trial and punishment faced by the actual killer to those who are participants with him in the crime and it seems to me, therefore, that, where a question as important as this is in issue, the correct starting point is the case of the actual killer. It seems to me plain that the reason that it was for so long stated by writers of authority that the defence of duress was not available in a charge or murder was because of the supreme importance that the law afforded to the protection of human life and that it seemed repugnant that the law should recognise in any individual in any circumstances, however extreme, the right to choose that one innocent person should be killed rather than another. In my opinion that is the question which we still must face. Is it right that the law should confer this right in any circumstances, however extreme? While I recognise fully the force of the reasoning which persuaded the majority of this House in *Lynch*'s case to reach the decision to which they came in relation to a person not the actual killer, it does not address directly this question in relation to the actual killer. I am not persuaded that there is good reason to alter the answer which Hale gave to this question. No development of the law or progress in legal thinking which has taken place since his day has, to my mind, demonstrated a reason to change this fundamental answer. In the circumstances which I have narrated of a report to Parliament from the Law Commission concerned, inter alia, with this very question, it would seem particularly inappropriate to make such a change now. For these reasons, in my opinion, the first certified question should be answered in the negative.

It follows that, in my opinion, the House should decline to follow the decision in *Lynch*'s case.

Note

1. In response to Question 2 (above, p. 247) Lord Mackay, that he would affirm the view of the Lord Chief Justice in the Court of Appeal that " ... where a person has been killed and that result is the result intended by another participant, the mere fact that the actual killer may be convicted only of the reduced charge of manslaughter for some reason special to himself does not, in my opinion, in any way result in a compulsory reduction for the other participant."

2. On Question 3 (above, p. 247) Lord Mackay confirmed that when duress was available as a defence the correct test was the partially objective test laid down in Graham (1982). In that case Lord Lane C.J. had said:

"As a matter of public policy, it seems to us essential to limit the defence of duress by means of an objective criterion formulated in the terms of reasonableness. Consistency of approach in defences to criminal liability is obviously desirable. Provocation and duress are analogous. In provocation the words or actions of one person break the self-control of another. In duress the words or actions of one person break the will of another. The law requires a defendant to have the self-control reasonably to be expected of the ordinary citizen in his situation. It should likewise require him to have the steadfastness reasonably to be expected of the ordinary citizen in his situation. So too with self-defence, in which the law permits the use of no more force than is reasonable in the circumstances" (but now see Scarlett, below, p. 268). And, in general, if a mistake is to excuse what would otherwise be criminal, the mistake must be a reasonable one. It follows that we accept counsel for the Crown's submission that the direction in this case was too favourable to the appellant. The Crown having conceded that the issue of duress was open to the appellant and was raised on the evidence, the correct approach on the facts of this case would have been as follows: (1) was the defendant, or may he have been, impelled to act as he did because, as a result of what he reasonably believed King had said or done, he had good cause to fear that if he did not so act King would kill him or (if this is to be added) cause him serious physical injury? (2) if so, have the prosecution made the jury sure that a sober person of reasonable firmness, sharing the characteristics of the defendant, would not have responded to whatever he reasonably believed King said or did by taking part in the killing? The fact that a defendant's will to resist has been eroded by the voluntary consumption of drink or drugs or both is not relevant to this test."

Question

Is the defence of duress available on a charge of attempted murder?

R. v. Gotts

[1992] 1 All E.R. 832

Lord Jauncey of Tullichettle. As the question is still open for decision by your Lordships it becomes a matter of policy how it should be answered. It is interesting to note that there is no uniformity of practice in other common law countries. The industry of Mr. Miskin who appeared with Mr. Farrer disclosed that in Queensland, Tasmania, Western Australia, New Zealand and Canada duress is not available as a defence to attempted murder but that it is available in almost all the states of the United States of America. The reason why duress has for so long been stated not to be available as a defence to a murder charge is that the law regards the sanctity of human life and the protection thereof as of paramount importance. Does that reason apply to attempted murder as well as to murder? As Lord Griffiths pointed out in the passage to which I have just referred, an intent to kill must be proved in the case of attempted murder but not necessarily in the case of murder. Is there logic in affording the defence to one who intends to kill but fails and denying it to one who mistakenly kills intending only to injure? If I may give two examples. (1a) A stabs B in the chest intending to kill him and leaves him for dead. By good luck B is found whilst still alive and rushed to hospital where surgical skill saves his life. (1b) C stabs D intending only to injure him and inflicts a near identical wound. Unfortunately D is not found until it is too late to save his life. I see no justification or logic or morality for affording a defence of duress to A who intended to kill when it is denied to C who did not so intend. (2a) E plants in a passenger aircraft a bomb timed to go off in mid-flight. Owing to bungling it explodes while the aircraft is still on the ground with the result that some 200 passengers suffer physical and mental injuries of which many are permanently disabling, but no one is killed. (2b) F plants a bomb in a light aircraft intending to disable the pilot before it takes off but in fact it goes off in mid-air killing the pilot who is the sole occupant of the airplane. It would in my view be both offensive to common sense and decency that E if he established duress should be acquitted and walk free without a stain on his character notwithstanding the appalling results which he has achieved, whereas F who never intended to kill should, if convicted in the absence of the defence, be sentenced to life imprisonment as a murderer.

It is of course true that withholding the defence in any circumstances will create some anomalies but I would agree with Lord Griffiths that nothing should be done to undermine in any way the highest duty of the law to protect the freedom and lives of those that live under it (see [1987] 1 All E.R. 771 at 789, [1987] A.C. 417 at 444). I can therefore see no justification in logic, morality or law in affording to an attempted murderer the defence which is withheld from a murderer. The intent required of an attempted murderer is more evil than that required of a murderer and the line which divides the two offences is seldom, if ever, of the deliberate making of the criminal. A man shooting to kill but missing a vital organ by a hair's breadth can justify his action no more than can the man who hits that organ. It is pure chance that the attempted murderer is not a murderer and I entirely agree with what Lord Lane C.J. said ([1991] 2 All E.R. 1 at 8, [1991] 1 Q.B. 660 at 667): ' . . . the fact that the attempt failed to kill should not make any difference.'

For the foregoing reasons I have no doubt that the Court of Appeal reached the correct conclusion and that the appeal should be dismissed.

Note

Despite a vigourous dissent by Lord Lowry, the majority supported Lord Jauncey. Lord Lowry argued that the authorities supported the view that duress was available as a defence to attempted murder and that a decision by their Lordships that it was no defence would, in effect, be a retrospective extension of criminal liability. If it was thought wrong that duress should be available as a defence to attempted murder, it should lie with Parliament to amend the law prospectively.

Question

Is duress available to a charge under section 18 of the Offences Against the Person Act 1861 (see below, p. 393)?

R. v. Shepherd

(1988) 86 Cr.App.R. 47 (C.A.)

S. was convicted of five offences of burglary. He had taken part in a series of shoplifting raids during which one member of the gang would distract the shopkeeper's attention while the others walked out with goods, usually cigarettes. S. said that he had gone willingly on the first expedition, but had then decided that he no longer wished to participate. P., another member of the gang with convictions for violence, had then threatened him and his family with violence if he did not continue. His story received some colour due to the fact that P. later received a prison sentence for an assault on S. within the precincts of the court while the case was awaiting trial.

The trial judge ruled that the defence of duress was unavailable to S. since his original participation in the joint venture had been voluntary.

Mustill L.J. At the conclusion of the argument we had arrived at the following opinion:

(1) Although it is not easy to rationalise the existence of duress as a defence rather than a ground of mitigation, it must in some way be founded on a concession to human frailty in cases where the defendant has been faced with a choice between two evils.

(2) The exception which exists where the defendant has voluntarily allied himself with the person who exercises the duress must be founded on the assumption that, just as he cannot complain if he had the opportunity to escape the duress and failed to take it, equally no concession to frailty is required if the risk of duress is freely undertaken.

(3) Thus, in some instances it will follow inevitably that the defendant has no excuse: for example, if he has joined a group of people dedicated to violence as a political end, or one which is overtly ready to use violence for other criminal ends. Members of so-called paramilitary illegal groups, or gangs of armed robbers, must be taken to anticipate what may happen to them if their nerve fails, and cannot be heard to complain if violence is indeed threatened.

(4) Other cases will be difficult. There is no need for recourse to extravagant examples. Common sense must recognise that there are certain kinds of criminal enterprises the joining of which, in the absence of any knowledge of

propensity to violence on the part of one member, would not lead another to suspect that a decision to think better of the whole affair might lead him into serious trouble. The logic which appears to underlie the law of duress would suggest that if trouble did unexpectedly materialise, and if it put the defendant into a dilemma in which a reasonable man might have chosen to act as he did, the concession to human frailty should not be denied to him.

Having arrived at these conclusions on the argument addressed to us, it appeared to us plain there had been a question which should properly have been put to the jury and that the appeal must accordingly be allowed. We intimated that this would be so, whilst taking the opportunity to put our reasons in writing.

Naturally a proper scepticism would have been in order when the defence came to be examined at the trial, for there were many aspects on which the appellant could have been pressed. In particular, his prior knowledge of P. would require investigation. At the same time the trial would not have been a foregone conclusion, since the concerted shoplifting enterprise did not involve violence to the victim either in anticipation or in the way it was actually put into effect. The members of the jury have had to ask themselves whether the appellant could be said to have taken the risk of P.'s violence simply by joining a shoplifting gang of which he was a member. Of course even if they were prepared to give the appellant the benefit of the doubt in this respect, an acquittal would be far from inevitable. The jury would have then to consider the nature and timing of the threats, and the nature and persistence of the offences, in order to decide whether the defendant was entitled to be exonerated. It may well be that, in the light of the evidence as it emerged, convictions would have followed. But the question was never put to the test. The issues were never investigated. The jury were left with no choice but to convict.

In these circumstances we saw no alternative but to hold that the convictions could not stand. The sentences necessarily fell away, leaving the fortunate appellant with no penalty attached to the first offence of which he was undeniably guilty, but which was not the subject of any charge.

That was the position at the conclusion of the argument. Since then we have been able to study a transcript of the ruling of the trial judge in *Sharp* (Kenneth Jones J.), a ruling which was approved on appeal (see (1987) 85 Cr.App.R. at

212, [1987] A.C. at 7F). It is sufficiently important in the present context to justify quotation at length:

"In my judgment there is no authority binding upon me on this point, but there are the strongest and most powerful pointers to what is the correct answer. In my judgment the law does not go so far as to embody that which was submitted by the Crown in the Court of Criminal Appeal in Northern Ireland in *Lynch's* case [1975] N.I. 35, namely that the defence of duress is not available to an accused who voluntarily joins in a criminal enterprise and is afterwards subject to threats of violence, but in my judgment the defence of duress is not available to an accused who voluntarily exposes and submits himself to illegal compulsion.

It is not merely a matter of joining in a criminal enterprise; it is a matter of joining in a criminal enterprise of such a nature that the defendant appreciated the nature of the enterprise itself and the attitudes of those in charge of it, so that when he was in fact subjected to compulsion he could fairly be said by a jury to have voluntarily exposed himself and submitted himself to such compulsion. Therefore on the facts advanced by or which are about to be advanced by Mr. Mylne, I hold that duress is not available as a defence to Sharp to the charge of murder, or indeed of manslaughter. Of course it follows that it would be a question of fact for the jury as to whether Sharp had voluntarily exposed and submitted himself to this illegal compulsion. The facts, as Mr. Mylne proposes to advance them, do not necessarily dispose of that matter. It is still a matter for the jury to decide—though as I am sure he will concede, the evidence lies very heavily against him in view of his client's admitted complicity in this offence, and indeed his client's view of the man who was in charge of it, namely Hussey. If the jury can find it possible to say that he, although joining in this criminal enterprise, did not voluntarily expose or submit himself to the possibility of coercion, compulsion by Hussey, then the jury would be putting him then in the position of the innocent bystander, and duress would be available to him as a defence. If the jury took the view on the totality of the evidence it has to be fairly and justly said that he voluntarily disposed and submitted himelf to illegal compulsion, then the defence of duress is not open to him. So much for the defence of duress."

This ruling, if we may say so, corresponds exactly with the view which we had independently formed. In the interests of accuracy it must be acknowledged that it was the ruling itself, rather than the whole of the passage in which it was expressed, which was the subject of the approval on appeal. Nevertheless the terms of the judgment delivered by the Lord Chief Justice were such as to make it clear, to our mind, that the approach of the trial judge was correct. In the context of that case, given the facts, such a conclusion was fatal to the appeal. Here, by contrast, it demonstrates that the issue ought to have been left to the jury.

In conclusion we should add that we have also examined the provisions of various penal statutes and codes emanating from other common law countries: for example, the Crime Act 1961, section 24 of New Zealand; the Model Penal Code, section 2.09(2) of the United States; and codes of Canada and various states in Australia. These are not identical in their terms, but they are all consistent with the view which we have expressed, as are the opinions set out in Law Commission Working Paper No. 83, paragraphs 2.35 to 2.38, and in articles including those by P. J. Rowe "Duress and Criminal Organisations" (1979), 42 M.L.R. 102, and R. S. O'Reagan, "Duress and Criminal Conspiracies" [1971] Crim.L.R. 35.

For these reasons therefore we consider that the conviction should be quashed.

Appeal allowed.
Conviction quashed.

(ii)   Duress of Circumstances

R. v. Martin

[1989] 1 All E.R. 652 (C.A.)

The defendant was convicted of driving a motor vehicle while disqualified.

Simon Brown J. The appellant now appeals against his conviction as of right on a pure point of law. The point is whether the defence of necessity is available to a charge of driving whilst disqualified when that driving occurs in circumstances such as the appellant was contending arose in his case. To those circumstances I shall come in a moment. In a private-room hearing before the appellant was arraigned, the judge held not. He concluded that, once it was established that the defendant was driving and that he was disqualified at the time, the offence was established. It was, in short, in those circumstances an absolute offence.

In consequence of that ruling the appellant pleaded guilty and merely prayed in aid as mitigation the circumstances on which he relied to establish the necessity of breaking the law. But for the ruling he would have contested the case.

The appeal is brought under s.2(1)(*b*) of the Criminal Appeal Act 1968, namely on the basis that the judgment of the court of trial should be set aside on the ground of a wrong decision on a question of law.

The circumstances which the appellant desired to advance by way of defence of necessity were essentially these. His wife has suicidal tendencies. On a number of occasions before the day in question she had attempted to take her own life. On the day in question her son, the appellant's stepson, had overslept. He had done so to the extent that he was bound to be late for work and at risk of losing his job unless, so it was asserted, the appellant drove him to work. The appellant's wife was distraught. She was shouting, screaming, banging her head against a wall. More particularly, it is said she was threatening suicide unless the appellant drove the boy to work.

The defence had a statement from a doctor which expressed the opinion that "in view of her mental condition it is likely that Mrs. Martin would have attempted suicide if her husband did not drive her son to work."

The appellant's case on the facts was that he genuinely, and he would suggest reasonably, believed that his wife would carry out that threat unless he did as she demanded. Despite his disqualification he therefore drove the boy. He was in fact apprehended by the police within about a quarter of a mile of the house.

Sceptically though one may regard that defence on the facts (and there were, we would observe, striking difficulties about the detailed evidence when it came finally to be given before the judge in mitigation), the sole question before this court is whether those facts, had the jury accepted they were or might be true, amounted in law to a defence. If they did, then the appellant was entitled to a trial of the issue before the jury. The jury would of course have had to be directed properly on the precise scope and nature of the defence, but the decision on the facts would have been for them. As it was, such a defence was pre-empted by the ruling. Should it have been?

In our judgment the answer is plainly not. The authorities are now clear. Their effect is perhaps most conveniently to be found in the judgment of this court in *R.* v. *Conway* [1988] 3 All E.R. 1025, [1988] 3 W.L.R. 1238. The decision reviews earlier relevant authorities.

The principles may be summarised thus: first, English law does, in extreme circumstances, recognise a defence of necessity. Most commonly this defence arises as duress, that is pressure on the accused's will from the wrongful threats or violence of another. Equally however it can arise from other objective dangers threatening the accused or others. Arising thus it is conveniently called "duress of circumstances."

Secondly, the defence is available only if, from an objective standpoint, the accused can be said to be acting reasonably and proportionately in order to avoid a threat of death or serious injury.

Thirdly, assuming the defence to be open to the accused on his account of the facts, the issue should be left to the jury, who should be directed to determine these two questions: first, was the accused, or may he have been, impelled to act as he did because as a result of what he reasonably believed to be the situation he had good cause to fear that otherwise death or serious physical injury would result; secondly, if so, would a sober person of reasonable firmness, sharing the characteristics of the accused, have responded to that situation by acting as the accused acted? If the answer to both those questions was Yes, then the jury would acquit; the defence of necessity would have been established.

That the defence is available in cases of reckless driving is established by *R.* v. *Conway* itself and indeed by an earlier decision of the court in *R.* v. *Willer* (1986) 83 Cr.App.R. 225. *R.* v. *Conway* is authority also for the proposition that the scope of the defence is no wider for reckless driving than for other serious offences. As was pointed out in the judgment, "reckless driving can kill" (see [1988] 3 All E.R. 1025 at 102, [1988] 3 W.L.R. 1238 at 1244).

We see no material distinction between offences of reckless driving and driving whilst disqualified so far as the application and scope of this defence is concerned. Equally we can see no distinction in principle between various threats of death; it matters not whether the risk of death is by murder or by suicide or indeed by accident. One can illustrate the latter by considering a disqualified driver being driven by his wife, she suffering a heart attack in remote countryside and he needing instantly to get her to hospital.

It follows from this that the judge quite clearly did come to a wrong decision on the question of law, and the appellant should have been permitted to raise this defence for what it was worth before the jury.

It is in our judgment a great pity that that course was not taken. It is difficult to believe that any jury would have swallowed the improbable story which this appellant desired to advance. There was, it emerged when evidence was given in mitigation, in the house at the time a brother of the boy who was late for work, who was licensed to drive, and available to do so; the suggestion was that he would not take his brother because of "a lot of aggravation in the house between them." It is a further striking fact that when apprehended by the police this appellant was wholly silent as to why on this occasion he had felt constrained to drive. But those considerations, in our judgment, were essentially for the jury, and we have concluded, although not without hesitation, that it would be inappropriate here to apply the proviso to s.2(1) of the 1968 Act.

In the result this appeal must be allowed and the conviction quashed.

Appeal allowed. Conviction quashed.

Question

Why is the Court of Appeal anxious to classify the defence in this case as a species of duress and not as a more general defence of necessity?

Was this a case of duress of circumstances?

C. Prevention of Crime, Self-Defence, Defence of Property

Criminal Law Act 1967, s.3

3.—(1) A person may use such force as is reasonable in the circumstances in the prevention of crime, or in effecting or assisting in the lawful arrest of offenders or of suspected offenders or of persons unlawfully at large.

(2) Subsection (1) above shall replace the rules of the common law on the question when force used for a purpose mentioned in the subsection is justified by that purpose.

Att.-Gen. for Northern Ireland's Reference (No. 1 of 1975)

[1977] A.C. 105 (H.L.)

[The accused has been charged with murder. He had shot the victim in the mistaken belief that the victim was a member of an illegal organisation—the I.R.A.]

264 *Defences*

Lord Diplock. [interpreting the Criminal Law Act (Northern Ireland) 1967, s.3 which is in the same terms as the Criminal Law Act 1967, s.3.] What amount of force is "reasonable in the circumstances" for the purpose of preventing crime is, in my view, always a question for the jury in a jury trial, never a "point of law" for the judge.

The form in which the jury would have to ask themselves the question in a trial for an offence against the person in which this defence was raised by the accused, would be: Are we satisfied that no reasonabe man (a) with knowledge of such facts as were known to the accused or *reasonably* believed by him to exist (b) in the circumstances and time available to him for reflection (c) could be of opinion that the prevention of the risk of harm to which others might be exposed if he suspect were allowed to escape justified exposing the suspect to the risk of harm to him that might result from the kind of force that the accused contemplated using?

To answer this the jury would have first to decide what were the facts that did exist and were known to the accused to do so and what were mistakenly believed by the accused to be facts. In respect of the latter the jury would have had to decide whether any *reasonable man on the material available to the accused* could have shared that belief. To select, as is done in paragraph 2(xiii) of the reference, two specific inferences of fact as to which it is said that the accused had no belief is merely to exclude them from the jury's consideration as being facts mistakenly believed by the accused to exist; but this does not preclude the jury from considering what inferences of fact a *reasonable* man would draw from the primary facts known to the accused.

The jury would have also to consider how the circumstances in which the accused had to make his decision whether or not to use force and the shortness of the time available to him for reflection, might affect the judgment of a reasonable man. In the facts that are to be assumed for the purposes of the reference there is material upon which a jury might take the view that the accused had reasonable grounds for apprehension of imminent danger to himself and other members of the patrol if the deceased were allowed to get away and join armed fellowmembers of the Provisional I.R.A. who might be lurking in the neighbourhood, and that the time available to the accused to make up his mind what to do was so short that even a reasonable man could only act intuitively. This being so, the jury in approaching the final part of the question should remind themselves that the postulated balancing of risk against risk, harm against harm, by the reasonable man is not undertaken in the calm analytical atmosphere of the courtroom after counsel with the benefit of hindsight have expounded at length the reasons for and against the kind and degree of force that was used by the accused; but in the brief second or two which the accused had to decide whether to shoot or not and under all the stresses to which he was exposed.

In many cases where force is used in the prevention of crime or in effecting an arrest there is a choice as to the degree of force to use. On the facts that are to be assumed for the purposes of the reference the only options open to the accused were either to let the deceased escape or to shoot at him with a service rifle. A reasonable man would know that a bullet from a self-loading rifle if it hit a human being, at any rate at the range at which the accused fired, would be likely to kill him or to injure him seriously. So in one scale of the balance the harm to which the deceased would be exposed if the accused aimed to hit him was predictable and grave and the risk of its occurrence high. In the other scale of the balance it would be open to the jury to take the view that it would not be unreasonable to assess the kind of harm to be averted by preventing the accused's escape as even graver—the killing or wounding of members of the patrol by terrorists in ambush, and the effect of this success by members of the Provisional I.R.A. in encouraging the continuance of the armed insurrection and all the misery and destruction of life and property that terrorist activity in Northern Ireland has entailed. *The jury would have to consider too what was the highest degree at which a reasonable man could have assessed the likelihood that such consequences might follow the escape of the deceased if the facts had been as the accused knew or believed them reasonably to be.*

Note

The words italicised should now be read in the light of *Beckford* (see above, p. 162. It is submitted that it suffices that the accused honestly held his mistaken view. It remains, of course, the position that the amount of force he uses in the circumstances which actually exist or which he mistakenly believes to exist, must be reasonable. What if the jury reach the conclusion he was right to use some force, but not as much as he, in fact, used?

Question

Where a court is hearing a murder charge and the defendant has pleaded self-defence or prevention of crime, the basic question for the court is whether the force used by the defendant was reasonable in the circumstances. We have seen from *Beckford* (above, p. 162) that the defendant is entitled to be judged on the circumstances he honestly thought to exist at the time. Thus if he is mistaken about the need for the use of force, the jury must still ask itself whether the force used would have been reasonable had the circumstances actually been as the defendant believed them to be. Should a similar approach be taken in relation to the amount of force used? In other words should the jury be asking itself whether the defendant honestly believed the amount of force he used was reasonable?

R. v. McInnes

[1971] 1 W.L.R. 1600 (C.A.)

[During the course of a fight between "skinheads" and "greasers" the accused stabbed and killed a member of the rival gang. At his trial he pleaded that it was an accident. He was convicted and in his appeal to the Court of Appeal he argued, *inter alia*, that the trial judge had not properly directed the jury on the issue of excessive force used in self-defence.]

Edmund-Davies L.J. The final criticism levelled against the summing-up is that the judge wrongly failed to direct the jury that, if death resulted from the use of excessive force by the accused in defending himself against the aggressiveness of the deceased, the proper verdict was one of not guilty of murder but guilty of manslaughter. Certainly no such direction was given, and the question that arises is whether its omission constitutes a defect in the summing-up.

The Privy Council decision in *Palmer* v. *The Queen* (1971) provides high persuasive authority which we, for our part, unhesitatingly accept, that there is certainly *no* rule that, in every case where self-defence is left to the jury, such a direction is called for.

But where self-defence fails on the ground that the force used went clearly beyond that which was reasonable in the light of the circumstances as they reasonably appeared to the accused, is it the law that the inevitable result must be that he can be convicted of manslaughter only, and not of murder? It seems that in Australia that question is answered in the affirmative ... but not, we think, in this country. On the contrary, if a plea of self-defence fails for the reason stated, it affords the accused no protection at all. But it is important to stress that the facts upon which the plea of self-defence is unsuccessfully sought to be based may nevertheless serve the defendant in good stead. They may, for example, go to show that he may have acted under provocation or that, although acting unlawfully, he may have lacked the intent to kill or cause serious bodily harm, and in that way render the proper verdict one of manslaughter.

The court elicited from defence counsel...that his researches had revealed no authority for the proposition he advanced, and which was described by the Court of Criminal Appeal in *Reg.* v. *Hassin* (1963) as "a novelty in present times." For our part, we think that at least persuasive authority to the contrary is not lacking. Thus, in *Palmer* v. *The Queen* (1971) Lord Morris of Borth-y-Gest said:

"There are no prescribed words which must be employed in or adopted in a summing up. All that is needed is a clear exposition, in relation to the particular facts of the case, of the conception of necessary self-defence. If there has been no attack, then clearly there will have been no need for defence. If there has been attack so that defence is reasonably necessary it will be recognised that a person defending himself cannot weigh to a nicety the exact measure of his necessary defensive action. If a jury thought that in a moment of unexpected anguish a person attacked had only done what he honestly and instinctively thought was necessary that would be most potent evidence that only reasonable defensive action had been taken. A jury will be told that the defence of self-defence, where the evidence makes its raising possible, will only fail if the prosecution show beyond doubt that what the accused did was not by way of self-defence. But their Lordships consider, in agreement with the approach in the *De Freitas* case (1960), that if the prosecution have shown that what was done was not done in self-defence then that issue is eliminated from the case. If the jury consider that an accused acted in self-defence or if the jury are in doubt as to this then they will acquit. The defence of self-defence either succeeds so as to result in an acquittal or it is disproved, in which case as a defence it is rejected. In a homicide case the circumstances may be such that it will become an issue as to whether there was provocation so that the verdict might be one of manslaughter. Any other possible issues will remain. If in any case the view is possible that the intent necessary to constitute the crime of murder was lacking then that matter would be left to the jury."

Section 3(1) of the Criminal Law Act 1967 provides that: "A person may use such force as is reasonable in the circumstances in the prevention of crime...," and in our judgment the degree of force permissible in self-defence is similarly limited. Deliberate stabbing was so totally unreasonable in the circumstances of this case, even on the defendant's version, that self-defence justifying a complete acquittal was not relied upon before us, and rightly so. Despite the high esteem in which we hold our Australian brethren, we respectfully reject as far as this country is concerned the refinement sought to be introduced that, if the accused, in defending himself during a fisticuffs encounter, drew out against his opponent (who he had no reason to think was armed) the deadly weapon which he had earlier unsheathed and then, "let him have it," the jury should have been directed that, even on those facts, it was open to them to convict of manslaughter. They are, in our view, the facts of this case. It follows that in our judgment no such direction was called for.

In the result, we hold that, upon abundant evidence and following a summing-up which is not open to substantial criticism, the jury arrived at a verdict which ought not to be disturbed. We accordingly dismiss this appeal.

Appeal dismissed.

Notes

1. In *Shannon* (1980) the Court of Appeal reaffirmed the view that although selfdefence either succeeded or failed, juries must be directed to take account of the circumstances in which the accused had to make his decision.

2. The Australian Courts have now abandoned as too complex their rule that use of excessive force by way of self-defence reduced a charge of murder to manslaughter; *Zekewic* (1987).

R. v. Scarlett

[1993] 4 All E.R. 629 (CA)

D was the landlord of a public house. After closing time on the evening in question, P, a heavily built man who had clearly been drinking, entered the bar and demanded to be served. D ordered him out and when P refused to go, pushed P into the lobby of the public house. P fell through the outer door of the lobby and down some steps. The fall caused him to sustain head injuries from which he later died. D was charged with manslaughter. The prosecution sought to prove constructive manslaughter which required proof that the victim died as a result of an unlawful act on the part of the defendant which was likely to cause some bodily harm (see further p. 334, below). The trial judge told the jury that if they came to the conclusion that D used excessive force to evict P, that would constitute an unlawful act (assault) and if they were satisfied that that act had caused P to fall and strike his head, D would be guilty of manslaughter. D was convicted and appealed.

Beldam L.J. The issue in R. v. *Williams* was whether the accused was entitled to be acquitted if he mistakenly believed that he was justified in using force. The court held that, even if the jury came to the conclusion that the mistake was an unreasonable one, if the defendant may genuinely have been labouring under it, he was entitled to rely upon it. The reason why he was entitled to be acquitted is because he did not intend to apply unlawful force. The principle we have quoted that the mental element necessary to constitute guilt of an assault is the intent to apply unlawful force to the victim was approved by the Board of the Privy Council in *Beckford* v. *R.* [1987] 3 All E.R. 425 at 431, [1988] A.C. 130 at 143.

If the mental element necessary to prove an assault is an intention to apply unlawful force to the victim, and the accused is to be judged according to his mistaken view of the facts whether that mistake was on an objective view reasonable or not, we can see no logical basis for distinguishing between a person who objectively is not justified in using force at all but mistakenly believes he is and another who is in fact justified in using force but mistakenly believes that the circumstances call for a degree of force objectively regarded as unnecessary.

Where, as in the present case, an accused is justified in using some force and can only be guilty of an assault if the force used is excessive, the jury ought to be directed that he cannot be guilty of an assault unless the prosecution prove that he acted with the mental element necessary to constitute his action an assault, that is 'that the defendant intentionally or recklessly applied force to the person of another' (see R. v. *Venna* [1975] 3 All E.R. 788 at 793, [1976] 1 Q.B. 421 at 429 *per* James L.J.).

Further they should be directed that the accused is not to be found guilty merely because he intentionally or recklessly used force which they consider to have been excessive. They ought not to convict him unless they are satisfied that the degree of force used was plainly more than was called for by the circumstances as he believed them to be and, provided he believed the circumstances called for the degree of force used, he is not to be convicted even if his belief was unreasonable.

In this case the learned judge gave no direction to the jury that the prosecution, to establish an assault, had to prove that the appellant intentionally or recklessly applied excessive force in seeking to evict the deceased. On the contrary the jury were simply left to say what in the circumstances they considered was reasonable force and directed that if they concluded that what was done involved an unnecessary and unreasonable degree of force they then only had to consider whether the act of unlawful and unnecessary force actually caused the deceased to fall down the steps. And again later:

"So you are left with the situation: how did he meet his death and are you sure that it was the accused's conduct which directly produced it by his unlawful act."

We are of the opinion that the directions to the jury in the circumstances of this case were inadequate to support a verdict of guilty of manslaughter. The appellant had given clear evidence that he only intended to use sufficient force to remove the deceased from the bar, an act he was lawfully entitled to do. It was not contended, nor were submissions made to the jury on the basis that he acted recklessly. The direction to the jury was based on the assertion that it was sufficient if they found the force used by the appellant excessive in the circumstances. The learned judge seems to have assumed that this was sufficient to prove that what the appellant did amounted to an assault.

Question

Why was no reference made in *Scarlett* to the cases of *Palmer* and *McInnes* either in the course of argument or in the judgment? Is it that they were considered irrelevant?

Self-defence and defence of property

In the large majority of cases where the accused acts to defend himself or his property, the would-be assailant will be attempting to commit a crime. Thus the situation will fall within the ambit of section 3 of the Criminal Law Act 1967. It is clear, however, that the law still recognises the existence of the common law defences of self-defence and defence of property and from time to time (as in *Bird* below) the court will be asked to decide whether any of the special rules relating to those defences still apply. On the whole, however, the courts are likely to try to unify all these varying defences under the principles governing section 3.

R. v. Bird

[1985] 2 All E.R. 513 (C.A.)

[B. was charged with unlawful wounding contrary to section 20 of the Offences Against the Person Act 1861. On appeal against conviction she argued that the judge was in error in directing the jury that self-defence could only be relied upon if the accused had demonstrated by her action that she did not want to fight. In the defence of self-defence at common law it was generally agreed that there was a duty to retreat first. This was stated in its modern form by Widgery L.J. in *Julien* (1969):

"The third point taken by counsel for the appellant is that the learned deputy chairman was wrong in directing the jury that before the appellant could use force in self-defence he was required to retreat. The submission here is that the obligation to retreat before using force in self-defence is an obligation which only arises in homicide cases. As the court understands it, it is submitted that if the injury results in death then the accused cannot set up self-defence except on the basis that he had retreated before he resorted to violence. On the other hand, it is said that where the injury does not result in death (as in the present case) the obligation to retreat does not arise. The sturdy submission is made that an Englishman is not bound to run away when threatened, but can stand his ground and defend himslf where he is. In support of this submission no authority is quoted, save that counsel for the appellant has been at considerable length and diligence to look at the textbooks on the subject, and has demonstrated to us that the textbooks in the main do not say that a preliminary retreat is a necessary prerequisite to the use of force in self-defence. Equally, it must be said that the textbooks do not state the contrary either; and it is, of course, well known to us all that for very many years it has been common form for judges directing juries where the issue of self-defence is raised in any case (be it a homicide case or not) that the duty to retreat arises. It is not, as we understand it, the law that a person threatened must take to his heels and run in the dramatic way suggested by counsel for the appellant; but what is necessary is that he should demonstrate by his actions that he does not want to fight. He must demonstrate that he is prepared to temporise and disengage and perhaps to make some physical withdrawal; and to the extent that that is necessary as a feature of the justification of self-defence, it is true, in our opinion, whether the charge is a homicide charge or something less serious. Accordingly, we reject counsel for the appellant's third submission."]

Lord Lane C.J. The matter is dealt with accurately and helpfully in Smith and Hogan *Criminal Law* (5th ed., 1983) p. 327 as follows:

"There were formerly technical rules about the duty to retreat before using force, or at least fatal force. This is now simply a factor to be taken into account in deciding whether it was necessary to use force, and whether the force was reasonable. If the only reasonable course is to retreat, then it would appear that to stand and fight must be to use unreasonable force. There is, however, no rule of law that a person attacked is bound to run away if he can; but it has been said that—'. . . what is necessary is that he should demonstrate by his actions that he does not want to fight. He must demonstrate that he is prepared to temporise and disengage and perhaps to make some physical withdrawal.' It is submitted that it goes too far to say that action of this kind is *necessary*. It is scarcely consistent with the rule that it is permissible to use force, not merely to counter an actual attack, but to ward off an attack honestly and reasonably believed to be imminent. A demonstration by D. [the defendant] at the time that he did not want to fight is, no doubt, the best evidence that he was acting reasonably and in good faith in self-defence; but it is no more than that. A person may in some circumstances so act without temporising, disengaging or withdrawing; and he should have a good defence."

We respectfully agree with that passage. If the defendant is proved to have been attacking or retaliating or revenging himself, then he was not truly acting in self-defence. Evidence that the defendant tried to retreat or tried to call off the fight may be a cast-iron method of casting doubt on the suggestion that he was the attacker or retaliator or the person trying to revenge himself. But it is not by any means the only method of doing that.

It seems to us therefore that in this case the trial judge (we hasten to add through no fault of his own), by using the word "necessary" as he did in the passages in the summing-up to which we have referred, put too high an obligation on the appellant.

Appeal allowed.

5. INFANCY

Children under 10 are conclusively presumed incapable of committing crimes. Children over 9, but under 14 were also presumed incapable of committing crimes, but here the presumption was rebuttable by proof that the child had a mischievous discretion, but now see *C (A Minor)* v. *D.P.P.* [1994] *The Times*, March 30 (D.C.), below.

C (A Minor) v. D.P.P.

(1994) Times L.R. March 30 (D.C.)

Lord Justice Mann, giving the judgment of the court, said that the appellant at the age of 12 was presumed to be *doli incapax* [incapable of committing a crime] until that presumption was rebutted by positive proof adduced by the prosecution that in fact he knew what he did was seriously wrong.

The justices had found that he had known that what he had done was seriously wrong. The damage to the motorcycle had been substantial and the appellant and his accomplice had run from the police.

The justices had drawn the inference from those two facts that he knew that he was in serious trouble because he had done something seriously wrong and had therefore convicted him.

It was submitted for the appellant that the justices were not entitled to draw such an inference. The act of running away was merely equivocal, as consistent with an appreciation of what he had done was naughty as with knowledge that it was seriously wrong. The damage to the motorcycle could not carry the matter any further.

The submission of the prosecution amounted to the proposition that the presumption might be rebutted by the very acts constituted by the alleged offence without any supervening evidence from the prosecution that the child appreciated that what he did was seriously wrong.

His Lordship said that the case law demonstrated that if the presumption were to be rebutted there had to be clear positive evidence that the defendant knew his act was seriously wrong not consisting merely in the evidence of the acts amounting to the offence itself.

Whatever had been the position in an earlier age when there was no system of universal compulsory education and when children did not grow up as quickly as they did nowadays, the presumption at the present time was a serious disservice to the law.

It meant that a child over 10 who committed an act of obvious dishonesty or even grave violence was to be acquitted unless the prosecution specifically proved by discrete evidence that he understood the obliquity of what he was doing.

Such an approach was unreal and contrary to common sense.

Aside from anything else, there would be cases where evidence of the kind required could not be obtained but, quite apart from pragmatic considerations, the presumption was in principle objectionable.

It was no part of the general law that a defendant should be proved to appreciate that his act was seriously wrong: that additional requirement where the presumption applied was out of step with the general law.

The requirement was, furthermore, conceptually obscure. The cases indicated that the presumption might be rebutted by proof that the child was of normal capacity for his age. If that was right the underlying premise was that a child of average or normal development was in fact taken to be *doli capax*, but the effect of the presumption was then that a defendant under 14 was assumed to possess subnormal mental capacity and for that reason be *doli incapax*. There could be no respectable justification for such a bizarre state of affairs.

The rule was also divisive because it attached criminal consequences to the acts of children coming from what used to be called good homes more readily than to the acts of others. It was perverse because it tended to absolve from criminal responsibility the very children most likely to commit criminal acts.

The youngster whose understanding of the difference between right and wrong was fragile or non-existent was more likely to get involved in criminal activity, yet the outdated and unprincipled presumption was tailored to secure his acquittal.

The prosecution were in effect required to prove as a condition of his guilt that he was morally responsible; but it was because he was morally irresponsible that he had commited the crime in the first place.

It was not surprising that the presumption took root in an era when the criminal law was altogether more draconian but the philosophy of criminal punishment had obviously changed out of all recognition since those days. The presumption had no utility whatever in the present era and ought to go.

The question was whether the court had authority to abolish it. Three arguments might be advanced to persuade the court that it ought not, or could not, abolish the rule:

1.   The court's decision would have retroactive effect since the law had not yet developed a practice of prospective rulings. Accordingly by holding that the presumption was no longer part of the criminal jurisprudence the court should be changing the legal rules effective at the time of the appellant's actual or putative crime and doing so retrospectively.

There would be manifest injustice were the court to extend the ambit of a criminal offence beyond its earlier limits and so pronounce a defendant guilty whose relevant actions were taken at a time when the definition of the offence in question did not touch them.

This was not such a case. There was no conceivable injustice to the appellant if the court consigned the presumption to legal history.

2.   The presumption was of such long standing that it should only be changed by Parliament, or at least a decision by the House of Lords.

Antiquity of itself conferred no virtue upon the legal *status quo*. The common law was not a system of rigid rules but of principles whose application might alter over time and should be renewed by succeeding generations of judges. In the present case, the conditions under which the presumption was developed in the earlier law now had no application.

3. The court was bound by the doctrine of precedent to adhere to the presumption.

The rules of *stare decisis* provided a crucial counterpoint to the law's capacity for change: apparently established principles were not to be altered save through the measured deliberation of a hierarchical system.

Although first instance courts did not, on the whole, effect root and branch changes to legal principle, the Divisional Court was in a peculiar position being a first instance court but an appellate court for cases like the present: and in such cases there was no appeal from its decisions save to the House of Lords.

All the cases cited in argument save two were either in the Divisional Court or at trial at first instance. It was clear on authority that the Divisional Court had power to depart from its own previous decisions.

All earlier decisions proceeded on the unargued premise that the presumption now in question was undoubtedly part of the fabric of English criminal law. The discard it therefore did not involve any disagreement with the express reasoning in those cases.

There was not the least impediment, in his Lordship's judgment, upon departing from the earlier Divisional Court authorities so far as they upheld the existence of the presumption: to do so was no affront to any principle of judicial comity, far less the doctrine of precedent.

The two cases in the Court of Appeal which were cited in argument proceeded upon the same unargued premise. That being so, the court was entitled to depart from the premise which lay behind the Court of Appeal's two decisions. To do so did not involve any departure from any adjudication which that court was required to make upon an issue in dispute before it.

In the circumstances, the presumption relied upon by the appellant was no longer part of the law of England and the appeal would therefore be dismissed.

Chapter 5

Attempts

1. THE ACTUS REUS OF ATTEMPTS

Attorney-General's Reference (No. 1 of 1992)

(1993) 96 Cr.App.R. 298

Following an evening's drinking, P walked home with D, a youth she had been friendly with for several years. On the way home he pulled her behind a hedge and lay full length on top of her. He threatened her with a knife if she did not remain quiet and she became unconscious. A local resident who had heard a disturbance, called the police. As the police arrived they heard screams and crying. They found P on her back, her breasts exposed and her skirt pulled up to her waist. Her knickers were later found in nearby undergrowth. The police said that they saw D kneeling near to the girl, though D said he was at least six feet away. His trousers were around his ankles and one of the officers noticed that his penis was not erect. Medical evidence disclosed recent bruising on the shaft of his penis which might indicate recent attempts to have intercourse and which could correspond with bruising found on P. D was charged with attempted rape.

Lord Taylor L.C. It is convenient at this point to set out the relevant provisions of the Criminal Attempts Act 1981. Section 1(1) provides as follows:

> "If, with intent to commit an offence to which this section applies, a person does an act which is more than merely preparatory to the commission of the offence, he is guilty of attempting to commit the offence."

Section 4(3) provides:

> "Where, in proceedings against a person for an offence under section 1 above, there is evidence sufficient in law to

support a finding that he did an act falling within subsection (1) of that section, the question whether or not his act fell within that subsection is a question of fact."

In his ruling the learned judge referred to those provisions of the Act. He also referred to the decisions of this Court in *Gullefer* (1990) 91 Cr.App.R. 356, [1990] 3 All E.R. 882 and *Jones (Kenneth)* (1990) 91 Cr.App.R. 351, [1990] 3 All E.R. 886, in which it was held that the words of the Act should be given their ordinary and natural meaning. The learned judge then reviewed the facts which have already been outlined, and concluded that there was evidence from which the jury could conclude that the respondent had done acts more than merely preparatory to the commission of the offence of rape. He said:

"That is evidence, in my judgment, from which the jury being properly directed can come to the conclusion that the defendant intended to have sexual intercourse with his victim at the very least whether she consented or not. Secondly, having regard also to the additional facts that the girl had been heard to scream and or moan in the moments before she was dragged inside the fence, she was as a matter of fact not consenting to what was happening to her at that time. Thirdly, there is evidence, in my judgment, that the defendant had done acts more than merely preparatory to the commission of the offence."

The learned judge then referred to a passage from the judgment of Lord Lane C.J. in *Gullefer*, including this sentence: (at pp. 358 and 885e):

"Was the appellant still in the stage of preparation to commit the substantive offence or was there a basis of fact which would entitle the jury to say that he had embarked on the [offence] itself?"

Finally the learned judge said this:

" ... I am satisfied that whether or not the defendant's penis was ever erect or even semi-erect, he had embarked upon the preparation of, he had embarked upon the commission of the offence itself but had not gone beyond the stage of attempt."

The case then proceeded. The respondent gave evidence and Mr Lakin for the defence was nearing the end of his final speech, when the learned judge intervened and caused the jury to retire. The judge then indicated that he had changed his mind and concluded that his earlier ruling was incorrect. The jury were then brought back to court and the learned judge directed them as follows:

> "The position is that I have ruled as a matter of law that what the prosecution can prove cannot in law amount to an attempted rape because, it seems to me, it is essential that for that offence to be proved, there must be some evidence of attempt, actual physical attempt at penetration. Of that there is no evidence."

Mr. Temple, on behalf of the Attorney-General, submits to us that the learned judge was correct in his first ruling and that the test he stated to the jury in directing them to acquit was wrong. That test, it is submitted, sought to resurrect one or two rival tests developed in the common law before the 1981 Act.

In *Jones*, and again in *Campbell* (1991) 93 Cr.App.R. 350, this Court made it clear that the words of the Act were to be applied in their plain and natural meaning, as the learned judge reminded himself in his first ruling. The words are not be interpreted so as to re-introduce either of the earlier common law tests. Indeed one of the objects of the Act was to resolve the uncertainty those tests created.

One of those tests was the so-called "last act" test, stated in *Eagleton* (1855) Dears C.C. 515, 169 E.R. 826, *i.e.* has the defendant with intent to commit the full offence, done the last act in his power towards committing that offence, or, as Lord Diplock put it in *D.P.P.* v. *Stonehouse* (1977) 65 Cr.App.R. 192, [1978] A.C. 55, has he "crossed the Rubicon and burnt his boats." The other test, derived from *Stephen's of the Criminal Law*, was, did the act done with the intent to commit the full offence form part of a series of acts which would constitute its actual commission if not interrupted.

In *Gullefer* Lord Lane C.J., after referring to those two approaches, said this (at pp. 358, 359 and 885e):

> "It seems to us that the words of the Act of 1981 seek to steer a midway course. They do not provide, as they might have done, that the *Eagleton* test is to be followed, or that, as Lord Diplock suggested, the defendant must have reached a point from which it was impossible for him to retreat before the *actus reus* of an attempt is proved. On the other hand the words give perhaps as clear a guidance as is possible in the circumstances on the point of time at which *Stephen's* 'series of acts' begin. It begins when the merely

preparatory acts come to an end and the defendant embarks upon the crime proper. When that is will depend of course upon the facts in any particular case."

Mr. Temple submits that here the test applied by the learned judge amounted to resurrecting the *Eagleton* test. It would be equivalent in the case of a charge of attempted murder by the use of a gun to saying that unless the trigger of the gun was actually pulled, there was insufficient evidence to go to the jury on that charge.

In our judgment the learned judge was correct in the ruling which he gave at first and fell into error in reconsidering it at the end of the case.

It is not, in our judgment, necessary, in order to raise to prima facie case of attempted rape, to prove that the defendant with the requisite intent had necessarily gone as far as to attempt physical penetration of the vagina. It is sufficient if there is evidence from which the intent can be inferred and there are proved acts which a jury could properly regard as more than merely preparatory to the commission of the offence. For example, and merely as an example, in the present case the evidence of the young woman's distress, of the state of her clothing, and the position in which she was seen, together with the respondent's acts of dragging her up the steps, lowering his trousers and interfering with her private parts, and his answers to the police, left it open to a jury to conclude that the respondent had the necessary intent and had done acts which were more than merely preparatory. In short that he had embarked on committing the offence itself.

Opinion accordingly.

Note

Note recent cases show how difficult it is to draw the line between acts which are merely preparatory to the commission of an offence and acts which constitute criminal attempts.

Gullefer (1987). G had placed a bet on a dog race. When he realised that his dog would not win, he ran on to the race track in order to distract the dogs. His intention was to cause the race stewards to declare the race null and void and so entitle those who had bet on the race to claim back their stakes. In fact the stewards did not declare the race to be null and void. G was charged with attempted theft. The Court of Appeal held that there was no evidence on which a jury could

find he was attemting to steal. There was much more he
needed to do. He was simply making preparations.

Jones (1990). J's mistress had left him in favour of
another man, F. J purchased several guns and shortened the
barrel of one. He went to where he knew he would find F
and got into F's car with him. He then pulled out the gun
with the shortened barrel and pointed it at F at close range. F
managed to get the gun away from J and threw it out of the
car. J was charged with attempted murder and argued that
there were still three things he had to do; (i) remove the
safety catch; (ii) put his finger on the trigger; (iii) pull the
trigger. The Court of Appeal, however, held there was
evidence upon which a jury could find J was attempting to
kill F.

Campbell (1991).   The police had received a tip that a post
office was to be robbed. They kept the post office under
surveillance and observed C acting suspiciously. He eventually walked towards the entrance and put his hand in his
pocket where the police thought he had a heavy object. They
arrested him outside the post office and he was charged with
attempted robbery. When searched he was found to be
carrying an imitation pistol. The Court of Appeal held that he
was still in the act of preparing to commit the crime of
robbery; he was not, as yet, on the job since he had not even
entered the building.

2.   MENS REA

R. v. Khan and Others

(1990) 91 Cr.App.R. 29

[Khan and several others were charged with rape and attempted rape of a
sixteen year old girl. In relation to the *mens rea* of rape and attempted rape
the judge gave the following direction to the jury. (The direction in respect of
rape was not challenged on appeal.)]

"Members of the jury, a man commits rape if he has
unlawful sexual intercourse with a woman who at the time
of the intercourse does not consent to it and also at that

time he knows that she does not consent to the intercourse, or is reckless as to whether she consents to it or not. Therefore, it must first be proved in this case that Miss Varndell did not in fact consent. If she did, or if in your view she may have done in relation to any of these defendants you may acquit them without considering the position further. If, however, you decide that she did not in fact consent, the next question is, did the defendant in question know that she was not consenting? If you are unsure about that go on to ask whether he was reckless as to whether the girl was consenting or not, and reckless in this context could be simply defined as it has been throughout the case as the state of mind of the particular defendant, that he could not care less either way whether she consented or not. If you are sure that was his state of mind then he was behaving recklessly and he would be guilty of the offence."

In relation to attempted rape he said:

"Now I turn to counts three, five, nine and eleven and again members of the jury count three is put quite starkly, and this means you are concerned with attempted rape. An attempt to commit a criminal offence is in law itself a crime. I have explained what rape amounts to. The question for you where attempted rape is the charge is to ask whether the defendant in question did more than merely prepare to commit the crime, but took a positive step that led directly to advance his objective. I should say, it matters not that he was not in the end capable of carrying out the final act. Thus, a lack of erection would not be fatal for a charge of attempted rape provided the defendant made a real effort to effect the crime and was only prevented by lack of erection that would amount to it in law. In this case Miss Varndell says each of the accused, except Mr Faiz, jabbed his erect penis against her vaginal area. If that is so, and it is only disputed in the case of Mr Faiz, you may think the defendant could not have done more to achieve penetration. Only the final act of inserting the penis remained to be done. It is your decision but in this case you may think that there was an attempt to have sexual intercourse with her in the legal sense and it has not I think really been argued to the contrary.

... As in the case of rape the principles relevant to consent apply in exactly the same way in attempted rape. I do not suppose you need me to go through it again. Apply the same principles as to rape."

On appeal against conviction.

Russell L.J. It is these last three sentences that counsel submits amount to a material misdirection, for it is argued that recklessness as a state of mind on the part of the offender has no place in the offence of attempted rape.

We remind ourselves first of the statutory definition of rape to be found in section 1(1) of the Sexual Offences (Amendment) Act 1976:

"1(1) For the purposes of section 1 of the Sexual Offences Act 1956 (which relates to rape) a man commits rape if—

(a) he has unlawful sexual intercourse with a woman who at the time of the intercourse does not consent to it; and

(b) at that time he knows that she does not consent to the intercourse or he is reckless as to whether she consents to it; ..."

Section 1(1) of the Criminal Attempts Act 1981 created a new statutory offence as follows.

"If with intent to commit an offence to which this section applies a person does an act which is more than prepatory to the commission of the offence his is guilty of attempting to commit the offence."

This section applies to rape.

The impact of the words of section 1 of the 1981 Act and in particular the words "with intent to committ an offence" has been the subject matter of much debate amongst distinguished academic writers. We were reffered to and we have read and considered an article by Professor Glanville Williams entitled "The Problem of Reckless Attempts" 1983 C.L.R. 365. The argument there advances is that recklessness can exist within the concept of attempt and support is derived from *R. v. Pigg* [1982] 2 All E.R. 591, [1982] 1 W.L.R. 762 albeit that authority was concerned with the law prior to the Criminal Attempts Act 1981. This approach also receives approval from Smith and Hogan Criminal Law 6th edition at pages 287 to 289.

Contrary views, however, have been expressed by Professor Griew and Mr Richard Buxton Q.C. who have both contended that the words "with intent to commit an offence" involve an intent as to every element constituting the crime.

Finally we have had regard to the observations of Mustill L.J. giving the judgment of the Court of Appeal Criminal Division in *R. v. Millard and Vernon* [1987] Crim L.R. 393. That was a case involving a charge of attempting to damage property, the Particulars of Offence reading:

"Gary Mann Millard and Michael Elliot Vernon, on 11th May 1985, without lawful excuse, attempted to damage a wooden wall at the Leeds Road Football Stand belonging to Huddersfield Town Association Football Club, intending to damage the said wall or being reckless as to whether the said would be damaged."

Mustill L.J. said:

"The appellants' case is simple. They submit that in ordinary speech the essence of an attempt is a desire to bring about a particular result, coupled with steps towards that end. The essence of recklessness is either indifference to a known risk or (in some circumstances) failure to advert to an obvious risk. The two states of mind cannot co-exist. Section 1(1) of the Criminal Attempts Act 1981 expressly demands that a person shall have an intent to commit an offence if he is to be guilty of an attempt to commit that offence. The word 'intent' may, it is true, have a specialised meaning in some contexts. But even if this can properly be attributed to the word where it is used in section 1(1) there is no warrant for reading it as embracing recklessness, nor for reading into it whatever lesser degree of *mens rea* will suffice for the particular substantive offence in question. For an attempt nothing but conscious volition will do. Accordingly that part of the particulars of offence which referred to recklessness was meaningless, and the parts of the direction which involved a definition of recklessness, and an implied invitation to convict if the jury found the appellants to have acted recklessly, were misleading. There was thus, so it was contended, a risk that the jury convicted on the wrong basis and the verdict cannot safely be allowed to stand.

At the conclusion of the argument it appeared to us that this argument was logically sound and that it was borne out by the authorities cited to us, especially *R.* v. *Whybrow* (1951) 35 Cr.App.R. 141, *Cunliffe* v. *Goodman* (1950) 2 K.B. 237, 253 and *Mohan* (1976) Q.B. 1, and that it was not inconsistent with anything in *Hyam* v. *Director of Public Prosecutions* (1975) A.C. 55. Our attention had however been drawn to a difference of opinion between commentators about the relationship between the *mens rea* in an attempt and the ingredients of the substantive offence, and we therefore reserved judgment so as to consider whether the question was not perhaps more difficult than it seemed.

In the event we have come to the conclusion that there does exist a problem in this field, and that it is by no means easy to solve; but also that it need not be solved for the purpose of deciding the present appeal.

In our judgment two different situations must be distinguished. The first exists where the substantive offence consists simply of the act which constitutes the *actus reus* (which for present purposes we shall call the 'result') coupled with some element of volition, which may or may not amount to a full intent. Here the only question is whether the 'intent' to bring about the result called for by section 1(1) is to be watered down to such a degree, if any, as to make it correspond with the *mens rea* of the substantive offence.

The second situation is more complicated. It exists where the substantive offence does not consist of one result and one *mens rea*, but rather involves not only the underlying intention to produce the result, but another state of mind directed to some circumstance or act which the prosecution must also establish in addition to proving the result.

The problem may be illustrated by reference to the offence of attempted rape. As regards the substantive offence the 'result' takes the shape of sexual intercourse with a woman. But the offence is not established without proof of an additional circumstance (namely that the woman did not consent), and a state of mind relative to that circumstance (namely that the defendant knew she did not consent, or was reckless as to whether she consented).

When one turns to the offence of attempted rape, one thing is obvious, that the result, namely the act of sexual intercourse, must be intended in the full sense. Also obvious is the fact that proof of an intention to have intercourse with a woman, together with an act towards that end, is not enough: the offence must involve proof of something about the woman's consent, and something about the defendant's state of mind in relation to that consent.

The problem is to decide precisely what that something is. Must the prosecution prove not only that the defendant intended the act, but also that he intended it to be nonconsensual? Or should the jury be directed to consider two different states of mind, intent as to the act and recklessness as to the circumstances? Here the commentators differ: contrast Smith and Hogan, Criminal Law, 5th Edition, pages 255 *et seq.*, with a note on the Act by Professor Griew in Current Law Statutes 1981."

We must now grapple with the very problem that Mustill L.J. identifies in the last paragraph of the passage cited.

In our judgment an acceptable analysis of the offence of rape is as follows:

(1) the intention of the offender is to have sexual intercourse with a woman;

(2) the offence is committed if, but only if, the circumstances are that:
(a) the woman does not consent; AND
(b) the defendant knows that she is not consenting or is reckless as to whether she consents.

Precisely the same analysis can be made of the offence of attempted rape:

(1) the intention of the offender is to have sexual intercourse with a woman;
(2) the offence is committed if, but only if, the circumstances are that:
(a) the woman does not consent; AND
(b) the defendant knows that she is not consenting or is reckless as to whether she consents.

The only difference between the two offences is that in rape sexual intercourse takes place, whereas in attempted rape it does not, although there has to be some act which is more than preparatory to sexual intercourse. Considered in that way, the intent of the defendant is precisely the same in rape and in attempted rape and the *mens rea* is identical, namely, an intention to have intercourse plus a knowledge of or recklessness as to the woman's absence of consent. No question of attempting to achieve a reckless state of mind arises; the attempt relates to the physical activity; the mental state of the defendant is the same. A man does not recklessly have sexual intercourse, nor does he recklessly attempt it. Recklessness in rape and attempted rape arises not in relation to the physical act of the accused but only in his state of mind when engaged in the activity of having or attempting to have sexual intercourse.

If this is the true analysis, as we believe it is, the attempt does not require any different intention on the part of the accused from that for the full offence of rape. We believe this to be a desirable result which in the instant case did not require the jury to be burdened with different directions as to the accused's state of mind, dependent upon whether the individual achieved or failed to achieve sexual intercourse.

We recognise, of course, that our reasoning cannot apply to all offences and all attempts. Where, for example, as in causing death by reckless driving or reckless arson, no state of mind other than recklessness is involved in the offence, there can be no attempt to commit it.

In our judgment, however, the words "with intent to commit an offence" to be found in section 1 of the 1981 Act mean, when applied to rape, "with intent to have sexual intercourse with a woman in circumstances where she does not consent and the defendant knows or could not care less about her absence of consent". The only "intent", giving that word its natural and ordinary meaning, of the rapist is to have sexual intercourse. He commits the offence because of the circumstances in which he manifests that intent,—*i.e.* when the woman is not consenting and he either knows it or could not care less about the absence of consent.

Accordingly we take the view that in relation to the four appellants the judge was right to give the directions that he did when inviting the jury to consider the charges of attempted rape.

Attorney-General's Reference (No. 3 of 1992)

[1994] 1 W.L.R. 409 (C.A.)

Shiemann J.   The point of law which has been referred to us was formulated as follows:

"Whether on a charge of attempted arson in the aggravated form contemplated by section 1(2) of the Criminal Damage Act 1971, in addition to establishing a specific intent to cause damage by fire, it is sufficient to prove that the defendant was reckless as to whether life would thereby be endangered."

Summary of the Relevant Facts

The acquittals which have given rise to this reference had the following background according to the prosecution evidence. Following previous attacks upon their property the complainants maintained a night-time watch over their premises from a motor car (a Ford Granda). In the early hours of the morning the defendants came upon the scene in a vehicle. Inside this car (a Sierra) was a milk crate containing a number of petrol bombs, matches, a petrol can and some rags. As the Sierra approached the complainants (four inside their car and two persons on the pavement talking to them) a lighted petrol bomb was thrown towards them from the Sierra. The Crown's case was that it was thrown at the Granada and it occupants. The petrol bomb in fact passed over the top of the Granada and smashed against the garden wall of a house a pavement's width away from the car. The Sierra accelerated away but crashed, and the defendants were arrested.

At the trial count 1 of the indictment alleged attempted aggravated arson, specifying in the particulars of offence, *inter alia*, an intent to endanger life. Count 2 alleged attempted aggravated arson, specifying in the particulars of offence, *inter alia*, recklessness as to whether life would be endangered. At the conclusion of the Crown's case the learned judge ruled that there was no evidence upon which the jury could find the necessary intent to endanger life required in count 1, and accordingly directed the jury to return "not guilty" verdicts in respect of that count. This reference is not concerned with that ruling, but with her directing an acquittal in relation to count 2. In essence her reasoning was that:

1. There can be no conviction of an attempt to commit an offence unless the defendant intends to commit that offence;
2. The evidence could not support an allegation that the defendants intended by the destruction of the car to endanger the life of its occupants, or the bystanders;
3. It is impossible to intend to be reckless as to whether the life of another would be endangered by damage to property and therefore
4. It is impossible in law to convict of an attempt to commit an aggravated arson if all that can be proved is that the defendant intended to damage property being reckless as to whether the life of another would be endangered by such damage.

The Substantive Offences

...

Schiemann J. then set out the statutory provisions relating to both criminal damage and aggravated criminal damage (see below, p. 401). He continued:

There are three further preliminary matters which need to be mentioned in this context as background, although none is contentious. First, it is common ground that the recklessness here referred to is what has become known as *Caldwell* [1982] A.C. 341 recklessness (see above, p. 133).

The second preliminary matter is this. It is clear that the prosecution are required to prove that the danger to life resulted from the destruction of or damage to property; it is not sufficient for the prosecution to prove that it resulted from the act of the defendant which caused the destruction or damage (*R. v. Steer* [1988] 1 A.C. 111; [1987] 2 All E.R. 833, H.L.).

The third preliminary matter is that, although in the present reference the question is posed in relation to arson, it has not been submitted that the presence or absence of fire makes any difference to the answer to the question posed which applies to any form of attempted criminal damage. So we omit any further reference to the element of fire in this judgment.

With those three preliminary matters out of the way, we turn to consider what again is uncontentious, namely what the prosecution need to prove in each case in order to secure a conviction for the completed offence of arson and aggravated arson.

So far as the completed single offence is concerned, the prosecution needs to prove:

1. Property belonging to another was damaged by the defendant.
2. The state of mind of the defendant was one of the following:

(a) He intended to damage such property

or

(b) He was reckless as to whether any such property would be damaged.

In the case of the completed aggravated offence the prosecution needs to prove:

1. The defendant in fact damaged property, whether belonging to himself or another;
2. That the state of mind of the defendant was one of the following:

(a) He intended to damage property, and intended by the damage to endanger the life of another

or

(b) He intended to damage property and was reckless as to whether the life of another would be thereby endangered

or

(c) He was reckless as to whether any property would be damaged and was reckless as to whether the life of another would be thereby endangered.

It is to be noted that the property referred to under 1. (to which we shall hereafter refer as the first named property) is not necessarily the same property as that referred to in 2. (to which we shall refer as the second named property), although it normally will be. Thus a man who—

1. owns a crane from which is suspended a heavy object and

2. cuts the rope (the first named property) which holds the object with the result that
3. The object falls and hits the roof of a passing car (the second named property) which roof
4. collapses killing the driver—

would be guilty if it could be shown that he damaged the rope, was reckless as to whether this would damage the car, and was reckless as to whether the life of the driver of the car would be endangered by the damage to the car.

All the foregoing is common ground. The problem which has given rise to this reference relates to an attempt to commit the aggravated offence in circumstances where the first named property is the same as the second named property—in the instant case a car. It amounts to this: whether, if the state of mind of the defendant was that postulated in 2(b) above, namely that he intended to damage property and was reckless as to whether the life of another would thereby be endangered, and whilst in that state of mind he did an act which was more than merely preparatory to the offence, he is guilty of attempting to commit that offence.

Schiemann J. set out the provisions of Section 1 of the Criminal Attempts Act 1981 and continued ...

Turning from the general to the particular, it is covenient to consider, first, attempting to commit the simple offence, which causes no problem, and then to pass on to attempting to commit the aggravated offence, which is what has given rise to this reference.

So far as attempting to commit the simple offence is concerned, in order to convict on such a charge it must be proved that the defendant—

(a) did an act which was more than merely preparatory to the commission of the offence

and

(b) he did an act intending to damage any property belonging to another.

One way of analysing the situation is to say that a defendant, in order to be guilty of an attempt, must be in one of the states of mind required for the commission of the full offence, and did his best, as far as he could, to supply what was missing from the completion of the offence. It is policy of the law that such people should be punished notwithstanding that in fact the intentions of such a defendant have not be fulfilled.

If the facts are that, although the defendant had one of the appropriate states of mind required for the complete offence, but the physical element required for the commission of the complete offence is missing, the defendant is not to be convicted unless it can be shown that he intended to supply that physical element. This was the state of affairs in *Millard & Vernon* (1987) C.L.R. 759, of which we have seen the transcript. There the defendants were convicted of attempting to damage property. The particulars of the offence were that they "attempted to damage a wooden wall at the ... stadium ... intending to damage the ... wall or being reckless as to whether the ... wall damaged." The trial judge directed the jury that recklessness was sufficient. Mustill L.J., delivering the judgment of the Court of Appeal, stated that:

"The result which would have been achieved if the offence had been taken to fruitition was damage to the stand ... the prosecution had to show ... that it was this state of affairs which each appellant had decided, so far as in him lay, to bring about."

In consequence, mere recklessness was not sufficient and the convictions were quashed.

We turn finally to the attempt to commit the aggravated offence. In the present case, what was missing to prevent a conviction for the completed offence was damage to the property referred to in the opening lines of section 1(2) of the 1981 Act, what in the example of a crane, which we gave earlier in this judgment, we referred to as "the first named property." Such damage is essential for the completed offence. If a defendant does not intend to cause such damage he cannot intend to commit the completed offence. At worst he is reckless as to whether the offence is committed. The law of attempt is concerned with those who are intending to commit crimes. If that intent cannot be shown, then there can be no conviction.

However, the crime here consisted of doing certain acts in a certain state of mind in circumstances where the first named property and the second named property were the same, in short where the danger to life arose from the damage to the property which the defendant intended to damage. The substantive crime is committed if the defendant damaged property in a state of mind where he was reckless as to whether the life of another would thereby be endangered. We see no reason why there should not be a conviction for attempt if the prosecution can show that he, in that state of mind, intended to damage the property by throwing a bomb at it. One analysis of this situation is to say that although the defendant was in an appropriate state of mind to render him guilty of the completed offence the prosecution had not proved the physical element of the completed offence, and therefore he is not guilty of the completed offence. If, on a charge of attempting to commit the offence, the prosecution can show not only the state of mind required for the completed offence but also that the defendant intended to supply the missing physical element of the completed offence, that suffices for a conviction. That can not be done merely by the prosecution showing him to be reckless. The defendant must intend to damage property, but there is no need for a graver mental state than is required for the full offence.

The learned trial judge in the present case, however, went further than this, and held that not merely must the defendant intend to supply all that was missing from the completed offence—namely, damage to the first named property—but also that recklessness as to the consequences of such damage for the lives of others was not enough to secure a conviction for attempt, although it was sufficient for the completed offence. She held that before a defendant could be convicted of attempting to commit the offence it had to be shown that he intended that the lives of others should be endangered by the damage which he intended.

She gave no policy for so holding, and there is no case which bound her so to hold. The most nearly relevant case is *R. v. Khan* [1990] 2 All E.R. 783, 91 Cr.App.R. 29. There the defendant was charged with attempted rape. He did not in fact penetrate the girl, but he did acts which were more than merely preparatory. The jury must have found that the girl did not in fact consent to sexual intercourse. The trial judge directed the jury that it sufficed if either the defendant knew the girl was not consenting or if he was reckless as to whether she consented or not. He was convicted and appealed, arguing that it was impossible to have an attempted reckless rape. This submission was rejected by the Court (see above, p. 285).

An attempt was made in argument to suggest that *Khan* was wrongly decided. No policy reasons were advanced for that view, and we do not share it. The result is one which accords with common sense, and does no violence to the words of the statute.

What was missing in *Khan* was the act of sexual intercourse, without which the offence was not complete. What was missing in the present case was damage to the first named property, without which the offence was not complete. The mental state of the defendant in each case contained everything which was required to render him guilty of the full offence. In order to succeed in a prosecution for attempt, it must be shown that the defendant intended to achieve that which was missing from the full offence. Unless that is shown, the prosecution have not proved that the defendant intended to commit the offence. Thus in *Khan* the prosecution had to show an intention to have sexual intercourse, and the remaining state of mind required for the offence of rape. In the present case, the prosecution had to show an intention to damage the first named property, and the remaining state of mind required for the offence of aggravated arson.

The learned judge in the instant case was faced, as we have been faced, not only with citations of views held by the Law Commission at one time on what should be the law of attempt, but also with various articles in legal journals and books commenting on those views. It is right to say that at one time it was proposed that intention should be required as to all the elements of an offence, thus making it impossible to secure a conviction of attempt in circumstances such as the present. However, this proposal has not prevailed, and has been overtaken by Khan, and a formulation of the draft code which does not incorporate the proposal.

While the learned judge in the instant case opined that Khan was distinguishable she did not indicate any policy reasons for distinguishing it. We see none, and none have been submitted to us directly.

We now remind ourselves of the precise question posed by the reference:

"Whether on a charge of attempted arson in the aggravated form contemplated by section 1(2) of the Criminal Damage Act 1971, in addition to establishing a specific intent to cause damage by fire, it is sufficient to prove that the defendant was reckless as to whether life would thereby be endangered."

We answer it in the affirmative. We add that, in circumstances where the first named property is not the same as the second named property, in addition to establishing a specific intent to cause damage to property, it is sufficient to prove that the defendant was reckless as to whether any second named property was damaged and reckless as to whether the life of another would be endangered by the damage to the second named property.

Judgment accordingly

3. ATTEMPTING THE IMPOSSIBLE

R. v. Shivpuri

[1986] 2 W.L.R. 988 (H.L.)

Lord Bridge of Harwich. My Lords, on 23 February 1984 the appellant was convicted at the Crown Court at Reading of two attempts to commit offences. The offences attempted were being knowingly concerned in dealing with (count 1) and in harbouring (count 2) a Class A controlled drug namely diamorphine, with intent to evade the prohibition of importation imposed by section 3(1) of the Misuse of Drugs Act 1971, contrary to section 170(1)(*b*) of the Customs and Excise Management Act 1979. On 5 November 1984 the Court of Appeal (Criminal Division) dismissed his appeals against conviction but certified that a point of law of general public importance was involved in their decision and granted leave to appeal to your Lordships' House. The certified question granted on 13 November 1984 reads:

"Does a person commit an offence under section 1 of the Criminal Attempts Act 1981 where, if the facts were as that person believed them to be, the full offence would have been committed by him, but where on the true facts the offence which that person set out to commit was in law impossible, *e.g.* because the substance imported and believed to be heroin was not heroin but a harmless substance?"

The facts plainly to be inferred from the evidence, interpreted in the light of the jury's guilty verdicts, may be shortly summarised. The appellant, on a visit to India, was approached by a man named Desai, who offered to pay him £1,000 if, on his return to England, he would receive a suitcase which a courier would deliver to him containing packages of drugs which the appellant was then to distribute according to instructions he would receive. The suitcase was duly delivered to him in Cambridge. On 30 November 1982, acting on instructions, the appellant went to Southall station to deliver a package of drugs to a third party. Outside the station he and the man he had met by appointment were arrested. A package containing a powdered substance was found in the appellant's shoulder bag. At the appellant's flat in Cambridge, he produced to customs officers the suitcase from which the lining had been ripped out and the remaining packages of the same powdered substance. In answer to questions by customs officers and in a long written statement the appellant made what amounted to a full confession of having played his part, as described, as recipient and distributor of illegally imported drugs. The appellant believed the drugs to be either heroin or cannabis. In due course the powdered substance in the several packages was scientifically analysed and found not to be a controlled drug but snuff or some similar harmless vegetable matter.

[Lord Bridge then considered an entirely separate ground of appeal, which was not raised in the Court of Appeal, before turning to the certified question. This concerned the interpretation of provisions of the drugs legislation and is not relevant here.]

. . . . . .

The certified question depends on the true construction of the Criminal Attempts Act 1981. That Act marked an important new departure since, by section 6, it abolished the offence of attempt at common law and substituted a new statutory code governing attempts to commit criminal offences. It was considered by your Lordships' House last year in *Anderton* v. *Ryan* (1985) after the decision in the Court of Appeal which is the subject of the present appeal. That might seem an appropriate starting point from which to examine the issues arising in this appeal. But your Lordships have been invited to exercise the power under the *Practice Statement (Judicial Precedent)* (1966) to depart from the reasoning in that decision if it proves necessary to do so in order to affirm the convictions appealed against in the instant case. I was not only a party to the decision in *Anderton* v. *Ryan*, I was also the author of one of the two opinions approved by the majority which must be taken to express the House's *ratio*. That seems to me to afford a sound reason why, on being invited to re-examine the language of the statute in its application to the facts of this appeal, I should initially seek to put out of mind what I said in *Anderton* v. *Ryan*. Accordingly I propose to approach the issue in the first place as an exercise in statutory construction, applying the language of the Act to the facts of the case, as if the matter were *res integra*. If this leads me to the conclusion that the appellant was not guilty of any attempt to commit a relevant offence, that will be the end of the matter. But if this initial exercise inclines me to reach a contrary conclusion, it will then be necessary to consider whether the precedent set by *Anderton* v. *Ryan* bars that conclusion or whether it can be surmounted either on the ground that the earlier decision is distinguishable or that it would be appropriate to depart from it under the Practice Statement.

[Section 1 of the Criminal Attempts Act 1981 was set out in full; see below, p. 386].

Applying this language to the facts of the case, the first question to be asked is whether the appellant intended to commit the offences of being knowingly concerned in dealing with and harbouring drugs of Class A or Class B with intent to evade the prohibition on their importation. Translated into more homely language the question may be rephrased without in any way altering its legal significance, in the following terms: did the appellant intend to receive and store (harbour) and in due course pass on to third parties (deal with) packages of heroin or cannabis which he knew had been smuggled into England from India? The answer is plainly yes, he did. Next, did he in relation to each offence, do an act which was more than merely preparatory to the commission of the offence? The act relied on in relation to harbouring was the receipt and retention of the packages found in the lining of the suitcase. The act relied on in relation to dealing was the meeting at Southall station with the intended recipient of one of the packages. In each case the act was clearly more than preparatory to the commission of the *intended* offence; it was not and could not be more than merely preparatory to the commission of the *actual* offence, because the facts were such that the commission of the actual offence was impossible. Here then is the nub of the matter. Does the "act which is more than merely preparatory to the commission of the offence" in section 1(1) of the Act of 1981 (the *actus reus* of the statutory offence of attempt) require any more than an act which is more than merely preparatory to the commission of the offence which the defendant intended to commit? Section 1(2) must surely indicate a negative answer; if it were otherwise, whenever the facts were such that the commission of the actual offence was impossible, it would be impossible to prove an act more than merely preparatory to the commission of that offence and subsections (1) and (2) would contradict each other.

This very simple, perhaps over-simple, analysis leads me to the provisional conclusion that the appellant was rightly convicted of the two offences of attempt· with which he was charged. But can this conclusion stand with *Anderton* v. *Ryan*? The appellant in that case was charged with an attempt to handle stolen goods. She bought a video recorder believing it to be stolen. On the facts as they were to be assumed it was not stolen. By a majority in the House decided that she was entitled to be acquitted. I have re-examined the case with care. If I could extract from the speech of Lord Roskill or from my own speech a clear and coherent principle distinguishing those cases of attempting the impossible which amount to offences under the statute from those which do not, I should have to consider carefully on which side of the line the instant case fell. But I have to confess that I can find no such principle.

Running through Lord Roskill's speech and my own in *Anderton* v. *Ryan* is the concept of "objectively innocent" acts which, in my speech certainly, are contrasted with "guilty acts." A few citations will make this clear. Lord Roskill said:

> "My Lords, it has been strenuously and ably argued for the respondent that these provisions involve that a defendant is liable to conviction for an attempt even where his actions are innocent but he erroneously believes facts which, if true, would make those actions criminal, and further, that he is liable to such conviction whether or not in the event his intended course of action is completed."

He proceeded to reject the argument.... I referred to the appellant's purchase of the video recorder and said:

> "Objectively considered, therefore, her purchase of the recorder was a perfectly proper commercial transaction."

A further passage from my speech proceeded, as:

> "The question may be stated in abstract terms as follows. Does section 1 of the Act of 1981 create a new offence of attempt where a person embarks on and completes a course of conduct which is objectively innocent, solely on the ground that the person mistakenly believes facts which, if true, would make that course of conduct a complete crime? If the question must be answered affirmatively it requires convictions in a number of surprising cases: the classic case, put by Bramwell B. in *Reg.* v. *Collins* (1864), of the man who takes away his own umbrella from a stand, believing it not to be his own and with intent to steal it; the case of the man who has consensual intercourse with a girl over 16 believing her to be under that age; the case of the art dealer who sells a picture which he represents to be and which is in fact a genuine Picasso, but which the dealer mistakenly believes to be a fake.
>
> The common feature of all these cases, including that under appeal, is that the mind alone is guilty, the act is innocent."

I then contrasted the case of the man who attempts to pick the empty pocket, saying:

"Putting the hand in the pocket is the guilty act, the intent to steal is the guilty mind, the offence is appropriately dealt with as an attempt, and the impossibility of committing the full offence for want of anything in the pocket to steal is declared by [subsection (2)] to be no obstacle to conviction."

If we fell into error, it is clear that our concern was to avoid convictions in situations which most people, as a matter of common sense, would not regard as involving criminality. In this connection it is to be regretted that we did not take due note of paragraph 2.97 of the Law Commission's report (Criminal Law: Attempt, and Impossibility in Relation to Attempt, Conspiracy and Incitement (1980) (Law Commission No. 102)) which preceded the enactment of the Act of 1981, which reads:

"If it is right in principle that an attempt should be chargeable even though the crime which it is sought to commit could not possibly be committed, we do not think that we should be deterred by the consideration that such a change in our law would also cover some extreme and exceptional cases in which a prosecution would be theoretically possible. An example would be where a person is offered goods at such a low price that he believes that they are stolen, when in fact they are not; if he actually purchases them, upon the principles which we have discussed he would be liable for an attempt to handle stolen goods. Another case which has been much debated is that raised in argument by Bramwell B. in *Reg.* v. *Collins* (1864). If A takes his own umbrella, mistaking it for one belonging to B and intending to steal B's umbrella, is he guilty of attempted theft? Again, on the principles which we have discussed he would in theory be guilty, but in neither case would it be realistic to suppose that a complaint would be made or that prosecution would ensue."

The prosecution in *Anderton* v. *Ryan* itself falsified the Commission's prognosis in one of the "extreme and exceptional cases." It nevertheless probably holds good for other such cases, particularly that of the young man having sexual intercourse with a girl over 16, mistakenly believing her to be under that age, by which both Lord Roskill and I were much troubled.

However that may be, the distinction between acts which are "objectively innocent" and those which are not is an essential element in the reasoning in *Anderton* v. *Ryan* and the decision, unless it can be supported on some other ground, must stand or fall by the validity of this distinction. I am satisfied on further consideration that the concept of "objective innocence" is incapable of sensible application in relation to the law of criminal attempts. The reason for this is that any attempt to commit an offence which involves "an act which is more than merely preparatory to the commission of the offence" but for any reason fails, so that in the event no offence is committed, must *ex hypothesi*, from the point of view of the criminal law, be "objectively innocent." What turns what would otherwise, from the point of view of the criminal law, be an innocent act into a crime is the intent of the actor to commit an offence. I say "from the point of view of the criminal law" because the law of tort must surely here be quite irrelevant. A puts his hand into B's pocket. Whether or not there is anything in the pocket capable of being stolen, if A intends to steal, his act is a criminal attempt; if he does not so intend, his act is innocent. A plunges a knife into a bolster in a bed. To avoid the complication of an offence of criminal damage, assume it to be A's bolster. If A believes the bolster to be his enemy B and intends to kill him, his act is an attempt to murder B; if he knows the bolster is only a bolster, his act is innocent. These considerations lead me to the conclusion that the distinction sought to be drawn in *Anderton* v. *Ryan* between innocent and guilty acts considered "objectively" and independently of the state of mind of the actor cannot be sensibly maintained.

Another conceivable ground of distinction which was to some extent canvassed in argument, both in *Anderton* v. *Ryan* and in the instant case, though no trace of it appears in the speeches in *Anderton* v. *Ryan*, is a distinction which would make guilt or innocence of the crime of attempt in a case of mistaken belief dependent on what, for want of a better phrase, I will call the defendant's dominant intention. According to the theory necessary to sustain this distinction, the appellant's dominant intention in *Anderton* v. *Ryan* was to buy a cheap video recorder; her belief that it was stolen was merely incidental. Likewise in the hypothetical case of attempted unlawful sexual intercourse, the young man's dominant intention was to have intercourse with the particular girl; his mistaken belief that she was under 16 was merely incidental. By contrast, in the instant case the appellant's dominant intention was to receive and distribute illegally imported heroin or cannabis.

Whilst I see the superficial attraction of this suggested ground of distinction, I also see formidable practical difficulties in its application. By what test is a jury to be told that a defendant's dominant intention is to be recognised and distinguished from his incidental but mistaken belief? But there is perhaps a more formidable theoretical difficulty. If this ground of distinction is relied on to support the acquittal of the appellant in *Anderton* v. *Ryan*, it can only do so on the basis that her mistaken belief that the video recorder was stolen played no significant part in her decision to buy it and therefore she may be acquitted of the intent to handle stolen goods. But this line of reasoning runs into head-on collision with section 1(3) of the Act of 1981. The theory produces a situation where, apart from the subsection, her intention would not be regarded as having amounted to any intent to commit an offence. Section 1(3)(*b*) then requires one to ask whether, if the video recorder had in fact been stolen, her intention would have been regarded as an intent to handle stolen goods. The answer must clearly be yes, it would. If she had bought the video recorder knowing it to be stolen, when in fact it was, it would have availed her nothing to say that her dominant intention was to buy a video recorder because it was cheap and that her knowledge that it was stolen was merely incidental. This seems to me fatal to the dominant intention theory.

I am thus led to the conclusion that there is no valid ground on which *Anderton* v. *Ryan* can be distinguished. I have made clear my own conviction, which as a party to the decision (and craving the indulgence of my noble and learned friends who agreed in it) I am the readier to express, that the decision was wrong. What then is to be done? If the case is indistinguishable, the application of the strict doctrine of precedent would require that the present appeal be allowed. Is it permissible to depart from precedent under the *Practice Statement (Judicial Precedent)* (1966) notwithstanding the especial need for certainty in the criminal law? The following considerations lead me to answer that question affirmatively. First, I am undeterred by the consideration that the decision in *Anderton* v. *Ryan* was so recent. The Practice Statement is an effective abandonment of our pretention to infallibility. If a serious error embodied in a decision of this House has distorted the law, the sooner it is corrected the better. Secondly, I cannot see how, in the very nature of the case, anyone could have acted in reliance on the law as propounded in *Anderton* v. *Ryan* in the belief that he was acting innocently and now find that, after all, he is to be held to have committed a criminal offence. Thirdly, to hold the House bound to follow *Anderton* v. *Ryan* because it cannot be distinguished and to allow the appeal in this case would, it seems to me, be tantamount to a declaration that the Act of

1981 left the law of criminal attempts unchanged following the decision in *Reg.* v. *Smith (Roger)* (1975). Finally, if, contrary to my present view, there is a valid ground on which it would be proper to distinguish cases similar to that considered in *Anderton* v. *Ryan*, my present opinion on that point would not foreclose the option of making such a distinction in some future case.

I cannot conclude this opinion without disclosing that I have had the advantage, since the conclusion of the argument in this appeal, of reading an article by Professor Glanville Williams entitled "The Lords and Impossible Attempts, or Quis Custodiet Ipsos Custodes?" [1986] C.L.J. 33. The language in which he criticises the decision in *Anderton* v. *Ryan* is not conspicuous for its moderation, but it would be foolish, on that account, not to recognise the force of the criticism and churlish not to acknowledge the assistance I have derived from it.

I would answer the certified question in the affirmative and dismiss the appeal.

[Lord Scarman delivered a speech in agreement with Lord Bridge.

The Lord Chancellor agreed with the speech of Lord Bridge, but added that had he been unable to depart from *Anderton* v. *Ryan*, he would be able to distinguish the cases.

Lord Elwyn-Jones and Lord Mackay of Clashfern agreed with the Lord Chancellor.]

Question

Albert comes from a country where sexual intercourse with a girl under the age of 21 is a criminal offence. He assumes that this is also the law in England, but nevertheless has intercourse with his 19-year-old girlfriend. Does he commit any criminal offence?

Chapter 6
Homicide

The *actus reus* for both murder and manslaughter is the unlawful killing of a human being; death occurring within a year and a day of the injury inflicted by the accused on the victim (see *Dyson*, above, p. 101). The distinction between the two lies in the *mens rea*.

1. MURDER

Refer to section 1 of the Homicide Act, below, p. 394. This section indicates that a killing does not amount to murder unless done with "malice aforethought (express or implied)." While the section states that express or implied malice is a requirement, it gives no clues as to their meanings.

R. v. Moloney

[1985] 1 All E.R. 1025 (H.L.)

[M. was charged with the murder of his stepfather, P. It was accepted by both sides that M. had shot and killed P. with a shotgun at about 4 a.m. following a party to celebrate P.'s wedding anniversary. M. and P. had both consumed much alcohol and had got into a heated discussion about M.'s future in the army. The other guests had all gone to bed by about 1 a.m. At 4 a.m. they were aroused by the sound of a gunshot. They discovered M. telephoning the police to say he had just "murdered" his stepfather. M. claimed that as the argument progressed P. challenged M. to see who could load and fire a shotgun the faster. M. had easily won and had pulled the trigger of the empty chamber, whereupon P. had taunted him by saying that he knew M. would not have the nerve to fire the gun. M. said that in his drunken state he responded by pulling the other trigger. His defence was that he in no way intended to harm, let alone kill, P.]

Lord Bridge. The judge correctly directed the jury that, in order to prove the appellant guilty of murder, "the prosecution have to prove that he intended either to kill his stepfather or to cause him some really serious bodily injury." But he had earlier given the following direction on intent:

"When the law requires that something must be proved to have been done with a particular intent, it means this: a

301

man intends the consequences of his voluntary act (a) when he desires it to happen, whether or not he foresees that it probably will happen, and (b) when he foresees that it will probably happen, whether he desires it or not."

[The jury convicted M. of murder. His appeal was dismissed by the Court of Appeal who certified that a point of law of general public importance was involved, namely:

"Is malice aforethought in the crime of murder established by proof that when doing the act which causes the death of another the accused either: (a) intends to kill or do serious harm; or (b) foresees that death of serious harm will probably occur, whether or not he desires either of those consequences?"]

Lord Bridge. The true and only basis of the appellant's defence that he was guilty not of murder but of manslaughter was encapsulated in the two sentences in his statement: "I didn't aim the gun. I just pulled the trigger and he was dead." The appellant amplified this defence in two crucial passages in his evidence. He said: "I never deliberately aimed at him and fired at him intending to hurt him or to aim close to him intending to frighten him." A little later he said he had no idea in discharging the gun that it would injure his father: "In my state of mind I never considered that the probable consequence of what I might do might result in injury to my father. I never conceived that what I was doing might cause injury to anybody. It was just a lark."

This being the evidence, the issue for the jury was a short and simple one. If they were sure that, at the moment of pulling the trigger which discharged the live cartridge, the appellant realised that the gun was pointing straight at his stepfather's head, they were bound to convict him of murder. If, on the other hand, they thought it might be true that, in the appellant's drunken condition and in the context of this ridiculous challenge, it never entered the appellant's head when he pulled the trigger that the gun was pointing at his father, he should have been acquitted of murder and convicted of manslaughter. . . .

The fact that, when the appellant fired the gun, the gun was pointing directly at his stepfather's head at a range of about six feet was not, and could not be, disputed. The sole issue was whether, when he pressed the trigger, this fact and its inevitable consequence were present to the appellant's mind. If they were, the inference was inescapable, using words in their ordinary, everyday meaning, that he intended to kill his stepfather. The undisputed facts that the appellant loved his stepfather and that there was no premeditation or rational motivation could not, as any reasonable juror would understand, rebut this inference. If, on the other hand, as the appellant was in substance asserting, it never crossed his mind, in his more or less intoxicated condition and when suddenly confronted by his stepfather's absurd challenge, that by pulling the trigger he might injure, let alone kill, his stepfather, no question of foresight of consequences arose for consideration. Whatever his state of mind, the appellant was undoubtedly guilty of a high degree of recklessness. But, so far as I know, no one has yet suggested that recklessness can furnish the necessary element in the crime of murder.

If the jury had not demonstrated, by the question they asked after four hours of deliberation, that the issue of intent was one they did not understand, there might be room for further argument as to the outcome of this appeal. As it is, the jury's question, the terms of the judge's further direction and the jury's decision, just over an hour later, to return a unanimous verdict of guilty of murder leave me in no doubt, with every respect to the trial judge, and the Court of Appeal, that this was an unsafe and unsatisfactory verdict.

That conclusion would be sufficient to dispose of this appeal. But, since I regard it as of paramount importance to the due administration of criminal justice that the law should indicate the appropriate direction to be given as to the mental element in the crime of murder, or indeed in any crime of specific intent, in terms which will be both clear to judges and intelligible to juries, I must first examine the present state of the law on that subject, and, if I find that it leads to some confusion, I must next consider whether it is properly within the judicial function of your Lordships' House to attempt some clarification and simplification. I emphasise at the outset that this is in no sense an academic, but is essentially a practical, exercise. . . .

The golden rule should be that, when directing a jury on the mental element necessary in a crime of specific intent, the judge should avoid any elaboration or paraphrase of what is meant by intent, and leave it to the jury's good sense to decide whether the accused acted with the necessary intent, unless the judge is convinced that, on the facts and having regard to the way the case has been presented to the jury in evidence and argument, some further explanation or elaboration is strictly necessary to avoid misunderstanding. In trials for murder or wounding with intent, I find it very difficult to visualise a case where any such explanation or elaboration could be required, if the offence consisted of a direct attack on the victim with a weapon, except possibly the case where the accused shot at A and killed B, which any first year law student could explain to a jury in the simplest of terms.

I do not, of course, by what I have said in the foregoing paragraph, mean to question the necessity, which frequently arises, to explain to a jury that intention is something quite distinct from motive or desire. But this can normally be quite simply explained by reference to the case before the court or, if necessary, by some homely example. A man who, at London airport, boards a plane which he knows to be bound for Manchester, clearly intends to travel to Manchester, even though Manchester is the last place he wants to be and his motive for boarding the plane is simply to escape pursuit. The possibility that the plane may have engine trouble and be diverted to Luton does not affect the matter. By boarding the Manchester plane, the man conclusively demonstrates his intention to go there, because it is a moral certainty that that is where he will arrive.

I return to the two uncertainties noted by the Criminal Law Revision Committee in the report referred to above as arising from *Hyam* v. *D.P.P.* which still remain unresolved. I should preface these observations by expressing my view that the differences of opinion to be found in the five speeches in *Hyam* v. *D.P.P.* have, as I believe, caused some confusion in the law in an area where, as I have already indicated, clarity and simplicity are, in my view, of paramount importance. I believe is also follows that it is within the judicial function of your Lordship's House to lay down new guidelines which will achieve those desiderata, if we can reach broad agreement what they should be. . . .

Starting from the proposition established by *R* v. *Vickers* (1957), as modified by *D.P.P.* v. *Smith* (1961), that the mental element in murder requires proof of an intention to kill or cause really serious injury, the first fundamental question to be answered is whether there is any rule of substantive law that foresight by the accused of one of those eventualities as a probable consequence of his voluntary act, where the probability can be defined as exceeding a certain degree, is equivalent or alternative to the necessary intention. I would answer this question in the negative. Here I derive powerful support from the speech of Lord Hailsham in *Hyam* v. *D.P.P.* (1974), where he said:

> "I do not, therefore, consider, as was suggested in argument, that the fact that a state of affairs is correctly foreseen as a highly probable consequence of what is done is the same thing as the fact that the state of affairs is intended."

And again:

> "...I do not think that foresight as such of a high degree of probability is at all the same thing as intention, and, in my view, it is not foresight but intention which constitutes the mental element in murder."

The irrationality of any such rule of substantive law stems from the fact that it is impossible to define degrees of probability, in any of the infinite variety of situations arising in human affairs, in precise or scientific terms. As Lord Reid said in *Southern Portland Cement Ltd* v. *Cooper* (1974):

> "Chance probability or likelihood is always a matter of degree. It is rarely capable of precise assessment. Many different expressions are in common use. It can be said that the occurrence of a future event is very likely, rather likely, more probable than not, not unlikely, quite likely, not improbable, more than a mere possibility, etc. It is neither practicable nor reasonable to draw a line at extreme probability."

I am firmly of opinion that foresight of consequences, as an element bearing on the issue of intention in murder, or indeed any other crime of specific intent, belongs not to the substantive law but to the law of evidence. Here again I am happy to find myself aligned with Lord Hailsham in *Hyam* v. *D.P.P.* (1974), where he said: "Knowledge or foresight is at the best material which entitles or compels a jury to draw the necessary inference as to intention." A rule of evidence which judges for more than a century found of the utmost utility in directing juries was expressed in the maxim, "A man is presumed to intend the natural and probable consequences of his acts." In *D.P.P.* v. *Smith* (1960) your Lordships' House, by treating this rule of evidence as creating an irrebuttable presumption and thus elevating it, in effect, to the status of a rule of substantive law, predictably provoked the intervention of Parliament by s.8 of the Criminal Justice Act 1967 to put the issue of intention back where it belonged, *viz.*, in the hands of the jury, "drawing such inferences from the evidence as appear proper in the circumstances." I do not by any means take the conjunction of the verbs "intended or foresaw" and "intend or foresee" in that section as an indication that Parliament treated them as synonymous; on the contrary, two verbs were needed to connote two different states of mind.

I think we should now no longer speak of presumptions in this context but rather of inferences. In the old presumption that a man intends the natural and probable consequences of his acts the important word is "natural." This word conveys the idea that in the ordinary course of events a certain act will lead to a certain consequence unless something unexpected supervenes to prevent it. One might almost say that, if a consequence is natural, it is really otiose to speak of it as also being probable.

Section 8 of the Criminal Justice Act 1967 leaves us at liberty to go back to the decisions before that of this House in *D.P.P.* v. *Smith* and it is here, I believe, that we can find a sure, clear, intelligible and simple guide to the kind of direction that should be given to a jury in the exceptional case where it is necessary to give guidance how, on the evidence, they should approach the issue of intent.

I know of no clearer exposition of the law than that in the judgment of the Court of Criminal Appeal (Lord Goddard C.J., Atkinson and Cassels JJ.) delivered by Lord Goddard C.J. in *R.* v. *Steane* (1947) where he said:

"No doubt, if the prosecution prove an act the natural consequence of which would be a certain result and no evidence or explanation is given, then a jury may, on a proper direction, find that the prisoner is guilty of doing the act with the intent alleged, but if, on the totality of the evidence, there is room for more than one view as to the intent of the prisoner, the jury should be directed that it is for the prosecution to prove the intent to a jury's satisfaction, and if, on a review of the whole evidence, they either think that the intent did not exist or they are left in doubt as to the intent, the prisoner is entitled to be acquitted."

In the rare cases in which it is necessary to direct a jury by reference to foresight of consequences, I do not believe it is necessary for the judge to do more than invite the jury to consider two questions. First, was death or really serious injury in a murder case (or whatever relevant consequence must be proved to have been intended in any other case) a natural consequence of the defendant's voluntary act? Secondly, did the defendant foresee that consequence as being a natural consequence of his act? The jury should then be told that if they answer Yes to both questions it is a proper inference for them to draw that he intended that consequence.

My Lords, I would answer the certified question in the negative. I would allow the appeal, set aside the verdict of murder, substitute a verdict of manslaughter and remit the case to the Court of Appeal, Criminal Division to determine the appropriate sentence. Having regard to the time the appellant has already spent in custody, the case should be listed for hearing at the earliest possible date.

Appeal allowed. Verdict of murder set aside and verdict of manslaughter substituted; case remitted to Court of Appeal, Criminal Division to determine appropriate sentence.

R. v. Hancock and Shankland

[1986] 2 W.L.R. 357 (H.L.)

Lord Scarman. My Lords, in this case the Director of Public Prosecutions appeals against the decision of the Court of Appeal (Criminal Division) quashing the respondents' convictions of murder and substituting verdicts of manslaughter. The appeal is brought to secure a ruling from the House upon the refusal of the Court of Appeal to accept as sound the guidelines formulated by this House in a recent case in which the House gave guidance as to the direction appropriate to be given by the judge to the jury in a murder trial in which the judge considers it necessary to direct the jury upon the issue of intent by reference to foresight of consequences. The case is *Reg.* v. *Moloney* (above, p. 301) and the guidance was in these terms:

"In the rare cases in which it is necessary to direct a jury by reference to foresight of consequences, I do not believe it is necessary for the judge to do more than invite the jury to consider two questions. First, was death or really serious injury in a murder case (or whatever relevant consequence must be proved to have been intended in any other case) a natural consequence of the defendant's voluntary act? Secondly, did the defendant foresee that consequence as being a natural consequence of his act? The jury should then be told that if they answer yes to both questions it is a proper inference for them to draw that he intended that consequence."

In the present case, the trial judge having based his direction to the jury on the guidance which I have quoted, the two accused (respondents to this appeal) were convicted of murder. The Court of Appeal quashed the convictions on the ground that the judge's guidance may well have misled the jury. The court refused leave to appeal but certified the following point of general public importance:

"Do the questions to be considered by a jury set out in the speech of Lord Bridge of Harwich in *Reg.* v. *Moloney* as a model direction require amplification?"

It will be observed that the questions which it was suggested in *Moloney* that the jury should ask themselves refer to a "natural" consequence, not a "natural and probable" consequence. The Director now appeals with the leave of the House.

The appeal is of importance for two reasons. First, of course, there is the need to settle a point of difference between this House and the Court of Appeal. The *Moloney* guidance was intended to be authoritative in the sense that it was given to be followed by judges in appropriate cases, *i.e.* those "exceptional" cases, as the House thought, where the foreseeability of death or serious bodily harm may be relevant to a decision as to the intent underlying the act of violence. The House realised and declared, however, that the guidance was no part of the *ratio decidendi* in the case.... The guidance was offered as an attempt in a practical way to clarify and simplify the task of the jury. It was not intended to prevent judges from expressing in other language, if they should deem it wise in a particular case, guidance designed to assist the jury to reach a conclusion on the facts in evidence....

The dangers inherent in general guidance for the assistance of juries in determining a question of fact lead me to the second reason for the importance of the appeal, namely that the cases to which the guidance was expressly limited by the House in *Moloney*, *i.e.* the "rare cases" in which it is necessary to direct a jury by reference to foresight of consequences, are unlikely to be so rare or so exceptional as the House believed. As the House then recognised, the guidelines as formulated are applicable to cases of any crime of specific intent, and not merely murder. But further and disturbingly, crimes of violence where the purpose is by open violence to protest, demonstrate, obstruct, or frighten are on the increase. Violence is used by some as a means of public communication. Inevitably there will be casualties: and inevitably death will on occasions result. If death results, is the perpetrator of the violent act guilty of murder? It will depend on his intent. How is the specific intent to kill or to inflict serious harm proved? Did he foresee the result of his action? Did he foresee it as probable? Did he foresee it as highly probable? If he did, is he guilty of murder? How is a jury to weigh up the evidence and reach a proper conclusion amidst these perplexities? The best guidance that can be given to a trial judge is to stick to his traditional function, *i.e.* to limit his direction to the applicable rule (or rules) of law, to emphasise the incidence and burden of proof, to remind the jury that they are the judges of fact, and against that background of law to discuss the particular questions of fact which the jury have to decide, indicating the inferences which they may draw if they think it proper from the facts which they find established. Should not appellate guidance emphasise the importance of particular facts and avoid generalisation? This is a question to be considered. The facts of this case would appear to indicate an affirmative answer.

... Reginald Dean Hancock and Russell Shankland were convicted of the murder of Mr. Wilkie. In the dark hours of the early morning of November 30, 1984 Mr. David Wilkie was driving his taxi along the Heads of the Valley Road. As he approached the bridge over the road at Rhymney he was killed when two lumps of concrete hit the car. The two lumps, a block and a post, had been dropped from the bridge as he approached it.

Mr. Wilkie's passenger was a miner going to work. Mr. Hancock and Mr. Shankland were miners on strike, and strongly objected to Mr. Wilkie's passenger going to work. That morning they had collected the block and the post from nearby, had brought them to the bridge under which the Heads of the Valley Road runs through a cutting, and had placed them on the parapet on the side facing towards the Rhymney roundabout. They then awaited the arrival of a convoy escorting the miner on his way to work. The convoy approached the bridge at about 5.15 a.m.: it consisted of a police motor-cycle, a police Land Rover, the taxi driven by Mr. Wilkie, and a police Sherpa van. The convoy was travelling from the Rhymney roundabout towards the bridge in the nearside lane of the carriageway. Estimates of its speed varied: it was put somewhere between 30 and 40 m.p.h. As the convoy neared the bridge, the concrete block struck the taxi's windscreen. The post struck the carriageway some 4ft. 8 ins. from the nearside verge. Before, however, the post subsided on the ground, it was hit by the taxi. The taxi skidded out of control, coming to rest on the embankment. Mr. Wilkie died from the injuries he received in the wrecking of the taxi by the two lumps of concrete.

The case for the prosecution was that the two concrete objects were either thrown from the bridge or pushed over its parapet in the path of the taxi at a time when the taxi could not avoid being struck by one or both of them. And, as the trial judge told the jury, the prosecution case could be compressed into one question and answer, the question being "what else could a person who pushed or threw such objects have intended but to cause really serious bodily harm to the occupants of the car?" The answer in the prosecution's submission was that a person acting in that way could in the circumstances have intended nothing less.

The defence was simple enough: that the two men intended to block the road, to stop the miner going to work, but not to kill or to do serious bodily harm to anyone. Hancock told Detective Chief Superintendent Caisley that he did not throw the two pieces of "masonry" over the bridge but merely "dropped" them. He told him that he dropped them on the side of the bridge "nearest to the roundabout where I could see them coming." At a later interview Hancock admitted "shoving" the block of concrete over the parapet of the bridge, but declared that he believed when he did so that he was standing "over the *middle* lane," *i.e.* not over the nearside lane, along which the convoy was moving. He said that he did not mean to do anyone damage—"just to frighten him [*i.e.* the miner going to work] more than anything." Shankland admitted that he was party to the plan to obstruct the road but denied that they intended to hurt anyone. Like Hancock, he emphasised that their plan was to drop the objects in the middle lane of the carriageway, *i.e.* clear of the lane alongside which the convoy was travelling, and that they believed that this was what they did.

Hancock and Shankland were prepared to plead guilty to manslaughter but the Crown decided to pursue the charge of murder. The issue was ultimately one of intention. Did they (or either of them) intend to kill or to cause anyone serious bodily harm?

The case called for a careful direction by judge to jury as to the state of mind required by law to be proved to their satisfaction before they could return a verdict of murder. The jury would also want his help in weighing up the evidence. The judge's direction as to the intention required by law was impeccable. He said:

> "If the prosecution has made you satisfied so as to be sure that Dean Hancock and Russell Shankland agreed that they would, in concert, push or throw missiles from the bridge, each having the intention either to kill or to cause really serious injury, then you will find each of them guilty of murder as the block was thrown or pushed by Dean Hancock in pursuance of the agreement."

When he came to help them on the facts, he offered guidance along the *Moloney* lines:

> "You may think that critical to the resolution of this case is the question of intent. In determining whether a person intended to kill or to cause really serious injury, you must have regard to all of the evidence which has been put before you, and draw from it such inferences as to you

seem proper and appropriate. You may or may not, for the purpose of considering what inferences to draw, find it helpful to ask: Was death or serious injury a natural consequence of what was done? Did a defendant foresee that consequence as a natural consequence? That is a possible question which you may care to ask yourselves. If you find yourselves not satisfied so as to be sure that there was an intent to kill or to cause really serious injury, then it is open to you to return a verdict of not guilty of murder, but guilty of manslaughter."

The jury was out for five hours. When they returned they told the judge that they had failed to reach agreement. The judge now gave them the option of a majority verdict. A few minutes later he received a note from the jury in these terms:

"Your Lordship,
With respect, the jury has discussed at great length the factual aspects of this case and feel, under the circumstances, confident in dealing with this matter. However, the precise legal definitions regarding the committing of murder and manslaughter are causing dissent because of lack of knowledge, particularly with regard to intent and foreseeable consequences."

The jury were plainly perplexed. The judge gave them a further direction but did not go beyond what he had already said in summing up. If they were puzzled by the way in which the judge had then dealt with the issue of intent, the second direction would not have helped them. Their problem was how to relate foresight to intention—a problem which they did not find solved by asking themselves the two questions relating to natural consequences and foresight which the judge had put to them.

In the Court of Appeal Lord Lane C.J. delivered the judgment of the court. The court found itself driven to the conclusion that the use by the judge of the *Moloney* guidelines may have misled the jury. The guidelines offered the jury no assistance as to the relevance or weight of the probability factor in determining whether they should, or could properly, infer from foresight of a consequence (in this case, of course, death or serious bodily harm) the intent to bring about that consequence. This was, in the court's view, a particularly serious omission because the case law, as Lord Bridge of Harwich in *Moloney* had recognised, indicated "that the probability of the consequence taken to have been foreseen must be little short of overwhelming before it will suffice to establish the necessary intent." In the court's view the judge's failure to explain the factor of probability was because he faithfully followed *Moloney*: "[he] was unwittingly led into misdirecting the jury by reason of the way in which the guidelines in *Moloney* were expressed:"

The question for the House is, therefore, whether the *Moloney* guidelines are sound. In *Moloney's* case the *ratio decidendi* was that the judge never properly put to the jury the defence, namely that the accused was unaware that the gun was pointing at his stepfather. The House, however, held it necessary in view of the history of confusion in this branch of the law to attempt to clarify the law relating to the establishment of the mental element necessary to constitute the crime of murder and to lay down guidelines for assisting juries to determine in what circumstances it is proper to infer intent from foresight. The House certainly clarified the law. First, the House cleared away the confusions which had obscured the law during the last 25 years laying down authoritatively that the mental element in murder is a specific intent, the intent to kill or to inflict serious bodily harm. Nothing less suffices: and the jury must be sure that the intent existed when the act was done which resulted in death before they can return a verdict of murder.

Secondly, the House made it absolutely clear that foresight of consequences is no more than evidence of the existence of the intent; it must be considered, and its weight assessed, together with all the evidence in the case. Foresight does not necessarily imply the existence of intention, though it may be a fact from which when considered with all the other evidence a jury may think it right to infer the necessary intent. Lord Hailsham of St. Marylebone L.C. put the point succinctly and powerfully in his speech in *Reg.* v. *Moloney*:

> "I conclude with the pious hope that your Lordships will not again have to decide that foresight and foreseeability are not the same thing as intention although either may give rise to an irresistible inference of such, and that matters which are essentially to be treated as matters of inference for a jury as to a subjective state of mind will not once again be erected into a legal presumption. They should remain, what they always should have been, part of the law of evidence and inference to be left to the jury after a proper direction as to their weight, and not part of the substantive law."

Thirdly, the House emphasised that the probability of the result of an act is an important matter for the jury to consider and can be critical in their determining whether the result was intended.

These three propositions were made abundantly clear by Lord Bridge of Harwich. His was the leading speech and received the assent of their other Lordships, Lord Hailsham of St. Marylebone L.C., Lord Fraser of Tullybelton. Lord EdmundDavies, and Lord Keith of Kinkel. His speech has laid to rest ghosts which had haunted the case law ever since the unhappy decision of your Lordships' House in *Reg.* v. *Smith* (1961) and which were given fresh vigour by the interpretation put by some upon the speeches of members of this House in *Reg.* v. *Hyam* (1975).

It is only when Lord Bridge of Harwich turned to the task of formulating guidelines that difficulty arises. It is said by the Court of Appeal that the guidelines by omitting any express reference to probability are ambiguous and may well lead a jury to a wrong conclusion. The omission was deliberate. Lord Bridge omitted the adjective "probable" from the timehonoured formula "foresight of the natural and probable consequences of his acts" because he thought that "if a consequence is natural, it is really otiose to speak of it as also being probable." But is it?

Lord Bridge of Harwich did not deny the importance of probability. He put it thus:

"But looking on their facts at the decided cases where a crime of specific intent was under consideration, including *Reg.* v. *Hyam* (1975) A.C. 55 itself, they suggest to me that the probability of the consequence taken to have been foreseen must be little short of overwhelming before it will suffice to establish the necessary intent."

In his discussion of the relationship between foresight and intention, Lord Bridge of Harwich reviewed the case law since the passing of the Homicide Act 1957 and concluded, at p. 928:

"foresight of consequences, as an element bearing on the issue of intention in murder, or indeed any other crime of specific intent, belongs, not to the substantive law, but to the law of evidence."

He referred to the rule of evidence that a man is presumed to intend the natural and probable consequences of his acts, and went on to observe that the House of Lords in *Smith's* case (1961) had treated the presumption as irrebuttable, but that Parliament intervened by section 8 of the Criminal Justice Act 1967 to return the law to the path from which it had been diverted, leaving the presumption as no more than an inference open to the jury to draw if in all the circumstances it appears to them proper to draw it.

Yet he omitted any reference in his guidelines to probability. He did so because he included probability in the meaning which he attributed to "natural." My Lords, I very much doubt whether a jury without further explanation would think that "probable" added nothing to "natural." I agree with the Court of Appeal that the probability of a consequence is a factor of sufficient importance to be drawn specifically to the attention of the jury and to be explained. In a murder case where it is necessary to direct a jury on the issue of intent by reference to foresight of consequences the probability of death or serious injury resulting from the act done may be critically important. Its importance will depend on the degree of probability: if the likelihood that death or serious injury will result is high, the probability of that result may, as Lord Bridge of Harwich noted and the Lord Chief Justice emphasised, be seen as overwhelming evidence of the existence of the intent to kill or injure. Failure to explain the relevance of probability may, therefore, mislead a jury into thinking that it is of little or no importance and into concentrating exclusively on the causal link between the act and its consequence. In framing his guidelines Lord Bridge of Harwich emphasised that he did not believe it necessary to do more than to invite the jury to consider his two questions. Neither question makes any reference (beyond the use of the word "natural") to probability. I am not surprised that when in this case the judge faithfully followed this guidance the jury found themselves perplexed and unsure. In my judgment, therefore, the *Moloney* guidelines as they stand are unsafe and misleading. They require a reference to probability. They also require an explanation that the greater the probability of a consequence the more likely it is that the consequence was foreseen and that if that consequence was foreseen the greater the probability is that that consequence was also intended. But juries also require to be reminded that the decision is theirs to be reached upon a consideration of all the evidence.

Accordingly, I accept the view of the Court of Appeal that the *Moloney* guidelines are defective. I am, however, not persuaded that guidelines of general application, albeit within a limited class of case, are wise or desirable. Lord Lane C.J. formulated in this case guidelines for the assistance of juries but for the reason which follows, I would not advise their use by trial judges when summing up to a jury.

I fear that their elaborate structure may well create difficulty. Juries are not chosen for their understanding of a logical and phased process leading by question and answer to a conclusion but are expected to exercise practical common sense. They want help on the practical problems encountered in evaluating the evidence of a particular case and reaching a conclusion. It is better, I suggest, notwithstanding my respect for the comprehensive formulation of the Court of Appeal's guidelines, that the trial judge should follow the traditional course of a summing up. He must explain the nature of the offence charged, give directions as to the law applicable to the particular facts of the case, explain the incidence and burden of proof, put both sides' cases making especially sure that the defence is put; he should offer help in understanding and weighing up all the evidence and should make certain that the jury understand that whereas the law is for him the facts are for them to decide. Guidelines, if given, are not to be treated as rules of law but as a guide indicating the sort of approach the jury may properly adopt to the evidence when coming to their decision on the facts.

In a case where foresight of a consequence is part of the evidence supporting a prosecution submission that the accused intended the consequence, the judge, if he thinks some general observations would help the jury, could well, having in mind section 8 of the Criminal Justice Act 1967, emphasise that the probability, however high, of a consequence is only a factor, though it may in some cases be a very significant factor, to be considered with all the other evidence in determining whether the accused intended to bring it about. The distinction between the offence and the evidence relied on to prove it is vital. Lord Bridge's speech in *Moloney* made the distinction crystal clear: it would be a disservice to the law to allow his guidelines to mislead a jury into overlooking it.

For these reasons I would hold that the *Moloney* guidelines are defective and should not be used as they stand without further explanation. The laying down of guidelines for use in directing juries in cases of complexity is a function which can be usefully exercised by the Court of Appeal. But it should be done sparingly, and limited to cases of real difficulty. If it is done, the guidelines should avoid generalisation so far as is possible and encourage the jury to exercise their common sense in reaching what is their decision on the facts. Guidelines are not rules of law: judges should not think that they must use them. A judge's duty is to direct the jury in law and to help them upon the particular facts of the case.

Accordingly, I would answer the certified question in the affirmative and would dismiss the appeal. I would propose that the costs of all parties be paid out of central funds.

Appeal dismissed.

R. v. Nedrick

[1986] 1 W.L.R. 1025 (C.A.)

[N. held a grudge against a woman and had poured paraffin through her letter box and on to the door itself, setting light to it. A child in the house was killed. N. said that he had not wanted anyone to die—he just wanted to wake the woman up and frighten her.]

Lord Lane C.J. What then do a jury have to decide so far as the mental element in murder is concerned? They simply have to decide whether the defendant intended to kill or do serious bodily harm. In order to reach that decision the jury must pay regard to all the relevant circumstances, including what the defendant himself said and did.

In the great majority of cases a direction to that effect will be enough, particularly where the defendant's actions amounted to a direct attack on his victim, because in such cases the evidence relating to the defendant's desire or motive will be clear and his intent will have been the same as his desire or motive. But in some cases, of which this is one, the defendant does an act which is manifestly dangerous and as a result someone dies. The primary desire or motive of the defendant may not have been to harm that person, or indeed anyone. In that situation what further directions should a jury be given as to the mental state which they must find to exist in the defendant if murder is to be proved?

We have endeavoured to crystallise the effect of their Lordships' speeches in *R. v. Moloney* and *R. v. Hancock* in a way which we hope may be helpful to judges who have to handle this type of case.

It may be advisable first of all to explain to the jury that a man may intend to achieve a certain result whilst at the same time not desiring it to come about. In *R. v. Moloney* [1985] 1 All E.R. 1025 at 1037, [1985] A.C. 905 at 926 Lord Bridge gave an illustration of the distinction:

"A man who, at London Airport, boards a plane which he knows to be bound for Manchester, clearly intends to travel to Manchester, even though Manchester is the last place he wants to be and his motive for boarding the plane is simply to escape pursuit."

The man who knowingly boards the Manchester aircraft wants to go there in the sense that boarding it is a voluntary act. His desire to leave London predominates over his desire not to go to Manchester. When he decides to board the aircraft, if not before, he forms the intention to travel to Manchester.

In *R.* v. *Hancock* the House decided that the *R.* v. *Moloney* guidelines require a reference to probability. Lord Scarman said ([1986] 1 All E.R. 641 at 651, [1986] A.C. 455 at 473):

"They also require an explanation that the greater the probability of a consequence the more likely it is that the consequence was foreseen and that if that consequence was foreseen the greater the probability is that that consequence was also intended."

When determining whether the defendant had the necessary intent, it may therefore be helpful for a jury to ask themselves two questions. (1) How probable was the consequence which resulted from the defendant's voluntary act? (2) Did he foresee that consequence?

If he did not appreciate that death or serious harm was likely to result from his act, he cannot have intended to bring it about. If he did, but thought that the risk to which he was exposing the person killed was only slight, then it may be easy for the jury to conclude that he did not intend to bring about that result. On the other hand, if the jury are satisfied that at the material time the defendant recognised that death or serious harm would be virtually certain (barring some unforeseen intervention) to result from his voluntary act, then that is a fact from which they may find it easy to infer that he intended to kill or do serious bodily harm, even though he may not have had any desire to achieve that result.

As Lord Bridge said in *R.* v. *Moloney* [1985] 1 All E.R. 1025 at 1036, [1985] A.C. 905 at 925:

"... the probability of the consequence taken to have been foreseen must be little short of overwhelming before it will suffice to establish the necessary intent."

Later he uses the expression "moral certainty" (see [1985] 1 All E.R. 1025 at 1037, [1985] A.C. 905 at 926) and says, "will lead to a certain consequence unless something unexpected supervenes to prevent it" (see [1985] 1 All E.R. 1025 at 1039, [1985] A.C. 905 at 929).

Where the charge is murder and in the rare cases where the simple direction is not enough, the jury should be directed that they are not entitled to infer the necessary intention unless they feel sure that death or serious bodily harm was a virtual certainty (barring some unforeseen intervention) as a result of the defendant's actions and that the defendant appreciated that such was the case.

Where a man realises that it is for all practical purposes inevitable that his actions will result in death or serious harm, the inference may be irresistible that he intended that result, however little he may have desired or wished it to happen. The decision is one for the jury to be reached on a consideration of all the evidence.

Appeal allowed.

Note

The foregoing cases state that murder requires intent. The intent required, however, is not confined to an intent to kill but also extends to an intent to cause grievous bodily harm. In *Vickers* ([1957] 2 All E.R. 741, C.C.A.) it was argued that the grievous bodily harm doctrine had been abolished by section 1 of the Homicide Act 1957, below, p. 394. The argument was that since such a killing was in the course or furtherance of another offence, *i.e.* the offence under section 18 of the Offences Against the Person Act 1861, below, p. 393, it could not amount to murder. The argument was rejected, the court holding that the section expressly retained "implied" malice and malice was to be implied where the defendant intends to cause grievous bodily harm. In *Hyam* ([1974] 2 All E.R. 41, H.L.) Lords Diplock and Kilbrandon doubted the correctness of *Vickers* but in *Cunningham* [(1981) 2 All E.R. 863, H.L.) the House of Lords confirmed that an intent to cause grievous bodily harm, where death results, suffices for murder.

Questions

1. Suppose X is in charge of an armoury containing 100 rifles. X knows that 99 of the rifles are loaded but does not know which is the one unloaded rifle. Seeing Y approach X takes down a rifle and aims it at Y. X does not care whether or not he has taken down one of the loaded rifles or an unloaded one. Indeed X hopes this will be Y's lucky day so that Y will get an awful fright but not be killed. It is not Y's lucky day and he is shot dead. Does X intend to kill Y?

2. Suppose 99 of the rifles are unloaded and one is loaded but X does not know which is the loaded rifle. Seeing Y approach he takes down a rifle and, hoping he has by chance selected the loaded rifle, he aims it at Y and pulls the trigger. The rifle is unloaded. Does X intend to kill Y?

2.   Voluntary Manslaughter (Provocation)

Manslaughter is said to be voluntary where although the defendant has the required intent for murder there are mitigating circumstances which justify a conviction for manslaughter. These are where the defendant kills under diminished responsibility (see above, p. 223); in pursuance of a suicide pact (not dealt with in this work); and under provocation which is the subject of this section.

Refer to section 3 of the Homicide Act 1957, below, p. 395.

R. v. Thornton

(1993) 96 Cr.App.R. 112 (C.A.)

[The appellant (W) married the deceased (H) in August 1988 and was thereafter subject to frequent violence at his hands at one stage leading to charges against H in May 1989. On June 10/11 following H was heard to say he would kill W. There was another row on June 13 and W went to the kitchen to seek something for her own protection. There W sharpened a carving knife and returned to the room where H was lying on the couch and asked him to come to bed. He declined and said he would kill her. W said she would kill H first. H sarcastically suggested she go ahead whereupon W stabbed him once in the stomach. W then called for an ambulance and the police. At this time she remarked to the police that she wanted to kill him and said to the ambulanceman attending H, "I don't know why you are bothering. Let him die." H died from the injury. Later W claimed that she had stabbed H only after he had threatened to kill her; but she meant to frighten and not to kill and thought that H would have deflected the blow.]

Beldam L.J. Against that background the appellant argues that the judge misdirected the jury on the question of provocation. His direction was as follows.

"I come now to the question of loss of control and provocation. It is my duty to mention this to you, members of the jury, [because] you will notice that [counsel] did not address you on the basis of provocation and it will I think be obvious to you why in a moment when you have heard what I have to say to you about it. Members of the jury, the word 'provocation' in ordinary language is used pretty freely and not always very appropriately."

The judge went on to give an example of the inappropriate use of the word "provocative." He continued:

"You are not being asked to consider 'Did he lead her a miserable life?', whether you think he did or not on the evidence, nor are you being asked yourself 'Does she deserve sympathy?', because that is not the issue in the case. For the purposes of the charge of murder, provocation consists of some act or series of acts done or words spoken or a continuation of words and acts which causes in the particular defendant a sudden and temporary loss of self-control and which would have caused a reasonable, sober person to lose her self-control and to behave as the defendant behaved. So there are two questions. The first question is whether the provocative conduct, such as it was, if there was any, caused the defendant to lose her self-control. There has to be a sudden loss of self-control. The defendant herself asserts that there was no sudden loss of self-control. Members of the jury, that no doubt is why [counsel] did not address you and invite you to consider provocation. But, even if that were the case, there would still be the second part. The second question is whether the provocative act would have caused a reasonable, sober person to lose her self-control and behave as the defendant behaved and on this, of course, you would take into account the whole picture, the whole story, everything that was said, possibly anything that was done, if there was anything done, on this night, according to the effect it would have on a reasonable, sober women in the position in which the defendant believed herself to be and, of course, a reasonable sober woman, like a reasonable, sober man, is expected to have ordinary powers of self-control, normal powers expected of a person of the sex and age of the particular defendant and sharing her characteristics as you have been able to discover them. Members of the jury, so far as this aspect is concerned, even if Mrs Thornton had lost her self-control, you would still have to ask whether a reasonable women in her position would have done what she did and, if you think (and this is for you to say) that she went out and found a knife and went back into the room and as a result of something said to her stabbed her husband as he lay defenceless on that settee deep into his stomach, it may be very difficult to come to the conclusion that that was, and I use the shorthand, a reasonable reaction. There are ... many unhappy, indeed miserable, husbands and wives. It is a fact of life. It has to be faced, members of the jury. But on the whole it is hardly reasonable, you may think, to stab them fatally when there are other alternatives available, like walking out or going upstairs."

The judge then reminded the jury that the burden was on the prosecution to prove that the appellant was not provoked or acting under provocation ...

Lord Gifford suggested that the legal concept of provocation did not require loss of self-control to be sudden, and that such a requirement had been incoporated into the law by a too literal adoption of the words used by Devlin J, in his summing up to the jury in *Duffy* [1949] 1 All E.R. 932, which was emphatically approved by Lord Goddard, C.J. on appeal. The passage in the summing up in that case from which the words are taken reads (at 932–933):

"Indeed, circumstances which induce a desire for revenge are inconsistent with provocation, since the conscious formulation of a desire for revenge means that a person has had time to think, to reflect, and that would negative a sudden temporary loss of self-control which is of the essence of provocation... Provocation being, therefore, as I have defined it, there are two things, in considering it, to which the law attaches great importance. The first of them is whether there was what is sometimes called time for cooling, that is, for passion to cool and for reason to regain dominion over the mind. That is why most acts of provocation are cases of sudden quarrels, sudden blows inflicted with an implement already in the hand, perhaps being used, or being picked up, where there has been no time for reflection."

The words "sudden and temporary loss of self-control" have ever since been regarded as appropriate to convey to a jury the legal concept of provocation first expressed by Tindal, C.J. in *Hayward* (1833) 6 C. & P. 157 at 159, 172 E.R. 1188 at 1189 in mitigation of the rigour of the law for acts committed—

"while smarting under a provocation so recent and so strong, that the prisoner might not be considered at the moment the master of his own understanding... "

Lord Gifford argued that Devlin J.'s words are no longer appropriate in the case of reaction by a person subjected to a long course of provocative conduct, including domestic violence, which may sap the resilience and resolve to retain self-control when the final confrontation erupts. In such circumstances it is misleading, he says, to talk of a sudden loss of control. He points to the words of section 3 of the Homicide Act 1957, which require the jury, in determining whether the provocation was sufficient to make a reasonable man do as the accused did, to take into account everything both done and said according to the effect it would have on a reasonable man. Lord Gifford also referred us to passages in the judgment in *D.P.P.* v. *Camplin* (1978) 67 Cr.App.R. 14, 23, (1978) A.C. 705, 721, where Lord Morris said:

"It seems to me that as a result of the changes effected by section 3 of the 1957 Act a jury is fully entitled to consider whether an accused person, placed as he was, only acted as even a resonable man might have acted if he had been in the accused's situation."

The changes in the law of provocation made by section 3 of the Homicide Act 1957 and the reasons for them are well known. It has never, so far as we are aware, been suggested that the distinction drawn by Devlin J. between a person who has time to think and reflect and regain self-control and a sudden temporary loss of self-control is no longer of significance. On the contrary, the distinction drawn by Devlin J. is just as, if not more, important in the kind of case to which Lord Gifford referred. It is within the experience of each member of the court that in cases of domestic violence which culminate in the death of a partner there is frequently evidence given of provocative acts committed by the deceased in the past, for it is in that context that the jury have to consider the accused's reaction. In every such case the question for the jury is whether at the moment the fatal blow was struck the accused had been deprived for that moment of the self-control which previously he or she had been able to exercise. The epithet "sudden and temporary" is one a jury are well able to understand and to recognise as expressing precisely the distinction drawn by Devlin J. We reject the suggestion that in using the phrase "sudden and temporary loss of control" there was any misdirection of the jury.

The other criticisms directed to this passage of the summing up are, we consider, without foundation. The jury were told in terms to take account of "the whole picture, the whole story" when considering if the provocative act would have caused a reasonable and sober person to lose her self-control and behave as the defendant behaved. It is not reasonable to suggest that, because the judge continued: "everything that was said, possibly anything that was done, if there was anything done, *on this night...*" the jury would have regarded those words as confining the whole picture, the whole story, to the night of the deceased's death.

Each case has to be considered against the background of its particular facts. So a direction to the jury that to find provocation they had to find in it something done on the morning of the killing was approved in *Brown* (1972) 56 Cr.App.R. 564, [1972] 2 Q.B. 229 and a direction that they could review the whole of the deceased's conduct throughout the tubulent years preceding the death was characterised as "too generous" in *Davies* (1975) 60 Cr.App.R. 253, [1975] Q.B. 691. Nor do we think that the judge was in error in referring to the fact that counsel for the appellant had not addressed them on provocation. The facts of this case were quite different to the facts of *Hopper* (1915) 11 Cr.App.R. 136, [1915] 2 K.B. 431, to which we were referred. In that case counsel for the defence had made it plain that he intended as an alternative to the defence of accident to invite the jury to acquit of murder but convict of manslaughter on the ground of provocation. The judge directed the jury to acquit the appellant or find him guilty of murder, taking the view that it was impossible to find a verdict of manslaughter. This court thought that the verdict of manslaughter was open to the jury and that it should have been left to them as a possible verdict. By his remarks to the jury in the present case, the judge was doing no more than telling the jury that counsel may not have felt able to advance the defence of provocation because of the clear evidence which the appellant herself had given, but notwithstanding that he directed them it was for them to say whether or not on the evidence the Crown had proved that she was not provoked . . .

Appeal dismissed

D.P.P. v. Camplin

[1978] A.C. 705 (H.L.)

[C., a 15-year-old boy, was charged with the murder of K. At his trial C. alleged that K. had forcibly buggered him and had then laughed at him, whereupon C. hit him over the head with a heavy chapati pan. The prosecution appealed to the House of Lords against the decision of the Court of Appeal to substitute a verdict of manslaughter for that of murder on the basis that C. had been provoked.]

Lord Diplock. The point of law of general public importance involved in the case has been certified as being:

"Whether, on the prosecution for murder of a boy of 15, where the issue of provocation arises, the jury should be directed to consider the question, under s.3 of the Homicide Act 1957, whether the provocation was enough to make a reasonable man do as he did by reference to a 'reasonable adult' or by reference to a 'reasonable boy of 15.' "

My Lords, the doctrine of provocation in crimes of homicide has always represented an anomaly in English law. In crimes of violence which result in injury short of death, the fact that the act of violence was committed under provocation, which has caused the accused to lose his self-control, does not affect the nature of the offence of which he is guilty: it is merely a matter to be taken into consideration in determining the penalty which it is appropriate to impose: whereas in homicide provocation effects a change in the offence itself from murder, for which the penalty is fixed by law (formerly death and now imprisonment for life), to the lesser offence of manslaughter, for which the penalty is in the discretion of the judge.

[Lord Diplock then reviewed the history of provocation showing how until 1957 the conduct of the deceased had to be of such a kind as was capable in law of constituting provocation and that this was a question of law for the judge. This meant that a trial judge could withdraw the issue of provocation from the jury on the basis that a reasonable man would not have reacted as the accused did. For example reasonable men were not provoked by words alone; they did not possess short tempers nor unusual characteristics; when provoked they tempered their reaction in proportion to the degree of provocation offered. He continued:]

My Lords, this was the state of law when *Bedder* (1954) fell to be considered by this House. The accused had killed a prostitute. He was sexually impotent. According to his evidence he had tried to have sexual intercourse with her and failed. She taunted him with his failure and tried to get away from his grasp. In the course of her attempts to do so she slapped him in the face, punched him in the stomach and kicked him in the groin, whereupon he took a knife out of his pocket and stabbed her twice and caused her death. The struggle that led to her death thus started because the deceased taunted the accused with his physical infirmity; but in the state of the law as it then was, taunts unaccompanied by any physical violence did not constitute provocation. The taunts were followed by violence on the part of the deceased in the course of her attempt to get away from the accused, and it may be that this subsequent violence would have a greater effect on the self-control of an impotent man already enraged by the taunts than it would have had on a person conscious of possessing normal physical attributes. So there might be some justification for the judge to instruct the jury to ignore the fact that the accused was impotent when they were considering whether the deceased's conduct amounted to such provocation as would cause a reasonable or ordinary person to lose his self-control. This indeed appears to have been the ground on which the Court of Appeal had approved the summing-up when they said:

"... no distinction is to be made in the case of a person who, though it may not be a matter of temperament is physically impotent, is conscious of that impotence, *and therefore mentally liable to be more excited unduly* if he is 'twitted' or attacked on the subject of that particular infirmity."

This statement, for which I have myself supplied the emphasis, was approved by Lord Simonds L.C. speaking on behalf of all the members of this House who sat on the appeal; but he also went on to lay down the broader proposition that:

> "It would be plainly illogical not to recognise an unusually excitable or pugnacious temperament in the accused as a matter to be taken into account but yet to recognise for that purpose some unusual physical characteristic, be it impotence or another."

[His Lordship read section 3 of the Homicide Act 1957, below, p. 395, and continued.]

My Lords, this section was intended to mitigate in some degree the harshness of the common law of provocation as it had been developed by recent decisions in this House. It recognises and retains the dual test: the provocation must not only have caused the accused to lose his self-control but also be such as might cause a reasonable man to react to it as the accused did. Nevertheless, it brings about two important changes in the law. The first is it abolishes all previous rules of law as to what can or cannot amount to provocation and in particular the rule of law that words unaccompanied by violence could not do so. Secondly it makes it clear that if there was any evidence that the accused himself at the time of the act which caused the death in fact lost his self-control in consequence of some provocation however slight it might appear to the judge, he was bound to leave to the jury the question, which is one of opinion not of law, whether a reasonable man might have reacted to that provocation as the accused did.

I agree with my noble and learned friend, Lord Simon of Glaisdale, that since this question is one for the opinion of the jury the evidence of witnesses as to how they think a reasonable man would react to the provocation is not admissible.

The public policy that underlay the adoption of the "reasonable man" test in the common law doctrine of provocation was to reduce the incidence of fatal violence by preventing a person relying on his own exceptional pugnacity or excitability as an excuse for loss of self-control. The rationale of the test may not be easy to reconcile in logic with more universal propositions as to the mental element in crime. Nevertheless it has been preserved by the 1957 Act but falls to be applied now in the context of a law of provocation that is significantly different from what it was before the Act was passed.

Although it is now for the jury to apply the "reasonable man" test, it still remains for the judge to direct them what, in the new context of the section, is the meaning of this apparently inapt expression, since powers of ratiocination bear no obvious relationships to powers of self-control. Apart from this the judge is entitled, if he thinks it helpful, to suggest considerations which may influence the jury in forming their own opinions as to whether the test is satisfied; but he should make it clear that these are not instructions which they are required to follow; it is for them and no one else to decide what weight, if any, ought to be given to them.

As I have already pointed out, for the purposes of the law of provocation the "reasonable man" has never been confined to the adult male. It means an ordinary person of either sex, not exceptionally excitable or pugnacious, but possessed of such powers of self-control as everyone is entitled to expect that his fellow citizens will exercise in society as it is today. A crucial factor in the defence of provocation from earliest times has been the relationship between the gravity of provocation and the way in which the accused retaliated, both being judged by the social standards of the day. When Hale was writing in the seventeenth century pulling a man's nose was thought to justify retaliation with a sword; when *Mancini* was decided by this House, a blow with a fist would not justify retaliation with a deadly weapon. But so long as words unaccompanied by violence could not in common law amount to provocation the relevant proportionality between provocation and retaliation was primarily one of degrees of violence. Words spoken to the accused before the violence started were not normally to be included in the proportion sum. But now that the law has been changed so as to permit of words being treated as provocation, even though unaccompanied by any other acts, the gravity of verbal provocation may well depend on the particular characteristics or circumstances of the person to whom a taunt or insult is addressed. To taunt a person because of his race, his physical infirmities or some shameful incident in his past may well be considered by the jury to be more offensive to the person addressed, however equable his temperament, if the facts on which the taunt is founded are true than it would be if they were not. It would stultify much of the mitigation of the previous harshness of the common law in ruling out verbal provocation as capable of reducing murder to manslaughter if the jury could not take into consideration all those factors which in their opinion would affect the gravity of taunts and insults when applied to the person to whom they are addressed. So to this extent at any rate the unqualified proposition accepted by this House in *Bedder* that for the purposes of the "reasonable man" test any unusual physical characteristics of the accused must be ignored requires revision as a result of the passing of the 1957 Act.

That he was only 15 years of age at the time of the killing is the relevant characteristic of the accused in the instant case. It is a characteristic which may have its effects on temperament as well as physique. If the jury think that the same power of selfcontrol is not to be expected in an ordinary, average or normal boy of 15 as in an older person, are they to treat the lesser powers of self-control possessed by an ordinary, average or normal boy of 15 as the standard of self-control with which the conduct of the accused is to be compared?

It may be conceded that in strict logic there is a transition between treating age as a characteristic that may be taken into account in assessing the gravity of the provocation addressed to the accused and treating it as a characteristic to be taken into account in determining what is the degree of self-control to be expected of the ordinary person with whom the accused's conduct is to be compared. But to require old heads on young shoulders is inconsistent with the law's compassion of human infirmity to which Sir Michael Foster ascribed the doctrine of provocation more than two centuries ago. The distinction as to the purpose for which it is legitimate to take the age of the accused into account involves considerations of too great nicety to warrant a place in deciding a matter of opinion, which is no longer one to be decided by a judge trained in logical reasoning but by a jury drawing on their experience of how ordinary human beings behave in real life.

There is no direct authority prior to the Act that states expressly that the age of the accused could not be taken into account in determining the standard of self-control for the purposes of the reasonable man test, unless this is implicit in the reasoning of Lord Simonds L.C. in *Bedder*. The Court of Appeal distinguished the instant case from that of *Bedder* on the ground that what it was there said must be ignored was an unusual characteristic that distinguished the accused from ordinary normal persons, whereas nothing could be more ordinary or normal than to be aged 15. The reasoning in *Bedder* would, I think, permit of this distinction between normal and abnormal characteristics, which may affect the powers of self-control of the accused; but for reasons that I have already mentioned the proposition stated in *Bedder* requires qualification as a consequence of changes in the law affected by the 1957 Act. To try to salve what can remain of it without conflict with the Act could in my view only lead to unnecessary and unsatisfactory complexity in a question which has now become a question for the jury alone. In my view *Bedder*, like *Mancini* and *Holmes*, ought no longer to be treated as an authority on the law of provocation.

In my opinion a proper direction to a jury on the question left to their exclusive determination by s.3 of the 1957 Act would be on the following lines. The judge should state what the question is, using the very terms of the section. He should then explain to them that the reasonable man referred to in the question is a person having the power of self-control to be expected of an ordinary person of the sex and age of the accused, but in other respects sharing such of the accused's characteristics as they think would affect the gravity of the provocation to him, and that the question is not merely whether such a person would in like circumstances be provoked to lose his self-control but also would react to the provocation as the accused did.

I accordingly agree with the Court of Appeal that the judge ought not to have instructed the jury to pay no account to the age of the accused even though they themselves might be of opinion that the degree of self-control to be expected in a boy of that age was less than in an adult. So to direct them was to impose a fetter on the right and duty of the jury which the 1957 Act accords to them to act on their own opinion on the matter.

I would dismiss this appeal.

R. v. Morhall

[1993] New L.J. 1441 (C.A.)

[The appellant was addicted to glue-sniffing. The deceased took the appellant to task over his addiction, nagged him about it and head butted him. A fight which ensued was broken up by a third party. But the deceased would not give up and followed the appellant to his bedroom from which banging and crashing was heard. During the fracas the appellant stabbed the deceased to death. The appellant was convicted of murder. The sole ground for his appeal concerned the direction of the trial judge relating to provocation.]

Lord Taylor (giving the judgement of the court, referred to *Camplin*, above, p. 323 and continued). This brings us to the crucial question in this case. What characteristics if any would it be inappropriate for the jury to take into account? In *Camplin* their Lordships gave examples of a number of characteristics which should be considered if the provocation related to them. They included age, sex, race, colour, ethnic origin, physical deformity or infirmity, impotence, some shameful incident in the past, an abscess on the cheek (where the provocation relied on was a blow to the face) or, in a female defendant, the conditions of pregnancy or menstruation.

However, it is to be noted that none of these characteristics is inconsistent with the general concept of a reasonable or ordinary person. Even a reasonable person may, in Lord Diplock's example, have something in his past of which he is ashamed and apart from that example, none of those given would be self-induced.

Where is the line to be drawn? Clearly *all* characteristics do not qualify for attribution to the hypothetical reasonable man. Some guidance is to be found in *R. v. McGregor* [1962] N.Z.L.R. 1069, in which North J. sought to explain the word "characteristics" used in a similar context in the New Zealand Crimes Act 1981. He said: "The legislature has given us no guide as to what limitations might be imposed but perforce there must be adopted a construction which will ensure regard being had to the characteristics of the offender without wholly extinguishing the ordinary man. The offender must be presumed to possess in general the power of self-control of the ordinary man, save in-so-far as his power of self-control is weakened because of some particular characteristic possessed by him. It is not every trait or disposition of the offender that can be invoked to modify the concept of the ordinary man. The characteristic must be something definite and of sufficient significance to make the offender a different person from the ordinary run of mankind, and have also a sufficient degree of permanence to warrant its being regarded as something constituting part of the individual's character or personality. A disposition to be unduly suspicious or to lose one's temper readily will not suffice, nor will a temporary or transitory state of mind such as a mood of depression, excitability or irascibility. These matters are either not of sufficient significance or not of sufficient permanency to be regarded as 'characteristics' which would enable the offender to be distinguished from the ordinary man ... still less can a self-induced transitory state be relied upon as where it arises from the consumption of liquor. The word 'characteristics' ... is wide enough to apply not only to physical qualities but also to mental qualities and such more intermediate attributes as colour, race and creed. It is to be emphasised that of whatever nature the characteristic may be, it must be such that it can fairly be said that the offender is thereby marked off or distinguished from the ordinary man of the community . . . In our opinion it is not enough to constitute a characteristic that the offender should merely in some general way be mentally deficient or weak-minded. To allow this to be said would, as we have earlier indicated, deny any real operation to the reference made in the section to the ordinary man and it would moreover go far towards the admission of a defence of diminished responsibility without any statutory authority in this country to sanction it. There must be something more, such as provocative words or acts directed to a particular phobia from which the offender suffers. Beyond that we do not think it is advisable that we should attempt to go."

That case was cited with approval as stating the position in English law by Lord Simon in *Camplin* and the particular passage was described as "impeccable" in *R.* v. *Newell* 71 Crim.App.R. 331 . . .

In the present case, the provocation relied on was specifically targeted at the appellant's addiction to glue-sniffing. Accordingly, the question is starkly raised as to whether that addiction should have been left to the jury as a characteristic which they could take into account as affecting the gravity of the provocation to the appellant.

Mr. Worsley contends that it should because, apart from the self-control of the reasonable man, all characteristics of a defendant relevant to the provocation alleged, must be left to the jury. For the Crown, it is submitted that characteristics which are repugnant to the concept of a reasonable man, do not qualify for consideration. Otherwise some remarkable results would follow.

Not only would a defendant who habitually abuses himself by sniffing glue to the point of addiction be entitled to have that characteristic taken into account in his favour by the jury. Logic would demand similar indulgence towards an alcoholic or a defendant who had illegally abused heroin, cocaine or crack to the point of addiction. Similarly, a paedophile up-braided for molesting children, would be entitled to have his characteristic weighed in his favour on the issue of provocation. Yet none of these addictions or propensities could sensibly be regarded as consistent with the reasonable man. It is to be noted and we emphasise that s. 3 refers to "a reasonable man", not just to a person with the self-control of a reasonable man. Whilst *Camplin* decided that the "reasonable man" should be invested with the defendant's characteristics, they surely cannot include characteristics repugnant to the concept of the reasonable man. Quite apart from the incongruity of regarding glue or drug addiction or paedophilia as characteristics of a reasonable man, the problem of getting a jury to consider how possession of any of those characteristics and being bated about it would affect the self-control of a reasonable man who ex hypothesi would not have such a characteristic, seems to us insuperable.

Physical deformity, whether from birth or by accident, colour, race, creed, impotence, homosexuality, are examples, but not an exhaustive list, of characteristics which are clearly consonant with the concept of a reasonable man and therefore, where they exist, they ought to be left to the jury to consider in accordance with Lord Diplock's suggested direction.

But the question raised in this case did not arise in *Camplin* and none of their Lordships considered characteristics inconsistent with a "reasonable man". In our judgment, it must be a matter for the judge as to whether any suggested characteristic is capable of being considered by the jury consistent with the concept of a reasonable man and capable of affecting the gravity of the provocation to the defendant. If he decides the characteristic is so capable he should leave it to the jury to decide whether it is in fact consistent with the reasonable man and whether, if so, it might have affected the gravity of the provocation to a reasonable man invested with it so as to cause him to lose his self-control and do as this defendant did.

In our judgment however, a self-induced addiction to glue-sniffing brought on by voluntary and persistent abuse of solvents is wholly inconsistent with the concept of a reasonable man. In effect, Mr Worsley's argument would stultify the test. It would result in the so-called reasonable man being a reincarnation of the appellant with his peculiar characteristics whether capable of being possessed by a reasonable man or not and whether acquired by nature or by his own abuse.

For these reasons we consider the judge was justified in giving his initial direction on provocation... This appeal is therefore dismissed.

R. v. Johnson

[1989] 2 All E.R. 839 (C.A.)

[J and R had been drinking at a night club. J became aggressive and offensive and threatened R and his lady friend with violence. J then made to leave but R followed him and a struggle ensued during which J produced a flick knife which he had been carrying, stabbed R and killed him. J's defence was self-defence which the jury, convicting J of murder, evidently rejected. The trial judge declined to leave the issue of provocation to the jury saying, "It is rather difficult to see how a man who excites provocative conduct can in turn rely on it as provocation in the criminal law."]

Watkins L.J.   We find it impossible to accept that the mere fact that a defendant caused a reaction in others, which in turn led him to lose his self-control, should result in the issue of provocation being kept outside a jury's consideration. Section 3 clearly provides that the question is whether things done or said or both provoked the defendant to lose his self-control. If there is any evidence that it may have done, the issue must be left to the jury. The jury would then have to consider all the circumstances of the incident, including all the relevant behaviour of the defendant, in deciding (a) whether he was in fact provoked and (b) whether the provocation was enough to make a reasonable man do what the defendant did.

Accordingly, whether or not there were elements in the appellant's conduct which justified the conclusion that he had started the trouble and induced others, including the deceased, to react in the way they did, we are firmly of the view that the defence of provocation should have been left to the jury.

Since it is not possible for us to infer from their verdict that the jury inevitably would have concluded that provocation as well as self-defence had been disproved, the verdict for murder will be set aside. A conviction for manslaughter on the basis of provocation will be substituted.

> *Appeal allowed. Verdict for murder quashed. Conviction for manslaughter substituted. Sentence of eight years' imprisonment imposed.*

Notes and Questions

1.   In *Newell* ((1980) 71 Cr.App.R. 331, C.A.), referred to in *Morhall*, N, a chronic alcoholic, was very depressed because his lady friend, with whom he had been living for some years and to whom he was strongly attached, left him. During a drinking bout with M, a friend, M made derogatory remarks about the lady friend. N allegedly lost his temper and killed M by inflicting 22 blows with a heavy ashtray. The trial judge asked the jury: "Would a sober man in relation to that drunken observation, batter his friend over the head with a nearly new two pound weight ashtray?" N was convicted of murder. His appeal was dismissed by the Court of Appeal, saying that a "characteristic" was relevant only if it had a sufficient degree of permanence and if the provocation was directed at that characteristic.

2.   Why was the age (15) of Camplin thought to be a relevant characteristic? Would not any reasonable man, of any age, be provoked by

being forcibly buggered and jeered at? Was the provocation directed at Camplin's age? Does it have to be?

3. Suppose that in *Newell* M had "twitted" N about his chronic alcoholism, causing N to lose his self-control and kill M. Assuming you are the trial judge, how would you direct the jury in such a case.

4. In *Camplin* Lord Diplock said that the trial judge should explain to the jury that the reasonable man referred to is a person having the power of self-control to be expected of an ordinary person of the sex and age of the accused sharing such of the accused's characteristics as the jury would think affect the gravity of the provocation on him. The reasonable man, he tells us, is not a drunken man nor is he exceptionally excitable or pugnacious.

5. Suppose that a father loses many a night's sleep because his baby cries persistently. Fatigued and driven to distraction he finally loses his self-control and kills the child. In *Doughty* ((1986) 83 Cr.App.R. 319, C.A.) it was held that the trial judge was wrong not to leave provocation to the jury on these facts. But was the loss of a few nights' sleep a characteristic of a sufficient degree of permanence? Was the provocation "directed at" that "characteristic?"

6. Suppose a mother is beset by a splitting headache. Her two-year-old son is enjoying himself by clattering pan lids together. Normally the mother would not be at all disturbed by the noise but her headache makes it intolerable. She loses her temper and kills the child. Provocation? Would it be different if the splitting headache was owing to a hangover following a protracted bout of drinking the night before?

3. INVOLUNTARY MANSLAUGHTER

The law relating to involuntary manslaughter is in the most urgent need of reform. Only criminal law examiners, who have found the larder of involuntary manslaughter providing them with a rich store of intricacies with which to baffle generations of students, might regret its reform.

Involuntary manslaughter is not a subject easy to present coherently, especially to the beginner. It takes three forms: (i) constructive manslaughter; (ii) gross negligence manslaughter; and (iii) reckless manslaughter. Under all three forms the defendant may be convicted of manslaughter, punishable by imprisonment for life, though the defendant did not in fact appreciate that his/her conduct might cause death or serious injury to the person.

Constructive manslaughter (sometimes referred to as unlawful act manslaughter) is typically committed where, say, the defendant intends no more than an assault occasioning actual bodily harm—a punch on the nose—but the punch causes the victim to lose his balance and in falling the victim strikes his head against the floor causing cranial fractures from which the victim dies. The intended result, occasioning actual bodily harm which carried five years' imprisonment, becomes manslaughter carrying imprisonment for life.

Constructive manslaughter is, in effect, the brother-in-law of the old felony-murder doctrine. This ordained that a killing in the course of a felony involving violence was murder even though the defendant had no intention to kill or cause serious bodily harm. This savage doctrine was abolished by the Homicide Act 1957, s. 1 (below, p. 394). But the Act left untouched the doctrine that a killing in the course of an unlawful act not amounting to a felony involving violence amounted to manslaughter. Perhaps logic ought to have dictated, even in 1957, that constructive manslaughter should have been abolished along with constructive murder. But there was then an important difference between murder and manslaughter; the former was punishable by death while the latter was not.

The story in relation to gross negligence manslaughter and reckless manslaughter is even more complex. Until *Caldwell* (above, p. 133) and *Lawrence* (below, p. 343) it had been generally assumed that, apart from unlawful act manslaughter, the only other form of manslaughter was manslaughter by gross negligence. Cases after *Caldwell* and *Lawrence* appeared to eschew gross negligence manslaughter in favour of reckless manslaughter, the test of recklessness being that espoused in *Caldwell* and *Lawrence*. At first sight this might seem to the student as a distinction without a difference. A person who is reckless in the *Caldwell/Lawrence* sense is surely grossly negligent. Well, not quite. Notice that in *Andrews* v. *D.P.P.* (below, p. 337) Lord Atkin, who approved gross negligence as a basis for liability for manslaughter, said that while the concept of recklessness "most nearly covered the case," [In what sense did Lord Atkin understand "recklessness" to mean?] it did not quite cover the case because the defendant might have appreciated the risk and have intended to avoid it but have shown such a high degree of negligence in the measures taken to avoid the risk as would justify a conviction for manslaughter.

But under the *Caldwell/Lawrence* test a person who considers the risk but decides, however foolishly, that there is none, is not reckless in the *Caldwell/Lawrence* sense and cannot be convicted of manslaughter. *Reid* (below, p. 344) appears to confirm this. The Court of Appeal has in the *Sulman & Others* cases (below, p. 399) has resiled from this position and has asserted that gross negligence in the appropriate test except, possibly, where the death is caused by bad driving.

A. Constructive Manslaughter

R. v. Lamb

[1967] 2 All E.R. 1282, C.A.

In jest the appellant pointed a revolver at his best friend who also regarded the matter as a joke. The revolver contained two live rounds but since neither was aligned with the barrel the appellant believed it was safe to pull the trigger. Unfortunately he did not realise that the magazine of a revolver rotates bringing the next chamber into play. The appellant pulled the trigger and shot his friend dead. On a charge of manslaughter the trial judge directed the jury that the pointing of a revolver and pulling of the trigger was an unlawful act even if there was no intention to injure or alarm. The appellant was convicted of manslaughter.

Sachs L.J. Counsel for the Crown, however, had at all times put forward the correct view that for the act to be unlawful it must constitute at least what he then termed 'a technical assault'. In this court, moreover, he rightly conceded that there was no evidence to go to the jury of any assault of any kind. Nor did he feel able to submit that the acts of the appellant were on any other ground unlawful in the criminal sense of that word. Indeed no such submission could in law be made: if, for instance, the pulling of the trigger had had no effect because the striking mechanism or the ammunition had been defective no offence would have been committed by the appellant. Another way of putting it is that *mens rea* being now an essential ingredient in manslaughter (compare *Andrews* v. *Director of Public Prosecutions* [[1937] A.C. 576 at 582, [1937] 2 All E.R. 552 at 555, 556; p. 439, above)] and *Church* [1966] 1 Q.B. at 70, [1965] 2 All E.R. at 76; p. 429] this could not in the present case be established in relation to the first ground except by proving that element of intent without which there can be no assault. It is perhaps as well to mention that when using the phrase 'unlawful in the criminal sense of that word' the court has in mind that it is long settled that it is not in point to consider whether an act is unlawful merely from the angle of civil liabilities. That was first made clear in *Franklin* [(1883) 15 Cox C.C. 163]. The relevant extracts from this and from later judgments are collected in *Russell on Crime* (11th ed., 1958) pp. 651–658. The whole of that part of the summing-up which concerned the first ground was thus vitiated by misdirections based on an erroneous concept of the law; and the strength with which that ground was put to the jury no doubt stemmed from the firm view of the trial judge, expressed more than once in the course of the discussion on law in relation to the undisputed facts: 'How can there be a defence to the charge of manslaughter? Manslaughter requires no intent.'. . .]His Lordship discussed the judge's direction on criminal negligence.] The general effect of the summing-up was thus to withdraw from the jury the defence put forward on behalf of the appellant. When the gravemen of a charge is criminal negligence—often referred to as recklessness—of an accused, the jury have to consider amongst other matters the state of his mind, and that includes the question of whether or not he thought that that which he was doing was safe. In the present case it would, of course, have been fully open to a jury. if properly directed, to find the accused guilty because they considered his view as to there being no danger was formed in a criminally negligent way. But he was entitled to a direction that the jury should take into account the fact that he had indisputably formed this view and that there was expert evidence as to this being an understandable view. Strong though the evidence of criminal negligence was, the appellant was entitled as of right to have his defence considered but he was not accorded this right and the jury was left without a direction on an essential matter. Those defects of themselves are such that the verdict cannot stand. . . .

Appeal allowed

D.P.P. v. Newbury

[1977] A.C. 500 (H.L.)

[Two boys (aged 15) pushed a piece of paving stone of a railway bridge into the path of an oncoming train. The guard in the train was killed and the boys were tried for and convicted of manslaughter. The House of Lords was asked whether an accused could be properly convicted of manslaughter, when his mind is not affected by drink or drugs, if he did not forsee that his act might cause harm to another.]

Lord Salmon. . . . The learned trial judge did not direct the jury that they should acquit the appellants unless they were satisfied beyond a reasonable doubt that the appellants had foreseen that they might cause harm to someone by pushing the piece of paving stone off the parapet into the path of the approaching train. In my view the learned trial judge was quite right not to give such a direction to the jury. The direction which he gave is completely in accordance with established law, which, possibly with one exception to which I shall presently refer, has never been challenged. In *R. v. Larkin* (1942), Humphreys J. said:

"Where the act which a person is engaged in performing is unlawful, then if at the same time it is a dangerous act, that is, an act which is likely to injure another person, and quite inadvertently the doer of the act causes death of that other person by that act then he is guilty of manslaughter."

I agree entirely with Lawton L.J. that that is an admirably clear statement of the law which has been applied many times. It makes it plain (a) that an accused is guilty of manslaughter if it is proved that he intentionally did an act which was unlawful and dangerous and that that act inadvertently caused death and (b) that it is unnecessary to prove that the accused knew that the act was unlawful or dangerous. This is one of the reasons why cases of manslaughter vary so infinitely in their gravity. They may amount to little more than pure inadvertence and sometimes to little less than murder.

I am sure that in *R. v. Church* (1966) Edmund-Davies J. in giving the judgment of the court, did not intend to differ from or qualify anything which had been said in *R. v. Larkin*, (1942). Indeed he was restating the principle laid down in that case by illustrating the sense in which the word "dangerous" should be understood. Edmund-Davies J. said, at p. 70:

"For such a verdict '(guilty of manslaughter)' inexorably to follow, the unlawful act must be such as all sober and reasonable people would inevitably recognise must subject the other person to, at least, the risk of some harm resulting therefrom, albeit not serious harm."

The test is still the objective test. In judging whether the act was dangerous the test is not did the accused recognise that it was dangerous but would all sober and reasonable people recognise its danger.

Notes and Questions

1. What was the unlawful act committed by Newbury and Jones? Must the unlawful act at least constitute an offence against the person?
2. In *Lamb* Sachs L.J. says it is now established that *mens rea* is an essential ingredient in manslaughter by unlawful act. What is the *mens rea*? May the defendant be convicted even though he does not realise the act is dangerous?
3. Constructive manslaughter requires an unlawful *act*. It has been held (*Lowe* [1973] Q.B. 702, C.A.) that this form of manslaughter cannot be committed by omission. But an omission may suffice for manslaughter by gross negligence which is next considered.

B. Gross Negligence Manslaughter

Andrews v. D.P.P.

[1937] A.C. 576 (H.L.)

[The appellant while driving his car ran down and killed a pedestrian. He was convicted of manslaughter.]

Lord Atkin ..."To substantiate that charge"—namely, manslaughter—Lord Ellenborough said, [in *Williamson* (1807)] "the prisoner must have been guilty of criminal misconduct, arising either from the grossest ignorance or the most criminal inattention." The word "criminal" in any attempt to define a crime is perhaps not the most helpful: but it is plain that the Lord Chief Justice meant to indicate to the jury a high degree of negligence. So at a much later date in *Rex v. Bateman* (1925) a charge of manslaughter was made against a qualified medical practitioner in similar circumstances to those of

Williamson's case. In a considered judgment of the Court the Lord Chief Justice, after pointing out that in a civil case once negligence is proved the degree of negligence is irrelevant, said, "In a criminal Court, on the contrary, the amount and degree of negligence are the determining question. There must be *mens rea*." After citing *Cashill* v. *Wright* (1856), a civil case, the Lord Chief Justice proceeds. "In explaining to juries the test which they should apply to determine whether the negligence, in the particular case, amounted or did not amount to a crime judges, have used many epithets such as 'culpable,' 'criminal,' 'gross,' 'wicked,' 'clear,' 'complete.' But whatever epithet be used and whether an epithet be used or not, in order to establish criminal liability the facts must be such that, in the opinion of the jury, the negligence of the accused went beyond a mere matter of compensation between subjects and showed such disregard for the life and safety of others as to amount to a crime against the State and conduct deserving punishment." Here again I think with respect that the expressions used are not, indeed they probably were not intended to be, a precise definition of the crime. I do not myself find the connotations of *mens rea* helpful in distinguishing between degrees of negligence, nor do the ideas of crime and punishment in themselves carry a jury much further in deciding whether in a particular case the degree of negligence shown is a crime and deserves punishment. But the substance of the judgment is most valuable, and in my opinion is correct. In practice it has generally been adopted by judges in charging juries in all cases of manslaughter by negligence, whether in driving vehicles or otherwise. The principle to be observed is that cases of manslaughter in driving motor cars are but instances of a general rule applicable to all charges of homicide by negligence. Simple lack of care such as will constitute civil liability is not enough: for purposes of the criminal law there are degrees of negligence; and a very high degree of negligence is required to be proved before the felony is established. Probably of all the epithets than can be applied, "reckless" most nearly covers the case. It is difficult to visualise a case of death caused by reckless driving in the connotation of that term in ordinary speech which would not justify a conviction of manslaughter; but it is probably not all-embracing, for "reckless" suggests an indifference to risk whereas the accused may have appreciated the risk and intended to avoid it and yet shown such a high degree of negligence in the means adopted to avoid the risk as would justify a conviction. If the principle of *Bateman's* case is observed it will appear that the law of manslaughter has not changed by the introduction of motor vehicles on the road. Death caused by their negligent driving, though unhappily much more frequent, is to be treated in law as death caused by any other form of negligence; and juries should be directed accordingly....

Appeal dismissed.

R. v. Sulman, R. v. Prentice, R. v. Adomako, R. v. Holloway

(1993) The Times, May 21, 1993 (C.A.)

[Judgment reserved from March 1 was being delivered on three appeals against conviction of manslaughter, which had been listed together and argued in succession.

Dr. Michael Charles Prentice, a pre-registration houseman, and Dr. Barry Sulman, a houseman, were convicted at Birmingham Crown Court (Mr. Justice Owen and a jury) of the manslaughter of Malcolm Savage, aged 16, at Peterborough General Hospital during injections. They were each sentenced to nine months imprisonment suspended for 12 months. Their convictions were quashed on appeal.

Dr. John Asare Adomako, an anaesthetist, was convicted at the Central Criminal Court (Mr. Justice Alliott and a jury) of the manslaughter of a patient, who had been totally paralysed by injections while undergoing an operation to repair a detached retina and suffered cardiac arrest after a tube inserted in his mouth enabling him to breathe became detached from the ventilator and he died from lack of oxygen. He was sentenced to six months imprisonment suspended for 12 months. His appeal failed.

Stephen John Holloway, a qualified electrician, was convicted on a re-trial at Maidstone Crown Court (Mr. Justice Boreham and a jury) of manslaughter of a man who was standing in stockinged feet on a not quite dry newly laid concrete floor and touched the metal sink top, which was live because of a faulty connection in a central heating system programmer the appellant had installed. He had received complaints about shocks which he had attributed to static. He was sentenced to nine months imprisonment suspended for two years. His conviction was quashed on appeal.]

The Lord Chief Justice giving the judgment of the court, said that essentially the question was that posed in *Archbold Criminal Pleading Evidence and Practice* (1992 edition, paragraph 19–97): whether gross negligence manslaughter had survived *R. v. Caldwell* ([1982] A.C. 341) and *R. v. Lawrence* ([1982] A.C. 510).

Their Lordships had been referred to a plethora of legal authority, going as far back as Bracton and Coke and as far abroad as the Commonwealth jurisdictions.

In their Lordships' view, however, it was necessary to cite only two authorities before the leading case, *Andrews* v. *D.P.P.* ([1937] A.C. 576): *R. v. Doherty* ((1887) 16 Cox C.C.

306, 309) and *R. v. Bateman* ((1925) 19 Cr.App.R. 8, 11). In *Andrews*, a case of motor manslaughter, Lord Atkin had quoted the passage from *Bateman* and (at p. 583) introduced the word "reckless" to denote the degree of negligence required.

Further, while he thought that "reckless" most nearly covered the case, he recognised it was not exhaustive; there was still scope for manslaughter by a high degree of negligence, even in the absence of indifference. He excluded "mere inadvertence" (p. 582) but he was not saying that all inadvertence fell short of creating criminal liability. On the contrary, he indicated that to establish guilt of manslaughter, the accused must be proved to have had "criminal disregard" for the safety of other (p. 582) and he gave as examples "the grossest ignorance or the most criminal inattention."

Where a duty of care was owed, the inattentive would often be negligent so as to be civilly liable even though, as a result of their inattention, they might not have adverted to the risk. But negligent inattention characterised as mere inadvertence did not create criminal liability. To do so, the inattention or inadvertence had to be, in the jury's view, grossly negligent.

In *R. v. Stone* ([1977] Q.B. 354, 362) Lord Justice Lane made clear that proof of foresight of the consequences was not necessary. What was necessary was proof of a high degree of negligence reflecting the *Andrews* approach. He said specifically (p. 363C) that it was to *Andrews* that one had to turn to discover the definition of the requisite degree of negligence.

After quoting from *Andrews* (p. 583) Lord Justice Lane went on: "It is clear from that passage that indifference to an obvious risk and appreciation of such risk, coupled with a determination nevertheless to run it, are both examples of recklessness ... Mere inadvertence is not enough. The defendant must be proved to have been indifferent to an obvious risk of injury to health, or actually to have foreseen the risk but to have determined nevertheless to run it."

The definition of recklessness by Lord Diplock in *Caldwell* and *Lawrence* involved two stages: the *actus reus* consisted of the defendant creating an obvious and serious risk. The *mens rea* was defined in the alternative as "without having given any thought to the possibility of there being any such risk or, having recognised that there was some risk involved, had nevertheless gone on to take it".

The wide Diplock meaning of recklessness had survived all attacks on it, most recently in *R. v. Reid* ([1992] 1 W.L.R. 793).

It was beyond doubt that, at least since 1982, the word "reckless" had caused the courts problems in regard to involuntary manslaughter which would not have occurred had the focus been on gross negligence rather than on recklessness.

His Lordship cited from *R. v. Seymour (Edward)* ([1983] 2 A.C. 493) and *Kong Cheuk Kwan v. The Queen* ((1985) 82 Cr.App.R. 18) and stated that their Lordships accepted the submission that Lord Roskill's sentence in *Seymour*, that "reckless" was to be given the same meaning in relation to all offences which involved recklessness as one of the elements unless Parliament had otherwise ordained, was *obiter* and should not be followed in regard to the class of manslaughter involved in the cases under appeal.

All counsel had submitted that the effect of the history which their Lordships had briefly outlined had been to create conflicting approaches and uncertainty about the appropriate tests and the proper jury direction in cases of involuntary manslaughter involving breach of duty.

The diversity of views was illustrated by the stances adopted in the appeals which had not been consistent even among counsel for the Crown on the one hand and those for the defence on the other.

Andrews had not been disapproved in any case their Lordships had seen, and it had been applied in *Stone*. There was no reason to doubt that *Andrews* was still good law and *Stone* had been referred to in argument and not disapproved in *Seymour*.

Leaving motor manslaughter aside, however, in their Lordships' judgment the proper test in manslaughter cases based on breach of duty was the gross negligence test established in *Andrews* and *Stone*. Their Lordships reached that conclusion principally because the line of cases from *Doherty* through *Bateman* to *Andrews* and *Stone* was, they believed, binding authority.

Second, they considered that the *Lawrence/Caldwell* recklessness approach was for reasons, some of which had been given, inappropriate in the present class of case.

Accordingly, except in motor manslaughter, the ingredients of involuntary manslaughter by breach of duty which needed to be proved were: (1) the existence of the duty; (2) a breach of the duty causing death; (3) gross negligence which the jury considered justified a criminal conviction.

The range of possible duties, breaches and surrounding circumstances was so varied that it was not possible to prescribe a standard jury direction appropriate in all cases. The judge should tailor his summing up to the specific circumstances of the particular case.

However, in accordance with the authorities reviewed and without purporting to give an exhaustive definition, their

Lordships considered proof of any of the following states of mind in the defendant might properly lead a jury to make a finding of gross negligence:

(a) indifference to an obvious risk of injury to health: (b) actual foresight of the risk coupled with the determination nevertheless to run it; (c) an appreciation of the risk coupled with an intention to avoid it but also coupled with such a high degree of negligence in the attempted avoidance as the jury considered justified the conviction; (d) inattention or failure to advert to a serious risk which went beyond "mere inadvertence" in respect of an obvious and important matter which the defendant's duty demanded he should address.

Their Lordships had borne in mind the *dicta* in *Seymour* (p. 216) and in *Kong Cheuk Kwan* (p. 26). They were to the effect that the word "reckless" was to be preferred to the word "negligence" with whatever epithet. However, in view of the different tests and meanings which had in various contexts been attached to reckless and recklessness their Lordships thought it preferable to avoid those words when directing juries as to involuntary manslaughter by breach of duty.

In each of the three appeals, criticism had been made in argument of the directions given by the judge. Before proceeding to the specific issues raised in each appeal, their Lordships wished to say that they had the greatest sympathy with the judges in having to decide how to direct the jury as to the true ingredients of involuntary manslaughter. It had been difficult for judges to know which line of authority to follow.

Their Lordships considered each appeal in detail and concluded that for reasons which they had set out, the appeals of Dr. Prentice and Dr. Sullman would be allowed, the appeal of Dr. Adomako would be dismissed and the appeal of Mr. Holloway would be allowed.

His Lordship, in concluding, said that, before parting with the cases, the state of the law of manslaughter prompted their Lordships to urge that the Law Commission take the opportunity to examine the subject in all its aspects as a matter of urgency. The appeals had exemplified the problems in the particular type of manslaughter.

A Note on Motor Manslaughter

Where death is caused by the driving of a motor vehicle the principles applicable to determine whether the motorist is guilty of manslaughter ought, in principle, to be the same as where death is caused by the use of a gun, a knife or, as in *Holloway*, by faulty electric wiring.

It is to be noted, however, that in the *Sulman, Prentice, Adomako* and *Holloway* cases the principles laid down are not necessarily applicable to cases where death is caused by the use of a motor vehicle. The Lord Chief Justice says, "Leaving motor manslaughter aside"—which suggests that some other test is applicable. Why should this be so and what is the other test that is applicable? To understand the answers it is perhaps best to look at the matter historically.

It has always been the law, and still is, that a motorist who kills may be convicted of manslaughter. In *Andrews*, above, p. 337, it will be noted that the conviction of the motorist for manslaughter was upheld and Lord Atkin said that death caused by negligent driving "is to be treated in law as death caused by any other form of negligence." But it was notoriously difficult to secure a conviction for manslaughter in such cases and in 1956 it was made an offence, punishable with five years' imprisonment, to cause death by driving a motor vehicle on a road "recklessly, or at speed or in a manner dangerous to the public."

In his speech in *Andrews* Lord Atkin referred to the offences of reckless and dangerous driving (these two offences existed at that time but the offence of causing death by such driving was not then in existence) as well as the offence of careless driving. To his mind they represented three degrees of negligence with careless driving at the lower end, reckless driving at the higher end of the spectrum and with dangerous driving between the two. Clearly the lack of care which suffices for careless driving would not, when death results, justify a conviction for manslaughter. Lord Atkin evidently thought that reckless driving which caused death would suffice for manslaughter. But what of dangerous driving which caused death? His Lordship thought it was possible to envisage cases where driving could be properly characterised as dangerous without demonstrating the very high degree of negligence necessary to support a conviction for manslaughter. So, and while the conviction was upheld in *Andrews*, Lord Atkin said the trial judge was wrong to direct the jury that if the death had been caused by dangerous driving then they could convict of manslaughter. Though causing death by reckless or dangerous driving carries the same maximum sentence, the former was regarded as more serious than the latter.

In practice juries rarely convicted motorists of manslaughter and usually preferred the option of causing death by dangerous (notice dangerous not reckless) driving. The courts experienced difficulty in articulating a satisfactory definition of dangerous driving (at one stage it was held to be an offence of strict liability so that a motorist could be convicted of causing death by dangerous driving without being in any way negligent!) and the legislature intervened to "solve" the problem by abolishing dangerous driving in the Criminal Law Act 1977.

The first case in which the House of Lords considered causing death by reckless driving was *Lawrence* ([1982] A.C. 510). This decision followed hard on the heels of *Caldwell*, above. p. 133, and was profoundly influenced by it. Driving was reckless, according to *Lawrence* if: (i) it created an obvious and serious risk of causing physical injury to another road user or of doing substantial damage to property; *and* (ii) the driver had *either* (a) given no thought to the possibility of there being any such risk, *or* (b) recognised that some such risk was involved but had gone on to take it. (Do you think that the definition of recklessness in *Lawrence* accords with Lord Atkin's formulation in *Andrews*?) Then in the following year in *Jennings* v. *United States Government* ([1983] A.C. 624) the House of Lords ruled, in extradition proceedings, that the offence of causing death by reckless driving was manslaughter even though it was also a statutory offence. Manslaughter and causing death by reckless driving were thus held to be coterminous though the former carried life imprisonment while the latter carries a maximum of five years' imprisonment.

The House of Lords subsequently sought in the cases of *Seymour* and *Kong Chenk Kwan* v. *R.*, referred to in *Sulman*, in effect, to replace gross negligence manslaughter by reckless manslaughter, the relevant definition of recklessness being provided by *Caldwell* and *Lawrence*. The question that needs to be addressed at this point is: does it make a scrap of difference? Is not a person who is reckless in the *Caldwell/Lawrence* sense also grossly negligent? Does it make any difference which test is applied?

In *Reid* ([1992] 1 W.L.R. 793) where the defendant was convicted of causing death by reckless driving the House of Lords reaffirmed the *Lawrence* test. In so doing, however, the House accepted that while a person was *Caldwell/Lawrence* reckless if owing to his incompetence he failed to recognise a risk of any injury to the person or of substantial damage to property, s/he was *not Caldwell/Lawrence* reckless if s/he recognised that there was such a risk and, owing to incompetence, thought that the measures taken would obviate it. Such a driver could neither be convicted of causing death by reckless driving nor of manslaughter. But Lord Atkin in *Andrews* appears to have thought otherwise. He there said: "Probably of all the epithets that can be applied, 'reckless' most nearly covers the case. It is difficult to visualise a case of death caused by reckless driving in the connotation of that term in ordinary speech which would not justify a conviction for manslaughter; but it is probably not all-embracing, for 'reckless' suggests an indifference to risk whereas the accused may have appreciated the risk and intended to avoid it and yet shown such a high degree of negligence in the means adopted to avoid the risk as would justify a conviction."

In the *Sulman* and other cases the Court of Appeal sought to rehabilitate gross negligence manslaughter. The Court of Appeal apparently agrees with Lord Atkin in thinking that conduct may be *Bateman/Andrews* grossly negligent though it is not *Caldwell/Lawrence* reckless. In view of the reaffirmation in *Reid* of *Lawrence* the Court of Appeal said that "leaving aside motor manslaughter" the appropriate test was gross negligence.

One further strand to the argument must be taken in. Following recommendations in the *North Report* (Road Traffic Law Review Report (H.M.S.O., 1988) the legislature once again changed the goalposts. The offence of reckless driving (and consequentially the offence of causing death by reckless driving) has been abolished. Dangerous driving (and causing death by dangerous driving) has been reintroduced. This time the legislation (the Road Traffic Act 1991 substituting provisions in the Road Traffic Act 1988) provides a definition of dangerous driving. It is driving which falls far below what would be expected of a competent and careful driver and such driving as would be obvious to a competent and careful driver would be dangerous.

The decision in *Reid* is thus no longer of any importance concerning causing death by reckless driving for there is no longer any such offence. *Reid*, however, remains authoritative in relation to motor manslaughter, if not, following the *Sulman* and other cases, applicable to manslaughter generally. The *Caldwell/Lawrence* test remains appropriate in cases of motor manslaughter but not in other cases.

Not surprisingly the Court of Appeal in *Sulman* urged the Law Commission to examine the subject of manslaughter in all its aspects as a matter of urgency.

Chapter 7

Non-Fatal Offences Against the Person

1. ASSAULT AND BATTERY

A. General Requirements of Assault and Battery

Collins v. Wilcock

[1984] 3 All E.R. 374 (D.C.)

[The respondent, a police officer, saw the appellant apparently soliciting for the purposes of prostitution. The police are empowered by statute to arrest a "common" prostitute and to establish that a woman is a common prostitute the police practice was to caution the woman on the first two occasions she was found to be soliciting and on the third to arrest her. The appellant was not a known prostitute; she was asked to get into the police car for questioning but refused and walked away. For the purpose of ascertaining the appellant's identity with a view to administering a caution the respondent took hold of the appellant by the arm. The appellant then became abusive and scratched the respondent's arm with her fingernails.

The appellant was convicted of assaulting a police officer in the execution of her duty, the magistrate holding that it was the duty of the respondent to make the relevant inquiries with a view to cautioning her, and that in putting out her arm to restrain the appellant the respondent was not acting unreasonably.]

Robert Goff L.J. The law draws a distinction, in terms more easily understood by philologists than by ordinary citizens, between an assault and a battery. An assault is an act which causes another person to apprehend the infliction of immediate, unlawful, force on his person; a battery is the actual infliction of unlawful force on another person. Both assault and battery are forms of trespass to the person. Another form of trespass to the person is false imprisonment, which is the unlawful imposition of constraint on another's freedom of movement from a particular place. The requisite mental element is of no relevance in the present case.

We are here concerned primarily with battery. The fundamental principle, plain and incontestable, is that every person's body is inviolate. It has long been established that any touching of another person, however slight, may amount to a battery. So Holt C.J. held in 1704 that 'the least touching of another in anger is a battery': see *Cole* v. *Turner* (1704) 6 Mod. Rep. 149, 90 E.R. 958. The breadth of the principle reflects the fundamental nature of the interest so protected; as Blackstone wrote in his Commentaries, 'the law cannot draw the line between different degrees of violence, and therefore totally prohibits the first and lowest stage of it; every man's person being sacred, and no other having a right to meddle with it, in any the slightest manner' (see 3 Bl Com. 120). The effect is that everybody is protected not only against physical injury but against any form of physical molestation.

But so widely drawn a principle must inevitably be subject to exceptions. For example, children may be subjected to reasonable punishment; people may be subjected to the lawful exercise of the power of arrest; and reasonable force may be used in self-defence or for the prevention of crime. But, apart from these special instances where the control or constraint is lawful, a broader exception has been created to allow for the exigencies of everyday life. Generally speaking, consent is a defence to battery; and most of the physical contacts of ordinary life are not actionable because they are impliedly consented to by all who move in society and so expose themselves to the risk of bodily contact. So nobody can complain of the jostling which is inevitable from his presence in, for example, a supermarket, an underground station or a busy street; nor can a person who attends a party complain if his hand is seized in friendship, or even if his back is (within reason) slapped ... Although such cases are regarded as examples of implied consent, it is more common nowadays to treat them as falling within a general exception embracing all physical contact which is generally acceptable in the ordinary conduct of daily life. We observe that, although in the past it has sometimes been stated that a battery is only committed where the action is 'angry, or revengeful, or rude, or insolent' ..., we think that nowadays it is more realistic, and indeed more accurate, to state the broad underlying principle, subject to the broad exception.

Among such forms of conduct, long held to be acceptable, is touching a person for the purpose of engaging his attention, though of course using no greater degree of physical contact than is reasonably necessary in the circumstances for the purpose. So, for example, it was held by the Court of Common Pleas in 1807 that a touch by a constable's staff on the shoulder of a man who had climbed on a gentleman's railing to gain a better view of a mad ox, the touch being only to engage the man's attention, did not amount to a battery (see *Wiffin* v. *Kincard* (1807)) 2 Bos. & P.N.R. 471, 127 E.R. 713 ... But a distinction is drawn between a touch to draw a man's attention, which is generally acceptable, and a physical restraint, which is not. So we find Parke B. observing in *Rawlings* v. *Till* (1837) 3 M. & W. 28 at 29, 150 E.R. 1042, with reference to *Wiffin* v. *Kincard*, that "There the touch was merely to engage a man's attention, not to put a restraint on his person." Furthermore, persistent touching to gain attention in the face of obvious disregard may transcend the norms of acceptable behaviour, and so be outside the exception. We do not say that more than one touch is never permitted; for example, the lost or distressed may surely be permitted a second touch, or possibly even more, on a reluctant or impervious sleeve or shoulder, as may a person who is acting reasonably in the exercise of a duty. In each case, the test must be whether the physical contract so persisted in has in the circumstances gone beyond generally acceptable standards of conduct; and the answer to that question will depend on the facts of the particular case.

The distinction drawn by Parke B. in *Rawlings* v. *Till* is of importance in the case of police officers. Of course, a police officer may subject another to restraint when he lawfully exercises his power of arrest ... But, putting such cases aside, police officers have for present purposes no greater rights than ordinary citizens. It follows that, subject to such cases, physical contact by a police officer with another person may be unlawful as a battery, just as it might be if he was an ordinary member of the public. But a police officer has his rights as a citizen, as well as his duties as a policeman. A police officer may wish to engage a man's attention, for example if he wishes to question him. If he lays his hand on the man's sleeve or taps his shoulder for that purpose, he commits no wrong. He may even do so more than once; for he is under a duty to prevent and investigate crime, and so his seeking further, in the exercise of that duty, to engage a man's attention in order to speak to him may in the circumstances be regarded as acceptable (see *Donnelly* v. *Jackman* [1970] 1 All E.R. 987). But if, taking into account the nature of his duty, his use of physical contact in the face of non-co-operation persists beyond generally acceptable standards of conduct, his action will become unlawful; and if a police officer restrains a man, for example by gripping his arm or his shoulder, then his action will also be unlawful, unless he is lawfully exercising his power of arrest. A police officer has no power to require a man to answer him, though he has the advantages of authority, enhanced as it is by the uniform which the state provides and requires him to wear, in seeking a response to his inquiry. What is not permitted, however, is the unlawful use of force or the unlawful threat (actual or implicit) to use force; and, excepting the lawful exercise of his power of arrest, the lawfulness of a police officer's conduct is judged by the same criteria as are applied to the conduct of any ordinary citizen of this country.

We have been referred by counsel to certain cases directly concerned with charges of assaulting a police officer in the execution of his duty, the crucial question in each case being whether the police officer, by using physical force on the accused in response to which the accused assaulted the police officer, was acting unlawfully and so not acting in the execution of his duty. In *Kenlin* v. *Gardiner* [1967] 2 Q.B. 510 it was held that action by police officers in catching hold of two schoolboys was performed not in the course of arresting them but for the purpose of detaining them for questioning and so was unlawful ...

In *Donnelly* v. *Jackman* the police officer wished to question the defendant about an offence which he had cause to believe that the defendant had committed. Repeated requests by the police officer to the defendant to stop and speak to him were ignored. The officer tapped him on the shoulder; he made it plain that he had no intention of stopping to speak to him. The officer persisted and again tapped the defendant on the shoulder, whereupon the defendant turned and struck him with some force. The justices convicted the defendant of assaulting the officer in the execution of his duty, and this court dismissed an appeal from that conviction by way of case stated. The court was satisfied that the officer had not detained the defendant, distinguishing *Kenlin* v. *Gardiner* as a case where the officers had in fact detained the boys (see [1970] 1 All E.R. 987 at 989, [1970] 1 W.L.R. 562 at 565). It appears that they must have considered that the justices were entitled to conclude that the action of the officer, in persistently tapping the defendant on the shoulder, did not in the circumstances of the case exceed the bounds of acceptable conduct, despite the fact that the defendant had made it clear that he did not intend to respond to the officer's request to stop and speak to him; we cannot help feeling that this is an extreme case.

Finally, in *Bentley* v. *Brudzinski* (1982) 75 Cr.App.Rep. 217 it was found by the justices that the police officer, having caught up with the defendant, said, "Just a minute"; then, not in any hostile way, but merely to attract attention, he placed his right hand on the defendant's left shoulder. The defendant then swore at the police officer and punched him in the face; and a struggle ensued. The justices considered that the act of the police officer amounted to unlawful attempt to stop and detain the defendant, and so dismissed an information against the defendant alleging that he assaulted the police officer in the execution of his duty. This court dismissed the prosecutor's appeal by way of case stated; it appears that they considered that, having regard to all the facts of the case as found by the justices, they were entitled to hold that the police officer's act was performed not merely to engage the attention of the defendant, but as part of a course of conduct in which the officer was attempting unlawfully to detain the defendant.

We now return to the facts of the present case. Before us, counsel for the respondent police officer sought to justify her conduct, first by submitting that, since the practice of cautioning women found loitering or soliciting in public places for the purposes of prostitution is recognised by section 2 of the 1959 Act, therefore it is implicit in the statute that police officers have a power to caution, and for that purpose they must have the power to stop and detain women in order to find out their names and addresses and, if appropriate, caution them. This submission, which accords with the opinion expressed by the magistrate, we are unable to accept. The fact that the statute recognises the practice of cautioning by providing a review procedure does not, in our judgment, carry with it an implication that police officers have the power to stop and detain women for the purpose of implementing the system of cautioning. If it had been intended to confer any such power on police officers that power could and should, in our judgment, have been expressly conferred by the statute.

Next, counsel for the respondent submitted that the purpose of the police officer was simply to carry out the cautioning procedure and that, having regard to her purpose, her action could not be regarded as unlawful. Again, we cannot accept that submission. If the physical contact went beyond what is allowed by law, the mere fact that the police officer has the laudable intention of carrying out the cautioning procedure in accordance with established practice cannot, we think, have the effect of rendering her action lawful. Finally, counsel for the respondent submitted that the question whether the respondent was or was not acting in the execution of her duty was a question of fact for the magistrate to decide; and that he was entitled, on the facts found by him, to conclude that the respondent had been acting lawfully. We cannot agree. The fact is that the respondent took hold of the appellant; and since her action went beyond the generally acceptable conduct of touching a person to engage his or her attention, it must follow, in our judgment, that her action constituted a battery on the appellant, and was therefore unlawful. It follows that the appellant's appeal must be allowed, and her conviction quashed . . .

Note

Robert Goff L.J. said in the above case that the law draws a distinction between assault and battery. What is the distinction? Suppose X aims to strike Y on the back but misses and that Y is unaware of this. Is X guilty of (i) assault; (ii) attempted assault; (iii) battery; (iv) attempted battery?

B.　Unlawfulness

As Robert Goff L.J. points out in *Collins* v. *Wilcock*, what would otherwise constitute an assault or a battery may be justified. Reasonable force may be used against another for the purpose of effecting an arrest, or in self-defence, or in the prevention of crime. In addition, and since assault requires an apprehension by the victim of an *unwanted* contact and battery requires an *unwanted* contact, it follows that if the victim consents to the contact, the contact should not be unlawful. But this requires two issues to be addressed: (i) what constitutes consent; and (ii) what restrictions the law places on conduct to which consent may be given.

Bolduc and Bird v. R.

(1967) 63 D.L.R. (2d.) 82 (Sup.Ct. of Canada)

[Bolduc was a qualified medical practitioner and Bird was a musician who claimed to be interested in entering the medical profession. Bolduc was due to perform a vaginal examination of the complainant. He introduced Bird to her as a medical student and asked if she minded if he remained during the examination. As she believed him to be a bona fide student she consented. When the true facts emerged Bolduc and Bird were convicted of an indecent assault. (In order to establish indecent assault, the prosecution must establish an assault.) On appeal to the Supreme Court of Canada from a decision of the Court of Appeal which had dismissed their first appeal:]

Hall J. The question for decision is whether on those facts and in the circumstances so described the appellants Bolduc and Bird were guilty of an indecent assault upon the person of the complainant contrary to s.141 of the *Criminal Code* which reads:

141(1) Every one who indecently assaults a female person is guilty of an indictable offence and is liable to imprisonment for five years and to be whipped.

(2) An accused who is charged with an offence under subsection (1) may be convicted if the evidence establishes that the accused did anything to the female person with her consent that, but for the consent, would have been an indecent assault, if her consent was obtained by false and fraudulent representation as to the nature and quality of the act.

With respect, I do not agree that an indecent assault was committed within the meaning of this section. What Bolduc did was unethical and reprehensible in the extreme and was something no reputable medical practitioner would have countenanced. However, Bolduc's unethical conduct and the fraud practised upon the complainant do not of themselves necessarily imply an infraction of s.141. It is common ground that the examination and treatment, including the insertion of the speculum were consented to by the complainant. The question is: "Was her consent obtained by false and fraudulent representations as to the nature and quality of the act?" Bolduc did exactly what the complainant understood he would do and intended that he should do, namely, to examine the vaginal tract and to cauterize the affected parts. Inserting the speculum was necessary for these purposes. There was no fraud on his part as to what he was supposed to do and in what he actually did. The complainant knew that Bird was present and consented to his presence. The fraud that was practised on her was not as to the nature and quality of what was to be done but was as to Bird's identity as a medical intern. His presence as distinct from some overt act by him was not an assault. However, any overt act either alone or in common with Bolduc would have transposed the situation into an unlawful assault, but Bird did not touch the complainant; he merely looked on and listened to Bolduc's comments on what was being done because of the condition then apparent in the vaginal tract. Bird was in a sense a "peeping Tom.". . .

The question of fraud vitiating a woman's consent in the case of rape or indecent assault was fully canvassed by Stephen J., in *R.* v. *Clarence* (1888), and by the High Court of Australia in *Papadimitropoulos* v. *The Queen* (1957), where the court, in concluding a full review of the relevant law and cases decided up to that ... time said [p. 261]:

To return to the central point; rape is carnal knowledge of a woman without her consent: carnal knowledge is the physical fact of penetration; it is the consent to that which is in question; such a consent demands a perception as to what is about to take place, as to the identity of the man and the character of what he is doing. But once the consent is comprehending and actual the inducing causes cannot destroy its reality ...

The complainant here knew what Bolduc was proposing to do to her, for this was one in a series of such treatments. Her consent to the examination and treatment was real and comprehending and it cannot, therefore, be said that her consent was obtained by false or fraudulent representations as to the nature and quality of the act to be done, for that was not the fraud practised on her. The fraud was as to Bird being a medical intern and it was not represented that he would do anything but observe. It was intended that the examination and treatment would be done by Bolduc and this he did without assistance or participation by Bird.

I would, accordingly, allow the appeals, quash the convictions and direct that a verdict of acquittal be entered for both appellants.

Notes and Questions

1. In *Clarence*, which the Supreme Court of Canada followed in *Bolduc & Bird*, Clarence, knowing that he was infected with gonorrhoea, had intercourse with his wife and infected her. His wife would not have consented to the intercourse had she known that he was infected. It was held that Clarence had not assaulted his wife.

2. Would the result have been different in *Bolduc & Bird* if the complainant, having been deceived into thinking that Bird was a medical student, had allowed Bird to conduct the vaginal examination? Can fraud ever vitiate consent?

3. Does a person whose consent has been secured by deception *really* consent?

R. v. Brown

[1993] 2 All E.R. 75 (H.L.)

[The appellants were homosexuals who willingly co-operated in the commission of acts of sado-masochism against each other, including whipping and caning, the application of stinging nettles to the genital area, and the insertion of map pins and fish hooks into the penis. This activity was carried out in private, there was no permanent injury, no infection and no evidence that any of the men required medical treatment.

The appellants were convicted of assault occasioning actual bodily harm contrary to section 47 and of malicious wounding contrary to section 20 of the

Offences against the Person Act 1861 (below, p. 393). Their convictions were upheld by the Court of Appeal which certified the following point of law for the House of Lords:

> "Where A wounds or assaults B occasioning him actual bodily harm in the course of a sado-masochistic encounter, does the prosecution have to establish lack of consent on the part of B before they can establish A's guilt under section 20 and section 47 of the 1861, Offences against the Person Act?"

The House of Lords, by three votes to two, answered the question in the negative.]

Lord Templeman ... In the present case each of the appellants intentionally inflicted violence upon another (to whom I refer as "the victim") with the consent of the victim and thereby occasioned actual bodily harm or in some cases wounding or grievous bodily harm. Each appellant was therefore guilty of an offence under section 47 or section 20 of the Act of 1861 unless the consent of the victim was effective to prevent the commission of the offence or effective to constitute a defence to the charge.

In some circumstances violence is not punishable under the criminal law. When no actual bodily harm is caused, the consent of the person affected precludes him from complaining. There can be no conviction for the summary offence of common assault if the victim has consented to the assault. Even when violence is intentionally inflicted and results in actual bodily harm, wounding or serious bodily harm the accused is entitled to be acquitted if the injury was a foreseeable incident of a lawful activity in which the person injured was participating. Surgery involves intentional violence resulting in actual or sometimes serious bodily harm but surgery is a lawful activity. Other activities carried on with consent by or on behalf of the injured person have been accepted as lawful notwithstanding that they involve actual bodily harm or may cause serious bodily harm. Ritual circumcision, tattooing, ear-piercing and violent sports including boxing are lawful activities.

In earlier days some other forms of violence were lawful and when they ceased to be lawful they were tolerated until well into the 19th century. Duelling and fighting were at first lawful and then tolerated provided the protagonists were voluntary participants. But where the results of these activities was the maiming of one of the participants, the defence of consent never availed the aggressor; see *Hawkins Pleas of the Crown* (8th ed., 1824), Chap. 15. A maim was bodily harm whereby a man was deprived of the use of any member of his body which he needed to use in order to fight but a bodily injury was not a maim merely because it was a disfigurement. The act of maim was unlawful because the King was deprived of the services of an able-bodied citizen for the defence of the realm. Violence which maimed was unlawful despite consent to the activity which produced the maiming. In these days there is no difference between maiming on the one hand and wounding or causing grievous bodily harm on the other hand except with regard to sentence.

When duelling became unlawful, juries remained unwilling to convict but the judges insisted that persons guilty of causing death or bodily injury should be convicted despite the consent of the victim.

Similarly, in the old days, fighting was lawful provided the protagonists consented because it was thought that fighting inculcated bravery and skill and physical fitness. The brutality of knuckle fighting however caused the courts to declare that such fights were unlawful even if the protagonists consented. Rightly or wrongly the courts accepted that boxing is a lawful activity.

In *R. v. Coney* (1882) 8 Q.B.D. 534, the court held that a prize-fight in public was unlawful ...

The conclusion is that a prize-fight being unlawful, actual bodily harm or serious bodily harm inflicted in the course of a prize-fight is unlawful notwithstanding the consent of the protagonists.

In *R. v. Donovan* [1934] 2 K.B. 498 the appellant in private beat a girl of seventeen for purposes of sexual gratification, it was said with her consent. Swift J. said, at 507 that:

"It is an unlawful act to beat another person with such a degree of violence that the infliction of bodily harm is a probable consequence, and when such an act is proved, consent is immaterial."

In *Attorney-General's Reference (No. 6 of 1980)* [1981] Q.B. 715 where two men quarrelled and fought with bare fists Lord Lane C.J., delivering the judgment of the Court of Appeal said, at 719:

"... It is not in the public interest that people should try to cause, or should cause, each other bodily harm for no good reason. Minor struggles are another matter. So, in our judgment, it is immaterial whether the act occurs in private or in public; it is an assault if actual bodily harm is intended and/or caused. This means that most fights will be unlawful regardless of consent. Nothing which we have said is intended to cast doubt upon the accepted legality of properly conducted games and sports, lawful chastisement or correction, reasonable surgical interference, dangerous exhibitions, etc. These apparent exceptions can be justified as involving the exercise of a legal right, in the case of chastisement or correction, or as needed in the public interest, in the other cases."

Duelling and fighting are both unlawful and the consent of the protagonists affords no defence to charges of causing actual bodily harm, wounding or grievous bodily harm in the course of an unlawful activity.

The appellants and their victims in the present case were engaged in consensual homosexual activities. The attitude of the public towards homosexual practices changed in the second half of this century. Change in public attitudes led to a change in the law.

The Wolfenden Report (Report of the Committee on Homosexual Offences and Prostitution (1957), Cmnd. 247) declared that the function of the criminal law in relation to homosexual behaviour 'is to preserve public order and decency, to protect the citizen from what is offensive or injurious, and to provide sufficient safeguards against exploitation and corruption of others, particularly those who are especially vulnerable because they are young, weak in body or mind, inexperienced, or in a state of special, physical, official or economic dependence'; paragraph 13 of Chapter 2.

In response to the Wolfenden Report and consistently with its recommendations, Parliament enacted section 1 of the Sexual Offences Act 1967 [His Lordship read section 1] . . .

By the Act of 1967, Parliament recognised and accepted the practice of homosexuality. Subject to exceptions not here relevant, sexual activities conducted in private between not more than two consenting adults of the same sex or different sexes are now lawful. Homosexual activities performed in circumstances which do not fall within section 1(1) of the Act of 1967 remain unlawful. Subject to the respect for private life embodied in the Act of 1967, Parliament has retained criminal sanctions against the practice, dissemination and encouragement of homosexual activities.

My Lords, the authorities dealing with the intentional infliction of bodily harm do not establish that consent is a defence to a charge under the Act of 1861. They establish that the courts have accepted that consent is a defence to the infliction of bodily harm in the course of some lawful activities. The question is whether the defence should be extended to the infliction of bodily harm in the course of sado-masochistic encounters. The Wolfenden Committee did not make any recommendations about sado-masochism and Parliament did not deal with violence in 1967. The Act of 1967 is of no assistance for present purposes because the present problem was not under consideration.

The question whether the defence of consent should be extended to the consequences of sado-masochistic encounters can only be decided by consideration of policy and public interest. Parliament can call on the advice of doctors, psychiatrists, criminologists, sociologists and other experts and can also sound and take into account public opinion. But the question must at this stage be decided by this House in its judicial capacity in order to determine whether the convictions of the appellants should be upheld or quashed.

Counsel for some of the appellants argued that the defence of consent should be extended to the offence of occasioning actual bodily harm under section 47 of the Act of 1861 but should not be available to charges of serious wounding and the inflicting of serious bodily harm under section 20. I do not consider that this solution is practicable. Sado-masochistic participants have no way of foretelling the degree of bodily harm which will result from their encounters. The differences between actual bodily harm and serious bodily harm cannot be satisfactorily applied by a jury in order to determine acquittal or conviction.

Counsel for the appellants argued that consent should provide a defence to charges under both section 20 and section 47 because, it was said, every person has a right to deal with his body as he pleases. I do not consider that this slogan provides a sufficient guide to the policy decision which must now be made. It is an offence for a person to abuse his own body and mind by taking drugs. Although the law is often broken, the criminal law restrains a practice which is regarded as dangerous and injurious to individuals and which if allowed and extended is harmful to society generally. In any event the appellants in this case did not mutilate their own bodies. They inflicted bodily harm on willing victims. Suicide is no longer an offence but a person who assists another to commit suicide is guilty of murder or manslaughter.

The assertion was made on behalf of the appellants that the sexual appetites of sadists and masochists can only be satisfied by the infliction of bodily harm and that the law should not punish the consensual achievement of sexual satisfaction. There was no evidence to support the assertion that sado-masochist activities are essential to the happiness of the appellants or any other participants but the argument would be acceptable if sado-masochism were only concerned with sex, as the appellants contend. In my opinion sado-masochism is not only concerned with sex. Sado-masochism is also concerned with violence. The evidence discloses that the practices of the appellants were unpredictably dangerous and degrading to body and mind and were developed with increasing barbarity and taught to persons whose consents were dubious or worthless.

A sadist draws pleasure from inflicting or watching cruelty. A masochist derives pleasure from his own pain or humiliation. The appellants are middle-aged men. The victims were youths some of whom were introduced to sado-masochism before they attained the age of 21. In his judgment in the Court of Appeal, Lord Lane C.J. said that two members of the group of which the appellants formed part, namely one Cadman and the appellant Laskey:

"... were responsible in part for the corruption of a youth K ... It is some comfort at least to be told, as we were, that K has now it seems settled into a normal hetrosexual relationship. Cadman had befriended K when the boy was 15 years old. He met him in a cafeteria and, so he says, found out that the boy was interested in homosexual activities. He introduced and encouraged K in "bondage affairs". He was interested in viewing and recording on videotape K and other teenage boys in homosexual scenes ... One cannot overlook the danger that the gravity of the assaults and injuries in this type of case may escalate to even more unacceptable heights."

[His Lordship referred to various of the sado-masochistic acts which had been performed, that while the appellants had not contracted AIDS two members of the group had died from AIDS, that the assertion that the instruments were sterile could not remove the risk of infection, that cruelty to humans had been supplemented by cruelty to animals in the form of bestiality, and that, given the nature of the acts, it was not surprising there had been no complaint to the police.]

In principle there is a difference between violence which is incidental and violence which is inflicted for the indulgence of cruelty. The violence of sado-masochistic encounters involves the indulgence of cruelty by sadists and the degradation of victims. Such violence is injurious to the participants and unpredictably dangerous. I am not prepared to invent a defence of consent for sado-masochistic encounters which breed and glorify cruelty and result in offences under sections 47 and 20 of the Act of 1861 ...

Notes and Questions

1. Dissenting in *Brown*, Lord Mustil emphasised that the appellants had been prosecuted under the Offences *against* the Person Act. He did not think that cases holding that prize-fighting was illegal were authorities for a general principle that consent could never be a defence when actual bodily harm was caused. What had led to the proscription of prize-fighting was that the activity was often accompanied by public disorder. The issue, his Lordship said, was not whether activities such as those indulged in by the appellants should *cease* to be criminal but whether the 1861 Act *made* then criminal. Leaving aside repugnance and moral objection (neither of which his Lordship thought sufficed for making conduct criminal) why should the conduct be made criminal?

2. Lord Templeman thought that the issue in the case could be determined only by considerations of "policy and public interest." Whose policy? What public interest?

3. Suppose you had been a Lord of Appeal in *Brown*. How would you have decided the case and why?

4. Suppose a husband has become HIV positive. He tells his wife of this but the wife nevertheless consents to sexual intercourse. The wife becomes HIV positive and both contract AIDS. This would amount, at the very least, to actual bodily harm. Following *Brown*, is the husband guilty of an assault occasioning actual bodily harm and the wife guilty of abetting him? Or is *Brown* distinguishable?

2. Assault Occasioning Actual Bodily Harm

See section 47 of the Offences against the Person Act 1861, below, p. 393.

"Actual bodily harm" is not defined in the Act. Any bodily harm, however trivial, would suffice. Pouring beer over the victim or spitting in his face would, as such, not constitute actual bodily harm but the merest bruising would suffice. In *Miller* ([1954] 2 All E.R. 529) it was held that any hurt of injury calculated to interfere with the health or comfort of the victim would suffice and would include hurt or injury resulting, not in any physical injury, but also in injury by shock to the state of mind of the victim.

In *Chan-Fook* [1993] *The Times*, November 19, however, the Court of Appeal held that merely transient emotions experienced by the victim (such as shock, fear, panic, hysteria) did not constitute actual bodily harm; the psychiatric injury must be one which would be recognised as such by clinicians.

See *R. v. Savage, R. v. Parmenter, infra.*

3. Malicious Wounding

See section 20 of the Offences against the Person Act 1861, below, p. 393.

The offence under section 20 is generally referred to as malicious wounding but, as reference to section 20 shows, it includes the malicious infliction of grievous bodily harm as well as wounding. A wounding requires a breach in the continuity of the whole skin. This sounds serious but is not as serious as it sounds. While an abrasion or a bruise which does not result in breaking the continuity of the whole skin will not suffice, a minor cut (even a pinprick) would suffice. A wounding falls within the section though the wound falls well short of grievous bodily harm. The offence, in effect, has a hole in the middle. The defendant may cause significant harm to the victim (say extensive bruising in a fight) which is much more serious than a trivial wound but less serious than the harm required to sustain a charge of inflicting grievous bodily harm. Such a defendant cannot be convicted under section 20 even though the harm caused is more serious than a wound but falls short of grievous bodily harm. This is because the 1861 Act was a scissors-and-paste job where the draftsman was required to restate the previous law and not to reform it. The law is clearly in need of rationalisation but, for the time being, we have to live with it as it is.

R. v. Savage, R. v. Parmenter

[1991] 4 All E.R. 698 (H.L.)

[The combined appeals in these two cases resolved many of the uncertainties concerning the offences under section 47 and section 20 as well as affirming what is the requisite *mens rea* for an assault.

The facts of *Savage* are as follows. Mrs. Savage was convicted on a single count of the unlawful wounding of Ms. Beal contrary to section 20 of the 1861 Act. Ms. Beal was a former girlfriend of Mrs. Savage's husband and there was no love lost between the two though neither had encountered the other until they ran into one another in a public house. Mrs. Beal made her way to the table where Ms. Beal was sitting and saying, "Nice to meet you darling," she threw the contents of a glass of beer over Ms. Beal. Unfortunately Mrs. Savage let go of the glass since it, or a piece of it, struck Ms. Beal and cut her wrist. The jury found either that Mrs. Savage had deliberately thrown not only the beer but also the glass at Ms. Beal or, alternatively, while deliberately throwing the beer over Ms. Beal the glass, or a piece of it, had accidentally slipped from Mrs. Savage's hand and had injured Ms. Beal's wrist but with no intention that the glass should injure or cut Ms. Beal.

The facts of *Parmenter* sufficiently appear in the speech of Lord Ackner.

In *Parmenter* it appeared that during the first three months of his life, Paul Parmenter, the defendant's son, was by the defendant caused injuries to the bony structures of his legs and right forearm. Charged with offences under s. 18 and s. 20 of the 1861 Act, his defence was that, being unfamiliar with the handling of babies, he did not realise that the way in which he had handled his son would cause injury. He was convicted of offences under s. 20.]

Lord Ackner: ...

II *Can a verdict of assault occasioning actual bodily harm be returned upon proof of an assault together with proof of the fact that actual bodily harm was occasioned by the assault, or must the prosecution also prove that the defendant intended to cause actual bodily harm or was reckless as to whether harm would be caused?*

Your Lordships are concerned with the mental element of a particular kind of assault, an assault "occasioning actual bodily harm." It is common ground that the mental element of assault is an intention to cause the victim to apprehend immediate and unlawful violence or recklessness whether such apprehension be caused (see *R. v. Venna* [1975] 3 All E.R. 788, [1976] Q.B. 421). It is of course common ground that Mrs. Savage committed an assault upon Miss Beal when she threw the contents of her glass of beer over her. It is also common ground that however the glass came to be broken and Miss Beal's wrist thereby cut, it was, on the finding of the jury, Mrs. Savages's handling of the glass which caused Miss Beal "actual bodily harm." Was the offence thus established or is there a further mental state that has to be established in relation to the bodily harm element of the offence? Clearly the section, by its terms, expressly imposes no such a requirement. Does it do so by necessary implication? It uses neither the word "intentionally" nor the word "maliciously." The words "occasioning actual bodily harm" are descriptive of the word "assault," by reference to a particular kind of consequence.

In neither *R. v. Savage* nor *R. v. Spratt* nor in *R. v. Parmenter* was the court's attention invited to the decision of the Court of Appeal in *R. v. Roberts* (1972) 56 Cr.App.R. 95. This is perhaps explicable on the basis that this case is not referred to in the index to *Archbold's Criminal Pleading, Evidence and Practice* (43rd ed., 1988). The relevant text, states (para. 20–117): "The mens rea required [for actual bodily harm] is that required for common assault," without any authority being provided for this proposition.

It is in fact *R. v. Roberts* which provides authority for this proposition. Roberts was tried on an indictment which alleged that he indecently assaulted a young woman. He was acquitted on that charge, but convicted of assault occasioning actual bodily harm to her. The girl's complaint was that while travelling in the defendant's car he sought to make advances towards her and then tried to take her coat off. This was the last straw and, although the car was travelling at some speed, she jumped out and sustained injuries. The defendant denied he had touched the girl. He had had an argument with her and in the course of that argument she suddenly opened the door and jumped out. In his direction to the jury the chairman of quarter sessions stated: "If you are satisfied that he tried to pull off her coat and as a result she jumped out of the moving car then your verdict is guilty."

It was contended on behalf of the appellant that this direction was wrong since the chairman had failed to tell the jury that they must be satisfied that the appellant foresaw that she might jump out of the car as a result of his touching her before they could convict. The court rejected that submission. The test was, said the court (at 102):

"Was it [the action of the victim which resulted in actual bodily harm] the natural result of what the alleged assailant said and did in the sense that it was something that could reasonably have been foreseen as the consequence of what he was saying or doing? As it was put in one of the old cases, it had got to be shown to be his act, and if of course the victim does something so "daft", in the words of the appellant in this case, or so unexpected not that this particular assailant did not actually foresee it but that no reasonable man could be expected to foresee it, then it is only in a very remote and unreal sense a consequence of his assault, it is really occasioned by a voluntary act on the part of the victim which could not reasonably be foreseen and which breaks the chain of causation between the assault and the harm or injury."

Accordingly, no fault was found in the following direction of the chairman to the jury (at 103):

"If you accept the evidence of the girl in preference to that of the man, that means that there was an assault occasioning actual bodily harm, that means that she did jump out as a direct result of what he was threatening her with, and what he was doing to her, holding her coat, telling her that he had beaten up girls who had refused his advances, and that means that through his acts he was in law and in fact responsible for the injuries which were caused to her by her decision, if it can be called that, to get away from his violence, his threats, by jumping out of the car."

Thus, once the assault was established, the only remaining question was whether the victim's conduct was the natural consequence of that assault. The words 'occasioning' raised solely a question of causation, an objective question which does not involve inquiring into the accused's state of mind.

In *R. v. Spratt* [1991] 2 All E.R. 210 at 219, [1900] 1 W.L.R. 1073 at 1082 McCowan L.J. said:

"However, the history of the interpretation of the 1861 Act shows that, whether or not the word "maliciously" appears in the section in question, the courts have consistently held that the mens rea of every type of offence against the person covers both actual intent and recklessness, in the sense of taking the risk of harm ensuing with foresight that it might happen."

My Lords, in my respectful view, the Court of Appeal in *R. v. Parmenter* was wrong in preferring the decision in *R. v. Spratt.* The decision in *R. v. Roberts* (1972) 56 Cr.App.R. 95 was correct. The verdict of assault occasioning actual bodily harm may be returned upon proof of an assault together with proof of the fact that actual bodily harm was occasioned by the assault. The prosecution are not obliged to prove that the defendant intended to cause some actual bodily harm or was reckless as to whether such harm would be caused.

III. *In order to establish an offence under section 20 of the 1861 Act, must the prosecution prove that the defendant actually foresaw that his act would cause harm, or is it sufficient to prove that he ought so to have foreseen?*

Although your Lordships' attention has been invited to a plethora of decided cases, the issue is a narrow one. Is the decision of the Court of Criminal Appeal in *R. v. Cunningham* [1957] 2 All E.R. 412, [1957] 2 Q.B. 396 still good law, subject only to a gloss placed upon it by the Court of Appeal, Criminal Division in *R. v. Mowatt* [1967] 3 All E.R. 47, [1968] 1 Q.B. 421, or does the later decision of your Lordships' House in *R. v. Caldwell* [1981] 1 All E.R. 961, [1982] A.C. 341 provide the answer to this question?

. . .

These three decisions require detailed consideration.

Before returning to the submission made by Mr. Sedley, to which I have referred above, I think it is now convenient to go back in time to the decisions of the Court of Appeal in *R. v. Mowatt* [1967] 3 All E.R. 47, [1968] 1 Q.B. 421, to which reference has already been made. The facts of that case were simple. On September 30, 1966 in the early hours of the morning the defendant and a companion stopped a third man in the street and asked him whether there was a pub anywhere nearby. The defendant's companion then snatched a £5 note from the third man's breastpocket and ran off. The third man chased him without success and returned to the defendant, grasping him by the lapels and demanding to know where his companion had gone. The defendant then struck the third man, knocking him down. Two police officers saw the defendant sit astride the third man and strike him repeated blows in the face, pull him to his feet and strike him again, knocking him down and rendering him almost unconscious. The defendant admitted inflicting the first blow but claimed it was self-defence. He was tried on an indictment which included a count for wounding with intent to do grievous bodily harm contrary to section 18 of the

Offences against the Person Act 1861. In summing up on this count the trial judge told the jury they were entitled to return a verdict of unlawful wounding under section 20 of the Act. However in his summing up, while explaining the meaning of the word "unlawfully" so far as it was relevant to the defence of self-defence, he gave no direction as to the meaning of "maliciously."

The importance of this case is that the Court of Appeal considered *R. v. Cunningham* and, although modifying or explaining an important feature of that decision, in no way queried its validity. The judgment of the Court of Appeal, to which I have already made references, was, as previously stated, given by Diplock L.J., as he then was. It is of course one of Mr. Sedley's points that, although *R. v. Mowatt* was not referred to in *R. v. Caldwell*, it was most unlikely that its existence was overlooked, particularly by Lord Diplock. Diplock L.J. observed that "unlawfully and maliciously" was a fashionable phrase of parliamentary draftsmen in 1861 (see [1967] 3 All E.R. 47 at 49, [1968] 1 Q.B. 421 at 425). It ran as a theme, with minor variations, through the Malicious Damage Act 1861, and the Offences against the Person Act 1861. He then referred to the "very special" facts in *R. v. Cunningham* and observed:

> "No doubt on these facts the jury should have been instructed that they must be satisfied before convicting the accused *that he was aware* that physical harm to some human being was a possible consequence of his unlawful act in wrenching off the gas meter. In the words of the court " 'maliciously' in a statutory crime postulates foresight of consequence" (see [1957] 2 All E.R. 412 at 414, [1957] 2 Q.B. 396 at 399), and on this proposition we do not wish to cast any doubt." (My emphasis)

Subsequently, he added ([1967] 3 All E.R. 47 at 50, [1968] 1 Q.B. 421 at 426):

> "In the offence under s. 20, and in the alternative verdict which may be given on a charge under s. 18—for neither of which is any specific intent required—the word "maliciously" does import on the part of the person who unlawfully inflicts the wound or other grievous bodily harm an *awareness* that his act may have the consequence of causing some physical harm to some other person. That is what is meant by "the particular kind of harm" in the citation from Professor Kenny's Outlines of Criminal Law (18th edn, 1962, para 158a, p. 202). It is quite unnecessary that the *accused* should have foreseen that his unlawful act

might cause physical harm of the gravity described in the section, i.e., a wound or serious physical injury. It is enough that *he* should have foreseen that some physical harm to some person, albeit of a minor character, might result." (My emphasis)

Mr Smedley submitted that in R. v. *Caldwell* your Lordships' House could have followed either of two possible paths to its conclusion as to the meaning of "recklessly" in the 1971 Act. These were: (a) to hold that R. v. *Cunningham* (and R. v. *Mowatt*) were wrongly decided and to introduce a single test, wherever recklessness was an issue; or (b) to accept that R. v. *Cunningham* (subject to the R. v. *Mowatt* "gloss" to which no reference was made) correctly states the law in relation to the Offences against the Persons Act 1861, because the word "maliciously" in that statute was a term of legal art which imported into the concept of recklessness a special restricted meaning, thus distinguishing it from "reckless" or "recklessly" in modern "revising" statutes then before the House, where those words bore their then popular or dictionary meaning.

I agree with Mr. Sedley that manifestly it was the latter course which the House followed. Therefore in order to establish an offence under section 20 the prosecution must prove either that the defendant intended or that he actually foresaw that his act would cause harm.

IV. *In order to establish an offence under section 20 is it sufficient to prove that the defendant intended or foresaw the risk of some physical harm or must he intend or foresee either wounding or grievous bodily harm?*

It is convenient to set out once again the relevant part of the judgment of Diplock L.J. in R. v. *Mowatt* [1967] 3 All E.R. 47 at 50, [1968] 1 Q.B. 421 at 426. Having considered Professor Kenny's statement, which I have quoted above, he then said:

"In the offence under s. 20 ... for ... which [no] specific intent is required—the word "maliciously" does import ... an awareness that his act may have the consequence of causing some physical harm to some other person. That is what is meant by the "particular kind of harm" in the citation from Professor Kenny's Outlines of Criminal Law (18th edn, 1962, para 158a, p 202). It is quite unnecessary that the accused should have foreseen that his unlawful act might cause physical harm of the gravity described in the section, i.e. a wound or serious physical injury. *It is enough that he should have foreseen that some physical harm to some person, albeit of a minor character, might result."* (My emphasis)

Mr. Sedley submits that this statement of the law is wrong. He contends that, properly construed, the section requires foresight of a wounding or grievous bodily harm. He drew your Lordships' attention to criticisms of *R. v. Mowatt* made by Professor Glanville-Williams and by Professor J.C. Smith in their textbooks and in articles or commentaries. They argue that a person should not be criminally liable for consequences of his conduct unless he foresaw a consequence falling into the same legal category as that set out in the indictment.

Such a general principle runs contrary to the decision in *R. v. Roberts* (1972) 56 Cr.App.R. 95, which I have already stated to be, in my opinion, correct. The contention is apparently based on the proposition that, as the actus reus of a section 20 offence is the wounding or the infliction of grievous bodily harm, the mens rea must consist of foreseeing such wounding or grievous bodily harm. But there is no such hard and fast principle. To take but two examples, the actus reus of murder is the killing of the victim, but foresight of grievous bodily harm is sufficient and, indeed, such bodily harm need not be such as to be dangerous to life. Again, in the case of manslaughter death is frequently the unforeseen consequence of the violence used.

The argument that, as sections 20 and 47 have both the same penalty, this somehow supports the proposition that the foreseen consequences must coincide with the harm actually done, overlooks the oft-repeated statement that this is the irrational result of this piecemeal legislation. The Act "is a rag-bag of offences brought together from a wide variety of sources with no attempt, as the draftsman frankly acknowledged, to introduce consistency as to substance or as to form" (see Professor J.C. Smith in his commentary on *R. v. Parmenter* ([1991] Crim. L.R. 43)).

If s. 20 was to be limited to cases where the accused does not desire but does foresee wounding or grievous bodily harm, it would have a very limited scope. The *mens rea* in a section 20 crime is comprised in the word "maliciously." As was pointed out by Lord Lane C.J. giving the judgment of the Court of Appeal in *R. v. Sullivan* [1981] Crim. L.R. 46, the "particular kind of harm" in the citation from Professor Kenny was directed to "harm to the person" as opposed to "harm to property." Thus it was not concerned with the degree of the harm foreseen. It is accordingly in my judgment wrong to look upon the decision in *R. v. Mowatt* [1967] 3 All E.R. 47, [1968] 1 Q.B. 421 as being in any way inconsistent with the decision in *R.* v. *Cunningham* [1957] 2 All E.R. 412, [1957] 2 Q.B. 396.

My Lords, I am satisfied that the decision in *R.* v. *Mowatt* was correct and that it is quite unnecessary that the accused should either have intended or have foreseen that his unlawful act might cause physical harm of the gravity described in section 20, *i.e.* a wound or serious physical injury. It is enough that he should have foreseen that some physical harm to some person, albeit of a minor character, might result.

In the result I would dismiss the appeal in *Savage's* case but allow the appeal in *Parmenter's* case, but only to the extent of substituting, in accordance with the provisions of section 3(2) of the Criminal Appeal Act 1968, verdicts of guilty of assault occasioning actual bodily harm contrary to section 47 of the 1861 Act for the four section 20 offences of which he was convicted.

4.   Causing Grievous Bodily Harm with Intent

See section 18 of the Offences against the Person Act 1861, below, p. 393.

Grievous bodily harm, according to *D.P.P.* v. *Smith* ([1961] A.C. 290, H.L.), "means no more and no less than 'really serious'" bodily harm.

Where a victim sustains serious bodily harm at the hands of D, D may be convicted either of the offence under section 20 (which carries five years' imprisonment) or of the offence under section 18 (which carries imprisonment for life). Commonly D is charged with both offences and it is left to the jury to decide which one is made out. The offences differ, however, in two respects. If D is charged under section 18 with "unlawfully wounding or causing grievous bodily harm with intent to cause grievous bodily harm" then it must be proved that D intended to cause serious bodily harm, and nothing short of intention will suffice. If D is charged under section 20 with "unlawfully and maliciously wounding or inflicting grievous bodily harm" D may be convicted where D recklessly brings about the harm. Indeed, as *R.* v. *Parmenter, R.* v. *Savage* shows, so long as the *actus reus* is made out (*i.e.* that the victim has sustained a wound or serious bodily harm) D may be convicted if he intended or foresaw some degree of harm to the victim.

The second respect in which the offences differ is that section 18 uses the word "cause" while s. 20 uses the word "inflict." "Inflict" might be thought to be narrower than "cause." In *Clarence*, above p. 352, the majority of the court held that an infliction required an assault and since *Clarence* had not assaulted his wife, he could not be convicted under s. 20. Assuming that the harm sustained (gonorrhoea) amounts to serious bodily harm and that *Clarence* intended to infect his wife, it would be clear that Clarence had caused that harm. In *Wilson and Jenkins* ([1983] 3 All E.R. 488), however, it was held by the House of Lords that "inflicts" does not require an assault. But the House went on to say that "inflict" was narrower than "cause" in that it required that the harm be directly brought about or, though not directly brought about, does directly result in force being applied to the body. Quite what this means is unclear.

Questions

1. What is the *mens rea* of an offence under (i) section 47; (ii) section 20; and (iii) section 18 of the Offences against the Person Act 1861?

2. During the course of an argument Al threw a punch at Ben. Of what offences might Al be convicted if:

(a) the punch left Ben severely winded;

(b) the punch broke two of Ben's ribs;

(c) the punch opened up several stiches in Ben's stomach of which Al was unaware and Ben lost two pints of blood;

(d) Al had no intention of making contact with the punch and intended only to frighten Ben. Ben, however, jumped backwards to avoid the punch, knocked over a tea-urn and severely scalded himself?

Chapter 8

Offences Under the Theft Act 1968

1. THEFT

A. Meaning of Appropriation

Refer to section 3 of the Theft Act 1968, below, p. 397.

R. v. Gomez

[1993] 1 All E.R. 1

Lord Keith of Kinkel. My Lords, this appeal raises the question whether two decisions of your Lordships' House upon the proper construction of certain provisions of the Theft Act 1968 are capable of being reconciled with each other, and, if so, in what manner. The two decisions are *Lawrence* v. *Comr. of Police for the Metropolis* [1971] 2 All E.R. 1253, [1972] A.C. 626 and *R.* v. *Morris* [1983] 3 All E.R. 288, [1984] A.C. 320. The question has given rise to much debate in subsequent cases and in academic writings.

The facts of this case are that the respondent, Edwin Gomez, was employed as assistant manager at a shop trading by retail in electrical goods. In September 1987 he was asked by an acquaintance called Jit Ballay to supply goods from the shop and to accept payment by two stolen building society cheques, one for £7,950 and the other for £9,250, which were undated and bore no payee's name. The respondent agreed, and prepared a list of goods to the value of £7,950 which he submitted to the manager, Mr. Gilberd, saying that it represented a genuine order by one Johal and asking him to authorise the supply of the goods in return for a building society cheque in that sum. Mr. Gilberd instructed the respondent to confirm with the bank that the cheque was acceptable, and the respondent later told him that he had done so and that such a cheque was "as good as cash". Mr. Gilberd agreed to the transaction, the respondent paid the cheque into the bank, and a few days later Ballay took possession of the goods, the respondent helping him to load them into his vehicle. Shortly afterwards a further consignment of goods to the value of £9,250 was ordered and supplied in similar fashion ... Mr. Gilberd agreed to this transaction without further inquiry. Later the two cheques were returned by the bank marked "Orders not to pay. Stolen cheque".

The respondent [was convicted on two counts of theft] and he was sentenced to two years' imprisonment on each count to run concurrently. The respondent appealed to the Court of Appeal, Criminal Division which ... quashed the convictions. Lord Lane C.J., delivering the judgment of the court, after considering *Lawrence* v. *Comr. of Police for the Metropolis* and *R.* v. *Morris*, said:

"What in fact happened was that the owner was induced by deceit to agree to the goods being transferred to Ballay. If that is the case, and if in these circumstances the [respondent] is guilty of theft, it must follow that anyone who obtains goods in return for a cheque which he knows will be dishonoured on presentation, or indeed by way of any other similar pretence, would be guilty of theft. That does not seem to be the law. *R.* v. *Morris* decides that when a person by dishonest deception induces the owner to transfer his entire proprietory interests that is not theft. There is no appropriation at the moment when he takes possession of the goods because he was entitled to do so under the terms of the contract of sale, a contract which is, it is true, voidable, but has not been avoided at the time the goods are handed over ... We therefore conclude that there was a de facto, albeit voidable, contract between the owners and Ballay, that it was by virtue of that contract that Ballay took possession of the goods, that accordingly the transfer of the goods to him was with the consent and express authority of the owner and that accordingly there was no lack of authorisation and no appropriation."

The court later granted a certificate ... that a point of law of general public importance was involved in the decision, namely:

"When theft is alleged and that which is alleged to be stolen passes to the defendant with the consent of the owner, but that consent has been obtained by a false representation, has, (a) an appropriation within the meaning of s. 1(1) of the Theft Act 1968 taken place, or (b) must such a passing of property necessarily involve an element of adverse [interference] with or usurpation of some right of the owner?"

The Crown now appeals, with leave granted here, to your Lordships' House.

The provisions of the 1968 Act principally relevant are these:

[His Lordship referred to sections 1(1), 3(1), 4(1), 7 and 15(1).]

It is to be observed that by section 26 of the Criminal Justice Act 1991 the maximum sentence for theft was reduced from ten to seven years. The section 15(1) penalty was left unchanged.

The facts in *Lawrence* v. *Comr. of Police for the Metropolis* section as set out in the speech of Viscount Dilhorne, were these:

"... the appellant was convicted on 2 December 1969 of theft contrary to s. 1(1) of the Theft Act 1968. On 1st September 1969 a Mr. Occhi, an Italian who spoke little English, arrived at Victoria Station on his first visit to this country. He went up to a taxi driver, the appellant, and showed him a piece of paper on which an address in Ladbroke Grove was written. The appellant said that it was very far and very expensive. Mr. Occhi got into the taxi, took £1 out of his wallet and gave it to the appellant who then, the wallet being still open, took a further £6 out of it. He then drove Mr. Occhi to Ladbroke Grove. The correct lawfule fare for the journey was in the region of 10s. 6d. The appellant was charged with and convicted for the theft of the £6."

The conviction was upheld by the Court of Appeal, Criminal Division, which in granting leave to appeal to your Lordships' House certified the following questions as involving a point of law of general public importance:

"(1) Whether section 1(1) of the Theft Act, 1968, is to be construed as though it contained the words 'without the consent of the owner' or words to that effect.

(2) Whether the provisions of section 15(1) and of section 1(1) of the Theft Act, 1968, are mutually exclusive in the sense that if the facts proved would justify a

conviction under section 15(1) there cannot lawfully be a conviction under Section 1(1) on those facts."

Viscount Dilhorne, whose speech was concurred in by Lord Donovan, Lord Pearson, Lord Diplock and Lord Cross of Chelsea, after stating the facts, and expressing some doubts as to what Mr. Occhi had meant when he said that he "permitted" the taxi driver to take the £6, continued:

"The main contention of the appellant in this House and in the Court of Appeal was that Mr. Occhi had consented to the taking of the £6 and that, consequently, his conviction could not stand. In my opinion, the facts of this case to which I have referred fall far short of establishing that Mr. Occhio had so consented. Prior to the passage of the Theft Act 1968, which made radical changes in and greatly simplified the law relating to theft and some other offences, it was necessary to prove that the property alleged to have been stolen was taken 'without the consent of the owner' (Larceny Act 1916, s. 1(1)). These words are not included in s. 1(1) of the Theft Act 1968, but the appellant contended that the subsection should be construed as if they were, as if they appeared after the world 'appropriates'. Section 1(1) provides: 'A person is guilty of theft if he dishonestly appropriates property belonging to another with the intention of permanently depriving the other of it; and "thief" and "steal" shall be construed accordingly.' I see no ground for concluding that the omission of the words 'without the consent of the owner' was inadvertent and not deliberate, and to read the subsection as if they were included is, in my opinion, wholly unwarranted. Parliament by the omission of these words has relieved the prosecution of the burden of establishing that the taking was without the owner's consent. That is no longer an ingredient of the offence. Megaw L.J., delivering the judgment of the Court of Appeal said that the offence created by s. 1(1) involved four elements: '(i) a dishonest (ii) appropriation (iii) of property belonging to another (iv) with the intention of permanently depriving the owner of it.' I agree. That there was appropriation in this case is clear. Section 3(1) states that any assumption by a person of the rights of an owner amounts to an appropriation. Here there was clearly such an assumption. That an appropriation was dishonest may be proved in a number of ways. In this case it was not contended that the appellant had not acted dishonestly ... Belief or the absence of belief that the owner had with such knowledge consented to the appropriation is relevant to the issue of dishonesty, not to the question whether or not there has been an appropriation. They may occur even though the owner has permitted or consented to the property being taken. So proof that Mr. Occhi had consented to the appropriation of £6 from his wallet without agreeing to paying a sum in excess of the legal fare does not suffice to show that there was not dishonesty in this case. There was ample evidence that there was. I now turn to the third element 'property belonging to another'. Counsel for the appellant contended that if Mr. Occhi consented to the appellant taking the £6, he consented to the property in the money passing from him to the appellant and that the appellant had not, therefore, appropriated property belonging to another. He argued that the old distinction between the offence of false pretences and larceny had been preserved. I am unable to agree with this. The new offence of obtaining property by deception created by s. 15(1) of the Theft Act 1968 also contains the words 'belonging to another'. 'A person who by any deception dishonestly obtains property belonging to another with the intention of permanently depriving the other of it . . .' commits that offence. 'Belonging to another' in s. 1(1) and in s. 15(1) in my view signifies no more than that, at the time of the appropriation or the obtaining, the property belonged to another with the words 'belonging to another' having the extended meaning given by s. 5. The short answer to this contention on behalf of the appellant is that the money in the wallet which he appropriated belonged to another, to Mr. Occhi. There was no dispute about the appellant's intention being permanently to deprive Mr. Occhi of the money. The four elements of the offence of theft as defined in the Theft Act 1968 were thus clearly established and, in my view, the Court of Appeal was right to dismiss the appeal."

In the result, each of the certified questions was answered in the negative.

It will be seen that Viscount Dilhorne's speech contains two clear pronouncements, first that it is no longer an ingredient of the offence of theft that the taking should be without the owner's consent and, second, that an appropriation may occur even though the owner has permitted or consented to the property being taken. The answer given to the first certified question was in line with those pronouncements, so even though Viscount Dilhorne was of opinion that the evidence fell short of establishing that Mr. Occhi had consented to the taking of the £6 it was a matter of decision that it made no difference whether or not he had so consented.

R. v. *Morris* involved two cases of price label switching in a supermarket. In the first case the defendant had removed the price label from a joint of meat and replaced it with a label showing a lesser price which he had removed from another joint. He was detected at the checkout point before he had paid for the joint and later convicted of theft contrary to section 1(1) of the 1968 Act. In the second case the defendant had in similar manner switched price labels on goods in a supermarket but was not arrested until after he had passed the checkout point and paid the lesser prices for the goods. He was charged with two counts of theft contrary to section 1(1) and one count of obtaining property by deception contrary to section 15(1). The jury convicted him on the counts of theft, but by direction of the recorder returned no verdict on the section 15(1) count. Appeals against conviction by both defendants were dismissed by the Court of Appeal, Criminal Division and by this House. Lord Roskill, in the course of a speech concurred in by Lord Fraser of Tullybelton, Lord Edmund-Davies, Lord Brandon of Oakbrook and Lord Brightman, referred to *Lawrence*'s case with apparent approval as having set out the four elements involved in the offence of theft and as having rejected the argument that they could not be theft within section 1(1) if the owner of the property had consented to the defendant's acts. He observed that in *Lawrence*'s case the House did not have to consider the precise meaning of "appropriation" in section 3(1) and continued:

"Counsel for the appellants submitted that the phrase in s. 3(1) 'any assumption by a person of *the rights* of an owner amounts to an appropriation' must mean any assumption of '*all* the rights of an owner'. Since neither appellant had at the time of the removal of the goods from the shelves and of the label switching assumed *all* the rights of the owner, there was no appropriation and therefore no theft. Counsel for the prosecution, on the other hand, contended that *the* rights in this context only meant *any* of the rights. An owner of goods has many rights: they have been described as 'a bundle or package of rights'. Counsel for the prosecution contended that on a fair reading of the subsection it cannot have been the intention that every one of the owner's rights had to be assumed by the alleged thief before an appropriation was proved and that essential ingredient of the offence of theft established. My Lords, if one reads the words 'the rights' at the opening of s. 3(1) literally and in isolation from the rest of the section, the submission of counsel for the appellants undoubtedly has force. But the later words 'any later assumption of a right'

... seem to me to militate strongly against the correctness of the submission. Moreover the provisions of s. 2(1)(*a*) also seem to point in the same direction. It follows therefore that it is enough for the prosecution if they have proved in these cases the assumption by the defendants of *any* of the rights of the owner of the goods in question, that is to say, the supermarket concerned, it being common ground in these cases that the other three of the four elements mentioned in Viscount Dilhorne's speech in *Lawrence's* case had been fully established. My Lords, counsel for the prosecution sought to argue that any removal from the shelves of the supermarket, even if unaccompanied by label-switching, was without more an appropriation. In one passage in his judgment in *Morris's* case Lord Lane CJ appears to have accepted the submission, for he said: '... It seems to us that in taking the article from the shelf the customer is indeed assuming one of the rights of the owner, the right to move the article from its position on the shelf to carry it to the checkout ...' With the utmost respect, I cannot accept this statement as correct. If one postulates an honest customer taking goods from a shelf to put in his or her trolley to take to the check-point there to pay the proper price. I am unable to see that any of these actions involves any assumption by the shopper of the rights of the super-market. In the context of s. 3(1), the concept of appropriation in my view involves not an act expressly or impliedly authorised by the owner but an act by way of adverse interference with or usurpation of those rights. When the honest shopper acts as I have just described, he or she is acting with the implied authority of the owner of the supermarket to take the goods from the shelf, put them in the trolley, take them to the check-point and there pay the correct price, at which moment the property in the goods will pass to the shopper for the first time. It is with the consent of the owners of the supermarket, be that consent express or implied, that the shopper does these acts and thus obtains at least control if not actual possession of the goods preparatory, at a later stage, to obtaining the property in them on payment of the proper amount at the check-point. I do not think that s. 3(1) envisages any such act as an 'appropriation', whatever may be the meaning of that word in other fields such as contract or sale of goods law. If, as I understood all your Lordships to agree, the concept of appropriation in s. 3(1) involves an element of adverse interference with or usurpation of some right of the owner, it is necessary next to consider whether that requirement is satisfied in either of these cases. As I have already said, in my view mere removal from the shelves without more is not an appropriation. Further, if a shopper with some perverted sense of humour, intending only to create confusion and nothing more, both for the super-market and for other shoppers, switches labels, I do not think that that act of label-switching alone is without more an appropriation, though it is not difficult to envisage some cases of dishonest label-switching which could be. In cases such as the present, it is in truth a combination of these actions, the removal from the shelf and the switching of the labels which evidences adverse interference with or usurpa-tion of the right of the owner. Those acts, therefore, amount to an appropriation and if they are accompanied by proof of the other three elements to which I have referred, the offence of theft is established. Further, if they are accompanied by other acts such as putting the goods so removed and relabelled into a receptacle, whether a trolley or the shopper's own bag or basket, proof of appropriation within s. 3(1) becomes overwhelming. It is the doing of one or more acts which individually or collectively amount to such adverse interference with or usurpation of the owner's rights which constitute appropriation under s. 3(1) and I do not think it matters [whether] there is more than one such act in which order the successive acts take place, or whether there is any interval of time between them. To suggest that it matters whether the mislabelling precedes or succeeds removal from the shelves is to reduce this branch of the law to an absurdity." (Lord Roskill's emphasis.)

The answer given to the question certified by the Court of Appeal was:

"... there is a dishonest appropriation for the purposes of the Theft Act 1968 where by the substitution of a price label showing a lesser price on goods for one showing a greater price, a defendant either by that act alone or by that act in conjunction with another act or other acts (whether done before or after the substitution of the labels) adversely interferes with or usurps the right of the owner to ensure that the goods concerned are sold and paid for at that greater price."

In my opinion Lord Roskill was undoubtedly right when he said in the course of the passage quoted that the assumption by the defendant of any of the rights of an owner could amount to an appropriation within the meaing of section 3(1), and that the removal of an article from the shelf and the changing of the price label on it constituted the assumption of one of the rights of the owner and hence an appropriation within the meaning of the subsection. But there are observations in the passage which, with the greatest possible respect to Lord Roskill, I must regard as unnecessary for the decision of the case and as being incorrect. In the first place, it seems to me that the switching of price labels on the article is in itself an assumption of one of the rights of the owner, whether or not it is accompanied by some other act such as removing the article from the shelf and placing it in a basket or trolley. No one but the owner has the right to remove a price label from an article or to place a price label upon it. If anyone else does so, he does an act, as Lord Roskill puts it, by way of adverse interference with or usurpation of that right. This is no less so in the case of the practical joker figured by Lord Roskill than in the case of one who makes the switch with dishonest intent. The practical joker, of course, is not guilty of theft because he has not acted dishonestly and does not intend to deprive the owner permanently of the article. So the label switching in itself constitutes an appropriation and so to have held would have been sufficient for the dismissal of both appeals. On the facts of the two cases it was unnecessary to decide whether, as argued by counsel for the prosecution, the mere taking of the article from the shelf and putting it in a trolley or other receptacle amounted to the assumption of one of the rights of the owner, and hence an appropriation. There was much to be said in favour of the view that it did, in respect that doing so gave the shopper control of the article and the capacity to exclude any other shopper from taking it. However, Lord Roskill expressed the opinion that it did not, on the ground that the concepts of appropriation in the context of section 3(1) "involves not an act expressly or impliedly authorised by the owner but an act by way of adverse interference with or usurpation of those rights." While it is correct to say that appropriation for purposes of section 3(1) includes the latter sort of act, it does not necessarily follow that no other act can amount to an appropriation and in particular that no act expressly or impliedly authorised by the owner can in any circumstances do so. Indeed, *Lawrence*'s case is a clear decision to the contrary since it laid down equivocally that an act may be an appropriation notwithstanding that it is done with the consent of the owner. It does not appear to me that any sensible distinction can be made in this context between consent and authorisation.

In the civil case of *Dobson* v. *General Accident Fire and Life Assurance Corp plc* [1989] 3 All E.R. 927, [1990] 1 Q.B. 274 a Court of Appeal consisting of Parker and Bingham L.J.J.

considered the apparent conflict between *Lawrence*'s case and
R. v. Morris and applied the former decision. The facts were
that the plaintiff had insured property with the defendant
company against, *inter alia*, "loss or damage caused by theft."
He advertised for sale a watch and ring at the total price of
£5,950. A rogue telephoned expressing an interest in buying
the articles and the plaintiff provisionally agreed with him
that the payment would be by a building society cheque in
the plaintiff's favour. The rogue called on the plaintiff the
next day and the watch and the ring were handed over to
him in exchange for a building society cheque for the agreed
amount. The plaintiff paid the cheque into his bank, which
informed him that it was stolen and worthless. The defendant
company denied liability under its policy of insurance on the
ground that the loss of the watch and ring was not caused by
theft within the meaning of the 1968 Act. The plaintiff
succeeded in the county court in an action to recover the
amount of his loss, and the decision was affirmed by the
Court of Appeal. One of the arguments for the defendants
was that there had been no theft because the plaintiff had
agreed to the transaction with the rogue and reliance was
placed on Lord Roskill's statement in *R. v. Morris* that
appropriation "involves not an act expressly or impliedly
authorised by the owner but an act by way of adverse
interference with or usurpation of those rights."
In dealing with this argument Parker L.J. said:

"The difficulties caused by the apparent conflict between
the decision in *Lawrence*'s case and *R. v. Morris* have
provided, not surprisingly, a basis for much discussion by
textbook writers and contributors of articles to law journals.
It is, however, clear that their Lordships in *R. v. Morris* did
not regard anything said in that case as conflicting with
Lawrence's case for it was specifically referred to in Lord
Roskill's speech, with which the other members of the
Appellate Committee all agreed, without disapproval or
qualification. The only comment made was that, in
Lawrence's case, the House did not have to consider the
precise meaning of 'appropriation' in s. 3(1) (see [1983] 3 All
E.R. 288 at 292, [1984] A.C. 320 at 331). With respect, I find
this comment hard to follow in the light of the first of the
questions asked in *Lawrence*'s case and the answer to it, the
passages from Viscount Dilhorne's speech already cited, the
fact that it was specifically argued that ' "appropriates" is
meant in a pejorative, rather than a neutral, sense in that
the appropriation is against the will of the owner' (see
[1972] A.C. 626 at 631 arg), and finally that dishonesty was

common ground. I would have supposed that *the* question in *Lawrence*'s case was whether appropriation necessarily involved an absence of consent." (Parker L.J.'s emphasis.)

Parker L.J. then said that he found difficulties in Lord Roskill's speech in *R. v. Morris* ...

Later Parker L.J. quoted this passage from the speech of Lord Roskill in *R. v. Morris*:

"... without going into further detail I respectfully suggest that it is on any view wrong to introduce into this branch of the criminal law questions whether particular contracts are void or voidable on the ground of mistake or fraud or whether any mistake is sufficiently fundamental to vitiate a contract. These difficult questions should so far as possible be confined to those fields of law to which they are immediately relevant and I do not regard them as relevant questions under the 1968 Act. After anxious consideration I have reached the conclusion that whatever *R. v. Morris* did decide it cannot be regarded as having overruled the very plain decision in *Lawrence*'s case that appropriation can occur even if the owner consents and that *R. v. Morris* itself makes it plain that it is no defence to say that the property passed under a voidable contract."

On this ground Parker L.J. dismissed the appeal.

Bingham L.J. plainly took the view that a customer in a supermarket assumes some of the rights of an owner when he takes goods into his possession and exercises control over them by putting them in a basket or trolley, and thus appropriates them. Later he mentioned that in Lord Roskill's speech in *R. v. Morris* no reference was made to Viscount Dilhorne's ruling in *Lawrence*'s case that appropriation might occur even though the owner has permitted or consented to the property being taken, and continued:

"I do not find it easy to reconcile this ruling of Viscount Dilhorne, which was as I understand central to the answer which the House of Lords gave to the certified question, with the reasoning of the House in *R. v. Morris*. Since, however, the House in *R. v. Morris* considered that there had plainly been an appropriation in *Lawrence*'s case, this must (I think) have been because the Italian student, although he had permitted or allowed his money to be taken, had not in truth consented to the taxi driver taking anything in excess of the correct far. This is not a wholly satisfactory reconciliation, since it might be said that a supermarket consents to customers taking goods from its shelves only when they honestly intend to pay and not otherwise. On the facts of the present case, however, it can be said, by analogy with *Lawrence*'s case, that although the plaintiff permitted and allowed his property to be taken by the rogue, he had not in truth consented to the rogue becoming owner without giving a valid draft drawn by the building society for the price. On this basis I conclude that the plaintiff is able to show an appropriation sufficient to satisfy s. 1(1) of the 1968 Act when the rogue accepted delivery of the articles."

It was argued for the respondent in the present appeal that *Dobson*'s case was wrongly decided. I disagree, and on the contrary find myself in full agreement with those parts of the judgment of Parker L.J. to which I have referred. As regards the attempted reconciliation by Bingham L.J. of the reasoning in *R. v. Morris* with the ruling in *Lawrence*'s case it appears to me that the suggested basis of reconciliation, which is essentially speculative, is unsound. The actual decision in *R. v. Morris* was correct, but it was erroneous, in addition to being unnecessary for the decision, to indicate that an act expressly or impliedly authorised by the owner could never amount to an appropriation. There is no material distinction between the facts in *Dobson*'s case and those in the present case. In each case the owner of the goods was induced by fraud to part with them to the rogue. *Lawrence*'s case makes it clear that consent to or authorisation by the owner of the taking by the rogue is irrelevant. The taking amounted to an appropriation with the meaning of section 1(1) of the 1968 Act. *Lawrence*'s case also make it clear that it is no less irrelevant that what happened may also have constituted the offence of obtaining property by deception under section 15(1) of the 1968 Act.

In my opinion it serves no useful at the present time to seek to construe the relevant provisions of the Theft Act by reference to the report which preceded it, namely the eighth report of the Criminal Law Revision Committee, *Theft and Related Offences* (Cmnd. 2977 (1966)). The decision in *Lawrence*'s case was a clear decision of this House upon the construction of the word "appropriates" in s. 1(1) of the 1968 Act, which had stood for 12 years when doubt was thrown upon it by obiter dicta in *R. v. Morris*. *Lawrence*'s case must be regarded as authoritative and correct, and there is no question of it now being right to depart from it.

It is desirable to say a few words about *R. v. Skipp* [1975] Crim. L.R. 114 and *R. v. Fritschy* [1985] Crim. L.R. 745. In the first case the defendant, posing as a haulage contractor, was instructed to collect consignments of goods from three different places and deliver them to a certain destination. He collected the goods and made off with them. The Court of Appeal, on his appeal against his conviction for theft upon one count covering all three consignments, on the ground that the count was bad for duplicity in that there were three separate appropriations, held that there had been no appropriation until the last of the goods were loaded, or probably until the defendant deviated from the route to the proper destination. In the second case the defendant was instructed by the owner to collect a quantity of krugerrands in London and deliver them to a safe deposit in Switzerland. Although the short report is not very clear on the matter, it seems that the defendant, having collected the coins, took them to Switzerland and there made away with them. The trial judge directed the jury that if at the time he collected the coins the defendant had formed the dishonest intention of keeping them for himself he was guilty of theft. The Court of Appeal overturned the resultant conviction for theft on the ground, following *R. v. Morris*, that there had been "no appropriation in England because the defendant had there taken possession of the krugerrands with the owner's authority. In my opinion both these cases were inconsistent with *Lawrence's* case and were wrongly decided . . ."

My Lords, for the reasons which I have given I would answer branch (a) of the certified question in the affirmative and branch (b) in the negative, and allow the appeal.

Appeal Allowed

Notes and Questions

1. The effect of *Gomez* appears to be that virtually all cases of obtaining by deception constitute theft. The only cases where a charge of theft would be inapt is where the property cannot be the subject matter of a charge of theft (*i.e.* land, things growing wild and wild creatures, see section 4 of the Theft Act, below, p. 397) but can be obtained by deception. This was not the result intended by the Criminal Law Reform Commission as its *Report* makes clear. Lord Keith, however, thought it would serve no useful function to refer to the *Report*. Was he right not to do so?

2. When did the theft (the appropriation) take place? Was it (i) when Mr. Gilberd (the manager) agreed to the transaction; or (ii) when Gomez paid the cheque into the bank; or (iii) when the property in the goods passed under the contract of sale; or (iv) when Ballay took possession of the goods?

3. The contract of sale in *Gomez* was voidable for fraud. On discovering the fraud the owner had two options available. Either he could avoid the contract and seek to recover his goods; or he could affirm the contract and sue the buyer for the price. Suppose that in *Gomez* the owner had chosen to affirm the contract. Could Gomez and Ballay still be convicted of theft notwithstanding that their title to the goods has never been challenged by the owner?

B. Dishonestly

A jury (or bench of magistrates) may not convict a defendant of theft unless the prosecution have proved that the defendant had acted dishonestly. "Dishonestly" receives a partial definition in section 2(1) of the Theft Act 1968, but the courts have accepted that there still remains a general jury issue of whether the defendant's conduct was "dishonest." In effect, this allows the tribunal of fact to decide whether the conduct in question merits a criminal sanction. In many cases the answer will be obvious, but certain situations might be viewed quite differently by different jurors. Consider the following situations. Do you consider the conduct of X, Y and Z to be (a) dishonest and/or (b) deserving of punishment?

(a) X works at a local shop. His employer has told him never to borrow money from the cash till. One rainy evening he is forced to work late and misses his last train home. He has insufficient money for a taxi fare and so he takes £5 from the till and leaves an IOU note. He has £50 at home from which he intends to repay the money on the following morning.

(b) Y works in a factory which makes paper. All employees are forbidden to remove paper for personal use. Y takes home some scrap paper for his children to draw on.

(c) Z has been instructed by his employer that he should always travel first class when on firm's business. Z believes this to be a waste of money and so always travels second class. However in order to appear to be following instructions he always claims the first class fare and donates the difference to charity.

For the purposes of the Theft Acts 1968 and 1978, should the jury be instructed that the defendant has acted dishonestly if they find:

(1) that the defendant believed that he was acting dishonestly;
(2) that ordinary decent people would think that the defendant was acting dishonestly;
(3) that the defendant knew that ordinary decent people would regard his conduct as dishonest?

R. v. Ghosh

[1982] 3 W.L.R. 110 (C.A.)

Lord Lane C.J. A little later *Reg.* v. *Feely* (1973) came before a court of five judges. The case is often treated as having laid down an objective test of dishonesty for the purpose of section 1 of the Theft Act 1968. But what it actually decided was (i) that it is for the jury to determine whether the defendant acted dishonestly and not for the judge, (ii) that the word "dishonestly" can only relate to the defendant's own state of mind, and (iii) that it is unnecessary and undesirable for judges to define what is meant by "dishonestly."

It is true that the court said:

"Jurors, when deciding whether an appropriation was dishonest can be reasonably expected to, and should, apply the current standards of ordinary decent people."

It is that sentence which is usually taken as laying down the objective test. But the passage goes on:

"In their own lives they have to decide what is and what is not dishonest. We can see no reason why, when in a jury box, they should require the help of a judge to tell them what amounts to dishonesty."

The sentence requiring the jury to apply current standards leads up to the prohibition on judges from applying *their* standards. That is the context in which the sentence appears. It seems to be reading too much into that sentence to treat it as authority for the view that "dishonesty can be established independently of the knowledge or belief of the defendant." If it could, then any reference to the state of mind of the defendant would be beside the point.

This brings us to the heart of the problem. Is "dishonestly" in section 1 of the Theft Act 1968 intended to characterise a course of conduct? Or is it intended to describe a state of mind? If the former, then we can well understand that it could be established independently of the knowledge or belief of the accused. But if, as we think, it is the latter, then the knowledge and belief of the accused are at the root of the problem.

Take for example a man who comes from a country where public transport is free. On his first day here he travels on a bus. He gets off without paying. He never had any intention of paying. His mind is clearly honest; but his conduct, judged objectively by what he has done, is dishonest. It seems to us that in using the word "dishonestly" in the Theft Act 1968, Parliament cannot have intended to catch dishonest conduct in that sense, that is to say conduct to which no moral obloquy could possibly attach. This is sufficiently established by the partial definition in section 2 of the Theft Act itself. All the matters covered by section 2(1) relate to the belief of the accused. Section 2(2) relates to his willingness to pay. A man's belief and his willingness to pay are things which can only be established subjectively. It is difficult to see how a partially subjective definition can be made to work in harness with the test which in all other respects is wholly objective.

If we are right that dishonesty is something in the mind of the accused (what Professor Glanville Williams calls "a special mental state"), then if the mind of the accused is honest, it cannot be deemed dishonest merely because members of the jury would have regarded it as dishonest to embark on that course of conduct.

So we would reject the simple uncomplicated approach that the test is purely objective, however attractive from the practical point of view that solution may be.

There remains the objection that to adopt a subjective test is to abandon all standards but that of the accused himself, and to bring about a state of affairs in which "Robin Hood would be no robber": *Reg.* v. *Greenstein.* This objection misunderstands the nature of the subjective test. It is no defence for a man to say "I knew that what I was doing is generally regarded as dishonest; but I do not regard it as dishonest myself. Therefore I am not guilty." What he is however entitled to say is "I did not know that anybody would regard what I was doing as dishonest." He may not be believed; just as he may not be believed if he sets up "a claim of right" under section 2(1) of the Theft Act 1968, or asserts that he believed in the truth of a misrepresentation under section 15 of the Act of 1968. But if he *is* believed, or raises a real doubt about the matter, the jury cannot be sure that he was dishonest.

In determining whether the prosecution has proved that the defendant was acting dishonestly, a jury must first of all decide whether according to the ordinary standards of reasonable and honest people what was done was dishonest. If it was not dishonest by those standards, that is the end of the matter and the prosecution fails.

If it was dishonest by those standards, then the jury must consider whether the defendant himself must have realised that what he was doing was by those standards dishonest. In most cases, where the actions are obviously dishonest by ordinary standards, there will be no doubt about it. It will be obvious that the defendant himself knew that he was acting dishonestly. It is dishonest for a defendant to act in a way which he knows ordinary people consider to be dishonest, even if he asserts or genuinely believes that he is morally justified in acting as he did. For example, Robin Hood or those ardent anti-vivisectionists who remove animals from vivisection laboratories are acting dishonestly, even though they may consider themselves to be morally justified in doing what they do, because they know that ordinary people would consider these actions to be dishonest.

Cases which might be described as borderline, such as *Boggeln* v. *Williams* (1978), will depend upon the view taken by the jury as to whether the defendant may have believed what he was doing was in accordance with the ordinary man's idea of honesty. A jury might have come to the conclusion that the defendant in that case was disobedient or impudent, but not dishonest in what he did.

R. v. Price

[1989] The Times, October 28 (C.A.)

[P was charged with obtaining services and property by deception, and forgery.]

Lord Lane C.J. said that: The defence of the appellant, who had made statements to the police and was not called to give evidence, was that he was the beneficiary of a trust fund that would produce £100,000 for him in due course.

One complaint of Mr. Barton on appeal was that no *Ghosh* direction so far as dishonesty was concerned was given.

It was by no means in every case that the *Ghosh* direction should be given. In the majority of cases it was unnecessary and, indeed, misleading to give that direction.

It was only desirable that it should be given when the defendant was saying: "I thought that what I was doing was honest but other people, and the majority of people might think it was not honest." That was the sort of situation in which the *Ghosh* direction was applicable.

In the instant case the simple question was: Did the appellant honestly believe that he was the beneficiary of a £100,000 trust fund? As the recorder directed the jury: "Was he dishonest ... Dishonesty: there is no need for me to explain it to you. You all know what honesty is and dishonesty is the opposite side of the coin."

Another complaint by Mr. Barton was that the recorder in his summing up said: "I do not know whether any of you remember the stories of Greyfriars School by Frank Richards, but in those stories there was a boy called Billy Bunter, and Billy Bunter was always expecting a postal order the next day.

"The only trouble with Billy Bunter was that the postal order had never arrived the next day and it went on and on never arriving—and the funds go on and on in this case never arriving—because Billy Bunter tried to persuade people to lend him money on the strength of the postal order that was due to arrive."

Mr. Barton suggested that that was an unfair comment. His Lordship disagreed. He suggested it was factually incorrect in that Billy Bunter's postal order did eventually arrive.

The fact remained that it was a homely illustration which the recorder thought would interest the jury and was an accurate illustration of how they were to approach the case.

The conviction was neither unsafe nor unsatisfactory.

2. BURGLARY

R. v. Collins

[1973] Q.B. 100 (C.A.)

Edmund Davies L.J.   gave the judgment of the court. This is about as extraordinary a case as my brethren and I have ever heard either on the bench or while at the bar. Stephen William George Collins was convicted on October 29, 1971, at the Essex Assizes of burglary with intent to commit rape and he was sentenced to 21 months' imprisonment. He is a 19-year-old youth, and he appeals against that conviction by the certificate of the judge. The terms in which that certificate is expressed reveal that the judge was clearly troubled about the case and the conviction.

Let me relate the facts. Were they put into a novel or portrayed on the stage, they would be regarded as being so improbable as to be unworthy of serious consideration and as verging at times on farce. At about 2 o'clock in the early morning of Saturday, July 24, 1971, a young lady of 18 went to bed at her mother's home in Colchester. She had spent the evening with her boyfriend. She had taken a certain amount of drink, and it may be that this fact affords some explanation of her inability to answer satisfactorily certain crucial questions put to her at the trial.

She has the habit of sleeping without wearing night apparel in a bed which is very near the lattice-type window of her room. At one stage in her evidence she seemed to be saying that the bed was close up against the window which, in accordance with her practice, was wide open. In the photographs which we have before us, however, there appears to be a gap of some sort between the two, but the bed was clearly quite near the window.

At about 3.30 or 4 o'clock she awoke and she then saw in the moonlight a vague form crouched in the open window. She was unable to remember, and this is important, whether the form was on the outside of the window sill or on that part of the sill which was inside the room, and for reasons which will later become clear, that seemingly narrow point is of crucial importance.

The young lady then realised several things: first of all that the form in the window was that of a male; secondly that he was a naked male; and thirdly that he was a naked male with an erect penis. She also saw in the moonlight that his hair was blond. She thereupon leapt to the conclusion that her boyfriend, with whom for some time she had been on terms of regular and frequent sexual intimacy, was paying her an ardent nocturnal visit. She promptly sat up in bed, and the man descended from the sill and joined her in bed and they had full sexual intercourse. But there was something about him which made her think that things were not as they usually were between her and her boyfriend. The length of his hair, his voice as they had exchanged what was described as "love talk," and other features led her to the conclusion that somehow there was something different. So she turned on the bed-side light, saw that her companion was not her boyfriend and slapped the face of the intruder, who was none other than the defendant. He said to her, "Give me a good time tonight," and got hold of her arm, but she bit him and told him to go. She then went into the bathroom and he promptly vanished.

The complainant said that she would not have agreed to intercourse if she had known that the person entering her room was not her boyfriend. But there was no suggestion of any force having been used upon her, and the intercourse which took place was undoubtedly effected with no resistance on her part.

The defendant was seen by the police at about 10.30 later that same morning. According to the police, the conversation which took place then elicited these points. He was very lustful the previous night. He had taken a lot of drink, and we may here note that drink (which to him is a very real problem) had brought this young man into trouble several times before, but never for an offence of this kind. He went on to say that he knew the complainant because he had worked around her house. On this occasion, desiring sexual intercourse—and according to the police evidence he added that he was determined to have a girl, by force if necessary, although that part of the police evidence he challenged—he went on to say that he walked around the house, saw a light in an upstairs bedroom, and he knew that this was the girl's bedroom. He found a step ladder, leaned it against the wall and climbed up and looked into the bedroom. He could see through the wide-open window a girl who was naked and asleep. So he descended the ladder and stripped off all his clothes, with the exception of his socks, because apparently he took the view that if the girl's mother entered the bedroom it would be easier to effect a rapid escape if he had his socks on than if he was in his bare feet. That is a matter about which we are not called upon to express any view, and would in any event find ourselves unable to express one.

Having undressed, he then climbed the ladder and pulled himself up on to the window sill. His version of the matter is that he was pulling himself in when she awoke. She then got up and knelt on the bed, she put her arms around his neck and body, and she seemed to pull him into the bed. He went on:

"I was rather dazed because I didn't think she would want to know me. We kissed and cuddled for about 10 or 15 minutes and then I had it away with her but found it hard because I had had so much to drink."

The Police officer said to the defendant:

"It appears that it was your intention to have intercourse with this girl by force if necessary, and it was only pure coincidence that this girl was under the impression that you were her boyfriend and apparently that is why she consented to allowing you to have sexual intercourse with her." It was alleged that he then said, "Yes, I feel awful about this. It is the worst day of my life, but I know it could have been worse."

Thereupon the officer said to him—and he challenges this: "What do you mean, you know it could have been worse?" to which he is alleged to have replied:

"Well, my trouble is drink and I got very frustrated. As I've told you, I only wanted to have it away with a girl and I'm only glad I haven't really hurt her."

Then he made a statement under caution, in the course of which he said:

"When I stripped off and got up the ladder I made my mind up that I was going to try and have it away with this girl. I feel terrible about this now, but I had too much to drink. I am sorry for what I have done."

In the course of his testimony, the defendant said that he would not have gone into the room if the girl had not knelt on the bed and beckoned him into the room. He said that if she had objected immediately to his being there or to his having intercourse he would not have persisted. While he was keen on having sexual intercourse that night, it was only if he could find someone who was willing. He strongly denied having told the police that he would, if necessary, have pushed over some girl for the purpose of having intercourse.

There was a submission of no case to answer on the ground that the evidence did not support the charge, particularly that ingredient of it which had reference to entry into the house "as a trespasser." But the submission was overruled, and, as we have already related, he gave evidence.

Now, one feature of the case which remained at the conclusion of the evidence in great obscurity is where exactly Collins was at the moment when, according to him, the girl manifested that she was welcoming him. Was he kneeling on the sill outside the window or was he already inside the room, having climbed through the window frame, and kneeling upon the inner sill? It was a crucial matter, for there were certainly three ingredients that it was incumbent upon the Crown to establish. Under section 9 of the Theft Act 1968, which renders a person guilty of burglary if he enters any building or part of a building as a trespasser and with the intention of committing rape, the entry of the accused into the building must first be proved. Well, there is no doubt about that, for it is common ground that he did enter this girl's bedroom. Secondly, it must be proved that he entered as a trespasser. We will develop that point a little later. Thirdly, it must be proved that he entered as a trespasser with intent at the time to commit rape therein.

The second ingredient of the offence—the entry must be as a trespasser—is one which has not, to the best of our knowledge, been previously canvassed in the courts. Views as to its ambit have naturally been canvassed by the textbook writers, and it is perhaps not wholly irrelevant to recall that those who were advising the Home Secretary before the Theft Bill was presented to Parliament had it in mind to get rid of some of the frequently absurd technical rules which had been built up in relation to the old requirement in burglary of a "breaking and entering." The cases are legion as to what this did or did not amount to, and happily it is not now necessary for us to consider them. But it was in order to get rid of those technical rules that a new test was introduced, namely, that the entry must be "as a trespasser."

What does that involve? According to the editors of *Archbold Criminal Pleading Evidence & Practice*, 37th ed. (1969), para. 1505:

"Any intentional, reckless or negligent entry into a building will, it would appear, constitute a trespass if the building is in the possession of another person who does not consent to the entry. Nor will it make any difference that the entry was the result of a reasonable mistake on the part of the defendant, so far as trespass is concerned."

If that be right, then it would be no defence for this man to say (and even were he believed in saying), "Well, I honestly thought that this girl was welcoming me into the room and I therefore entered, fully believing that I had her consent to go in." If *Archbold* is right, he would nevertheless be a trespasser, since the apparent consent of the girl was unreal, she being mistaken as to who was at her window. We disagree. We hold that, for the purposes of section 9 of the Theft Act, a person entering a building is not guilty of trespass if he enters without knowledge that he is trespassing or at least without acting recklessly as to whether or not he is unlawfully entering.

A view contrary to that of the editors of *Archbold* was expressed in Professor Smith's book on *The Law of Theft*, 1st ed. (1968), where, having given an illustration of an entry into premises, the author comments, at paragraph 462:

"It is submitted that ... D should be acquitted on the ground of lack of *mens rea*. Though, under the civil law, he entered as a trespasser, it is submitted that he cannot be convicted of the criminal offence unless he knew of the facts which caused him to be a trespasser or, at least, was reckless."

The matter has also been dealt with by Professor Griew, who in paragraph 4–05 of his work *The Theft Act 1968* has this passage:

"What if D wrongly believes that he is not trespassing? His belief may rest on facts which, if true, would mean that he was not trespassing: for instance, he may enter a building by mistake, thinking that it is the one he has been invited to enter. Or his belief may be based on a false view of the legal effect of the known facts: for instance, he may misunderstand the effect of a contract granting him a right of passage through a building. Neither kind of mistake will protect him from tort liability for trespass. In either case, then, D satisfies the literal terms of section 9(1): he 'enters ... as a trespasser.' But for the purposes of criminal liability a man should be judged on the basis of the facts as he believed them to be, and this should include making allowances for a mistake as to rights under the civil law.

This is another way of saying that a serious offence like
burglary should be held to require mens rea in the fullest
sense of the phrase: D should be liable for burglary only if
he knowingly trespasses or is reckless as to whether he
trespasses or not. Unhappily it is common for Parliament to
omit to make clear whether mens rea is intended to be an
element in a statutory offence. It is also, though not
equally, common for the courts to supply the mental
element by construction of the statute."

We prefer the view expressed by Professor Smith and
Professor Griew to that of the editors of *Archbold*. In the
judgment of this court there cannot be a conviction for
entering premises "as a trespasser" within the meaning of
section 9 of the Theft Act unless the person entering does so
knowing that he is a trespasser and nevertheless deliberately
enters, or, at the very least, is reckless as to whether or not
he is entering the premises of another without the other
party's consent.

Having so held, the pivotal point of this appeal is whether
the Crown established that this defendant at the moment that
he entered the bedroom knew perfectly well that he was not
welcome there or, being reckless as to whether he was
welcome or not, was nevertheless determined to enter. That
in turn involves consideration as to where he was at the time
that the complainant indicated that she was welcoming him
into her bedroom. If, to take an example that was put in the
course of argument, her bed had not been near the window
but was on the other side of the bedroom, and he (being
determined to have her sexually even against her will)
climbed through the window and crossed the bedroom to
reach her bed, then the offence charged would have been
established. But in this case, as we have related, the layout of
the room was different, and it became a point of nicety which
had to be conclusively established by the Crown as to where
he was when the girl made welcoming signs, as she
unquestionably at some stage did.

How did the judge deal with this matter? We have to say
regretfully that there was a flaw in his treatment of it.
Referring to section 9, he said:

"There are three ingredients. First is the question of entry.
Did he enter into that house? Did he enter as a trespasser?
This is to say, was the entry, if you are satisfied there was
an entry, intentional or reckless? And, finally, and you may
think this is the crux of the case as opened to you by Mr.
Irwin, if you are satisfied that he entered as a trespasser,
did he have the intention to rape this girl?"

The judge then went on to deal in turn with each of these three ingredients. He first explained what was involved in "entry" into a building. He then dealt with the second ingredient. But here he unfortunately repeated his earlier observation that the question of entry as a trespasser depended on "was the entry intentional or reckless?" We have to say that this was putting the matter inaccurately. This mistake may have been derived from a passage in the speech of counsel for the Crown when replying to the submission of "no case." Mr. Irwin at one stage said: "Therefore, the first thing that the Crown have got to prove, my Lords, is that there has been a trespass which may be an intentional trespass, or it may be a reckless trespass." Unfortunately the judge regarded the matter as though the second ingredient in the burglary charged was whether there had been an intentional or reckless entry, and when he came to develop this topic in his summing up that error was unfortunately perpetuated. The judge told the jury:

"He had no right to be in that house, as you know, certainly from the point of view of the girl's parent. But if you are satisfied about entry, did he enter intentionally or recklessly? What the prosecution say about that is, you do not really have to consider recklessness because when you consider his own evidence he intended to enter that house, and if you accept the evidence I have just pointed out to you, he in fact did so. So, at least, you may think, it was intentional. At the least, you may think it was reckless because as he told you he did not know whether the girl would accept him."

We are compelled to say that we do not think the judge by these observations made sufficiently clear to the jury the nature of the second test about which they had to be satisfied before this young man could be convicted of the offence charged. There was no doubt that his entry into the bedroom was "intentional." But what the accused had said was, "She knelt on the bed, she put her arms around me and then I went in." If the jury thought he might be truthful in that assertion, they would need to consider whether or not, although entirely surprised by such a reception being accorded to him, this young man might not have been entitled reasonably to regard her action as amounting to an invitation to him to enter. If she in fact appeared to be welcoming him, the Crown do not suggest that he should have realised or even suspected that she was so behaving because, despite the moonlight, she thought he was someone else. Unless the jury were entirely satisfied that the defendant made an effective and substantial entry into the bedroom without the complainant doing or saying anything to cause him to believe that she was consenting to his entering it, he ought not to be convicted of the offence charged. The point is a narrow one, as narrow maybe as the window sill which is crucial to this case. But this is a criminal charge of gravity and, even though one may suspect that his intention was to commit the offence charged, unless the facts show with clarity that he in fact committed it he ought not to remain convicted....

We have to say that this appeal must be allowed on the basis that the jury were never invited to consider the vital question whether this young man did enter the premises as a trespasser, that is to say knowing perfectly well that he had no invitation to enter or reckless of whether or not his entry was with permission. The certificate of the judge, as we have already said, demonstrated that he felt there were points involved calling for further consideration. That consideration we have given to the best of our ability. For the reasons we have stated, the outcome of the appeal is that this young man must be acquitted of the charge preferred against him. The appeal is accordingly allowed and his conviction quashed.

Appeal allowed.

Notes and Questions

1. In *Brown* [1985] Crim. L.R. 212, C.A., it was said that while an entry must be "effective" it did not have to be "substantial". There was held to be an entry by Brown who was found standing on the pavement outside a shop and bending through the broken shop window rummaging among the goods inside. Suppose the goods inside the window had been out of Brown's reach. Would the entry still be "effective?"

2. Could Collins have been convicted of (i) attempted burglary; or (ii) attempted rape?

Chapter 9

Statutes on Criminal Law

Accessories and Abettors Act 1861

As to abettors in misdemeanours

8. Whosoever shall aid, abet, counsel, or procure the commission of any misdemeanour whether the same be a misdemeanour at common law or by virtue of any Act passed or to be passed, shall be liable to be tried, indicted, and punished as a principal offender.

Offences Against the Person Act 1861

Shooting or attempting to shoot, or wounding, with intent to do grievous bodily harm, or to resist apprehension

18. Whosoever shall unlawfully and maliciously by any means whatsoever wound or cause any grievous bodily harm to any person, with intent to do some grievous bodily harm to any person, or with intent to resist or prevent the lawful apprehension or detainer of any person, shall be guilty of [an offence], and being convicted thereof shall be liable ... to [imprisonment] for life.

Inflicting bodily injury, with or without weapon

20. Whosoever shall unlawfully and maliciously wound or inflict any grievous bodily harm upon any other person, either with or without any weapon or instrument, shall be guilty of [an offence], and being convicted thereof shall be liable ... to [a term of imprisonment not exceeding five years].

Assault occasioning bodily harm, common assault

47. Whosoever shall be convicted on indictment of any assault occasioning actual bodily harm shall be liable ... to [imprisonment for five years].

Sexual Offences Act 1956

Rape

1.—(1) It is [an offence] for a man to rape a woman.
(2) A man who induces a married woman to have sexual intercourse with him by impersonating her husband commits rape.

Indecent assault on a woman

14.—(1) It is an offence, subject to the exception mentioned in subsection (3) of this section, for a person to make an indecent assault on a woman.

(2) A girl under the age of sixteen cannot in law give any consent which would prevent an act being an assault for the purposes of this section.

(3) Where a marriage is invalid under section two of the Marriage Act, 1949, or section one of the Age of Marriage Act, 1929 (the wife being a girl under the age of sixteen), the invalidity does not make the husband guilty of any offence under this section by reason of her incapacity to consent while under that age, if he believes her to be his wife and has reasonable cause for the belief.

(4) A woman who is a defective cannot in law give any consent which would prevent an act being an assault for the purposes of this section, but a person is only to be treated guilty of an indecent assault on a defective by reason of that incapacity to consent, if that person knew or had reason to suspect her to be a defective.

Indecent assault on a man

15.—(1) It is an offence for a person to make an indecent assault on a man.

(2) A boy under the age of sixteen cannot in law give any consent which would prevent an act being an assault for the purposes of this section.

(3) A man who is a defective cannot in law give any consent which would prevent an act being an assault for the purposes of this section, but a person is only to be treated as guilty of an indecent assault on a defective by reason of that incapacity to consent, if that person knew or had reason to suspect him to be a defective.

(4) ...

(5) For the purposes of the last foregoing subsection a person shall be presumed, unless the contrary is proved, to have been under the age of seventeen, at the time of the offence charged if he is stated in the charge or indictment, and appears to the court, to have been so.

Abduction of unmarried girl under sixteen from parent or guardian

20.—(1) It is an offence for a person acting without lawful authority or excuse to take an unmarried girl under the age of sixteen out of the possession of her parent or guardian against his will.

(2) In the foregoing subsection "guardian" means any person having the lawful care or charge of the girl.

Homicide Act 1957

Abolition of "constructive malice"

1.—(1) Where a person kills another in the course or furtherance of some other offence, the killing shall not amount to murder unless done with the same malice aforethought (express or implied) as is required for a killing to amount to murder when not done in the course or furtherance of another offence.

(2) For the purposes of the foregoing subsection, a killing done in the course or for the purpose of resisting an officer of justice, or of resisting or

avoiding or preventing a lawful arrest, or of effecting or assisting an escape or rescue from legal custody, shall be treated as a killing in the course or furtherance of an offence.

Persons suffering from diminished responsibility

2.—(1) Where a person kills or is a party to the killing of another, he shall not be convicted of murder if he was suffering from such abnormality of mind (whether arising from a condition of arrested or retarded development of mind or any inherent causes or induced by disease or injury) as substantially impaired his mental responsibility for his acts and omissions in doing or being a party to the killing.

(2) On a charge of murder, it shall be for the defence to prove that the person charged is by virtue of this section not liable to be convicted of murder.

(3) A person who but for this section would be liable, whether as principal or as accessory, to be convicted of murder shall be liable instead to be convicted of manslaughter.

(4) The fact that one party to a killing is by virtue of this section not liable to be convicted of murder shall not affect the question whether the killing amounted to murder in the case of any other party to it.

Provocation

3. Where on a charge of murder there is evidence on which the jury can find that the person charged was provoked (whether by things done or by things said or by both together) to lose his self-control, the question whether the provocation was enough to make a reasonable man do as he did shall be left to be determined by the jury; and in determining that question the jury shall take into account everything both done and said according to the effect which, in their opinion, it would have on a reasonable man.

Indecency with Children Act 1960

Indecent conduct towards young child

1.—(1) Any person who commits an act of gross indecency with or towards a child under the age of fourteen, or who incites a child under that age to such an act with him or another, shall be liable on conviction on indictment to imprisonment for a term not exceeding two years, or on summary conviction to imprisonment for a term not exceeding six months, to a fine not exceeding [four hundred pounds] or to both.

Criminal Law Act 1967

Use of force in making arrest, etc.

3.—(1) A person may use such force as is reasonable in the circumstances in the prevention of crime, or in effecting or assisting in the lawful arrest of offenders or suspected offenders or of persons unlawfully at large.

Penalties for assisting offenders

4.—(1) Where a person has committed an arrestable offence, any other person who, knowing or believing him to be guilty of the offence or of some other arrestable offence, does without lawful authority or reasonable excuse any act with intent to impede his apprehension or prosecution shall be guilty of an offence.

(2) If on the trial of an indictment for an arrestable offence the jury are satisfied that the offence charged (or some other offence of which the accused might on that charge be found guilty) was committed, but find the accused not guilty of it, they may find him guilty of any offence under subsection (1) above of which they are satisfied he is guilty in relation to the offence charged (or that other offence).

(For meaning of arrestable offence see H.S.B., p. 104).

Criminal Justice Act 1967

Proof of criminal intent

8. A court or jury, in determining whether a person has committed an offence:

- (a) shall not be bound in law to infer that he intended or foresaw a result of his actions by reason only of its being a natural and probable consequence of those actions; but
- (b) shall decide whether he did intend or foresee that result by reference to all the evidence, drawing such inferences from the evidence as appear proper in the circumstances.

Theft Act 1968

Definition of "theft"

Basic definition of theft

1.—(1) A person is guilty of theft if he dishonestly appropriates property belonging to another with the intention of permanently depriving the other of it; and "thief" and "steal" shall be construed accordingly.

(2) It is immaterial whether the appropriation is made with a view to gain, or is made for the thief's own benefit.

(3) The five following sections of this Act shall have effect as regards the interpretation and operation of this section (and, except as otherwise provided by this Act, shall apply only for purposes of this section).

"Dishonestly"

2.—(1) A person's appropriation of property belonging to another is not to be regarded as dishonest—

- (a) if he appropriates the property in the belief that he has in law the right to deprive the other of it, on behalf of himself or of a third person; or
- (b) if he appropriates the property in the belief that he would have the other's consent if the other knew of the appropriation and the circumstances of it; or

   (c) (except where the property came to him as trustee or personal representative) if he appropriates the property in the belief that the person to whom the property belongs cannot be discovered by taking reasonable steps.

(2) A person's appropriation of property belonging to another may be dishonest notwithstanding that he is willing to pay for the property.

"Appropriates"

3.—(1) Any assumption by a person of the rights of an owner amounts to an appropriation, and this includes, where he has come by the property (innocently or not) without stealing it, any later assumption of a right to it by keeping or dealing with it as owner.

(2) Where property or a right or interest in property is or purports to be transferred for value to a person acting in good faith, no later assumption by him of rights which he believed himself to be acquiring shall, by reason of any defect in the transferor's title, amount to theft of the property.

"Property"

4.—(1) "Property" includes money and all other property, real or personal, including things in action and other intangible property.

(2) A person cannot steal land, or things forming part of land and severed from it by him or by his directions, except in the following cases, that is to say—

   (a) when he is a trustee or personal representative, or is authorised by power of attorney, or as liquidator of a company, or otherwise, to sell or dispose of land belonging to another, and he appropriates the land or anything forming part of it by dealing with it in breach of the confidence reposed in him; or

   (b) when he is not in possession of the land and appropriates anything forming part of the land by severing it or causing it to be severed, or after it has been severed; or

   (c) when, being in possession of the land under a tenancy he appropriates the whole or part of any fixture or structure let to be used with the land.

For purposes of this subsection "land" does not include incorporeal hereditaments; "tenancy" means a tenancy for years or any less period and includes an agreement for such a tenancy, but a person who after the end of a tenancy remains in possession as statutory tenant or otherwise is to be treated as having possession under the tenancy, and "let" shall be construed accordingly.

(3) A person who picks mushrooms growing wild on any land, or who picks flowers, fruit or foliage from a plant growing wild on any land, does not (although not in possession of the land) steal what he picks, unless he does it for reward or for sale or other commercial purpose.

For purposes of this subsection "mushroom" includes any fungus, and "plant" includes any shrub or tree.

(4) Wild creatures, tamed or untamed, shall be regarded as property; but a person cannot steal a wild creature not tamed nor ordinarily kept in captivity, or the carcase of any such creature unless either it has been reduced into possession by or on behalf of another person and possession of it has not since been lost or abandoned, or another person is in course of reducing it into possession.

"Belonging to another"

5.—(1) Property shall be regarded as belonging to any person having possession or control of it, or having in it any proprietary right or interest (not being an equitable interest arising only from an agreement to transfer or grant an interest).

(2) Where property is subject to a trust, the persons to whom it belongs shall be regarded as including any person having a right to enforce the trust, and an intention to defeat the trust shall be regarded accordingly as an intention to deprive of the property any person having that right.

(3) Where a person receives property from or on account of another, and is under an obligation to the other to retain and deal with that property or its proceeds in a particular way, the property or proceeds shall be regarded (as against him) as belonging to the other.

(4) Where a person gets property by another's mistake, and is under an obligation to make restoration (in whole or in part) of the property or its proceeds or of the value thereof, then to the extent of that obligation the property or proceeds shall be regarded (as against him) as belonging to the person entitled to restoration, and an intention not to make restoration shall be regarded accordingly as an intention to deprive that person of the property or proceeds.

(5) Property of a corporation sole shall be regarded as belonging to the corporation notwithstanding a vacancy in the corporation.

"With the intention of permanently depriving the other of it"

6.—(1) A person appropriating property belonging to another without meaning the other permanently to lose the thing itself is nevertheless to be regarded as having the intention of permanently depriving the other of it if his intention is to treat the thing as his own to dispose of regardless of the other's rights: and a borrowing or lending of it may amount to so treating it if, but only if, the borrowing or lending is for a period and in circumstances making it equivalent to an outright taking or disposal.

(2) Without prejudice to the generality of subsection (1) above, where a person, having possession or control (lawfully or not) of property belonging to another, parts with the property under a condition as to its return which he may not be able to perform, this (if done for purposes of his own and without the other's authority) amounts to treating the property as his own to dispose of regardless of the other's rights.

Theft, robbery, burglary, etc.

Theft

7. A person guilty of theft shall on conviction on indictment be liable to imprisonment for a term not exceeding seven years.

Robbery

8.—(1) A person is guilty of robbery if he steals, and immediately before or at the time of doing so, and in order to do so, he uses force on any person or puts or seeks to put any person in fear of being then and there subjected to force.

(2) A person guilty of robbery, or of an assault with intent to rob, shall on conviction on indictment be liable to imprisonment for life.

Burglary

9.—(1) A person is guilty of burglary if—

(a) he enters any building or part of a building as a trespasser and with intent to commit any such offence as is mentioned in subsection (2) below; or

(b) having entered any building or part of a building as a trespasser he steals or attempts to steal anything in the building or that part of it or inflicts or attempts to inflict on any person therein any grievous bodily harm.

(2) The offences referred to in subsection (1)(*a*) above are offences of stealing anything in the building or part of a building in question, of inflicting on any person therein any grievous bodily harm or raping any woman therein, and of doing unlawful damage to the building or anything therein.

(3) A person guilty of burglary shall on conviction on indictment be liable to imprisonment for a term not exceeding;

(a) where the offence was committed in respect of a building or part of a building which is a dwelliung, fourteen years;

(b) in any other case, ten years.

(4) References in subsections (1) and (2) above to a building, and the reference in subsection (3) to a building which is a dwelling, shall apply also to an inhabited vehicle or vessel, and shall apply to any such vehicle or vessel when the person having a habitation in it is not there as well as at times when he is.

Abstracting of electricity

13. A person who dishonestly uses without due authority, or dishonestly causes to be wasted or diverted, any electricity shall on conviction on indictment be liable to imprisonment for a term not exceeding five years.

Obtaining property by deception

15.—(1) A person who by any deception dishonestly obtains property belonging to another, with the intention of permanently depriving the other of it, shall on conviction on indictment be liable to imprisonment for a term not exceeding ten years.

(2) For purposes of this section a person is to be treated as obtaining property if he obtains ownership, possession or control of it, and "obtain" includes obtaining for another or enabling another to obtain or to retain.

(3) Section 6 above shall apply for purposes of this section, with the necessary adaptation of the reference to appropriating, as it applies for purposes of section 1.

(4) For purposes of this section "deception" means any deception (whether deliberate or reckless) by words or conduct as to fact or as to law, including a deception as to the present intentions of the person using the deception or any other person.

Obtaining pecuniary advantage by deception

16.—(1) A person who by any deception dishonestly obtains for himself or another any pecuniary advantage shall on conviction on indictment be liable to imprisonment for a term not exceeding five years.

(2) The cases in which a pecuniary advantage within the meaning of this section is to be regarded as obtained for a person are cases where—

  (a) [*Repealed by Theft Act 1978, s.5(5).*]
  (b) he is allowed to borrow by way of overdraft, or to take out any policy of insurance or annuity contract, or obtains an improvement of the terms on which he is allowed to do so; or
  (c) he is given the opportunity to earn remuneration or greater remuneration in an office or employment, or to win money by betting.

(3) For purposes of this section "deception" has the same meaning as in section 15 of this Act.

. . .

Blackmail

21.—(1) A person is guilty of blackmail if, with a view to gain for himself or another or with intent to cause loss to another, he makes any unwarranted demand with menaces; and for this purpose a demand with menaces is unwarranted unless the person making it does so in the belief—

  (a) that he has reasonable grounds for making the demand; and
  (b) that the use of the menaces is a proper means of reinforcing the demand.

(2) The nature of the act or omission demanded is immaterial, and it is also immaterial whether the menaces relate to action to be taken by the person making the demand.

(3) A person guilty of blackmail shall on conviction on indictment be liable to imprisonment for a term not exceeding fourteen years.

Handling stolen goods

22.—(1) A person handles stolen goods if (otherwise than in the course of the stealing) knowing or believing them to be stolen goods he dishonestly receives the goods, or dishonestly undertakes or assists in their retention, removal, disposal or realisation by or for the benefit of another person, or if he arranges to do so.

(2) A person guilty of handling stolen goods shall on conviction on indictment be liable to imprisonment for a term not exceeding fourteen years.

Scope of offences relating to stolen goods

24.—(1) The provisions of this Act relating to goods which have been stolen shall apply whether the stealing occurred in England or Wales or elsewhere, and whether it occurred before or after the commencement of this Act, provided that the stealing (if not an offence under this Act) amounted to an offence where and at the time when the goods were stolen; and reference to stolen goods shall be construed accordingly.

(2) For purposes of those provisions references to stolen goods shall include, in addition to the goods originally stolen and parts of them (whether in their original state or not)—

(a) any other goods which directly or indirectly represent or have at any time represented the stolen goods in the hands of the thief as being the proceeds of any disposal or realisation of the whole or part of the goods stolen or of goods so representing the stolen goods; and

(b) any other goods which directly or indirectly represent or have at any time represented the stolen goods in the hands of a handler of the stolen goods or any part of them as being the proceeds of any disposal or realisation of the whole or part of the stolen goods handled by him or of goods so representing them.

(3) But no goods shall be regarded as having continued to be stolen goods after they have been restored to the person from whom they were stolen or to other lawful possession or custody, or after that person and any other person claiming through him have otherwise ceased as regards those goods to have any right to restitution in respect of the theft.

(4) For purposes of the provisions of this Act relating to goods which have been stolen (including subsections (1) to (3) above) goods obtained in England or Wales or elsewhere either by blackmail or in the circumstances described in section 15(1) of this Act shall be regarded as stolen; and "steal," "theft" and "thief" shall be construed accordingly.

Going equipped for stealing, etc.

25.—(1) A person shall be guilty of an offence if, when not at his place of abode, he has with him any article for use in the course of or in connection with any burglary, theft or cheat.

(2) A person guilty of an offence under this section shall on conviction on indictment be liable to imprisonment for a term not exceeding three years.

(3) Where a person is charged with an offence under this section, proof that he had with him any article made or adapted for use in committing a burglary, theft or cheat shall be evidence that he had it with him for such use.

(4) Any person may arrest without warrant anyone who is, or whom he, with reasonable cause, suspects to be, committing an offence under this section.

(5) For the purposes of this section an offence under section 12(1) of this Act of taking a conveyance shall be treated as theft, and "cheat" means an offence under section 15 of this Act.

Criminal Damage Act 1971

Destroying or damaging property

1.—(1) A person who without lawful excuse destroys or damages any property belonging to another intending to destroy or damage any such property or being reckless as to whether any such property would be destroyed or damaged shall be guilty of an offence.

(2) A person who without lawful excuse destroys or damages any property, whether belonging to himself or another—

(a) intending to destroy or damage any property or being reckless as to whether any property would be destroyed or damaged; and

(b) intending by the destruction or damage to endanger the life of another or being reckless as to whether the life of another would be thereby endangered;

shall be guilty of an offence.

(3) An offence committed under this section by destroying or damaging property by fire shall be charged as arson.

Sexual Offences (Amendment) Act 1976

Meaning of "rape" etc.

1.—(1) For the purposes of section 1 of the Sexual Offences Act 1956 (which relates to rape) a man commits rape if—

(a) he has unlawful sexual intercourse with a woman who at the time of the intercourse does not consent to it; and

(b) at that time he knows that she does not consent to the intercourse or he is reckless as to whether she consents to it;

references to rape in other enactments (including the following provisions of this Act) shall be construed accordingly.

(2) It is hereby declared that if at a trial for a rape offence the jury has to consider whether a man believed that a woman was consenting to sexual intercourse, the presence or absence of reasonable grounds for such a belief is a matter to which the jury is to have regard, in conjunction with any other relevant matters, in considering whether he so believed.

Theft Act 1978

Obtaining services by deception

1.—(1) A person who by any deception dishonestly obtains services from another shall be guilty of an offence.

(2) It is an obtaining of services where the other is induced to confer a benefit by doing some act, or causing or permitting some act to be done, on the understanding that the benefit has been or will be paid for.

Evasion of liability by deception

2.—(1) Subject to subsection (2) below, where a person by any deception—

(a) dishonestly secures the remission of the whole or part of any existing liability to make a payment, whether his own liability or another's; or

(b) with intent to make permanent default in whole or in part on any existing liability to make a payment, or with intent to let another do so, dishonestly induces the creditor or any person claiming payment on behalf of the creditor to wait for payment (whether or not the due date for payment is deferred) or to forgo payment; or

(c) dishonestly obtains any exemption from or abatement of liability to make a payment,

he shall be guilty of an offence.

(2) For the purposes of this section "liability" means legally enforceable liability; and subsection (1) shall not apply in relation to liability that has not

been accepted or established to pay compensation for a wrongful act or omission.

(3) For purposes of subsection (1)(*b*) a person induced to take in payment a cheque or other security for money by way of conditional satisfaction of a pre-existing liability is to be treated not as being paid but as being induced to wait for payment.

(4) For purposes of subsection (1)(*c*) "obtains" includes obtaining for another or enabling another to obtain.

Making off without payment

3.—(1) Subject to subsection (3) below, a person who, knowing that payment on the spot for any goods supplied or service done is required or expected from him, dishonestly makes off without having paid as required or expected and with intent to avoid payment of the amount due shall be guilty of an offence.

(2) For purposes of this section "payment on the spot" includes payment at the time of collecting goods on which work has been done or in respect of which service has been provided.

(3) Subsection (1) above shall not apply where the supply of the goods or the doing of the service is contrary to law, or where the service done is such that payment is not legally enforceable.

(4) Any person may arrest without warrant anyone who is, or whom he, with reasonable cause, suspects to be, committing or attempting to commit an offence under this section.

Supplementary

5.—(1) For the purposes of sections 1 and 2 above "deception" has the same meaning as in section 15 of the Theft Act 1968, that is to say, it means any deception (whether deliberate or reckless), by words or conduct as to fact or as to law, including a deception as to the present intentions of the persons using the deception or any other person; and section 18 of that Act (liability of company officers for offences by the company) shall apply in relation to sections 1 and 2 above as it applies in relation to section 15 of that Act.

Criminal Attempts Act 1981

Attempting to commit an offence

1.—(1) If, with intent to commit an offence to which this section applies, a person does an act which is more then merely preparatory to the commission of the offence, he is guilty of attempting to commit the offence.

(2) A person may be guilty of attempting to commit an offence to which this section applies even though the facts are such that the commission of the offence is impossible.

(3) In any case where—

(a) apart from this subsection a person's intention would not be regarded as having amounted to an intent to commit an offence; but

(b) if the facts of the case had been as he believed them to be, his intention would be so regarded,

then, for the purposes of subsection (1) above, he shall be regarded as having had an intent to commit that offence.

(4) This section applies to any offence which, if it were completed, would be triable in England and Wales as an indictable offence, other than—

- (a) conspiracy (at common law or under section 1 of the Criminal Law Act 1977 or any other enactment);
- (b) aiding, abetting, counselling, procuring or suborning the commission of an offence;
- (c) offences under section 4(1) (assisting offenders) or 5(1) (accepting or agreeing to accept consideration for not disclosing information about an arrestable offence) of the Criminal Law Act 1967.

Trial and penalties

4.—(1) A person guilty by virtue of section 1 above of attempting to commit an offence shall—

- (a) if the offence is murder or any other offence the sentence for which is fixed by law, be liable on conviction on indictment to imprisonment for life; and
- (b) if the offence attempted is indictable but does not fall within paragraph (a) above, be liable on conviction on indictment to any penalty to which he would have been liable on conviction on indictment of that offence; and
- (c) if the offence attempted is triable either way, be liable on summary conviction to any penalty to which he would have been liable on summary conviction of that offence.

(2) In any case in which a court may proceed to summary trial of an information charging a person with an offence and an information charging him with an offence under section 1 above of attempting to commit it or an attempt under a special statutory provision, the court may, without his consent, try the informations together.

(3) Where, in proceedings against a person for an offence under section 1 above, there is evidence sufficient in law to support a finding that he did an act falling within subsection (1) of that section, the question whether or not his act fell within that subsection is a question of fact.

(4) Where, in proceedings against a person for an attempt under a special statutory provision, there is evidence sufficient in law to support a finding that he did an act falling within subsection (3) of section 3 above, the question whether or not his act fell within that subsection is a question of fact.

Conspiracy

Extension of definition of the offence of conspiracy

5.—(1) For subsection (1) of section 1 of the Criminal Law Act 1977 (definition of the offence of conspiracy) there shall be substituted the following subsection)—

"(1) Subject to the following provisions of this Part of this Act, if a person agrees with any other person or persons that a course of conduct shall be pursued which, if the agreement is carried out in accordance with their intentions, either—

- (a) will necessarily amount to or involve the commission of any offence or offences by one or more of the parties to the agreement, or

(b)   would do so but for the existence of facts which render the commission of the offence or any of the offences impossible,

he is guilty of conspiracy to commit the offence or offences in question."

(2) This section shall not apply where an agreement was entered into before the commencement of this Act unless the conspiracy continued to exist after that date.

Criminal Justice Act 1988

Common assault and battery shall be summary offences

39. Common assault and battery shall be summary offences and a person guilty of either of them shall be liable to a fine not exceeding level 5 on the standard scale, to imprisonment for a term not exceeding six months, or to both.

PART THREE

CONTRACT

Chapter 1

Offer and Acceptance

1. THE INGREDIENTS OF A CONTRACT

Carlill v. Carbolic Smoke Ball Company

[1893] 1 Q.B. 256 (C.A.)

[The defendants were the sellers of a medical preparation picturesquely described as the "Carbolic Smoke Ball." They placed an advertisement in the *Pall Mall Gazette* stating that they would pay £100 to anyone who bought and used the ball according to their directions and who still contracted influenza. They mentioned that £1,000 had been deposited with their bankers to show their sincerity in the matter. Despite using the ball as prescribed, the plaintiff contracted 'flu. She thereupon sued the defendants for her £100.]

Bowen L.J. We were asked to say that this document was a contract too vague to be enforced.

The first observation which arises is that the document itself is not a contract at all, it is only an offer made to the public. The defendants contend next, that it is an offer the terms of which are too vague to be treated as a definite offer, inasmuch as there is no limit of time fixed for the catching of the influenza, and it cannot be supposed that the advertisers seriously meant to promise to pay money to every person who catches the influenza at any time after the inhaling of the smoke ball. It was urged also, that if you look at this document you will find much vagueness as to the persons with whom the contract was intended to be made—that, in the first place, its terms are wide enough to include persons who may have used the smoke ball before the advertisement was issued; at all events, that it is an offer to the world in general, and, also, that it is unreasonable to suppose it to be a definite offer, because nobody in their senses would contract themselves out of the opportunity of checking the experiment which was going to be made at their own expense. It is also

409

contended that the advertisement is rather in the nature of a puff or a proclamation than a promise or offer intended to mature into a contract when accepted. But the main point seems to be that the vagueness of the document shows that no contract whatever was intended. It seems to me that in order to arrive at a right conclusion we must read this advertisement in its plain meaning, as the public would understand it. It was intended to be issued to the public and to be read by the public. How would an ordinary person reading this document construe it? It was intended unquestionably to have some effect, and I think the effect which it was intended to have, was to make people use the smoke ball, because the suggestions and allegations which it contains are directed immediately to the use of the smoke ball as distinct from the purchase of it. It did not follow that the smoke ball was to be purchased from the defendants directly, or even from agents of theirs directly. The intention was that the circulation of the smoke ball should be promoted, and that the use of it should be increased. The advertisement begins by saying that a reward will be paid by the Carbolic Smoke Ball Company to any person who contracts the increasing epidemic after using the ball. It has been said that the words do not apply only to persons who contract the epidemic after the publication of the advertisement, but include persons who had previously contracted the influenza. I cannot so read the advertisement. It is written in colloquial and popular language, and I think that it is equivalent to this: "100*l*. will be paid to any person who shall contract the increasing epidemic after having used the carbolic smoke ball three times daily for two weeks." And it seems to me that the way in which the public would read it would be this, that if anybody, after the advertisement was published, used three times daily for two weeks the carbolic smoke ball, and then caught cold, he would be entitled to the reward. Then again it was said: "How long is this protection to endure? Is it to go on for ever, or for what limit of time?" I think that there are two constructions of this document, each of which is good sense, and each of which seems to me to satisfy the exigencies of the present action. It may mean that the protection is warranted to last during the epidemic, and it was during the epidemic that the plaintiff contracted the disease. I think, more probably, it means that the smoke ball will be a protection while it is in use. That seems to me the way in which an ordinary person would understand an advertisement about medicine, and about a specific against influenza. It could not be supposed that after you have left off using it you are still to be protected for ever, as if there was to be a stamp set upon your forehead that you were never to catch influenza because you had once used the carbolic smoke ball. I think the immunity is to last during the use of the ball. That is the way in which I should naturally read it, and it seems to be that the subsequent language of the advertisement supports that construction. It says: "During the last epidemic of influenza many thousand carbolic smoke balls were sold, and in no ascertained case was the disease contracted by those using" (not "who had used") "the carbolic smoke ball," and it concludes with saying that one smoke ball will last a family several months (which imports that it is to be efficacious while it is being used), and that the ball can be refilled at a cost of 5s. I, therefore, have myself no hesitation in saying that I think, on the construction of this advertisement, the protection was to enure during the time that the carbolic smoke ball was being used. My brother, the Lord Justic who preceded me, thinks that the contract would be sufficiently definite if you were to read it in the sense that the protection was to be warranted during a reasonable period after use. I have some difficulty myself on that point; but it is not necessary for me to consider it further, because the disease here was contracted during the use of the carbolic smoke ball.

Was it intended that the 100*l*. should, if the conditions were fulfilled, be paid? The advertisement says that 1000*l*. is lodged at the bank for the purpose. Therefore, it cannot be said that the statement that 100*l*. would be paid was intended to be a mere puff. I think it was intended to be understood by the public as an offer which was to be acted upon.

But it was said there was no check on the part of the persons who issued the advertisement, and that it would be an insensate thing to promise 100*l*. to a person who used the smoke ball unless you could check or superintend his manner of using it. The answer to that argument seems to me to be that if a person chooses to make extravagant promises of this kind he probably does so because it pays him to make them, and, if he has made them, the extravagance of the promises is no reason in law why he should not be bound by them.

It was also said that the contract is made with all the world—that is, with everybody; and that you cannot contract with everybody. It is not a contract made with all the world. There is the fallacy of the agreement. It is an offer made to all the world; and why should not an offer be made to all the world which is to ripen in to a contract with anybody who comes forward and performs the condition? It is an offer to become liable to any one who, before it is retracted, performs the condition, and, although the offer is made to the world, the contract is made with that limited portion of the public who come forward and perform the condition on the faith of the advertisement. It is not like cases in which you offer to negotiate, or you issue advertisements that you have got a stock of books to sell, or houses to let, in which case there is no offer to be bound by any contract. Such advertisements are offers to negotiate—offers to receive offers—offers to chaffer as, I think, some learned judge in one of the cases has said. If this is an offer to be bound, then it is a contract the moment the person fulfils the condition. That seems to me to be sense, and it is also the ground on which all these advertisement cases have been decided during the century; and it cannot be put better than in Willes, J.'s, judgment in *Spencer* v. *Harding* (1870). "In the advertisement cases," he says "there never was any doubt that the advertisement amounted to a promise to pay the money to the person who first gave information. To difficulty suggested was that it was a contract with all the world. But that, of course, was soon overruled. It was an offer to become liable to any person who before the offer should be retracted should happen to be the person to fulfil the contract, of which the advertisement was an offer or tender. That is not the sort of difficulty which presents itself here. If the circular had gone on, 'and we undertake to sell to the highest bidder,' the reward cases would have applied, and there would have been a good contract in respect of the persons." As soon as the highest bidder presented himself says, Wills, J., the person who was to hold the vinculum juris on the other side of the contract was ascertained, and it became settled.

Then it was said that there was no notification of the acceptance of the contract. One cannot doubt that, as an ordinary rule of law, an acceptance of an offer made ought to be notified to the person who makes the offer, in order that the two minds may come together. Unless this is done the two minds may be apart and there is not that consensus which is necessary according to the English law—I say nothing about the laws of other countries—to make a contract. But there is this clear gloss to be made upon that doctrine, that a notification of acceptance is required for the benefit of the person who makes the offer, the person who makes the offer may dispense with notice to himself if he thinks it desirable to do so, and I suppose there can be no doubt that where a person in an offer made by him to another person, expressly or impliedly intimates a particular mode of acceptance as sufficient to make the bargain binding, it is only necessary for the other person to whom such offer is made to follow the indicated method of acceptance and if the person making the offer, expressly or impliedly intimates in his offer that it will be sufficient to act on the proposal without communicating acceptance of it to himself, performance of the condition is a sufficient acceptance without notification.

That seems to me to be the principle which lies at the bottom of the acceptance cases, of which two instances are the wellknown judgment of Mellish, L.J., in *Harris's Case* (1873), and the very instructive judgment of Lord Blackburn in *Brogden v. Metropolitan Ry. Co.* (1877), in which he appears to me to take exactly the line I have indicated.

Now, if that is the law, how are we to find out whether the person who makes the offer does intimate that notification of acceptance will not be necessary in order to constitute a binding bargain? In many cases you look to the offer itself. In many cases you extract from the character of the transaction that notification is not required, and in the advertisement cases it seems to me to follow as an inference to be drawn from the transaction itself that a person is not to notify his acceptance of the offer before he performs the condition, but that if he performs the condition notification is dispensed with. It seems to me that from the point of view of common sense no other idea could be entertained. If I advertise to the world that my dog is lost, and that anybody who brings the dog to a particular place will be paid some money, are all the police or the persons whose business it is to find lost dogs to be expected to sit down and write me a note saying that they have accepted my proposal? Why, of course, they at once look after the dog, and as soon as they find the dog they have performed the condition. The essence of the transaction is that the dog should be found, and it is not necessary under such circumstances, as it seems to me, that in order to make the contract binding there should be any notification of acceptance. It follows from the nature of the thing that the performance of the condition is sufficient acceptance without the notification of it, and a person who makes an offer in an advertisement of that kind makes an offer which must be read by the light of that common sense reflection. He does, therefore, in his offer impliedly indicate that he does not require notification of the acceptance of the offer.

A further argument for the defendants was that this was a nudum pactum—that there was no consideration for the promise—that taking the influenza was only a condition, and that the using the smoke ball was only a condition, and that there was no consideration at all; in fact, that there was no request, express or implied, to use the smoke ball.... The short answer, to abstain from academical discussion, is, it seems to me, that there is here a request to use involved in the offer. Then as to the alleged want of consideration. The definition of "consideration" ... which is cited and adopted by Tindal, C.J., in the case of *Laythoarp* v. *Bryant* (1836), is this: "Any act of the plaintiff from which the defendant derives a benefit or advantage, or any labour, detriment, or inconvenience sustained by the plaintiff, provided such act is performed or such inconvenience suffered by the plaintiff, with the consent, either express or implied, of the defendant." Can it be said here that if the person who reads this advertisement applies thrice daily, for such time as may seem to him tolerable, the carbolic smoke ball to his nostrils for a whole fortnight, he is doing nothing at all—that it is a mere act which is not to count towards consideration to support a promise (for the law does not require us to measure the adequacy of the consideration). Inconvenience sustained by one party at the request of the other is enough to create a consideration. I think therefore, that it is consideration enough that the plaintiff took the trouble of using the smoke ball. But I think also that the defendants received a benefit from this user, for the use of the smoke ball was contemplated by the defendants as being indirectly a benefit to them, because the use of the smoke balls would promote their sale.

... Here, ... if you once make up your mind that there was a promise made to this lady who is the plaintiff, as one of the public—a promise made to her that if she used the smoke ball three times daily for a fortnight and got the influenza, she should have 100*l.*, it seems to me that her using the smoke ball was sufficient consideration. I cannot picture to myself the view of the law on which the contrary could be held when you have once found who are the contracting parties. If I say to a person, "If you use such and such a medicine for a week I will give you 5*l.*," and he uses it, there is ample consideration for the promise.

[Lindley and A.L. Smith L.JJ. delivered concurring judgments.]

Questions

1. This leading case is quoted at length for its importance not only to the problems of offer and acceptance but also for its discussion of many other issues. What other issues do arise in the case?

2. An example of a similar range of problems arising in a modern context is *Esso Petroleum Ltd.* v. *Commissioners of Customs and Excise* (1976) see below, p. 450.

3. What sort of contract was involved in *Carlill*? If the company made an offer here, how could they have revoked it?

4. Compare the "reward" cases of *Williams* v. *Carwardine* (1833) and *R.* v. *Clarke* (1927) (Australia). What problems of revocation arise in this type of case? See, *e.g. Errington* v. *Errington* (1952).

5. What if the plaintiff had only seen the advertisement after she had bought the smoke ball?

2. OFFER AND INVITATION TO TREAT

Pharmaceutical Society of Great Britain v. Boots Cash Chemists (Southern) Ltd.

[1953] 1 Q.B. 401 (C.A.)

[It was an offence for Boots to sell certain medicines except under the supervision of a registered pharmacist. Two customers in a "self service" shop placed such medicines selected from the open shelves in the wire baskets provided. A pharmacist was available to supervise the transaction at the cash desk. The problem at issue was, therefore, when did the contract of sale take place?]

Somervell L.J. The point taken by the plaintiffs is this: it is said that the purchase is complete if and when a customer going round the shelves takes an article and puts it in the receptacle which he or she is carrying, and that therefore, if that is right, when the customer comes to the pay desk, having completed the tour of the premises, the registered pharmacist, if so minded, has no power to say: "This drug ought not to be sold to this customer." Whether and in what circumstances he would have that power we need not inquire, but one can, of course, see that there is a difference if supervision can only be exercised at a time when the contract is completed.

I agree with the Lord Chief Justice in everything that he said, but I will put the matter shortly in my own words. Whether the view contended for by the plaintiffs is a right view depends on what are the legal implications of this layout—the invitation to the customer. Is a contract to be regarded as being completed when the article is put into the receptacle, or is this to be regarded as a more organised way of doing what is done already in many types of shops—and a bookseller is perhaps the best example—namely, enabling customers to have free access to what is in the shop, to look at the different articles, and then, ultimately, having got the ones which they wish to buy, to come up to the assistant saying "I want this"? The assistant in 999 times out of 1,000 says "That is all right," and the money passes and the transaction is completed. I agree with what the Lord Chief Justice has said, and with the reasons which he has given for his conclusion that in the case of an ordinary shop, although goods are displayed and it is intended that customers should go and choose what they want, the contract is not completed until, the customer having indicated the articles which he needs, the shop-keep, or someone on his behalf, accepts that offer. The the contract is completed. I can see no reason at all, that being clearly the normal position, for drawing any different implication as a result of this layout.

The Lord Chief Justice, I think, expressed one of the most formidable difficulties in the way of the plaintiffs' contention when he pointed out that, if the plaintiffs are right, once an article has been placed in the receptacle the customer himself is bound and would have no right, without paying for the first article, to substitute an article which he saw later of a similar kind and which he perhaps preferred. I can see no reason for implying from this self-service arrangement any implication other than that which the Lord Chief Justice found in it, namely, that it is a convenient method of enabling customers to see what there is and choose, and possibly put back and substitute, articles which they wish to have, and then to go up to the cashier and offer to buy what they have so far chosen. On that conclusion the case fails, because it is admitted that there was supervision in the sense required by the Act and at the appropriate moment of time. For these reasons, in my opinion, the appeal should be dismissed.

[Birkett and Romer L.JJ. concurred.]

Questions

1. What of advertisements and displays? See *Partridge* v. *Crittenden* (1968); *Fisher* v. *Bell* (1961).

2. Jane visits a motorway service area where she selects a hot meal from the counter. After waiting in the queue at the cash desk, she decides she is not hungry after all. Is she obliged to pay?

3. Who makes the offer and who accepts at an auction? See *Harris* v. *Nickerson* (1873); *Warlow* v. *Harrison* (1859); Sale of Goods Act 1979, s.57(2).

3.   OFFERS AND COUNTER-OFFERS

Stevenson v. McLean

(1880) 5 Q.B.D. 346 (Q.B.D.)

[The parties were negotiating about the sale of a quantity of iron. The defendant wrote: " ... I would now sell for 40s. net cash, open till Monday." The plaintiffs telegraphed in reply, "Please wire whether you would accept forty for delivery over two months, or if not, longest limit you would give." The defendant, after receipt of this telegram sold the iron to a third party. The plaintiff's, not yet having received a reply to their telegram, telegraphed an acceptance of the offer to sell at 40s. cash. The plaintiff's sued the defendant for breach of contract; the defendant alleged that the plaintiffs had made a counter offer which entitled the defendant to regard the original offer as no longer open.]

Lush J. Looking at the form of the telegram, the time when it was sent, and the state of the iron market, I cannot think this is its fair meaning. The plaintiff Stevenson said he meant it only as an inquiry, expecting an answer for his guidance, and this, I think, is the sense in which the defendant ought to have regarded it.

It is apparent throughout the correspondence, that the plaintiffs did not contemplate buying the iron on speculation, but that their acceptance of the defendant's offer depended on their finding some one to take the warrants off their hands. All parties knew that the market was in an unsettled state, and that no one could predict at the early hour when the telegram was sent how the prices would range during the day. It was reasonable that, under these circumstances, they should desire to know before business began whether they were to be at liberty in case of need to make any and what concession as to the time or times of delivery, which would be the time or times of payment, or whether the defendant was determined to adhere to the terms of his letter; and it was highly unreasonable that the plaintiffs should have intended to close the negotiation while it was uncertain whether they could find a buyer or not, having the whole of the business hours of the day to look for one. The, again, the form of the telegram is one of inquiry. It is not "I offer forty for delivery over two months," which would have likened the case to *Hyde* v. *Wrench* [see below].... Here there is no counter proposal. The words are, "Please wire whether you would accept forty for delivery over two months, or, if not, the longest limit you would give." There is nothing specific by way of offer or rejection, but a mere inquiry, which should have been answered and not treated as a rejection of the offer. This ground of objection therefore fails.

Hyde v. Wrench

(1840) 3 Beav. 334 (Rolls Court)

[The defendant offered to sell his farm for £1,000. The plaintiff made an offer of £950 which was refused. The plaintiff then wrote saying that he was prepared to pay £1000 and attempted to enforce the contract of sale at that price. The court held that there was no longer an offer which he could accept.]

The Master of the Rolls [Lord Langdale]. Under the circumstances stated in this bill, I think there exists no valid binding contract between the parties for the purchase of the property. The Defendant offered to sell it for £1000, and if that had been at once unconditionally accepted, there would undoubtedly have been a perfect binding contract; instead of that, the Plaintiff made an offer of his own, to purchase the property for £950, and he thereby rejected the offer previously made by the Defendant. I think that it was not afterwards competent for him to revive the proposal of the Defendant, by tendering an acceptance of it; and that, therefore, there exists no obligation of any sort between the parties; the demurrer must be allowed.

Butler Machine Tool Co. Ltd. v. Ex-Cell-O Corporation

[1979] 1 All E.R. 965 (C.A.)

[The sellers offered to sell one of their machines to the plaintiff on their standard terms, printed on the quotation, which were stated to prevail over any terms and conditions in the buyer's order. The buyer replied by placing an order stated to be on their own terms, which *inter alia* contained a crucial price variation clause in conflict with the seller's terms. The sellers acknowledge receipt of the order on the buyer's form. The problem was, on whose terms had the contract been concluded?]

Lawton L.J. The modern commercial practice of making quotations and placing orders with conditions attached, usually in small print, is indeed likely, as in this case, to produce a battle of forms. The problem is how should that battle be conducted? The view taken by the judge was that the battle should extend over a wide area and the court should do its best to look into the minds of the parties and make certain assumptions. In my judgment, the battle has to be conducted in accordance with set rules. It is a battle more on classical 18th century lines when convention decided who had the right to open fire first rather than in accordance with the modern concept of attrition.

The rules relating to a battle of this kind have been known for the past 130-odd years. They were set out by the ten Master of the Rolls, Lord Langdale, in *Hyde* v. *Wrench* (1840) . . .

When those rules are applied to this case, in my judgment, the answer is obvious. The sellers started by making an offer. That was in their quotation. The small print was headed by the following words:

"GENERAL. All orders are accepted only upon and subject to the terms set out in our quotation and the following conditions. These terms and conditions shall prevail over any terms and conditions in the Buyer's order."

That offer was not accepted. The buyers were only prepared to have one of these very expensive machines on their own terms. Their terms had very material differences in them from the terms put forward by the sellers. They could not be reconciled in any way. In the language of art 7 of the Uniform Law on the Formation of Contracts for the International Sale of Goods they did materially alter the terms set out in the offer made by the sellers.

As I understand *Hyde* v. *Wrench* and the cases which have followed, the consequence of placing the order in that way, if I may adopt Megaw J's words, was to kill the quotation. It follows that the court has to look at what happened after the buyers made their counter-offer. By letter dated 4th June 1969 the sellers acknowledged receipt of the counter-offer and they went on in this way: "Details of this order have been passed to our Halifax works for attention and a formal acknowledgement of order will follow in due course." That is clearly a reference to the printed tear-off-slip which was at the bottom of buyers' counter-offer. By letter dated 5th June 1969 the sales office manager at the sellers' Halifax factory completed that tear-off slip and sent it back to the buyers. . . .

As I pointed out in the course of argument to counsel for the sellers, if the letter of 5th June which accompanied the form acknowledging the terms which the buyers had specified had amounted to a counter-offer, then in my judgment the parties never were *ad idem*. It cannot be said that the buyers accepted the counter-offer by reason of the fact that ultimately they took physical delivery of the machine. By the time they took physical delivery of the machine, they had made it clear by correspondence that they were not accepting that there was any price escalation clause in any contract which they had made with the plaintiffs.

[Lord Denning M.R. and Bridge L.J. gave concurring judgments, although Lord Denning took the opportunity to criticise the traditional analysis of offer and acceptance as applied to a modern situation such as the "Battle of the Forms" cases.]

Byrne v. Van Tienhoven

(1880) 5 C.P.D. 344 (Common Pleas)

[The defendants in Cardiff posted a letter to New York offering to sell 1,000 boxes of tinplates. On October 8 they posted a letter revoking the offer. On October 11 the plaintiffs received the first letter and telegraphed their acceptance. The second letter arrived on October 20. Had there been a revocation of the offer?]

Lindley J There is no doubt that an offer can be withdrawn before it is accepted, and it is immaterial whether the offer is expressed to be open for acceptance for a given time or not: *Routledge* v. *Grant* (1828). For the decision of the present case, however, it is necessary to consider two other questions, *viz.*: 1. Whether a withdrawal of an offer has any effect until it is communicated to the person to whom the offer has been sent? 2. Whether posting a letter of withdrawal is a communication to the person to whom the letter is sent?

[The court held that a revocation to be effective must be communicated. It was not fatal to a contract that *both* parties were no longer consenting *ad idem*. This is an example of the "objective" approach of English contract law.]

I pass, therefore, to the next question, viz., whether posting the letter of revocation was a sufficient communication of it to the plaintiff. The offer was posted on the 1st October, the withdrawal was posted on the 8th, and did not reach the plaintiff until after he had posted his letter of the 11th, accepting the offer. It may be taken as now settled that where an offer is made and accepted by letters sent through the post, the contract is completed the moment the letter accepting the offer is posted ... even although it never reaches its destination. When, however, these authorities are looked at, it will be seen that they are based upon the principle that the writer of the offer has expressly or impliedly assented to treat an answer to him by a letter duly posted as a sufficient acceptance and notification to himself, or, in other words, he has made the post office his agent to receive the acceptance and notification of it. But this principle appears to me to be inapplicable to the case of the withdrawal of an offer. In this particular case I can find no evidence of any authority in fact given by the plaintiffs to the defendants to notify a withdrawal of their offer by merely posting a letter; and there is no legal principle or decision which compels me to hold, contrary to the fact, that the letter of the 8th of October is to be treated as communicated to the plaintiff on that day or on any day before the 20th, when the letter reached them. But before that letter had reached the plaintiffs, they had accepted the offer, both by telegram and by post; and they had themselves resold the tin plates at a profit. In my opinion the withdrawal by the defendants on the 8th of October of their offer of the 1st was inoperative; and a complete contract binding on both parties was entered into on the 11th of October, when the plaintiffs accepted the offer of the 1st, which they had no reason to suppose had been withdrawn. Before leaving this part of the case it may be as well to point out the extreme injustice and inconvenience which any other conclusion would produce. If the defendants' contention were to prevail no person who had received an offer by post and had accepted it would know his position until he had waited such a time as to be quite sure that a letter withdrawing the offer had not been posted before his acceptance of it. It appears to me that both legal principles, and practical convenience require that a person who has accepted an offer not known to him to have been revoked, shall be in a position safely to act upon the footing that the offer and acceptance constitute a contract binding on both parties.

Judgment was given for the plaintiffs.

Question

What if a party only hears a rumour that the potential seller has changed his mind? See *Dickinson* v. *Dodds* (1876).

4. ACCEPTANCE

Felthouse v. Bindley

(1862) 142 E.R. 1037 (Common Pleas)

[The plaintiff, Paul Felthouse, was anxious to buy a horse forming part of the farming stock which his nephew, John Felthouse, wished to sell. A misunderstanding arose as to the price, John thinking he had sold the horse for 30 guineas, Paul thinking he had bought it for £30. Accordingly, Paul wrote to John on January 2 offering to split the difference and added, "If I hear no more about him, I consider the horse mine at £30.15s." John did not reply, but he did tell the auctioneer, Brindley, to withdraw the horse from the sale. Brindley mistakenly sold the horse to another. Paul sued Brindley, claiming that at the time of the auction on February 25, the horse already belonged to him.]

Willes, J. I am of opinion that the rule to enter a nonsuit should be made absolute.... It is clear that there was no complete bargain on the 2nd of January: and it is also clear that the uncle had no right to impose upon the nephew a sale of his horse for 30l.15s. unless he chose to comply with the condition of writing to repudiate the offer. The nephew might, no doubt, have bound his uncle to the bargain by writing to him: the uncle might also have retracted his offer at any time before acceptance. It stood an open offer and so things remained until the 25th of February, when the nephew was about to sell his farming stock by auction. The horse in question being catalogued with the rest of the stock, the auctioneer (the defendant) was told that it was already sold. It is clear, therefore, that the nephew in his own mind intended his uncle to have the horse at the price which he (the uncle) had named,—30l.15s.: but he had not communicated such his intention to his uncle, or done anything to bind himself. Nothing, therefore, had been done to vest the property in the

horse in the plaintiff down to the 25th February, when the
horse was sold by the defendant. . . .

Keating, J. I am of the same opinion. Had the question
arisen as between the uncle and the nephew, there would
probably have been some difficulty. But, as between the uncle
and the auctioneer, the only question we have to consider is
whether the horse was the property of the plaintiff at the time
of the sale on the 25th of February. It seems to me that
nothing had been done at that time to pass the property out
of the nephew and vest it in the plaintiff.

[*Byles J.* concurred.]

Question

Suppose the auctioneer had not sold the horse, but the uncle had refused
to accept delivery of the horse. Could the nephew have sued for breach of
contract?

Entores Ltd. v. Miles Far East Corporation

[1955] 2 Q.B. 327 (C.A.)

[The plaintiffs in London telexed the defendant's agents in Holland making
an offer. The agents sent an acceptance by telex which was received in
London. An issue arose of where the contract had been made, this in turn
depended upon at what point there had been acceptance of the offer.]

Lord Denning M.R. When a contract is made by post it is
clear law throughout the common law countries that the
acceptance is complete as soon as the letter is put into the
post box, and that is the place where the contract is made.
But there is no clear rule about contracts made by telephone
or by Telex. Communications by these means are virtually
instantaneous and stand on a different footing.

The problem can only be solved by going in stages. Let me
first consider a case where two people make a contract by
word of mouth in the presence of one another. Suppose, for
instance, that I shout an offer to a man across a river or a
courtyard but I do not hear his reply because it is drowned by
an aircraft flying overhead. There is no contract at that
moment. If he wishes to make a contract, he must wait till the

aircraft is gone and then shout back his acceptance so that I can hear what he says. Not until I have his answer am I bound....

Now take a case where two people make a contract by telephone. Suppose, for instance, that I make an offer to a man by telephone and, in the middle of his reply, the line goes "dead" so that I do not hear his words of acceptance. There is no contract at that moment. The other man may not know the precise moment when the line failed. But he will know that the telephone conversation was abruptly broken off: because people usually say something to signify the end of the conversation. If he wishes to make a contract, he must therefore get through again so as to make sure that I heard. Suppose next, that the line does not go dead, but it is nevertheless so indistinct that I do not catch what he says and I ask him to repeat it. He then repeats it and I hear his acceptance. The contract is made, not on the first time when I do not hear, but only the second time when I do hear. If he does not repeat it, there is no contract. The contract is only complete when I have his answer accepting the offer.

Lastly, take the Telex. Suppose a clerk in a London office taps out on the teleprinter an offer which is immediately recorded on a teleprinter in a Manchester office, and a clerk at that end taps out an acceptance. If the line goes dead in the middle of the sentence of acceptance, the teleprinter motor will stop. There is then obviously no contract. The clerk at Manchester must get through again and send his complete sentence. But it may happen that the line does not go dead, yet the message does not get through to London. Thus the clerk at Manchester may tap out his message of acceptance and it will not be recorded in London because the ink at the London end fails, or something of that kind. In that case, the Manchester clerk will not know of the failure but the London clerk will know of it and will immediately send back a message "not receiving." Then, when the fault is rectified, the Manchester clerk will repeat his message. Only then is there a contract. If he does not repeat it, there is no contract. It is not until his message is received that the contract is complete.

In all the instances I have taken so far, the man who sends the message of acceptance knows that it has not been received or he has reason to know it. So he must repeat it. But, suppose that he does not know that his message did not get home. He thinks it has. This may happen if the listener on the telephones does not catch the words of acceptance, but nevertheless does not trouble to ask for them to be repeated: or the ink on the teleprinter fails at the receiving end, but the clerk does not ask for the message to be repeated: so that the man who sends an acceptance reasonably believes that his message has been received. The offeror in such circumstances is clearly bound, because he will be estopped from saying that he did not receive the message of acceptance. It is his own fault that he did not get it. But if there should be a case where the offeror without any fault on his part does not receive the message of acceptance—yet the sender of it reasonably believes it has got home when it has not—then I think there is no contract.

My conclusion is, that the rule about instantaneous communications between the parties is different from the rule about the post. The contract is only complete when the acceptance is received by the offeror: and the contract is made at the place where the acceptance is received.

In a matter of this kind, however, it is very important that the countries of the world should have the same rule. I find that most of the European countries have substantially the same rule as that I have stated. Indeed, they apply it to contracts by post as well as instantaneous communications. But in the United States of America it appears as if instantaneous communications are treated in the same way as postal communications. In view of this divergence, I think that we must consider the matter on principle: and so considered, I have come to the view I have stated, and I am glad to see that Professor Winfield in this country (55 Law Quarterly Review, 514), and Professor Williston in the United States of America (Contracts, para. 82, p. 239), take the same view.

Applying the principles which I have stated, I think that the contract in this case was made in London where the acceptance was received.

Notes

The House of Lords approved this decision in *Brinkibon Ltd.* v. *Stahag Stahl* (1982).

Lord Denning has taken the view that the conventional analysis of situations into offer and acceptance is not always appropriate. See *Butler Machine Tool Co. Ltd.* v. *Ex-Cell-O Corporation* (above, p. 418); *Gibson* v. *Manchester City Council* (1979). There are certainly cases where it can become very strained. An example is the problem of cross offers (see *Tinn* v. *Hoffman* (1873)) or the peculiar facts of *Clarke* v. *Dunraven* (1897).

Questions

1. What is the legal effect of a "telemessage"?
2. Suppose the agents had replied by telephone, but it was a message dictated on to the plaintiff's answering machine. Would there have been a valid acceptance? If so, when would it be effective?

Chapter 2

Consideration

1. THE MEANING OF CONSIDERATION

Chappell & Co. v. Nestlé

[1960] A.C. 87 (H.L.)

[As part of a sale's promotion Nestlé's offered a record for sale at a price of 1s. 6d. plus three wrappers from their bars of chocolate. An issue arose as to whether the wrappers were part of the consideration for the contract.]

Lord Somervell of Harrow. I think they are part of the consideration. They are so described in the offer. "They," the wrappers, "will help you to get smash hit recordings." They are so described in the record itself—"all you have to do to get such new record is to send three wrappers from Nestlé's 6d. milk chocolate bars, together with postal order for 1s. 6d." This is not conclusive but, however described, they are, in my view, in law part of the consideration. It is said that when received the wrappers are of no value to Nestlé's. This I would have thought irrelevant. A contracting party can stipulate for what consideration he chooses. A peppercorn does not cease to be good consideration it if is established that the promisee does not like pepper and will throw away the corn. As the whole object of selling the record, if it was a sale, was to increase the sales of the chocolate, it seems to me wrong not to treat the stipulated evidence of such sales as part of the consideration. For these reasons I would allow the appeal.

[Lords Reid and Tucker delivered speeches allowing the appeal.]

Bainbridge v. Firmstone

(1838) 112 E.R. 1019 (Q.B.D.)

[The plaintiff, at the request of the defendant, allowed the defendant to weigh two of the plaintiff's boilers. The defendant promised to return the boilers in perfect condition, which he failed to do. The plaintiff sued, but the defendant claimed there was no consideration for his promise.]

Lord Denman C.J. It seems to me that the declaration is well enough. The defendant had some reason for wishing to weigh the boilers; and he could do so only by obtaining permission from the plaintiff, which he did obtain by promising to return them in good condition. We need not enquire what benefit he expected to derive. The plaintiff might have given or refused leave.

Patteson J. The consideration is, that the plaintiff, at the defendant's request, had consented to allow the defendant to weigh the boilers. I suppose the defendant thought he had some benefit; at any rate, there is a detriment to the plaintiff from his parting with the possession for even so short a time.

Williams and *Coleridge J.J.s.* concurred.

Notes

For a further discussion of consideration, see *Carlill* v. *Carbolic Smoke Ball Co.* (above, p. 413). On the requirement often stated that, "consideration must move from the promisee," see *Tweddle* v. *Atkinson* (1861) and Chapter 7.

2. CONSIDERATION AND THE TIME OF THE AGREEMENT

Lampleigh v. Braithwait

(1615) 80 E.R. 255 (Common Bench)

[Thomas Braithwait who had killed a man asked Anthony Lampleigh to obtain a pardon for him from the King. Lampleigh went to considerable trouble at his own expense, and Braithwait then promised him £100 for his troubles which he failed to pay. Lampleigh sued, Braithwait alleged that the consideration was passed and that there was therefore no contract.]

First, it was agreed, that a meer voluntary curtesie will not have a consideration to uphold an assumpsit. But if that curtesie were moved by a suit or request of the party that gives the assumpsit, it will bind, for the promise, though it follows, yet it is not naked, but couples itself with the suit before, and the merits of the party procured by that suit, which is the difference.

Judgment given for Anthony Lampleigh.

Note

A more recent illustration of the same principle is to be found in *Re Casey's Patents, Stewart v. Casey* (1893) (H.S.B., p. 441).

Roscorla v. Thomas

(1842) 114 E.R. 496 (Q.B.)

[The defendant sold the plaintiff a horse without, it seems, any warranty that it was sound. Subsequently the defendant claimed that it was "sound and free from vice." The plaintiff sued on the grounds that it was in fact "vicious, restive, ungovernable, and ferocious."]

Lord Denman C.J. This was an action of assumpsit for breach of warranty of the soundness of a horse. The first count of the declaration, upon which alone the question arises, stated that, in consideration that the plaintiff, at the request of the defendant, had bough of the defendant a horse for the sum of 301., the defendant promised that it was sound and free from vice. And it was objected, in arrest of judgment, that the precedent executed consideration was insufficient to support the subsequent promise. And we are of opinion that the objection must prevail.

It may be taken as a general rule, subject to exceptions not applicable to this case, that the promise must be coextensive with the consideration. In the present case, the only promise that would result from the consideration, as stated, and be coextensive with it, would be to deliver the horse upon request. The precedent sale, without a warranty, though at the request of the defendant, imposes no other duty or obligation upon him. It is clear, therefore, that the consideration stated would not raise an implied promise by the defendant that the horse was sound or free from vice.

But the promise in the present case must be taken to be, as in fact it was, express: and the question is, whether that fact will warrant the extension of the promise beyond that which would be implied by law; and whether the consideration, though insufficient to raise an implied promise, will nevertheless support an express one. And we think that it will not.

The cases in which it has been held that, under certain circumstances, a consideration insufficient to raise an implied promise will nevertheless support an express one, will be found. . . . They are cases of voidable contracts subseqently ratified, of debts barred by operation of law, subsequently revived, and of equitable and moral obligations, which, but for some rule of law, would of themselves have been sufficient to raise an implied promise. All these cases are distinguishable from, and indeed inapplicable to, the present, which appears to us to fall within the general rule, that a consideration past and executed will support no other promise than such as would be implied by law.

Judgment for the defendant.

Note

A modern illustration of the same principle is *Re McArdle* (1951).

Question

What if the defendant had made the statement about the horse *before* the plaintiff had agreed to buy it?

3. PERFORMANCE OF AN EXISTING DUTY

Ward v. Byham

[1956] 2 All E.R. 318 (C.A.)

[The defendant, who was the father of the plaintiff's illegitimate child, wrote to her saying that he would provide £1 a week maintenance "providing you can prove that she will be well looked after and happy and also that she is allowed to decide for herself whether or not she wishes to come and live with you." The father appealed against the court's judgment for the mother.]

Lord Denning. The mother now brings this action, claiming that the father should pay her £1 per week, even though she herself has married. The only point taken before us in answer to the claim is that it is said that there was no consideration for the promise by the father to pay £1 a week, because, when she looked after the child, the mother was only doing that which she was legally bound to do, and that is no consideration in law.

. . .

By statute the mother of an illegitimate child is bound to maintain it, whereas the father is under no such obligation (see s.42 of the National Assistance Act, 1948). If she is a single woman the mother can apply to the magistrates for an affiliation order against the father, and it might be thought that consideration could be found in this case by holding that the mother must be taken to have agreed not to bring affiliation proceedings against the father. In her evidence the mother said, however, that she never at any time had any intention of bringing affiliation proceedings. It is now too late for her to bring them, because she has married and is no longer a single woman.

I approach the case, therefore, on the footing that, in looking after the child, the mother is only doing what she is legally bound to do. Even so, I think that there was sufficient consideration to support the promise. I have always though that a promise to perform an existing duty, or the performance of it, should be regarded as good consideration, because it is a benefit to the person to whom it is given. Take this very case. It is as much a benefit for the father to have the child looked after by the mother as by a neighbour. If he gets the benefit for which he stipulated, he ought to honour his promise, and he ought not to avoid it by saying that the mother was herself under a duty to maintain the child.

I regard the father's promise in this case as what is sometimes called a unilateral contract, a promise in return for an act, a promise by the father to pay £1 a week in return for the mother's looking after the child. Once the mother embarked on the task of looking after the child, there was a binding contract. So long as she looked after the child, she would be entitled to £1 a week. . . .

[*Morris and Parker L.JJ.* concurred.]

Notes

Forebearance to sue is also capable of amounting to consideration. Lord Denning's view of performance of an existing duty as consideration was not consistent with much of the case law on the subject. Contrast, *e.g. Collins* v. *Godefroy* (1831) with *Glasbrook Bros.* v. *Glamorgan County Council* (1925). Does Lord Denning's view gain support from *Williams* v. *Roffey Bros.* (below)? The performance of a contractual duty owed to a third party can amount to consideration, see *Scotson* v. *Pegg* (1861); *New Zealand Shipping Co. Ltd.* v. *Satterthwaite & Co. Ltd.* (1975). The point was authoratatively confirmed by the Privy Council in *Pau On* v. *Lau Yiu Long* (1980). What is the basis for allowing performance of a duty owed to a third party to amount to consideration? Why should cases of statutory duty be treated differently?

Williams v. Roffey Bros. & Nicholls (Contractors) Ltd.

[1990] 1 All E.R. 512 (C.A.)

[The plaintiff had contracted to carry out certain carpentry work for the defendants. Before the work was completed it became clear that the plaintiff was in difficulties and would not be able to complete the work punctually. The defendants accordingly offered the plaintiff payment in addition to the agreed contract price in return for completing the work on time. Naturally consideration had to be found for the defendants' promise. In *Stilk* v. *Myrick* (H.S.B. 444) two seamen deserted on a voyage and the captain promised the remaining crew extra wages if they would work the ship back short-handed. They did so but were subsequently refused the extra money. It was held that the crew were doing no more than their duty in meeting the normal contingencies of a sea voyage. Lord Ellenborough expressly stated that he based his decision on lack of consideration.]

Purchas L.J. Evidence given by Mr. Cottrell, the defendants' surveyor, established that, to their knowledge, the original contract price was too low to enable to plaintiff to operate satisfactorily and at a profit by something a little over £3,780. It was also known that the plaintiff was falling short in the supervision of his own labour force with the result that productivity fell and his financial difficulties had been aggravated. A further difficulty, which the judge found had arisen by the time of the meeting in April, was that the plaintiff had been paid for more than 80 per cent. of the work but had not completed anything like this percentage. These facts were all obviously known to the plaintiff as well as the defendants. Also known to the defendants through Mr Cottrell, and probably also appreciated by the plaintiff, was that the carpentry work to be executed by the plaintiff was on what was known as "the critical path of the defendants' global operations". Failure to complete this work by the plaintiff, in accordance with the contract, would seriously prejudice the defendants as main contractors vis-à-vis the owners for whom they were working.

In these circumstances there were clearly incentives to both parties to make a further arrangement in order to relieve the plaintiff of his financial difficulties and also to ensure that the plaintiff was in a position, or alternatively was willing, to continue with the sub-contract works to a reasonable and timely completion. Against this context the judge found that on 9 April 1986 a meeting took place between the plaintiff and a man called Hooper, the plaintiff's surveyor, on the one hand, and Mr. Cottrell and Mr. Roffey, the defendants' managing director, on the other hand. The arrangement was that the defendants would pay the plaintiff an extra £10,300 by way of increasing the lump sum for the total work. It was further agreed that the sum of £10,300 was to be paid at the rate of £575 per flat on the completion of each flat. This arrangement was beneficial to both sides. By completing one flat at a time rather than half completing all the flats the plaintiff was able to receive monies on account and the defendants were able to direct their other trades to do work in the completed flats which otherwise would have been held up until the plaintiff had completed his work.

The point of some difficulty which arises on this appeal is whether ... the agreement reached on 9 April failed for lack of consideration within the principle established by the old cases of *Stilk* v. *Myrick* (1809), approving *Harris* v. *Watson* (1791).

. . . . . .

In my judgment, therefore, the rule in *Stilk* v. *Myrick* remains valid as a matter of principle, namely that a contract not under seal must be supported by consideration. Thus, where the agreement on which reliance is placed provides that an extra payment is to be made for work to be done by the payee which he is already obliged to perform, then unless some other consideration is detected to support the agreement to pay the extra sum that agreement will not be enforceable. *Harris* v. *Watson* and *Stilk* v. *Myrick* involved circumstances of a very special nature, namely the extraordinary conditions existing at the turn of the eighteenth century under which seamen had to serve their contracts of employment on the high seas. There were strong public policy grounds at that time to protect the master and owners of a ship from being held to ransom by disaffected crews. Thus, the decision that the promise to pay extra wages even in the circumstances established in those cases was not supported by consideration is readily understandable. Of course, conditions today on the high seas have changed dramatically and it is at least questionable, counsel for the plaintiff submitted, whether these cases might not well have been decided differently if they were tried today. The modern cases tend to depend more on the defence of duress in a commercial context rather than lack of consideration for the second agreement. In the present case, the question of duress does not arise. The initiative in coming to the agreement of 9 April came from Mr. Cottrell and not from the plaintiff. It would not, therefore, lie in the defendants' mouth to assert a defence of duress. Nevertheless, the court is more ready in the presence of this defence being available in the commercial context to look for mutual advantages which would amount to sufficient consideration to support the second agreement under which the extra money is paid. Although the passage cited below from the speech of Lord Hailsham L.C. in *Woodhouse A.C. Israel Cocoa Ltd. S.A.* v. *Nigerian Produce Marketing Co. Ltd.* (1972) was strictly *obiter dicta* I respectfully adopt it as an indication of the approach to be made in modern times. The case involved an agreement to vary the currency in which the buyer's obligation should be met, which was subsequently affected by a depreciation in the currency involved. The case was decided on an issue of estoppel but Lord Hailsham L.C. commented on the other issue, namely the variation of the original contract in the following terms:

"If the exchange letter was not variation, I believe it was nothing. The [buyers] asked for a variation in the mode of discharge of a contract of sale. If the proposal meant what they claimed, and was accepted and acted on, I venture to think that the [vendors] would have been bound by their acceptenace at least until they gave reasonable notice to terminate, and I imagine that a modern court would have found no difficulty in discovering consideration for a such a promise. Businessmen know their own business best even when they appear to grant an indulgence, and in the present case I do not think that there would have been insuperable difficulty in spelling out consideration from the earlier correspondence."

In the light of those authorities the question now must be addressed: was there evidence on which the judge was entitled to find that there was sufficient consideration to support the agreement of 9 April, as set out in the passage from his judgment already set out in the judgment of Glidewell L.J.? The references to this problem in *Chitty on Contracts* are not wholly without some conflict among themselves. The learned editors turn to the question of consideration to support an agreement to vary an existing contract (para. 1491):

"In many cases, consideration can be found in the mutual abandonment of existing rights or the conferment of new benefits by each party on the other."

Reference is made to the *Woodhouse A.C. Israel Cocoa* case, to which I have already referred:

"For example, an alteration of the money of account in a contract proposed or made by one party and accepted by the other is binding on both parties, since either may benefit from the variation ... However, an agreement whereby one party undertakes an additional obligation, but the other party is merely bound to perform his existing obligations, or an agreement whereby one party undertakes an additional obligation, but for the benefit of that party alone, will not be effective to vary the contract, as no consideration is present."

These statements are based on *Stilk* v. *Myrick* and *Syros Shipping Co. S.A.* v. *Elaghill Trading Co., The Proodos C* (1981). Reference is also made to an earlier passage (para. 185) in the textbook where *Stilk* v. *Myrick* is considered at some length. On the other hand the learned editors make this proposition (para. 173):

"The requirement that consideration must remove from the promisee is most generally satisfied where some detriment is suffered by him: *e.g.* where he parts with money or goods, or renders services, in exchange for the promise. But the requirement may equally well be satisfied where the promisee confers a benefit on the promisor without *in fact* suffering any detriment. For example, in *De la Bere* v. *Pearson Ltd.* (1908) the defendants owned a newspaper and invited readers to apply for financial advice on the terms that the defendants should be entitled to publish the readers' letters and their own replies." (Chitty's emphasis.)

This is an accurate recital of the facts in *De la Bere* v. *Pearson Ltd.* but when the argument and judgments are read the case turned on issues other than consideration, namely remoteness of damage etc. So the case is doubtful support for the proposition made in this paragraph.

The question must be posed: what consideration has moved from the plaintiff to support the promise to pay the extra £10,300 added to the lump sum provision? In the particular circumstances which I have outlined above, there was clearly a commercial advantage to both sides from a pragmatic point of view in reaching the agreement of 9 April. The defendants were on risk that as a result of the bargain they had struck the plaintiff would not or indeed possibly could not comply with his existing obligations without further finance. As a result of the agreement the defendants secured their position commercially. There was, however, no obligation added to the contractual duties imposed on the plaintiff under the original contract. Prima facie this would appear to be a classic *Stilk* v. *Myrick* case. It was, however, open to the plaintiff to be in deliberate breach of the contract in order to "cut his losses" commercially. In normal circumstances the suggestion that a contracting party can rely on his own breach to establish consideration is distinctly unattractive. In many cases it obviously would be and if there was any element of duress brought on the other contracting party under the modern development of this branch of the law the proposed breaker of the contract would not benefit. With some hesitation and comforted by the passage from the speech of Lord Hailsham L.C., to which I have referred, I consider that the modern approach to the question of consideration would be that there were benefits by each party to a contract of variation even though one party did not suffer a detriment this would not be fatal to the establishing of sufficient consideration to support the agreement. If both parties benefit from an agreement it is not necessary that each also suffers a detriment. In my judgment, on the facts as found by the judge, he was entitled to reach the conclusion that consideration existed and in those circumstances I would not disturb that finding. This is sufficient to determine the appeal. The judge found as a fact that the flats were "substantially completed" and that payment was due to the plaintiff in respect of the number of flats substantially completed, which left an outstanding amount due from the defendants to the plaintiff in the absence of the payment of which the plaintiff was entitled to remove from the site. For these reasons and for the reasons which have already been given by Glidewell L.J., I would dismiss this appeal.

Note

None of the judges in the Court of Appeal thought they were overruling *Stilk* v. *Myrick*, but can this case really be distinguished? What impact might its reasoning have on, for example, the law relating to part-payment of a debt? Is this a case where a court has reached a decision without a full awareness of its implications? If the case is correctly decided, would its practical impact often be limited by considerations of duress? See below, p. 549.

4. PART PAYMENT OF A DEBT

Foakes v. Beer

(1884) 9 App.Cas. 605 (H.L.)

[Mrs. Beer had obtained judgment against Dr. Foakes for £2090 19s. She subsequently agreed in a written memorandum that she would not "take any proceedings whatever on the judgment" if he would pay the money by instalments. By statute, a judgment debt bears interest until it is fully paid, but the agreement made no reference to interest. Dr. Foakes paid off the entire judgment and Mrs. Beer then claimed the interest as well. The House of Lords was divided on the issue of whether the agreement should properly be understood to mean that the claim to interest was waived by Mrs. Beer. They were nevertheless unanimous that, even if this were so, such an agreement would be unenforceable for lack of consideration.]

Earl of Selbourne L.C. [Having doubted whether the agreement was intended to reserve Mrs. Beer's claim to interest, continued:] But the question remains, whether the agreement is capable of being legally enforced. Not being under seal, it cannot be legally enforced against the respondent, unless she received consideration for it from the appellant, or unless, though without consideration, it operates by way of accord and satisfaction, so as to extinguish the claim for interest. What is the consideration? On the face of the agreement none is expressed, except a present payment of £500, on account and in part of the larger debt then due and payable by law under the judgment. The appellant did not contract to pay the future instalments of £150 each, at the times therein mentioned; much less did he give any new security, in the shape of negotiable paper, or in any other form. The promise de futuro was only that of the respondent, that if the half-yearly payments of £150 each were regularly paid, she would "take no proceedings whatever on the judgment." No doubt if the appellant had been under no antecedent obligation to pay the whole debt, his fulfilment of the condition might have imported some consideration on his part for that promise. But he was under that antecedent obligation; and payment at those deferred dates, by the forbearance and indulgence of the creditor, of the residue of the principal debt and costs, could not (in my opinion) be a consideration for the relinquishment of interest and discharge of the judgment, unless the payment of the £500, at the time of signing the agreement, was such a consideration. As to accord and satisfaction, in point of fact there could be no complete satisfaction, so long as any future instalment remained payable; and I do not see how any mere payments on account could operate in law as a satisfaction *ad interim*, conditionally upon other payments being afterwards duly made, unless there was a consideration sufficient to support the agreement while still unexecuted. Nor was anything, in fact, done by the respondent in this case, on the receipt of the last payment, which could be tantamount to an acquittance, if the agreement did not previously bind her.

The question, therefore, is nakedly raised by this appeal, whether your Lordships are now prepared, not only to overrule, as contrary to law, the doctrine stated by Sir Edward Coke to have been laid down by all the judges of the Common Pleas in *Pinnel's Case* in 1602, and repeated in his note to Littleton, sect.344(2), but to treat a prospective agreement, not under seal, for satisfaction of a debt, by a series of payments on account to a total amount less than the whole debt, as binding in law, provided those payments are regularly made; the case not being one of a composition with a common debtor, agreed to, inter se, by several creditors. . . . The doctrine itself, as laid down by Sir Edward Coke, may have been criticised, as questionable in principle, by some persons whose opinions are entitled to respect, but it has never been judicially overruled; on the contrary I think it has always, since the sixteenth century, been accepted as law. If so, I cannot think that your Lordships would do right, if you were now to reverse, as erroneous, a judgment of the Court of Appeal, proceeding upon a doctrine which has been accepted as part of the law of England for 280 years. . . .

The distinction between the effect of a deed under seal, and that of an agreement by parol, or by writing not under seal, may seem arbitrary, but it is established in our law; nor is it really unreasonable or practically inconvenient that the law should require particular solemnities to give to a gratuitous contract the force of a binding obligation. If the question be (as, in the actual state of the law, I think it is), whether consideration is, or is not, given in a case of this kind, by the debtor who pays down part of the debt presently due from him, for a promise by the creditor to relinquish, after certain further payments on account, the residue of the debt, I cannot say that I think consideration is given, in the sense in which I have always understood that word as used in our law. It might be (and indeed I think it would be) an improvement in our law, if a release or acquittance of the whole debt, on payment of any sum which the creditor might be content to receive by way of accord and satisfaction (though less than the whole), were held to be, generally, binding, though not under seal; nor should I be unwilling to see equal force given to a prospective agreement, like the present, in writing though not under seal; but I think it impossible, without refinements which practically alter the sense of the word, to treat such a release or acquittance as supported by any new consideration proceeding from the debtor. . . .

Lord Blackburn. [Having also considered the intention of the parties as evidenced in the memorandum, turned to the question of whether payment of a lesser sum is good satisfaction for a debt:]

This is a question, I think, of difficulty.

In Coke, Littleton 212 b, Lord Coke says: "where the condition is for payment of £20, the obligor or feoffor cannot at the time appointed pay a lesser sum in satisfaction of the whole, because *it is apparent* that a lesser sum of money *cannot* be a satisfaction of a greater. . . . If the obligor or feoffor pay a lesser sum either before the day or at another place than is limited by the condition, and the obligee or feoffor receiveth it, this is a good satisfaction." For this he cites *Pinnel's Case* (1602). That was an action on a bond for £16, conditioned for the payment of £8 10s. on the 11th of November 1600. Plea that defendant, at plaintiff's request, before the said day, to wit, on the 1st of October, paid to the plaintiff £5 2s. 2d., which the plaintiff accepted in full satisfaction of the £8 10s. The plaintiff had judgment for the insufficient pleading. But though this was so, Lord Coke reports that it was resolved by the whole Court of Common Pleas "that payment of a lesser sum on the day in satisfaction of a greater cannot be any satisfaction for the whole, because it appears to the judges that by no possibility a lesser sum can be a satisfaction to the plaintiff for a greater sum: but the gift of a horse, hawk, or robe, &c., in satisfaction is good, for it shall be intended that a horse, hawk, or robe, &c., might be more beneficial to the plaintiff than the money, in respect of some circumstance, or otherwise the plaintiff would not have accepted of it in satisfaction. But when the whole sum is due, by no intendment the acceptance of parcel can be a satisfaction to the plaintiff; but in the case at bar it was resolved that the payment and acceptance of parcel before the day in satisfaction of the whole would be a good satisfaction in regard of circumstance of time; for peradventure parcel of it before the day would be more beneficial to him than the whole at the day, and the value of the satisfaction is not material; so if I am bound in £20 to pay you £10 at Westminster, and you request me to pay you £5 at the day at

York, and you will accept it in full satisfaction for the whole £10, it is a good satisfaction for the whole, for the expenses to pay it at York is sufficient satisfaction."

There are two things here resolved. First, that where a matter paid and accepted in satisfaction of a debt certain might by any possibility be more beneficial to the creditor than his debt, the Court will not inquire into the adequacy of the consideration. If the creditor, without any fraud, accepted it in satisfaction when it was not a sufficient satisfaction it was his own fault. And that payment before the day might be more beneficial, and consequently that the plea was in substance good, and this must have been decided in the case.

There is a second point stated to have been resolved, viz.: "That payment of a lesser sum on the day cannot be any satisfaction of the whole, because it appears to the judges that by no possibility a lesser sum can be a satisfaction to the plaintiff for a greater sum." This was certainly not necessary for the decision of the case; but though the resolution of the Court of Common Pleas was only a dictum, it seems to me clear that Lord Coke deliberately adopted the dictum, and the great weight of his authority makes it necessary to be cautious before saying that what he deliberately adopted as law was a mistake. . . .

For instance, in *Sibree* v. *Tripp* (1846) Parke, B. says, "It is clear if the claim be a liquidated and ascertained sum, payment of part cannot be satisfaction of the whole, although it may, under certain circumstances, be evidence of a gift of the remainder." And Alderson, B. in the same case says, "It is undoubtedly true that payment of a portion of a liquidated demand, in the same manner as the whole liquidated demand which ought to be paid, is payment only in part, because it is not one bargain, but two; viz. payment of part, and an agreement without consideration to give up the residue. The Courts might very well have held the contrary, and have left the matter to the agreement of the parties, but undoubtedly the law is so settled." After such strong expressions of opinion, I doubt much whether any judge sitting in a Court of the first instance would be justified in treating the question as open. But as this has very seldom, if at all, been the ground of the decision even in a Court of the first instance, and certainly never been the ground of a decision in the Court of Exchequer Chamber, still less in this House, I did think it open in your Lordships' House to reconsider this question. And, notwithstanding the very high authority of Lord Coke, I think it is not the fact that to accept prompt payment of a part only of a liquidated demand, can never be more beneficial than to insist on payment of the whole. And if it be not the fact, it cannot be apparent to the judges.

[His Lordship then considered various earlier authorities.]

What principally weighs with me in thinking that Lord Coke made a mistake of fact is my conviction that all men of business, whether merchants or tradesmen, do every day recognise and act on the ground that prompt payment of a part of their demand may be more beneficial to them than it would be to insist on their rights and enforce payment of the whole. Even where the debtor is perfectly solvent, and sure to pay at last, this often is so. Where the credit of the debtor is doubtful it must be more so. I had persuaded myself that there was no such long-continued action on this dictum as to render it improper in this House to reconsider the question. I had written my reasons for so thinking; but as they were not satisfactory to the other noble and learned Lords who heard the case, I do not now repeat them nor persist in them.

I assent to the judgment proposed, though it is not that which I had originally thought proper.

[Lords Watson and Fitsgerald also agreed that there was no consideration provided by Dr. Foakes.]

Notes

Composition agreements with creditors are an exception to the principle that payment of a lesser sum is satisfaction for a debt. See also *Hirachand Punamchand* v. *Temple* (1911).

Question

Would this case be decided by a court in the same way today?

5.   PROMISSORY ESTOPPEL

Central London Property Trust Ltd. v. High Trees House Ltd.

[1947] K.B. 130 (K.B.D.)

[In September 1939 the plaintiffs had leased a block of flats to the defendants. Because of the subsequent wartime conditions many of the flats were unoccupied and the landlords agreed in 1940 to accept half-rent only. By 1945 all the flats were let and so the plaintiffs claimed the full rent for the last two quarters of 1945. The defendants pleaded in the alternative that either the agreement of 1940 operated throughout the entire remaining period of the lease or that the plaintiffs were estopped from demanding or had waived their rights to demand rent at the full rate for the period before 1945.]

Denning J. stated the facts and continued: If I were to consider this matter without regard to recent developments in the law, there is no doubt that had the plaintiffs claimed it, they would have been entitled to recover ground rent at the rate of 2,500*l*. a year from the beginning of the term, since the lease under which it was payable was a lease under seal which, according to the old common law, could not be varied by an agreement by parol (whether in writing or not), but only by deed. Equity, however stepped in, and said that if there has been a variation of a deed by a simple contract (which in the case of a lease required to be in writing would have to be evidenced by writing), the courts may give effect to it as is shown in *Berry* v. *Berry* (1929). That equitable doctrine, however, could hardly apply in the present case because the variation here might be said to have been made without consideration. With regard to estoppel, the representation made in relation to reducing the rent, was not a representation of an existing fact. It was a representation, in effect, as to the future, namely, that payment of the rent would not be enforced at the full rate but only at the reduced rate. Such a representation would not give rise to an estoppel, because, as was said in *Jorden* v. *Money* (1854), a representation as to the future must be embodied as a contract or be nothing.

But what is the position in view of developments in the law in recent years? The law has not been standing still since *Jorden* v. *Money*. There has been a series of decisions over the last fifty years which, although they are said to be cases of estoppel are not really such. They are cases in which a promise was made which was intended to create legal relations and which, to the knowledge of the person making the promise, was going to be acted on by the person to whom it was made, and which was in fact so acted on. In such cases the courts have said that the promise must be honoured. . . . As I have said they are not cases of estoppel in the strict sense. They are really promises—promises intended to be binding, intended to be acted on, and in fact acted on. *Jorden* v. *Money* can be distinguished, because there the promisor made it clear that she did not intend to be legally bound, whereas in the cases to which I refer the proper inference was that the promisor did intend to be bound. In each case the court held the promise to be binding on the party making it, even though under the old common law it might be difficult to find any consideration for it. The courts have not gone so far as to give a cause of action in damages for the breach of such a promise, but they have refused to allow the party making it to act inconsistently with it. It is in that sense, and that sense only, that such a promise gives rise to an estoppel. The decisions are a natural result of the fusion of law and equity: for the cases of *Hughes* v. *Metropolitan Ry. Co.* (1877) [His Lordship also referred to two other cases] afford a sufficient basis for saying that a party would not be allowed in equity to go back on such a promise. In my opinion, the time has now come for the validity of such a promise to be recognized. The logical consequence, no doubt is that a promise to accept a smaller sum in discharge of a larger sum, if acted upon, is binding notwithstanding the absence of consideration: and if the fusion of law and equity leads to this result, so much the better. That aspect was not considered in *Foakes* v. *Beer* (1884). At this time of day however, when law and equity have been joined together for over seventy years, principles must be reconsidered in the light of their combined effect. It is to be noticed that in the Sixth Interim Report of the Law Revision Committee, paras. 35, 40, it is recommended that such a promise as to which I have referred, should be enforceable in law even though no consideration for it has been given by the promisee. It seems to me that, to the extent I have mentioned, that result has now been achieved by the decisions of the courts.

I am satisfied that a promise such as that to which I have referred is binding and the only question remaining for my consideration is the scope of the promise in the present case. I am satisfied on all the evidence that the promise here was that the ground rent should be reduced to 1,250*l*. a year as a temporary expedient while the block of flats was not fully, or substantially fully let, owing to the conditions prevailing. That means that the reduction in the rent applied throughout the years down to the end of 1944, but early in 1945 it is plain that the flats were fully let, and, indeed the rents received from them (many of them not being affected by the Rent Restrictions Acts), were increased beyond the figure at which it was originally contemplated that they would be let. At all events the rent from them must have been very considerable. I find that the conditions prevailing at the time when the reduction in rent was made, had completely passed away by the early months of 1945. I am satisfied that the promise was understood by all parties only to apply under the conditions prevailing at the time when it was made, namely, when the flats were only partially let, and that it did not extend any further than that. When the flats became fully let, early in 1945, the reduction ceased to apply.

In those circumstances, under the law as I hold it, it seems to me that rent is payable at the full rate for the quarters ending September 29 and December 25, 1945.

If the case had been one of estoppel, it might be said that in any event the estoppel would cease when the conditions to which the representation applied came to an end, or it also might be said that it would only come to an end on notice. In either case it is only a way of ascertaining what is the scope of the representation. I prefer to apply the principle that a promise intended to be binding, intended to be acted on an in fact acted on, is binding so far as its terms properly apply. Here it was binding as covering the period down to the early part of 1945, and as from that time full rent is payable.

I therefore give judgment for the plaintiff company for the amount claimed.

Judgment for plaintiffs.

Note

A lucid account of the background and development of the *High Trees* doctrine, as seen through the eyes of its creator, can be found in Part Five of Denning, *The Discipline of Law* (Butterworths, 1979).

Question

How, if at all, does the principle in *High Trees* differ from that laid down in *Hughes* v. *Metropolitan Railway Co.*?

6. THE DEVELOPMENT OF PROMISSORY ESTOPPEL

D & C Builders Ltd. v. Rees

[1966] 2 Q.B. 617 (Q.B.D.)

Lord Denning M.R. The plaintiffs are a little company. "D" stands for Donaldson, a decorator, "C" for Casey, a plumber. They are jobbing builders. The defendant has a shop where he sells builders' materials.

In the spring of 1964 the defendant employed the plaintiffs to do work at his premises, 218, Brick Lane. The plaintiffs did the work and rendered accounts in May and June, which came to £746 13s. 1d. altogether. The defendant paid £250 on account. In addition the plaintiffs made an allowance of £14 off the bill. So in July 1964 there was owing to the plaintiffs the sum of £482. 13s. 1d. At this stage there was no dispute as to the work done. But the defendant did not pay.

On August 31, 1964, the plaintiffs wrote asking the defendant to pay the remainder of the bill. He did not reply. On October 19, 1964, they wrote again, pointing out that the "outstanding account of £480 is well overdue." Still the defendant did not reply. He did not write or telephone for more than three weeks. Then on Friday, November 13, 1964, the defendant was ill with influenza. His wife telephoned the plaintiffs. She spoke to Casey. She began to make complaints about the work: and then said: "My husband will offer you £300 in settlement. That is all you'll get. It is to be in satisfaction." Casey said he would have to discuss it with Donaldson. The two of them talked it over. Their company was in desperate financial straits. If they did not have the £300, they would be in a state of bankruptcy. So they decided to accept the £300 and see what they could do about the rest afterwards. Thereupon Donaldson telephoned to the defendant's wife. He said to her: "£300 will not even clear our commitments on the job. We will accept £300 and give you a year to find the balance." She said: "no, we will never have enough money to pay the balance. £300 is better than nothing." He said: "we have no choice but to accept." She said: "Would you like the money by cash or by cheque. If it is cash, you can have it on Monday. If by cheque, you can have it tomorrow (Saturday)."

On Saturday, November 14, 1964, Casey went to collect the money. He took with him a receipt prepared on the company's paper with the simple words: "Received the sum of £300 from Mr. Rees." She gave him a cheque for £300 and asked for a receipt. She insisted that the words "in completion of the account" be added. Casey did as she asked. He added the words to the receipt. So she had the clean receipt: "Received the sum of £300 from Mr. Rees in completion of the account. Paid, M. Casey." Casey gave in evidence his reason for giving it: "If I did not have the £300 the company would have gone bankrupt. The only reason we took it was to save the company. She knew the position we were in."

The plaintiffs were so worried about their position that they went to their solicitors. Within a few days, on November 23, 1964, the solicitors wrote complaining that the defendant had "extricated a receipt of some sort or other" from them. They said they were treating the £300 as a payment on account. On November 28, 1964, the defendant replied alleging bad workmanship. He also set up the receipt which Casey gave to his wife, adding: "I assure you she had no gun on her." The plaintiffs brought this action for the balance. The defendant set up a defence of bad workmanship and also that there was a binding settlement. The question of settlement was tried as a preliminary issue.

The judge made these findings:

"I concluded that by the middle of August the sum due to the plaintiffs was ascertained and not then in dispute. I also concluded that there was no consideration to support the agreement of November 13 and 14. It was a case of agreeing to take a lesser sum when a larger sum was already due to the plaintiffs. It was not a case of agreeing to take a cheque for a smaller amount instead of receiving cash for a larger amount. The payment by cheque was an incidental arrangement."

He decided, therefore, the preliminary issue in favour of the plaintiffs. The defendant appeals to this court. He says that there was here an accord and satisfaction—an *accord* when the plaintiffs agreed, however reluctantly, to accept $300 in settlement of the account—and *satisfaction* when they accepted the cheque for £300 and it was duly honoured. The defendant relies on *Sibree* v. *Tripp* (1846) and *Goddard* v. *O'Brien* (1882) as authorities in his favour.

This case is of some consequence: for it is a daily occurrence that a merchant or tradesman, who is owed a sum of money, is asked to take less. The debtor says he is in difficulties. He offers a lesser sum in settlement, cash down. He says he cannot pay more. The creditor is considerate. He accepts the proffered sum and forgives him the rest of the debt. The question arises: Is the settlement binding on the creditor? The answer is that, in point of law, the creditor is not bound by the settlement. He can the next day sue the debtor for the balance: and get judgment. The law was so stated by Lord Coke in *Pinnel's Case* (1602)—and accepted by the House of Lords in *Foakes* v. *Beer* (1884).

Now, suppose that the debtor, instead of paying the lesser sum in cash, pays it by cheque. He makes out a cheque for the amount. The creditor accepts the cheque and cashes it. Is the position any different? I think not. No sensible distinction can be taken between payment of a lesser sum by cash and payment of it by cheque. The cheque, when given, is conditional payment. When honoured, it is actual payment. It is then just the same as cash. If a creditor is not bound when he receives payment by cash, he should not be bound when he receives payment by cheque. This view is supported by the leading case of *Cumber* v. *Wane* (1721), which has suffered many vicissitudes but was, I think, rightly decided in point of law.

Sibree v. *Tripp* (1846) is easily distinguishable. There the plaintiffs brought an action for £500. It was settled by the defendant giving three promissory notes amounting in all to £250. Those promissory notes were given upon a new contract, in substitution for the debt sued for, and not as conditional payment. The plaintiff's only remedy thenceforward was on the notes and not on the debt.

Goddard v. *O'Brien* (1882) is not so easily distinguishable. There a creditor was owed £125 for some slates. He met the debtor and agreed to accept £100 in discharge of it. The debtor gave a cheque for £100. The creditor gave a written receipt "in settlement on the said cheque being honoured." The cheque was clearly given by way of conditional payment. It was honoured. The creditor sued the debtor for the balance of £25. He lost because the £100 was paid by cheque and not by cash. The decision was criticised by Fletcher Moulton L.J. in *Hirachand Punamchand* v. *Temple* (1911), and by the editors of *Smith's Leading Cases*, 13th ed. (1929), Vol. 1, p. 380. It was, I think, wrongly decided. In point of law payment of a lesser sum, whether by cash or by cheque, is no discharge of a greater sum.

This doctrine of the common law has come under heavy fire. It was ridiculed by Sir George Jessel in *Couldery* v. *Bartram* (1881). It was said to be mistaken by Lord Blackburn in *Foakes* v. *Beer*. It was condemned by the Law Revision Committee (1945 Cmd. 5449), paras. 20 and 21. But a remedy has been found. The harshness of the common law has been relieved. Equity has stretched out a merciful hand to help the debtor. The courts have invoked the broad principle stated by Lord Cairns in *Hughes* v. *Metropolitan Railway Co.* (1877).

> "It is the first principle upon which all courts of equity proceed, that if parties, who have entered into definite and distinct terms involving certain legal results, afterwards by their own act or with their own consent enter upon a course of negotiation which has the effect of leading one of the parties to suppose that *the strict rights arising under the contract will not be enforced*, or will be kept in suspense, or held in abeyance, the person who otherwise might have enforced those rights *will not be allowed to enforce them when it would be inequitable having regard to the dealings which have taken place between the parties*."

It is worth noticing that the principle may be applied, not only so as to suspend strict legal rights, but also so as to preclude the enforcement of them.

This principle has been applied to cases where a creditor agrees to accept a lesser sum in discharge of a greater. So much so that we can now say that, when a creditor and a debtor enter upon a course of negotiation, which leads the debtor to suppose that, on payment of the lesser sum, the creditor will not enforce payment of the balance, and on the faith thereof the debtor pays the lesser sum and the creditor accepts it as satisfaction: then the creditor will not be allowed to enforce payment of the balance when it would be inequitable to do so. This was well illustrated during the last war. Tenants went away to escape the bombs and left their houses unoccupied. The landlords accepted a reduced rent for the time they were empty. It was held that the landlords could not afterwards turn round and sue for the balance, see *Central London Property Trust Ltd.* v. *High Trees House Ltd.* (1947). This caused at the time some eyebrows to be raised in high places. But they have been lowered since. The solution was so obviously just that no one could well gainsay it.

In applying this principle, however, we must note the qualification: The creditor is only barred from his legal rights when it would be *inequitable* for him to insist upon them. Where there has been a *true accord*, under which the creditor voluntarily agrees to accept a lesser sum in satisfaction, and the debtor *acts upon* that accord by paying the lesser sum and the creditor accepts it, then it is inequitable for the creditor afterwards to insist on the balance. But he is not bound unless there has been truly an accord between them.

In the present case, on the facts as found by the judge, it seems to me that there was no true accord. The debtor's wife held the creditor to ransom. The creditor was in need of money to meet his own commitments, and she knew it. When the creditor asked for payment of the £480 due to him, she said to him in effect: "We cannot pay you the £480. But we will pay you £300 if you will accept it in settlement. If you do not accept it on those terms, you will get nothing. £300 is better than nothing." She had no right to say any such thing. She could properly have said: "We cannot pay you more than £300. Please accept it on account." But she had no right to insist on his taking it in settlement. When she said: "We will pay you nothing unless you accept £300 in settlement," she was putting undue pressure on the creditor. She was making a threat to break the contract (by paying nothing) and she was doing it so as to compel the creditor to do what he was unwilling to do (to accept £300 in settlement): and she succeeded. He complied with her demand. That was on recent authority a case of intimidation: see *Rookes* v. *Barnard* (1964) and *Stratford (J.T.) & Son Ltd.* v. *Lindley* (1964). In these circumstances there was no true accord so as to found a defence of accord and satisfaction: see *Day* v. *McLea* (1889). There is also no equity in the defendant to warrant any departure from the due course of law. No person can insist on a settlement procured by intimidation.

In my opinion there is no reason in law or equity why the creditor should not enforce the full amount of the debt due to him. I would, therefore, dismiss this appeal.

[Dankwerts and Winn L.JJ. gave judgments also dismissing the appeal.]

Note

In *Woodhouse Ltd.* v. *Nigerian Produce Ltd.* (1972), Lord Hailsham commented:

"I desire to add that the time may soon come when the whole sequence of cases based on promissory estoppel since the war, beginning with *Central London Property Trust Ltd.* v. *High Trees House Ltd.* (1947) may need to be reviewed and reduced to a coherent body of doctrine by the courts. I do not mean to say that any are to be regarded with suspicion. But as is common with an expanding doctrine they do raise problems of coherent exposition which have never been systematically explored."

Pending such a systematic judicial exposition, or legislative intervention, some aspects of the scope of the doctrine remain uncertain.

For example, are obligations merely suspended or extinguished by the doctrine? Must the promisee, in order to be able to rely on the doctrine, act to his detriment or is it sufficient that he simply acts in reliance upon the promise? The dicta of Lord Denning in such cases as *D & C Builders* v. *Rees* (above), *Alan* v. *El Nasr* (1972) and *Brikom Investments* v. *Carr* (1979) go further in their claims for the doctrine than some other judicial pronouncements. The House of Lords in particular seemed to take a more traditional line in *Tool Metal Manufacturing Co. Ltd.* v. *Tungsten Electric* (1955). In *Ajayi* v. *R. T. Briscoe* (1964) Lord Hodson put the matter thus:

"Their Lordships are of opinion that the principle of law as defined by Bowen L.J. has been confirmed by the House of Lords in the case of *Tool Metal Manufacturing Co. Ltd.* v. *Tungsten Electric Co. Ltd.* (1955) where the authorities were reviewed and no encouragement was given to the view that the principle was capable of extension so as to create rights in the promisee for which he had given no consideration. The principle, which has been described as quasi estoppel and perhaps more aptly as promissory estoppel, is that when one party to a contract in the absence of fresh consideration agrees not to enforce his rights an equity will be raised in favour of the other party. This equity is, however, subject to the qualifications (1) that the other party has altered his position, (2) that the promisor can resile from his promise on giving reasonable notice, which need not be a formal notice, giving the promisee a reasonable opportunity of resuming his position, (3) the promise only becomes final and irrevocable if the promisee cannot resume his position."

If the House of Lords made a systematic explanation of the issues left open by the doctrine of promissory estoppel, how would they resolve them?

Chapter 3

Intention to Create Legal Relations

Esso Petroleum Ltd. v. Commissioners of Customs and Excise

[1976] 1 W.L.R. 1 (H.L.)

[As part of a sales promotion scheme Esso Petroleum displayed posters at their garages inviting customers to collect a set of coins commemorating the English squad for the World Cup. The posters stated, "One coin given with every four gallons of petrol." The Commissioners claimed that the coins were chargeable to purchase tax on the grounds that they had been sold to the customers. Esso asserted that the coins were not sold but distributed as free gifts. It therefore became relevant to consider (a) whether the coins were the subject of a legal contract, and (b) whether such a contract was a "sale."]

Viscount Dilhorne. If the coins were a free gift to every customer who purchased four gallons of petrol or multiples of that quantity, then the appeal must be dismissed. If, on the other hand, a legal contract was entered into between the customer and the dealer which, in addition to the supply of petrol, involved the dealer in a legally binding obligation to transfer a coin or coins to the customer, and if that legal contract amounted to a sale, then the appeal must be allowed.

Was there any intention on the part of the garage proprietor and also on the part of the customer who bought four gallons, or multiples of that quantity, of petrol to enter into a legally binding contract in relation to a coin or coins? In *Rose and Frank Co.* v. *J.R. Crompton and Brothers Ltd.* (1923), Scrutton L.J. said:

"Now it is quite possible for parties to come to an agreement by accepting a proposal with the result that the agreement concluded does not give rise to legal relations. The reason of this is that the parties do not intend that their agreement shall give rise to legal relations. This intention may be implied from the subject matter of the agreement, but it may also be expressed by the parties. In social and family relations such an intention is readily implied, while in business matters the opposite result would ordinarily follow."

And Atkin L.J. said:

"To create a contract there must be a common intention of the parties to enter into legal obligations, mutually communicated expressly or impliedly."

The facts of that case were very different from those of this. In that case there was an agreement dealing with business matters. In this case the question has to be considered whether there was any agreement as to a coin or coins between the garage proprietor and the customer and also, if there was, was it intended on both sides to be one having legal relations? If a coin was just to be given to the motorist, it would not be necessary for there to have been any agreement between him and the garage proprietor with regard to it.

In *Edwards* v. *Skyways Ltd.* (1964), where the facts were also very different from those in this case and where the plaintiff was seeking to recover the amount of an *ex gratia* payment, Megaw J. referred to these passages in *Rose and Frank Co.* v. *J.R. Crompton and Brothers Ltd.* and said:

"In the present case, the subject matter of the agreement is business relations, not social or domestic matters. There was a meeting of minds—an intention to agree. There was, admittedly, consideration for the company's promise. I accept the propositions of counsel for the plaintiff that in a case of this nature the onus is on the party who asserts that no legal effect was intended, and the onus is a heavy one."

I do not wish in any way to criticise or qualify these statements, but I do not feel that they provide a sound foundation for the decision of this appeal.

True it is that the respondents are engaged in business. True it is that they hope to promote the sale of their petrol, but it does not seem to me necessarily to follow or to be inferred that there was any intention on their part that their dealers should enter into legally binding contracts with regard to the coins; or any intention on the part of the dealers to enter into any such contract or any intention on the part of the purchaser of four gallons of petrol to do so.

If in this case on the facts of this case the conclusion is reached that there was any such intention on the part of the customer, of the dealer and of the respondents, it would seem to exclude the possibility of any dealer ever making a free gift to any of his customers however negligible its value to promote his sales.

If what was described as being a gift, which would be given if something was purchased, was something of value to the purchaser, then it could readily be inferred that there was a common intention to enter into legal relations. But here, whatever the cost of production, it is clear that the coins were of little intrinsic value.

I do not consider that the offer of a gift of a free coin is properly to be regarded as a business matter in the sense in which that word was used by Scrutton L.J. in the passage cited above. Nor do I think that such an offer can be comprehended within the "business relations" which were in the *Skyways* case, as Megaw J. said: "the subject-matter of the agreement." I see no reason to imply any intention to enter into contractual relations from the statements on the posters that a coin would be given if four gallons of petrol were bought.

Nor do I see any reason to impute to every motorist who went to a garage where the posters were displayed to buy four gallons of petrol any intention to enter into a legally binding contract for the supply to him of a coin. On the acceptance of his offer to purchase four gallons there was no doubt a legally binding contract for the supply to him of that quantity of petrol. but I see again no reason to conclude that because such an offer was made by him, it must be held that, as the posters were displayed, his offer included an offer to take a coin. The gift of a coin might lead to a motorist returning to the garage to obtain another one, but I think the facts in this case negative any contractual intention on his part and on the part of the dealer as to the coin and suffice to rebut any presumption there may be to the contrary.

If, however, there was any contract relating to the coin or coins, the consideration for the entry into that contract was not the payment of any money but the entry into a contract to purchase four gallons or multiples of that quantity of petrol, in which case the contract relating to the coin or coins cannot be regarded as a contract of sale.

I therefore, while of opinion that there was no legally binding contract as to the coins and so that it has not been established that they were produced for sale, am also of opinion that if there was any such contract it was not one for sale.

In my opinion this appeal should be dismissed.

Lord Simon of Glaisdale. I am, however, my Lords, not prepared to accept that the promotion material put out by Esso was not envisaged by them as creating legal relations between the garage proprietors who adopted it and the motorists who yielded to its blandishments. In the first place, Esso and the garage proprietors put the material out for their commercial advantage, and designed it to attract the custom of motorists. The whole transaction took place in a setting of business relations. In the second place, it seems to me in general undesirable to allow a commercial promoter to claim that what he has done is a mere puff, not intended to create legal relations (*cf. Carlill* v. *Carbolic Smoke Ball Co.* (1893)). The coins may have been themselves of little intrinsic value; but all the evidence suggests that Esso contemplated that they would be attractive to motorists and that there would be a large commercial advantage to themselves from the scheme, an advantage to which the garage proprietors also would share. Thirdly, I think that authority supports the view that legal relations were envisaged. In *Rose and Frank Co.* v. *J.R. Crompton and Brothers Ltd.* (1923) Scrutton L.J. said:

[His Lordship cited the same passage as above.]

In the same case Atkin L.J. said:

"To create a contract there must be a common intention of the parties to enter into legal obligations, mutually communicated expressly or impliedly. Such an intention ordinarily will be inferred when parties enter into an agreement which in other respects conforms to the rules of law as to the formation of contracts. It may be negatived impliedly by the nature of the agreed promise or promises, as in the case of offer and acceptance of hospitality, or of some agreements made in the course of family life between members of a family as in *Balfour* v. *Balfour* (1919)."

In *Edwards* v. *Skyways Ltd.* (1964) Megaw J. quoted these passages and added:

[His Lordship cited the same passage as above.]

I respectfully agree. And I venture to add that it begs the question to assert that no motorist who bought petrol in consequence of seeing the promotion material prominently displayed in the garage forecourt would be likely to bring an action in the county court if he were refused a coin. He might be a suburban Hampden who was not prepared to forgo what he conceived to be his rights or to allow a tradesman to go back on his word.

Notes

Purely domestic or social relations will not generally give rise to legal relations, as Lord Atkin observed in his citation of *Balfour* v. *Balfour* (1919). This is, however, only a starting point in the analysis of the situation not a conclusive rule. Compare, for example, *Merritt* v. *Merritt* (1970), *Jones* v. *Padavatton* (1969) and *Simpkins* v. *Pays* (1955).

Questions

1. Lord Russell of Killowen agreed with Viscount Dilhorne; Lord Wilberforce took the same view as Lord Simon on this issue.

Which view do you think is to be preferred?

2. Despite the fact that it is reached in a commercial setting, a collective agreement between an employer and a trade union will not generally give rise to legal relations (see *Ford Motor Co. Ltd.* v. *Amalgamated Union of Engineering and Foundry Workers* (1969) (H.S.B., p. 459); Trade Union and Labour Relations Act 1974, s.18).

Why should this be so?

Chapter 4

Contractual Terms

1. INCORPORATION OF TERMS

Parker v. South Eastern Railway Co.

(1877) 2 C.P.D. 416

[The plaintiff deposited a bag in the defendant's cloakroom, paid the 2d. charge and received a ticket in return. The front of the ticket detailed the opening hours of the office and also the words: "See back." On the back was a clause limiting the company's liability in the case of loss to £10. A placard hung up in the cloakroom contained the same condition. The bag was lost by the defendant. The plaintiff claimed £24.10s., the value of the lost bag. The defendant claimed liability was limited to £10. The defendant appealed to the Court of Appeal against the trial judge's direction to the jury.]

Mellish L.J. In this case we have to consider whether a person who deposits in the cloakroom of a railway company, articles which are lost through the carelessness of the company's servants, is prevented from recovering, by a condition on the back of the ticket, that the company would not be liable for the loss of goods exceeding the value of £10. It was argued on behalf of the railway company that the company's servants were only authorised to receive goods on behalf of the company upon the terms contained in the ticket; and a passage from Mr. Justice Blackburn's judgment in *Harris* v. *Great Western Ry. Co.* (1876) was relied on in support of their contention: "I doubt much—inasmuch as the railway company did not authorise their servants to receive goods for deposit on any other terms, and as they had done nothing to lead the plaintiff to believe that they had given such authority to their servants so as to preclude them from asserting, as against her, that the authority was so limited—whether the true rule of law is not that the plaintiff must assent to the contract intended by the defendants to be authorised, or treat

455

the case as one in which there was no contract at all, and consequently no liability for safe custody." I am of opinion that this objection cannot prevail. It is clear that the company's servants did not exceed the authority given them by the company. They did the exact thing they were authorised to do. They were authorised to receive articles on deposit as bailees on behalf of the company, charging 2*d.* for each article, and delivering a ticket properly filled up to the person leaving the article. This is exactly what they did in the present cases, and whatever may be the legal effect of what was done, the company must, in my opinion, be bound by it. The directors may have thought, and no doubt did think, that the delivering the ticket to the person depositing the article would be sufficient to make him bound by the conditions contained in the ticket, and if they were mistaken in that, the company must bear the consequence.

The question then is, whether the plaintiff was bound by the conditions contained in the ticket. In an ordinary case, where an action is brought on a written agreement which is signed by the defendant, the agreement is proved by proving his signature, and, in the absence of fraud, it is wholly immaterial that he has not read the agreement and does not know its contents. The parties may, however, reduce their agreement into writing, so that the writing constitutes the sole evidence of the agreement, without signing it; but in that case there must be evidence independently of the agreement itself to prove that the defendant has assented to it. In that case, also, if it is proved that the defendant has assented to the writing constituting the agreement between the parties, it is, in the absence of fraud, immaterial that the defendant had not read the agreement and did not know its contents. Now if in the course of making a contract one party delivers to another a paper containing writing, and the party receiving the paper knows that the paper contains conditions which the party delivering it intends to constitute the contract, I have no doubt that the party receiving the paper does, by receiving and keeping it, assent to the conditions contained in it, although he does not read them, and does not know what they are. I hold therefore that the case of *Harris* v. *Great Western Ry. Co.* (1876) was rightly decided, because in that case the plaintiff admitted, on cross-examination, that he believed there were some conditions on the ticket. On the other hand, the case of *Henderson* v. *Stevenson* (1875) is a conclusive authority that if the person receiving the ticket does not know that there is any writing upon the back of the ticket, he is not bound by a condition printed on the back.

The facts in the cases before us differ from those in both
Henderson v. *Stevenson* and *Harris* v. *Great Western Ry. Co.*
because in both the cases which have been argued before us,
though the plaintiffs admitted that they knew there was
writing on the back of the ticket, they swore not only that
they did not read it, but that they did not know or believe
that the writing contained conditions, and we are to consider
whether, under those circumstances, we can lay down as a
matter of law either that the plaintiff is bound or that he is
not bound by the conditions contained in the ticket, or
whether his being bound depends on some question of fact to
be determined by the jury, and if so, whether, in the present
case, the right question was left to the jury.

Now, I am of opinion that we cannot lay down, as a matter
of law, either that the plaintiff was bound or that he was not
bound by the conditions printed on the ticket, from the mere
fact that he knew that there was writing on the ticket, but did
not know that the writing contained conditions. I think there
may be cases in which a paper containing writing is delivered
by one party to another in the course of a business
transaction, where it would be quite reasonable that the party
receiving it should assume that the writing contained in it no
condition, and should put it in his pocket unread. For
instance, if a person driving through a turnpike-gate received
a ticket upon paying the toll, he might reasonably assume
that the object of the ticket was that by producing it he might
be free from paying toll at some other turnpike-gate, and
might put it in his pocket unread. On the other hand, if a
person who ships goods to be carried on a voyage by sea
receives a bill of lading signed by the master, he would
plainly be bound by it, although afterwards in an action
against the shipowner for the loss of the goods, he might
swear that he had never read the bill of lading, and that he
did not know that it contained the terms of the contract of
carriage, and that the shipowner was protected by the
exceptions contained in it. Now the reason why the person
receiving the bill of lading would be bound seems to me to be
that in the great majority of cases persons shipping goods do
know that the bill of lading contains the terms of the contract
of carriage; and the shipowner, or the master delivering the
bill of lading, is entitled to assume that the person shipping
goods has that knowledge. It is, however, quite possible to
suppose that a person who is neither a man of business nor a
lawyer might on some particular occasion ship goods without
the least knowledge of what a bill of lading was, but in my
opinion such a person must bear the consequences of his own

exceptional ignorance, it being plainly impossible that business could be carried on if every person who delivers a bill of lading had to stop to explain what a bill of lading was.

Now the question we have to consider is whether the railway company were entitled to assume that a person depositing luggage, and receiving a ticket in such a way that he could see that some writing was printed on it, would understand that the writing contained the conditions of contract, and this seems to me to depend upon whether people in general would in fact, and naturally, draw that inference. The railway company, as it seems to me, must be entitled to make some assumptions respecting the person who deposits luggage with them: I think they are entitled to assume that he can read, and that he understands the English language, and that he pays such attention to what he is about as may be reasonably expected from a person in such a transaction as that of depositing luggage in a cloakroom. The railway company must, however, take mankind as they find them, and if what they do is sufficient to inform people in general that the ticket contains conditions, I think that a particular plaintiff ought not to be in a better position than other persons on account of his exceptional ignorance or stupidity or carelessness. But if what the railway company do is not sufficient to convey to the minds of people in general that the ticket contains conditions, then they have received goods on deposit without obtaining the consent of the persons depositing them to the conditions limiting their liability. I am of opinion, therefore, that the proper direction to leave to the jury in these cases is, that if the person receiving the ticket did not see or know that there was any writing on the ticket, he is not bound by the conditions; that if he knew there was writing, and knew or believed that the writing contained conditions, then he is bound by the conditions; that if he knew there was writing on the ticket, but did not know or believe that the writing contained conditions, nevertheless he would be bound, if the delivering of the ticket to him in such a manner that he could see there was writing upon it, was, in the opinion of the jury, reasonable notice that the writing contained conditions.

I have lastly to consider whether the direction of the learned judge was correct, namely, "Was the plaintiff, under the circumstances, under any obligation, in the exercise of reasonable and proper caution, to read or to make himself aware of the condition?" I think that this direction was not strictly accurate, and was calculated to mislead the jury. The plaintiff was certainly under no obligation to read the ticket, but was entitled to leave it unread if he pleased, and the question does not appear to me to direct the attention of the jury to the real question, namely, whether the railway company did what was reasonably sufficient to give the plaintiff notice of the condition.

On the whole, I am of opinion that there ought to be a new trial.

[Baggallay L.J. concurred, but Bramwell L.J. took the view that the question was one of law and judgment ought to be entered for the defendant.]

Note

An example of failure to incorporate a term in the context of a ticket case is *Chapelton* v. *Barry U.D.C.* (1940) (H.S.B., p. 464).

Questions

1. Mellish L.J. states that the defendant could assume the plaintiff understands English. Could as much reliance be placed on this dictum now as in 1877?

2. It is very common for a notice to incorporate by reference terms that are fully set out elsewhere in a comprehensive document. A rather extreme illustration of this is to be found in *Thompson* v. *L.M. & S. Railway* (1930). Would this case be followed today?

Interfoto Picture Library Ltd. v. Stiletto Visual Programmes Ltd.

[1989] 1 Q.B. 433 (C.A.)

The defendants were an advertising agency who required photographs of the 1950s for a presentation. They telephoned the plaintiffs, who ran a picture library, and asked them if they had any suitable photographs. The parties had never dealt with each other before. The plaintiffs dispatched 47 transparencies to the defendants packed in a bag with a delivery note which set out clearly that the pictures were to be returned by March 19th, and contained various other terms. One of these terms stated that unless the pictures were returned within 14 days there would be holding fee of £5 plus VAT per day for each transparency returned after that time. The defendants accepted delivery but it was unlikely that they had read any of the conditions printed on the delivery note. The defendants did not use the transparencies, put them to one side and forgot about them. After the pictures were returned to the plaintiffs on April 2nd, the defendants were presented with a bill for £3,783.50 based upon the holding fee and the pictures' late return. The trial judge gave judgment for the plaintiffs. The defendants appealed on the grounds that the term had not been incorporated into the contract.]

Dillon L.J.   This sort of question was posed, in relation to printed conditions, in the ticket cases, such as *Parker* v. *South Eastern Railway Co.* (1877), in the last century. At that stage the printed conditions were looked at as a whole and the question considered by the courts was whether the printed conditions as a whole had been sufficiently drawn to a customer's attention to make the whole set of conditions part of the contract; if so the customer was bound by the printed conditions even though he never read them.

More recently the question has been discussed whether it is enough to look at a set of printed conditions as a whole. When for instance one condition in a set is particularly onerous does something special need to be done to draw customers' attention to that particular condition? In an *obiter dictum* in *J. Spurling Ltd.* v. *Bradshaw* (1956) (cited in *Chitty on Contracts*, 25th ed. (1983), Vol. 1, p. 408) Denning L.J. stated:

> "Some clauses which I have seen would need to be printed in red ink on the face of the document with a red hand pointing to it before the notice could be held to be sufficient."

Then in *Thornton* v. *Shoe Lane Parking Ltd.* (1971) [and see below, p. 464] both Lord Denning M.R. and Megaw L.J. held as one of their grounds of decision, as I read their judgments, that where a condition is particularly onerous or unusual the party seeking to enforce it must show that that condition, or an unusual condition of that particular nature, was fairly brought to the notice of the other party. Lord Denning M.R., at pp. 169h–170d, restated and applied what he had said in the *Spurling* case, and held that the court should not hold any man bound by such a condition unless it was drawn to his attention in the most explicit way. Megaw L.J. deals with the point, at pp. 172–173, where he said:

> "I agree with Lord Denning M.R. that the question here is of the particular condition on which the defendants seek to rely, and not of the conditions in general. When the conditions sought to be attached all constitute, in Lord Dunedin's words [in *Hood* v. *Anchor Line (Henderson Brothers) Ltd.*] (1918) 'the sort of restriction . . . that is usual,' it may

not be necessary for a defendant to prove more than that the intention to attach *some* conditions has been fairly brought to the notice of the other party. But at least where the particular condition relied on involves a sort of restriction that is not shown to be usual in that class of contract, a defendant must show that his intention to attach an unusual condition *of that particular nature* was fairly brought to the notice of the other party. How much is required as being, in the words of Mellish L.J. [in *Parker* v. *South Eastern Railway Co.*], 'reasonably sufficient to give the plaintiff notice of the condition,' depends upon the nature of the restrictive condition. In the present case what has to be sought in answer to the third question is whether the defendant company did what was reasonable fairly to bring to the notice of the plaintiff, at or before the time when the contract was made, the existence of this particular condition. This condition is that part of the clause—a few words embedded in a lengthy clause—which Lord Denning M.R. has read, by which, in the midst of provisions as to damage to property, the defendants sought to exempt themselves from liability for any personal injury suffered by the customer while he was on their premises. Be it noted that such a condition is one which involves the abrogation of the right given to a person such as the plaintiff by statute, the Occupiers' Liability Act 1957. True, it is open under that statute for the occupier of property by a contractual term to exclude that liability. In my view, however, before it can be said that a condition of that sort, restrictive of statutory rights, has been fairly brought to the notice of a party to a contract there must be some clear indication which would lead an ordinary sensible person to realise, at or before the time of making the contract, that a term of that sort, relating to personal injury, was sought to be included. I certainly would not accept that the position has been reached today in which it is to be assumed as a matter of general knowledge, custom, practice, or whatever is the phrase that is chosen to describe it, that when one is invited to go upon the property of another for such purposes as garaging a car, a contractual term is normally included that if one suffers any injury on those premises as a result of negligence on the part of the occupiers of the premises they shall not be liable."

Counsel for the plaintiffs submits that *Thornton* v. *Shoe Lane Parking Ltd.* (1971) was a case of an exemption clause and that what their Lordships said must be read as limited to exemption clauses and in particular exemption clauses which would deprive the party on whom they are imposed of statutory rights. But what their Lordships said was said by way of interpretation and application of the general statement of the law by Mellish L.J. in *Parker* v. *South Eastern Railway Co.*, and the logic of it is applicable to any particularly onerous clause in a printed set of conditions of the one contracting party which would not be generally known to the other party.

Condition 2 of these plaintiffs' conditions is in my judgment a very onerous clause. The defendants could not conceivably have known, if their attention was not drawn to the clause, that the plaintiffs were proposing to charge a "holding fee" for the retention of the transparencies at such a very high and exorbitant rate.

At the time of the ticket cases in the last century it was notorious that people hardly ever troubled to read printed conditions on a ticket or delivery note or similar document. That remains the case now. In the intervening years the printed conditions have tended to become more and more complicated and more and more one-sided in favour of the party who is imposing them, but the other parties, if they notice that there are printed conditions at all, generally still tend to assume that such conditions are only concerned with ancillary matters of form and are not of importance. In the ticket cases the courts held that the common law required that reasonable steps be taken to draw the other parties' attention to the printed conditions or they would not be part of the contract. It is, in my judgment, a logical development of the common law into modern conditions that it should be held, as it was in *Thornton* v. *Shoe Lane Parking Ltd.* (1971), that, if one condition in a set of printed conditions is particularly onerous or unusual, the party seeking to enforce it must show that that particular condition was fairly brought to the attention of the other party.

In the present case, nothing whatever was done by the plaintiffs to draw the defendants' attention particularly to condition 2; it was merely one of four columns' width of conditions printed across the foot of the delivery note. Consequently condition 2 never, in my judgment, became part of the contract between the parties.

I would therefore allow this appeal and reduce the amount of the judgment which the judge awarded against the defendants to the amount which he would have awarded on a *quantum meruit* on his alternative findings, *i.e.* the reasonable charge of £3.50 per transparency per week for the retention of the of the transparencies beyond a reasonable period, which he fixed at 14 days from the date of their receipt by the defendants.

Question

Bingham L.J. concurred in upholding the defendants' appeal and suggested another ground for disallowing the plaintiffs' claim. What might that have been?

L'Estrange v. Graucob

[1934] 2 K.B. 394 (D.C.)

[The plaintiff signed an order form for the purchase of a cigarette vending machine which, when delivered, did not work properly. The defendants had acknowledged the order by signing a printed order confirmation agreeing to the terms in the order form. In small print, on brown paper, there was a term printed to the effect that, "any express or implied condition, statement, or warranty, statutory or otherwise not stated herein is hereby excluded." The sellers relied on this clause to exempt themselves from liability. The plaintiff asserted that she had not read the form when she signed it, knew nothing of its contents and the smallness of the print made if difficult to read.]

Maugham L.J   I regret the decision to which I have come, but I am bound by legal rules and cannot decide the case on other considerations.

The material question is whether or not there was a contract in writing between the plaintiff and the defendants in the terms contained in the brown paper document. In the case of a formal contract between seller and buyer, such as a deed, there is a presumption which puts it beyond doubt that the parties intended that the document should contain the terms of their contract. The brown paper document is not a formal instrument of that character, yet, in my opinion, having been signed it may well constitute a contract in writing. A reference to any of the textbooks dealing with the law of contract will provide many cases of the verbal acceptance of a written offer, in which the courts have held that the written offer and the acceptance, even though only verbal, together constituted a contract in writing, which could not be altered by extraneous evidence. The rule may not operate equitably in all cases, but it is unquestionably binding in law.

. . . . . .

I deal with this case on the footing that when the order confirmation was signed by the defendants confirming the order form which had been signed by the plaintiff, there was then a signed contract in writing between the parties. If that is so, then, subject to certain contingencies, there is no doubt that it was wholly immaterial whether the plaintiff read the small print or not. There can be no dispute as to the soundness in law of the statement of Mellish L.J. in *Parker* v. *South Eastern Ry. Co.*, (1877) which has been read by my learned brother, to the effect that where a party has signed a written agreement it is immaterial to the question of his liability under it that he has not read it and does not know its contents. That is true in any case in which the agreement is held to be an agreement in writing.

Scrutton L.J. ... When a document containing contractual terms is signed, then, in the absence of fraud, or, I will add, misrepresentation, the party signing it is bound, and it is wholly immaterial whether he has read the document or not.

Judgment entered for the defendants.

Notes

With some notable exceptions, such as contracts of guarantee or for the disposition of an interest in land, it is not a formal requirement of the law that a contract be in writing. Similarly, as here, a signed document can be legally binding even if it is not emblazoned with words to the effect that, "This is a Contractual Document." For an example of the way in which the possible unfairness of the principle can be avoided, see, *e.g. Curtis* v. *Chemical Cleaning and Dyeing Co.* (1951) (H.S.B. 596).

Much legislative and judicial ingenuity has been used over the last 50 years to mitigate the possibly harsh effect of the rule in *L'Estrange* v. *Graucob.* Examples are restrictions on the exclusion of certain terms (Unfair Contract Terms Act 1977, s.6., Sched. 2), or the elaborate protection given to purchasers under credit agreements provided by the Consumer Credit Act 1974. The latter Act, for example, provides for the size of type and paper to be regulated in hire-purchase transactions.

The inclusion of "unfair" terms exempting or qualifying liability received its most thoroughgoing legislative treatment in the Unfair Contract Terms Act 1977, and see generally, below, pp. 580, 587, 623.

Thornton v. Shoe Lane Parking

[1971] 2 Q.B. 163 (C.A.)

[The plaintiff drove up to the barrier of a car park and a machine automatically produced a ticket as he did so. The ticket referred to various exempting terms which could be inspected in a display panel attached to a pillar opposite the ticket machine. One of these "conditions" stated that the defendants were not liable for any injury to a customer occurring on the premises. After parking his car in the car park, the plaintiff was injured in an accident for which the defendants were partly responsible. The defendants sought to rely upon the exempting "condition." See also above, p. 460].

Lord Denning M.R. We have been referred to the ticket cases of former times from *Parker* v. *South Eastern Railway Co.* (1877) to *McCutcheon* v. *David MacBrayne Ltd.* (1964). They were concerned with railways, steamships and cloakrooms where booking clerks issued tickets to customers who took them away without reading them. In those cases the issue of the ticket was regarded as an *offer* by the company. If the customer took it and retained it without objection, his act was regarded as an *acceptance* of the offer: see ... *Thompson* v. *London, Midland and Scottish Railway Co.* (1930). These cases were based on the theory that the customer, on being handed the ticket, could refuse it and decline to enter into a contract on those terms. He could ask for his money back. That theory was, of course, a fiction. No customer in a thousand ever read the conditions. If he had stopped to do so, he would have missed the train or the boat.

None of those cases has any application to a ticket which is issued by an automatic machine. The customer pays his money and gets a ticket. He cannot refuse it. He cannot get his money back. He may protest to the machine, even swear at it. But it will remain unmoved. He is committed beyond recall. He was committed at the very moment when he put his money into the machine. The contract was concluded at that time. It can be translated into offer and acceptance in this way: the offer is made when the proprietor of the machine holds it out as being ready to receive the money. The acceptance takes place when the customer puts his money into the slot. The terms of the offer are contained in the notice placed on or near the machine stating what is offered for the money. The customer is bound by those terms as long as they are sufficiently brought to his notice beforehand, but not otherwise. He is not bound by the terms printed on the ticket if they differ from the notice, because the ticket comes too late. The contract has already been made: see *Olley* v. *Marlborough Court Ltd.* (1949). The ticket is no more than a voucher or receipt for the money that has been paid (as in the deckchair case, *Chapelton* v. *Barry Urban District Council* (1940)) on terms which have been offered and accepted before the ticket is issued.

In the present case the offer was contained in the notice at the entrance giving the charges for garaging and saying "at owner's risk," *i.e.* at the risk of the owner so far as damage to the car was concerned. The offer was accepted when Mr. Thornton drove up to the entrance and, by the movement of his car, turned the light from red to green, and the ticket was thrust at him. The contract was then concluded, and it could not be altered by any words printed on the ticket itself. In particular, it could not be altered so as to exempt the company from liability for personal injury due to their negligence.

Assuming, however, that an automatic machine is a booking clerk in disguise—so that the old-fashioned ticket cases still apply to it. We then have to go back to the three questions put by Mellish L.J. in *Parker* v. *South Eastern Railway Co.* (1877). Telescoping the three questions, they come to this: the customer is bound by the exempting condition if he knows that the ticket is issued subject to it; or, if the company did what was reasonably sufficient to give him notice of it.

Mr. Machin admitted here that the company did not do what was reasonably sufficient to give Mr. Thornton notice of the exempting condition. That admission was properly made. I do not pause to inquire whether the exempting condition is void for unreasonableness. All I say is that it is so wide and so destructive of rights that the court should not hold any man bound by it unless it is drawn to his attention in the most explicit way. It is an instance of what I had in mind in *J. Spurling Ltd.* v. *Bradshaw* (1956). In order to give sufficient notice, it would need to be printed in red ink with a red hand pointing to it—or something equally startling.

But, although reasonable notice of it was not given, Mr. Machin said that this case came within the second question propounded by Mellish L.J., namely that Mr. Thornton "knew or believed that the writing contained conditions." There was no finding to that effect. The burden was on the company to prove it, and they did not do so. Certainly there was no evidence that Mr. Thornton knew of this exempting condition. He is not, therefore, bound by it.

Mr. Machin relied on a case in this court last year—*Mendelssohn* v. *Normand Ltd.* (1970). Mr. Mendelssohn parked his car in the Cumberland Garage at Marble Arch, and was given a ticket which contained an exempting condition. There was no discussion as to whether the condition formed part of the contract. It was conceded that it did. That is shown by the report in the Law Reports at p. 180. Yet the garage company were not entitled to rely on the exempting condition for the reasons there given.

That case does not touch the present, where the whole question is whether the exempting condition formed part of the contract. I do not think it did. Mr. Thornton did not know of the condition, and the company did not do what was reasonably sufficient to give him notice of it.

I do not think the garage company can escape liability by reason of the exemption condition. I would, therefore, dismiss the appeal.

[Megaw L.J. and Sir Gordon Wilmer also gave judgments dismissing the appeal.]

Questions

1. What were the reasons which prevented the garage company relying on the exempting condition in *Mendelssohn* v. *Mormand Ltd.* (1970)?

2. Would it have made any difference if Mr. Thornton had used the car park on previous occasions?

2. IMPLYING TERMS

British Crane Hire v. Ipswich Plant Hire

[1975] Q.B. 303 (C.A.)

[The defendants, who were themselves a plant hire company, hired a crane from the plaintiffs. Subsequently, the crane sank into the marshy ground where it was being used and considerable expense was incurred in retrieving it. Whether the plaintiffs or the defendants should bear this loss depended upon the incorporation of certain terms in the contract between the parties.]

Lord Denning M.R. The judge found that the printed conditions were not incorporated into the contract. The plaintiffs appeal from that finding. The facts are these: the arrangements for the hire of the crane were all on the telephone. The plaintiffs agreed to let the defendants this crane. It was to be delivered on the Sunday. The hiring charges and transport charges were agreed. Nothing was said about conditions. There was nothing in writing. But soon after the crane was delivered, the plaintiffs, in accordance with their practice, sent forward a printed form to be signed by the hirer. It set out the order, the work to be done, and the hiring fee, and that it was subject to the conditions set out on the back of the form. The defendants would ordinarily have sent the form back signed: but this time they did not do so. The accident happened before they signed it. So they never did so. But the plaintiffs say that nevertheless, from the previous course of dealing, the conditions on the form govern the relationship between the parties. They rely on . . .

[Lord Denning set out two of the terms which had the effect of making the hirer responsible for the recovery of the crane from soft ground.]

In support of the course of dealing, the plaintiffs relied on two previous transactions in which the defendants had hired cranes from the plaintiffs.

One was February 20, 1969; and the other October 6, 1969. Each was on a printed form which set out the hiring of a crane, the price, the site, and so forth; and also setting out the conditions the same as those here. There were thus only two transactions many months before and they were not known to the defendants' manager who ordered this crane. In the circumstances I doubt whether those two would be sufficient to show a course of dealing.

In *Hollier* v. *Rambler Mortors (A.M.C.) Ltd.* (1972) Salmon L.J. said he knew of no case

"in which it has been decided or even argued that a term could be implied into an oral contract on the strength of a course of dealing (if it can be so called) which consisted at the most of three or four transactions over a period of five years."

That was a case of a private individual who had had his car repaired by the defendants and had signed forms with conditions on three or four occasions. The plaintiff there was not of equal bargaining power with the garage company which repaired the car. The conditions were not incorporated.

But here the parties were both in the trade and were of equal bargaining power. Each was a firm of plant hirers who hired out plant. The defendants themselves knew that firms in the plant-hiring trade always imposed conditions in regard to the hiring of plant: and that their conditions were on much the same lines. The defendants' manager, Mr. Turner (who knew the crane), was asked about it. He agreed that he had seen these conditions or similar ones in regard to the hiring of plant. He said that most of them were, to one extent or another, variations of a form which he called "the Contractors' Plant Association form." The defendants themselves (when they let out cranes) used the conditions of that form. The conditions on the plaintiffs' form were in rather different words, but nevertheless to much the same effect. . . .

It is clear that both parties knew quite well that conditions were habitually imposed by the supplier of these machines; and both parties knew the substance of those conditions. In particular that if the crane sank in soft ground it was the hirer's job to recover it: and that there was an indemnity clause. In these circumstances, I think the conditions on the form should be regarded as incorporated into the contract. I would not put it so much on the course of dealing, but rather on the common understanding which is to be derived from the conduct of the parties, namely, that the hiring was to be on the terms of the plaintiff's usual conditions.

As Lord Reid said in *McCutcheon* v. *David MacBrayne Ltd.* (1964) quoting from the Scottish textbook, *Gloag on Contract*, 2nd ed. (1929),

"The judicial task is not to discover the actual intentions of each party; it is to decide what each was reasonably entitled to conclude from the attitude of the other."

It seems to me that, in view of the relationship of the parties, when the defendants requested this crane urgently and it was supplied at once—before the usual form was received—the plaintiffs were entitled to conclude that the defendants were accepting it on the terms of the plaintiffs' own printed conditions—which would follow in a day or two. It is just as if the plaintiffs had said: "We will supply it on our usual conditions," and the defendants said "Of course, that is quite understood."

Even though the judge did not find that the conditions were incorporated, he held that there was an implied term that the hirer should return the chattel to the owner at the end of the hiring. Mr. McCowan pointed out that that implied term was not distinctly pleaded or relied upon. But, nevertheless, there is much to be said for it. When a machine is let out on hire for use on marshy land, and both parties know that it may sink into a marsh, then it seems to me that, if it sinks into the marsh, it is the hirer's job to recover it, so as to restore it to the owner at the end of the hiring. Take a motor car which is let out on hire, and by reason of a gale, or an icy road, it goes off the road into a ditch. It is the hirer's job to get it back on to the road and restore it at the end of the hiring. Just as when he takes it on a long journey and falls ill a long distance away. It still is his duty to get it back and restore it to the owner at the end of the hiring. Of course, if it is lost or damaged and he can prove that it was not due to any fault on his part, he would not be liable. A bailee is not liable for loss or damage which he can prove occurred without any default on his part: but the return of the vehicle is different. It is the duty of the hirer to return the vehicle at the end of the hiring to the owner, and to pay the cost of doing so. Although he is not liable for loss or damage occurring without his fault, nevertheless he is liable to do what is reasonable to restore the property to the owner.

So, apart from the express conditions, it may well be, if it had been pleaded, that the plaintiffs could have recovered from the second mishap on an implied term.

[Megaw and Sachs L.JJ. concurred in dismissing the appeal.]

Question

What is the relevance, if any, of the fact that the parties were stated to be of equal bargaining power?

The Moorcock

(1889) 14 P.D. 64 (C.A.)

[The defendants contracted to allow the plaintiff to discharge his vessel at their jetty. Both parties knew that the vessel would ground at low tide. Whilst unloading, the vessel did settle on the bottom and was damaged by a ridge of hard ground under the mud. The contract did not expressly provide that it was a safe anchorage.]

Bowen L.J. The question which arises here is whether when a contract is made to let the use of this jetty to a ship which can only use it, as is known by both parties, by taking the ground, there is any implied warranty on the part of the owners of the jetty, and if so, what is the extent of the warranty. Now, an implied warranty, or, as it is called, a covenant in law, as distinguished from an express contract or express warranty, really is in all cases founded on the presumed intention of the parties, and upon reason. The implication which the law draws from what must obviously have been the intention of the parties, the law draws with the object of giving efficacy to the transaction and preventing such a failure of consideration as cannot have been within the contemplation of either side; and I believe if one were to take all the cases, and they are many, of implied warranties or covenants in law, it will be found that in all of them the law is raising an implication from the presumed intention of the parties with the object of giving to the transaction such efficacy as both parties must have intended that at all events it should have. In business transactions such as this, what the law desires to effect by the implication is to give such business efficacy to the transaction as must have been intended at all events by both parties who are business men; not to impose on one side all the perils of the transaction, or to emancipate one side from all the chances of failure, but to make each party promise in law as much, at all events, as it must have been in the contemplation of both parties that he should be responsible for in respect of those perils or chances.

[Lord Esher M.R. and Fry L.J. concurred in affirming judgment for the plaintiff, in that the defendants had impliedly represented that reasonable care had been taken to ascertain that the river bottom was not in such condition as to cause damage to the vessel.]

Note

The reasoning of *The Moorcock* was considered and affirmed by the House of Lords in the leading case of *Liverpool Corporation* v. *Irwin* (1976). They did, however, reject Lord Denning's view that a term could be implied simply on the grounds that it was just and reasonable under the circumstances (see below).

Shell v. Lostock Garages

[1977] 1 All E.R. 481 (C.A.)

[The parties had entered into a "solus" agreement whereby Lostock Garages agreed to buy their petrol exclusively from Shell. In the course of a petrol price war, Shell reduced the price of their petrol to neighbouring garages but not to the defendant. It therefore became uneconomical for the defendant to carry on trading. When Shell sought an injunction restraining Lostock Garages from buying their petrol elsewhere, the defendant claimed as part of their defence that there was an implied term in the agreement that Shell would not abnormally discriminate against Lostock Garages in their pricing of petrol.]

Lord Denning M.R. This submission makes it necessary once again to consider the law as to implied terms. I ventured with some trepidation to suggest that terms implied by law could be brought within one comprehensive category, in which the courts could imply a term such as was just and reasonable in the circumstances: see *Greaves & Co. (Contractors) Ltd.* v. *Baynham Meikle & Partners; Liverpool City Council* v. *Irwin.* But, as I feared, the House of Lords have rejected it as quite unacceptable. As I read the speeches, there are two broad categories of implied terms.

(i) *The first category*

The first category comprehends all those relationships which are of common occurrence, such as the relationship of seller and buyer, owner and hirer, master and servant, landlord and tenant, carrier by land or by sea, contractor for building works, and so forth. In all those relationships the courts have imposed obligations on one party or the other, saying they are implied terms. These obligations are not founded on the intention of the parties, actual or presumed, but on more general considerations: see *Luxor (Eastbourne) Ltd.* v. *Cooper (1941), per* Lord Wright; *Lister* v. *Romford Ice and Cold Storage Co., per* Viscount Simonds and Lord Tucker (both of whom give interesting illustrations); *Liverpool City Council* v. *Irwin, per* Lord Cross of Chelsea and Lord Edmund-Davies. In such relationships the problem is not solved by asking: what did the parties intend? or, would they have unhesitatingly agreed to it, if asked? It is to be solved by asking: has the law already defined the obligation or the extent of it? If so, let it be followed. If not, look to see what would be reasonable in the general run of such cases (see *per* Lord Cross of Chelsea) and then say what the obligation shall be. The House in *Liverpool City Council* v. *Irwin* went through that very process. They examined the existing law of landlord and tenant, in particular that relating to easements, to see if it contained the solution to the problem; and, having found that it did not, they imposed an obligation on the landlord to use reasonable care. In these relationships the parties can exclude or modify the obligation by express words, but unless they do so, the obligation is a legal incident of the relationship which is attached by the law itself and not by reason of any implied term.

Likewise, in the general law of contract, the legal effect of frustration does not depend on an implied term. It does not depend on the presumed intention of the parties, nor on what they would have answered, if asked, but simply on what the court itself declares to amount to a frustration: see *Davis Contractors* v. *Fareham Urban District Council* (1956), *per* Lord Radcliffe; *Ocean Tramp Tankers Corpn.* v. *V/O Sovfracht, The Eugenia* (1964).

(ii) *The second category*

The second category comprehends those cases which are not within the first category. These are cases, not of common occurrence, in which from the particular circumstances a term is to be implied. In these cases the implication is based on an intention imputed to the parties from their actual circumstances: see *Luxor (Eastbourne) Ltd.* v. *Cooper* (1941), *per* Lord Wright. Such an imputation is only to be made when it is necessary to imply a term to give efficacy to the contract and make it a workable agreement in such manner as the parties would clearly have done if they had applied their mind to the contingency which has arisen. These are the "officious bystander" type of case: see *Lister* v. *Romford Ice & Cold Storage Co* (1957), *per* Lord Tucker. In such cases a term is not to be implied on the ground that it would be reasonable, but only when it is necessary and can be formulated with a sufficient degree of precision. This was the test applied by the majority of this court in *Liverpool City Council* v. *Irwin* (1976); and they were emphatically upheld by the House on this point; see *per* Lord Cross of Chelsea and Lord Edmund-Davies.

There is this point to be noted about *Liverpool City Council* v. *Irwin*. In this court the argument was only about an implication in the second category. In the House of Lords that argument was not pursued. It was only the first category.

Into which of the two categories does the present case come? I am tempted to say that a solus agreement between supplier and buyer is of such common occurrence nowadays that it could be put into the first category; so that the law could imply a term based on general considerations. But I do not think this would be found acceptable. Nor do I think the case can be brought within the second category. If Shell had been asked at the beginning: "Will you agree not to discriminate abnormally against the buyer?" I think they would have declined. It might be a reasonable term, but it is not a necessary term. Nor can it be formulated with sufficient precision. On this point I agree with Kerr J. It should be noticed that in *Esso Petroleum Co Ltd.* v. *Harper's Garage (Stourport) Ltd.* (1968) Mocatta J. also refused to make such an implication and there was no appeal from his decision.

In the circumstances, I do not think any term can be implied.

[Ormrod L.J. agreed that no term could be implied.]

Bridge L.J. [dissented, stating:] It is clearly not possible to imply in this agreement a term which would inhibit Shell altogether from discriminating against Lostock. It is recognised that, in the course of normal trading, oil companies like Shell in fact negotiate marginally different rates of rebate with different dealers with whom they enter into solus agreements. In some agreements, we are told, an express term is introduced to the effect that no other buyer shall be given more favourable terms than the contracting party. But it does not follow that in the absence of any such express term Shell must be at liberty to discriminate against Lostock to any degree. An extreme example will serve to illustrate that such a freedom on the part of the plaintiffs would lead to absurdity. Suppose that an oil company concludes a five-year solus agreement with A at a normal rate of rebate. If on the very next day the company were to conclude two other five-year solus agreements with B and C, A's nearest competitors, giving them in each case a rebate at a rate 10p per gallon higher than the rate of rebate given to A, this would make it manifestly impossible for A to trade on the terms expressly agreed. To say that in those circumstances A must still be bound by his contract would be an absurdity. Obviously the parties as reasonable men cannot have intended such an absurdity. Accordingly it seems to me to follow that the necessary foundation for the application of the classic doctrine on which terms are implied in contracts is here present. That doctrine, as I understand it, requires that terms should be implied to prevent contractual absurdities which reasonable parties cannot have intended.

The extreme difficulty which this case presents is that of defining appropriately the degree of discrimination which any implied term is to preclude. If one were to say that Shell must not discriminate abnormally, unfairly, or unreasonably, none of those criteria indicate where the line is to be drawn with any precision. If any term is to be implied, it may be appropriate to define it by reference to the necessary effect of the discrimination on Lostock. If the effect of the discrimination is, so long as it continues, such as to render it commercially impracticable for Lostock to continue to trade on the express contractual terms, then, in my judgment, one could say with confidence that the limitation to be imposed by implication on Shell's freedom to discriminate has been exceeded.

Note

Many terms are implied by statute, as for example ss.12 to 15 of the Sale of Goods Act 1979 (see p. 626), or the Supply of Goods and Services Act 1982 which extends analogous protection for the consumer to contracts for services.

Question

Of the two views presented, which most accurately reflects the legitimate expectations of reasonable business people?

3. REPRESENTATIONS AND TERMS

City and Westminster Properties (1934) Ltd. v. Mudd

[1959] Ch. 129 (Ch.)

[The defendant leased a shop from the plaintiffs annexed to which was a small room in which, as the plaintiffs knew, the defendant slept. A subsequent lease was negotiated which contained a clause restricting use to business purposes only. The plaintiffs had, however, made an oral undertaking to the defendant that if he signed the lease notwithstanding this clause, he could still sleep on the premises. Although the defendant thereupon signed the agreement, the plaintiffs later sued for breach of the covenant relating to use of the premises.]

Harman J. [Having rejected various other defence claims continued] There remains the so-called question of estoppel. This, in my judgment, is a misnomer and the present case does not raise the controversial issue of the *Central London Property Trust Ltd.* v. *High Trees House Ltd.* (1947) decision. This is not a case of a representation made after contractual relations existed between the parties to the effect that one party to the contract could not rely on his rights. If the defendant's evidence is to be accepted, as I hold it is, it is a case of a promise made to him before the execution of the lease that, if he would execute it in the form put before him, the landlord would not seek to enforce against him personally the covenant about using the property as a shop only. The defendant says that it was in reliance on the promise that he executed the lease and entered on the onerous obligations contained in it. He says, moreover, that but for the promise made he would not have executed the lease, but would have moved to other premises available to him at the time. If these be the facts, there was a clear contract acted upon by the defendant to his detriment and from which the plaintiffs cannot be allowed to resile.

... The plea that this was a mere licence retractable at the plaintiffs' will does not bear examination. The promise was that so long as the defendant personally was tenant, so long would the landlords forbear to exercise the rights which they would have if he signed the lease. He did sign the lease on this promise and is therefore entitled to rely on it so long as he is personally in occupation of the shop.

Judgment for the defendant.

Notes

This case provides a striking example of how the device of a "collateral" contract can override even the terms of a formal signed document (*cf. L'Estrange* v. *Graucob*, above).

For further examples of a collateral contract, see *De Lassalle* v. *Guildford* (1901) (H.S.B., p. 472); *Shanklin Pier Ltd.* v. *Detel Products Ltd.* (1951).

If no collateral contract can be discovered by the court, it may sometimes be difficult to ascertain whether a statement is a term of the contract or merely a representation. Contrast, for example, *Oscar Chess* v. *Williams* (1957) with *Dick Bentley Productions Ltd.* v. *Harold Smith (Motors) Ltd.* (1965) (H.S.B., p. 462). The importance of the distinction lies in the remedy available, which may be either for breach of contract or misrepresentation (see Chap. 5).

Question

If the promise made by the plaintiffs had contractual force, what was the consideration which the defendant gave for it?

4. THE RELATIVE IMPORTANCE OF CONTRACTUAL TERMS

A/S Awilco v. Fulvia SpA di Navigazione of Cagliari; The Chikuma

[1981] 1 All E.R. 652 (H.L.)

[A charterparty, in a form commonly used, provided that unless "punctual and regular payment" of the hire charge was made, the owners were entitled to withdraw the vessel from the charterers. On one occasion the charterers paid in a way that effectively gave the owners an overdraft facility for the amount of the monthly hire as opposed to an equivalent to an unconditional cash payment. If the owners had wished to draw on the money immediately, it would probably have cost them no more than $100 in interest charges in the context of a monthly payment from the charterers of nearly $69,000 and a charterparty of several years' duration. The owners claimed, nevertheless, that because of the technical failure to make an unconditional payment, they had not been punctually paid and were entitled to withdraw the ship.]

Lord Bridge. It has often been pointed out that ship-owners and charterers bargain at arm's length. Neither class has such a preponderance of bargaining power as to be in a position to oppress the other. They should be in a position to look after themselves by contracting only on terms which are acceptable to them. Where, as here, they embody in their contracts common form clauses, it is, to my mind, of overriding importance that their meaning and legal effect should be certain and well understood. The ideal at which the courts should aim, in construing such clauses, is to produce a result such that in any given situation both parties seeking legal advice as to their rights and obligations can expect the same clear and confident answer from their advisers and neither will be tempted to embark on long and expensive litigation in the belief that victory depends on winning the sympathy of the court. This ideal may never be fully attainable, but we shall certainly never even approximate to it unless we strive to follow clear and consistent principles and steadfastly refuse to be blown off course by the supposed merits of individual cases.

[Lords Diplock, Simon, Edmund-Davies and Scarman concurred in giving judgment in favour of the owners.]

Notes

Although their Lordships did not actually use the terminology of "conditions" and "warranties," the effect of the decision is that the "punctual and regular payment" clause in such a charterparty is a "condition," which is strictly construed.

Even, however, in commercial matters the courts have sometimes taken a more flexible approach to the importance of terms as illustrated by the next case.

Hong Kong Fir Shipping Co. Ltd. v. Kawasaki Kisen Kaisha Ltd.

[1962] 2 Q.B. 26 (H.L.)

[The plaintiffs chartered a ship to the defendants for two years, by an agreement which stated that the ship was "in every way fitted for ordinary

cargo service." In fact the engines were elderly and the crew required to
maintain them incompetent. The result was that several months of the charter
were wasted in delays. The defendants accordingly claimed that the
agreement was at an end and repudiated the charter. The plaintiffs, whose
ship it was, sued for damages for wrongful repudiation. The precise status of
this "seaworthiness clause" therefore had to be considered.]

Lord Diplock. [Having stated that contractual undertakings
cannot all be categorised as either "conditions" or "warranties" continued] Lawyers tend to speak of this classification as if it were comprehensive, partly for the historical
reasons which I have already mentioned and partly because
Parliament itself adopted it in the Sale of Goods Act 1893 as
respects a number of implied terms in contracts for the sale of
goods and has in that Act used the expressions "condition"
and "warranty" in that meaning. But it is by no means true of
contractual undertakings in general at common law.

No doubt there are many simple contractual undertakings,
sometimes express but more often because of their very
simplicity ("It goes without saying") to be implied, of which it
can be predicated that every breach of such an undertaking
must give rise to an event which will deprive the party not in
default of substantially the whole benefit which it was
intended that he should obtain from the contract. And such a
stipulation, unless the parties have agreed that breach of it
shall not entitle the non-defaulting party to treat the contract
as repudiated, is a "condition." So too there may be other
simple contractual undertakings of which it can be predicated
that *no* breach can give rise to an event which will deprive the
party not in default of substantially the whole benefit which it
was intended that he should obtain from the contract; and
such a stipulation, unless the parties have agreed that breach
of it shall entitle the nondefaulting party to treat the contract
as repudiated, is a "warranty."

There are, however, many contractual undertakings of a
more complex character which cannot be categorised as being
"conditions" or "warranties," if the late-nineteenth-century
meaning adopted in the Sale of Goods Act 1893 and used by
Bowen L.J. in *Bentsen* v. *Taylor, Sons & Co.* (1893) be given to
those terms. Of such undertakings all that can be predicated
is that some breaches will and others will not give rise to an
event which will deprive the party not in default of
substantially the whole benefit which it was intended that he
should obtain from the contract; and the legal consequences
of a breach of such an undertaking, unless provided for
expressly in the contract, depend upon the nature of the
event to which the breach gives rise and do not follow

automatically from a prior classification of the undertaking as a "condition" or a "warranty." For instance, to take Bramwell B.'s example in *Jackson* v. *Union Marine Insurance Co. Ltd.* (1874) itself, breach of an undertaking by a shipowner to sail with all possible dispatch to a named port does not necessarily relieve the charterer of further performance of his obligation under the charterparty, but if the breach is so prolonged that the contemplated voyage is frustrated it does have this effect.

. . . . . .

As my brethren have already pointed out, the shipowners' undertaking to tender a seaworthy ship has, as a result of numerous decisions as to what can amount to "unseaworthiness," become one of the most complex of contractual undertakings. It embraces obligations with respect to every part of the hull and machinery, stores and equipment and the crew itself. It can be broken by the presence of trivial defects easily and rapidly remediable as well as by defects which must inevitably result in a total loss of the vessel.

Consequently the problem in this case is, in my view, neither solved nor soluble by debating whether the shipowner's express or implied undertaking to tender a seaworthy ship is a "condition" or a "warranty." It is like so many other contractual terms an undertaking one breach of which may give rise to an event which relieves the charterer of further performance of his undertakings if he so elects and another breach of which may not give rise to such an event but entitle him only to monetary compensation in the form of damages. It is, with all deference to Mr. Ashton Roskill's skilful argument, by no means surprising that among the many hundreds of previous cases about the shipowner's undertaking to deliver a seaworthy ship there is none where it was found profitable to discuss in the judgments the question whether that undertaking is a "condition" or a "warranty"; for the true answer, as I have already indicated, is that it is neither, but one of that large class of contractual undertakings one breach of which may have the same effect as that ascribed to a breach of "condition" under the Sale of Goods Act 1893 and a different breach of which may have only the same effect as that ascribed to a breach of "warranty" under that Act.

. . . . . .

What the judge had to do in the present case, as in any other case where one party to a contract relies upon a breach by the other party as giving him a right to elect to rescind the contract, and the contract itself makes no express provision as to this, was to look at the events which had occurred as a result of the breach at the time at which the charterers purported to rescind the charterparty and to decide whether the occurrence of those events deprived the charterers of substantially the whole benefit which it was the intention of the parties as expressed in the charterparty that the charterers should obtain from the further performance of their own contractual undertakings.

One turns therefore to the contract, the Baltime 1939 charter, of which Sellers L.J. has already cited the relevant terms. Clause 13, the "due diligence" clause, which exempts the shipowners from responsibility for delay or loss or damage to goods on board due to unseaworthiness, unless such delay or loss or damage has been caused by want of due diligence of the owners in making the vessel seaworthy and fitted for the voyage, is in itself sufficient to show that the mere occurrence of the events that the vessel was in some respect unseaworthy when tendered or that such unseaworthiness had caused some delay in performance of the charterparty would not deprive the charterer of the whole benefit which it was the intention of the parties he should obtain from the performance of his obligations under the contract—for he undertakes to continue to perform his obligations notwithstanding the occurrence of such events if they fall short of frustration of the contract and even deprives himself of any remedy in damages unless such events are the consequence of want of due diligence on the part of the shipowner.

The question which the judge had to ask himself was, as he rightly decided, whether or not at the date when the charterers purported to rescind the contract, namely, June 6, 1957, or when the shipowners purported to accept such rescission, namely August 8, 1957, the delay which had already occurred as a result of the incompetence of the engine-room staff, and the delay which was likely to occur in repairing the engines of the vessel and the conduct of the shipowners by that date in taking steps to remedy these two matters, were, when taken together, such as to deprive the charterers of substantially the whole benefit which it was the intention of the parties they should obtain from further use of the vessel under the charterparty.

In my view, in his judgment—on which I would not seek to improve—the judge took into account and gave due weight to all the relevant considerations and arrived at the right answer for the right reasons.

Judgment for the plaintiffs.

Note

In substance, the "innominate term" predates the *Hong Kong Fir* case even though that case was the first to discuss it. An earlier example is *Aerial Advertising Co.* v. *Batchelor's Peas Ltd.* (1938). The advantages of flexibility in regarding a term as "innominate" have to be set against the uncertainty which is thereby produced. Cases which seem to follow the *Hong Kong Fir* approach such as *Cehave N.V.* v. *Bremer Handelsgeselschaft mbH (The Hansa Nord)* (1976) and *Reardon Smith Line* v. *Hansen Tangen* (1976) can be contrasted with *The Mihalis Angelos* (1971) where the House of Lords affirmed the value of the distinction between "conditions" and "warranties" (H.S.B., pp. 473–478).

Chapter 5

Misrepresentation

1. THE MEANING OF MISREPRESENTATION

Bisset v. Wilkinson

[1927] A.C. 177 (P.C.)

[Bisset was selling two plots of land in New Zealand to Wilkinson for the purpose of sheep farming. In the course of negotiations, Bisset expressed the view that if the land were worked properly it could carry 2,000 sheep. Both parties knew that the land concerned had never been used for sheep-farming. The issue arose of whether or not this was an actionable misrepresentation.]

Lord Merrivale. In an action for rescission, as in an action for specific performance of an executory contract, when misrepresentation is the alleged ground of relief of the party who repudiates the contract, it is, of course, essential to ascertain whether that which is relied upon is a representation of a specific fact, or a statement of opinion, since an erroneous opinion stated by the party affirming the contract, though it may have been relied upon and have induced the contract on the part of the party who seeks rescission, gives no title to relief unless fraud is established. The application of this rule, however, is not always easy, as is illustrated in a good many reported cases, as well as in this. A representation of fact may be inherent in a statement of opinion and, at any rate, the existence of the opinion in the person stating it is a question of fact. In *Karberg's Case* Lindley L.J., in the course of testing a representation which might have been, as it was said to be by interested parties, one of opinion or belief, used this inquiry: "Was the statement of expectation a statement of things not really expected?" The Court of Appeal applied this test and rescinded the contract which was in question. In *Smith* v. *Land and House Property Corporation* (1884) there came in question a vendor's description of the tenant of the property sold as "a most desirable tenant"—a statement of his opinion, as was argued on his behalf in an action to enforce the contract of sale. This description was held by the Court of Appeal to be a misrepresentation of fact, which, without proof of fraud, disentitled the vendor to specific performance of the contract of purchase. "It is often fallaciously assumed," said Bowen L.J., "that a statement of opinion cannot involve the statement of fact. In a case where the facts are equally well known to both parties, what one of them says to the other is frequently nothing but an expression of opinion. The statement of such opinion is in a sense a statement of fact, about the condition of the man's own mind, but only of an irrelevant fact, for it is of no consequence what the opinion is. But if the facts are not equally well known to both sides, then a statement of opinion by one who knows the facts best involves very often a statement of a material fact, for he impliedly states that he knows facts which justify his opinion.

[His Lordship considered the particular facts of this case.]

As was said by *Sim J.*: "In ordinary circumstances, any statement made by an owner who has been occupying his own farm as to its carrying capacity would be regarded as a statement of fact. ... This, however, is not such a case. ... In these circumstances ... the defendants were not justified in regarding anything said by the plaintiff as to the carrying capacity as being anything more than an expression of his opinion on the subject." In this view of the matter their Lordships concur.

Judgment for the appellant, Bisset.

Note

The statement in *Bisset* v. *Wilkinson* was regarded under the circumstances merely as an expression of opinion. In *Smith* v. *Land and House Property Corporation* (1884) the statement was in reality one of fact because the vendors were well aware that the tenant paid only "by driblets under pressure." There was therefore an implied statement of fact in the vendors assertion which was quite untrue, namely that they knew facts which justified their opinion.

2.   SILENCE AS MISREPRESENTATION

Wales v. Wadham

[1977] 2 All E.R. 125

[Mr. Wales and his wife, who were in the process of obtaining a divorce, entered into a compromise agreement whereby in return for a capital payment of £13,000 she agreed not to make a claim for maintenance. She had previously stated her intention not to remarry, and did not inform her husband that she had, by the time of the agreement, changed her mind on this issue. The husband would have had no obligation to maintain his wife after her remarriage. Mr. Wales subsequently brought an action for rescission of the agreement.]

Tudor Evans J. I must now consider the husband's submission that the wife's statement to him that she would not remarry amounts to a misrepresentation which induced him to enter the contract. It is the husband's case that had he been aware of the true fact he would never have made the offer to pay £13,000. This was intended to commute his liability for periodical payments, a liability which, in the event, he would never have had. In order to prove a fraudulent misrepresentation, the husband must show that the wife made a statement of fact which was false to her knowledge or that she was reckless as to its truth, and that such misrepresentation was intended to, and did, cause the husband to enter the contract. It is submitted that even if the wife's statement that she would never remarry was honestly held, she was under a duty to tell the husband of her changed circumstances, but that she failed to do so. Counsel has referred me to *With* v. *O'Flanagan* (1936) in the Court of Appeal. In that case, during course of negotiations for the sale of a medical practice, the vendor made representations to the purchaser about the existing nature of the practice which, by the time when the contract was signed, were untrue. The value of the practice had declined in the meantime because of the vendor's inability to attend to it through illness. Lord Wright M.R. quoted, with approval, observations of Fry J. in *Davies* v. *London and Provincial Marine Insurance Co.* (1878) where he said:

"So, again, if a statement has been made which is true at the time, but which during the course of negotiations becomes untrue, then the person who knows that it has become untrue is under an obligation to disclose to the other the change of circumstances."

The representations in both of these cases related to existing fact and not to a statement of intention in relation to future conduct. A statement of intention is not a representation of existing fact, unless the person making it does not honestly hold the intention he is expressing, in which case there is a misrepresentation of fact in relation to the state of that person's mind. That does not arise on the facts as I have found them. On the facts of this case, the wife made an honest statement of her intention which was not a representation of fact, and I can find no basis for holding that she was under a duty in the law of contract to tell the husband of her change of mind. Counsel for the wife submits that, apart from any other consideration, the wife's objection to remarriage after divorce and her specific statements to the husband that she would not remarry, do not have the quality of representations in the sense that at her age she could not seriously be taken as representing that she would never change her mind. I accept that submission. It seems to me that when after a marriage which had lasted for some 26 years the wife told the husband she would never marry again she was not representing to the husband that, she then being barely 50, she would never change her mind. The wife's objections to remarriage on religious grounds could not, in themselves, amount to a representation. They were simply general opinions expressed during the existence of the marriage, and not in any way made in contemplation by either party of a contract. With respect to the specific statements, as I have said, I am satisfied that the wife made them in an attempt to save her marriage and I am satisfied she was not representing that she would never change her mind. . . .

I must now consider the submission of the husband that the contract in this case was one requiring uberrima fides. Such contracts are an exception to the common law rule that a party may remain silent about material facts when negotiating a contract, and that such silence does not amount to a misrepresentation. I have been referred to *Bell* v. *Lever Bros Ltd.* (1932), where Lord Thankerton said:

"The most familiar of these exceptions is found in the case of policies of insurance, as to which Blackburn J. says, in *Fletcher* v. *Krell*, 'mercantile custom has established the rule with regard to concealment of material facts in policies of assurance, but in other cases there must be an allegation of moral guilt or fraud.' Other exceptions are found in case of trustee and cestui que trust and of a company issuing a prospectus and an applicant for shares, but the number of exceptions is limited, and no authority has been cited which extends the exceptions to cover a case such as the present."

Further examples are contracts of partnership and suretyship but there is no case in which the principle has been extended to contracts between a husband and wife, although counsel for the husband has referred to a number of authorities in the 19th century concerned with deeds of separation, in which he submits the duty to disclose has been recognised. I shall refer to these cases at a later stage. The first submission is that the contract in the present case is similar to a contract of insurance. It is pointed out that contracts of insurance are speculative in nature in the sense that an insurer can only compute his risk on the basis of what he is told by the proposed assured. I have been referred to an early case, *Carter* v. *Boehm* (1766), where Lord Mansfield C.J. said:

"Insurance is a contract upon speculation. The special facts, upon which the contingent chance is to be computed, lie most commonly in the knowledge of the *insured* only: the under-writer trusts to his representation, and proceeds upon confidence that he does not keep back any circumstance in his knowledge, to mislead the underwriter into a belief that the circumstance does not exist ..."

It is said that the husband in the present case was computing or compromising in a single sum a future and uncertain liability to maintain the wife and that the likelihood of the wife's remarriage was a material fact in the computation which should have been disclosed. I cannot accept that there is any analogy between a contract of insurance and the contract in the present case. In contracts of insurance, the material facts on which the insurer decides whether to assume the risk and, if so, on what terms, lie exclusively within the knowledge of the insured. Contracts requiring uberrima fides are based on the fact that, from the very necessity of the case, only one party possesses knowledge of all the material facts. In the case of life assurance, for example, only the proposed assured can know the state of his health, past or present. The contract in the present case was one in which material facts on both sides were withheld. Neither side made full disclosure. The husband admitted in cross-examination that he did not disclose his income. ... On the wife's side, she did not disclose that between the end of October 1972, when the husband made the offer, and February 1973, when counsel agreed the terms in settlement of all the wife's claims for ancillary relief for maintenance, that she had an arrangement to marry Mr. Wadham. No questions were asked of the wife's financial position nor whether she intended to marry at any time in the future. It seems to me that the negotiations and the agreement reached was a compromise without full disclosure on either side. I can find no similarity at all to a contract of insurance.

Judgment for the wife.

Question

Was the judge in this case correct to distinguish the decision in *With* v. *O'Flanagan*? Does not a statement of intention reflect the present state of a person's mind just as much when the person holds the intention he is expressing?

3. TERMS AND NEGLIGENT MISREPRESENTATION

Esso Petroleum Co. Ltd. v. Mardon

[1976] 2 All E.R. 5 (C.A.)

[Esso had bought a site for development as a petrol station. Their very experienced sales representative assured the defendant that the garage would have a throughput of petrol of some 200,000 gallons per year. The defendant doubted this but ultimately, in reliance upon the representative's estimate, signed the tenancy agreement. In fact, the petrol sales were less than half the estimate. In the resulting litigation the defendant counterclaimed against Esso on the basis of the negligent statement made by their representative.]

Lord Denning M.R. . . .

Collateral warranty

Ever since *Heilbut Symons & Co.* v. *Buckleton* (1913) we have had to contend with the law as laid down by the House of Lords that an innocent misrepresentation gives no right to damages. In order to escape from that rule, the pleader used to allege—I often did it myself—that the misrepresentation was fraudulent, or alternatively a collateral warranty. At the trial we nearly always succeeded on collateral warranty. We had to reckon, of course, with the dictum of Lord Moulton that "such collateral contracts must from their very nature be rare." But more often than not the court elevated the innocent misrepresentation into a collateral warranty; and thereby did justice—in advance of the Misrepresentation Act 1967. I remember scores of cases of that kind, especially on the sale of a business. A representation as to the profits that had been made in the past was invariably held to be a warranty. Besides that experience, there have been many cases since I have sat in this court where we have readily held a representation—which induces a person to enter into a contract—to be a warranty sounding in damages. I summarised them in *Dick Bentley Productions Ltd.* v. *Harold Smith (Motors) Ltd.* (1965) when I said:

> "Looking at the cases once more, as we have done so often, it seems to me that if a representation is made in the course of dealings for a contract for the very purpose of inducing the other party to act on it, and it actually induces him to act on it by entering into the contract, that is prima facie ground for inferring that the representation was intended as a warranty. It is not necessary to speak of it as being collateral. Suffice it that the representation was intended to be acted on and was in fact acted on."

Counsel for Esso retaliated, however, by citing *Bisset* v. *Wilkinson* where the Privy Council said that a statement by a New Zealand farmer that an area of land "would carry 2,000 sheep" was only an expression of opinion. He submitted that the forecast here of 200,000 gallons was an expression of opinion and not a statement of fact; and that it could not be interpreted as a warranty or promise.

Now, I would quite agree with counsel for Esso that it was not a warranty—in this sense—that it did not *guarantee* that the throughput *would be* 200,000 gallons. But, nevertheless, it was a forecast made by a party, Esso, who had special knowledge and skill. It was the yardstick ... by which they measured the worth of a filling station. They knew the facts. They knew the traffic in the town. They knew the throughput of comparable stations. They had much experience and expertise at their disposal. They were in a much better position than Mr. Mardon to make a forecast. It seems to me that if such a person makes a forecast—intending that the other should act on it and he does act on it—it can well be interpreted as a warranty that the forecast is sound and reliable in this sense that they made it with reasonable care and skill. It is just as if Esso said to Mr. Mardon: "Our forecast of throughput is 200,000 gallons. You can rely on it as being a sound forecast of what the service station should do.

The rent is calculated on that footing." If the forecast turned out to be an unsound forecast, such as no person of skill or experience should have made, there is a breach of warranty. Just as there is a breach of warranty when a forecast is made "expected to load" by a certain date if the maker has no reasonable grounds for it: see *Samuel Sanday* v. *Keighley Maxted & Co.* (1922), or bunkers "expected 600/700 tons": see *The Pantanassa* (1958) by Diplock J. It is very different from the New Zealand case where the land had never been used as a sheep farm and both parties were equally able to form an opinion as to its carrying capacity.

In the present case it seems to me that there was a warranty that the forecast was sound, that is that Esso had made it with reasonable care and skill. That warranty was broken. Most negligently Esso made a "fatal error" in the forecast they stated to Mr. Mardon, and on which he took the tenancy. For this they are liable in damages. The judge, however, declined to find a warranty. So I must go further.

Negligent misrepresentation

Assuming that there was no warranty, the question arises whether Esso are liable for negligent mis-statement under the doctrine of *Hedley Byrne & Co. Ltd.* v. *Heller & Partners Ltd.* (1964). It has been suggested that *Hedley Byrne* cannot be used so as to impose liability for negligent pre-contractual statements; and that, in a pre-contract situation, the remedy (at any rate before the 1967 Act) was only in warranty or nothing. Thus in *Hedley Byrne* itself Lord Reid said: "Where there is a contract there is no difficulty as regards the contracting parties: the question is whether there is a warranty." And in *Oleificio Zucchi SPA* v. *Northern Sales Ltd.* (1965) McNair J. said: " . . . as at present advised, I consider the submission advanced by the buyers—that the ruling in [*Hedley Byrne*] applies as between contracting parties, is without foundation." As against these, I took a different view in *McInerny* v. *Lloyds Bank Ltd.* (1974), when I said: ". . . if one person, by a negligent misstatement, induces another to enter into a contract—with himself or a third person—he may be liable in damages."

It follows that I cannot accept counsel for Esso's proposition. It seems to me that *Hedley Byrne*, properly understood, covers this particular proposition: if a man, who has or professes to have special knowledge or skill, makes a representation by virtue thereof to another—be it advice, information or opinion—with the intention of inducing him to enter into a contract with him, he is under a duty to use reasonable care to see that the representation is correct, and that the advice, information or opinion is reliable. If he negligently gives unsound advice or misleading information or expresses an erroneous opinion, and thereby induces the other side into a contract with him, he is liable in damages. This proposition is in line with what I said in *Candler* v. *Crane Christmas & Co.* (1951), which was approved by the majority of the Privy Council in *Mutual Life & Citizens' Assurance Ltd.* v. *Evatt*, (1971). And the judges of the Commonwealth have shown themselves quite ready to apply *Hedley Byrne* between contracting parties: see, in Canada, *Sealand of the Pacific Ltd.* v. *Ocean Cement Ltd.* (1973) and, in New Zealand, *Capital Motors Ltd.* v. *Beecham* (1975).

Applying this principle, it is plain that Esso professed to have—and did in fact have—special knowledge or skill in estimating the throughput of a filling station. They made the representation—they forecast a throughput of 200,000 gallons—intending to induce Mr. Mardon to enter into a tenancy on the faith of it. They made it negligently. It was a "fatal error." And thereby induced Mr. Mardon to enter into a contract of tenancy that was disastrous to him. For this misrepresentation they are liable in damages.

[Ormrod and Shaw L.JJ. concurred in giving judgment for the defendant on the counterclaim.]

Question

Even though there may be a cause of action in both contract and tort in these circumstances, why might a litigant prefer to bring his action under the Misrepresentation Act 1967?

4. MISREPRESENTATION AND THE MISREPRESENTATION ACT 1967

Howard Marine & Dredging Co. Ltd. v. A. Ogden and Son (Excavations) Ltd.

[1978] Q.B. 574 (C.A.)

[Ogdens wished to hire some barges for removing large quantities of clay. The carrying capacity of the barges to be used was crucial as this would affect, for example, how quickly the job could be done. They approached Howards, who hired out barges, and on enquiring as to their capacity received an oral reply from their representative Mr. O'Loughlin which proved to be incorrect in that it was too high. The mistake arose from the maker's reliance on the entry in Lloyds Register (which was usually accurate) instead of checking the ship's documents which were in their possession. When the error became apparent, Ogdens refused to make further hire payments. Howards, the plaintiffs, withdrew the barges and claimed for hire payments. Ogdens counterclaimed on the grounds of misrepresentation.]

Lord Denning M.R. (dissenting):

The collateral oral warranties

Ogdens submitted that, in the two telephone conversations in April 1974, Howards gave oral warranties as to the carrying capacity of the barges: and that, on the faith of these warranties, they tendered for the main excavation contract and entered into it: that the warranties are therefore binding on Howards on the authority of such cases as *Shanklin Pier Ltd.* v. *Detel Products Ltd.* (1951) and *Wells (Merstham) Ltd.* v. *Buckland Sand and Silica Ltd.* (1965). Further, that at the interview of July 11, 1974, Howards gave a further oral warranty as to the carrying capacity of the barges: and that, on the faith of it, they did order the barges and took them on hire under the charterparties.

On this point we were, as usual, referred to *Heilbut, Symons & Co.* v. *Buckleton* (1913). That case has come under considerable criticism lately, particularly in view of the contemporaneous decision of the House of Lords in *Schawel* v. *Reade* (1912). . . . Much of what was said in *Heilbut, Symons & Co.* v. *Buckleton* is now out of date, as I mentioned in *J. Evans & Sons (Portsmouth) Ltd.* v. *Andrea Merzario Ltd.* (1976) and *Esso Petroleum Co. Ltd.* v. *Mardon* (1976). No doubt it is still true to say, as Holt C.J. said: "an affirmation at the time of the sale is a warranty, provided it appears as evidence to be so intended"—which I take to mean intended to be binding.

Applying this test, I cannot regard any of the oral representations made in April 1974 as contractual warranties. Ogdens invited offers from five different owners of barges. These five made separate offers. Howards made their written offer "subject to availability and contract": which shows that they were not binding themselves to anything at that stage. It cannot be supposed that in the telephone conversations they were binding themselves contractually to anything. Nor would I regard the statement at the interview of July 11, 1974, as a contractual warranty. It was made three months before the barges were delivered. And meanwhile there was the "on-hire condition survey": and the exchange of the draft charterparties—in which you would expect any contractual terms to be included.

I agree with the judge that there were no collateral warranties here.

Negligent misrepresentations

Ogdens contended next that the representations by Howards, as to the carrying capacity of the barges, were made negligently: and that Howards are liable in damages for negligent misrepresentation on the principles laid down in *Hedley Byrne & Co. Ltd.* v. *Heller & Partners Ltd.* (1964).

This raises the vexed question of the scope of the doctrine of *Hedley Byrne*. It was much discussed in the Privy Council in *Mutual Life and Citizens' Assurance Co. Ltd.* v. *Evatt* (1971) and in this court in *Esso Petroleum Co. Ltd.* v. *Mardon* (1976). To my mind one of the most helpful passages is to be found in the speech of Lord Pearce in *Hedley Byrne & Co. Ltd.* v. *Heller & Partners Ltd.* (1964):

> "... To import such a duty (of care) the representation must normally, I think, concern a business or professional transaction whose nature makes clear the gravity of the inquiry and the importance and influence attached to the answer.... A most important circumstance is the form of the inquiry and of the answer."

To this I would add the principle stated by Lord Reid and Lord Morris of Borth-y-Gest in the Privy Council case, *Mutual Life and Citizens' Assurance Co. Ltd.* v. *Evatt* (1971), which I would adopt in preference to that stated by the majority:

> "... when an inquirer consults a business man in the course of his business and makes it plain to him that he is seeking considered advice and intends to act on it in a particular way ... his action in giving such advice ... (gives rise to) ... a legal obligation to take such care as is reasonable in the whole circumstances."

Those principles speak of the "gravity of the inquiry" and the seeking of "considered advice." Those words are used so as to exclude representations made during a casual conversation in the street; or in a railway carriage; or an impromptu opinion given offhand; or "off the cuff" on the telephone. To put it more generally, the duty if one of honesty and no more whenever the opinion, information or advice is given in circumstances in which it appears that it is unconsidered and it would not be reasonable for the recipient to act on it without taking further steps to check it. . . .

Applying this test, it seems to me that at these various conversations Mr. O'Loughlin was under a duty to be honest, but no more. Take the first two conversations. They were on the telephone. The callers from the north wanted to know what was the capacity of the barges. Mr. O'Loughlin answered it offhand as best he could, without looking up the file. If they had wanted considered advice, they should have written a letter and got it in writing. Take the last conversation. It was on an occasion when Mr. O'Loughlin went up to the north to discuss all sorts of things. In the course of it, he was asked again the capacity of the barges. He had not got the file with him, so he answered as best he could from memory. To my mind in those circumstances it was not reasonable for Ogdens to act on his answers without checking them. They ought either to have got him to put in writing—that would have stressed the gravity and importance of it—or they ought to have got expert advice on their own behalf—especially in a matter of such importance to them. So I agree with the judge that there was not such a situation here as to give rise to a duty of care: or to make Howards liable for negligent misrepresentation at common law.

The Misrepresentation Act 1967

Alternatively Ogdens claim damages for innocent mis-representation under the Misrepresentation Act 1967. It says in section 2: . . . [see p. 621]

This enactment imposes a new and serious liability on anyone who makes a representation of fact in the course of negotiations for a contract. If that representation turns out to be mistaken—then however innocent he may be—his is just as liable as if he made it fraudulently. But how different from times past! For years he was not liable in damages at all for innocent misrepresentation: see *Heilbut, Symons & Co.* v. *Buckleton* (1913). Quite recently he was made liable if he was proved to have made it negligently: see *Esso Petroleum Co. Ltd.* v. *Mardon* (1976). But now with this Act he is made liable—unless he proves—and the burden is on him to prove—that he had reasonable ground to believe and did in fact believe that it was true.

Section 2(1) certainly applies to the representation made by Mr. O'Loughlin on July 11, 1974, when he told Ogdens that each barge could carry 1,600 tonnes. The judge found that it was a misrepresentation: that he said it with the object of getting the hire contract for Howards. They got it: and, as a result, Ogdens suffered loss. But the judge found that Mr. O'Loughlin was not negligent: and so Howards were not liable for it.

The judge's finding was criticised before us: because he asked himself the question: was Mr. O'Loughlin negligent? Whereas he should have asked himself: did Mr. O'Loughlin have reasonable ground to believe that the representation was true? I think that criticism is not fair to the judge. By the word "negligent" he was only using shorthand for the longer phrase contained in section 2(1) which he had before him. And the judge, I am sure, had the burden of proof in mind: for he had come to the conclusion that Mr. O'Loughlin was not negligent. The judge said in effect: "I am satisfied that Mr. O'Loughlin was not negligent": and being so satisfied, the burden need not be further considered. . . .

. . . . . .

It seems to me that when one examines the details, the judge's view was entirely justified. He found that Mr. O'Loughlin's state of mind was this: Mr. O'Loughlin had examined Lloyd's Register and had seen there that the deadweight capacity of each barge was 1,800 tonnes. That figure stuck in his mind. The judge found that "the 1,600 tonnes was arrived at by knocking off what he considered a reasonable margin for fuel, and so on, from the 1,800 tonnes summer deadweight figure in Lloyd's Register, which was in the back of his mind." The judge said that Mr. O'Loughlin had seen at some time the German shipping documents and had seen the deadweight figure of 1,055.135 tonnes: but it did not register. All that was in his mind was the 1,800 tonnes in Lloyd's Register which was regarded in shipping circles as the Bible. That afforded reasonable ground for him to believe that the barges could each carry 1,600 tonnes pay load: and that is what Mr. O'Loughlin believed.

So on this point, too, I do not think we should fault the judge. It is not right to pick his judgment to pieces—by subjecting it—or the shorthand note—to literal analysis. Viewing it fairly, the judge (who had section 2(1) in front of him) must have been of opinion that the burden of proof was discharged.

The exception clause

If I be wrong so far, however, there remains the exception clause in the charterparty. It was, as I have said, included throughout all the negotiations: and no objection was ever taken to it. The important words are:

"... charterers' acceptance of handing over the vessel shall be conclusive that [she is] ... in all respects fit for the intended and contemplated use by the charterers and in every other way satisfactory to them."

In the old days we used to construe such an exception clause strictly against the party relying on it: but there is no need—and I suggest no warrant—any longer for construing it so strictly. The reason is that now by section 3 of the Misrepresentation Act 1967 the provision is of no effect except to the extent that the court may allow reliance on it as being fair and reasonable in the circumstances of the case. Under this section the question is not whether the provision itself is reasonable: but only whether "reliance on its [is] fair and reasonable in the circumstances of the case."

If the clause itself is reasonable, that goes a long way towards showing that the reliance on it is fair and reasonable. It seems to me that the clause was itself fair and reasonable. The parties here were commercial concerns and were of equal bargaining power. The clause was not foisted by one on the other in a standard printed form. It was contained in all the drafts which passed between them, and it was no doubt given close consideration by both sides, like all the other clauses, some of which were amended and others not. It was a clause common in charterparties of this kind: and is familiar in other commercial contracts, such as construction and engineering contracts.... It is specially applicable in cases where the contractor has the opportunity of checking the position for himself. It tells him that he should do so: and that he should not rely on any information given beforehand, for it may be inaccurate. Thus it provides a valuable safeguard against the consequences of innocent misrepresentation.

... I would do nothing to impair its efficacy. I would allow Howards to rely on it.

Bridge L.J. [Having also rejected the collateral warranty argument, and after citing section 2(1) of the Act continued:]

The first question then is whether Howards would be liable in damages in respect of Mr. O'Loughlin's misrepresentation if it had been made fraudulently, that is to say, if he had known that it was untrue. An affirmative answer to that question is inescapable. The judge found in terms that what Mr. O'Loughlin said about the capacity of the barges was said with the object of getting the hire contract for Howards, in other words, with the intention that it should be acted on. This was clearly right. Equally clearly the misrepresentation was in fact acted on by Ogdens. It follows, therefore, on the plain language of the statute that, although there was no allegation of fraud, Howards must be liable unless they proved that Mr. O'Loughlin had reasonable ground to believe what he said about the barges' capacity.

It is unfortunate that the judge never directed his mind to the question whether Mr. O'Loughlin had any reasonable ground for his belief. The question he asked himself, in considering liability under the Misrepresentation Act 1967, was whether the innocent misrepresentation was negligent. He concluded that if Mr. O'Loughlin had given the inaccurate information in the course of the April telephone conversations he would have been negligent to do so but that in the circumstances obtaining at the Otley interview in July there was no negligence. I take it that he meant by this that on the earlier occasions the circumstances were such that he would have been under a duty to check the accuracy of his information, but on the later occasions he was exempt from any such duty. I appreciate the basis of this distinction, but it seems to me, with respect, quite irrelevant to any question of liability under the statute. If the representee proves a misrepresentation which, if fraudulent, would have sounded in damages, the onus passes immediately to the representor to prove that he had reasonable ground to believe the facts represented. In other words the liability of the representor does not depend upon his being under a duty of care the extent of which may vary according to the circumstances in which the representation is made. In the course of nego-tiations leading to a contract the statute imposes an absolute obligation not to state facts which the representor cannot prove he had reasonable ground to believe.

Although not specifically posing the question of whether he had reasonable ground for his belief, the judge made certain findings about Mr. O'Loughlin's state of mind. He said:

> "Mr. O'Loughlin looked at the documents of the ships he was in charge of including HB2 and HB3's German documents. He is not a master of maritime German. He saw, but did not register, the deadweight figure of 1,055.135 tonnes. Being in the London office he went to the City and looked up Lloyd's Register. There he noted that the summer loading deadweight figure for B41 and B45, described as TM sand carriers, was 1,800 tonnes. This figure stayed in his mind. But it was one of Lloyd's Register's rare mistakes."

[Having considered the evidence in the case.]

I am fully alive to the dangers of trial by transcript and it is to be assumed that Mr. O'Loughlin was perfectly honest throughout. But the question remains whether his evidence, however benevolently viewed, is sufficient to show that he had an objectively reasonable ground to disregard the figure in the ship's documents and to prefer the Lloyd's Register figure. I think it is not. ... Accordingly I conclude that Howards failed to prove that Mr. O'Loughlin had reasonable ground to believe the truth of his misrepresentation to Mr. Redpath.

Having reached a conclusion favourable to Ogdens on the issue of liability under the Misrepresentation Act 1967, I do not find it necessary to express a concluded view on the issue of negligence at common law. As at present advised I doubt if the circumstances surrounding the misrepresentation at the Otley interview were such as to impose on Howards a common law duty of care for the accuracy of the statement. If there was such a duty, I doubt if the evidence established a breach of it.

[His Lordship then considered the exception clause:]

A clause of this kind is to be narrowly construed. It can only be relied on as conclusive evidence of the charterers' satisfaction in relation to such attributes of the vessel as would be apparent on an ordinary examination of the vessel. I do not think deadweight capacity is such an attribute. It can only be ascertained by an elaborate calculation or by an inspection of the ship's documents. But even if, contrary to this view, the clause can be read as apt to exclude liability for the earlier misrepresentation, Howards still have to surmount the restriction imposed by section 3 of the Misrepresentation Act 1967, which provides: ... [See p. 621.]

What the judge said in this matter was: "If the wording of the clause is apt to exempt from responsibility for negligent misrepresentation as to carrying capacity, I hold that such exemption is not fair and reasonable." The judge having asked himself the right question and answered it as he did in the exercise of the discretion vested in him by the Act, I can see no ground on which we could say that he was wrong.

I would accordingly allow the appeal to the extent of holding that Ogdens establish liability against Howards under section 2(1) of the Misrepresentation Act 1967 for any damages they suffered as a result of Mr. O'Loughlin's misrepresentation at the Otley interview in the terms as found by the judge.

[*Shaw L.J.* expressed the view that there was a cause of action in negligence at common law, but otherwise concurred with Bridge L.J.]

Judgment for the defendants.

Question

There were three main claims in the defendant's counterclaim. What were they? On which one did they ultimately succeed?

Note

For an example of a clause in a common form contract purporting to restrict liability for misrepresentation which was considered not to be fair and reasonable, see *Walker* v. *Boyle* (1982) (H.S.B., p. 492).

It now appears that a plaintiff's damages in a claim under the 1967 Act could be reduced by contributory negligence, *Gran Gelato Ltd.* v. *Richcliffe (Group) Ltd.* (1992).

For a case where an action for misrepresentation may be more beneficial to a plaintiff than a claim for breach of a contractual term see *Naughton* v. *O'Callaghan* (1990).

Chapter 6
Mistake

1. MISTAKE AS TO THE EXISTENCE OF THE SUBJECT-MATTER

Lever Brothers Ltd. v. Bell

[1931] 1 K.B. 557

[The facts are set out later at p. 500.]

Wright J. The mistake here invoked is of that type which has often been discussed, and has been described by various terms—for instance, as being mistake of subject-matter, or substance, or essence, or fundamental basis. However described, what is meant is some mistake or misapprehension as to some facts (which term here includes particular private rights, as held in *Cooper* v. *Phibbs* (1867)), which, by the common intention of the parties, whether expressed or more generally implied, constitute the underlying assumption without which the parties would not have made the contract they did. The simplest and oldest illustration of such mistake is where the parties contracted to sell and buy a specific chattel which at the date of the contract, though both parties thought it existing, had ceased to exist: in that event, however absolute the terms of the contract, there is in law no binding contract, and this principle is now embodied in the Sale of Goods Act, 1893, s.6. The principle was applied in a sense to the sale of a cargo sold c.i.f. which had, before the date of the contract, owing to sea damage, been properly sold by the shipmaster at a port of refuge, and hence became, without the knowledge of either party, incapable of delivery, though it may be that it still existed: *Couturier* v. *Hastie* (1852). The contract in such cases is void.... In ... *Scott* v. *Coulson* (1903), there was a contract for the sale of a life policy, but before that the assured had died, both parties to the contract being in ignorance of that fact. This transaction was set aside, and Vaughan Williams L.J. thus stated his conclusion: "If we are to take it that it was common ground that, at the date of the contract for the sale of this policy, both the parties to the contract supposed the assured to be alive, it is true that both parties entered into this contract upon the basis of a common affirmative belief that the assured was alive; but as it turned out that this was a common mistake, the contract was one which cannot be enforced. This is so as law; and the plaintiffs do not require to have recourse to equity to rescind the contract, if the basis which both parties recognized as the basis is not true."

Note

The case was subsequently appealed to the House of Lords, see below.

2.   MISTAKE AS TO QUALITY

Bell v. Lever Brothers

[1932] A.C. 161 (H.L.)

[Lever Brothers appointed Bell as managing director of a company in which they had a controlling interest at an annual salary of £8,000 for a period of five years. Because of a merger Bell's services were no longer required and Lever Brothers paid him £30,000 compensation for his loss of employment. They subsequently discovered that during his employment he had committed various acts which would have entitled them to terminate his employment without any compensation at all, although it was also found that Bell had not been fraudulent in failing to reveal these actions. Lever Brothers sued for rescission of the agreement and for the recovery of the £30,000. One of the bases for this claim was that there was a common mistake rendering the contract void.]

Lord Atkin. Two points present themselves for decision. Was the agreement of March 19, 1929, void by reason of a mutual mistake of Mr. D'Arcy Cooper and Mr. Bell?

Could the agreement of March 19, 1929, be avoided by reason of the failure of Mr. Bell to disclose his misconduct in regard to the cocoa dealings?

My Lords, the rules of law dealing with the effect of mistake on contract appear to be established with reasonable clearness. If mistake operates at all it operates so as to negative or in some cases to nullify consent. The parties may be mistaken in the identity of the contracting parties, or in the existence of the subject-matter of the contract at the date of the contract, or in the quality of the subject-matter of the contract. These mistakes may be by one party, or by both, and the legal effect may depend upon the class of mistake above mentioned. Thus a mistaken belief by A. that he is contracting with B., whereas in fact he is contracting with C., will negative consent where it is clear that the intention of A. was to contract only with B. So the agreement of A. and B. to purchase a specific article is void if in fact the article had perished before the date of sale. In this case, though the parties in fact were agreed about the subject-matter, yet a consent to transfer or take delivery of something not existent is deemed useless, the consent is nullified. As codified in the Sale of Goods Act the contract is expressed to be void if the seller was in ignorance of the destruction of the specific chattel. I apprehend that if the seller with knowledge that a chattel was destroyed purported to sell it to a purchaser, the latter might sue for damages for non-delivery though the former could not sue for non-acceptance, but I know of no case where a seller has so committed himself. This is a case where mutual mistake certainly and unilateral mistake by the seller of goods will prevent a contract from arising. Corresponding to mistake as to the existence of the subject-matter is mistake as to title in cases where, unknown to the parties, the buyer is already the owner of that which the seller purports to sell to him. The parties intended to effectuate a transfer of ownership: such a transfer is impossible: the stipulation is naturali ratione inutilis. This is the case of *Cooper* v. *Phibbs* (1867) where A. agreed to take a lease of a fishery from B., though contrary to the belief of both parties at the time A. was tenant for life of the fishery and B. appears to have had no title at all. To such a case Lord Westbury applied the principle that if parties contract under a mutual mistake and misapprehension as to their relative and respective rights the result is that the agreement is liable to be set aside as having proceeded upon a common mistake. Applied to the context the statement is only subject to the criticism that the agreement would appear to be void rather than voidable. Applied to mistake as to rights generally it would appear to be too wide. Even where the vendor has no title, though both parties think he has, the correct view would appear to be that there is a contract: but that the vendor has either committed a breach of a stipulation as to title, or is not able to perform his contract. The contract is unenforceable by him but is not void.

Mistake as to quality of the thing contracted for raises more difficult questions. In such a case a mistake will not affect assent unless it is the mistake of both parties, and is as to the existence of some quality which makes the thing without the quality essentially different from the thing as it was believed to be. Of course it may appear that the parties contracted that the article should possess the quality which one or other or both mistakenly believed it to possess. But in such a case there is a contract and the inquiry is a different one, being whether the contract as to quality amounts to a condition or a warranty, a different branch of the law. The principles to be applied are to be found in two cases which, as far as my knowledge goes, have always been treated as authoritative expositions of the law. The first is *Kennedy* v. *Panama Royal Mail Co.* (1867).

In that case the plaintiff had applied for shares in the defendant company on the faith of a prospectus which stated falsely but innocently that the company had a binding contract with the Government of New Zealand for the carriage of mails. On discovering the true facts the plaintiff brought an action for the recovery of the sums he had paid on calls. The defendants brought a cross action for further calls. Blackburn J., in delivering the judgment of the Court (Cockburn C.J., Blackburn, Mellor and Shee JJ.), said: "The only remaining question is one of much greater difficulty. It was contended by Mr. Mellish, on behalf of Lord Gilbert Kennedy, that the effect of the prospectus was to warrant to the intended shareholders that there really was such a contract as is there represented, and not merely to represent that the company *bona fide* believed it; and that the difference in substance between shares in a company with such a contract and shares in a company whose supposed contract was not binding, was a difference in substance in the nature of the thing; and that the shareholder was entitled to return the shares as soon as he discovered this, quite independently of fraud, on the ground that he had applied for one thing and got another. And, if the invalidity of the contract really made the shares he obtained different things in substance from those which he applied for, this would, we think, be good law. The case would then resemble *Gompertz* v. *Bartlett* (1853) and *Gurney* v. *Womersley* (1854), where the person who had honestly sold what he thought a bill without recourse to him, was nevertheless held bound to return the price on its turning out that the supposed bill was a forgery in the one case, and void under the stamp laws in the other; in both cases the ground of this decision being that the thing handed over was not the thing paid for. A similar principle was acted on in *Ship's Case* (1865). There is, however, a very important difference between cases where a contract may be rescinded on account of fraud, and those in which it may be rescinded on the ground that there is a difference in substance between the thing bargained for and that obtained. It is enough to show that there was a fraudulent representation as to any part of that which induced the party to enter into the contract which he seeks to rescind; but where there has been an innocent misrepresentation or misapprehension, it does not authorize a rescission unless it is such as to show that there is a complete difference in substance between what was supposed to be and what was taken, so as to constitute a failure of consideration. For example, where a horse is bought under a belief that it is sound, if the purchaser was induced to buy by a fraudulent representation as to the horse's soundness, the contract may be rescinded. If it was induced by an honest misrepresentation as to its soundness, though it may be clear that both vendor and purchaser thought that they were dealing about a sound horse and were in error, yet the purchaser must pay the whole price unless there was a warranty; and even if there was a warranty, he cannot return the horse and claim back the whole price, unless there was a condition to that effect in the contract: *Street* v. *Blay* (1831)."

The Court came to the conclusion in that case that, though there was a misapprehension as to that which was a material part of the motive inducing the applicant to ask for the shares, it did not prevent the shares from being in substance those he applied for.

The next case is *Smith* v. *Hughes* (1871), the well known case as to new and old oats. . . .

[See p. 520. Lord Atkin gave the facts and quoted from the judgments in that case.]

The Court ordered a new trial. It is not quite clear whether they considered that if the defendant's contention was correct, the parties were not ad idem or there was a contractual condition that the oats sold were old oats. In either case the defendant would succeed in defeating the claim.

In these cases I am inclined to think that the true analysis is that there is a contract, but that the one party is not able to supply the very thing whether goods or services that the other party contracted to take; and therefore the contract is unenforceable by the one if executory, while if executed the other can recover back money paid on the ground of failure of the consideration.

We are now in a position to apply to the facts of this case the law as to mistake so far as it has been stated. It is essential on this part of the discussion to keep in mind the finding of the jury acquitting the defendants of fraudulent misrepresentation or concealment in procuring the agreements in question. Grave injustice may be done to the defendants and confusion introduced into the legal conclusion, unless it is quite clear that in considering mistake in this case no suggestion of fraud is admissible and cannot strictly be regarded by the judge who has to determine the legal issues raised. The agreement which is said to be void is the agreement contained in the letter of March 19, 1929, that Bell would retire from the Board of the Niger Company and its subsidiaries, and that in consideration of his doing so Levers would pay him as compensation for the termination of his agreements and consequent loss of office the sum of 30,000*l*. in full satisfaction and discharge of all claims and demands of any kind against Lever Brothers, the Niger Company or its subsidiaries. The agreement, which as part of the contract was terminated, had been broken so that it could be repudiated. Is an agreement to terminate a broken contract different in kind from an agreement to terminate an unbroken contract, assuming that the breach has given the one party the right to declare the contract at an end? I feel the weight of the plaintiffs' contention that a contract immediately determinable is a different thing from a contract for an unexpired term, and that the difference in kind can be illustrated by the immense price of release from the longer contract as compared with the shorter. And I agree that an agreement to take an assignment of a lease for five years is not the same thing as to take an assignment of a lease for three years, still less a term for a few months. But, on the whole, I have come to the conclusion that it would be wrong to decide that an agreement to terminate a definite specified contract is void if it turns out that the agreement had already been broken and could have been terminated otherwise. The contract released is the identical contract in both cases, and the party paying for release gets exactly what he bargains for. It seems immaterial that he could have got the same result in another way, or that if he had known the true facts he would not have entered into the bargain. A. buys B.'s horse; he thinks the horse is sound and he pays the price of a sound horse; he would certainly not have bought the horse if he had known as the fact is that the horse is unsound. If B. has made no representation as to soundness and has not contracted that the horse is sound, A. is bound and cannot recover back the price. A. buys a picture from B.; both A. ad B. believe it to be the work of an old master, and a high price is paid. It turns out to be a modern copy. A. has no remedy in the absence of representation or warranty. A. agrees to take on lease or to buy from B. an unfurnished dwelling-house. The house is in fact uninhabitable. A. would never have entered into the bargain if he had known the fact. A. has no remedy, and the position is the same whether B. knew the facts or not, so long as he made no representation or gave no warranty. A. buys a roadside garage business from B. abutting on a public thoroughfare: unknown to A., but known to B., it has already been decided to construct a byepass road which will divert substantially the whole of the traffic from passing A.'s garage. Again A. has no remedy. All these cases involve hardship on A. and benefit B., as most people would say, unjustly. They can be supported on the ground that it is of paramount importance that contracts should be observed, and that if parties honestly comply with the essentials of the formation of contracts—*i.e.* agree in the same terms on the same subject-matter—they are bound, and must rely on the stipulations of the contract for protection from the effect of facts unknown to them.

This brings the discussion to the alternative mode of expressing the result of a mutual mistake. It is said that in such a case as the present there is to be implied a stipulation in the contract that a condition of its efficacy is that the facts should be as understood by both parties—namely, that the contract could not be terminated till the end of the current term. The question of the existence of conditions, express or implied, is obviously one that affects not the formation of contract, but the investigation of the terms of the contract when made. A condition derives its efficacy from the consent of the parties, express or implied. They have agreed, but on what terms. One term may be that unless the facts are or are not of a particular nature, or unless an event has or has not happened, the contract is not the take effect. With regard to future facts such a condition is obviously contractual. Till the event occurs the parties are bound. Thus the condition (the exact terms of which need not here be investigated) that is generally accepted as underlying the principle of the frustration cases is contractual, an implied condition. Sir John Simon formulated for the assistance of your Lordships a proposition which should be recorded: "Whenever it is to be inferred from the terms of a contract or its surrounding circumstances that the consensus has been reached upon the basis of a particular contractual assumption, and that assumption is not true, the contract is avoided: *i.e.* it is void *ab initio* if the assumption is of present fact and it ceases to bind if the assumption is of future fact."

I think few would demur to this statement, but its value depends upon the meaning of "a contractual assumption," and also upon the true meaning to be attached to "basis," a metaphor which may mislead. When used expressly in contracts, for instance, in policies of insurance, which state that the truth of the statements in the proposal is to be the basis of the contract of insurance, the meaning is clear. The truth of the statements is made a condition of the contract, which failing, the contract is void unless the condition is waived. The proposition does not amount to more than this that, if the contract expressly or impliedly contains a term that a particular assumption is a condition of the contract, the contract is avoided if the assumption is not true. But we have not advanced far on the inquiry how to ascertain whether the contract does contain such a condition. Various words are to be found to define the state of things which made a condition. "In the contemplation of both parties fundamental to the continued validity of the contract," "a foundation essential to its existence," "a fundamental reason for making it," are phrases found in the important judgment of Scrutton L.J. in the present case. The first two phrases appear to me to be unexceptionable. They cover the case of a contract to serve in a particular place, the existence of which is fundamental to the service, or to procure the services of a professional vocalist, whose continued health is essential to performance. But "a fundamental reason for making a contract" may, with respect, be misleading. The reason of one party only is presumably not intended, but in the cases I have suggested above, of the sale of a horse or of a picture, it might be said that the fundamental reason for making the contract was the belief of both parties that the horse was sound or the picture an old master, yet in neither case would the condition as I think exist. Nothing is more dangerous than to allow oneself liberty to construct for the parties contracts which they have not in terms made by importing implications which would appear to make the contract more businesslike or more just. The implications to be made are to be no more than are "necessary" for giving business efficacy to the transaction, and it appears to me that, both as to existing facts and future facts, a condition would not be implied unless the new state of facts makes the contract something different in kind from the contract in the original state of facts. Thus, in *Krell* v. *Henry* (1903), Vaughan Williams L.J. finds that the subject of the contract was "rooms to view the procession": the postponement, therefore, made the rooms not rooms to view the procession. This also is the test finally chosen by Lord Sumner in *Bank Line* v. *Arthur Capel & Co.* (1919), agreeing with Lord Dunedin in *Metropolitan Water Board* v. *Dick Kerr* (1918), where, dealing with the criterion for determining the effect of interruption in "frustrating" a contract, he says: "An interruption may be so long as to destroy the identity of the work or service, when resumed, with the work or service when interrupted." We there get a common standard for mutual mistake, and implied conditions whether as to existing or as to future facts. Does the state of the new facts destroy the identity of the subject-matter as it was in the original state of facts? To apply the principle to the infinite combinations of facts that arise in actual experience will continue to be difficult, but if this case results in establishing order into what has been a somewhat confused and difficult branch of the law it will have served a useful purpose.

I have already stated my reasons for deciding that in the present case the identity of the subject-matter was not destroyed by the mutual mistake, if any, and need not repeat them.

[Lord Atkin then went on to hold that there was no duty on Bell to disclose the improper transactions. The relationship of employer and employee is not of the kind mentioned at p. 485 as being of *uberrimae fidei* (of the utmost good faith).]

The result is that in the present case servants unfaithful in some of their work retain large compensation which some will think they do not deserve. Nevertheless it is of greater importance that well established principles of contract should be maintained than that a particular hardship should be redressed; and I see no way of giving relief to the plaintiffs in the present circumstances except by confiding to the Courts loose powers of introducing terms into contracts which would only serve to introduce doubt and confusion where certainty is essential.

[Lord Blanesburgh and Lord Thankerton agreed with Lord Atkin in giving judgment for the defendant Bell.

Viscount Hailsham and Lord Warrington dissented on the grounds that the erroneous assumption of the parties was indeed fundamental, "as fundamental to the bargain as any error one can imagine."]

Note

Of the nine judges who were at different times involved in the case, six disagreed with the majority in the House of Lords.

Questions

1. Was the conclusion which Lord Atkin came to in the final paragraph of his judgment really so inevitable? Were the principles enunciated in his judgment correctly applied to the facts?
2. Would *Bell's* case be decided in the same way today?

Associated Japanese Bank (International) Ltd. v. Crédit du Nord SA and another

[1988] 3 All E.R. 902 (Q.B.D.)

[The plaintiff bank had entered into an agreement with B. for the lease of certain machines. The defendant bank had guaranteed B.'s obligations under the arrangement. Unknown to both the plaintiff and the defendant, B. had acted fraudulently and the machines which were the subject-matter of the transaction did not actually exist. The plaintiff nevertheless sued the defendant under the guarantee. The common mistake of the parties therefore became a central issue in the case.]

Steyn J. Throughout the law of contract two themes regularly recur: respect for the sanctity of contract and the need to give effect to the reasonable expectations of honest men. Usually, these themes work in the same direction. Occasionally, they point to opposite solutions. The law regarding common mistake going to the root of a contract is a case where tension arises between the two themes. That is illustrated by the circumstances of this extraordinary case....

Mistake

The common law regarding mutual or common mistake

There was a lively debate about the common law rules governing a mutual or common mistake of the parties as to some essential quality of the subject-matter of the contract. Counsel for CDN submitted that *Bell* v. *Lever Bros. Ltd.* (1932) authoritatively established that a mistake by both parties as to the existence of some quality of the subject-matter of the contract, which makes the subject-matter of the contract without the quality essentially different from the subject-matter as it was believed to be, renders the contract void ab initio. Counsel for AJB contested this proposition. He submitted that at common law a mistake even as to an essential quality of the subject-matter of the contract will not affect the contract unless it resulted in a total failure of consideration. It was not clear to me that this formulation left any meaningful and independent scope for the application of common law rules in this area of the law. In any event, it is necessary to examine the legal position in some detail.

The landmark decision is undoubtedly *Bell* v. *Lever Bros. Ltd.* Normally a judge of first instance would simply content himself with applying the law stated by the House of Lords.

There has, however, been substantial controversy about the rule established in that case. It seems right therefore to examine the effect of that decision against a somewhat wider framework. In the early history of contract law, the common law's preoccupation with consideration made the development of a doctrine of mistake impossible. Following the emergence in the nineteenth century of the theory of consensus ad idem it became possible to treat misrepresentation, undue influence and mistake as factors vitiating consent. Given that the will theory in English contract law was cast in objective form, judging matters by the external standard of the reasonable man, both as to contract formation and contractual interpretation, it nevertheless became possible to examine in what circumstances mistake might nullify or negative consent. But even in late Victorian times there was another powerful policy consideration militating against upsetting bargains on the ground of unexpected circumstances which occurred before or after the contract. That was the policy of caveat emptor which held sway outside the field of contract law subsequently codified by the Sale of Goods Act in 1893. Nevertheless, principles affecting the circumstances in which consent may be vitiated gradually emerged. The most troublesome areas proved to be two related areas, *viz*, common mistake as to an essential quality of the subject-matter of the contract and post-contractual frustration. Blackburn J., an acknowledged master of the common law, who yielded to no one in his belief in the sanctity of contract, led the way in both areas.

In *Taylor* v. *Caldwell* (1863) Blackburn J. first stated the doctrine of frustration in terms which eventually led to the adoption of the "radical change in obligation" test of commercial frustration in modern law: see *Davis Contractors Ltd.* v. *Fareham U.D.C.* (1956); *National Carriers Ltd.* v. *Panalpina (Northern) Ltd.* (1981). In the field of mistake as to the essential quality of the subject-matter Blackburn J. also gave the lead. In *Kennedy* v. *Panama New Zealand and Australian Royal Mail Co. Ltd.* (1867) the issue was whether a contract for the purchase of shares was vitiated by an untrue representation that the company had secured a contract to carry mail for the New Zealand government. The court upheld the contract. In passing it must be noted that the case was decided on a restrictive approach as to the circumstances in which a contract can be rescinded for innocent misrepresentation; that, of course, was remedied in due course by equity. But in the present context the importance of the case lies in the remarks of Blackburn J. about mistakes as to quality (at 586–590). Given the fact that there was no direct authority on the point (and certainly none which could not be explained on other grounds) he turned to the civil law. He referred to the civilian doctrine of error in substantia. That doctrine seeks to categorise mistakes into two categories, *viz*, mistakes as to the substance of the subject-matter or mistakes as to attributes (sometimes classified as mistakes in motive). Blackburn J., delivering the judgment of the court, held (at 588):

> "... the principle of our law is the same as that of the civil law; and the difficulty in every case is to determine whether the mistake or misapprehension is as to the substance of the whole consideration, going, as it were, to the root of the matter, or only to some point, even though a material point, an error as to which does not affect the substance of the whole consideration."

That test did not avail the plaintiff, for it was held that he got what he bought.

None of the cases between the decisions in *Kennedy* v. *Panama New Zealand and Australian Royal Mail Co. Ltd.* and *Bell* v. *Lever Bros. Ltd.* significantly contributed to the development of this area of the law. But *Bell* v. *Lever Bros. Ltd.* was a vitally important case. The facts of that case are so well known as to require no detailed exposition. Lever Bros. had, in the modern phrase, given two employees "golden handshakes" of £30,000 and £20,000 in consideration of early termination of their service contracts. Subsequently, Lever Bros discovered that the contracts of service had been voidable by reason of the two employees' breach of fiduciary duties in trading for their own account. Lever Bros. argued that the contracts pursuant to which the service agreements were terminated were void ab initio for common mistake, and sought recovery of the sums paid to the employees. The claim succeeded at first instance and in the Court of Appeal but by a three to two majority the House of Lords held that the claim failed. Lord Atkin held:

> "... a mistake will not affect assent unless it is the mistake of both parties, and is as to the existence of some quality which makes the thing without the quality essentially different from the thing as it was believed to be."

In my view none of the other passages in Lord Atkin's speech detract from that statement of the law. Lord Thankerton came to a similar conclusion. He held that common mistake "can only properly relate to something which both must necessarily have accepted in their minds as an essential and integral part

of the subject-matter" (see [1932] A.C. 161 at 235, [1931] All
E.R. Rep. 1 at 36).

That seems to me exactly the same test as Lord Atkin
enunciated. Clearly, Lotd Atkin did not conceive of any
difference between his formulation and that of Lord Thankerton, for he observed:

> "To apply the principle to the infinite combinations of facts
> that arise in actual experience will continue to be difficult,
> but if this case results in establishing order into what has
> been a somewhat confused and difficult branch of the law it
> will have served a useful purpose."

Lord Blanesburgh's speech proceeded on different lines. It
must not be forgotten that the issue of common mistake was
only put forward at the eleventh hour. Lord Blanesburgh
would have refused the necessary amendment, but he
expressed his "entire accord" with the substantive views of
Lord Atkin and Lord Thankerton (see [1932] A.C. 161 at
198–199, [1931] All E.R. Rep. 1 at 18–19). The majority were
therefore in agreement about the governing principle.

It seems to me that the better view is that the majority in
Bell v. *Lever Bros. Ltd.* had in mind only mistake at common
law. That appears to be indicated by the shape of the
argument, the proposed amendment placed before the House
of Lords (see [1932] A.C. 161 at 191, [1931] All E.R. Rep. 1 at
15) and the speeches of Lord Atkin and Lord Thankerton.
But, if I am wrong on this point, it is nevertheless clear that
mistake at common law was in the forefront of the analysis in
the speeches of the majority.

The law has not stood still in relation to mistake in equity.
Today, it is clear that mistake in equity is not circumscribed
by common law definitions. A contract affected by mistake in
equity is not void but may be set aside on terms: see *Solle* v.
Butcher (1949) [and see below p. 494]; *Magee* v. *Pennine
Insurance Co. Ltd.* (1969); *Grist* v. *Bailey* (1966). It does not
follow, however, that *Bell* v. *Lever Bros. Ltd.* is no longer an
authoritative statement of mistake at common law. On the
contrary, in my view the principles enunciated in that case
clearly still govern mistake at common law. It is true that in
Solle v. *Butcher* (1949) Denning L.J. interpreted *Bell* v. *Lever
Bros. Ltd.* differently. He said that a common mistake, even
on a most fundamental matter, does not make the contract
void at law. That was an individual opinion. Neither Bucknill
L.J. (who agreed in the result) nor Jenkins L.J. (who
dissented) even mentioned *Bell* v. *Lever Bros. Ltd.* In *Magee* v.
Pennine Insurance Co. Ltd. (1969) Lord Denning M.R. returned
to the point. About *Bell* v. *Lever Bros. Ltd.* he simply said: "I

do not propose ... to go through the speeches in that case. They have given enough trouble to commentators already." He then repeated his conclusion in *Solle* v. *Butcher*. Winn L.J. dissented. Fenton Atkinson L.J. agreed in the result but it is clear from his judgment that he did not agree with Lord Denning M.R.'s interpretation of *Bell* v. *Lever Bros. Ltd.* (see [1969] 2 All E.R. 891 at 896, [1969] 2 Q.B. 507 at 517–518). Again, Lord Denning M.R.'s observation represented only his own view. With the profoundest respect to the former Master of the Rolls, I am constrained to say that in my view his interpretation of *Bell* v. *Lever Bros. Ltd.* does not do justice to the speeches of the majority.

When Lord Denning M.R. referred in *Magee* v. *Pennine Insurance Co. Ltd.* to the views of commentators he may have had in mind comments in Cheshire and Fifoot *Law of Contract* (6th edn., 1964) p. 196. In substance the argument was that the actual decision in *Bell* v. *Lever Bros. Ltd.* contradicts the language of the speeches. If the test was not satisfied there, so the argument runs, it is difficult to see how it could ever be satisfied: see the latest edition of this valuable textbook for the same argument (Cheshire, Fifoot and Furmston *Law of Contract* (11th edn., 1986) pp. 225–226). This is a point worth examining because at first glance it may seem persuasive. *Bell* v. *Lever Bros. Ltd.* was a quite exceptional case; all their Lordships were agreed that common mistake had not been pleaded and would have required an amendment in the House of Lords if it were to succeed. The speeches do not suggest that the employees were entitled to keep both the gains secretly made and the golden handshakes. The former were clearly recoverable from them. Nevertheless, the golden handshakes were very substantial. But there are indications in the speeches that the so-called "merits" were not all in favour of Lever Bros. The company was most anxious, because of a corporate merger, to terminate the two service agreements. There was apparently a doubt whether the voidability of the service agreements if revealed to the company *at the time of the severance contract* would have affected the company's decision. Lord Thankerton said:

"... I do not find sufficient material to compel the inference that the appellants, at the time of the contract, regarded the indefeasibility of the service agreements as an essential and integral element in the subject-matter of the bargain."

Lord Atkin clearly regarded it as a hard case on the facts, but concluded "on the whole" that the plea of common mistake must fail (see [1932] A.C. 161 at 223, [1931] All E.R. Rep. 1 at

30). It is noteworthy that Lord Atkin commented on the scarcity of evidence as to the subsidiaries from the boards of which the two employees resigned (see [1932] A.C. 161 at 212, [1931] All E.R. Rep. 1 at 25). Lord Blanesburgh's speech was directed to his conclusion that the amendment ought not to be allowed. He did, however, make clear that "the mistake must go to the whole consideration," and pointed to the advantages (other than the release from the service agreements) which Lever Bros. received (see [1932] A.C. 161 at 181, 197, [1931] All E.R. Rep. 1 at 10, 18). Lord Blanesburgh emphasised that Lever Bros. secured the *future* co-operation of the two employees for the carrying through of the amalgamation (see [1932] A.C. 161 at 181, [1931] All E.R. Rep. 1 at 10). And the burden, of course, rested squarely on Lever Bros. With due deference to the distinguished authors who have argued that the actual decision in *Bell* v. *Lever Bros. Ltd.* contradicts the principle enunciated in the speeches it seems to me that their analysis is altogether too simplistic, and that the actual decision was rooted in the particular facts of the case. In my judgment there is no reason to doubt the substantive reasons emerging from the speeches of the majority.

No one could fairly suggest that in this difficult area of the law there is only one correct approach or solution. But a narrow doctrine of common law mistake (as enunciated in *Bell* v. *Lever Bros. Ltd.*), supplemented by the more flexible doctrine of mistake in equity (as developed in *Solle* v. *Butcher* and later cases), seems to me to be an entirely sensible and satisfactory state of the law: see *Sheikh Bros. Ltd.* v. *Ochsner* (1957). And there ought to be no reason to struggle to avoid its application by artificial interpretations of *Bell* v. *Lever Bros. Ltd.*

It might be useful if I now summarised what appears to me to be a satisfactory way of approaching this subject. Logically, before one can turn to the rules as to mistake, whether at common law or in equity, one must first determine whether the contract itself, by express or implied condition precedent or otherwise, provides who bears the risk of the relevant mistake. It is at this hurdle that many pleas of mistake will either fail or prove to have been unnecessary. Only if the contract is silent on the point is there scope for invoking mistake. That brings me to the relationship between common law mistake and mistake in equity. Where common law mistake has been pleaded, the court must first consider this plea. If the contract is held to be void, no question of mistake in equity arises. But, if the contract is held to be valid, a plea of mistake in equity may still have to be considered: see *Grist* v. *Bailey* (1966) and the analysis in *Anson's Law of Contract* (26th edn., 1984) pp. 290–291. Turning now to the approach to common law mistake, it seems to me that the following propositions are valid although not necessarily all entitled to be dignified as propositions of law.

The first imperative must be that the law ought to uphold rather than destroy apparent contracts. Second, the common law rules as to a mistake regarding the quality of the subject-matter, like the common law rules regarding commercial frustration, are designed to cope with the impact of unexpected and wholly exceptional circumstances on apparent contracts. Third, such a mistake in order to attract legal consequences must substantially be shared by both parties, and must relate to facts as they existed at the time the contract was made. Fourth, and this is the point established by *Bell* v. *Lever Bros. Ltd.*, the mistake must render the subject-matter of the contract essentially and radically different from the subject-matter which the parties believed to exist. While the civilian distinction between the substance and attributes of the subject-matter of a contract has played a role in the development of our law (and was cited in the speeches in *Bell* v. *Lever Bros. Ltd.*), the principle enunciated in *Bell* v. *Lever Bros Ltd.* is markedly narrower in scope than the civilian doctrine. It is therefore no longer useful to invoke the civilian distinction. The principles enunciated by Lord Atkin and Lord Thankerton represent the ratio decidendi of *Bell* v. *Lever Bros. Ltd.* Fifth, there is a requirement which was not specifically discussed in *Bell* v. *Lever Bros. Ltd.* What happens if the party who is seeking to rely on the mistake had no reasonable grounds for his belief? An extreme example is that of the man who makes a contract with minimal knowledge of the facts to which the mistake relates but is content that it is a good speculative risk. In my judgment a party cannot be allowed to rely on a common mistake where the mistake consists of a belief which is entertained by him without any reasonable grounds for such belief: *cf. McRae* v. *Commonwealth Disposals Commission* (1951) 84 C.L.R. 377 at 408. That is not because principles such as estoppel or negligence require it, but simply because policy and good sense dictate that the positive rules regarding common mistake should be so qualified. Curiously enough this qualification is similar to the civilian concept where the doctrine of error in substantia is tempered by the principles governing culpa in contrahendo. More importantly, a recognition of this qualification is consistent with the approach in equity where fault on the part of the party adversely affected by the mistake will generally preclude the granting of equitable relief: see *Solle* v. *Butcher* [1949] 2 All E.R. 1107 at 1120, [1950] 1 K.B. 671 at 693.

[Applying these principles to the facts of the case Steyn J. dismissed the plaintiff's claim.]

3. MISTAKE AND EQUITY

Solle v. Butcher

[1950] 1 K.B. 671 (C.A.)

[A. agreed to let a flat to B. for seven years at a rent of £250 a year. Both parties assumed that the Rent Acts did not apply to the property. In fact, it was so subject and the maximum rent permitted was only £140. The plaintiff sued to recover the amount of rent paid out over and above the rate of £140 per year; the defendant counterclaimed for rescission of the agreement on the grounds of mistake. One of the results of the application of the Rent Acts was that notice to increase the rent from the permitted amount of £140 could not be given during the currency of the contractual tenancy. The landlord therefore stood to lose after both parties had entered an agreement under a serious misapprehension as to the nature of the property.]

Denning L.J. In this plight the landlord seeks to set aside the lease. He says, with truth, that it is unfair that the tenant should have the benefit of the lease for the outstanding five years of the term at 140*l.* a year, when the proper rent is 250*l.* a year. If he cannot give a notice of increase now, can he not avoid the lease? The only ground on which he can avoid it is on the ground of mistake. It is quite plain that the parties were under a mistake. They thought that the flat was not tied down to a controlled rent, whereas in fact it was. In order to see whether the lease can be avoided for this mistake it is necessary to remember that mistake is of two kinds: the first, mistake which renders the contract void, that is, a nullity from the beginning, which is the kind of mistake which was dealt with by the courts of common law; and, secondly, mistake which renders the contract not void, but voidable, that is, liable to be set aside on such terms as the court thinks fit, which is the kind of mistake which was dealt with by the courts of equity. Much of the difficulty which has attended this subject has arisen because before the fusion of law and equity, the courts of common law, in order to do justice in the case in hand, extended this doctrine of mistake beyond its proper limits and held contracts to be void which were really only voidable, a process which was capable of being attended with much injustice to third persons who had bought goods or otherwise committed themselves on the faith that there was a contract. In the well-known case of *Cundy* v. *Lindsay* (1878), Cundy suffered such an injustice. He bought the handkerchiefs from the rogue, Blenkarn, before the Judicature Acts came into operation. Since the fusion of law and equity, there is no reason to continue this process, and it will be found that only those contracts are now held void in which the mistake was such as to prevent the formation of any contract at all.

Let me first consider mistakes which render a contract a nullity. All previous decisions on this subject must now be read in the light of *Bell* v. *Lever Bros. Ltd.* (1932). The correct interpretation of that case, to my mind, is that, once a contract has been made, that is to say, once the parties, whatever their inmost states of mind, have to all outward appearances agreed with sufficient certainty in the same terms on the same subject-matter, then the contract is good unless and until it is set aside for failure of some condition on which the existence of the contract depends, or for fraud, or on some equitable ground. Neither party can rely on his own mistake to say it was a nullity from the beginning, no matter that it was a mistake which to his mind was fundamental, and no matter that the other party knew that he was under a mistake. *A fortiori*, if the other party did not know of the mistake, but shared it. The cases where goods have perished at the time of sale, or belong to the buyer, are really contracts which are not void for mistake but are void by reason of an implied condition precedent, because the contract proceeded on the basic assumption that it was possible of performance. So far as cases later than *Bell* v. *Lever Bros. Ltd.* (1932) are concerned, I do not think that *Sowler* v. *Potter* (1940) can stand with *King's Norton Metal Co. Ltd.* v. *Edridge* (1897), which shows that the doctrine of French law as enunciated by Pothier is no part of English law. Nor do I think that the contract in *Nicholson and Venn* v. *Smith-Marriott* (1947) was void from the beginning.

Applying these principles, it is clear that here there was a contract. The parties agreed in the same terms on the same subject-matter. It is true that the landlord was under a mistake which was to him fundamental: he would not for one moment have considered letting the flat for seven years if it meant that he could only charge 140*l.* a year for it. He made the fundamental mistake of believing that the rent he could charge was not tied down to a controlled rent; but, whether it was his own mistake or a mistake common to both him and the tenant, it is not a ground for saying that the lease was from the beginning a nullity. Any other view would lead to remarkable results, for it would mean that, in the many cases where the parties mistakenly think a house is outside the Rent Restriction Acts when it is really within them, the tenancy would be a nullity, and the tenant would have to go; with the result that the tenants would not dare to seek to have their rents reduced to the permitted amounts lest they should be turned out.

Let me next consider mistakes which render a contract voidable, that is, liable to be set aside on some equitable ground. Whilst presupposing that a contract was good at law, or at any rate not void, the court of equity would often relieve a party from the consequences of his own mistake, so long as it could do so without injustice to third parties. The court, it was said, had power to set aside the contract whenever it was of opinion that it was unconscientious for the other party to avail himself of the legal advantage which he had obtained: *Torrance* v. *Bolton* (1872) *per* James L.J.

The court had, of course, to define what it considered to be unconscientious, but in this respect equity has shown a progressive development. It is now clear that a contract will be set aside if the mistake of the one party has been induced by a material misrepresentation of the other, even though it was not fraudulent or fundamental; or if one party, knowing that the other is mistaken about the terms of an offer, or the identity of the person by whom it is made, lets him remain under his delusion and concludes a contract on the mistaken terms instead of pointing out the mistake. That is, I venture to think, the ground on which the defendant in *Smith* v. *Hughes* (1871) would be exempted nowadays, and on which, according to the view by Blackburn J. of the facts, the contract in *Lindsay* v. *Cundy* (1878), was voidable and not void; and on which the lease in *Sowler* v. *Potter* (1940), was, in my opinion, voidable and not void.

A contract is also liable in equity to be set aside if the parties were under a common misapprehension either as to facts or as to their relative and respective rights, provided that the misapprehension was fundamental and that the party seeking to set it aside was not himself at fault. That principle was first applied to private rights as long ago as 1730 in *Landsdown* v. *Lansdown* (1730). There were four brothers, and the second and third of them died. The eldest brother entered on the lands of the deceased brothers, but the youngest brother claimed them. So the two rival brothers consulted a friend who was a local schoolmaster. The friend looked up a book which he then had with him called the Clerk's Remembrancer and gave it as his opinion that the lands belonged to the youngest brother. He recommended the two of them to take further advice, which at first they intended to do, but they did not do so; and, acting on the friend's opinion, the elder brother agreed to divide the estate with the younger brother, and executed deeds and bonds giving effect to the agreement. Lord Chancellor King declared that the documents were obtained by a mistake and by a misrepresentation of the law by the friend, and ordered them to be given up to be cancelled. He pointed out that the maxim ignorantia juris non excusat only means that ignorance cannot be pleaded in excuse of crimes. Eighteen years later, in the time of Lord Hardwicke, the same principle was applied in *Bingham* v. *Bingham* (1748).

If and in so far as those cases were compromises of disputed rights, they have been subjected to justifiable criticism, but, in cases where there is no element of compromise, but only of mistaken rights, the House of Lords in 1867 in the great case of *Cooper* v. *Phibbs* (1867), affirmed the doctrine there acted on as correct. In that case an uncle had told his nephew, not intending to misrepresent anything, but being in fact in error, that he (the uncle) was entitled to a fishery; and the nephew after the uncle's death, acting in the belief of the truth of what the uncle had told him, entered into an agreement to rent the fishery from the uncle's daughters, whereas it actually belonged to the nephew himself. The mistake there as to the title to the fishery did not render the tenancy agreement a nullity. If it had done, the contract would have been void at law from the beginning and equity would have had to follow the law. There would have been no contract to set aside and no terms to impose. The House of Lords, however, held that the mistake was only such as to make it voidable, or, in Lord Westbury's words, "liable to be set aside" on such terms as the court thought fit to impose; and it was so set aside.

The principle so established by *Cooper* v. *Phibbs* (1867), has been repeatedly acted on: see, for instance, *Earl Beauchamp* v. *Winn* (1873), and *Huddersfield Banking Co. Ltd.* v. *Lister* (1895). It is no way impaired by *Bell* v. *Lever Bros. Ltd.* (1932), which was treated in the House of Lords as a case at law depending on whether the contract was a nullity or not. If it had been considered on equitable grounds, the result might have been different. In any case, the principle of *Cooper* v. *Phibbs* has been fully restored by *Norwich Union Fire Insurance Society Ltd.* v. *William H. Price, Ltd.* (1934).

Applying that principle to this case, the facts are that the plaintiff, the tenant, was a surveyor who was employed by the defendant, the landlord, not only to arrange finance for the purchase of the building and to negotiate with the rating authorities as to the new rateable values, but also to let the flats. He was the agent for letting, and he clearly formed the view that the building was not controlled. He told the valuation officer so. He advised the defendant what were the rents which could be charged. He read to the defendant an opinion of counsel relating to the matter, and told him that in his opinion he could charge 250*l*. and that there was no previous control. He said that the flats came outside the Act and that the defendant was "clear." The defendant relied on what the plaintiff told him, and authorised the plaintiff to let at the rentals which he had suggested. The plaintiff not only let the four other flats to other people for a long period of years at the new rentals, but also took one himself for seven years at 250*l*. Now he turns round and says, quite unashamedly, that he wants to take advantage of the mistake to get the flat at 140*l*. a year for seven years instead of the 250*l*. a year, which is not only the rent he agreed to pay but also the fair and economic rent; and it is also the rent permitted by the Acts on compliance with the necessary formalities. If the rules of equity have become so rigid that they cannot remedy such an injustice, it is time we had a new equity, to make good the omission of the old. But, in my view, the established rules are amply sufficient for this case.

On the defendant's evidence, which the judge preferred, I should have thought there was a good deal to be said for the view that the lease was induced by an innocent material misrepresentation by the plaintiff. It seems to me that the plaintiff was not merely expressing an opinion on the law: he was making an unambiguous statement as to private rights; and a misrepresentation as to private rights is equivalent to a misrepresentation of fact for this purpose: *MacKenzie* v. *Royal Bank of Canada* (1934). But it is unnecessary to come to a firm conclusion on this point, because, as Bucknill L.J. has said, there was clearly a common mistake, or, as I would prefer to describe it, a common misapprehension, which was fundamental and in no way due to any fault of the defendant; and *Cooper* v. *Phibbs* (1867), affords ample authority for saying that, by reason of the common misapprehension, this lease can be set aside on such terms as the court thinks fit.

. . . . . .

The terms will be complicated by reason of the Rent Restriction Acts, but it is not beyond the wit of man to devise them. Subject to any observations which the parties may desire to make, the terms which I suggest are these: the lease should only be set aside if the defendant is prepared to give an undertaking that he will permit the plaintiff to be a licensee of the premises pending the grant of a new lease. Then, whilst the plaintiff is a licensee, the defendant will in law be in possession of the premises, and will be able to serve on the plaintiff, as prospective tenant, a notice under s.7, sub-s.4, of the Act of 1938 increasing the rent to the full permitted amount. The defendant must further be prepared to give an undertaking that he will serve such a notice within three weeks from the drawing up of the order, and that he will, if written request is made by the plaintiff, within one month of the service of the notice, grant him a new lease at the full permitted amount of rent, not, however, exceeding 250*l.* a year, for a term expiring on September 29, 1954, subject in all other respects to the same covenants and conditions as in the rescinded lease. If there is any difference of opinion about the figures stated in the notice, that can, of course, be adjusted during the currency of the lease. If the plaintiff does not choose to accept the licence or the new lease, he must go out. He will not be entitled to the protection of the Rent Restriction Acts because, the lease being set aside, there will be no initial contractual tenancy from which a statutory tenancy can spring.

[Bucknill L.J. concurred in giving judgment in the terms indicated by Denning L.J. Jenkins L.J. dissented.]

Notes

For a similar approach to problems of mistake, see *Grist* v. *Bailey* (1967) and *Magee* v. *Pennine Insurance Co. Ltd.* (1969) (H.S.B., p. 500). Would the well-known case of *Leaf* v. *International Galleries* (1950) (H.S.B., pp. 490, 499) now be disposed of using the court's equitable jurisdiction?

4. MISTAKE AS TO THE AGREEMENT BETWEEN THE PARTIES

Smith v. Hughes

(1871) L.R. 6 Q.B. 507 (Q.B.)

[The defendant was shown a sample of oats by the plaintiff. He wanted old oats as the plaintiff apparently knew. The defendant agreed to buy them, labouring under the misapprehension that they were old oats, which was the only kind he had any use for. There was no evidence of fraud, but there was a conflict of evidence over whether or not the parties had specifically referred to "old oats" or just "oats." When he realised the mistake, the defendant refused to accept the oats and the plaintiff sued for the price. The judge directed the jury to consider two questions. First, had the parties used the word "old" of the oats? If so, judgment for the defendant. If not, then secondly, did they believe that the plaintiff believed the defendant to believe, or to be under the impression, that he was contracting for old oats? If so, again there would be judgment for the defendant. The jury found for the defendant, and the plaintiff appealed on the grounds that the judge had misdirected the jury.]

Cockburn C.J. It is to be regretted that the jury were not required to give specific answers to the questions so left to them. For, it is quite possible that their verdict may have been given for the defendant on the first ground; in which case there could, I think, be no doubt as to the propriety of the judge's direction; whereas now, as it is possible that the verdict of the jury—or at all events of some of them—may have proceeded on the second ground, we are called upon to consider and decide whether the ruling of the learned judge with reference to the second question was right.

For this purpose we must assume that nothing was said on the subject of the defendant's manager desiring to buy *old* oats, nor of the oats having been said to be old; while, on the other hand, we must assume that the defendant's manager believed the oats to be old oats, and that the plaintiff was conscious of the existence of such belief, but did nothing, directly or indirectly, to bring it about, simply offering his oats and exhibiting his sample, remaining perfectly passive as to what was passing in the mind of the other party. The question is whether, under such circumstances, the passive acquiescence of the seller in the self-deception of the buyer will entitle the latter to avoid the contract. I am of opinion that it will not.

The oats offered to the defendant's manager were a specific parcel, of which the sample submitted to him formed a part. He kept the sample for 24 hours, and had, therefore, full opportunity of inspecting it and forming his judgment upon it. Acting on his own judgment, he wrote to the plaintiff, offering him a price. Having this opportunity of inspecting and judging of the sample, he is practically in the same position as if he had inspected the oats in bulk. It cannot be said that, if he had gone and personally inspected the oats in bulk, and then, believing—but without anything being said or done by the seller to bring about such a belief—that the oats were old, had offered a price for them, he would have been justified in repudiating the contract, because the seller, from the known habits of the buyer, or other circumstances, had reason to infer that the buyer was ascribing to the oats a quality they did not possess, and did not undeceive him.

I take the true rule to be, that where a specific article is offered for sale, without express warranty, or without circumstances from which the law will imply a warranty—as where, for instance, an article is ordered for a specific purpose—and the buyer has full opportunity of inspecting and forming his own judgment, if he chooses to act on his own judgment, the rule caveat emptor applies. If he gets the article he contracted to buy, and that article corresponds with what it was sold as, he gets all he is entitled to, and is bound by the contract. Here the defendant agreed to buy a specific parcel of oats. The oats were what they were sold as, namely, good oats according to the sample. The buyer persuaded himself they were old oats, when they were not so; but the seller neither said nor did anything to contribute to his deception. He has himself to blame. The question is not what a man of scrupulous morality or nice honour would do under such circumstances.

The case put of the purchase of an estate, in which there is a mine under the surface, but the fact is unknown to the seller, is one in which a man of tender conscience or high honour would be unwilling to take advantage of the ignorance of the seller; but there can be no doubt that the contract for the sale of the estate would be binding. . . .

Now, in this case, there was plainly no legal obligation in the plaintiff in the first instance to state whether the oats were new or old. He offered them for sale according to the sample, as he had a perfect right to do, and gave the buyer the fullest opportunity of inspecting the sample, which, practically, was equivalent to an inspection of the oats themselves. What, then, was there to create any trust or confidence between the parties, so as to make it incumbent on the plaintiff to communicate the fact that the oats were not, as the defendant assumed them to be, old oats? If, indeed, the buyer, instead of acting on his own opinion, had asked the question whether the oats were old or new, or had said anything which intimated his understanding that the seller was selling the oats as old oats, the case would have been wholly different; or even if he had said anything which shewed that he was not acting on his own inspection and judgment, but assumed as the foundation of the contract that the oats were old, the silence of the seller, as a means of misleading him, might have amounted to a fraudulent concealment, such as would have entitled the buyer to avoid the contract. Here, however, nothing of the sort occurs. The buyer in no way refers to the seller, but acts entirely on his own judgment. . . .

It only remains to deal with an argument which was pressed upon us, that the defendant in the present case intended to buy old oats, and the plaintiff to sell new, so the two minds were not ad idem; and that consequently there was no contract. This argument proceeds on the fallacy of confounding what was merely a motive operating on the buyer to induce him to buy with one of the essential conditions of the contract. Both parties were agreed as to the sale and purchase of this particular parcel of oats. The defendant believed the oats to be old, and was thus induced to agree to buy them, but he omitted to make their age a condition of the contract. All that can be said is, that the two minds were not ad idem as to the age of the oats; they certainly were ad idem as to the sale and purchase of them. Suppose a person to buy a horse without a warranty, believing him to be sound, and the horse turns out unsound, could it be contended that it would be open to him to say that, as he had intended to buy a sound horse, and the seller to sell an unsound one, the contract was void, because the seller must have known from the price the buyer was willing to give, or from his general habits as a buyer of horses, that he thought the horse was sound? The cases are exactly parallel.

The result is that, in my opinion, the learned judge of the county court was wrong in leaving the second question to the jury, and that consequently, the case must go down to a new trial.

Blackburn J. The jury were directed that, if they believed the word "old" was used, they should find for the defendant—and this was right; for if that was the case, it is obvious that neither did the defendant intend to enter into a contract on the plaintiff's terms, that is, to buy this parcel of oats without any stipulation as to their quality; nor could the plaintiff have been led to believe he was intending to do so.

But the second direction raises the difficulty. I think that, if from that direction the jury would understand that they were first to consider whether they were satisfied that the defendant intended to buy this parcel of oats on the terms that it was part of his contract with the plaintiff that were old oats, so as to have the warranty of the plaintiff to that effect, they were properly told that, if that was so, the defendant could not be bound to a contract without any such warranty unless the plaintiff was misled. But I doubt whether the direction would bring to the minds of the jury the distinction between agreeing to take the oats under the belief that they were old, and agreeing to take the oats under the belief that the plaintiff contracted that they were old.

The difference is the same as that between buying a horse believed to be sound, and buying one believed to be warranted sound; but I doubt if it was made obvious to the jury, and I doubt this the more because I do not see much evidence to justify a finding for the defendant on this latter ground if the word "old" was not used. There may have been more evidence than is stated in the case; and the demeanour of the witnesses may have strengthened the impression produced by the evidence there was; but it does not seem a very satisfactory verdict if it proceeded on this latter ground. I agree, therefore, in the result that there should be a new trial.

New Trial ordered.

Notes

Whilst an agreement mistake as to the quality of the subject-matter will not normally be sufficient, it may be otherwise if the mistake of quality was so great that it really amounted to a mistake of identity, see *Nicholson & Venn* v. *SmithMarriott* (1947) (H.S.B. 505).

Although it may not always be very apparent, there is a distinction drawn between mistake as to a quality and mistake as to the subject-matter. The latter provides a basis for operative mistake. Examples are the decisions in *Scriven Bros. & Co.* v. *Hindley & Co.* (1913) and *Raffles* v. *Wichelhaus* (1864) (H.S.B. 504).

Question

What is the *ratio decidendi* of *Smith* v. *Hughes*? What of Denning L.J.'s approach to the case in *Solle* v. *Butcher* (above, p. 517)?

5. MISTAKE AS TO IDENTITY

Cundy v. Lindsay

(1878) 3 App.Cas. 459 (H.L.)

[A respectable firm of merchants called "Blenkiron & Co." carried on business at 123 Wood Street, London. A rogue called Blenkarn hired a room, also in Wood Street and placed an order for handkerchiefs with Lindsay & Co. The order came in a letter which gave the Wood Street address and was signed in such a way that it could have been read as "Bleniron & Co." The plaintiffs delivered the handkerchiefs, the rogue failed to pay. Before the fraud was discovered Cundy had bought the goods in good faith from Blenkarn. Lindsay sued Cundy for conversion. The question therefore arose as to the status of the agreement between Lindsay and the rogue. If it was only voidable, title has passed to Cundy. If it was void, Lindsay had never lost title to the goods.]

Lord Cairns L.C. Now, my Lords, there are two observations bearing upon the solution of that question which I desire to make. In the first place, if the property in the goods in question passed, it could only pass by way of contract; there is nothing else which could have passed the property. The second observation is that, your Lordships are not here embarrassed by any conflict of evidence, or any evidence whatever as to conversations or as to acts done, the whole history of the whole transaction lies upon paper. The principal parties concerned, the Respondents and *Blenkarn*, never came in contact personally—everything that was done was done by writing. What has to be judged of, and what the jury in the present case had to judge of, was merely the conclusion to be derived from that writing, as applied to the admitted facts of the case.

Now, my Lords, discharging that duty and answering that inquiry, what the jurors have found is in substance this: it is not necessary to spell out the words, because the substance of it is beyond all doubt. They have found that by the form of the signatures to the letters which were written by *Blenkarn*, by the mode in which his letters and his applications to the Respondents were made out, and by the way in which he left uncorrected the mode and form in which, in turn, he was addressed by the Respondents that by all those means he led, and intended to lead, the Respondents, to believe, and they did believe, that the person with whom they were communicating was not *Blenkarn*, the dishonest and irresponsible man, but was a well known and solvent house of *Blenkiron & Co.*, doing business in the same street. My Lords, those things are found as matters of fact, and they are placed beyond the range of dispute and controversy in the case.

If that is so, what is the consequence? It is that *Blenkarn*—the dishonest man, as I call him—was acting here just in the same way as if he had forged the signature of *Blenkiron & Co.*, the respectable firm, to the applications for goods, and as if, when, in return, the goods were forwarded and letters were sent, accompanying them, he had intercepted the goods and intercepted the letters, and had taken possession of the goods, and of the letters which were addressed to, and intended for, not himself but, the firm of *Blenkiron & Co.* Now, my Lords, stating the matter shortly in that way, I ask the question, how is it possible to imagine that in that state of things any contract could have arisen between the Respondents and *Blenkarn*, the dishonest man? Of him they knew nothing, and of him they never thought. With him they never intended to deal. Their minds never, even for an instant of time rested upon him, and as between him and them there was no *consensus* of mind which could lead to any agreement or any contract whatever. As between him and them there was merely the one side to a contract, where, in order to produce a contract, two sides would be required. With the firm of *Blenkiron & Co.* of course there was no contract, for as to them the matter was entirely unknown, and therefore the pretence of a contract was a failure.

The result, therefore, my Lords, is this, that your Lordships have not here to deal with one of those cases in which there is *de facto* a contract made which may afterwards be impeached and set aside, on the ground of fraud; but you have to deal with a case which ranges itself under a completely different chapter of law, the case namely in which the contract never comes into existence. My Lords, that being so, it is idle to talk of the property passing. The property remained, as it originally had been, the property of the Respondents, and the title which was attempted to be given to the Appellants was a title which could not be given to them.

My Lords, I therefore move your Lordships that this appeal be dismissed with costs, and the judgment of the Court of Appeal affirmed.

[Lords Hatherley, Penzance and Gordon concurred.]

Question

Compare the view of Lord Denning at p. 516. Which view is to be preferred?

Lewis v. Averay

[1972] 1 Q.B. 198 (C.A.)

[A rogue offered to buy the plaintiff's car, falsely claiming to be Richard Green, an actor who portrayed the part of Robin Hood. In support of his claim he produced a pass to Pinewood Studios with his name and photograph on it. After paying with a worthless cheque, he sold the car to an innocent purchaser, Averay. When Lewis discovered what had happened, he sued Averay for conversion. The central issue which faced the court was therefore identical to that which arose in *Cundy* v. *Lindsay*.]

Lord Denning M.R. The real question in the case is whether on May 8, 1969, there was a contract of sale under which the property in the car passed from Mr. Lewis to the rogue. If there was such a contract, then, even though it was voidable for fraud, nevertheless Mr. Averay would get a good title to the car. But if there was no contract of sale by Mr. Lewis to the rogue—either because there was, on the face of it, no agreement between the parties, or because any apparent agreement was a nullity and void ab initio for mistake, then no property would pass from Mr. Lewis to the rogue. Mr. Averay would not get a good title because the rogue had no property to pass to him.

There is no doubt that Mr. Lewis was mistaken as to the identity of the person who handed him the cheque. He thought that he was Richard Greene, a film actor of standing and worth: whereas in fact he was a rogue whose identity is quite unknown. It was under the influence of that mistake that Mr. Lewis let the rogue have the car. He would not have dreamed of letting him have it otherwise.

What is the effect of this mistake? There are two cases in our books which cannot, to my mind, be reconciled the one with the other. One of them is *Phillips* v. *Brooks Ltd.* (1919) where a jeweller had a ring for sale. The other is *Ingram* v. *Little* (1961) where two ladies had a car for sale. In each case the story is very similar to the present. A plausible rogue comes along. The rogue says he likes the ring, or the car, as the case may be. He asks the price. The seller names it. The rogue says he is prepared to buy it at that price. He pulls out a cheque book. He writes or prepares to write, a cheque for the price. The seller hesitates. He has never met this man before. He does not want to hand over the ring or the car not knowing whether the cheque will be met. The rogue notices the seller's hesitation. He is quick with his next move. He says to the jeweller in *Phillips* v. *Brooks*: "I am Sir George Bullough of 11 St. James's Square"; or to the ladies in *Ingram* v. *Little* "I am P. G. M. Hutchinson of Stanstead House, Stanstead Road, Caterham"; or to the post-graduate student in the present case: "I am Richard Greene, the film actor of the Robin Hood series." Each seller checks up the information. The jeweller looks up the directory and finds there is a Sir George Bullough at 11 St. James's Square.

The ladies check up too. They look at the telephone directory and find there is a "P. G. M. Hutchinson of Stanstead House, Stanstead Road, Caterham." The post-graduate student checks up too. He examines the official pass of the Pinewood Studios and finds that it is a pass for "Richard A. Green" to the Pinewood Studios with this man's photograph on it. In each case the seller feels that this is sufficient confirmation of the man's identity. So he accepts the cheque signed by the rogue and lets him have the ring, in the one case, and the car and logbook in the other two cases. The rogue goes off and sells the goods to a third person who buys them in entire good faith and pays the price to the rogue. The rogue disappears. The original seller presents the cheque. It is dishonoured. Who is entitled to the goods? The original seller? Or the ultimate buyer? The courts have given different answers. In *Phillips* v. *Brooks*, the ultimate buyer was held to be entitled to the ring. In *Ingram* v. *Little* the original seller was held to be entitled to the car. In the present case the deputy county court judge has held the original seller entitled.

It seems to me that the material facts in each case are quite indistinguishable the one from the other. In each case there was, to all outward appearance, a contract: but there was a mistake by the seller as to the identity of the buyer. This mistake was fundamental. In each case it led to the handing over of the goods. Without it the seller would not have parted with them.

This case therefore raises the question: What is the effect of a mistake by one party as to the identity of the other? It has sometimes been said that if a party makes a mistake as to the identity of the person with whom he is contracting there is no contract, or, if there is a contract, it is a nullity and void, so that no property can pass under it. This has been supported by a reference to the French jurist Pothier; but I have said before, and I repeat now, his statement is no part of English law. . . .

For instance, in *Ingram* v. *Little* (1961) the majority of the court suggested that the difference between *Phillips* v. *Brooks* (1919) and *Ingram* v. *Little* was that in *Phillips* v. *Brooks* the contract of sale was concluded (so as to pass the property to the rogue) before the rogue made the fraudulent misrepresentation . . .: whereas in *Ingram* v. *Little* the rogue made the fraudulent misrepresentation before the contract was concluded. My own view is that in each case the property in the goods did not pass until the seller let the rogue have the goods.

Again it has been suggested that a mistake as to the identity of a person is one thing: and a mistake as to his attributes is another. A mistake as to identity, it is said, avoids a contract: whereas a mistake as to attributes does not. But this is a distinction without a difference. A man's very name is one of his attributes. It is also a key to his identity. If then, he gives a false name, is it a mistake as to his identity?

or a mistake as to his attributes? These fine distinctions do no good to the law.

As I listened to the argument in this case, I felt it wrong that an innocent purchaser (who knew nothing of what passed between the seller and the rogue) should have his title depend on such refinements. After all, he has acted with complete circumspection and in entire good faith: whereas it was the seller who let the rogue have the goods and thus enabled him to commit the fraud. I do not, therefore, accept the theory that a mistake as to identity renders a contract void. I think the true principle is that which underlies the decision of this court in *King's Norton Metal Co. Ltd. v. Edridge Merrett & Co. Ltd.* (1897) and of Horridge J. in *Phillips* v. *Brooks* (1919), which has stood for these last 50 years. It is this: When two parties have come to a contract—or rather what appears, on the face of it, to be a contract—the fact that one party is mistaken as to the identity of the other does not mean that there is no contract, or that the contract is a nullity and void from the beginning. It only means that the contract is voidable, that is, liable to be set aside at the instance of the mistaken person, so long as he does so before the third parties have in good faith acquired rights under it.

Applied to the cases such as the present, this principle is in full accord with the presumption stated by Pearce L.J. and also Devlin L.J. in *Ingram* v. *Little* (1961). When a dealing is had between a seller like Mr. Lewis and a person who is actually there present before him, then the presumption in law is that there is a contract, even though there is a fraudulent impersonation by the buyer representing himself as a different man than he is. There is a contract made with the very person there, who is present in person. It is liable no doubt to be avoided for fraud, but it is still a good contract under which title will pass unless and until it is avoided. In support of that presumption, Devlin L.J. quoted, at p. 66, not only the English case of *Phillips* v. *Brooks,* but other cases in the United States where "the courts hold that if A appeared in person before B, impersonating C, an innocent purchaser from A gets the property in the goods against B." That seems to me to be right in principle in this country also.

In this case Mr. Lewis made a contract of sale with the very man the rogue, who came to the flat. I say that he "made a contract" because in this regard we do not look into his intentions, or into his mind to know what he was thinking or into the mind of the rogue. We look to the outward appearances. On the face of the dealing, Mr. Lewis made a contract under which he sold the car to the rogue, delivered the car and the logbook to him, and took a cheque in return.

The contract is evidenced by the receipts which were signed. It was, of course, induced by fraud. The rogue made false representations as to his identity. But it was still a contract, though voidable for fraud. It was a contract under which this property passed to the rogue, and in due course passed from the rogue to Mr. Averay, before the contract was avoided.

Though I very much regret that either of these good and reliable gentleman should suffer, in my judgment it is Mr. Lewis who should do so. I think the appeal should be allowed and judgment entered for the defendant.

[Phillimore L.J. concurred stating that he thought the case was on all fours with *Phillips* v. *Brooks*. Megaw L.J. concurred stating that the plaintiff had merely made a mistake as to an attribute of the rogue, his credit worthiness.]

Questions

How can *Cundy* v. *Lindsay* and *Lewis* v. *Averay* be distinguished? Are Lord Denning's dicta compatible with the decision in the earlier case?

6. Non est Factum

Saunders v. Anglia Building Society

[1971] A.C. 1004 (H.L.)

[Mrs. Gallie, a 78-year-old widow, was deceived by her nephew, Wally Parkin, into assigning the leasehold interest in her house to a dishonest acquaintance of the nephew, one Lee. She had thought she was merely making a gift of the house to Parkin to enable him to raise money, something she was content to do. The dishonest Lee then mortgaged the house to a building society but defaulted on the mortgage payments. When the building society, who of course were unaware of the way Mr. Lee had obtained title to the property, sought possession of the house they were met by the defence of *non est factum*.]

Lord Pearson. I must, however, deal specifically with the broad principle stated by the Master of the Rolls as his conclusion from his investigation of the law, at pp. 36–37:

"... whenever a man of full age and understanding, who can read and write, signs a legal document which is put before him for signature—by which I mean a document which, it is apparent on the fact of it, is intended to have legal consequences—then, if he does not take the trouble to read it, but signs it as it is, relying on the word of another as to its character or contents or effect, he cannot be heard to say that it is not his document. By his conduct in signing it he has represented, to all those into whose hands it may come, that it is his document: and once they act upon it as being his document, he cannot go back on it, and say it was a nullity from the beginning."

In applying the principle to the resent case, the Master of the Rolls said, at p. 37:

"... Mrs. Gallie cannot in this case say that the deed of assignment was not her deed. She signed it without reading it, relying on the assurance of Lee that it was a deed of gift to Wally. It turned out to be a deed of assignment to Lee. But it was obviously a legal document. She signed it: and the building society advanced money on the faith of it being her document. She cannot now be allowed to disavow her signature."

There can be no doubt that this statement of principle by the Master of the Rolls is not only a clear and concise formulation but also a valuable guide to the right decision to be given by a court in any ordinary case. The danger of giving an undue extension to the plea of *non est factum* has been pointed out in a number of cases. For instance in *Muskham Finance Ltd.* v. *Howard* (1963) Donovan L.J. delivering the judgment of the court said:

"The plea of *non est factum* is a plea which must necessarily be kept within narrow limits. Much confusion and uncertainty would result in the field of contract and elsewhere if a man were permitted to try to disown his signature simply by asserting that he did not understand that which he had signed."

. . . . . .

The principle stated by the Master of the Rolls can and should be applied so as to confine the scope of the plea of *non est factum* within narrow limits. It rightly prevents the plea from being successful in the normal case of a man who, however much he may have been misinformed about the nature of a deed or document, could easily have ascertained its true nature by reading it and has taken upon himself the risk of not reading it.

I think, however, that unless the doctrine of *non est factum*, as it has been understood for at least a hundred years, is to be radically transformed, the statement of principle by the

Master of the Rolls, taken just as it stands, is too absolute and rigid and needs some amplification and qualification. Doubts can be raised as to the meaning of the phrase "a man of full age and understanding, who can read and write." There are degrees of understanding and a person who is a great expert in some subjects may be like a child in relation to other subjects. Does the phrase refer to understanding of things in general, or does it refer to capacity for understanding (not necessarily in more than a general and elementary way) legal documents and property transactions and business transactions?

In my opinion, the plea of *non est factum* ought to be available in a proper case for the relief of a person who for permanent or temporary reasons (not limited to blindness or illiteracy) is not capable of both reading and sufficiently understanding the deed or other document to be signed. By "sufficiently understanding" I mean understanding at least to the point of detecting a fundamental difference between the actual document and the document as the signer had believed it to be. There must be a proper case for such relief. There would not be a proper case if (a) the signature of the document was brought about by negligence of the signer in failing to take precautions which he ought to have taken, or (b) the actual document was not fundamentally different from the document as the signer believed it to be. I will say something later about negligence and about fundamental difference.

In the present case the plaintiff was not at the material time a person who could read, because on the facts found she had broken her spectacles and could not effectively read without them. In any case her evidence (unless it was deliberately false, which has not been argued) shows that she had very little capacity for understanding legal documents and property transactions, and I do not think a reasonable jury would have found that she was negligent. In my opinion, it would not be right to dismiss the plaintiff's appeal on the ground that the principle stated by the Master of the Rolls is applicable to her case. I do not think it is.

The principle as stated is limited to a case in which it is apparent on the fact of the document that it is intended to have legal consequences. That allows for possible success of the plea in a case such as *Lewis* v. *Clay* (1897) where Clay had been induced to sign promissory notes by the cunning deception of a false friend, who caused him to believe that he was merely witnessing the friend's signature on several private and highly confidential documents, the material parts of which had been covered up.

I wish to reserve the question whether the plea of *non est factum* would ever be rightly successful in a case where (1) it is apparent on the face of the document that it is intended to have legal consequences; (2) the signer of the document is able to read and sufficiently understand the document; (3) the document is fundamentally different from what he supposes it to be; (4) he is induced to sign it without reading it. It seems unlikely that the plea ought ever to succeed in such a case, but it is advisable to rule out the wholly exceptional and unpredictable case.

I have said above that the statement of principle by the Master of the Rolls needs to be amplified and qualified unless the doctrine of *non est factum*, as it has been understood for at least at hundred years, is to be radically transformed. What is the doctrine, and should it be radically transformed?

As to the early history, the authorities referred to in the judgment of Byles J. in *Foster* v. *Mackinnon* (1869) (and also referred to in *Holdsworth's History of English Law*, Vol. 8, pp. 50–51) were cited in the argument of this appeal. Having considered them I think they show that the law relating to the plea of *non est factum* remained in an undeveloped state until the judgment in *Foster* v. *Mackinnon*, and the modern development began with that judgment. It was the judgment of the court (Bovill C.J., Byles, Keating and Montague Smith JJ.) delivered by Byles J. He said, at p. 711:

"It seems plain, on principle and on authority, that, if a blind man, or a man who cannot read, or who for some reason (not implying negligence) forbears to read, has a written contract falsely read over to him, the reader misreading to such a degree that the written contract is of a nature altogether different from the contract pretended to be read from the paper which the blind or illiterate man afterwards signs; then, at least if there be no negligence, the signature so obtained is of no force. And it is invalid not merely on the ground of fraud, where fraud exists, but on the ground that the mind of the signer did not accompany the signature; in other words, that he never intended to sign, and therefore in contemplation of law never did sign, the contract to which his name is appended."

In my opinion, the essential features of the doctrine are contained in that passage and the doctrine does not need any radical transformation. A minor comment is that the phrase "who for some reason (not implying negligence) forbears to read" is (to use a currently fashionable word) too "permissive" in its tone. If a person forbears to read the document, he nearly always should be reckoned as negligent or otherwise debarred from succeeding on the plea of *non est factum*.

The passage which I have set out from Byles J.'s judgment, though I think it contains the essential features, was only a brief summary in a leading judgment, and there are further developments which need to be considered.

Ascertainment of the intention: I think the doctrine of *non est factum* inevitably involves applying the subjective rather than the objective test to ascertain the intention. It takes the intention which a man has in his own mind rather than the intention which he manifests to others (the intention which as reasonable men they would infer from his words and conduct).

There are, however, some cases in which the subjective test of intention can be applied so as to produce the same result as would be produced by the objective test. Suppose a man signs a deed without knowing or inquiring or having any positive belief or formed opinion, as to its nature or effect: he signs it because his solicitor or other trusted adviser advises him to do so. Then his intention is to sign the deed that is placed before him, whatever it may be or do. That is the intention in his own mind as well as the intention which by signing he manifests to others. Examples of this will be found in *Hunter* v. *Walters* (1871); *National Provincial Bank of England* v. *Jackson* (1886); *King* v. *Smith* (1900). In *King* v. *Smith*, Farwell J., at p. 430, cited and relied upon a passage in the judgment of Mellish L.J. in *Hunter* v. *Walters* (1871) where he said:

"When a man knows that he is conveying or doing something with his estate, but does not ask what is the precise effect of the deed, because he is told it is a mere form, and has such confidence in his solicitor as to execute the deed in ignorance, then, in my opinion, a deed so executed, although it may be voidable upon the ground of fraud, is not a void deed."

Farwell J. said that Mr. King "had absolute confidence in his solicitor, and executed any deed relating to his property that Eldred put before him."

I think this principle affords a solution to a problem that was raised in the course of the argument. Suppose that the very busy managing director of a large company has a pile of documents to be signed in a few minutes before his next meeting, and his secretary has arranged them for maximum speed with only the spaces for signature exposed, and he "signs them blind," as the saying is, not reading them or even looking at them. He may be exercising a wise economy of his time and energy. There is the possibility of some extraneous document, involving him in unexpected personal liability, having been fraudulently inserted in the pile, but this possibility is so improbable that a reasonable man would disregard it: *Bolton* v. *Stone* (1951). Such conduct is not negligence in any ordinary sense of the word. But the person who signs documents in this way ought to be held bound by them, and ought not to be entitled to avoid liability so as to shift the burden of loss on to an innocent third party. The whole object of having documents signed by him is that he makes them his documents and takes responsibility for them. He takes the chance of a fraudulent substitution. I think the right view of such a case is that the person who signs intends to sign the documents placed before him, whatever they may be, and so there is no basis on which he could successfully plead *non est factum*.

Negligence: It is clear that by the law as it was laid down in *Foster* v. *Mackinnon* (1869) a person who had signed a document differing fundamentally from what he believed it to be would be disentitled from successfully pleading *non est factum* if his signing of the document was due to his own negligence. The word "negligence" in this connection had no special technical meaning. It meant carelessness and in each case it was a question of fact for the jury to decide whether the person relying on the plea had been negligent or not. In *Foster* v. *Mackinnon* the Lord Chief Justice had told the jury that, if the indorsement was not the defendant's signature, or if, being his signature, it was obtained upon a fraudulent representation that it was a guarantee, and the defendant signed it without knowing that it was a bill, and under the belief that it was a guarantee and if the defendant was not guilty of any negligence in so signing the paper, the defendant was entitled to the verdict. On appeal this direction was held to be correct. In *Vorley* v. *Cooke* (1857) Stuart V.-C. said:

"It cannot be said that Cooke's conduct was careless or rash. He was deceived, as anyone with the ordinary amount of intelligence and caution would have been deceived, and he is therefore entitled to be relieved."

Whatever may be thought of the merits of the decision in that case, this passage illustrates the simple approach to the question whether the signer of the deed had been negligent or not. Similarly, in *Lewis* v. *Clay* (1898), Lord Russell of Killowen C.J. left to the jury the question: "Was the defendant, in signing his name as he did, recklessly careless, and did he thereby enable Lord William Nevill to perpetrate the fraud?"

......

The degree of difference required: The judgments in the older cases used a variety of expressions to signify the degree or kind of difference that, for the purposes of the plea of *non est factum*, must be shown to exist between the document as it was and the document as it was believed to be. More recently there has been a tendency to draw a firm distinction between (a) a difference in character or class, which is sufficient for the purposes of the plea, and (b) a difference only in contents, which is not sufficient. This distinction has been helpful in some cases, but, as the judgments of the Court of Appeal have shown, it would produce wrong results if it were applied as a rigid rule for all cases. In my opinion, one has to use a more general phrase, such as "fundamentally different" or "radically different" or "totally different."

I would dismiss the appeal.

[Lords Reid, Hodson, Wilberforce and Viscount Dilhorne concurred in the view that Mrs. Gallie had not established her plea of *non est factum*.]

Note

Even though a plea of *non est factum* may fail, a defendant may still successfully plead that the transaction be set aside on the basis of undue influence. See, *e.g. Avon Finance Co. Ltd.* v. *Bridger* (1985) and below, p. 553.

Chapter 7
Privity

Tweddle v. Atkinson

(1861) 1 B. & S. 393 (Q.B.)

[As part of a marriage settlement William Guy and John Tweddle agreed with each other that they would provide a sum of money for William Tweddle. Guy died without having paid the money so William Tweddle sued his executors for the £200 which he considered had been promised to him.]

Crompton J. It is admitted that the plaintiff cannot succeed unless this case is an exception to the modern and well established doctrine of the action of assumpsit. At the time when the cases which have been cited were decided the action of assumpsit was treated as an action of trespass upon the case, and therefore in the nature of a tort; and the law was not settled, as it now is, that natural love and affection is not a sufficient consideration for promise upon which an action may be maintained; nor was it settled that promisee cannot bring an action unless the consideration for the promise moved from him. The modern cases have, in effect, overruled the old decisions; they shew that the consideration must move from the party entitled to sue upon the contract. It would be a monstrous proposition to say that a person was a party to the contract for the purpose of suing upon it for his own advantage, and not a party to it for the purpose of being sued. It is said that the father in the present case was agent for the son in making the contract, but that argument ought also to make the son liable upon it. I am prepared to overrule the old decisions, and to hold that, by reason of the principles which now govern the action of assumpsit, the present action is not maintainable.

[Wightman and Blackburn JJ. concurred in giving judgment for the defendant.]

Dunlop v. Selfridge

[1915] A.C. 847 (H.L.)

[Dunlop, the plaintiffs who were the appellants in the House of Lords, sold tyres to Dew & Co. under a contract which stated that the buyers would not sell the tyres below a certain price and that a similar term would be part of any agreement between *Dew & Co.* and subsequent purchasers. *Dew & Co.* sold tyres to Selfridge, the respondents, who also agreed not to sell below the fixed price and to pay Dunlop £5 for every tyre sold in breach of this agreement. Selfridge did later supply tyres to customers below the fixed price, and Dunlop sued for damages and an injunction in an attempt to restrain them from doing so.]

Viscount Haldane L.C. My Lords, in the law of England certain principles are fundamental. One is that only a person who is a party to a contract can sue on it. Our law knows nothing of a jus quaesitum tertio arising by way of contract. Such a right may be conferred by way of property, as, for example, under a trust, but it cannot be conferred on a stranger to a contract as a right to enforce the contract in personam. A second principle is that if a person with whom a contract not under seal has been made is to be able to enforce it consideration must have been given by him to the promisor or to some other person at the promisor's request. These two principles are not recognized in the same fashion by the jurisprudence of certain Continental countries or of Scotland, but here they are well established. A third proposition is that a principal not named in the contract may sue upon it if the promisee really contracted as his agent. But again, in order to entitle him so to sue, he must have given consideration either personally or through the promisee, acting as his agent in giving it.

My Lords, in the case before us, I am of opinion that the consideration, the allowance of what was in reality part of the discount to which Messrs. Dew, the promisees, were entitled as between themselves and the appellants, was to be given by Messrs. Dew on their own account, and was not in substance, any more than in form, an allowance made by the appellants. The case for the appellants is that they permitted and enabled Messrs. Dew, with the knowledge and by the desire of the respondents, to sell to the latter on the terms of the contract of January 2, 1912. But it appears to me that even if this is so the answer is conclusive. Messrs. Dew sold to the respondents goods which they had a title to obtain from the appellants independently of this contract. The consideration by way of discount under the contract of January 2 was to come wholly out of Messrs. Dew's pocket, and neither directly nor indirectly out of that of the appellants. If the appellants enabled them to sell to the respondents on the terms they did, this was not done as any part of the terms of the contract sued on.

No doubt it was provided as part of these terms that the appellants should acquire certain rights, but these rights appear on the face of the contract as jura quaesita tertio, which the appellants could not enforce. Moreover, even if this difficulty can be got over by regarding the appellants as the principals of Messrs. Dew in stipulating for the rights in question, the only consideration disclosed by the contract is one given by Messrs. Dew, not as their agents, but as principals acting on their own account.

. . . . . .

Lord Dunedin. My Lords, I confess that this case is to my mind apt to nip any budding affection which one might have had for the doctrine of consideration. For the effect of that doctrine in the present case is to make it possible for a person to snap his fingers at a bargain deliberately made, a bargain not in itself unfair, and which the person seeking to enforce it has a legitimate interest to enforce. Notwithstanding these considerations I cannot say that I have ever had any doubt that the judgment of the Court of Appeal was right.

My Lords, I am content to adopt from a work of Sir Frederick Pollock, to which I have often been under obligation, the following words as to consideration: "An act or forbearance of one party, or the promise thereof, is the price for which the promise of the other is bought, and the promise thus given for value is enforceable." (Pollock on Contracts, 8th ed., p. 175.)

Now the agreement sued on is an agreement which on the face of it is an agreement between Dew and Selfridge. But speaking for myself, I should have no difficulty in the circumstances of this case in holding it proved that the agreement was truly made by Dew as agent for Dunlop, or in other words that Dunlop was the undisclosed principal, and as such can sue on the agreement. None the less, in order to enforce it he must show consideration, as above defined, moving from Dunlop to Selfridge.

In the circumstances, how can he do so? The agreement in question is not an agreement for sale. It is only collateral to an agreement for sale; but that agreement for sale is an agreement entirely between Dew and Selfridge. The tyres, the property in which upon the bargain is transferred to Selfridge, were the property of Dew, not of Dunlop, for Dew under his agreement with Dunlop held these tyres as proprietor, and not as agent. What then did Dunlop do, or forbear to do, in a question with Selfridge? The answer must be, nothing. He did not do anything, for Dew, having the right of property in the tyres, could give a good title to any one he liked, subject, it might be, to an action of damages at the instance of Dunlop for breach of contract, which action, however, could never create a vitium reale in the property of the tyres. He did not forbear in anything, for he had no action against Dew which he gave up, because Dew had fulfilled his contract with Dunlop in obtaining, on the occasion of the sale, a contract from Selfridge in the terms prescribed.

To my mind, this ends the case. That there are methods of framing a contract which will cause persons in the position of Selfridge to become bound, I do not doubt. But that has not been done in this instance; and as Dunlop's advisers must have known of the law of consideration, it is their affair that they have not so drawn the contract.

I think the appeal should be dismissed.

Lord Parker of Waddington. My Lords, even assuming that the undertaking upon which this action is funded was given by the respondents to Messrs. A. J. Dew & Co. as agents for the appellants, and was intended to enure for their benefit, the appeal cannot succeed unless the undertaking was founded on a consideration moving from the appellants, and in my opinion there was no such consideration. The appellants did not give or give up anything on the strength of the undertaking. They had sold tyres to Messrs. A.J. Dew & Co. on the terms that the latter should not resell them at prices less than those specified in the appellants' price list, except that Messrs. A.J. Dew & Co. were to be at liberty to allow to persons legitimately engaged in the motor trade a certain discount off such price list, if they, as agents for the appellants, obtained from such persons a written undertaking such as that upon which this action is founded. In reselling these tyres to the respondents, and obtaining from the respondents the undertaking in question, Messrs. A.J. Dew & Co. admittedly committed no breach of contract. The sale was, of course, a good consideration for the undertaking moving from Messrs. A.J. Dew & Co., but the appellants, in whose favour the undertaking was given, being in the position of volunteers not parties to the contract of sale, cannot sue on it. The case was argued on behalf of the appellants as though what was done by Messrs. A.J. Dew & Co. would have been unlawful but for the leave and licence of the appellants, and that such leave and licence, though general in form, must be taken as given on the occasion of each sale, in consideration of the undertaking. I cannot accept this contention. In the first place, it is wrong to speak of an exception from a restrictive contract as importing any leave or licence at all. But for any contract to the contrary, Messrs. A.J. Dew & Co. were entitled to resell the goods supplied to them by the appellants upon any terms they might think fit, and in reselling as they did there was no breach of any restrictive contract. Even, however, if the sale can be considered as lawful only by licence of the appellants, the licence was given once for all in their contract to Messrs. A.J. Dew & Co., and was not given as part of the terms upon which any particular sale was allowed.

The appeal fails on this ground and should be dismissed with costs.

[Lords Atkinson, Sumner and Parmoor all gave speeches dismissing Dunlop's appeal.]

Note

The area of resale price maintenance is now governed by the Resale Prices Act 1976, which places severe restrictions on such agreements (see H.S.B., p. 514).

Question

Lord Dunedin comments that the contract could have been framed in such a way as to bind Selfridge. How could this have been done?

Beswick v. Beswick

[1968] A.C. 58 (H.L.)

[Peter Beswick, who was elderly and in poor health, sold his business to his nephew, John, on terms that Peter would receive a weekly payment for the rest of his life, and in the event of his death, his widow was to receive £5 per week. Peter died soon afterwards but John only made one payment to the widow. She thereupon sued the nephew (i) as administratix of her husband's estate, and (ii) in her personal capacity. In the Court of Appeal, Lord Denning M.R. and Dankwerts L.J. considered that section 56 of the Law of Property Act 1925 had abrogated the rule in *Tweddle* v. *Atkinson*, so enabling the widow to bring a claim under (ii). Section 56(1) of the Act states, "A person may take an immediate or other interest in land or other property, or the benefit of any condition, ... covenant or agreement ... respecting land or other property, although he may not be named as a party to the conveyance or other instrument ..." Section 205 of the Act contains a definition of "property" as including "any thing in action, and any interest in real or personal property" "unless the context otherwise requires."]

Lord Pearce. My Lords, if the annuity had been payable to a third party in the lifetime of Beswick senior and there had been default, he could have sued in respect of the breach. His administratrix is now entitled to stand in his shoes and to sue in respect of the breach which has occurred since his death.

It is argued that the estate can only recover nominal damages and that no other remedy is open, either to the estate or to the personal plaintiff. Such a result would be wholly repugnant to justice and commonsense. And if the argument were right it would show a very serious defect in the law.

In the first place, I do not accept the view that damages must be nominal. Lush L.J. in *Lloyds's* v. *Harper* said:

"Then the next question which, no doubt, is a very important and substantial one, is, that Lloyd's having sustained no damage themselves, could not recover for the losses sustained by third parties by reason of the default of Robert Henry Harper as an underwriter. That, to my mind, is a startling and alarming doctrine, and a novelty, because I consider it to be an established rule of law that where a contract is made with A for the benefit of B, A can sue on the contract for the benefit of B, and recover all that B could have recovered if the contract had been made with B himself."

... I agree with the comment of Windeyer J. in the case of *Coulls* v. *Bagot's Executor and Trustee Co. Ltd.* in the High Court of Australia that the words of Lush L.J. cannot be accepted without qualification and regardless of context and also with his statement:

"I can see no reason why in such cases the damages which A would suffer upon B's breach of his contract to pay C $500 would be merely nominal: I think that in accordance with the ordinary rules for the assessment of damages for breach of contract they could be substantial. They would not necessarily be $500; they could I think be less or more."

In the present case I think that the damages, if assessed, must be substantial. It is not necessary, however, to consider the amount of damages more closely since this is a case in which, as the Court of Appeal rightly decided, the more appropriate remedy is that of specific performance.

The administratrix is entitled, if she so prefers, to enforce the agreement rather than accept its repudiation, and specific performance is more convenient than an action for arrears of payment followed by separate actions as each sum falls due. Moreover, damages for breach would be a less appropriate remedy since the parties to the agreement were intending an annuity for a widow; and a lump sum of damages does not accord with this. And if (contrary to my view) the argument that a derisory sum of damages is all that can be obtained by right, the remedy of damages in this case is manifestly useless.

The present case presents all the features which led the equity courts to apply their remedy of specific performance. The contract was for the sale of a business. The defendant could on his part clearly have obtained specific performance of it if Beswick senior or his administratrix had defaulted. Mutuality is a ground in favour of specific performance.

Moreover, the defendant on his side has received the whole benefit of the contract and it is a matter of conscience for the court to see that he now performs his part of it. Kay J. said in *Hart* v. *Hart*:

"... when an agreement for valuable consideration ... has been partially performed, the court ought to do its utmost to carry out that agreement by a decree for specific performance."

What, then, is the obstacle to granting specific performance?

It is argued that since the widow personally has no rights which she personally could enforce the court will not make an order which will have the effect of enforcing those rights. I can find no principle to this effect. The condition as to payment of an annuity to the widow personally was valid. The estate (though not the widow personally) can enforce it. Why should the estate be barred from exercising its full contractual rights merely because in doing so it secures justice for the widow who, by a mechanical defect of our law, is unable to assert her own rights? Such a principle would be repugnant to justice and fulfil no other object than that of aiding the wrongdoer. I can find no ground on which such a principle should exist.

. . . . . .

In my opinion, the plaintiff as administratrix is entitled to a decree of specific performance.

It is not, therefore, strictly necessary to deal with the respondent's argument that the plaintiff is entitled at common law or, by reason of section 56 of the Law of Property Act, 1925, to sue in her personal capacity. The learned Master of the Rolls expressed the view that at common law the widow was entitled to sue personally; but this view was not argued before your Lordships. He distinguished *Tweddle* v. *Atkinson* (1861). In *Smith and Snipes Hall Farm Ltd.* v. *River Douglas Catchment Board* (1949) and *White* v. *John Warwick & Co. Ltd.* (1953) the same learned judge had given his reasons for thinking that *Tweddle* v. *Atkinson* was wrongly decided and was out of line with the law as it had been settled in previous centuries. On the other hand, in *Coulls* v. *Bagot's Executor and Trustee Co. Ltd.* (1967) a survey of the cases from Tudor times led Windeyer J. to a different conclusion, namely that:

"The law was not in fact 'settled' either way during the two hundred years before 1861. But it was, on the whole, moving towards the doctrine that was to be then and thereafter taken as settled."

But the greatest difficulty in the way of the widow's right to sue personally is that two cases in this House, *Dunlop Pneumatic Tyre Co. Ltd.* v. *Selfridge & Co. Ltd.* (1915) and *Midland Silicones Ltd.* v. *Scruttons Ltd.*, (1962) clearly accepted the principle that a third party cannot sue on a contract to which he was not a party.

The majority of the Court of Appeal expressed the view that this principle had been abolished by section 56 of the Law of Property Act. If, however, a far reaching and substantial alteration had been intended by Parliament, one would expect it to be expressed in clear terms. Yet the terms of section 56(1) are far from clear and appear to be simply an enlargement of a section passed 80 years before. Further, section 56 is to be found in a part of the Act devoted to the technicalities of conveyancing rather than the creation of rights. The cross heading of that part of the Act is "Conveyances and other Instruments." And the second part of the section deals with a small question of formality. The important innovations in the law of property were contained in the two Acts of 1922 and 1924, but this alleged innovation was not among them. It first appears in the 1925 Law of Property Act. That was a consolidation Act and therefore, one should not find a substantial innovation in it. . . .

[Lords Reid, Halson, Guest and Upjohn delivered judgments also dismissing the defendant's appeal and granting a decree of specific performance.]

Jackson v. Horizon Holidays

[1975] 1 W.L.R. 1468 (C.A.)

[The plaintiffs contracted with the defendants for a holiday in Ceylon for himself, his wife and children. When they arrived they discovered that the plumbing was inadequate, the room had mould growing up the walls and the food was distasteful. Clearly there was a breach of contract. The difficulty was that the "damage" extended not only to the plaintiff but also to his family who were not parties to the contract. The issue arose as to how such damage was to be treated.]

Lord Denning M.R. On this question a point of law arises. The judge said that he could only consider the mental distress to his wife and children. He said:

"The damages are the plaintiff's ... I can consider the effect upon his mind of the wife's discomfort, vexation, and the like, although I cannot award a sum which represents her own vexation."

Mr. Davies, for Mr. Jackson, disputes that proposition. He submits that damages can be given not only for the leader of the party—in this case, Mr. Jackson's own distress, discomfort and vexation—but also for that of the rest of the party.

We have had an interesting discussion as to the legal position when one person makes a contract for the benefit of a party. In this case it was a husband making a contract for the benefit of himself, his wife and children. Other cases readily come to mind. A host makes a contract with a restaurant for a dinner for himself and his friends. The vicar makes a contract for a coach trip for the choir. In all these cases there is only one person who makes the contract. It is the husband, the host or the vicar, as the case may be. Sometimes he pays the whole price himself. Occasionally he may get a contribution from the others. But in any case it is he who makes the contract. It would be a fiction to say that the contract was made by all the family, or all the guests, or all the choir, and that he was only an agent for them. Take this very case. It would be absurd to say that the twins of three years old were parties to the contract or that the father was making the contract on their behalf as if they were principals. It would equally be a mistake to say that in any of these instances there was a trust. The transaction bears no resemblance to a trust. There was no trust fund and no trust property. No, the real truth is that in each instance, the father, the host or the vicar, was making a contract himself for the benefit of the whole party. In short, a contract by one for the benefit of third persons.

What is the position when such a contract is broken? At present the law says that the only one who can sue is the one who made the contract. None of the rest of the party can sue, even though the contract was made for their benefit. But when that one does sue, what damages can he recover? Is he limited to his own loss? Or can he recover for the others? Suppose the holiday firm puts the family into a hotel which is only half built and the visitors have to sleep on the floor? Or suppose the restaurant is fully booked and the guests have to go away, hungry and angry, having spent so much on fares to get there? Or suppose the coach leaves the choir stranded halfway and they have to hire cars to get home? None of them individually can sue. Only the father, the host or the vicar can sue. He can, of course, recover his own damages. But can he not recover for the others? I think he can. The case comes within the principle stated by Lush L.J. in *Lloyds's* v. *Harper* (1880):

> "I consider it to be an established rule of law that where a contract is made with A. for the benefit of B., A. can sue on the contract for the benefit of B., and recover all that B. could have recovered if the contract had been made with B. himself."

It has been suggested that Lush L.J. was thinking of a contract in which A was trustee for B. But I do not think so. He was a common lawyer speaking of common law. His words were quoted with considerable approval by Lord Pearce in *Beswick* v. *Beswick* (1968). I have myself often quoted them. I think they should be accepted as correct, at any rate so long as the law forbids the third persons themselves from suing for damages. It is the only way in which a just result can be achieved. Take the instance I have put. The guests ought to recover from the restaurant their wasted fares. The choir ought to recover the cost of hiring the taxis home. Then is no one to recover from them except the one who made the contract for their benefit? He should be able to recover the expense to which he has been put, and pay it over to them. Once recovered, it will be money had and received to their use. (They might even if desired, be joined as plaintiffs). If he can recover for the expense, he should also be able to recover for the discomfort, vexation and upset which the whole party have suffered by reason of the breach of contract, recompensing them accordingly out of what he recovers.

Applying the principles to this case, I think that the figure of £1,100 was about right. It would, I think, have been excessive if it had been awarded only for the damage suffered by Mr. Jackson himself. But when extended to his wife and children, I do not think it is excessive. People look forward to a holiday. They expect the promises to be fulfilled. When it fails, they are greatly disappointed and upset. It is difficult to assess in terms of money; but it is the task of the judges to do the best they can. I see no reason to interfere with the total award of £1,100. I would therefore dismiss the appeal.

[Orr and James L.JJ. agreed in giving judgment for the plaintiff.]

Note

In *Woodar Investment Development Ltd.* v. *Wimpey Construction UK Ltd.* (1980) the case of *Jackson* was criticised by the House of Lords. Lord Wilberforce commented:

"I am not prepared to dissent from the actual decision in that case. It may be supported either as a broad decision on the measure of damages (*per* James L.J.) or possibly as an example of a type of contract—examples of which are persons contracting for family holidays, ordering meals in restaurants for a party, hiring a taxi for a group—calling for special treatment. As I suggested in *New Zealand Shipping Co. Ltd.* v. *A.M. Satterthwaite & Co. Ltd.* (1975) there are many situations of daily life which do not fit neatly into conceptual analysis, but which require some flexibility in the law of contract. *Jackson's* case may well be one."

He then went on to criticise reliance upon the passage from Lush L.J. in *Lloyds's* v. *Harper* (1880).

Lord Russel of Killowen stated:

"I do not criticize the outcome of that case: the plaintiff had bought and paid for a high class family holiday: he did not get it, and therefore he was entitled to substantial damages for the failure to supply *him* with one. It is to be observed that the order of the Court of Appeal as drawn up did not suggest that any part of the damages awarded to him were "for the use and benefit of" any member of his family. It was a special case quite different from the instant case on the Transworld point. I would not, my Lords, wish to leave the *Jackson* case without adverting with respectful disapproval to the reliance there placed by Lord Denning M.R.—not for the first time—on an extract taken from the judgment of Lush L.J. in *Lloyd's* v. *Harper* (1880). That case was plainly a case in which a trustee or agent was enforcing the right of a beneficiary or principal, there being therefore a fiduciary relationship. Lord Denning in *Jackson's* case said . . .:

"The case comes within the principle stated by Lush L.J. in *Lloyd's* v. *Harper* (1880): 'I consider it to be an established rule of law that where a contract is made with A. for the benefit of B., A. can sue on the contract for the benefit of B. and recover all that B. could have recovered if the contract had been made with B. himself.' ""

Lord Denning continued: "It has been suggested that Lush L.J. was thinking of a contract in which A was trustee for B. But I do not think so. He was a common lawyer speaking of common law." I have already indicated that in all the other judgments the matter proceeded upon a fiduciary relationship between A and B: and Lush L.J. in the same passage makes it plain that he does also; for he says:

> "It is true that the person [B] who employed him [the broker A] has a right, if he pleases, to take action himself and sue upon the contract made by the broker for him, for he [B] *is a principal party to the contract*."

To ignore that passage is to divorce the passage quoted by Lord Denning from the fiduciary context in which it was uttered, the context of principal and agent, a field with which it may be assumed Lush L.J. was familiar. I venture to suggest that the brief quotation should not be used again as support for a proposition which Lush L.J. cannot have intended to advance.

More recently the House of Lords in *Linden Gardens* v. *Lenesta Sludge* (1993) regarded it as "apparently established" that a contracting party in a case like *Jackson* can recover for the unhappiness suffered by the plaintiff's family (*per* Lord Brown-Wilkinson [1993] 3 All E.R. at 434j).

Chapter 8

Duress, Undue Influence and Illegality

1. DURESS

A. Threats

Barton v. Armstrong

[1975] 2 W.L.R. 1050 (P.C.)

[Armstrong threatened Barton, the appellant, with death if the latter would not agree to buy out Armstrong's interest in a business. Barton executed the deed but subsequently brought an action against Armstrong on the grounds that the transaction should be set aside because of the threats. There was evidence that Barton in fact executed the deed because he thought it was a satisfactory business arrangement. On this basis the trial judge dismissed the claim because he found that the threats were not the predominant reason why the appellant had entered the agreement. The Court of Appeal of New South Wales also dismissed the appeal and held that the appellant was not entitled to succeed unless he established that, but for the threats, he would not have signed the agreement. In this he had failed. The appellant appealed to the Privy Council.]

Lord Cross. Their Lordships turn now to consider the question of law which provoked a difference of opinion in the Court of Appeal Division. It is hardly surprising that there is no direct authority on the point, for if A threatens B with death if he does not execute some document and B, who takes A's threats seriously, executes the document it can be only in the most unusual circumstances that there can be any doubt whether the threats operated to induce him to execute the document. But this is a most unusual case and the findings of fact made below do undoubtedly raise the question whether it was necessary for Barton in order to obtain relief to establish that he would not have executed the deed in question but for the threats. In answering this question in favour of Barton, Jacobs J.A. relied both on a number of old common law authorities on the subject of "duress" and also—by way of analogy—on later decisions in equity with regard to the avoidance of deeds on the ground of fraud. Their Lordships do not think that the common law authorities are of any real assistance for it seems most unlikely that the authors of the statements relied on had the sort of problem which has arisen here in mind at all. On the other hand they think that the conclusion to which Jacobs J.A. came was right and that it is supported by the equity decisions. The scope of common law duress was very limited and at a comparatively early date equity began to grant relief in cases where the disposition in question had been procured by the exercise of pressure which the Chancellor considered to be illegitimate—although it did not amount to common law duress. There was a parallel development in the field of dispositions induced by fraud. At common law the only remedy available to the man defrauded was an action for deceit but equity in the same period in which it was building up the doctrine of "undue influence" came to entertain proceedings to set aside dispositions which had been obtained by fraud: see *Holdsworth, A History of English Law*, vol. V (1924), pp. 328–329. There is an obvious analogy between setting aside a disposition for duress or undue influence and setting it aside for fraud. In each case—to quote the words of Holmes J. in *Fairbanks* v. *Snow* (1887)—"the party has been subjected to an improper motive for action." Again the similarity of the effect in law of metus and dolus in connection with dispositions of property is noted by Stair in his *Institutions of the Law of Scotland*, New ed. (1832), Book IV, title 40.25. Had Armstrong made a fraudulent misrepresentation to Barton for the purpose of inducing him to execute the deed of January 17, 1967, the answer to the problem which has arisen would have been clear. If it were established that Barton did not allow the representation to affect his judgment then he could not make it a ground for relief even though the representation was designed and known by Barton to be designed to affect his judgment. If on the other hand Barton relied on the misrepresentation Armstrong could not have defeated his claim to relief by showing that there were other more weighty causes which contributed to his decision to execute the deed, for in this field the court does not allow an examination into the relative importance of contributory causes.

"Once make out that there has been anything like deception, and no contract resting in any degree on that foundation can stand": *per* Lord Cranworth L.J. in *Reynell* v. *Sprye* (1852)—see also the other cases referred to in *Cheshire and Fifoot's Law of Contract*, 8th ed. (1972), pp. 250–251. Their Lordship think that the same rule should apply in cases of duress and that if Armstrong's threats were "a" reason for Barton's executing the deed he is entitled to relief even though he might well have entered into the contract if Armstrong had uttered no threats to induce him to do so.

[Their Lordships went on to decide that the onus was on the respondent, Armstrong, to prove that the threats did not contribute to the appellant's decision to sign the deed. The proper inference from the facts was that, although the appellant might have executed the deed anyway, the threats contributed to the decision. The deeds were accordingly executed under duress.]

Judgment for the appellant.

[Lord Kilbrandon and Sir Garfield Barwick agreed. Lords Wilberforce and Simon dissented on the basis that there was no justification for interfering with the lower court's findings of fact.]

B. Economic Duress

Pau On v. Lau Yiu Long

[1980] A.C. 614 (P.C.)

Lord Scarman. Duress, whatever form it takes, is a coercion of the will so as to vitiate consent. Their Lordships agree with the observation of Kerr J. in *Occidental Worldwide Investment Corporation* v. *Skibs A/S Avanti* (1976) that in a contractual situation commercial pressure is not enough. There must be present some factor "which could in law be regarded as a coercion of his will so as to vitiate his consent." This conception is in line with what was said in this Board's decision in *Barton* v. *Armstrong* (1976) by Lord Wilberforce and Lord Simon of Glaisdale—observations with which the majority judgment appears to be in agreement. In determining whether there was a coercion of will such that there was no true consent, it is material to inquire whether the person alleged to have been coerced did or did not protest; whether, at the time he was allegedly coerced into making the contract, he did or did not have an alternative course open to him such as an adequate legal remedy; whether he was independently advised; and whether after entering the contract he took steps to avoid it. All these matters are, as was recognised in *Maskell* v. *Horner* (1915), relevant in determining whether he acted voluntarily or not.

[Their Lordships noted that the facts in this case disclosed commercial pressure, not coercion.]

It is therefore, unnecessary for the Board to embark upon an inquiry into the question whether English law recognises a category of duress known as "economic duress." But, since the question has been fully argued in this appeal, their Lordships will indicate very briefly the view which they have formed. At common law money paid under economic compulsion could be recovered in an action for money had and received *Astley* v. *Reynolds* (1731). The compulsion had to be such that the party was deprived of "his freedom of exercising his will". It is doubtful, however, whether at common law any duress other than duress to the person sufficed to render a contract voidable: see *Blackstone's Commentaries*, Book 1, 12th ed. pp. 130–131 and *Skeate* v. *Beale* (1841). American law (*Williston on Contracts*, 3rd ed.) now recognises that a contract may be avoided on the ground of economic duress. The commercial pressure alleged to constitute such duress must, however, be such that the victim must have entered the contract against his will, must have had no alternative course open to him, and must have been confronted with coercive acts by the party exerting the pressure: *Williston on Contracts*, 3rd ed., vol. 13 (1970), section 1603. American judges pay great attention to such evidential matters as the effectiveness of the alternative remedy available, the fact or absence of protest, the availability of independent advice, the benefit received, and the speed with which the victim has sought to avoid the contract. Recently two English judges have recognised that commercial pressure may constitute duress the pressure of which can render a contract voidable: Kerr J. in *Occidental Worldwide Investment Corporation* v. *Skibs A/S Avanti* (1976) and Mocatta J. in *North*

Ocean Shipping Co. Ltd. v. *Hyundai Construction Co. Ltd.* (1979). Both stressed that the pressure must be such that the victim's consent to the contract was not a voluntary act on his part. In their Lordship's view, there is nothing contrary to principle in recognising economic duress as a factor which may render a contract voidable, provided always that the basis of such recognition is that it must amount to a coercion of will, which vitiates consent. It must be shown that the payment made or the contract entered into was not a voluntary act.

Notes

The growth of the doctrine of economic duress is a good example of the courts developing a traditional common law concept and applying it to modern conditions. The House of Lords explicitly recognised the doctrine in *Universe Tankships of Monrovia* v. *International Transport Workers Federation* (1983), note in particular the judgments of Lords Diplock and Scarman.

The ambit of the doctrine will no doubt be developed further in subsequent cases. In *North Ocean Shipping Co. Ltd.* v. *Hyundai Construction Co. Ltd., The Atlantic Baron* (1979) (H.S.B., p. 489) and *Alec Lobb Ltd.* v. *Total Oil G.B. Ltd.* (1983) the plea of economic duress failed on the facts. *Atlas Express Ltd.* v. *Kafco (Importers and Distributors) Ltd.* (1989) presents an interesting recent illustration of the plea in action. Here a small company entered into an agreement with a national firm of carriers for the delivery of their merchandise at an agreed rate of carriage. Later the carriers sought to impose a minimum charge per load which was substantially higher than the amount previously agreed. Because the defendant company was unable to find an alternative carrier and was heavily dependant on their contract with the outlets to whom delivery was being made they agreed to the new terms but later refused to pay the new rate. On these facts the court upheld the defendant's plea of economic duress. An alternative basis for the decision was that there was no consideration for the new agreement. The plaintiff's claim based upon the new terms was accordingly dismissed.

2.   Undue Influence

Barclays Bank v. O'Brien

[1993] 4 All E.R. 417 (H.L.)

Lord Browne-Wilkinson. My Lords, in this appeal your Lordships for the first time have to consider a problem which has given rise to reported decisions of the Court of Appeal on no less than 11 occasions in the last eight years and which has led to a difference of judicial view. Shortly stated the question is whether a bank is entitled to enforce against a wife an obligation to secure a debt owed by her husband to the bank where the wife has been induced to stand as surety for her husband's debt by the undue influence or misrepresentation of the husband.

The facts

The facts of the present case are very fully set out in the judgment of Scott L.J. in the Court of Appeal. I will only state them in summary form. Mr. and Mrs. O'Brien were husband and wife. The matrimonial home, 151 Farnham Lane, Slough, was in their joint names subject to a mortgage of approximately £25,000 to a building society. Mr. O'Brien was a chartered accountant and had an interest in a company, Heathrow Fabrications Ltd. The company's bank account was at the Woolwich branch of Barclays Bank. In the first three months of 1987 the company frequently exceeded its overdraft facility of £40,000 and a number of its cheques were dishonoured on presentation. In discussions in April 1981 between Mr. O'Brien and the manager of the Woolwich branch, Mr. Tucker, Mr. O'Brien told Mr. Tucker that he was remortgaging the matrimonial home: Mr. Tucker made a note that Mrs. O'Brien might be a problem. The overdraft limit was raised at that stage to £60,000 for one month. Even though no additional security was provided, by June 15, 1987 the company's overdraft had risen to £98,000 and its cheques were again being dishonoured.

On June 22, 1987 Mr. O'Brien and Mr. Tucker agreed (1) that the company's overdraft limit would be raised to £135,000 reducing to £120,000 after three weeks, (2) that Mr. O'Brien would guarantee the company's indebtedness and (3) that Mr. O'Brien's liability would be secured by a second charge on the matrimonial home.

The necessary security documents were prepared by the bank. They consisted of an unlimited guarantee by Mr. O'Brien of the company's liability and a legal charge by both Mr. and Mrs. O'Brien of the matrimonial home to secure any liability of Mr. O'Brien to the bank. Mr. Tucker arranged for the documents, together with a side letter, to be sent to the Burnham branch of the bank for execution by Mr. and Mrs. O'Brien. In a covering memorandum Mr. Tucker requested the Burnham branch to advise the O'Briens as to the current level of the facilities afforded to the bank (£107,000) and the projected increase to £135,000. The Burnham branch was also asked to ensure that the O'Briens were "fully aware of the nature of the documentation to be signed and advised that if they are in any doubt they should contact their solicitors before signing."

Unfortunately the Burnham branch did not follow Mr. Tucker's instructions. On July 1, Mr. O'Brien alone signed the guarantee and legal charge at the Burnham branch, the document simply being produced for signature and witnessed by a clerk. On the following day Mrs. O'Brien went to the branch with her husband. There were produced for signature by Mrs. O'Brien the legal charge on the matrimonial home together with a side letter, which reads:

"We hereby agree acknowledge and confirm as follows: (1) That we have each received from you a copy of the guarantee dated 3 July 1987 (a copy of which is attached hereto) under which Nicholas Edward O'Brien guarantees the payment and discharge of all moneys and liabilities now or hereafter due owing or incurred by Heathrow Fabrications Ltd. to you. (2) That the liability of the said Nicholas Edward O'Brien to you pursuant to the said guarantee is and will be secured by the legal charge dated 3 July 1987 over the property described above made between (1) Nicholas Edward O'Brien (2) Nicholas Edward O'Brien and Bridget Mary O'Brien and (3) Barclays Bank Plc. (3) That you recommended that we should obtain independent legal advice before signing this letter."

In fact the Burnham branch gave Mrs. O'Brien no explanation of the effect of the documents. No one suggested that she should take independent legal advice. She did not read the documents or the side letter. She simply signed the legal charge and side letter and her signature was witnessed by the clerk. She was not given a copy of the guarantee.

The company did not prosper and by October 1987 its indebtedness to the bank was over £154,000. In November 1987 demand was made against Mr. O'Brien under his guarantee. When the demand was not met possession proceedings under the legal charge were brought by the bank against Mr. and Mrs. O'Brien. Mrs. O'Brien seeks to defend these proceedings by alleging that she was induced to execute the legal charge on the matrimonial home by the undue influence of Mr. O'Brien and by his misrepresentation.

. . .

Policy considerations

The large number of cases of this type coming before the courts in recent years reflects the rapid changes in social attitudes and the distribution of wealth which have recently occurred. Wealth is now more widely spread. Moreover a high proportion of privately owned wealth is invested in the matrimonial home. Because of the recognition by society of the equality of the sexes, the majority of matrimonial homes are now in the joint names of both spouses. Therefore in order to raise finance for the business enterprises of one or other of the spouses, the jointly owned home has become a main source of security. The provision of such security requires the consent of both spouses.

In parallel with these financial developments, society's recognition of the equality of the sexes has led to a rejection of the concept that the wife is subservient to the husband in the management of the family's finances. A number of the authorities reflect an unwillingness in the court to perpetuate law based on this outmoded concept. Yet, as Scott L.J. in the Court of Appeal rightly points out, although the concept of the ignorant wife leaving all financial decisions to the husband is outmoded, the practice does not yet coincide with the ideal (see [1992] 4 All E.R. 983 at 1008; [1993] Q.B. 109 at 139). In a substantial proportion of marriages it is still the husband who has the business experience and the wife is willing to follow his advice without bringing a truly independent mind and will to bear on financial decisions. The number of recent cases in this field shows that in practice many wives are still subjected to, and yield to, undue influence by their husbands. Such wives can reasonably look to the law for some protection when their husbands have abused the trust and confidence reposed in them.

On the other hand, it is important to keep a sense of balance in approaching these cases. It is easy to allow sympathy for the wife who is threatened with the loss of her home at the suit of a rich bank to obscure an important public interest, *viz.* the need to ensure that the wealth currently tied up in the matrimonial home does not become economically sterile. If the rights secured to wives by the law renders vulnerable loans granted on the security of matrimonial homes, institutions will be unwilling to accept such security, thereby reducing the flow of loan capital to business enterprises. It is therefore essential that a law designed to protect the vulnerable does not render the matrimonial home unacceptable as security to financial institutions.

With these policy considerations in mind I turn to consider the existing state of the law. The whole of the modern law is derived from the decision of the Privy Council in *Turnbull & Co.* v. *Duval* (1902) which, as I will seek to demonstrate, provides an uncertain foundation. Before considering that case however, I must consider the law of undue influence which (though not directly applicable in the present case) underlies both *Turnbull* v. *Duval* and most of the later authorities.

Undue influence

A person who has been induced to enter into a transaction by the undue influence of another (the wrongdoer) is entitled to set that transaction aside as against the wrongdoer. Such undue influence is either actual or presumed. In *Bank of Credit and Commerce International SA* v. *Aboody* (1988) the Court of Appeal helpfully adopted the following classification.

Class 1: actual undue influence. In these cases it is necessary for the claimant to prove affirmatively that the wrongdoer exerted undue influence on the complainant to enter into the particular transaction which is impugned.

Class 2: presumed undue influence. In these cases the complainant only has to show, in the first instance, that there was a relationship of trust and confidence between the complainant and the wrongdoer of such a nature that it is fair to presume that the wrongdoer abused that relationship in procuring the complainant to enter into the impugned transaction. In class 2 cases therefore there is no need to produce evidence that actual undue influence was exerted in relation to the particular transaction impugned: once a confidential relationship has been proved, the burden then shifts to the wrongdoer to prove that the complainant entered into the impugned transaction freely, for example by showing that the complainant had independent advice. Such a confidential relationship can be established in two ways, viz:

Class 2A. Certain relationships (for example solicitor and client, medical advisor and patient) as a matter of law raise the presumption that undue influence has been exercised.

Class 2B. Even if there is no relationship falling within class 2A, if the complainant proves the de facto existence of a relationship under which the complainant generally reposed trust and confidence in the wrongdoer, the existence of such relationship raises the presumption of undue influence. In a class 2B case therefore, in the absence of evidence disproving undue influence, the complainant will succeed in setting aside the impugned transaction merely by proof that the complainant reposed trust and confidence in the wrongdoer without having to prove that the wrongdoer exerted actual undue influence or otherwise abused such trust and confidence in relation to the particular transaction impugned.

As to dispositions by a wife in favour of her husband, the law for long remained in an unsettled state. In the nineteenth century some judges took the view that the relationship was such that it fell into class 2A, i.e. as a matter of law undue influence by the husband over the wife was presumed. It was not until the decisions in *Howes* v. *Bishop* (1909) and *Bank of Montreal* v. *Stuart* (1911) that it was finally determined that the relationship of husband and wife did not as a matter of law raise a presumption of undue influence within class 2A. It is to be noted therefore that when *Turnbull* v. *Duval* was decided in 1902 the question whether there was a class 2A presumption of undue influence as between husband and wife was still unresolved.

An invalidating tendency?

Although there is no class 2A presumption of undue influence as between husband and wife, it should be emphasised that in any particular case a wife may well be able to demonstrate that *de facto* she did leave decisions on financial affairs to her husband thereby bringing herself within class 2B, *i.e.* that the relationship between husband and wife in the particular case was such that the wife reposed confidence and trust in her husband in relation to their financial affairs and therefore undue influence is to be presumed. Thus, in those cases which still occur where the wife relies in all financial matters on her husband and simply does what he suggests, a presumption of undue influence within class 2B can be established solely from the proof of such trust and confidence without proof of actual undue influence.

In the appeal in *CIBC Mortgages plc* v. *Pitt* (1993) (judgment in which is to be given immediately after that in the present appeal) [see below, p. 565] Mr. Price Q.C. for the wife argued that in the case of transactions between husband and wife there was an "invalidating tendency," *i.e.* although there was no class 2A presumption of undue influence, the courts were more ready to find that a husband had exercised undue influence over his wife than in other cases. Scott L.J. in the present case also referred to the law treating married women "more tenderly" than others. This approach is based on dicta in early authorities. In *Grigby* v. *Cox* (1750) Lord Hardwicke L.C. whilst rejecting any presumption of undue influence, said that a court of equity "will have more jealousy" over dispositions by a wife to a husband. In *Yerkey* v. *Jones* (1939)

Dixon J. refers to this "invalidating tendency." He also refers (at 677) to the court recognising "the opportunities which a wife's confidence in her husband gives him of unfairly or improperly procuring her to become surety."

In my judgment this special tenderness of treatment afforded to wives by the courts is properly attributable to two factors. First, many cases may well fall into the class 2B category of undue influence because the wife demonstrates that she placed trust and confidence in her husband in relation to her financial affairs and therefore raises a presumption of undue influence. Second, the sexual and emotional ties between the parties provide a ready weapon for undue influence; a wife's true wishes can easily be overborne because of her fear of destroying or damaging the wider relationship between her and her husband if she opposes his wishes.

For myself, I accept that the risk of undue influence affecting a voluntary disposition by a wife in favour of a husband is greater than in the ordinary run of cases where no sexual or emotional ties affect the free exercise of the individual's will.

Undue influence, misrepresentation and third parties

Up to this point I have been considering the right of a claimant wife to set aside a transaction as against the wrongdoing husband when the transaction has been procured by his undue influence. But in surety cases the decisive question is whether the claimant wife can set aside the transaction, not against the wrongdoing husband, but against the creditor bank. Of course, if the wrongdoing husband is acting as agent for the creditor bank in obtaining the surety from the wife, the creditor will be fixed with the wrongdoing of its own agent and the surety contract can be set aside as against the creditor. Apart from this, if the creditor bank has notice, actual or constructive, of the undue influence exercised by the husband (and consequentially of the wife's equity to set aside the transaction) the creditor will take subject to that equity and the wife can set aside the transaction against the creditor (albeit a purchaser for value) as well as against the husband: see *Bainbrigge* v. *Browne* (1881) and *BCCI* v. *Aboody* (1990). Similarly, in cases such as the present where the wife has been induced to enter into the transaction by the husband's misrepresentation, her equity to set aside the transaction will be enforceable against the creditor if either the husband was acting as the creditor's agent or the creditor had actual or constructive notice.

. . .

[His Lordship considered the authority of *Turnbull* v. *Duval*.]

Accordingly, the present law is built on the unsure foundations of *Turnbull* v. *Duval*. Like most law founded on obscure and possibly mistaken foundations it has developed in an artificial way, giving rise to artifical distinctions and conflicting decisions. In my judgment your Lordships should seek to restate the law in a form which is principled, reflects the current requirements of society and provides as much certainty as possible.

Conclusions

(a) Wives. My starting point is to clarify the basis of the law. Should wives (and perhaps others) be accorded special rights in relation to surety transactions by the recognition of a special equity applicable only to such persons engaged in such transactions? Or should they enjoy only the same protection as they would enjoy in relation to their other dealings? In my judgment, the special equity theory should be rejected. First, I can find no basis in principle for affording special protection to a limited class in relation to one type of transaction only. Second, to require the creditor to prove knowledge and understanding by the wife in all cases is to reintroduce by the back door either a presumption of undue influence of class 2A (which has been decisely rejected) or the Romilly heresy (which has long been treated as bad law). Third, although Scott LJ found that there were two lines of cases one of which supported the special equity theory, on analysis although many decisions are not inconsistent with that theory the only two cases which support it are *Yerkey* v. *Jones* and the decision of the Court of Appeal in the present case. Finally, it is not necessary to have recourse to a special equity theory for the proper protection of the legitimate interests of wives as I will seek to show.

In my judgment, if the doctrine of notice is properly applied, there is no need for the introduction of a special equity in these types of cases. A wife who has been induced to stand as a surety for her husband's debts by his undue influence, misrepresentation or some other legal wrong has an equity as against him to set aside that transaction. Under the ordinary principles of equity, her right to set aside that transaction will be enforceable against third parties (e.g. against a creditor) if either the husband was acting as the third party's agent or the third party had actual or constructive notice of the facts giving rise to her equity.

Although there may be cases where, without artificiality, it can properly be held that the husband was acting as the agent of the creditor in procuring the wife to stand as surety, such cases will be of very rare occurrence. The key to the problem is to identify the circumstances in which the creditor will be taken to have had notice of the wife's equity to set aside the transaction.

The doctrine of notice lies at the heart of equity. Given that there are two innocent parties, each enjoying rights, the earlier right prevails against the later right if the acquirer of the later right knows of the earlier right (actual notice) or would have discovered it had he taken proper steps (constructive notice). In particular, if the party asserting that he takes free of the earlier rights of another knows of certain facts which put him on inquiry as to the possible existence of the rights of that other and he fails to make such inquiry or take such other steps as are reasonable to verify whether such earlier right does or does not exist, he will have constructive notice of the earlier right and take subject to it. Therefore where a wife has agreed to stand surety for her husband's debts as a result of undue influence or misrepresentation, the creditor will take subject to the wife's equity to set aside the transaction if the circumstances are such as to put the creditor on inquiry as to the circumstances in which she agreed to stand surety.

It is at this stage that, in my view, the "invalidating tendency" or the law's "tender treatment" of married women, becomes relevant. As I have said above in dealing with undue influence, this tenderness of the law towards married women is due to the fact that, even today, many wives repose confidence and trust in their husbands in relation to their financial affairs. This tenderness of the law is reflected by the fact that voluntary dispositions by the wife in favour of her husband are more likely to be set aside than other dispositions by her: a wife is more likely to establish presumed undue influence of class 2B by her husband than by others because, in practice, many wives do repose in their husbands trust and confidence in relation to their financial affairs. Moreover the informality of business dealings between spouses raises a substantial risk that the husband has not accurately stated to the wife the nature of the liability she is undertaking, i.e. he has misrepresented the position, albeit negligently.

Therefore, in my judgment a creditor is put on inquiry when a wife offers to stand surety for her husband's debts by the combination of two factors: (a) the transaction is on its face not to the financial advantage of the wife; and (b) there is a substantial risk in transactions of that kind that, in procuring the wife to act as surety, the husband has committed a legal or equitable wrong that entitles the wife to set aside the transaction.

It follows that, unless the creditor who is put on inquiry takes reasonable steps to satisfy himself that the wife's agreement to stand surety has been properly obtained, the creditor will have constructive notice of the wife's rights.

What, then are the reasonable steps which the creditor should take to ensure that it does not have constructive notice of the wife's rights, if any? Normally the reasonable steps necessary to avoid being fixed with constructive notice consist of making inquiry of the person who may have the earlier right (i.e. the wife) to see if whether such right is asserted. It is plainly impossible to require of banks and other financial institutions that they should inquire of one spouse whether he or she has been unduly influenced or misled by the other. But in my judgment the creditor, in order to avoid being fixed with constructive notice, can reasonably be expected to take steps to bring home to the wife the risk she is running by standing as surety and to advise her to take independent advice. As to past transactions, it will depend on the facts of each case whether the steps taken by the creditor satisfy this test. However for the future in my judgment a creditor will have satisfied these requirements if it insists that the wife attend a private meeting (in the absence of the husband) with a representative of the creditor at which she is told of the extent of her liability as surety, warned of the risk she is running and urged to take independent legal advice. If these steps are taken in my judgment the creditor will have taken such reasonable steps as are necessary to preclude a subsequent claim that it had constructive notice of the wife's rights. I should make it clear that I have been considering the ordinary case where the creditor knows only that the wife is to stand surety for her husband's debts. I would not exclude exceptional cases where a creditor has knowledge of further facts which render the presence of undue influence not only possible but probable. In such cases, the creditor to be safe will have to insist that the wife is separately advised.

I am conscious that in treating the creditor as having constructive notice because of the risk of class 2B undue influence or misrepresentation by the husband I may be extending the law as stated by Fry J. in *Bainbrigge* v. *Browne* (1881) and the Court of Appeal in *BCCI* v. *Aboody*. Those cases suggest that for a third party to be affected by constructive notice of presumed undue influence the third party must actually know of the circumstances which give rise to a presumption of undue influence. In contrast, my view is that the risk of class 2B undue influence or misrepresentation is sufficient to put the creditor on inquiry. But my statement accords with the principles of notice: if the known facts are such as to indicate the possibility of an adverse claim that is sufficient to put a third party on inquiry.

If the law is established as I have suggested, it will hold the balance fairly between on the one hand the vulnerability of the wife who relies implicitly on her husband and, on the other hand, the practical problems of financial institutions asked to accept a secured or unsecured surety obligation from the wife for her husband's debts. In the context of suretyship, the wife will not have any right to disown her obligations just because subsequently she proves that she did not fully understand the transaction: she will, as in all other areas of her affairs, be bound by her obligations unless her husband has, by misrepresentation, undue influence or other wrong, committed an actionable wrong against her. In the normal case, a financial institution will be able to lend with confidence in reliance on the wife's surety obligation provided that it warns her (in the absence of the husband) of the amount of her potential liability and of the risk of standing surety and advises her to take independent advice.

. . .

(b) Other persons. I have hitherto dealt only with the position where a wife stands surety for her husband's debts. But in my judgment the same principles are applicable to all other cases where there is an emotional relationship between cohabitees. The "tenderness" shown by the law to married women is not based on the marriage ceremony but reflects the underlying risk of one cohabitee exploiting the emotional involvement and trust of the other. Now that unmarried cohabitation, whether heterosexual or homosexual, is widespread in our society, the law should recognise this. Legal wives are not the only group which are now exposed to the emotional pressure of cohabitation. Therefore if, but only if, the creditor is aware that the surety is cohabiting with the principal debtor, in my judgment the same principles should apply to them as apply to husband and wife.

In addition to the cases of cohabitees, the decision of the Court of Appeal in *Avon Finance Co. Ltd.* v. *Bridger* (1985) shows (rightly in my view) that other relationships can give rise to a similar result. In that case a son, by means of misrepresentation, persuaded his elderly parents to stand surety for his debts. The surety obligation was held to be unenforceable by the creditor inter alia because to the bank's knowledge the parents trusted the son in their financial dealings. In my judgment that case was rightly decided: in a case where the creditor is aware that the surety reposes trust and confidence in the principal debtor in relation to his financial affairs, the creditor is put on inquiry in just the same way as it is in relation to husband and wife.

Summary

I can therefore summarise my views as follows. Where one cohabitee has entered into an obligation to stand as surety for the debts of the other cohabitee and the creditor is aware that they are cohabitees: (1) the surety obligation will be valid and enforceable by the creditor unless the suretyship was procured by the undue influence, misrepresentation or other legal wrong of the principal debtor; (2) if there has been undue influence, misrepresentation or other legal wrong by the principal debtor, unless the creditor has taken reasonable steps to satisfy himself that the surety entered into the obligation freely and in knowledge of the true facts, the creditor will be unable to enforce the surety obligation because he will be fixed with constructive notice of the surety's right to set aside the transaction; (3) unless there are special exceptional circumstances, a creditor will have taken such reasonable steps to avoid being fixed with constructive notice if the creditor warns the surety (at a meeting not attended by the principal debtor) of the amount of her potential liability and of the risks involved and advises the surety to take independent legal advice.

I should make it clear that in referring to the husband's debts I include the debts of a company in which the husband (but not the wife) has a direct financial interest.

The decision of this case

Applying those principles to this case, to the knowledge of the bank Mr. and Mrs. O'Brien were man and wife. The bank took a surety obligation from Mrs. O'Brien, secured on the matrimonial home, to secure the debts of a company in which Mr. O'Brien was interested but in which Mrs. O'Brien had no direct pecuniary interest. The bank should therefore have been put on inquiry as to the circumstances in which Mrs. O'Brien had agreed to stand as surety for the debt of her husband. If the Burnham branch had properly carried out the instructions from Mr. Tucker of the Woolwich branch, Mrs. O'Brien would have been informed that she and the matrimonial home were potentially liable for the debts of a company which had an existing liability of £107,000 and which was to be afforded an overdraft facility of £135,000. If she had been told this, it would have counteracted Mr. O'Brien's misrepresentation that the liability was limited to £60,000 and would last for only three weeks. In addition according to the side letter she would have been recommended to take independent legal advice.

Unfortunately Mr. Tucker's instructions were not followed and to the knowledge of the bank (through the clerk at the Burnham branch) Mrs. O'Brien signed the documents without any warning of the risks or any recommendation to take legal advice. In the circumstances the bank (having failed to take reasonable steps) is fixed with constructive notice of the wrongful misrepresentation made by Mr. O'Brien to Mrs. O'Brien. Mrs. O'Brien is therefore entitled as against the bank to set aside the legal charge on the matrimonial home securing her husband's liability to the bank.

[*Lords Templeman, Lowry, Slynn and Woolf all concurred.*]

Note

In *CIBC Mortgages plc* v. *Pitt* (1993) the wife's claim to have a security set aside on the grounds of undue influence failed. Lord Browne-Wilkinson, again giving the decision of the House of Lords, explained:

"What distinguishes the case of the joint advance from the surety is that, in the latter, there is not only the possibility of undue influence having been exercised but also the increased risk of it having in fact been exercised because, at least on its face, the guarantee by a wife of her husband's debts is not for her financial benefit. It is the combination of these two factors that puts the creditor on inquiry."

In this case their Lordships took the view that there was nothing to suggest that the loan was other than a normal advance for the couple's joint benefit. The lender accordingly had no actual or constructive notice of the husband's undue influence.

3. ILLEGALITY

Pearce v. Brooks

(1866) L.R. 1 Ex. 213 (Exchequer Chamber)

[The plaintiff sued the defendant on what was an early example of a hire purchase agreement. The defendant alleged that the plaintiff could not recover on the basis, in effect, that the contract was tainted with illegality.

One of the issues that arose was whether it must be proved in such a case that the plaintiff expected to be paid out of the proceeds of the immoral act, or whether it was enough simply that it was known that the defendant would apply the article for an immoral purpose.]

Bramwell B. There is no doubt that the woman was a prostitute; no doubt to my mind that the plaintiffs knew it; there was cogent evidence of the fact, and the jury have so found. The only fact really in dispute is for what purpose was the brougham hired, and if for an immoral purpose, did the plaintiff's know it? At the trial I doubted whether there was evidence of this, but, for the reasons I have already stated, I think the jury were entitled to infer, as they did, that it was hired for the purposes of display, that is, for the purpose of enabling the defendant to pursue her calling, and that the plaintiffs knew it.

That being made out, my difficulty was, whether, though the defendant hired the brougham for that purpose, it could be said that the plaintiffs let it for the same purpose. In one sense, it was not for the same purpose. If a man were to ask for duelling pistols, and to say: "I think I shall fight a duel tomorrow," might not the seller answer: "I do not want to know your purpose; I have nothing to do with it; that is your business: mine is to sell the pistols, and I look only to the profit of trade." No doubt the act would be immoral, but I have felt a doubt whether it would be illegal; and I should still feel it, but that the authority of *Cannan* v. *Bryce* (1819) *M'Kinnell* v. *Robinson* (1838) concludes the matter. In the latter case the plea does not say that the money was lent on the terms that the borrower should game with it; but only that it was borrowed by the defendant, and lent by the plaintiff "for the purpose of the defendant's illegally playing and gaming therewith." The case was argued by Mr. Justice Crompton against the plea, and by Mr. Justice Wightman in support of it; and the considered judgment of the Court was delivered by Lord Abinger, who says ... : "As the plea states that the money for which the action is brought was lent for the purpose of illegally playing and gaming therewith, at the illegal game of 'Hazard,' this money cannot be recovered back, on the principle, not for the first time laid down, but fully settled in the case of *Cannan* v. *Bryce*. This principle is that the repayment of money, lent for the express purpose of accomplishing an illegal object, cannot be enforced." This Court, then, following *Cannan* v. *Bryce*, decided that it need not be part of the bargain that the subject of the contract should be used unlawfully, but that it is enough if it is handed over for the purpose that the borrower shall so apply it. We are, then, concluded by authority on the point; and, as I have no doubt that the finding of the jury was right, the rule must be discharged.

[Pollock C.B., Martin and Pigott BB. concurred in giving judgment for the defendant.]

Note

The intricacies of the law relating to illegality, and its effects on the rights of the contracting parties, are somewhat complex (see for example, H.S.B., pp. 528–538). Even if the agreement does contain an "illegal" element, a plaintiff is not necessarily without remedy. For example, it may be possible to "sever" the offending element or find a collateral contract as in *Strongman* (1945) v. *Simcock* (1955). A further example is set out below.

Shelley v. Paddock

[1979] 1 Q.B. 120 (Q.B.)

[Miss Shelley, the plaintiff, wished to buy a house in Spain. She entered into an agreement with the defendants, who in fact did not have authority to sell and were acting fraudulently, for the purchase of a house and duly paid over the purchase price. In fact, such a payment was illegal, being in breach of the then existing exchange control legislation which required Treasury consent for such a transaction. The plaintiff was completely unaware of this requirement and had acted quite innocently. The defendants were unable to convey a title to the house, and Miss Shelley brought an action in the tort of deceit for the return of the purchase price of £9,400. The defendants claimed, *inter alia*, that the plaintiff was unable to recover the payment because the agreement by which she had paid the money was an illegal transaction.]

Bristow J. [having outlined the facts continued] At any rate, what she did clearly was a breach of section 5 of the Exchange Control Act 1947. What is the effect of this?

The first expression of the principle of law with which we have to deal to which reference is made when this sort of problem arises was enunciated by Lord Mansfield as long ago as the 1770s. The case in which he enunciated it was *Holman* v. *Johnson* (1775):

"The objection, that a contract is immoral or illegal as between plaintiff and defendant, sounds at all times very ill in the mouth of the defendant. It is not for his sake, however, that the objection is ever allowed; but it is founded in general principles of policy, which the defendant has the advantage of, contrary to the real justice, as between him and the plaintiff, by accident, if I may say so. The principle of public policy is this; ex dolo malo non oritur actio. No court will lend its aid to a man who founds his cause of action upon an immoral or illegal act. If, from the plaintiff's own stating or otherwise, the cause of action appears to arise ex turpi causa, or the transgression of a positive law of this country, there the court says he has no right to be assisted. It is upon that ground the court goes; not for the sake of the defendant, but because they will not lend their aid to such plaintiff. So if the plaintiff and defendant were to change sides, and the defendant was to bring his action against the plaintiff, the latter would then have the advantage of it; for where both are equally in fault, potior est conditio defendentis."

The Latin is perhaps not unimportant in appreciating the principle and the reason for it. "Dolo malo" can be translated accurately as "a dirty trick." "Turpis" means shameful, wicked, disgraceful. Both the Latin words involve the stigma of blameworthy conduct.

The application of the principle between 1775 and 1977 has been the subject of a vast wealth of judicial authority, which is examined in all the textbooks. I do not propose to try to make any elaborate review of the authorities. Among other cases, there are cases in which a plaintiff who, in order to maintain his action, has disclosed that he has been involved in a breach of the Exchange Control Act 1947, and has been told that he cannot recover because of this principle. But in nearly all the cases, and certainly in the exchange control cases, the breach of the Exchange Control Act 1947 has been deliberate. If, as I find in this case, the plaintiff genuinely had not any idea that there was such a thing, does her innocence in this respect make any difference? Clearly, where somebody deliberately breaks the law, it would be absurd for the courts to lend their assistance to that person to establish rights which result from a deliberate breach of the law. Nearly all the cases involve perfectly deliberate breaches of the law at the time the transaction was entered into from which the rights sought to be established depend. I asked Mr. Barker whether there were any cases in which somebody who genuinely did not know that they were breaking the law had been held unable to succeed because of this principle. There is such a case, decided in the Court of Appeal in 1963. It is *J.M. Allan (Merchandising) Ltd.* v. *Cloke* (1963). It is the only case where a plaintiff did not know when the transaction was entered into that it was being entered into in breach of the law. It is a case which is of course binding upon me. But in that case the contract in breach of the law which was entered into was the hiring of a roulette outfit, wheel plus cloth plus croupier's rake, for the express purpose of what was in fact an illegal way of playing roulette. So that you had a continuing contract under which the hirer was seeking to recover the rent of the outfit, and although the court expressly held that both parties did not realise that the particular game for which the outfit was hired was illegal, for the court to enforce that contract once it was known it was illegal would clearly have been against public policy, just as in any other of the cases where a deal is entered into with knowledge that it is illegal.

The facts in this case are very different. The plaintiff does not sue on the contract. She says: "I have been defrauded. I sue in tort. It is true that I paid money in breach of the Exchange Control Act 1947"—she does not say that, but I do—"and I am asking for damages from the people who defrauded me, not for my money back."

In my judgment, there is nothing in the wealth of authority which has arisen on this principle, and nothing in the decision of the Court of Appeal in *J.M. Allan (Merchandising) Ltd.* v. *Cloke*—by which I am bound and which I respectfully regard as entirely correct and in accordance with principle—which prevents me from asking myself: given that the plaintiff did not know, how does the principle encapsulated in the Latin "dolus malus" or "turpis causa" apply to her? In my judgment, public policy does not require, and the law as I understand it and the principle enunciated by Lord Mansfield does not require, that the court shall not lend its assistance to the plaintiff in order to give her compensation for the wrong committed to her by the fraud of the defendants. In my judgment, she is entitled to succeed in this action. She is entitled to recover as damages for fraud the equivalent of what she paid the defendants, that is to say £9,400.

[The Court also awarded the plaintiff her expenses in making two abortive trips to Spain and £500 for her mental and physical suffering caused by the defendants' fraudulent conduct.]

Note

Bristow J.'s decision was subsequently upheld by the Court of Appeal (1980).

Chapter 9

Discharge

1. PERFORMANCE

A. Exact and Substantial Performance

Cutter v. Powell

(1795) 101 E.R. 573 (K.B.)

[Cutter agreed to serve as second mate on a ship bound from Kingston, Jamaica, to Liverpool. The agreement between the parties stated "Ten days after the ship 'Governor Parry', myself master, arrives at Liverpool, I promise to pay to Mr. T. Cutter the sum of thirty guineas, provided he proceeds, continues and does his duty as second mate in the said ship from hence to the port of Liverpool, Kingston July 31, 1793." Unfortunately Cutter died on the voyage before reaching Liverpool. His widow sued for the wages he had earned up to the date of his death; the defendant claimed that the agreement was one entire contract which had not been performed.]

Lord Kenyon Ch.J. I should be extremely sorry that in the decision of this case we should determine against what had been the received opinion in the mercantile world on contracts of this kind, because it is of great importance that the laws by which the contracts of so numerous and so useful a body of men as the sailors are supposed to be guided should not be overturned. Whether these kind of notes are much in use among the seamen, we are not sufficiently informed; and the instances now stated to us from Liverpool are too recent to form any thing like usage. But it seems to me at present that the decision of this case may proceed on the particular words of this contract and the precise facts here stated, without touching marine contracts in general. That where the parties have come to an express contract none can be implied has prevailed so long as to be reduced to an axiom in the law. Here the defendant expressly promised to pay the intestate thirty guineas, provided he proceeded, continued and did his duty as second mate in the ship from Jamaica to Liverpool; and the accompanying circumstances disclosed in the case are that the common rate of wages is four pounds per month, when the party is paid in proportion to the time he serves: and that this voyage is generally performed in two months. Therefore if there had been no contract between these parties, all that the intestate could have recovered on a quantum meruit for the voyage would have been eight pounds, whereas here the defendant contracted to pay thirty guineas provided the mate continued to do his duty as mate during the whole voyage, in which case the latter would have received nearly four times as much as if he were paid for the number of months he served. He stipulated to receive the larger sum if the whole duty were performed, and nothing unless the whole of that duty were performed: it was a kind of insurance. On this particular contract my opinion is formed at present; at the same time I must say that if we were assured that these notes are in universal use, and that the commercial world have received and acted upon them in a different sense, I should give up my own opinion.

[Ashurst, Grose and Lawrence JJ. concurred.]

Question

If the facts of *Cutter* v. *Powell* were to recur today, how would the court approach the problem?

Hoenig v. Isaacs

[1952] 2 All E.R. 176 (C.A.)

[An interior decorator agreed to decorate and furnish a flat for £750. The defendant paid £400 on account but refused to pay the remaining £350 on the grounds that the design and workmanship was faulty. It was found by the official referee that there were defects but the cost of remedying these came to some £56. The plaintiff claimed the £350; the official referee held there had been substantial compliance, and awarded him £294, being the balance claimed less the cost of rectifying the defects. The defendant appealed.]

Somervell L.J., stated the facts and continued. Counsel for the defendant submits that the decision of the official referee is wrong in law. He submits that this is an entire contract which, on the findings of fact, has not been performed. On the wellknown principle applied to the facts of that case in *Cutter* v. *Powell* he submitted that the plaintiff cannot, therefore, recover on his contract. He was not concerned to dispute that on this basis the plaintiff might on the facts of this case be entitled to recover on a quantum meruit. Such a claim has never been put forward. If it were, he submits that the amount recoverable would be the fair value of what was done and delivered. The learned official referee found that there had been a substantial compliance with the contract. Counsel submits that, if his first point is right, this does not enable the plaintiff to succeed. If necessary, he submits that on his findings of fact the learned official referee was wrong as a matter of law in holding that there had been substantial compliance. [His Lordship referred to the official referee's findings as to the wardrobe door, the bookshelf, and the bookcase, and continued:] If any issue arises whether the breaches were substantial, I think it must be based on the items to which I have referred, bearing in mind, of course, that there were some additional minor defects.

The official referee regarded the principle laid down in *H. Dakin & Co. Ltd.* v. *Lee* (1916) as applicable. The contract in that case was for repairs to a house. The official referee before whom the case came in the first instance found that the work as completed did not accord with the contract in certain respects. He proceeded to hold that the plaintiff could not recover any part of the contract price or any sum in respect of the contract work. This decision was reversed in the Divisional Court and their decision was affirmed by this court. In support of the official referee's decision it was argued that the plaintiff could not recover either on the contract or on a quantum meruit. No new contract on the latter basis could be implied from the fact that the defendant by continuing to live in her house had enjoyed the benefit of what had been done.

In *Eshelby* v. *Federated European Bank, Ltd.* (1932) *Greer, L.J.* clearly felt some difficulty about *H. Dakin & Co. Ltd.* v. *Lee* (1916) as possibly inconsistent with *Cutter* v. *Powell* (1975), and the cases following that decision and deciding that where work is to be done for a sum named neither that sum nor any part of it can be recovered while the work remains undone. We were referred to a number of these cases and I have considered those authorities and others. Each case turns on the construction of the contract. In *Cutter* v. *Powell* the condition for the promissory note sued on was that the sailor should proceed to continue and do his duty as second mate in the ship from Jamaica to the port of Liverpool. The sailor died before the ship reached Liverpool and it was held his estate could not recover either on the contract or on a quantum meruit. It clearly decided that his continuing as mate during the whole voyage was a condition precedent to payment. It did not decide that if he had completed the main purpose of the contract, namely, serving as mate for the whole voyage, the defendant could have repudiated his liability by establishing that in the course of the voyage the sailor had, possibly through inadvertence, failed on some occasion in his duty as mate whereby some damage had been caused. In these circumstances, the court might have applied the principle applied to ordinary contracts for freight. The shipowner can normally recover nothing unless the goods are carried to their agreed destination. On the other hand, if this is done, his claim is not defeated by the fact that some damage has been done to the goods in transit which has resulted from a breach of the contract. The owner of the goods has his remedy by cross-action: *Dakin* v. *Oxley* (1864). The damage might, of course, be so great as to raise the question whether what was agreed to be carried had substantially arrived (*ibid.*). *Sinclair* v. *Bowles* (1829) is often cited as an illustration of the *Cutter* v. *Powell* principle. The plaintiff had undertaken to repair chandeliers and make them "complete" or "perfect." This he, quite plainly on the evidence and findings of the jury, failed to do. It may, perhaps, be regarded as a case where, on the construction of the contract, having regard to the subject-matter, there was no scope for terms collateral to the main purpose.

The principle that fulfilment of every term is not necessarily a condition precedent in a contract for a lump sum is usually traced back to a short judgment of Lord Mansfield, C.J., in *Boone* v. *Eyre* (1779)—the sale of the plantation with its slaves. Lord Mansfield said . . . :

> ". . . where mutual covenants go to the whole of the consideration on both sides, they are mutual conditions, the one precedent to the other. But where they go only to a part, where a breach may be paid for in damages, there the defendant has a remedy on his covenant, and shall not plead it as a condition precedent."

One is very familiar with the application of this principle in the law relating to the sale of goods. Quoad stipulations which are conditions, the *Cutter* v. *Powell* principle is applicable. If they are not all performed the other party can repudiate, but there will not have been, as there was in *Cutter* v. *Powell*, a partial performance. But there may be other terms, collateral to the main purpose, the breach of which in English law gives rise to a claim for damages, but not to a right to reject the goods and treat the contract as repudiated: see definition of warranty, Sale of Goods Act, 1893, s.62.

In a contract to erect buildings on the defendant's land for a lump sum, the builder can recover nothing on the contract if he stops before the work is completed in the ordinary sense—in other words, abandons the contract. He is also usually in a difficulty in recovering on a quantum meruit because no new contract can be inferred from the mere fact that the defendant remains in possession of his land: *Sumpter* v. *Hedges* (1898). In *Appelby* v. *Myers* (1867) while the work was in progress the premises and the work so far done on them were destroyed by fire and the court held both parties excused. At the end of his judgment Blackburn, J., after referring to *Cutter* v. *Powell, Sinclair* v. *Bowles* (1829), and that line of cases, said ... :

" ... the plaintiffs, having contracted to do an entire work for a specific sum, can recover nothing unless the work be done ... "

in *H. Dakin & Co. Ltd.* v. *Lee* Lord Cozens-Hardy, M.R., I think, had this principle in mind when he said ...

"The work was finished—and when I say this I do not wish to prejudice matters, but I cannot think of a better word to use at the moment."

The question here is whether in a contract for work and labour for a lump sum payable on completion the defendant can repudiate liability under the contract on the ground that the work though "finished" or "done" is in some respects not in accordance with the contract. *H. Dakin & Co. Ltd.* v. *Lee* (1916) is, of course, binding on us, but counsel for the defendant submitted that it was an exception to a general rule applying to contracts such as that in issue here and should be confined within as narrow limits as possible. I agree with the learned editor of the notes to *Cutter* v. *Powell* in *Smith's Leading Cases*, ... that *H. Dakin & Co. Ltd.* v. *Lee*, so far from being an exception, re-affirmed the true position on the construction of this class of contract on which doubts had been thrown by taking certain observations out of their context.

. . . . . .

The learned official referee regarded *H. Dakin & Co. Ltd.* v. *Lee* as laying down that the price must be paid subject to set-off or counterclaim if there was a substantial compliance with the contract. I think on the facts of this case where the work was finished in the ordinary sense, though in part defective this is right. It expresses in a convenient epithet what is put from another angle in the Sale of Goods Act, 1893. The buyer cannot reject if he proves only the breach of a term collateral to the main purpose. I have, therefore, come to the conclusion that the first point of counsel for the defendant fails.

The learned official referee found that there was substantial compliance. Bearing in mind that there is no appeal on fact, was there evidence on which he could so find? The learned official referee having, as I hold, properly directed himself, this becomes, I think, a question of fact. The case on this point was, I think, near the border line, and if the finding had been the other way I do not think we could have interfered. Even if I had felt we could interfere, the defendant would be in a further difficulty. The contract included a number of chattels. If the defendant wished to repudiate his liability under the contract he should not, I think, have used those articles, which he could have avoided using. On this view, though it is not necessary to decide it, I think he put himself in the same position as a buyer of goods who by accepting them elects to treat a breach of condition as a breach of warranty.

I now come to the final question, the measure of damages. It seems from the argument that the defendant regards the price of £750 as excessive irrespective of any relief by way of reduction of price or on his counterclaim. He was anxious to put the plaintiff in the position of having to sue on a quantum meruit for the value of the work done and he was anxious to tender evidence designed, no doubt, to show that the work done was worth much less than £750. The learned official referee excluded this evidence. The measure he applied was the cost of putting the work in accordance with the contract and on this basis such evidence was rightly excluded. The defendant is bound, he held, to pay for the furniture supplied less the cost of putting right the defects. This I think is, as the learned official referee thought, in accordance with *H. Dakin & Co. Ltd.* v. *Lee.* Lord Cozens-Hardy, M.R., there said ... :

> "the builders are entitled to recover the contract price, less so much as it is found ought to be allowed in respect of the items which the official referee has found to be defective."

This seems to follow what was said by Parke B., in *Mondel* v. *Steel* (1841). In dealing with the procedural point he said ... that the defendant need not bring a cross-action but can diminish the price.

> "... by showing how much less the subject-matter of the contract was worth, by reason of the breach of contract."

I therefore think the appeal must be dismissed.

[Denning and Romer L.JJ. concurred in dismissing the appeal.]

Note

A case to contrast with the above is *Bolton* v. *Mahadeva* (1972). The cost of remedying defects was there £174 in the context of a price of £560 to install central heating. The Court of Appeal refused to allow the plaintiff's claim for payment of the agreed lump sum since they did not regard the performance as substantial.

B. Acceptance of Part Performance

Sumpter v. Hedges

[1898] 1 Q.B. 673 (C.A.)

[The plaintiff, a builder, agreed to erect certain buildings on the defendant's land for £565. After completing £333 worth of work he abandoned the contract, and the defendant had to complete the work himself. The builder sued the defendant on a *quantum meruit*.]

Collins L.J. I agree. I think the case is really concluded by the finding of the learned judge to the effect that the plaintiff had abandoned the contract. If the plaintiff had merely broken his contract in some way so as not to give the defendant the right to treat him as having abandoned the contract, and the defendant had then proceeded to finish the work himself, the plaintiff might perhaps have been entitled to sue on a quantum meruit on the ground that the defendant had taken the benefit of the work done. But this is not the present case. There are cases in which, though the plaintiff has abandoned the performance of a contract, it is possible for him to raise the inference of a new contract to pay for the work done on a quantum meruit from the defendant's having taken the benefit of that work, but, in order that that may be done, the circumstances must be such as to give an option to the defendant to take or not to take the benefit of the work done. It is only where the circumstances are such as to give that option that there is any evidence on which to ground the inference of a new contract. Where, as in the case of work done on land, the circumstances are such as to give the defendant no option whether he will take the benefit of the work or not, then one must look to other facts than the mere taking the benefit of the work in order to ground the inference of a new contract. In this case I see no other facts on which such an inference can be founded. The mere fact that a defendant is in possession of what he cannot help keeping, or even has done work upon it, affords no ground for such an inference. He is not bound to keep unfinished a building which in an incomplete state would be nuisance on his land. I am therefore of opinion that the plaintiff was not entitled to recover for the work which he had done.

[Smith and Chitty L.JJ. concurred in dismissing the appeal.]

C. Vicarious Performance

British Waggon Co. v. Lea

(1880) 5 Q.B.D. 149 (Q.B.)

[The plaintiffs let a number of railway wagons to the defedants under a contract which required the latter to keep them in good repair. Consequent upon the liquidation of the plaintiffs' company, the task of maintaining the wagons was assigned to another company. The defendants resisted an action for the rent on the trucks on the grounds that the plaintiffs were, in effect, in breach of contract in not themselves maintaining the trucks.]

Cockburn C.J. The main contention on the part of the defendants, however, was that, as the Parkgate Company had, by assigning the contracts, and by making over their repairing stations to the British Company, incapacitated themselves to fulfil their obligation to keep the waggons in repair, that company had no right, as between themselves and the defendants, to substitute a third party to do the work they had engaged to perform, nor were the defendants bound to accept the party so substituted as the one to whom they were to look for performance of the contract; the contract was therefore at an end.

[His Lordship considered an authority involving the repair of a carriage.]

In like manner, where goods are ordered of a particular manufacturer, another, who has succeeded to his business, cannot execute the order, so as to bind the customer, who has not been made aware of the transfer of the business, to accept the goods. The latter is entitled to refuse to deal with any other than the manufacturer whose goods he intended to buy. For this *Boulton* v. *Jones* (1857) is a sufficient authority. The case of *Robson* v. *Drummond* (1831) comes nearer to the present case, but is, we think, distinguishable from it. We entirely concur in the principle on which the decision in *Robson* v. *Drummond* rests, namely, that where a person contracts with another to do work or perform service, and it can be inferred that the person employed has been selected with reference to his individual skill, competency, or other personal qualification, the inability or unwillingness of the party so employed to execute the work or perform the service is a sufficient answer to any demand by a stranger to the original contract of the performance of it by the other party, and entitles the latter to treat the contract as at an end, notwithstanding that the person tendered to take the place of the contracting party may be equally well qualified to do the service. Personal performance is in such a case of the essence of the contract, which, consequently, cannot in its absence be enforced against an unwilling party. But this principle appears to us inapplicable in the present instance, inasmuch as we cannot suppose that in stipulating for the repair of these waggons by the company—a rough description of work which ordinary workmen conversant with the business would be perfectly able to execute—the defendants attached any importance to whether the repairs were done by the company, or by any one with whom the company might enter into a subsidiary contract to do the work. All that the hirers, the defendants, cared for in this stipulation was that the waggons should be kept in repair; it was indifferent to them by whom the repairs should be done. Thus if, without going into liquidation, or assigning these contracts, the company had entered into a contract with any competent party to do the repairs, and so had procured them to be done, we cannot think that this would have been a departure from the Berms of the contract to keep the waggons in repair. ...

Much work is contracted for, which it is known can only be executed by means of subcontracts; much is contracted for as to which it is indifferent to the party for whom it is to be done, whether it is done by the immediate party to the contract, or by someone in his behalf. In all these cases the maxim Qui facit per alium facit per se applies.

Judgment for the plaintiff.

2. AGREEMENT

In Chapter 2 we have seen how the doctrine of consideration and promissory estoppel affect the formation and operation of a contract. The law will not generally enforce a gratuitous promise, or permit reliance upon an equally gratuitous waiver of the other party's obligations. Similar principles apply, albeit at a different stage, to the discharge of a contract by agreement. They are not, therefore, dealt with at length again here (see H.S.B., pp. 547–550).

An illuminating example is provided by *Charles Rickards Ltd.* v. *Oppenhaim* (1950). The defendant ordered a body to be built on a car chassis, the work to be completed within "six or seven months." At the end of this time the work was not finished, but he agreed to wait another three months. On this aspect of the case see below:

Charles Rickards Ltd. v. Oppenhaim

[1950] 1 K.B. 616

Denning L.J. If this had been originally a contract without any stipulation as to time and, therefore, with only the implication of reasonable time, it may be that the plaintiffs could have said that they had fulfilled the contract; but in my opinion the case is very different when there was an initial contract, making time of the essence of the contract: "within six or at the most, seven months." I agree that that initial time was waived by reason of the requests that the defendant made after March, 1948, for delivery; and that, if delivery had been tendered in compliance with those requests, the defendant could not have refused to accept the coach-body. Suppose, for instance, that delivery had been tendered in April, May, or June, 1948: the defendant would have had no answer. It would be true that the plaintiffs could not aver and prove they were ready and willing to deliver in accordance with the original contract. They would have had, in effect, to rely on the waiver almost as a cause of action. At one time there would have been theoretical difficulties about their doing that. It would have been said that there was no consideration; or, if the contract was for the sale of goods, that there was nothing in writing to support the variation. There is the well-known case of *Plevins* v. *Downing* (1876), coupled with what was said in *Besseler, Waechter, Glover & Co.* v. *South Derwent Coal Co. Ltd.* (1938), which gave rise to a good deal of difficulty on that score; but all those difficulties were swept away now. If the defendant, as he did, led the plaintiffs to believe that he would not insist on the stipulation as to time, and that, if they carried out the work, he would accept it, and they did it, he could not afterwards set up the stipulation as to the time against them. Whether it be called waiver or forbearance on his part, or an agreed variation or substituted performance, does not matter. It is a kind of estoppel. By his conduct he evinced an intention to affect their legal relations. He made, in effect, a promise not to insist on his strict legal rights. That promise was intended to be acted on, and was in fact acted on. He cannot afterwards go back on it. I think not only that that follows from *Panoutsos* v. *Raymond Hadley Corporation of New York* (1917), a decision of this court, but that it was also anticipated in *Bruner* v. *Moore* (1904). It is a particular application of the principle which I endeavoured to state in *Central London Property Trust Ltd.* v. *High Trees House Ltd.* (1947).

[In fact, the car was not delivered within even the extended time and the defendant thereupon gave reasonable notice that unless it was ready by a certain date, he would not accept it. It was not ready, and by his actions the defendant had once again made time of the essence in the contract. The plaintiffs were therefore in clear breach of contract and the action failed.]

Note

See also, for an example of discharge by "accord and satisfaction," *British Russian Gazette Ltd.* v. *Associated Newspapers Ltd.* (1933) (H.S.B., p. 550).

3. BREACH

Photo Production Ltd. v. Securicor

[1980] A.C. 827 (H.L.)

[Securicor had been employed to provide a night patrol service to their client's factory. In the course of such a visit one of Securicor's employees decided to light a small fire. It became a big one. The result was £615,000 worth of damage to the factory, although it was found that the employee did not intend to burn down the premises and that Securicor had not been negligent in employing or supervising him. The fee for the provision of the service was only £8.15s. a week. When sued, Securicor relied upon an exemption clause which stated:]

"Under no circumstances shall the company [Securicor] be responsible for any injurious act or default by any employee of the company unless such act or default could have been foreseen and avoided by the exercise of due diligence on the part of the company as his employer, nor, in any event, shall the company be held responsible for (a) any loss suffered by the customer through burglary, theft, fire or any other cause, except in so far as such loss is solely attributable to the negligence of the company's employees acting within the court of their employment ... "

The Court of Appeal, following the *Harbutt's Plasticine* case gave judgment for the plaintiffs on the grounds that there had been a fundamental breach of the contract which brought it to an end, so preventing reliance upon the exemption clause. In the alternative, the clause could not be construed to apply to the events which had actually occurred. The defendants appealed.]

Lord Wilberforce ...

[After stating that the *ratio decidendi* of the *Suisse Atlantique* case (1967) was accurately summarised in the headnote, which stated, "the question whether an exceptions clause was applicable where there was a fundamental breach of contract was one of the true construction of the contract," continued:]

1. The doctrine of "fundamental breach" in spite of its imperfections and doubtful parentage has served a useful purpose. There was a large number of problems, productive of injustice, in which it was worse than unsatisfactory to leave exception clauses to operate. Lord Reid referred to these in the *Suisse Atlantique* case (1967), pointing out at the same time that the doctrine of fundamental breach was a dubious specific. But since then Parliament has taken a hand: it has passed the Unfair Contract Terms Act 1977. This Act applies to consumer contracts and those based on standard terms and enables exception clauses to be applied with regard to what is just and reasonable. It is significant that Parliament refrained from legislating over the whole field of contract. After this Act, in commercial matters generally, when the parties are not of unequal bargaining power, and when risks are normally borne by insurance, not only is the case for judicial intervention undemonstrated, but there is everything to be said, and this seems to have been Parliament's intention, for leaving the parties free to apportion the risks as they think fit and for respecting their decisions.

At the stage of negotiations as to the consequences of a breach, there is everything to be said for allowing the parties to estimate their respective claims according to the contractual provisions they have themselves made, rather than for facing them with a legal complex so uncertain as the doctrine of fundamental breach must be. What, for example, would have been the position of the respondents' factory if instead of being destroyed it had been damaged, slightly or moderately or severely? At what point does the doctrine (with what logical justification I have not understood) decide, ex post facto, that the breach was (factually) fundamental before going on to ask whether legally it is to be regarded as fundamental? How is the date of "termination" to be fixed? Is it the date of the innocent party's election, or some other date? All these difficulties arise from the doctrine and are left unsolved by it.

At the judicial stage there is still more to be said for leaving cases to be decided straightforwardly on the parties have bargained for rather than upon analysis, which becomes progressively more refined, of decisions in other cases leading to inevitable appeals. The learned judge was able to decide this case on normal principles of contractual law with minimal citation of authority. I am sure that most commercial judges have wished to be able to do the same: see *Trade and Transport Inc.* v. *Ilno Kaiun Kaisha Ltd.* (1973), *per* Kerr J. In my opinion they can and should.

2.   The case of *Harbutt* (1970) must clearly be overruled. It would be enough to put that upon its radical inconsistency with the *Suisse Atlantique* case (1967). But even if the matter were res integra I would find the decision to be based upon unsatisfactory reasoning as to the "termination" of the contract and the effect of "termination" on the plaintiffs' claim for damage. I have, indeed been unable to understand how the doctrine can be reconciled with the well accepted principle of law, stated by the highest modern authority, that when in the context of a breach of contract one speaks of "termination," what is meant is no more than that the innocent party or, in some cases, both parties, are excused from further performance. Damages, in such cases, are then claimed under the contract, so what reason in principle can there be for disregarding what the contract itself says about damages—whether it "liquidates" them, or limits them, or excludes them? These difficulties arise in part from uncertain or inconsistent terminology. A vast number of expressions are used to describe situations where a breach has been committed by one party of such a character as to entitle the other party to refuse further performance: discharge, rescission, termination, the contract is at an end, or dead, or displaced clauses cannot survive, or simply go. I have come to think that some of these difficulties can be avoided; in particular the use of "rescission," even if distinguished from rescission ab initio, as an equivalent for discharge, though justifiable in some contexts (see *Johnson* v. *Agnew* (1980)) may lead to confusion in others. To plead for complete uniformity may be to cry for the moon. But what can and ought to be

avoided is to make use of these confusions in order to produce a concealed and unreasoned legal innovation to pass, for example, from saying that a party, victim of a breach of contract, is entitled to refuse further performance, to saying that he may treat the contract as at an end, or as rescinded, and to draw from this the proposition, which is not analytical but one of policy, that all or (arbitrarily) some of the clauses of the contract lose, automatically, their force, regardless of intention.

If this process is discontinued the way is free to use such words as "discharge" or "termination" consistently with principles as stated by modern authority which *Harbutt's* case (1970) disregards. I venture with apology to relate the classic passages. In *Heyman* v. *Darwins Ltd.* (1942) Lord Porter said:

> "To say that the contract is rescinded or has come to an end or has ceased to exist may in individual cases convey the truth with sufficient accuracy, but the fuller expression that the injured party is thereby absolved from future performance of his obligations under the contract is a more exact description of the position. Strictly speaking, to say that on acceptance of the renunciation of a contract the contract is rescinded is incorrect. In such a case the injured party may accept the renunciation as a breach going to the root of the whole of the consideration. By that acceptance he is discharged from further performance and may bring an action for damages, but the contract itself is not rescinded."

And similarly Lord MacMillan ... : see also *Boston Deep Sea Fishing and Ice Co.* v. *Ansell* (1888), *per* Bowen L.J. In *Lep Air Services Ltd.* v. *Rolloswin Investments Ltd.* (1973), my noble and learned friend, Lord Diplock, drew a distinction (relevant for that case) between primary obligations under a contract, which on "recission" generally come to an end, and secondary obligations which may then arise. Among the latter he includes an obligation to pay compensation, *i.e.* damages. And he states in terms that this latter obligation "is just as much an obligation arising from the contract as are the primary obligations that it replaces." My noble and learned friend has developed this line of thought in an enlightening manner in his opinion which I have now had the benefit of reading.

These passages I believe to state correctly the modern law of contract in the relevant respects: they demonstrate that the whole foundation of *Harbutt's* case (1970) is unsound.

......

3. I must add to this, by way of exception to the decision not to "gloss" the *Suisse Atlantique* (1967) a brief observation

on the deviation cases, since some reliance has been placed upon them, particularly upon the decision of this House in *Hain Steamship Co. Ltd.* v. *Tate and Lyle Ltd.* (1936) (so earlier than the *Suisse Atlantique*) in the support of the *Harbutt* doctrine. I suggested in the *Suisse Atlantique* that these cases can be regarded as proceeding upon normal principles applicable to the law of contract generally viz., that it is a matter of the parties' intentions whether and to what extent clauses in shipping contracts can be applied after a deviation, *i.e.* a departure from the contractually agreed voyage or adventure. It may be preferable that they should be considered as a body of authority sui generis with special rules derived from historical and commercial reasons. What on either view they cannot do is to lay down different rules as to contracts generally from those later stated by this House in *Heyman* v. *Darwins Ltd.* (1942). . . .

4. It is not necessary to review fully the numerous cases in which the doctrine of fundamental breach has been applied or discussed. Many of these have now been superseded by the Unfair Contract Terms Act 1977. Others, as decisions, may be justified as depending upon the construction of the contract (see *Levison* v. *Patent Steam Carpet Cleaning Co. Ltd.* (1978)) in the light of well known principles such as that stated in *Alderslade* v. *Hendon Laundry Ltd.* (1945).

In this situation the present case has to be decided. As a preliminary the nature of the contract has to be understood. Securicor undertook to provide a service of periodical visits for a very modest charge which works out at 26p per visit. It did not agree to provide equipment, it would have no knowledge of the value of the plaintiffs' factory: that and the efficacy of their fire precautions, would be known to the respondents. In these circumstances nobody could consider it unreasonable that as between these two equal parties the risk assumed by Securicor should be a modest one, and that the respondents should carry the substantial risk of damage or destruction.

The duty of Securicor was, as stated, to provide a service. There must be implied an obligation to use due care in selecting their patrolmen, to take care of the keys and, I would think, to operate the service with due and proper regard to the safety and security of the premises. The breach of duty committed by Securicor lay in a failure to discharge this latter obligation. Alternatively it could be put upon a vicarious responsibility for the wrongful act of Musgrove—viz., starting a fire on the premises: Securicor would be responsible for this upon the principle stated in *Morris* v. *C.W. Martin & Sons Ltd.* (1966). This being the breach, does condition 1 apply? It is drafted in strong terms, "Under no circumstances" ... "any injurious act or default by any employee." These words have to be approached with the aid of the cardinal rules of construction that they must be read contra proferentem and that in order to escape from the consequences of one's own wrongdoing, or that of one's servant, clear words are necessary. I think that these words are clear. The respondents in fact relied upon them for an argument that since they exempted from negligence they must be taken as not exempting from the consequence of deliberate acts. But this is a perversion of the rule that if a clause can cover something other than negligence, it will not be applied to negligence. Whether, in addition to negligence, it covers other, *e.g.* deliberate, acts, remains a matter of construction requiring, of course, clear words. I am of opinion that it does, and being free to construe and apply the clause, I must hold that liability is excluded. On this part of the case I agree with the judge and adopt his reasons for judgment. I would allow the appeal.

[Lords Keith and Scarman agreed with Lord Wilberforce. Lords Diplock and Salmon gave judgments also allowing the appeal.]

Ailsa Craig Fishing Co. Ltd. v. Malvern Fishing Co. Ltd.

[1983] 1 All E.R. 101 (H.L.)

[Here Securicor agreed to provide security services for certain vessels moored in Aberdeen harbour. As a result of their failure to perform the contract two ships sank. They sought to rely on a limitation clause which greatly restricted their liability to pay damages in such an event. The Scottish Court of Session held that Securicor's liability was limited by the clause even though there had been a total failure by them to perform the contract. There was an appeal to the House of Lords.]

Lord Wilberforce. My Lords, the only questions for decision in these appeals are (i) whether the liability of the respondents, Securicor (Scotland) Ltd, under a short-term contract made on December 31, 1971, has been effectively limited by a special condition in that contract, and if so (ii) [what were the damages].

Whether a condition limiting liability is effective or not is a question of construction of that condition in the context of the contract as a whole. If it is to exclude liability for negligence, it must be most clearly and unambiguously expressed, and, in such a contract as this, must be construed contra proferentem. I do not think that there is any doubt so far. But I venture to add one further qualification, or at least clarification: one must not strive to create ambiguities by strained construction, as I think the appellants have striven to do. The relevant words must be given, if possible, their natural, plain meaning. Clauses of limitation are not regarded by the courts with the same hostility as clauses of exclusion; this is because they must be related to other contractual terms, in particular to the risks to which the defending party may be exposed, the remuneration which he receives and possibly also the opportunity of the other party to insure.

It is clear, on the findings of Lord Ordinary (Wylie), that the respondents were negligent as well as in material breach of their contractual obligations. The negligence consisted in a total or partial failure to provide the service contract for, viz "continuous security cover for your [the appellants'] vessels from 1900 hours on 31/12/71 until 0700 hours on 5/1/72" over the increased area specified in the contract. It is arguable, in my opinion, that the failure was not total, in that some security against some risks was provided, though not that which was necessary to prevent the actual damage which occurred. But I do not think that it makes a difference as regards the applicability of the clause of limitation whether this is right or not, and since their Lordships in the Inner House were of opinion that the failure was total, I will proceed on the assumption that this was so.

The clause of limitation was as follows (condition 2(f) of the special conditions of the contract):

> "If, pursuant to the provisions set out herein, any liability on the part of the Company shall arise (whether under the express or implied terms of this Contract, or at Common law, or in any other way) to the customer for any loss or damage of whatever nature arising out of or connected with the provision of, or purported provision of, or failure in provision of, the services covered by this Contract, such liability shall be limited to the payment by the Company by way of damages of a sum [alternatives are then stated to which I shall refer later]."

This clause is on the face of it clear. It refers to failure in provision of the services covered by the contract. There is no warrant as a matter of construction for reading "failure" as meaning "partial failure," *i.e.* as excluding "total failure" and there is no warrant in authority for so reading the word as a matter of law.

[Lords Elynn-Jones, Salmon, Fraser and Lowry all concurred in dismissing the appeal.]

George Mitchell (Chesterhall) Ltd. v. Finney Lock Seeds

[1983] 1 All E.R. 108 (C.A.)

Lord Denning M.R. Some farmers, called George Mitchell (Chesterhall) Ltd, ordered 30lb of cabbage seed. It was supplied. It looked just like cabbage seed. No one could say it was not. The farmers planted it over 63 acres. Six months later there appeared out of the ground a lot of loose green leaves. They looked like cabbage leaves but they never turned in. They had no hearts. They were not "cabbages" in our common parlance because they had no hearts. The crop was useless for human consumption. Sheep or cattle might eat it if hungry enough. It was commercially useless. The price of the seed was £192. The loss to the farmers was over £61,000. They claimed damages from the seed merchants, Finney Lock Seeds Ltd. The judge awarded them that sum with interest. The total comes to nearly £100,000.

The seed merchants appeal to this court. They say that they supplied the seed on a printed clause by which their liability was limited to the cost of the seed, that is £192. They rely much on two recent cases in the House of Lords: *Photo Production Ltd. v. Securicor Transport Ltd* (1980) and *Ailsa Craig Fishing Co. Ltd. v. Malvern Fishing Co. Ltd.* (1983) (the two *Securicor* cases).

For the last 25 years these farmers, and other farmers in the maritime belt, have got their seed from Finneys who get it from Holland. Finneys had a respresentative, Mr Wing. He called on the farmers each year. At Christmas 1973 he came. They gave him an order by word of mouth for 30lb of Finneys Late Dutch Special Cabbage Seed. There was no order in writing. In February 1974 the seeds arrived. The invoice gave the date of despatch as 14 February 1974:

"30lbs Cabbage Finneys Late Dutch Special £192.00 ... IMPORTANT.—For Seeds Act statutory declarations, Conditions of Sale etc., see reverse."

Then on the back there were in small printed [*sic*] many conditions of sale. Included in them was the clause relied on by Finneys. They say that their liability was limited to the return of the price, £192, and that they are not liable for the £61,000 claimed.

Are the conditions part of the contract?

The farmers were aware that the sale was subject to some conditions of sale. All seed merchants have conditions of sale. They were on the back of the catalogue. They were also on the back of the invoice each year. So it would seem that the farmers were bound at common law by the terms of them. The infererence from the course of dealing would be that the farmers had accepted the conditions as printed, even though they had never read them and did not realise that they contained a limitation on liability.

But, in view of modern developments, it is to be noticed that the conditions were not negotiated at all between any representative bodies. They were not negotiated by the National Farmers' Union. They were introduced by the seed merchants by putting them in their catalogue and invoice, and never objected to by the farmers.

It is also to be noticed that the farmers never thought of insuring against any breach of contract by the seedsmen. It would be difficult to get any quotation. It might be possible for the seed merchants to insure themselves, something in the nature of a product liability insurance. Some seed merchants do so.

The printed condition here

The limitation clause here is of long standing in the seed trade. It has been in use for many years. The material part of it is as follows:

"All Seeds, Bulbs, Corms, Tubers, Roots, Shrubs, Trees and Plants (hereinafter referred to as 'Seeds or Plants') offered for sale or sold by us to which the Seeds Act 1920 or the Plant Varieties and Seeds Act 1964 as the case may be and the Regulations thereunder apply have been tested in accordance with the provisions of the same. In the event of any seeds or plants sold or agreed to be sold by us not complying with the express terms of the contract of sale or with any representation made by us or by any duly authorised agent or representative on our behalf prior to, at the time of, or in any such contract, or any seeds or plants proving defective in varietal purity *we will, at our option, replace the defective seeds or plants, free of charge to the buyer or will refund all payments made to us by the buyer in respect of the defective seeds or plants and this shall be the limit of our obligation. We hereby exclude all liability for any loss or damage arising from the use of any seeds or plants supplied by us and for any consequential loss or damage arising out of such use* or any failure in the performance of or any defect in any seeds or plants supplied by us *or for any other loss or damage whatsoever save for, at our option, liability for any such replacement or refund as aforesaid.* In accordance with the established custom of the Seed Trade any express or implied condition, statement or warranty, statutory or otherwise, not stated in these Conditions is hereby excluded. *The price of any seeds or plants sold or offered for sale by us is based upon the foregoing limitations upon our liability. The price of such seeds or plants would be much greater if a more extensive liability were required to be undertaken by us.*" (My emphasis.)

The natural meaning

There was much discussion before us as to the construction of that condition. I am much impressed by the words I have emphasised. Taking the clause in its natural plain meaning, I think it is effective to limit the liability of the seed merchants to a return of the money or replacement of the seeds. The explanation they give seems fair enough. They say that it is so as to keep the price low, and that if they were to undertake any greater liability the price would be much greater.

After all, the seed merchants did supply seeds. True, they were the wrong kind altogether. But they were seeds. On the natural interpretation, I think the condition is sufficient to limit the seed merchants to a refund of the price paid or replacement of the seeds.

The hostile meaning

Before the decisions of the House of Lords in the two *Securicor* cases, I would have been inclined to decide the case as the judge did. I would have been "hostile" to the clause. I would have said that the goods supplied here were different *in kind* from those that were ordered, and that the seed merchants could not avail themselves of the limitation clause. But in the light of the House of Lords cases, I think that that approach is not available.

I am particularly impressed by the words of Lord Wilberforce in the *Ailsa Craig* case (1983) where he said:

"... one must not strive to create ambiguities by strained construction, as I think the appellants have striven to do. The relevant words must be given, if possible, their natural, plain meaning. Clauses of limitation are not regarded by the courts with the same hostility as clauses of exclusion; this is because they must be related to other contractual terms, in particular to the risks to which the defending party may be exposed, the remuneration which he receives and possibly also the opportunity of the other party to insure."

To my mind these two cases have revolutionised our approach to exemption clauses. In order to explain their importance, I propose to take you through the story.

The heyday of freedom of contract

None of you nowadays will remember the trouble we had, when I was called to the Bar, with exemption clauses. They were printed in small print on the back of tickets and order forms and invoices. They were contained in catalogues or timetables. They were held to be binding on any person who took them without objection. No one ever did object. He never read them or knew what was in them. No matter how unreasonable they were, he was bound. All this was done in the name of "freedom of contract." But the freedom was all on the side of the big concern which had the use of the printing press. No freedom for the little man who took the ticket or order form or invoice. The big concern said, "Take it or leave it." The little man had no option but to take it. The big concern could and did exempt itself from liability in its own interest without regard to the little man. It got away with it time after time. When the courts said to the big concern, "You must put it in clear words," the big concern had no hesitation in doing so. It knew well that the little man would never read the exemption clauses or understand them.

It was a bleak winter for our law of contract. It is illustrated by two cases, *Thompson* v. *London Midland and Scottish Rly. Co.* (1930) (in which there was exemption from liability, not on the ticket, but only in small print at the back of the timetable, and the company were held not liable) and *L'Estrange* v. *F. Graucob Ltd.* (1934) (in which there was complete exemption in small print at the bottom of the order form, and the company were held not liable). [See p. 463.]

The secret weapon

Faced with this abuse of power, by the strong against the weak, by the use of the small print of the conditions, the judges did what they could to put a curb on it. They still had before them the idol, "freedom of contract." They still knelt down and worshipped it, but they concealed under their cloaks a secret weapon. They used it to stab the idol in the back. This weapon was called "the true construction of the contract." They used it with great skill and ingenuity. They used it so as to depart from the natural meaning of the words of the exemption clause and to put on them a strained and unnatural construction. In case after case, they said that the words were not strong enough to give the big concern exemption from liability, or that in the circumstances the big concern was not entitled to rely on the exemption clause. If a ship deviated from the contractual voyage, the owner could not rely on the exemption clause. If a warehouseman stored the goods in the wrong warehouse, he could not pray in aid the limitation clause. If the seller supplied goods difference in kind from those contracted for, he could not rely on any exemption from liability. If a shipowner delivered goods to a person without production of the bill of lading, he could not escape responsibility by reference to an exemption clause. In short, whenever the wide words, in their natural meaning, would give rise to an unreasonable result, the judges either rejected them as repugnant to the main purpose of the contract or else cut them down to size in order to produce a reasonable result. This is illustrated by these cases in the House of Lords: *Glynn* v. *Margetson & Co.* (1893), *London and North Western Rly. Co.* v. *Neilson* (1922), *Cunard Steamship Co. Ltd.* v. *Buerger* (1927); and by these in the Privy Council: *Canada Steamship Lines Ltd.* v. *R.* (1952), *Sze Hai Tong Bank Ltd.* v. *Rambler Cycle Co. Ltd.* (1959); and innumerable cases in the Court of Appeal, culminating in *Levison* v. *Patent Steam Carpet Cleaning Co. Ltd.* (1978). But when the clause was itself reasonable and gave rise to a reasonable result, the judges upheld it, at any rate when the clause did not exclude liability entirely but only limited it to a reasonable amount. So, where goods were deposited in a cloakroom or sent to a laundry for cleaning, it was quite reasonable for the company to limit their liability to a reasonable amount, having regard to the small charge made for the service. These are illustrated by *Gibaud* v. *Great Eastern Rly. Co.* (1921), *Alderslade* v. *Hendon Laundry Ltd.* (1945) and *Gillespie Bros. & Co. Ltd.* v. *Roy Bowles Transport Ltd.* (1973).

Fundamental breach

No doubt had ever been cast thus far by anyone. But doubts arose when in this court, in a case called *Karsales (Harrow) Ltd.* v. *Wallis* (1956), we ventured to suggest that if the big concern was guilty of a breach which went to the "very root" of the contract, sometimes called a "fundamental breach," or at other times a "total failure" of its obligations, then it could not rely on the printed clause to exempt itself from liability. This way of putting it had been used by some of the most distinguished names in the law such, as Lord Dunedin in *W. & S. Pollock & Co.* v. *Macrae* (1922) Lord Atkin and Lord Wright in *Hain Steamship Co. Ltd.* v. *Tate & Lyle Ltd.* (1936) and Devlin J. in *Smeaton Hanscomb & Co. Ltd.* v. *Sassoon I Setty Son & Co. (No. 1)* (1953). But we did make a mistake, in the eyes of some, in elevating it, by inference, into a "rule of law." That was too rude an interference with the idol of "freedom of contract." We ought to have used the secret weapon. We ought to have said that in each case, on the "true construction of the contract" in that case, the exemption clause did not avail the party where he was guilty of a fundamental breach or a breach going to the root. That is the lesson to be learnt from the "indigestible" speeches in *Suisse Atlantique Société d'Armement Maritime SA* v. *NV Rotterdamsche Kolen Centrale* (1967). They were all *obiter dicta*. The House were dealing with an agreed damages clause and not an exemption clause and the point had never been argued in the courts below at all. It is noteworthy that the House did not overrule a single decision of the Court of Appeal. Lord Wilberforce appears to have approved them. ... At any rate, he cast no doubt on the actual decision in any case.

The change in climate

In 1969 there was a change in climate. Out of winter into spring. It came with the first report of the Law Commission on Exemption Clauses in Contracts (Law Com No. 24) which was implemented in the Supply of Goods (Implied Terms) Act 1973. In 1975 there was a further change. Out of spring into summer. It came with their second report on Exemption Clauses (Law Com No. 69) which was implemented by the Unfair Contract Terms Act 1977. No longer was the big concern able to impose whatever terms and conditions it liked in a printed form, no matter how unreasonable they might be. These reports showed most convincingly that the courts could and should only enforce them if they were fair and reasonable in themselves and it was fair and reasonable to allow the big concern to rely on them. So the idol of "freedom of contract" was shattered. In cases of personal injury or death, it was not permissible to exclude or restrict liability at all. In consumer contracts any exemption clause was subject to the test of reasonableness.

These reports and statutes have influenced much the thinking of the judges. At any rate, they influenced me as you will see if you read *Gillespie Bros & Co. Ltd.* v. *Roy Bowles*

Transport Ltd. (1973) and *Photo Production Ltd.* v. *Securicor Transport Ltd.* (1978):

> "Thus we reach, after long years, the principle which lies behind all our striving: the court will not allow a party to rely on an exemption or limitation clause in circumstances in which it would not be fair or reasonable to allow reliance on it; and, in considering whether it is fair and reasonable, the court will consider whether it was in a standard form, whether there was equality of bargaining power, the nature of the breach, and so forth."

The effect of the changes

What is the result of all this? To my mind it heralds a revolution in our approach to exemption clauses; not only where they exclude liability altogether and also where they limit liability; not only in the specific categories in the Unfair Contract Terms Act 1977, but in other contracts too. Just as in other fields of law we have done away with the multitude of cases on "common employment," "last opportunity," "invitees" and "licensees" and so forth, so also in this field we should do away with the multitude of cases on exemption clauses. We should no longer have to go through all kinds of gymnastic contortions to get round them. We should no longer have to harass our students with the study of them. We should set about meeting a new challenge. It is presented by the test of reasonableness.

The two Securicor cases

The revolution is exemplified by the recent two *Securicor* cases in the House of Lords (*Photo Production Ltd.* v. *Securicor Transport Ltd.* (1980) and *Ailsa Craig Fishing Co. Ltd.* v. *Malvern Fishing Co. Ltd.* (1983)). In each of them the Securicor company provided a patrolman to keep watch on premises so as to see that they were safe from intruders. They charged very little for the service. In the *Photo Production* case it was a factory with a lot of paper in it. The patrolman set light to it and burnt down the factory. In the *Ailsa Craig* case it was a quay at Aberdeen where ships were berthed. The patrolman went off for the celebrations on New Year's Eve. He left the ships unattended. The tide rose. A ship rose with it. Its bow got "snubbed" under the deck of the quay. It sank. In each case the owners were covered by insurance. The factory owners had their fire insurance. The shipowners had their hull insurance. In each case the Securicor company relied on a limitation clause. Under it they were protected from liability beyond a limit which was quite reasonable and their insurance cover was limited accordingly. The issue in practical terms was: which of the insurers should bear the loss? The question in legal terms in each case was whether Securicor could avail themselves of the limitation clause. In each case the House held that they could.

In the first case the House made it clear that the doctrine of "fundamental breach" was no longer applicable. They replaced it by the test of reasonableness. That was the test applied by the trial judge MacKenna J. which I myself quoted with approval. He said:

> "Condition 1, as I construe it, is, I think, a reasonable provision. ... Either the owner of the premises, or the person providing the service, must bear the risk. Why should the parties not agree to its being borne by the [owner of the premises]? He is certain to be insured against fire and theft, and is better able to judge the cover needed than the party providing the service.... That is only another way of shifting the risk from the party who provides the service to the party who received it. There is, as I have said, nothing unreasonable, nothing impolitic, in such a contract."

His judgment was approved by the House of Lords, who themselves held that the limitation clause was valid because it was a reasonable way of opportioning the risks, as between the insurers on either side. I would set out two passages to prove it. Lord Wilberforce said ...:

> "Securicor undertook to provide a service of periodical visits for a very modest charge which works out at 26p per visit. It did not agree to provide equipment. It would have no knowledge of the value of Photo Productions' factory; that, and the efficacy of their fire precautions, would be known to Photo Productions. In these circumstances nobody could consider it unreasonable that as between these two equal parties the risk assumed by Securicor should be a modest one, and that Photo Productions should carry the substantial risk of damage or destruction."

And Lord Diplock said:

> "For the reasons given by Lord Wilberforce it seems to me that this apportionment of the risk of the factory being damaged or destroyed by the injurious act of an employee of Securicor while carrying out a visit to the factory is one which reasonable businessmen in the position of Securicor

and Photo Productions might well think was the most economical. An analogous apportionment of risk is provided for by the Hague Rules in the case of goods carried by sea under bills of lading."

I do hope, however, that we shall not often have to consider the new-found analysis of contractual obligations into "primary obligations," "secondary obligations," "general secondary obligations" and "anticipatory secondary obligations." No doubt it is logical enough, but it is too esoteric altogether. It is fit only for the ratified atmosphere of the House of Lords. Not at all for the chambers of the practitioner. Let alone for the student at the university.

In the second case the House made a distinction between clauses which excluded liability altogether, and those which only limited liability to a certain sum. Exclusion clauses were to be construed strictly contra proferentem, whereas limitation clauses were to be construed naturally. This must be because a limitation clause is more likely to be reasonable than an exclusion clause. If you go by the plain, natural meaning of the words (as you should do) there is nothing to choose between them. As Lord Sumner said fifty years ago in *Atlantic Shipping and Trading Co.* v. *Louis Dreyfus & Co.* (1922):

"There is no difference in principle between words which save them from having to pay at all and words which save them from paying as much as they would otherwise have had to pay."

If you read the speeches in the *Ailsa Craig* case, it does look as if the House of Lords were relying on the reasonableness of the limitation clause. They held it was applicable even though the failure of the Securicor company was a "total failure" to provide the service contracted for. They also said, obiter, that they would construe an exclusion clause much more strictly, just as was done in the old cases decided in the winter time. But I would suggest that the better reason is because it would not be fair or reasonable to allow the propounder of them to rely on them in the circumstances of the case.

The Supply of Goods (Implied Terms) Act 1973

In any case the contract for these cabbage seeds was governed by s.4 of the Supply of Goods (Implied Terms) Act 1973: see now s.55(4) as set out in para. 11 of Sch. 1 to the Sale of Goods Act 1979. That section says that in the case of a contract of sale of goods any term "is ... not enforceable to the extent that it is shown that it would not be fair or reasonable to allow reliance on the term." That provision is exactly in accord with the principle which I have advocated above. So the ultimate question, to my mind, in this case is just this: to what extent would it be fair or reasonable to allow the seed merchants to rely on the limitation clause?

Fair and reasonable

There is only one case in the books so far on this point. It is *R.W. Green Ltd.* v. *Cade Bros. Farm* (1978). There Griffiths J held that it was fair and reasonable for seed potato merchants to rely on a limitation clause which limited their liability to the contract price of the potatoes. That case was very different from the present. The terms had been evolved over twenty years. The judge said ...: "They are therefore not conditions imposed by the strong upon the weak; but are rather a set of trading terms upon which both sides are apparently content to do business." The judge added ...: "No moral blame attaches to either party; neither of them knew, nor could be expected to know, that the potatoes were infected." In that case the judge held that the clause was fair and reasonable and that the seed merchants were entitled to rely on it.

Our present case is very much on the borderline. There is this to be said in favour of the seed merchants. The price of this cabbage seed was small: £192. The damages claimed are high: £61,000. But there is this to be said on the other side. The clause was not negotiated between persons of equal bargaining power. It was inserted by the seed merchants in their invoices without any negotiation with the farmers.

To this I would add that the seed merchants rarely, if ever, invoked the clause. Their very frank director said: "The trade does not stand on the strict letter of the clause. ... Almost invariably when a customer justifiably complains, the trade pays something more than a refund." The papers contain many illustrations where the clause was not invoked and a settlement was reached.

Next, I would point out that the buyers had no opportunity at all of knowing or discovering the seed was not cabbage seed, whereas the sellers could and should have known that it was the wrong seed altogether. The buyers were not covered by insurance against the risk. No could they insure. But, as to the seed merchants, the judge said:

"I am entirely satisfied that it is possible for seedsmen to insure against this risk. I am entirely satisfied that the cost of so doing would not materially raise the price of seeds on the market. I am entirely satisfied that the protection of this clause for the purposes of protecting against the very rare case indeed, such as the present, is not reasonably required. If and in so far as it may be necessary to consider the matter, I am also satisfied that it is possible for seedsmen to test seeds before putting them on to the market."

To that I would add this further point. Such a mistake as this could not have happened without serious negligence on the part of the seed merchants themselves or their Dutch suppliers. So serious that it would not be fair to enable them to escape responsibility for it.

In all the circumstances I am of opinion that it would not be fair or reasonable to allow the seed merchants to rely on the clause to limit their liability.

I would dismiss the appeal accordingly.

[Oliver and Kerr L.JJ also gave judgments dismissing the appeal. The decision of the Court of Appeal was later affirmed by the House of Lords, [1983] 2 All E.R. 737.]

Note

As regards exemption clauses, reference should also be made to the discussion of incorporation at p. 455 and the terms of the Unfair Contract Terms Act 1977 at p. 623.

4. FRUSTRATION

Krell v. Henry

[1903] 2 K.B. 740 (C.A.)

[The defendant made a written agreement for the hire of a suite of rooms overlooking the coronation procession of Edward VII. The agreement did not expressly mention the procession, but both parties understood that this was the reason for the hire. The procession was cancelled, but the plaintiff nevertheless sued for the balance of the hire fee. The plaintiff appealed to the Court of Appeal against the trial judge's judgment for the defendant.]

Vaughan Williams L.J. The real question in this case is the extent of the application in English law of the principle of the Roman law which has been adopted and acted on in many English decisions, and notably in the case of *Taylor* v. *Caldwell* (1863). That case at least makes it clear that "where, from the nature of the contract, it appears that the parties must from the beginning have known that it could not be fulfilled unless, when the time for the fulfilment of the contract arrived, some particular specified thing continued to exist, so that when entering into the contract they must have contemplated such continued existence as the foundation of what was to be done; there, in the absence of any express or implied warranty that the thing shall exist, the contract is not to be considered a positive contract, but as subject to an implied condition that the parties shall be excused in case, before breach, performance becomes impossible from the perishing of the thing without default of the contractor." Thus far it is clear that the principle of the Roman law has been introduced into the English law. The doubt in the present case arises as to how far this principle extends. The Roman law dealt with obligationes de certo corpore. Whatever may have been the limits of the Roman law, the case of *Nickoll* v. *Ashton* (1901) makes it plain that the English law applies the principle not only to cases where the performance of the contract becomes impossible by the cessation of existence of the thing which is the subject-matter of the contract, but also to cases where the event which renders the contract incapable of performance is the cessation or non-existence of an express condition or state of things, going to the root of the contract, and essential to its performance. It is said, on the one side, that the specified thing, state of things, or condition the continued existence of which is necessary for the fulfilment of the contract, so that the parties entering into the contract must have contemplated the continued existence of that thing, condition, or state of things as the foundation of what was to be done under the contract, is limited to things which are either the subject-matter of the contract or a condition or state of things, present or anticipated, which is expressly mentioned in the contract. But, on the other side, it is said that the condition or state of things need not be expressly specified, but that it is sufficient if that condition or state of things clearly appears by extrinsic evidence to have been assumed by the parties to be the foundation or basis of the contract, and the event which causes the impossibility is of such a character that it cannot reasonably be supposed to have been in the contemplation of the contracting parties when the contract was made. In such a case the contracting parties will not be held bound by the general words which, though large enough to include, were not used with reference to a possibility of a particular event rendering performance of the contract impossible. I do not think that the principle of the civil law as introduced into the English law is limited to cases in which the event causing the impossibility of performance is the destruction or non-existence of some thing which is the subject-matter of the contract or of some condition or state of things expressly specified as a condition of it. I think that you first have to ascertain, not necessarily from the terms of the contract, but, if required, from necessary inferences, drawn from surrounding circumstances recognised by both contracting parties, what is the substance of the contract, and then to ask the question whether that substantial contract needs for its foundation the assumption of the existence of a particular state of things. If it does, this will limit the operation of the general words, and in such case, if the contract becomes impossible of performance by reason of the non-existence of the state of things assumed by both contracting parties as the foundation of the contract, there will be no breach of the contract thus limited. Now what are the facts of the present case?

[His Lordship stated them.]

In my judgment the use of the rooms was let and taken for the purpose of seeing the Royal procession. It was not a demise of the rooms, or even an agreement to let and take the rooms. It is a licence to use rooms for a particular purpose and none other. And in my judgment the taking place of those processions on the days proclaimed along the proclaimed route, which passed 56A, Pall Mall, was regarded by both contracting parties as the foundation of the contract; and I think that it cannot reasonably be supposed to have been in the contemplation of the contracting parties, when the contract was made, that the coronation would be held on the proclaimed days, or the processions not take place on those days along the proclaimed route; and I think that the words imposing on the defendant the obligation to accept and pay for the use of the rooms for the named days, although general and unconditional, were not used with reference to the possibility of the particular contingency which afterwards occurred. It was suggested in the course of the argument that if the occurrence, on the proclaimed days, of the coronation and the procession in this case were the foundation of the contract, and if the general words are thereby limited or qualified, so that in the event of the non-occurrence of the coronation and procession along the proclaimed route they would discharge both parties from further performance of the contract, it would follow that if a cabman was engaged to take

some one to Epsom on Derby Day at a suitable enhanced
price for such a journey, say 10*l*., both parties to the contract
would be discharged in the contingency of the race at Epsom
for some reason becoming impossible; but I do not think this
follows, for I do not think that in the cab case the happening
of the race would be the foundation of the contract. No doubt
the purpose of the engager would be to go to see the Derby,
and the price would be proportionately high; but the cab had
no special qualifications for the purpose which led to the
selection of the cab for this particular occasion. Any other cab
would have done as well. Moreover, I think that, under the
cab contract, the hirer, even if the race went off, could have
said, "Drive me to Epsom; I will pay you the agreed sum; you
have nothing to do with the purpose for which I hired the
cab," and that if the cabman refused he would have been
guilty of a breach of contract, there being nothing to qualify
his promise to drive the hirer to Epsom on a particular day.
Whereas in the case of the coronation, there is not merely the
purpose of the hirer to see the coronation procession, but it is
the coronation procession and the relative position of the
rooms which is the basis of the contract as much for the lessor
as the hirer; and I think that if the King, before the coronation
day and after the contract, had died, the hirer could not have
insisted on having the rooms on the days named. It could not
in the cab case be reasonably said that seeing the Derby race
was the foundation of the contract, as it was of the licence in
this case. Whereas in the present case, where the rooms were
offered and taken; by reason of their peculiar suitability from
the position of the rooms for a view of the coronation
procession, surely the view of the coronation procession was
the foundation of the contract, which is a very different thing
from the purpose of the man who engaged the cab—namely,
to see the race—being held to be the foundation of the
contract. Each case must be judged by its own circumstances.
In each case one must ask oneself, first, what, having regard
to all the circumstances, was the foundation of the contract?
Secondly, was the performance of the contract prevented?
Thirdly, was the event which prevented the performance of
the contract of such a character that it cannot reasonably be
said to have been in the contemplation of the parties at the
date of the contract? If all these questions are answered in the
affirmative (as I think they should be in this case), I think
both parties are discharged from further performance of the
contract. I think that the coronation procession was the
foundation of this contract, and that the non-happening of it
prevented the performance of the contract; and, secondly, I
think that the non-happening of the procession, to use the

words of Sir James Hannen in *Baily* v. *De Crespigny* (1869) was an event "of such a character that it cannot reasonably be supposed to have been in the contemplation of the contracting parties when the contract was made, and that they are not to be held bound by general words which, though large enough to include, were not used with reference to the possibility of the particular contingency which afterwards happened." The test seems to be whether the event which causes the impossibility was or might have been anticipated and guarded against. It seems difficult to say, in a case where both parties anticipate the happening of an event, which anticipation is the foundation of the contract, that either party must be taken to have anticipated, and ought to have guarded against, the event which prevented the performance of the contract. In both *Jackson* v. *Union Marine Insurance Co.* (1874) and *Nickoll* v. *Ashton* (1901) the parties might have anticipated as a possibility that perils of the sea might delay the ship and frustrate the commercial venture: in the former case the carriage of the goods to effect which the charterparty was entered into; in the latter case the sale of the goods which were to be shipped on the steamship which was delayed. But the Court held in the former case that the basis of the contract was that the ship would arrive in time to carry out the contemplated commercial venture, and in the latter that the steamship would arrive in time for the loading of the goods the subject of the sale. I wish to observe that cases of this sort are very different from cases where a contract or warranty or representation is implied, such as was implied in *The Moorcock* (1889), and refused to be implied in *Hamlyn* v. *Wood* (1891). But *The Moorcock* is of importance in the present case as shewing that whatever is the suggested implication—be it condition, as in this case, or warranty or representation—one must, in judging whether the implication ought to be made, look not only at the words of the contract, but also at the surrounding Dacts and the knowledge of the parties of those facts. There seems to me to be ample authority for this proposition.

[His Lordship cited the relevant authorities.]

I see no difficulty whatever in the case. It is not essential to the application of the principle of *Taylor* v. *Caldwell* that the direct subject of the contract should perish or fail to be in existence at the date of performance of the contract. It is sufficient if a state of things or condition expressed in the

contract and essential to its performance perishes or fails to be
in existence at that time. In the present case the condition
which fails and prevents the achievement of that which was,
in the contemplation of both parties, the foundation of the
contract, is not expressly mentioned either as a condition of
the contract or the purpose of it; but I think for the reasons
which I have given that the principle of *Taylor* v. *Caldwell*
(1863) ought to be applied. This disposes of the plaintiff's
claim for 50*l.* unpaid balance of the price agreed to be paid for
the use of the rooms.

Judgment for the defendant.

Note

For an example of a "coronation case" in which it was held that the
contract had not been frustrated, contrast *Herne Bay Steam Boat Company* v.
Hutton (1903).

Fibrosa Spolka Akcyjna v. Fairbairn Lawson Combe Barbour Ltd.

[1943] A.C. 32 (H.L.)

[Fairbairn agreed to make some machinery for Fibrosa (a Polish company) in
July 1939 for a price of £4,800. Of this amount £1,600 was payable in advance
although only £1,000 was in fact paid over by Fibrosa. By September 1940 the
place of delivery in Poland was under German occupation and the contract
was therefore frustrated. Fibrosa claimed the return of their £1,000. The Court
of Appeal rejected the claim relying on the authority of *Chandler* v. *Webster*
(1904). This, another "coronation case," had stated that where money was
payable before the frustrating event, it could not be recovered on the grounds
that frustration only operated from the time of the frustrating event. It did
not therefore affect rights which had accrued before this. Fibrosa appealed to
the House of Lords.]

Viscount Simon L.C.

[Having considered the implications of *Chandler* v. *Webster* continued:]

If we are to approach this problem anew, it must be
premised that the first matter to be considered is always the
terms of the particular contract. If, for example, the contract is
"divisible" in the sense that a sum is to be paid over in
respect of completion of a defined portion of the work, it may

well be that the sum is not returnable if completion of the whole work is frustrated. If the contract itself on its true construction stipulates for a particular result which is to follow in regard to money already paid, should frustration afterwards occur, this governs the matter. The ancient and firmly established rule that freight paid in advance is not returned if the completion of the voyage is frustrated: *Byrne* v. *Schiller* (1871) should, I think, be regarded as a stipulation introduced into such contracts by custom, and not as the result of applying some abstract principle. And so, a fortiori, if there is a stipulation that the prepayment is "out and out." To take an example, not from commerce, but from sport, the cricket spectator who pays for admission to see a match cannot recover the entrance money on the ground that rain has prevented play if, expressly or by proper implication, the bargain with him is that no money will be returned. In as much as the effect of frustration may be explained as arising from an implied term: see *Joseph Constantine Steamship Line, Ltd.* v. *Imperial Smelting Corporation Ltd.* (1942); it is tempting to speculate whether a further term could be implied as to what was to happen, in the event of frustration, to money already paid, but, if the parties were assumed to have discussed the point when entering into the contract, they could not be supposed to have agreed on a simple formula which would be fair in all circumstances, and all that could be said is that, in the absence of such agreement, the law must decide. The question now to be determined is whether, in the absence of a term in the contract dealing with the matter, the rule which is commonly called the rule in *Chandler* v. *Webster* (1904) should be affirmed.

[His Lordship considered the case noting that it had been criticised.]

The locus classicus for the view which has hitherto prevailed is to be found in the judgment of Collins M.R. in *Chandler* v. *Webster*. It was of a considered judgment, but it is hardly necessary to say that I approach this pronouncement of the then Master of the Rolls with all the respect due to so distinguished a common lawyer. When his judgment is studied, however, one cannot but be impressed by the circumstances that he regarded the proposition that money in such cases could not be recovered back as flowing from the decision in *Taylor* v. *Caldwell* (1863). *Taylor* v. *Caldwell*, however, was not a case in which any question arose whether money could be recovered back, for there had been no payment in advance, and there is nothing in the judgment of Blackburn J., which, at any rate in terms, affirms the general proposition that "the loss lies where it falls." The application by Collins M.R. of *Taylor* v. *Caldwell* to the actual problem with which he had to deal in *Chandler* v. *Webster* deserves close examination. He said: "The plaintiff contends that he is entitled to recover the money which he had paid on the ground that here has been a total failure of consideration. He says that the condition on which he paid the money was that the procession should take place, and that, as it did not take place, there has been a total failure of consideration. That contention does no doubt raise a question of some difficulty, and one which has perplexed the courts to a considerable extent in several cases. The principle on which it has been dealt with is that which was applied in *Taylor* v. *Caldwell*—namely, that where, from causes outside the volition of the parties, something which was the basis of, or essential to the fulfilment of, the contract has become impossible, so that, from the time when the fact of that impossibility has been ascertained, the contract can no further be performed by either party, it remains a perfectly good contract up to that point, and everything previously done in pursuance of it must be treated as rightly done, but the parties are both discharged from further performance of it. If the effect were that the contract were wiped out altogether, no doubt the result would be that money paid under it would have to be repaid as on a failure of consideration. But that is not the effect of the doctrine; it only releases the parties from further performance of the contract. Therefore the doctrine of failure of consideration does not apply."

It appears to me that the reasoning in this crucial passage is open to two criticisms: (*a*) The claim of a party, who has paid money under a contract, to get the money back, on the ground that the consideration for which he paid it has totally failed, is not based on any provision contained in the contract, but arises because, in the circumstances that have happened, the law gives a remedy in quasi-contract to the party who has not got that for which he bargained. It is a claim to recover money to which the defendant has no further right because in the circumstances that have happened the money must be regarded as received to the plaintiff's use. It is true that the effect of frustration is that, while the contract can no further be performed, "it remains a perfectly good contract up to that point, and everything previously done in pursuance of it must be treated as rightly done," but it by no means follows that the situation existing at the moment of frustration is one which leaves the party that has paid money and has not received the stipulated consideration without any remedy. To claim the return of money paid on the ground of total failure of consideration is not to vary the terms of the contract in any way. The claim arises not because the right to be repaid is one of the stipulated conditions of the contract, but because, in the circumstances that have happened, the law gives the remedy. It is the failure to distinguish between the action of assumpsit for money had and received in a case where the consideration has wholly failed, and an action on the contract itself, which explains the mistake which I think has been made in applying English law to this subject-matter. Thus, in *Blakeley* v. *Muller & Co.* (1903), Lord Alverstone C.J. said, "I agree that *Taylor* v. *Caldwell* applies, but the consequence of that decision is that neither party here could have sued on the contract in respect of anything which was to be done under it after the procession had been abandoned." That is true enough, but it does not follow that because the plaintiff cannot sue "on the contract" he cannot sue dehors the contract for the recovery of a payment in respect of which consideration has failed. In the same case, Wills J. relied on *Appleby* v. *Myers* (1867) where a contract was made for the erection by A. of machinery on the premises of B., to be paid for on completion. There was no prepayment and in the course of the work the premises were destroyed by fire. It was held that both parties were excused from further performance, and that no liability accrued on either side, but the liability referred to was liability under the contract, and the learned judge seems to have thought that no action to recover money in such circumstances as the present could be conceived of unless there was a term of the contract, express or implied, which so provided. Once it is realized that the action to recover money for a consideration that has wholly failed rests, not on a contractual bargain between the parties, but, as Lord Sumner said in *Sinclair* v. *Brougham* (1914), "upon a notional or imputed promise to repay," or (if it is preferred to omit reference to a fictitious promise) upon an obligation to repay arising from the circumstances, the difficulty in the way of holding that a prepayment made under a contract which has been frustrated can be recovered back appears to me to disappear. (*b*) There is, no doubt, a distinction between cases in which a contract is "wiped out altogether," *e.g.* because it is void as being illegal from the start or as being due to fraud which the innocent party has elected to treat as avoiding the contract, and cases in which intervening impossibility "only releases the parties from further performance of the contract." But does the distinction between these two classes of case justify the deduction of Collins M.R. that "the doctrine of failure of consideration does not apply" where the contract remains a perfectly good contract up to the date of frustration? This conclusion seems to be derived from the view that, if the contract remains good and valid up to the moment of frustration, money which has already been paid under it cannot be regarded as having been paid for a consideration which has wholly failed. The party that has paid the money has had the advantage, whatever it may be worth, of the promise of the other party. That is true, but it is necessary to draw a distinction. In English law, an enforceable contract may be formed by an exchange of a promise for a promise, or by the exchange of a promise for an act—I am excluding contracts under seal—and thus, in the law relating to the formation of contract, the promise to do a thing may often be the consideration, but when one is considering the law of failure of consideration and of the quasi-contractual right to recover money on that ground, it is, generally speaking, not the promise which is referred to as the consideration, but the performance of the promise. The money was paid to secure performance and, if performance fails the inducement which brought about the payment is not fulfilled.

If this were not so, there could never be any recovery of money, for failure of consideration, by the payer of the money in return for a promise of future performance, yet there are endless examples which show that money can be recovered, as for a complete failure of consideration, in cases where the promise was given but could not be fulfilled.... A simple illustration of the same result is an agreement to buy a horse, the price to be paid down, but the horse not to be delivered and the property not to pass until the horse had been shod. If the horse dies before the shoeing, the price can unquestionably be recovered as for a total failure of consideration, notwithstanding that the promise to deliver was given. This is the case of a contract de certo corpore where the certum corpus perishes after the contract is made, but, as Vaughan Williams L.J.'s judgment in *Krell* v. *Henry* (1903) explained, the same doctrine applies "to cases where the event which renders the contract incapable of performance is the cessation or non-existence of an express condition or state of things, going to the root of the contract, and essential to its performance." I can see no valid reason why the right to recover prepaid money should not equally arise on frustration arising from supervening circumstances as it arises on frustration from destruction of particular subject-matter. The conclusion is that the rule in *Chandler* v. *Webster* (1904) is wrong, and that the appellants can recover their 1000*l.*

While this result obviates the harshness with which the previous view in some instances treated the party who had made a prepayment, it cannot be regarded as dealing fairly between the parties in all cases, and must sometimes have the result of leaving the recipient who has to return the money at a grave disadvantage. He may have incurred expenses in connection with the partial carrying out of the contract which are equivalent, or more than equivalent, to the money which he prudently stipulated should be prepaid, but which he now has to return for reasons which are no fault of his. He may have to repay the money, though he has executed almost the whole of the contractual work, which will be left on his hands. These results follow from the fact that the English common law does not undertake to apportion a prepaid sum in such circumstances. ... It must be for the legislature to decide whether provision should be made for an equitable apportionment of prepaid moneys which have to be returned by the recipient in view of the frustration of the contract in respect of which they were paid. I move that the appeal be allowed, and that judgment be entered for the appellants.

[Lords Atkin, Russel, MacMillan, Wright, Roche and Porter concurred.]

Notes

The legislature's response to Viscount Simon's criticisms was the Law Reform (Frustrated Contracts) Act 1943, for which see p. 619. Since, however, this Act does not apply to every contract and may be excluded by the parties themselves, the common law remains important.

The somewhat complex provisions of this Act are subjected to a detailed and helpful commentary in the judgment of Robert Goff J. in *BP Exploration* v. *Hunt (No. 2)* (1979).

Question

How would the cases of *Cutter* v. *Powell* (see p. 570), and *Fibrosa* be decided under the terms of the 1943 Act?

Chapter 10

Remedies

1. REMOTENESS OF DAMAGE

Victoria Laundry (Windsor) Ltd. v. Newman Industries Ltd.

[1949] 2 K.B. 528 (C.A.)

[The plaintiffs, who were launderers and dyers, required a larger boiler to expand their business. The defendants agreed to install a boiler on June 5, 1946, but in breach of contract it was not delivered until November 8, 1946. The plaintiffs claimed under two heads: (i) £16 a week damages for loss of profits for the extra custom they could have taken on, and (ii) £262 a week which they could have obtained under certain lucrative contracts with the Ministry of Supply.]

Asquith L.J. [delivering the judgment of the court (Tucker, Asquith and Singleton L.JJ.)] The authorities on recovery of loss of profits as a head of damage are not easy to reconcile. At one end of the scale stand cases where there has been nondelivery or delayed delivery of what is on the face of it obviously a profit-earning chattel; for instance, a merchant or passenger ship: see *Fletcher* v. *Tayleur* (1855); *In re Trent and Humber Company, ex parte Cambrian Steam Packet Company* (1868); or some essential part of such a ship; for instance, a propeller, in *Wilson* v. *General Ironscrew Company* (1887), or engines, *Saint Line* v. *Richardson* (1940). In such cases loss of profit has rarely been refused. A second and intermediate class of case in which loss of profit has often been awarded is where ordinary mercantile goods have been sold to a merchant with knowledge by the vendor that the purchaser wanted them for resale; at all events, where there was no market in which the purchaser could buy similar goods against the contract on the seller's default, see, for instance, *Borries* v. *Hutchinson* (1865). At the other end of the scale are cases where the defendant is not a vendor of the goods, but a carrier, see, for instance, *Hadley* v. *Baxendale* (1854) and *Gee* v.

Lancashire and Yorkshire Railway (1860). In such cases the courts have been slow to allow loss of profit as an item of damage. This was not, it would seem, because a different principle applies in such cases, but because the application of the same principle leads to different results. A carrier commonly knows less than a seller about the purposes for which the buyer or consignee needs the goods, or about other "special circumstances" which may cause exceptional loss if due delivery is withheld.

Three of the authorities call for more detailed examination. First comes *Hadley* v. *Baxendale* (1854) itself. Familiar though it is, we should first recall the memorable sentence in which the main principles laid down in the case are enshrined: "Where two parties have made a contract which one of them has broken, the damages which the other party ought to receive in respect of such breach of contract should be such as may fairly and reasonably be considered as either arising naturally, *i.e.* according to the usual course of things, from such breach of contract itself, or such as may reasonably be supposed to have been in the contemplation of both parties, at the time they made the contract, as the probable "result of the breach of it." The limb of this sentence prefaced by "either" embodies the so-called "first" rule that prefaced by "or" the "second." In considering the meaning and application of these rules, it is essential to bear clearly in mind the facts on which *Hadley* v. *Baxendale* (1854) proceeded. The head-note is definitely misleading in so far as it says that the defendant's clerk, who attended at the office, was told that the mill was stopped and that the shaft must be delivered immediately. The same allegation figures in the statement of facts which are said ... to have "appeared" at the trial before Crompton J. If the Court of Exchequer had accepted these facts as established, the court must, one would suppose, have decided the case the other way round; must, that is, have held the damage claimed was recoverable under the second rule. But it is reasonably plain from Alderson B's judgment that the court rejected this evidence, for ... he says: "We find that the only circumstances here communicated by the plaintiffs to the defendants at the time when the contract was made were that the article to be carried was the broken shaft of a mill and that the plaintiffs were the millers of that mill," and it is on this basis of fact that he proceeds to ask, "How do these circumstances show reasonably that the profits of the mill must be stopped by an unreasonable delay in the delivery "of the broken shaft by the carrier to the third person?"

British Columbia Sawmills v. *Nettleship* (1868) annexes to the principle laid down in *Hadley* v. *Baxendale* (1854) a rider to the effect that where knowledge of special circumstances is relied on as enhancing the damage recoverable that knowledge must have been brought home to the defendant at the time of the contract and in such circumstances that the defendant impliedly undertook to bear any special loss referable to a breach in those special circumstances. The knowledge which was lacking in that case on the part of the defendant was knowledge that the particular box of machinery negligently lost by the defendants was one without which the rest of the machinery could not be put together and would therefore be useless.

Cory v. *Thames Ironworks Company* (1868)—a case strongly relied on by the plaintiffs—presented the peculiarity that the parties contemplated respectively different profit-making uses of the chattel sold by the defendant to the plaintiff. It was the hull of a boom derrick, and was delivered late. The plaintiffs were coal merchants, and the obvious use, and that to which the defendants believed it was to be put, was that of a coal store. The plaintiffs, on the other hand, the buyers, in fact intended to use it for transhipping coals from colliers to barges, a quite unprecedented use for a chattel of this kind, one quite unsuspected by the sellers and one calculated to yield much higher profits. The case accordingly decides, *inter alia*, what is the measure of damage recoverable when the parties are not *ad idem* in their contemplation of the use for which the article is needed. It was decided that in such a case no loss was recoverable beyond what would have resulted if the intended use had been that reasonably within the contemplation of the defendants, which in that case was the "obvious" use. This special complicating factor, the divergence between the knowledge and contemplation of the parties respectively, has somewhat obscured the general importance of the decision, which is in effect that the facts of the case brought it within the first rule of *Hadley* v. *Baxendale* (1854) and enabled the plaintiff to recover loss of such profits as would have arisen from the normal and obvious use of the article. The "natural consequence," said Blackburn J., of not delivering the derrick was that 420*l.* representing those normal profits was lost. Cockburn C.J., interposing during the argument, made the significant observation: "No doubt in order to recover damage arising from a special purpose the buyer must have communicated the special purpose to the seller; but there is one thing which must always be in the knowledge of both parties, which is that the thing is bought for the purpose of being in some way or other profitably applied." This observation is apposite to the present case.

These three cases have on many occasions been approved by the House of Lords without any material qualification.

What propositions applicable to the present case emerge from the authorities as a whole, including those analysed above? We think they include the following:—

(1) It is well settled that the governing purpose of damages is to put the party whose rights have been violated in the same position so far as money can do so, as if his rights had been observed: (*Sally Wertheim* v. *Chicoutimi Pulp Company* (1911)). This purpose, if relentlessly pursued, would provide him with a complete indemnity for all loss *de facto* resulting from a particular breach, however improbable, however unpredictable. This, in contract at least, is recognised as too harsh a rule. Hence,

(2) In cases of breach of contract the aggrieved party is only entitled to recover such part of the loss actually resulting as was at the time of the contract reasonably forseeable as liable to result from the breach.

(3) What was at that time reasonably so foreseeable depends on the knowledge then possessed by the parties or, at all events, by the party who later commits the breach.

(4) For this purpose, knowledge "possessed" is of two kinds; one imputed, the other actual. Everyone, as a reasonable person, is taken to know the "ordinary course of things" and consequently what loss is liable to result from a breach of contract in that ordinary course. This is the subject-matter of the "first rule" in *Hadley* v. *Baxendale*. But to this knowledge, which a contract-breaker is assumed to possess whether he actually possesses it or not, there may have to be added in a particular case knowledge which he actually possesses, of special circumstances outside the "ordinary course of things," of such a kind that a breach in those special circumstances would be liable to cause more loss. Such a case attracts the operation of the "second rule" so as to make additional loss also recoverable.

(5) In order to make the contract-breaker liable under either rule it is not necessary that he should actually have asked himself what loss is liable to result from a breach. As has often been pointed out, parties at the time of contracting contemplate not the breach of the contract, but its performance. It suffices that, if he had considered the question, he would as a reasonable man have concluded that the loss in question was liable to result (see certain observations of Lord du Parcq in the recent case of *A/B Karlshamns Oljefabriker* v. *Monarch Steamship Company Limited* (1949)).

(6) Nor, finally, to make a particular loss recoverable, need it be proved that upon a given state of knowledge the

defendant could, as a reasonable man, foresee that a breach must necessarily result in that loss. It is enough if he could foresee it was likely so to result. It is indeed enough, to borrow from the language of Lord du Parcq in the same case, ... if the loss (or some factor without which it would not have occurred) is a "serious possibility" or a "real danger." For short, we have used the word "liable" to result. Possibly the colloquialism "on the cards" indicates the shade of meaning with some approach to accuracy.

If these, indeed, are the principles applicable, what is the effect of their application to the facts of this case?

[The court held that the defendants, as an engineering company who were not therefore mere "laymen" in the matter, could reasonably foresee that loss of business profits would result from the delay in delivery. They were not, however, aware of the especially lucrative supply contract and so were not liable for the loss of profits on those contracts.]

Note

The principles of the rule in *Hadley* v. *Baxendale* were subsequently considered by the House of Lords in *Koufos* v. *C. Czarnikow Ltd. (The Heron II)* (1969). The judgments, although refining it somewhat, appear to leave the principles of the rule essentially intact.

2. QUANTIFICATION

Chaplin v. Hicks

[1911] 2 K.B. 786 (C.A.)

[The defendant agreed with the plaintiff that if she attended an audition along with 49 other actresses she would have the chance of being one of the 12 chosen for employment as an actress. The plaintiff, in breach of contract, failed to give her a reasonable opportunity to attend but claimed that only nominal damages could be recovered for a loss of such a speculative kind.]

Vaughan Williams L.J. It was said that the plaintiff's chance of winning a prize turned on such a number of contingencies that it was impossible for any one, even after arriving at the conclusion that the plaintiff had lost her opportunity by the breach, to say that there was any assessable value of that loss. It is said that in a case which involves so many contingencies it is impossible to say what was the plaintiff's pecuniary loss. I am unable to agree with that contention. I agree that the presence of all the contingencies upon which the gaining of the prize might depend makes the calculation not only difficult but incapable of being carried out with certainty or precision. The proposition is that, whenever the contingencies on which the result depends are numerous and difficult to deal with, it is impossible to recover any damages for the loss of the chance or opportunity of winning the prize. In the present case I understand that there were 50 selected competitors, of whom the plaintiff was one, and 12 prizes, so that the average chance of each competitor was about one in four. Then it is said that the questions which might arise in the minds of the judges are so numerous that it is impossible to say that the case is one in which it is possible to apply the doctrine of averages at all. I do not agree with the contention that, if certainty is impossible of attainment, the damages for a breach of contract are unassessable. I agree, however, that damages might be so unassessable that the doctrine of averages would be inapplicable because the necessary figures for working upon would not be forthcoming; there are several decisions, which I need not deal with, to that effect. I only wish to deny with emphasis that, because precision cannot be arrived at, the jury has no function in the assessment of damages.

In early days when it was necessary to assess damages, no rules were laid down by the Courts to guide juries in the assessment of damages for breach of contract; it was left to the jury absolutely. But in course of time judges began to give advice to juries; as the stress of commerce increased, let us say between the reigns of Queen Elizabeth and Queen Victoria, rule after rule was suggested by way of advice to juries by the judges when damages for breach of contract had to be assessed. But from first to last there were, as there are now, many cases in which it was difficult to apply definite rules. In the case of a breach of a contract for the delivery of goods the damages are usually supplied by the fact of there being a market in which similar goods can be immediately bought, and the difference between the contract price and the price given for the substituted goods in the open market is the measure of damages; that rule has been always recognised. Sometimes, however, there is no market for the particular class of goods; but no one has ever suggested that, because there is no market, there are no damages. In such a case the jury must do the best they can, and it may be that the amount of their verdict will really be a matter of guesswork. But the fact that damages cannot be assessed with certainty does not relieve the wrongdoer of the necessity of paying damages for his breach of contract. I do not wish to lay down any such rule as that a judge can in every case leave it to the jury to assess damages for a breach of contract. There are cases, no doubt, where the loss is so dependent on the mere unrestricted volition of another that it is impossible to say that there is any assessable loss resulting from the breach. In the present case there is no such difficulty. It is true that no market can be said to exist. None of the 50 competitors could have gone into the market and sold her right; her right was a personal right and incapable of transfer. But a jury might well take the view that such a right, if it could have been transferred, would have been of such a value that every one could recognise that a good price could be obtained for it. My view is that under such circumstances as those in this case the assessment of damages was unquestionably for the jury. The jury came to the conclusion that the taking away from the plaintiff of the opportunity of competition, as one of a body of 50, when 12 prizes were to be distributed, deprived the plaintiff of something which had a momentary value. I think that they were right and that this appeal fails.

Note

For another example of the courts' willingness to award damages in cases where exact quantification is difficult or impossible, see *Jackson* v. *Horizon Holidays* above, p. 546.

3. AGREED DAMAGES AND PENALTIES

Dunlop Pneumatic Tyre Co. Ltd. v. New Garage and Motor Co. Ltd.

[1915] A.C. 79 (H.L.)

Lord Dunedin.   I do not think it is advisable to attempt any detailed review of the various cases, but I shall content myself with stating succinctly the various propositions which I think are deducible from the decisions which rank as authoritative—

1.   Though the parties to a contract who use the words "penalty" or "liquidated damages" may prima facie be supposed to mean what they say, yet the expression used is not conclusive. The Court must find out whether the payment

stipulated is in truth a penalty or liquidated damages. This doctrine may be said to be found *passim* in nearly every case.

2. The essence of a penalty is a payment of money stipulated as *in terrorem* of the offending party; the essence of liquidated damages is a genuine covenanted pre-estimate of damage (*Clydebank Engineering and Shipbuilding Co.* v. *Don Jose Ramos Yzquierdo y Castanedo* (1905)).

3. The question whether a sum stipulated is penalty or liquidated damages is a question of construction to be decided upon the terms and inherent circumstances of each particular contract, judged of as at the time of the making of the contract, not as at the time of the breach (*Public Works Commissioner* v. *Hill* (1906) and *Webster* v. *Bosanquet* (1912)).

4. To assist this task of construction various tests have been suggested, which if applicable to the case under consideration may prove helpful, or even conclusive. Such are:

(*a*) It will be held to be penalty if the sum stipulated for is extravagant and unconscionable in amount in comparison with the greatest loss that could conceivably be proved to have followed from the breach. (Illustration given by Lord Halsbury in *Clydebank Case*).

(*b*) It will be held to be a penalty if the breach consists only in not paying a sum of money, and the sum stipulated is a sum greater than the sum which ought to have been paid (*Kemble* v. *Farren* (1829)). This though one of the most ancient instances is truly a corollary to the last test. Whether it had its historical origin in the doctrine of the common law that when A. promised to pay B. a sum of money on a certain day and did not do so, B. could only recover the sum with, in certain cases, interest, but could never recover further damages for non-timeous payment, or whether it was a survival of the time when equity reformed unconscionable bargains merely because they were unconscionable—a subject which much exercised Jessel M.R. in *Wallis* v. *Smith* (1882)—is probably more interesting than material.

(*c*) There is a presumption (but no more) that it is penalty when "a single lump sum is made payable by way of compensation, on the occurrence of one or more or all of several events, some of which may occasion serious and others but trifling damage" (Lord Watson in *Lord Elphinstone* v. *Monkland Iron and Coal Co.* (1886)).

On the other hand:

(*d*) It is no obstacle to the sum stipulated being a genuine pre-estimate of damage, that the consequences of the breach are such as to make precise pre-estimation almost an impossibility. On the contrary, that is just the situation when it is probable that pre-estimated damage was the true bargain between the parties (*Clydebank Case*, Lord Halsbury; *Webster* v. *Bosanquet*, Lord Mersey (1912)).

4. MITIGATION

Pilkington v. Wood

[1953] Ch. 770 (Ch.)

[The plaintiff's solicitor, the defendant, who had acted for him in the purchase of a house, had negligently and in breach of contract failed to notice that there was a defect in the title to the property. The only issue was as to the measure of damages.]

Harman J. It would appear then at first sight that the measure of the defendant's liability is the diminution in value of the property; that is to say, the difference between the value in 1950, the date of the plaintiff's purchase of the property with a good title and with the title which it in fact had.

The defendant, however, argues that it is the duty of the plaintiff before suing him in damages to seek to recover damages against his vendor Colonel Wilks under the covenant for title implied by reason of the conveyance as beneficial owner. It is said that this duty arises because of the obligation which rests on a person injured by a breach of contract to mitigate the damages. This suggestion seems to me to carry the doctrine of mitigation a stage further than it has been carried in any case to which I have been referred. The classic statement of the doctrine is that of Lord Haldane in *British Westinghouse Electric and Manufacturing Co. Ld.* v. *Underground Electric Railways Company of London Ld.* (1912) The Lord Chancellor expressed it thus:

> "The quantum of damage is a question of fact, and the only guidance the law can give is to lay down general principles which afford at times but scanty assistance in dealing with particular cases. The judges who give guidance to juries in these cases have necessarily to look at their special character, and to mould, for the purposes of different kinds of claim, the expression of the general principles which apply to them, and this is apt to give rise to an appearance

of ambiguity. Subject to these observations I think that there are certain broad principles which are quite well settled. The first is that, as far as possible, he who has proved a breach of a bargain to supply what he contracted to get is to be placed, as far as money can do it, in as good a situation as if the contract had been performed. The fundamental basis is thus compensation for pecuniary loss naturally flowing from the breach; but this first principle is qualified by a second, which imposes on a plaintiff the duty of taking all reasonable steps to mitigate the loss consequent on the breach, and debars him from claiming any part of the damage which is due to his neglect to take such steps. In the words of James L.J. in *Dunkirk Colliery Co.* v. *Lever* (1878), 'the person who has broken the contract is not to be exposed to additional cost by reason of the plaintiffs not doing what they ought to have done as reasonable men, and the plaintiffs not being under any obligation to do anything otherwise than in the ordinary course of business.' "

For the present purpose it seems to me that it is apposite to state the plaintiff's rights in the words of Scrutton L.J. in *Payzu Ld.* v. *Saunders* (1919) thus: "he can recover no more than he would have suffered if he had acted reasonably, because any further damages do not reasonably follow from the defendant's breach. ...."

Ought then the plaintiff as a reasonable man to enter on the litigation suggested? It was agreed that the defendant must offer him an indemnity against the costs, and it was suggested on the defendant's behalf that if an adequate indemnity were offered, if, secondly, the proposed defendant appeared to be solvent, and if, thirdly, there were a good prima facie right of action against that person, it was the duty of the injured party to embark on litigation in order to mitigate the damage suffered. This is a proposition which, in such general terms, I am not prepared to accept, nor do I think I ought to entertain it here, because I am by no means certain that the foundations for it exist.

It may be conceded that the indemnity offered would be adequate and that Colonel Wilks is a man of substance. It was clear, however, that he would resist any claim and would in his turn claim over against his solicitors, for that was his attitude in the witness-box.

About the third condition much more doubt exists.

[His Lordship discussed the point.]

I do not propose to attempt to decide whether an action against Colonel Wilks would lie or be fruitful. I can see it would be one attended with no little difficulty. I am of opinion that the so-called duty to mitigate does not go so far as to oblige the injured party, even under an indemnity, to embark on a complicated and difficult piece of litigation against a third party. The damage to the plaintiff was done once and for all *directly* the voidable conveyance to him was executed. This was the direct result of the negligent advice tendered by his solicitor, the defendant, that a good title had been shown; and, in my judgment, it is no part of the plaintiff's duty to embark on the proposed litigation in order to protect his solicitor from the consequences of his own carelessness.

Chapter 11

Selected Statutes

LAW REFORM (FRUSTRATED CONTRACTS) ACT 1943

Adjustment of rights and liabilities of parties to frustrated contracts

1.—(1) Where a contract governed by English law has become impossible of performance or been otherwise frustrated, and the parties thereto have for that reason been discharged from the further performance of the contract, the following provisions of this section shall, subject to the provisions of section 2 of this Act, have effect in relation thereto.

(2) All sums paid or payable to any party in pursuance of the contract before the time when the parties were so discharged (in this Act referred to as "the time of discharge") shall, in the case of sums so paid, be recoverable from him as money received by him for the use of the party by whom the sums were paid, and, in the case of sums so payable, cease to be so payable:

Provided that, if the party to whom the sums were so paid or payable incurred expenses before the time of discharge in, or for the purpose of, the performance of the contract, the court may, if it considers it just to do so having regard to all the circumstances of the case, allow him to retain or, as the case may be, recover the whole or any part of the sums so paid or payable, not being an amount in excess of the expenses so incurred.

(3) Where any party to the contract has, by reason of anything done by any other party thereto in, or for the purpose of, the performance of the contract, obtained a valuable benefit (other than a payment of money to which the last foregoing subsection applies) before the time of discharge, there shall be recoverable from him by the said party such sum (if any), not exceeding the value of the said benefit to the party obtaining it, as the court considers just, having regard to all the circumstances of the case and, in particular,—

    (a)   the amount of any expenses incurred before the time of discharge by the benefited party in, or for the purpose of, the performance of the contract, including any sums paid or payable by him to any other party in pursuance of the contract and retained or recoverable by that party under the last foregoing subsection, and

    (b)   the effect, in relation to the said benefit, of the circumstances giving rise to the frustration of the contract.

(4) In estimating, for the purposes of the foregoing provisions of this section, the amount of any expenses incurred by any party to the contract, the court may, without prejudice to the generality of the said provisions, include such sums as appears to be reasonable in respect of overhead expenses and in respect of any work or services performed personally by the said party.

(5) In considering whether any sum ought to be recovered or retained under the foregoing provisions of this section by any party to the contract, the court shall not take into account any sums which have, by reason of the circumstances giving rise to the frustration of the contract, become payable to that party under any contract of insurance unless there was an obligation to insure imposed by an express term of the frustrated contract or by or under any enactment.

(6) Where any person has assumed obligations under the contract in consideration of the conferring of a benefit by any other party to the contract upon any other person, whether a party to the contract or not, the court may, if in all the circumstances of the case it considers it just to do so, treat for the purposes of subsection (3) of this section any benefit so conferred as a benefit obtained by the person who has assumed the obligations as aforesaid.

Provision as to application of this Act

2.—(1) This Act shall apply to contracts, whether made before or after the commencement of this Act, as respects which the time of discharge is on or after the first day of July, 1943, but not to contracts as respects which the time of discharge is before the said date.

(2) This Act shall apply to contracts to which the Crown is a party in like manner as to contracts between subjects.

(3) Where any contract to which this Act applies contains any provision which, upon the true construction of the contract, is intended to have effect in the event of circumstances arising which operate, or would but for the said provision operate, to frustrate the contract, or is intended to have effect whether such circumstances arise or not, the court shall give effect to the said provision and shall only give effect to the foregoing section of this Act to such extent, if any, as appears to the court to be consistent with the said provision.

(4) Where it appears to the court that a part of any contract to which this Act applies can properly be severed from the remainder of the contract, being a part wholly performed before the time of discharge, or so performed except for the payment in respect of that part of the contract of sums which are or can be ascertained under the contract, the court shall treat that part of the contract as if it were a separate contract and had not been frustrated and shall treat the foregoing section of this Act as only applicable to the remainder of that contract.

(5) This Act shall not apply—

  (a) to any charterparty, except a time charterparty or a charterparty by way of demise, or to any contract (other than a charterparty) for the carriage of goods by sea; or

  (b) to any contract of insurance, save as is provided by subsection (5) of the foregoing section; or

  (c) to any contract to which section 7 of the Sale of Goods Act, 1893 (which avoids contracts for the sale of specific goods which perish before the risk has passed to the buyer) applies, or to any other contract for the sale, or for the sale and delivery, of specific goods, where the contract is frustrated by reason of the fact that the goods have perished.

MISREPRESENTATION ACT 1967

Removal of certain bars to rescission for innocent misrepresentation

1.— Where a person has entered into a contract after a misrepresentation has been made to him, and—

(a) the misrepresentation has become a term of the contract; or

(b) the contract has been performed;

or both, then, if otherwise he would be entitled to rescind the contract without alleging fraud, he shall be so entitled, subject to the provisions of this Act, notwithstanding the matters mentioned in paragraphs (a) and (b) of this section.

Damages for misrepresentation

2.—(1) Where a person has entered into a contract after a misrepresentation has been made to him by another party thereto and as a result thereof he has suffered loss, then, if the person making the misrepresentation would be liable to damages in respect thereof had the misrepresentation been made fraudulently, that person shall be so liable notwithstanding that the misrepresentation was not made fraudulently, unless he proves that he had reasonable ground to believe and did believe up to the time the contract was made that the facts represented were true.

(2) Where a person has entered into a contract after a misrepresentation has been made to him otherwise than fraudulently, and he would be entitled, by reason of the misrepresentation, to rescind the contract, then, if it is claimed, in any proceedings arising out of the contract, that the contract ought to be or has been rescinded the court or arbitrator may declare the contract subsisting and award damages in lieu of rescission, if of opinion that it would be equitable to do so, having regard to the nature of the misrepresentation and the loss that would be caused by it if the contract were upheld, as well as to the loss that rescission would cause to the other party.

(3) Damages may be awarded against a person under subsection (2) of this section whether or not he is liable to damages under subsection (1) thereof, but where he is so liable any award under the said subsection (2) shall be taken into account in assessing his liability under the said subsection (1).

Avoidance of certain provisions excluding liability for misrepresentation

3.—If a contract contains a term which would exclude or restrict—

(a) any liability to which a party to a contract may be subject by reason of any misrepresentation made by him before the contract was made; or

(b) any remedy available to another party to the contract by reason of such a misrepresentation,

that term shall be of no effect except in so far as it satisfies the requirement of reasonableness as stated in section 11(1) of the Unfair Contract Terms Act 1977; and it is for those claiming that the term satisfies that requirement to show that it does.

UNSOLICITED GOODS AND SERVICES ACT 1971

Rights of recipient of unsolicited goods

1.—(1) In the circumstances specified in the following subsection, a person who after the commencement of this Act receives unsolicited goods, may as between himself and the sender, use, deal with or dispose of them as if they were an unconditional gift to him, and any right of the sender to the goods shall be extinguished.

(2) The circumstances referred to in the preceding subsection are that the goods were sent to the recipient with a view to his acquiring them, that the recipient has no reasonable cause to believe that they were sent with a view to their being acquired for the purposes of a trade or business and has neither agreed to acquire nor agreed to return them, and either—

    (a)   that during the period of six months beginning with the day on which the recipient received the goods the sender did not take possession of them and the recipient did not unreasonably refuse to permit the sender to do so; or

    (b)   that not less than 30 days before the expiration of the period aforesaid the recipient gave notice to the sender in accordance with the following subsection, and that during the period of 30 days beginning with the day on which the notice was given the sender did not take possession of the goods and the recipient did not unreasonably refuse to permit the sender to do so.

(3) A notice in pursuance of the preceding subsection shall be in writing and shall—

    (a)   state the recipient's name and address and, if possession of the goods in question may not be taken by the sender at that address, the address at which it may be so taken;

    (b)   contain a statement, however expressed, that the goods are unsolicited,

and may be sent by post.

(4) In this section "sender," in relation to any goods, includes any person on whose behalf or with whose consent the goods are sent, and any other person claiming through or under the sender or any such person.

Demands and threats regarding payment

2.—(1) A person who, not having reasonable cause to believe there is a right to payment, in the course of any trade or business makes a demand for payment, or asserts a present or prospective right to payment, for what he knows are unsolicited goods sent (after the commencement of this Act) to another person with a view to his acquiring them, shall be guilty of an offence and on summary conviction shall be liable to a fine not exceeding [level 4 on the standard scale].

(2) A person who, not having reasonable cause to believe there is a right to payment, in the course of any trade or business and with a view to obtaining any payment for what he knows are unsolicited goods sent as aforesaid—

    (a)   threatens to bring any legal proceedings; or

    (b)   places or causes to be placed the name of any person on a list of defaulters or debtors or threatens to do so; or

(c)   invokes or causes to be invoked any other collection procedure or threatens to do so,

shall be guilty of an offence and shall be liable on summary conviction to a fine not exceeding [level 5 on the standard scale].

UNFAIR CONTRACT TERMS ACT 1977

Negligence liability

2.—(1)   A person cannot by reference to any contract term or to a notice given to persons generally or to particular persons exclude or restrict his liability for death or personal injury resulting from negligence.

(2)   In the case of other loss or damage, a person cannot so exclude or restrict his liability for negligence except in so far as the term or notice satisfies the requirement of reasonableness.

(3)   Where a contract term or notice purports to exclude or restrict liability for negligence a person's agreement to or awareness of it is not of itself to be taken as indicating his voluntary acceptance of any risk.

Liability arising in contract

3.—(1)   This section applies as between contracting parties where one of them deals as consumer or on the other's written standard terms of business.

(2)   As against that party, the other cannot by reference to any contract term—

(a)   when himself in breach of contract, exclude or restrict any liability of his in respect of the breach; or

(b)   claim to be entitled—

(i)   to render a contractual performance substantially different from that which was reasonably expected of him, or

(ii)   in respect of the whole or any part of his contractual obligation, to render no performance at all,

except in so far (in any of the cases mentioned above in this subsection) the contract term satisfies the requirement of reasonableness.

Sale and hire-purchase

6.—(1)   Liability for breach of the obligations arising from—

(a)   section 12 of the Sale of Goods Act 1979 (seller's implied undertakings as to title, etc.);

(b)   section 8 of the Supply of Goods (Implied Terms) Act 1973 (the corresponding thing in relation to hire-purchase),

cannot be excluded or restricted by reference to any contract term.

(2)   As against a person dealing as consumer, liability for breach of the obligations arising from—

(*a*)   section 13, 14 or 15 of the 1979 Act (seller's implied undertakings as to conformity of goods with description or sample, or as to their quality or fitness for a particular purpose);

(*b*)   section 9, 10 or 11 of the 1973 Act (the corresponding things in relation to hire-purchase),

cannot be excluded or restricted by reference to any contract term.

(3)   As against a person dealing otherwise than as consumer, the liability specified in subsection (2) above can be excluded or restricted by reference to a contract term, but only in so far as the term satisfies the requirement of reasonableness.

(4)   The liabilities referred to in this section are not only the business liabilities defined by section 1(3), but include those arising under any contract of sale of goods or hire-purchase agreement.

. . .

The "reasonableness" test

11.—(1)   In relation to a contract term, the requirement of reasonableness for the purposes of this Part of this Act, section 3 of the Misrepresentation Act 1967 and section 3 of the Misrepresentation Act (Northern Ireland) 1967 is that the term shall have been a fair and reasonable one to be included having regard to the circumstances which were, or ought reasonably to have been, known to or in the contemplation of the parties when the contract was made.

(2)   In determining for the purposes of section 6 or 7 above whether a contract term satisfies the requirement of reasonableness, regard shall be had in particular to the matters specified in Schedule 2 to this Act; but this subsection does not prevent the court or arbitrator from holding, in accordance with any rule of law, that a term which purports to exclude or restrict any relevant liability is not a term of the contract.

(3)   In relation to a notice (not being a notice having contractual effect), the requirement of reasonableness under this Act is that it should be fair and reasonable to allow reliance on it, having regard to all the circumstances obtaining when the liability arose or (but for the notice) would have arisen.

(4)   Where by reference to a contract term or notice a person seeks to restrict liability to a specified sum of money, and the question arises (under this or any other Act) whether the term or notice satisfies the requirement of reasonableness, regard shall be had in particular (but without prejudice to subsection (2) above in the case of contract terms) to—

(*a*)   the resources which he could expect to be available to him for the purpose of meeting the liability should it arise; and

(*b*)   how far it was open to him to cover himself by insurance.

(5)   It is for those claiming that a contract term or notice satisfies the requirement of reasonableness to show that it does.

"Dealing as consumer"

12.—(1)   A party to a contract "deals as consumer" in relation to another party if—

(*a*)   he neither makes the contract in the course of a business nor holds himself out as doing so; and

(*b*)   the other party does make the contract in the course of a business; and

(*c*)   in the case of a contract governed by the law of sale of goods or hire-purchase, or by section 7 of this Act, the goods passing under or in pursuance of the contract are of a type ordinarily supplied for private use or consumption.

(2) But on a sale by auction or by competitive tender the buyer is not in any circumstances to be regarded as dealing as consumer.

(3) Subject to this, it is for those claiming that a party does not deal as consumer to show that he does not.

Varieties of exemption clause

13.—(1) To the extent that this Part of this Act prevents the exclusion or restriction of any liability it also prevents—

(a) making the liability or its enforcement subject to restrictive or onerous conditions;

(b) excluding or restricting any right or remedy in respect of the liability, or subjecting a person to any prejudice in consequence of his pursuing any such right or remedy;

(c) excluding or restricting rules of evidence or procedure;

and (to that extent) sections 2 and 5 to 7 also prevent excluding or restricting liability by reference to terms and notices which exclude or restrict the relevant obligation or duty.

(2) But an agreement in writing to submit present or future differences to arbitration is not to be treated under this Part of this Act as excluding or restricting any liability.

. . .

Schedule 2

"Guidelines" for Application of Reasonableness Test

The matters to which regard is to be had in particular for the purposes of sections 6(3), 7(3) and (4), 20 and 21 are any of the following which appear to be relevant—

(a) the strength of the bargaining positions of the parties relative to each other, taking into account (among other things) alternative means by which the customer's requirements could have been met;

(b) whether the customer received an inducement to agree to the term, or in accepting it had an opportunity of entering into a similar contract with other persons, but without having to accept a similar term;

(c) whether the customer knew or ought reasonably to have known of the existence and extent of the term (having regard, among other things, to any custom of the trade and any previous course of dealing between the parties);

(d) where the term excludes or restricts any relevant liability if some condition is not complied with, whether it was reasonable at the time of the contract to expect that compliance with that condition would be practicable;

(e) whether the goods were manufactured, processed or adapted to the special order of the customer.

Sale of Goods Act 1979

Goods which have perished

6. Where there is a contract for the sale of specific goods, and the goods without the knowledge of the seller have perished at the time when the contract is made, the contract is void.

Implied terms about title, etc.

12.—(1) In a contract of sale, other than one to which subsection (3) below applies, there is an implied condition on the part of the seller that in the case of a sale he has a right to sell the goods, and in the case of an agreement to sell he will have such a right at the time when the property is to pass.

(2) In a contract of sale, other than one to which subsection (3) below applies, there is also an implied warranty that—

    (a)   the goods are free, and will remain free until the time when the property is to pass, from any charge or encumbrance not disclosed or known to the buyer before the contract is made, and

    (b)   the buyer will enjoy quiet possession of the goods except so far as it may be disturbed by the owner or other person entitled to the benefit of any charge or encumbrance so disclosed or known.

(3) This subsection applies to a contract of sale in the case of which there appears from the contract or is to be inferred from its circumstances an intention that the seller should transfer only such title as he or a third person may have.

(4) In a contract to which subsection (3) above applies there is an implied warranty that all charges or encumbrances known to the seller and not known to the buyer have been disclosed to the buyer before the contract is made.

(5) In a contract to which subsection (3) above applies there is also an implied warranty that none of the following will disturb the buyer's quiet possession of the goods, namely—

    (a)   the seller;

    (b)   in a case where the parties to the contract intend that the seller should transfer only such title as a third person may have, that person;

    (c)   anyone claiming through or under the seller or that third person otherwise than under a charge or encumbrance disclosed or known to the buyer before the contract is made.

(6) . . .

Sale by description

13.—(1) Where there is a contract for the sale of goods by description, there is an implied condition that the goods will correspond with the description.

(2) If the sale is by sample as well as by description it is not sufficient that the bulk of the goods corresponds with the sample if the goods do not also correspond with the description.

(3) A sale of goods is not prevented from being a sale by description by reason only that, being exposed for sale or hire, they are selected by the buyer.

(4) . . .

Implied terms about quality or fitness

14.—(1) Except as provided by this section and section 15 below and subject to any other enactment, there is no implied condition or warranty about the quality or fitness for any particular purpose of goods supplied under a contract of sale.

(2) Where the seller sells goods in the course of a business, there is an implied condition that the goods supplied under the contract are of merchantable quality, except that there is no such condition—

(*a*)   as regards defects specifically drawn to the buyer's attention before the contract is made; or

(*b*)   if the buyer examines the goods before the contract is made, as regards defects which that examination ought to reveal.

(3) Where the seller sells goods in the course of a business and the buyer, expressly or by implication, makes known—

(*a*)   to the seller, or

(*b*)   where the purchase price or part of it is payable by instalments and the goods were previously sold by a credit-broker to the seller, to that credit-broker,

any particular purpose for which the goods are being bought, there is an implied condition that the goods supplied under the contract are reasonably fit for that purpose, whether or not that is a purpose for which such goods are commonly supplied, except where the circumstances show that the buyer does not rely, or that it is unreasonable for him to rely, on the skill or judgment of the seller or credit-broker.

(4) An implied condition or warranty about quality or fitness for a particular purpose may be annexed to a contract of sale by usage.

(5) The preceding provisions of this section apply to a sale by a person who in the course of a business is acting as agent for another as they apply to a sale by a principal in the course of a business, except where that other is not selling in the course of a business and either the buyer knows that fact or reasonable steps are taken to bring it to the notice of the buyer before the contract is made.

(6) Goods of any kind are of merchantable quality within the meaning of subsection (2) above if they are as fit for the purpose or purposes for which goods of that kind are commonly bought as it is reasonable to expect having regard to any description applied to them, the price (if relevant) and all the other relevant circumstances.

(7)   . . .

(8)   . . .

Sale by sample

15.—(1) A contract of sale is a contract for sale by sample where there is an express or implied term to that effect in the contract.

(2) In the case of a contract for sale by sample there is an implied condition—

(*a*)   that the bulk will correspond with the sample in quality;

(*b*)   that the buyer will have a reasonable opportunity of comparing the bulk with the sample;

(c)   that the goods will be free from any defect, rendering them unmerchantable, which would not be apparent on reasonable examination of the sample.

(3) In subsection (2)(c) above "unmerchantable" is to be construed in accordance with section 14(6) above.

(4) ...

...

Auction sales

57.—(1) Where the goods are put up for sale by auction in lots, each lot is prima facie deemed to be the subject of a separate contract of sale.

(2) A sale by auction is complete when the auctioneer announces its completion by the fall of the hammer, or in other customary manner; and until the announcement is made any bidder may retract his bid.

(3) A sale by auction may be notified to be subject to a reserve or upset price, and a right to bid may also be reserved expressly by or on behalf of the seller.

(4) Where a sale by auction is not notified to be subject to a right to bid by or on behalf of the seller, it is not lawful for the seller to bid himself or to employ any person to bid at the sale, or for the auctioneer knowingly to take any bid from the seller or any such person.

(5) A sale contravening subsection (4) above may be treated as fraudulent by the buyer.

(6) Where, in respect of a sale by auction, a right to bid is expressly reserved (but not otherwise) the seller or any one person on his behalf may bid at the auction.

Minors' Contracts Act 1987

2. Guarantees

Where—

(a)   a guarantee is given in respect of an obligation of a party to a contract made after the commencement of this Act, and

(b)   the obligation is unenforceable against him (or he repudiates the contract) because he was a minor when the contract was made,

the guarantee shall not for that reason alone be unenforceable against the guarantor.

3. Restitution

Where—

(a)   a person ("the plaintiff") has after the commencement of this Act entered into a contract with another ("the defendant"), and

(b)   the contract is unenforceable against the defendant (or he repudiates it) because he was a minor when the contract was made,

the court may, if it is just and equitable to do so, require the defendant to transfer to the plaintiff any property acquired by the defendant under the contract, or any property representing it.

(2) Nothing in this section shall be taken to prejudice any other remedy available to the plaintiff.

LAW OF PROPERTY (MISCELLANEOUS PROVISIONS) ACT 1989

Contracts for sale etc of land to be made by signed writing

2.—(1) A contract for the sale or other disposition of an interest in land can only be made in writing and only by incorporating all the terms which the parties have expressly agreed in one document or, where contracts are exchanged, in each.

(2) The terms may be incorporated in a document either by being set out in it or by reference to some other document.

(3) The document incorporating the terms or, where contracts are exchanged, one of the documents incorporating them (but not necessarily the same one) must be signed by or on behalf of each party to the contract.

(4) Where a contract for the sale or other disposition of an interest in land satisfies the conditions of this section by reason only of the rectification of one or more documents in pursuance of an order of a court, the contract shall come into being, or be deemed to have come into being, at such time as may be specified in the order.

(5) This section does not apply in relation to—

(a) a contract to grant such a lease as is mentioned in section 54(2) of the Law of Property Act 1925 (short leases);

(b) a contract made in the course of a public auction; or

(c) a contract regulated under the Financial Services Act 1986;

and nothing in this section affects the creation or operation of resulting, implied or constructive trusts.

(6) In this section—

"disposition" has the same meaning as in the Law of Property Act 1925;

"interest in land" means any estate, interest or charge in or over land or in or over the proceeds of sale of land.

(7) Nothing in this section shall apply in relation to contracts made before this section comes into force.

(8) ... [This subsection repeals the Law of Property Act 1925, s.40.]

Index